CONTENTS

Chapter 1

"IT'S GOING TO CHANGE YOUR LIFE"

Chapter 2

NURSERY NECESSITIES: CRIBS, DRESSERS & MORE

Chapter 3

BABY BEDDING & DECOR

Chapter 4

THE REALITY LAYETTE: LITTLE CLOTHES FOR LITTLE PRICES

BABY
Bargains®

As Seen on Oprah

Secrets to saving 20% to 50% on baby furniture, equipment, maternity wear and much, much more!

Money-Back Guarantee

Denise & Alan Fields
Authors of the best-seller, Bridal Bargains

Copyright Page and Carbon-Neutral Credits

Saxophone, lead guitar and breast-feeding by Denise Fields
Drums, rhythm guitar and father stuff by Alan Fields
Congas on "Grandparents" by
Max & Helen Coopwood, Howard & Patti Fields
Cover/interior design and keyboard solo by Epicenter Creative
Screaming guitar solos on "(Let's Go) Perego" by Jack and Ben Fields
Additional guitar work on "Diaper Changing Blues" by Todd Snider
Backing vocals on "(She's Got A) LATCH Car Seat" by Ric Ocasek
Band photography by Moses Street

To order this book, call 1-800-888-0385. Or send $17.95 plus $3 shipping to Windsor Peak Press, 436 Pine Street, Boulder, CO 80302. Questions or comments? Please call the authors at (303) 442-8792. Or fax them a note at (303) 442-3744. Or write to them at the above address in Boulder, Colorado. E-mail the authors at authors@babybargains.com.

Learn more about this book online at
BabyBargains.com
Distributed to the book trade by Ingram
Publisher Services, 866-400-5351.

Library Cataloging in Publication Data

Fields, Denise
Fields, Alan
  Baby Bargains: Secrets to saving 20% to 50% on baby furniture, equipment, clothes, toys, maternity wear and much, much more/ Denise & Alan Fields
  640 pages.
  Includes index.
  ISBN 978-1-889392-44-8
  1. Child Care—Handbooks, manuals, etc. 2. Infants' supplies—Purchasing—United States, Canada, Directories. 3. Children's paraphernalia—Purchasing—Handbooks, manuals. 4. Product Safety—Handbooks, manuals. 5. Consumer education.
  649'.122'0296—dc20. 2014.

Version 10.1

Chapter 5

MATERNITY/NURSING CLOTHES

Chapter 6

FEEDING BABY: BREASTFEEDING, BOTTLES, HIGH CHAIRS

Chapter 7

Around the House: Monitors, Diaper Pails, Safety & More

Chapter 8

Car Seats

Chapter 9

STROLLERS, DIAPER BAGS AND OTHER TO GO GEAR

Chapter 10

CARRIERS

Chapter 11

CONCLUSION: WHAT DOES IT ALL MEAN?

Icons

 Getting Started

 Money-Saving Secrets

 Sources

 Best Buys

 Best Online Sources

 The Name Game

 What Are You Buying?

 Do it By Mail

 Safe & Sound

 Email from the Real World

 Smart Shopper

 More Money Buys You . . .

 Wastes of Money

 Bottom Line

CHAPTER 1

"It's Going to Change Your Life!"

Inside this chapter

That had to be the silliest comment we heard while we were pregnant with our first baby. Believe it or not, we even heard this refrain more often than "Are you having a boy or a girl?" and "I'm sorry. Your insurance doesn't cover that." For the friends and relatives of first-time parents out there, we'd like to point out that this is a pretty silly thing to say. Of course, we knew that a baby was going to change our lives. What we didn't realize was how much a baby was going to change our pocketbook.

Oh sure, we knew that we'd have to buy triple our weight in diapers and be subjected to dangerously high levels of Nickelodeon. What we didn't expect was the endless pitches for cribs, gear, toys, clothing and other items parents are required to purchase by FED-ERAL BABY LAW.

We quickly learned that having a baby is like popping on the Juvenile Amusement Park Ride from Consumer Hell. Once that egg is fertilized, you're whisked off to the Pirates of the Crib ride. Then it's on to marvel at the little elves in StrollerLand, imploring you to buy brands with names you can't pronounce. Finally, you take a trip to Magic Car Seat Mountain, where the confusion is so real, it's scary.

Consider us your tour guides—the Yogi Bear to your Boo Boo Bear, the Fred to your Ethel, the . . . well, you get the idea. Before we enter BabyLand, let's take a look at the Four Truths That No One Tells You About Buying Stuff For Baby.

The Four Truths That No One Tells You About Buying Stuff for Baby

1 **BABIES DON'T CARE IF THEY'RE WEARING DESIGNER CLOTHES OR SLEEPING ON DESIGNER SHEETS.** Let's be realistic. Babies just want to be comfortable. They can't even distinguish between the liberals and conservatives on "Meet the Press," so how would they ever be able to tell the difference between Baby Gucci crib bedding and another less famous brand that's just as comfortable, but 70% less expensive? Our focus is on making your baby happy—at a price that won't break the bank.

2 **YOUR BABY'S SAFETY IS MUCH MORE IMPORTANT THAN YOUR CONVENIENCE.** Here are the scary facts: 74,100 children under age five were injured (requiring emergency room visits) by nursery products in 2011 (the latest year figures are available). During a recent three-year period, those same baby products caused 114 deaths per year. (Source: 2012 Consumer Product Safety Commission report based on 2011 data).

Each chapter of this book has a section called "Safe & Sound" to arm you with in-depth advice on keeping your baby out of trouble. We'll tell you which products we think are dangerous and how to safely use other potentially hazardous products.

3 **MURPHY'S LAW OF BABY TOYS SAYS YOUR BABY'S HAPPINESS WITH A TOY IS INVERSELY RELATED TO THE TOY'S PRICE.** Buy a $200 shiny new wagon with anti-lock brakes, and odds are baby just wants to play with the box it came in. In recognition of this reality, we've included "wastes of money" in each chapter that will steer you away from frivolous items.

4 **IT'S GOING TO COST MORE THAN YOU THINK.** Whatever amount of money you budget for your baby, get ready to spend more. Here's a breakdown of the average costs of bringing a baby into the world today:

The Average Cost of Having a Baby

(based on industry estimates for a child from birth to age one)

Crib, mattress, dresser, rocker	$1420
Bedding / Decor	$350
Baby Clothes	$655
Disposable Diapers	$750
Maternity / Nursing Clothes	$1300
Nursery items, high chair, toys	$545
Baby Food / Formula	$1015
Stroller, Car Seats, Carrier	$730
Miscellaneous	$620
TOTAL	**$7,385**

The above figures are based on a survey of 1000 readers, buying name brand products at regular retail prices.

Bedding/Decor includes not only bedding items but also lamps, wallpaper, and so on for your baby's nursery. Baby Food/Formula assumes mom breastfeeds for the first six months and then feeds baby jarred baby food ($385) and formula ($630) until age one. If you plan to bottle-feed instead of breastfeed, add another $630 on to that figure. (Of course, the goal is to breastfeed your baby as long as possible—one year is a good target.)

Sure, you do get an automatic tax write-off for that bundle of joy, but that only amounts to about $3900 this year (plus you also get up to an additional $3000 child care tax credit, depending on your income). But those tax goodies won't nearly offset the actual cost of raising a child. And as you probably realize, our cost chart is missing some expensive "extras" . . . like medical bills, childcare, saving for college and more. Here's an overview of what can add to the tab.

Scary Number: The Cost of Raising Baby to 18

$234,900. That's what the federal government says it costs to raise a child born in 2013 to age 18. Those costs include food, transportation, housing, clothes and child care.

But let's talk about child care. Critics say the federal government grossly underestimates this cost (the feds say parents spend $2040 to $5090 on child care each year for the first two years).

So what does child care really cost? According to the National Association of Child Care Resource and Referral Agencies, the average annual bill for center care ranges from $4,600 in Mississippi to $15,000 in Massachusetts (2012 statistics).

College is another expense the government leaves out of their figures. The College Board estimates that four years at a public college averages $68,524 (tuition, fees, room and board). At a private college, that same figure is $154,356. Given current rates of return, that means you have to put away $5200+ a year every year for 18 years to afford that public school.

The take-home message: raising a baby ain't cheap. It's important to start saving your pennies now, so you can start saving for those important items (college, etc.) down the road.

Reality Check: Does it Really Cost that Much to Have a Baby?

Now that we've thoroughly scared you enough to inquire whether the stork accepts returns, we should point out that children do NOT have to cost that much. Even if we focus just on the first year, you don't have to spend $7385 on baby gear. And that's what this book is all about: how to save money and still buy the best. Follow all the tips in this book, and we estimate the first year will cost you $4323. Yes, that's a savings of $3092!

Now, at this point, you might be saying "That's impossible! I suppose you'll recommend shopping garage sales and dollar stores." On the contrary, we'll show you how to get *quality* name brands and safe products at discount prices. Most importantly, you will learn how not to WASTE your money on dubious gear. And much more. Yes, we've got the maximum number of bargains allowed by federal law.

A word on bargain shopping: when interviewing hundreds of parents for this book, we realized bargain seekers fall into two frugal camps. There's the "do-it-yourself" crowd and the "quality at a discount" group. As the name implies, "do-it-yourselfers" are resourceful folks who like to take second-hand products and refurbish them. Others use creative tricks to make homemade versions of baby care items like baby wipes and diaper rash cream.

While that's all well and good, we fall more into the second camp of bargain hunters, the "quality at a discount" group. We love discovering a name brand stroller for 75% off on Craigslist. Or the hidden discount line of a name brand furniture brand, sold at 20% discount. We also realize savvy parents save money by not *wasting* it on inferior goods or useless items.

While we hope that *Baby Bargains* pleases both groups of bargain hunters, the main focus of this book is not on do-it-yourself projects. Our emphasis is on identifying best buys for the dollar and not wasting your money, as well as on the best discount online sources.

What? There's No Advertising in This Book?

Yes, it's true. This book contains zero percent advertising. We have never taken any money to recommend a product or company. We make our living off the sales of this and other books, ebooks and web site subscriptions. **No company recommended in this book paid any consideration or was charged any fee to be mentioned.** (In fact, some companies probably would offer us money to leave them *out* of the book, given our comments about their products or services).

We also do not accept samples or other freebies from companies we review—if we are doing a first-hand inspection of a product, we purchase it on our own at regular retail prices. When we visit factories or other company facilities, we pay for our own travel expenses. As consumer advocates, we believe these policies help to ensure objectivity.

We also are parents of two kids. Although our children are now well past their baby years, we still demo products like baby monitors here at the home office (keeping an eye on our faithful dog, Shadow).

Of course, given the sheer volume of baby stuff, there's no way we can test everything personally. To solve that dilemma, we rely on reader feedback to help us figure out which are the best products to recommend. We receive over 200 emails a day from parents; this helps us spot overall trends on which brands/products parents love. And which ones they want to destroy with a rocket launcher.

Parents post reviews of products to our web site, message boards and blog. (Our message boards log 1000 posts a day). Full disclosure: we do monetize some links posted by readers to our message boards in order to pay for bandwidth and server infrastructure.

Of course, one bad review from one parent doesn't mean we won't recommend a product—we combine multiple review sources to come up with an overall picture as to which products and brands are best.

The prices you see in our book were accurate as of press time. We aim to print actual selling prices (versus suggested retail prices) in our book—we do this by surveying stores and web sites. While the publisher makes every effort to ensure their accuracy, errors and omissions may exist. That's why we update this book with every new printing—make sure you are using the most recent version (go to BabyBargains.com and click on Book and then Which Version?).

Our door is always open—we want to hear your opinions. Email us at authors@BabyBargains.com or call us at (303) 442-8792 to ask a question, report a mistake, or just give us your thoughts.

So, Who Are You Guys Anyway?

Why do a book on saving money on baby products? Don't new parents throw caution to the wind when buying for their baby, spending whatever it takes to ensure their baby's safety and comfort?

Ha! When our first child was born, we quickly realized how darn expensive this guy was. Sure, as a new parent, you know you've got to buy a car seat, crib, clothes and diapers . . . but have you walked into one of those baby "superstores" lately? It's a blizzard of baby stuff, with a bewildering array of "must have" gear, gadgets and gizmos, all claiming to be the best thing for parents since sliced bread.

Becoming a parent in this day and age is both a blessing and curse. The good news: parents today have many more choices for baby products than past generations. The *bad* news: parents today have many more choices for baby products than past generations.

Our mission: make sense of this stuff, with an eye on cutting costs. As consumer advocates, we've been down this road before. We researched bargains and uncovered scams in the wedding business when we wrote *Bridal Bargains*. Then we penned an exposé on new homebuilders in *Your New House*.

Yet, we found the baby business to be perplexing in different ways—instead of outright fraud or scam artists, we've instead discovered some highly questionable products that don't live up to their hype—and others that are outright dangerous. We were surprised to learn that most juvenile items face little (or no) government scrutiny, leaving parents to sort out true usefulness and safety from sales hype.

So, we've gone on a quest to find the best baby products, at prices that won't send you to the poor house. Sure, we've sampled many of these items first hand. But this book is much more than our experiences—we interviewed over 15,000 new parents to learn their experiences with products. Our message boards have over 42,000 members, buzzing with all sorts of product feedback and advice. We also attend juvenile product trade shows to quiz manufacturers and retailers on what's hot and what's not. The insights from retailers are especially helpful, since these folks are on the front lines, seeing which items unhappy parents return.

Our focus is on safety and durability: which items stand up to real

The 7 Commandments of Baby Bargains

Yes, we've come down from the mountain to share with you our SEVEN commandments of *Baby Bargains*—the keys to saving every parent should know. Let's review:

1 SAFETY IS JOB ONE. As a parent, your baby's safety is paramount. We never compromise safety for a bargain—that's why hand-me-down cribs or used car seats are not a good idea. Good news: you can subscribe to our free blog to get an email or instant message when a baby product is recalled. Go to BabyBargains.com/ blog and enter your email address in the box at the right.

2 FOCUS ON THE BASICS. Big box baby stores are so overwhelming, with a blizzard of baby products. Key on the basics: setting up a safe place for baby to sleep (the nursery) and safe transport (car seats). Many items like high chairs, toys, and so on are not needed immediately.

3 WEED OUT THE FLUFF. Our advice: take an experienced mom with you when you register. A mom with one or two kids can help you separate out needed items from the fluff!

world conditions and which don't. Interestingly, we found many products for baby are sold strictly on price . . . and sometimes a great "bargain" broke, fell apart or shrunk after a few uses. Hence, you'll note some of our top recommendations aren't always the lowest in price. To be sensitive to those on really tight budgets, we try to identify "good, better and best" bets in different price ranges.

We get questions: Top 6 Questions & Answers

From the home office here in Boulder, CO, here are the top five questions we get asked here at *Baby Bargains*:

1 **HOW DO I KNOW IF I HAVE THE CURRENT EDITION?** We strive to keep *Baby Bargains* as up-to-date as possible. As such, we update it periodically with new editions. But if you just borrowed this book from a friend, how do you know how old it is? First, look at the copyright page. There at the bottom you will see a version number (such as 10.0). The first number (the 10 in this case) means

4 **TWO WORDS: FREE MONEY.** As a parent, you NEVER pass up free money! From tax deductions to tax credits, being a parent means freebies. And don't overlook your employer: take advantage of benefits like dependent care accounts—using PRE-TAX dollars to pay for child care will save you HUNDREDS if not THOUSANDS of dollars.

5 **MORE FREEBIES.** Many companies throw swag at new parents, hoping they will become future customers. We keep an updated freebie list on our web site—get free diapers, bottles, and more. Go to BabyBargains.com/freebies for the latest update!

6 **SHOP AT STORES THAT DO NOT HAVE "BABY" IN THEIR NAME.** Costco for diapers? Pet web sites for safety gates? IKEA for high chairs? Yes! Yes! Yes! You can save 30% or more by not buying items at baby stores.

7 **ONLINE SHOPPING SAVVY.** Let's face It: as a new mom and dad, you probably won't have much time to hit the mall. The web is a savior—but how do you master the deals? One smart tip: ALWAYS use coupon codes for discounts or FREE shipping before you order. We keep a list (updated daily!) of the best coupon codes on our Bargain Alert Forum on our free message boards (BabyBargains.com).

What you need, when

Yes, buying for baby can seem overwhelming, but there is a silver lining: you don't need ALL this stuff immediately when baby is born. Let's look at what items you need quickly and what you can wait on. This chart indicates usage of certain items for the first 12 months of baby's life:

			Months of Use		
Item	**Birth**	**3**	**6**	**9**	**12+**
Nursery Necessities					
Cradle/bassinet					
Crib/Mattress					
Dresser					
Glider Rocker					
Bedding: Cradle					
Bedding: Crib					
Clothing					
Caps/Hats					
Blanket Sleepers					
Layette Gowns					
Booties					
All other layette					
Around the House					
Baby Monitor					
Baby Food (solid)					
High Chairs					
Places to Go					
Infant Car Seat					
Convertible Car Seat*					
Full-size Stroller/Stroller Frame					
Umbrella Stroller					
Front Carrier					
Backpack Carrier					
Safety items					

*You can use a convertible car seat starting immediately with that first ride home from the hospital. However, it is our recommendation that you use an infant car seat for the first six months or so, then, when baby grows out of it, buy the convertible car seat.

you have the 10th edition. The second number indicates the printing—every time we reprint the book, we make minor corrections, additions and changes. Version 10.0 is the initial printing of the 10th edition, version 10.1 is the first reprint of the 10th edition and so on.

So, how can you tell if your book is current or woefully out-of-date? Go to our web page at BabyBargains.com and click on Book and then "Which version?"—this shows the most current version. (One clue: look at the book's cover. We note the edition number on each cover. And we change the color of the cover with each edition.) We update this book every two years (roughly). About 30% to 40% of the content will change with each edition. Bottom line: if you pick up a copy of this book that is one or two editions old, you will notice a significant number of changes.

2 **I AM LOOKING FOR A SPECIFIC PRODUCT BUT I DON'T KNOW WHERE TO START! HELP!** Yep, this book is 600+ pages long and we realize it can be a bit intimidating. But you have a friend in the index—flip to the back of the book to look up just about anything. You can look up items by category, brand name and more. If that doesn't work, try the table of contents. We sort the book into major topic areas (strollers, car seats, etc).

FYI: some companies have sub-brands—we list these aliases alphabetically and refer you to the main company review (for example, Baby Cache cribs are made by Munire; we discuss Baby Cache in Munire's review.)

3 **WHY DO YOU CHARGE A SEPARATE FEE FOR YOUR WEB SITE?** There are two parts to our web site at BabyBargains.com: free and paid (subscriber's only).

The free side includes our blog, which tracks the latest news on baby gear, safety recalls and more. Our message boards are also free (and ad-free). We also post "bonus material" online for free—these are reviews of smaller companies that didn't fit in our book.

The paid or subscriber side of our web site (called Reviews) includes all the reviews you see in this book, plus a few online exclusives (example: baby food processors).

We charge for a separate subscription fee because we know some folks prefer online access to the book; and others want both online and offline access. Bandwidth and web programming are expensive, so in order to maintain a quality digital experience without any advertising, we charge a small subscription fee.

While the reviews online basically duplicate what we have in book form, we are able to update the web site reviews with any changes that happen after we go to press (pricing, recalls, new products, etc).

FYI: We sell a bundle of both the print book and web site access at a discounted price online. If you purchased the book in a bookstore and discover you'd also like a web site subscription, email us a copy of your receipt (authors@babybargains.com) with the magic words (We love Baby Bargains!) and we'll send you a discount code.

4 **CAN I ASK A QUESTION?** Sure, our door is always open—email us at authors@babybargains.com. We value your feedback, so feel free to tell us how to make our book or web site better.

5 **WHY DO YOU SOMETIMES RECOMMEND A MORE EXPENSIVE PRODUCT THAN A CHEAPER OPTION?** Yes, this is a book about bargains, but sometimes we will pick a slightly more expensive item in a category if we believe it is superior in quality or safety. In some cases, it makes sense to invest in better-quality products that will last through more than one child. And don't forget about the hassle of replacing a cheap product that breaks in six months.

To be sure, however, we recognize that many folks are on tight budgets. To help, we offer "Good, Better, Best" product suggestions that are typically sorted by price (good is most affordable, best is usually more expensive). Don't torture yourself if you can't afford the "best" in every category; a "good" product will be just as, well, good.

Another note: remember that our brand reviews cover many options in a category, not just the cheapest. Don't be dismayed if we give an expensive brand an "A" rating—such ratings are often based on quality, construction, innovation and more. Yes, we will try to identify the best values in a category as well. But we realize that some folks want to spend more on certain items (car seats, for example)—hence we try to identify the best of the best, not just the cheapest.

Why does our advice sometimes conflict with other publications like *Consumer Reports*? Simple reason: we have different research methods. Most *Consumer Reports* reviews are based on lab tests; we relied on more on parent feedback, culled from hundreds (and sometimes thousands) of reviews and emails. That's our secret sauce.

More often than not, our picks and *Consumer Reports* usually match; when we don't agree, we try to point out the differences, both in our book and blog. Of course, we review and rate many more baby products than *Consumer Reports*, as our focus is just baby gear. We know you want in-depth info to make the best decisions . . . that's why we're here.

6 **WHAT OTHER PARENTING BOOKS DO YOU PUBLISH?** Yes, we do have three other best-selling books: *Expecting 411, Baby 411* and *Toddler 411*. Co-authored by an award-winning pediatrician, these books answer your questions about pregnancy, your baby's sleep, nutrition and more. See the back of this book for details.

Get social

Social media sites like Groupon.com are an important new tool in the bargain hunter's toolbox. In case you're new to this world, let's go over a couple of tips on how to use social media to rack up baby bargains.

◆ **Deal of the day sites.** Localized to major cities, sites like Groupon.com post discounted deals every day—restaurants, retail stores, magazine subscriptions and more. When it comes to baby stuff, we've seen 50% off coupons to local baby stores, discounts from local baby proofers and more. Here's how it works: deals change by the day, you buy the certificate the day it appears on Groupon, typically within six hours or before it sells out. Then you take the certificate to the store, restaurant or other location and use it like a prepaid gift card. Share the deal on your Facebook or Twitter page.

◆ **Go deeper.** Of course, there is more than just Groupon! We have a list of deal of the day sites on our web site at BabyBargains.com/deals. We also recommend checking out DailyDeals.Oohey.com, which aggregates deals from Groupon and several other sites.

◆ **Don't forget:** regular web sites offer deals of the day. Examples include Target, Garnet Hill, Amazon and more. These are typically limited time specials on a small selection of items. Example: TinySoles.com has a Daily Deal. When we last looked at the site, a Pediped shoe for toddlers that retailed for $45 was on sale for $27. Many of these sites post their deals on their Facebook and Twitter feeds—like or subscribe to keep tabs on sales.

◆ **Cash Back/Rewards sites.** If you are a heavy online shopper, consider signing up with an online cash back or rewards site. Ebates.com is probably the most well known—you earn cash back when you shop any one of 1200 web sites. Ebates also sends out coupons and promo codes for major sites. Upromise.com is a similar site that helps you pay for a child's college tuition. A great site that compares rebates from various sites is eReward.com.

What's New in This Edition?

Welcome to the 10th edition—this year marks our 20th year of covering the baby biz. Yes, we started writing this book way back in the Clinton administration!

As always, we've added dozens of brand reviews for cribs, car seats and strollers. New this year: more eco-friendly baby products. We focus on green cribs and nursery furniture, with an expanded look at eco-friendly crib mattresses.

We've beefed up our car seat reviews with the government's ease of use ratings. And the booster seat reviews now include whether the seat is recommended by the Insurance Institute for Highway Safety.

Look for expanded reviews of carriers in this book, with a model-by-model look at the top brands. We've increased our coverage of video baby monitors, with new reviews of models that are much better than in years' past.

Of course, we've kept the features you love about *Baby Bargains*, including those nifty comparison charts that sum up our picks and our ever-popular baby registry at-a-glance (Appendix B).

Don't forget to check out our extensive online offerings—click on the Bargain forum on our message boards (shortcut: BabyBargains.com/coupons) to get news on the latest discount codes and more. Our "Bargain Alert" message board has dozens of posts by readers each day, sharing deals, steals and more.

E-books, PDF's and more

Baby Bargains is more than just a book. Got a Kindle? Nook? iPad? You can now read our book as an ebook on these devices. Bonus: the Apple iBook version of this book is enhanced with color photography and how-to videos. This works exclusively on iPads.

Want to get an updated chapter from this book? You can download a PDF of our latest research direct from our web page. That way if you just want to read about the latest strollers, you can get just that chapter for much less than buying the entire book again. Or you can subscribe to our online reviews for just 30 days to get updates.

Check our web page at BabyBargains.com for the latest news on all these new versions of *Baby Bargains*. Or email us at authors@BabyBargains.com if you have a question or suggestion.

Let's Go Shopping!

Now that all the formal introductions are done, let's move on to the good stuff. As your tour guides to BabyLand, we'd like to remind you of one key rule: the Baby Biz is just that—business.

The juvenile products industry is a $9.8 BILLION DOLLAR business. While all those baby stores may want to help you, they are first and foremost in business to make a profit. As a consumer, you should arm yourself with the knowledge necessary to make smart decisions. So let's get rolling!

CHAPTER 2

Nursery Necessities:
Cribs, Dressers & More

Inside this chapter

How can you save 20% to 50% off cribs, dressers, and other furniture for your baby's room? In this chapter, you'll learn these secrets, plus discover smart shopper tips that help clarify all those confusing crib options and features. Then, you'll learn which juvenile furniture has safety problems and where to go online to find the latest recall info. Next, we'll rate and review over 40 top brands of cribs, focusing on quality and value. Finally, you'll learn which crib mattress is best, how to get a deal on a dresser, and several more items to consider for your baby's room.

Getting Started:
When Do You Need This Stuff?

So, you want to buy a crib for Junior? And, what the heck, why not some other furniture, like a dresser to store all those baby gifts and a changing table for, well, you know. Just pop down to the store, pick out the colors, and set a delivery date, right?

Not so fast, o' new parental one. Once you get to that baby store, you'll discover that most don't have all those nice cribs and furniture *in stock*. No, that would be too easy, wouldn't it? You will quickly learn that you have to *special order* much of that booty.

To be fair, we should note that in-stock items vary from store to store. Some (especially the larger chain stores) may stock a fair number of cribs. Yet Murphy's Law says the last in-stock crib you want was just sold five minutes ago. And while stores may stock a good number of cribs, dressers are another story—these bulky items almost always must be special-ordered.

So, let's cut to chase: when should you order nursery furniture? The answer depends on WHERE you plan to buy furniture. *If you choose an independent baby store, order at your 20th week of pregnancy.* Yes, it really takes 10-14 weeks on average to have specialty-store nursery furniture ordered and delivered (we figured you want it there a few weeks before baby arrives!).

Major caveat: some brands take as long as 16 weeks to order . . . ask your local retailer for advice, as lead times for brands can shift.

What about chain stores like Babies R Us? You need less time than specialty stores, but it isn't lighting quick either. Babies R Us says IF the furniture is in stock at their warehouse, it takes seven to 21 business days to be delivered to a store. If the furniture is NOT in stock, you'll have to wait for four to six weeks. Bottom line: *if you choose a chain store, order at your 25th week of pregnancy.* That way you have left plenty of time, even if the furniture is on a six-week delay.

Why does it take so long to get nursery furniture? Most furniture today is made in Asia (primarily China). Manufacturers wait until they receive enough orders of a certain collection before they go into production. Then the furniture is loaded into a shipping container and sent on a four-to-six week ocean journey to the U.S. Assuming all goes well (no hurricanes, port strikes, etc.), the furniture is delivered to a manufacturer's distribution center. From there, it is trucked to the retailer.

Yes, you might get lucky and find your nursery furniture in stock at a manufacturer or retailer's warehouse. But don't bet on it.

We should note that some parents wait until after a baby is born to take delivery of nursery furniture. Why? Certain religious and ethnic customs say it is bad luck to have any baby gear in the house before baby is born. These families will order baby furniture, but not have it delivered until baby is born—needless to say, if you go this route, you have to find a retailer willing to store your furniture until that time.

First-time parent question: so, how long will baby use a crib? Answer: it depends. Most babies will use a crib for two or three years. Yes, some babies are out of the crib by 18 months, while others may be pushing four years. One key factor: when does baby learn they can climb out of the crib? Once that happens, the crib days are numbered, as you can understand. Of course, there may be other factors that push baby out of a crib—if you are planning to have a second child and want the crib for the new baby, it may be time to transition to a "big boy/girl" bed. We discuss more about the transition out of a crib in our other book, *Toddler 411*. See the back of this book for more info.

Cribs: Sources to Find

This year, more than one million households plan to buy infant/nursery furniture, according to a survey by *Kids Today*. That translates into $1.8 billion in sales of infant furniture—yes, this is big business. In their quest for the right nursery, parents have four basic sources for finding a crib, each with its own advantages and drawbacks:

1 **INDEPENDENT BABY SPECIALTY STORES.** Indie baby specialty stores are pretty self-explanatory—shops that specialize in the retailing of baby furniture, strollers, and accessories. Independents come in all sizes: some are small boutiques; others are as large as a chain superstore. A good number of indie retailers have joined together in "buying groups" to get volume discounts on items from suppliers—these groups include Baby Furniture Plus (babyfurnitureplus.com), Baby News (BabyNewsStores.com), NINFRA (ninfra. com) and USA Baby (USAbaby.com). Other good resources to find a specialty store near you are BabyProductExperts.com and Brixy.com.

Like other independent stores, many baby specialty shops have been hard hit by the expansion of national chains like Babies R Us. Yet, those that have survived do so by emphasizing service and products you can't find at the chains. Of course, quality of service can vary widely from store to store . . . but just having a breathing human to ask a question of is a nice plus.

The problems with specialty stores? Readers complain the stores only carry expensive brands. One parent told us the only baby specialty store in her town doesn't carry any cribs under $600. We understand the dilemma faced by mom and pop retailers—in order to provide all that service, they have to make a certain profit margin on furniture and other products. And that margin is easier to get on high-end goods. That's all well and good, but failing to carry products in entry-level price points only drives parents to the chains.

Another gripe with some indie stores: some shops can be downright hostile to you if they think you are price-shopping. A reader said she found this out when comparing high-end nursery furniture in her town. "When I asked to price cribs and dressers at two baby stores, I met with resistance and hostility. At one store, I was asked if I was a 'spy' for their competition! The store managers at both baby stores I visited said they didn't want people to comparison shop them on price, yet both advertise they will 'meet or beat' the competition's prices."

The bottom line: despite the hassles, if you have a locally owned baby store in your town, give them a shot. Don't assume chains always have lower prices and better selection. See the box nearby

The Best Baby Stores in America

Who are the best independent baby stores in America? In researching this book, we have visited hundreds of baby stores from coast to coast during the past 15 years. Along the way, we've met some of the smartest retailers In the U.S.—folks we often turn to to find out what's REALLY happening in the baby gear biz. Which cribs, strollers and car seats are selling and winning raves from parents . . . and what are the bombs.

Readers often tell us they want to support indie stores—but which ones are most reputable? If you are tired of the chains, we offer our list of stores to check out.

A few notes: just in case you are wondering, NO retailers paid us to be on this list. We don't take advertising, commissions or fees to recommend stores in our book or blog. The retailers we think are best earned it the old fashioned way—by focusing on their customers.

We compiled this list from reader feedback and store visits; we also asked baby gear manufacturers to name their top retailers. This list focuses on baby stores in major metro areas (with a few exceptions). Most of these stores sell baby furniture/products in a wide range of prices; these aren't expensive boutiques, but mainstream retailers.

So . . . drum roll . . . here are the Best Baby Stores in America (in alphabetical order):

Baby Furniture Plus (North and South Carolina)
Baby Super Mart (Broomall, PA)
Baby's & Kid's 1st (Houston, TX)
Behr's (Metro NY)
Berg's Baby & Teen (Cleveland, OH)
Cribs to College Bedrooms (Naperville, IL)
Galt Toys + Galt Baby (Chicago)
Georgia Baby and Kids (Atlanta)
Great Beginnings (Washington DC: Maryland, Virginia)
Ideal Baby & Kids (Miami); also known as La Ideal.
Juvenile Shop (Sherman Oaks, CA)
Kids Stuff Superstores (South Dakota, Nebraska)
Lazar's (Chicago)
Magic Beans (Boston metro, Connecticut)
Planet Kids (New York City)
Treasures Room (St Louis)

for our picks of the top indie baby stores in the U.S.

2 **THE CHAINS.** There are two types of chains that sell baby products: specialty chains like Babies R Us and Buy Buy Baby who focus on juvenile products and discounters like Walmart, Target, and Kmart that have small baby departments. We'll discuss each in-depth later in this chapter. The selection at chains can vary widely—some carry more premium brands, but most concentrate on mass-market names to appeal to price-conscious shoppers. Service? Fuggedaboutit—often, you'll be lucky to find someone to help you check out, much less answer questions.

In recent years, we've seen a third type of chain enter the baby market: specialty chains such as Pottery Barn Kids (PBK) and Restoration Hardware. The former has stores that sell some baby furniture; the latter (Restoration Hardware) has an online-only baby boutique.

3 **ONLINE.** Long before the web, companies tried to sell furniture via mail order, albeit with mixed results. Perhaps the best example is JCPenney (jcpenney.com), whose mail-order catalog (and now web site) specializes in affordable cribs and dressers. Despite the challenge of shipping bulky items like dressers, web sites and specialty retailers are still piling into the online nursery niche. We'll discuss the pros and cons if this approach later in the chapter.

Some web sites try a hybrid approach: online and retail. The RightStart.com has nine stores including a Denver flagship that has nursery furniture displays. You can see it in the store and then have it drop-shipped to your home.

Even if you decide to order your entire nursery online, there are several roadblocks. Given the weight and bulk of cribs and dressers, only a few (mostly lower-end) brands are typically sold online. Shipping charges can be exorbitant—and that assumes you can get items shipped at all (most sites don't ship furniture to Hawaii, Alaska, Canada or military addresses). With shipping, you then have the issue of damage, delays and worse. Given the limitations of drop-shipped furniture delivery, it is more realistic to use online sites to buy accessories (lamps, rockers, décor) for your nursery rather than an entire furniture suite.

4 **REGULAR FURNITURE STORES.** You don't have to go to a "baby store" to buy juvenile furniture. Many regular furniture stores sell name-brand cribs, dressers and other nursery items. Since these stores have frequent sales, you may be able to get a better price than at a juvenile specialty store. On the other hand, the salespeople may not be as knowledgeable about brand and safety issues.

What Are You Buying?

Ok, let's break this down. Outfitting a nursery usually means buying three basic furniture items: a crib, dresser (which doubles as a place to change baby's diaper) and rocker. Here's a quick discussion of each.

◆ **Crib.** Crib prices start at $100 for an inexpensive crib at a discounter like Walmart. The mid-range for cribs is probably best typified by what you see at chains stores such as Babies R Us and Baby Depot—most of their cribs are in the $250 to $600 range (the stores seem to be a bit more pricey while their online sites offer more lower price options). Specialty stores and catalogs tend to carry upper-end cribs that run $400 to $1000. And what about the top end? We'd be remiss not to mention the modern-design and solid wood cribs, which run $1000 to $2000.

Surprise! The vast majority of cribs don't come with mattresses; those are sold separately ($60 to $350). Bedding is also extra ($100 to $500). We'll discuss mattresses later in this chapter; bedding gets its own entire chapter (Chapter 3).

◆ **Dresser.** Most nurseries need a place to store clothes, diapers, supplies and so on. Known in the baby biz as case pieces (because they are, uh, a case), dressers range from simple, ready-to-assemble four-drawer chests to elaborate armoires (and their smaller cousins, chiffarobes).

Now, there is no federal law that says you MUST buy a dresser or armoire that exactly matches the finish of your crib. Some folks simply re-purpose a dresser from another room to baby's nursery—or pick up a dresser second-hand or at a discount from a regular furniture store. That's fine, of course.

But . . . we realize the allure of matching nursery furniture convinces many new parents to pony up the bucks. So here are some general price guidelines: a ready-to-assemble dresser from IKEA or a discount store runs $150 to $200.

Now, if you'd like to have something fancier (and already assembled), prices for dressers range from $200 to $800 in chain stores. Step into a specialty store and you'll find plenty of fancy dressers, armoires and chiffarobes . . . for $500 to $1000 and higher.

Most dressers also double as a place to change baby—some have tops specifically designed for that purpose. These changer tops remove after baby is done with diapers (usually right before college). So most parents today do not need to buy a separate changing table.

◆ **Rocker.** A place to sit and nurse baby is an important part of any nursery's function—so the next question is . . . where to sit? Again, you can re-purpose a rocker from grandma's house or pick up one secondhand. If you have the room, a small loveseat or over-sized chair is a workable solution for nursing baby.

Brand new "glider-rockers" run the gamut from wooden chairs with thin pads to fully upholstered models. And the price range reflects this: you can spend as little as $100 to $200 for a rocker from Target or Walmart . . . as much as $1300 for a tricked out leather model from a specialty store. Most folks probably buy a basic model from chain stores like Babies R Us for about $300. Yes, ottomans are a nice extra—but cost $100 to $300 more.

Glider rockers get their own section later in this chapter.

The Grand Total. As you can see, the bare-bones budget for a nursery would be $600 (simple crib, mattress, basic dresser and rocker). The mid-range would run about $1100 . . . and on the designer end, you could easily spend $2000 to $3000 on nursery furniture.

And these figures are BEFORE you get to any of the other décor items: bedding, lamps, paint, artwork, curtains, etc.

More Money Buys You . . .

Here's a little secret expensive crib makers don't want you to hear: ALL new cribs (no matter what price) sold in the U.S. or Canada must meet federal safety standards. Yes, the governments of both the U.S. and Canada strictly regulate crib safety and features—that's one reason why most cribs have the same basic design, no matter the brand or price. So, whether you buy a $150 crib special at a discount store or a $1500 wrought iron crib at a posh specialty boutique, either way you get a crib that meets federal safety requirements.

Now, that said, when you spend more money, there are some perks. The higher the price-tag of the crib (generally), the fancier the design (thicker corner posts, designer colors, etc.). That's nice, but is it really necessary? No—a basic, safe crib in a simple finish is all a baby needs.

The biggest sales pitch for cribs is convertibility: more expensive cribs are convertible. They morph into beds for older kids: toddler bed (basically, a crib with one side removed and a short rail), day bed (no rail) and (finally) full-sized bed. That latter uses the sides of the crib to become a headboard and footboard—some cribs even transform into queen-size adult beds.

Convertible cribs are pitched to parents as "lifetime cribs" (your child will take the bed to college with them, we suppose) and smart investments, because it "grows with your child." Here's what the pitch leaves out: to convert the crib, you often have to buy a conversion kit (sold separately, naturally). And think about the SIZE of

Three Golden Rules of Buying Nursery Furniture

◆ **Don't over buy**—think about your needs first. Here's a common first time parent mistake: rushing out to a local baby store and falling in love with that fancy cognac finish on a chif-farobe. Instead, think about what you really NEED. Start with the size of your baby's nursery—most secondary bedrooms in a typical suburban home are small (10' x12' is common). That barely leaves room for a crib, dresser and rocker. Don't let a baby store sell you on a double dresser PLUS an armoire when you don't have room. For urban apartment dwellers, space is at a premium. Closets need to be tricked out to provide maximum storage. Expect furniture to do double duty.

◆ **Three words: set a budget.** Don't waste your time with designer furniture if you haven't done the math. As you saw from the discussion on the last few pages, a three-piece nursery set (crib, dresser, rocker) runs anywhere from $600 . . . up to $3000. Pick a budget and stick with it. Then read the brand reviews later in this chapter—you'll quickly realize which ones are in your budget and which aren't! Again, it pays to think outside the box: can you re-purpose a dresser from another room? Get a hand-me-down rocker from a friend or off Craigslist?

◆ **Decide on nursery style.** There are two theories of nursery design: either a baby's room should look, well, baby-ish . . . or it should be more adult-looking, able to adapt as the child grows. There is no right or wrong answer. If you subscribe to the baby-theme, then go with a simple (non-convertible) crib and dresser that you will later swapped out for a twin bed and computer desk/hutch. If you prefer the other path, then buy a convertible crib (which converts to a full size bed) and dresser that can do double duty. Some brands have dressers that are first a changing area for diapers . . . and then convert to a computer area complete with pull out keyboard drawer.

the average kids' bedroom these days: most can barely squeeze in a TWIN bed and dresser . . . a full or queen size bed is often impossible. We'll discuss this issue more, later in the chapter.

Some crib extras also have dubious value—take the under-crib storage drawer. Often seen on cribs that run $500 or more, this feature appeals to parents who have a storage crunch in their home (you can put blankets, extra clothes in the drawer). The problem? The drawer usually doesn't have a top. So, anything inside will be a dust magnet.

Ok, so now you know the typical prices of nursery furniture . . . and what more money really buys you. How do you decide what is best for your baby's nursery? See the previous box for our Three Golden Rules of Buying Nursery Furniture.

Safe & Sound

Here's a fact to keep you up at night: cribs are the third-biggest cause of injuries and deaths among all nursery products. In the latest year for which statistics are available, 12,200 injuries and 49 deaths were blamed on cribs and mattresses.

You may recall the massive safety recalls of cribs during the past decade. That's because the government changed the safety standards for cribs in 2011, outlawing previously legal drop-size cribs. These new rules also mandated strength requirements for side rails.

Even with the new safety rules, there are some basic guidelines when it comes to buying safe nursery furniture. Here's an overview:

◆ **Don't buy a used or old crib.** Let's put that into bold caps: DON'T BUY A USED OR OLD CRIB. And don't take a hand-me-down from a well-meaning friend or relative. Why? Because old cribs account for most of the injuries and deaths when it comes to cribs. Surprisingly, these old cribs may not be as old as you think—cribs made before 2011 don't meet current standards.

Most folks realize that cribs made in the 70's and 80's aren't safe . . . but that never seems to stop a well-meaning relative to bring down a "family heirloom" crib from the attic. These are death traps. spindles that are too far apart, cutouts in the headboard, and other hazards that could entrap your baby. Decorative trim (like turned posts) that looks great on adult beds are a major no-no for cribs—they present a strangulation hazard. (Note: cribs with TALL posts are fine; it is the shorter posts that are prohibited—see the graphic on the next page).

Some old cribs have lead paint, a dangerous peril for a teething baby. Another hazard to hand-me-down cribs (regardless of age):

missing parts and directions. It only takes one missing screw or bolt to make an otherwise safe crib into a danger. Without directions, you can incorrectly assemble the crib and create additional safety hazards. So, even if your friend wants to give/sell you a recent model crib, you could still have problems if parts or directions are missing.

It may seem somewhat ironic that a book on baby bargains would advise you to go out and spend your hard earned money on a new crib. True, we find great bargains on Craigslist and second-hand stores. However, you have to draw the line at your baby's safety. Certain second-hand items are great deals—toys and clothes come to mind. However, cribs (and, as you'll read later, car seats) are no-no's, no matter how tempting the bargains.

And second hand stores have a spotty record when it comes to selling safe products. A recent report from the CPSC said that a whopping two-thirds of all U.S. thrift/second-hand stores sell baby products that have been recalled, banned or do not meet current safety standards (specifically 12% of stores stocked old cribs). Even though recently strengthened laws prevent the resale of banned products like drop-side cribs, some second-hand stores still sell these items, either knowingly or unknowingly in violation of the law.

Readers often ask us why we don't give tips for evaluating old or hand-me-down cribs. The reason is simple: it's hard to tell whether an old crib is dangerous just by looking at it. Cribs don't always have "freshness dates"—some manufacturers don't stamp the date of manufacture on their cribs. Was the crib made before or after the current safety standards went into effect in 2011? Often, you can't tell.

Today's safety regulations are so specific (example: strength of

No corner post extensions

No decorative cut-outs on the headboard or footboard

Drop-sides now banned

Smooth corners

Slat space 2-3/8 inches

Snug mattress fit

Mattress support hangers are secured

Older cribs typically have many hazards. Here's a graphic of what is dangerous. Note: all new cribs sold today are required by law to NOT have any of these features.

side slats) that you just can't judge a crib's safety with a cursory examination. Another problem: if the brand name is rubbed off, it will be hard to tell if the crib has been involved in a recall. Obtaining replacement parts is also difficult for a no-name crib.

What about floor model cribs? Is it safe to buy a crib that has been used as a floor sample in a baby store? Yes—as long as it is in good working condition, has no missing/broken parts, etc. Floor model cribs CAN take a tremendous amount of abuse from parents, who shake them to check stability and so on. As a result, the bolts that hold the crib together can loosen. Obviously, that can be fixed (just have the store tighten the bolts) . . . and as a result, we think floor model cribs are fine. That isn't what we mean by avoiding a "used" crib!

What if a relative insists you should use that "family heirloom" crib we mentioned earlier? We've spoken to dozens of parents who felt pressured into using an old crib by a well-meaning relative. There's a simple answer: don't do it. As a parent, you sometimes have to make unpopular decisions that are best for your child's safety. This is just the beginning.

◆ **Cribs with fold-down rails.** A handful of cribs have fold-down rails— the upper one-third of the railing is hinged and folds down. These are also called swing gate cribs (see picture).

One major crib maker uses these rails for some of their models: Baby's Dream. While we like the quality of Baby's Dream's furniture overall, we do not recommend any crib with a fold down rail. Why? Older babies who can stand (which happens around a year of age) can get a foothold on the hinged rail to climb out of the crib, injuring themselves as they fall to the floor.

A reader in Seattle, WA recently emailed us with exactly that story: her 13 month old son fractured his fibula (calf bone) after falling out of his Baby's Dream drop-gate crib. "We liked how the drop gate was easy to operate and worked better for a shorter person," she said. "However, we didn't foresee that the drop gate would provide a ledge for him to prop his foot on and fall out."

We should point out that even though swing gate cribs ARE legal (they meet the new safety standard), we don't personally recommend them based on our own research and opinion.

◆ **Inspect monthly.** Many cribs that were recalled in the past year had defective hardware or spindles that broke. While drop-side cribs (which had more hardware failures than static side cribs) are no longer on the market, all cribs should be inspected monthly. Make sure all bolts are tightened, no slats are loose, etc.

The new 2011 crib safety standards require hardware that doesn't need to be retightened—however, wood furniture is wood furniture. Changes in humidity or temperatures in a nursery may still require hardware or bolts to be tightened from time to time.

If a part has broken on your crib, immediately stop using it. Don't attempt to repair it yourself—and never use a crib with missing, broken or loose parts.

◆ **Lead paint.** The lead paint scare of 2007 is still fresh in the minds of many consumers—and that concern has translated into fears of cribs made in China. So, here's the scoop:

While there have been numerous toys and other children's products recalled for lead paint, there was only one nursery furniture recall for this reason (Munire recalled 3000 cribs and 5000 matching dressers for lead paint in 2008). Most nursery furniture companies have their paint and stains independently tested to verify they are lead-free—one (Sorelle) even posts its test results online. Yet, as the Munire recall shows, even a diligent company can have lapses.

Still, we realize some folks still don't trust China and want to avoid Chinese-made furniture. To help, we have a box on later in this chapter in the brand reviews that lists all the nursery furniture makers who make their furniture in countries other than China.

◆ **Formaldehyde.** Most of us are familiar with this chemical from those middle school biology classes. A gas at room temperature, formaldehyde is an organic compound that was classified as a probable human carcinogen back in 1987. It is linked to increased risk of childhood asthma and allergies.

Of course, you probably don't plan to be dissecting frogs in your child's nursery, so there's no need to worry about formaldehyde, right? Wrong—formaldehyde sneaks into your house in other ways. It is found in furniture, specifically the glue in engineered wood products like particle board, chip board and some types of medium density fiberboard (MDF).

The Environmental Protection Agency regulates the amount of formaldehyde that can off-gas from furniture and other wood products. And some states (California) have even stricter limits. In fact, the state of California sued five baby furniture makers in 2008 for unsafe levels of formaldehyde. The suit was prompted by a report from Environment California, which found certain furniture items from Child Craft, Delta, Stork Craft, South Shore and Dorel had unsafe levels of the chemical.

So how can you avoid this hazard in your nursery? One alternative is to stick with solid wood furniture, but this can be pricey (that's why furniture makers use engineered wood like MDF and particle board: it's cheaper). A second recommendation is to consider furniture that is GREENGUARD certified (greenguard.org). In order to pass this certification process, furniture must meet strict chemical emission limits.

Yes, it is an environmental paradox: engineered wood products like MDF are better for the environment, since you don't have to cut down a tree to make a dresser. But the resin that holds MDF together can contain formaldehyde, which contributes to bad indoor air quality. To get around this conundrum, some eco-friendly nursery companies claim they use MDF that has low-emission glue. While this is hard to verify this, this might be something to consider if you have a history of allergies and/or asthma in your family.

Another obvious tip: if your freshly-delivered nursery furniture has a strong chemical smell, let it air out before baby arrives. If it continues to stink, don't use it.

◆ **Stripped screws.** Cheap cribs often have screws that attach directly to the wood of the headboard. The problem? The screws can strip over time (especially if the crib is assembled several times) and that can weaken the crib's support . . . which is very dangerous. If you ever discover you are not able to tighten the screws or bolts used to hold your crib together, immediately stop using it. When you are crib shopping, look at how the mattress support is attached to the headboards—look for metal screwed into metal.

◆ **Be aware of the hazards of putting a baby in an adult bed.** Co-sleeping is where a baby shares a bed with adults. While common in other parts of the world, co-sleeping is controversial here in the U.S.—on one side are attachment parenting advocates who insist it is safe, a big convenience for nursing moms and an important part of parent/child emotional bonds.

On the other side are safety advocates, including the Consumer Product Safety Commission and the American Academy of Pediatrics. A CPSC report blamed 122 infant deaths in a previous three-year period on co-sleeping. Of those deaths, many were caused when a child's head became entrapped between the adult bed and another object (a headboard, footboard, wall, etc). Other deaths were caused by falls or suffocation in bedding. The American Academy of Pediatrics agreed with the CPSC's concerns, issuing a recommendation against co-sleeping in 2005 and again in 2011.

We have an expanded discussion of this debate in our other book, *Baby 411*. Our basic advice: the safest place for a baby to sleep is a separate sleep space (a crib or bassinet that meets current safety standards).

◆ **When assembling a crib, make sure ALL the bolts and screws are tightened**. A recent report on *Good Morning America* pointed out how dangerous it can be to put your baby in a miss-assembled crib—a child died in a Child Craft crib when he became trapped in a side rail that wasn't properly attached to the crib. How did that happen? The parent didn't tighten the screws that held the side rail to the crib. Cribs (including the Child Craft one here in question) are safe when assembled correctly; just be sure to tighten those bolts!

◆ **Recalls: where to find information.** The U.S. Consumer Product Safety Commission has a toll-free hotline at (800) 638-2772 and web site (cpsc.gov) for the latest recall information on cribs and other juvenile items. Both are easy to use—you can also report any potential hazard you've discovered or an injury to your child caused by a product. FYI: The CPSC takes care of all juvenile product recalls, except for car seats—that's the purview of the National Highway Traffic Safety Administration (nhtsa.gov).

Here's a great new feature on SaferProducts.gov: you can now search for reports of injuries or problems for any product or brand. Filed by consumers, these reports sometimes include company responses.

A great "all-in-one" site for recalls is Recalls.gov. Also: subscribe to our blog—we will send you an email or text message when a product is recalled. Go to BabyBargains.com/blog and enter your email at the box at the right and hit subscribe. It's free!

◆ **Safety is more than a crib.** Be sure to have a smoke and carbon monoxide detector for your baby's nursery. And if you haven't had your home tested for radon yet, this would be a good time. (We discuss radon and other environmental hazards in our book, *Toddler 411*. See the back of this book for details).

 Smart Shopper Tips

Smart Shopper Tip #1
The Art and Science of Selecting the Right Crib.

"How do you evaluate a crib? They all look the same to me. What really makes one different from another?"

Selecting a good crib is more than just picking out the style and finish. You should look under the hood, so to speak. Here are our nine key points to look for when shopping for a crib:

◆ **Brand reputation.** Later in this chapter, we will rate and review the biggest crib brands. Our advice: stick with a brand that gets a B or better rating. We formulate these ratings from parent feedback (some of which is posted on our web site, where readers rate and review various crib brands) as well as our analysis of a brand's track record. We look at recall history, customer service, delivery reliability and overall quality to assign a rating.

◆ **Mattress support.** Look underneath that mattress and see what is holding it up. The best cribs use a metal spring platform or a grid of wooden slats. Other cribs use cheap vinyl straps or a piece of particle board. We think the last two are inferior—vinyl straps aren't as secure as metal springs or wood slats; and concerns have been raised over formaldehyde emissions with particle board (see earlier discussion).

◆ **Static side rails.** All cribs sold in the U.S. and Canada are now stationary or static side cribs. In years past, cribs with drop sides (where one side lowers to give assess to the baby) were linked to numerous safety recalls. Although you won't see drop-side cribs sold in stores, there are still many listed for sale on Craigslist and in second-hand stores—we say avoid them.

One exception to the no-drop side rule: one crib maker, Baby's Dream, still offers some cribs with a fold-down rail. Instead of lowering, the rail has a hinge that allows the top portion to fold down. The CPSC deems these rails to be safe; we aren't big fans of fold-down rails for reasons we outlined earlier in this chapter.

◆ **Hardware/bolts: hidden or exposed?** Some cribs have visible bolts that attach the crib rails to the headboard; others are hidden. Is there a difference in safety or durability? No, it's just aesthetics. The more money you spend, the more likely the hardware/bolts will be hidden.

◆ **How stable is the crib?** Because all cribs sold today have stationary sides, this is less of an issue than in years past. Stationary cribs by virtue of have no moving parts, tend to be more stable then the drop-side cribs of years past. And yes, more expensive cribs are typically heavier with thicker posts and slats than low-priced options—and that makes them more stable.

◆ **How do you move the crib?** Few cribs sold today have wheels. When you move a crib, it is a two-person job. And some cribs weigh in excess of 100 pounds. Never drag a crib across the carpet, as you can damage it. One idea: if your crib has legs or bun feet, use Magic Sliders (magicsliders.com, $7) to make it easier to move a crib to clean or vacuum behind it.

◆ *How easy is it to assemble?* Ask to see those instructions—most stores should have a copy lying around. Make sure they are not indecipherable. Yes, some stores offer set-up and delivery, but with chain superstores, you are typically on your own. Sadly, some crib makers don't put a high priority on easy-to-understand assembly instructions—check first before you buy! The good news: some crib makers now have instructions you can download from their web sites.

◆ *Compare the overall safety features of the crib.* In a section earlier in this book, we discuss crib safety in more detail.

◆ *Which wood is best?* Most cribs are made of hardwoods: birch, beech, mahogany, etc. In recent years, crib makers have also made some models in pine. The problem? Pine is a softwood that isn't as durable as hardwood—it tends to nick, scratch and damage.

FYI: there are many types of pine—some are harder (and more durable) than others. Unfortunately, furniture makers don't tell you they are using red pine (the hardest) versus Eastern White pine (the softest).

To be clear, pine isn't a safety hazard . . . it just isn't as durable. Sometimes this is a price trade-off—later in this chapter, we'll recommend a couple of affordable crib models, two of which are made of pine. For cribs under $200, most of your choices will be pine.

So, which wood is best? If the budget allows, we recommend you go with a hardwood crib—it doesn't matter whether it is birch, beech, mahogany or even ramin (also called rubberwood). The latter is an Asian hardwood that is often seen in low-price cribs.

Another recent trend: modern furniture made of medium-density fiberboard (MDF) with a glossy lacquer finish. Made of wood fibers and resin, MDF has a smooth, grain-free surface, which enables manufacturers to add that high-gloss finish.

We aren't fans of composite wood—MDF simply isn't as durable as hardwood. Yes, we realize fans of modern furniture are more sold on the aesthetic . . . MDF looks cool. But as we discussed earlier, MDF and other engineered wood have been blamed for outgassing of formaldehyde and other chemical emissions that lead to bad indoor air quality.

Another quick point: don't confuse *finish* with wood. Some stores and web sites tout "cherry" cribs when they are actually referring to the finish, not the actual wood. It may be a "cherry" stain, but the wood is probably not.

Smart Shopper Tip #2
Cyber-Nursery: Ordering furniture online

"We don't have any good baby stores nearby, so I want to order furniture online. How do you buy items sight unseen and make sure they arrive in one piece?"

Sure, you can buy just about everything today online, but when it comes to nursery furniture, we have two words of advice: be wary.

Despite the fact that most stores selling nursery items have online sites offering furniture, our readers report that the actual experience of buying a crib or dresser online leaves them frustrated.

You probably guessed the reason: bulk. Cribs and dressers are heavy and bulky—this makes them expensive to ship and susceptible to damage. If there is a problem, you have to deal with a customer service agent half way across the country.

Our advice: order from a local store and have the items delivered/set-up. If the store doesn't have items in stock, see if they have a "site to store" shipping option—you order online, but the item is delivered to a local store where you pick it up. This helps eliminate shipping damage.

Wastes of Money

1 **Low quality "baby" furniture that won't last.** Baby furniture stores (both chains and independents) are sometimes guilty of selling very poor quality furniture. Take a dresser, for example. Many dressers made by juvenile furniture companies have stapled drawers, veneer construction (instead of solid wood), cheap drawer glides and worse. Now, that wouldn't be so bad if such dressers were low in price. But often you see these dressers going for $500 and up in baby stores—basically, you are paying a premium to merely match the color of your crib. While we don't see a problem buying low-end "disposable" furniture at a good price (IKEA is a prime example), paying a fortune for a poorly made dresser is ridiculous. In this chapter, we will point out brand names that provide more quality for the dollar. Look for solid wood construction, dovetail drawers, and smooth drawer glides if you want that dresser to last.

2 **Under-crib drawers.** It sounds like a great way to squeeze out a bit more storage in a nursery—the drawer that slides out from under a crib. Getting a crib with such a feature usually costs an extra $100 or $150. The problem? Most of these drawers do NOT have tops . . . therefore anything kept in there will get dusty in a hurry. So that nixes storing extra blankets or clothes. We say skip the extra expense of an under-crib drawer.

3 **THE TODDLER BED.** Some crib makers tout cribs that convert to toddler beds. This is accomplished by removing the side rail and adding a smaller toddler rail. Smaller than a twin bed, a toddler bed uses the crib mattress and is pitched as a transition between the crib and a big boy/girl bed. But, guess what? Most kids can go straight from a crib to a regular twin bed with no problem whatsoever. The toddler bed is a waste of money, in our opinion.

4 **CRADLE.** Most pediatricians recommend "rooming in" with your newborn to help with breastfeeding. But where will the baby sleep? Cradles and bassinets are one option, but can be pricey. Cradles (basically a mini crib that rocks) run up to $400, while separate bassinets (a basket on a stand) can cost $200. A more affordable solution: just set up the crib in your room. After you establish that breastfeeding rhythm, the baby and crib can move to the nursery. If you don't have room in your master bedroom to set up the crib, consider a playpen with bassinet feature like the Graco Pack N Play. We'll discuss the best buys on bassinets at the end of this chapter; playpens like the Pack N Play are reviewed in Chapter 7, Around the House.

5 **CRIBS WITH "SPECIAL FEATURES."** Some stores carry unique styles of cribs and that might be tempting for parents looking to make a statement for their nursery. An example: round or elliptical cribs. The only problem: special cribs like this may require additional expenses, such as custom-designed mattresses or bedding. And since few companies make bedding for these cribs, your choices are limited. The best advice: make sure you price out the total investment (crib, mattress, bedding) before falling in love with an unusual style.

6 **CHANGING TABLES.** Separate changing tables are a big waste of money. Don't spend $90 to $200 on a piece of furniture you won't use again after your baby gives up diapers. A better bet: buy a dresser that can do double duty as a changing table. Many dressers you'll see in baby stores are designed with this extra feature—just make sure the height is comfortable for both you and your spouse. Other parents we interviewed did away with the changing area altogether—they used a crib, couch or countertop to do diaper changes.

E-Mail from The Real World
Spending $385 for a $50 dresser

A reader in Ohio shared her frustration with a dresser bought online that had significant shipping damage:

"I ordered a three drawer combo dresser from a well-known baby gear web site. It had all of the things suggested in your book and was $385. The manufacturer is Angel Line. The item arrived with split wood on the corner, a knob missing, a missing wall strap and one of the drawers didn't shut completely and was crooked. I called the site and they said I had to contact the manufacturer directly to get the problem resolved. It took four calls and the best I could get was another knob and drawer sent to me with corners that did not fit together. So, I essentially paid $400 for something that looks like a dresser that's $50 at a garage sale."

Top 8 Things Baby Stores Won't Tell You About Buying Nursery Furniture

◆ *Our store may disappear before your nursery furniture arrives.* It's a sad fact: baby stores come and go. Most retailers that close do so reputably—they don't take special orders for merchandise they can't fill. A handful are not so honest . . . they take deposits up until the day the landlord padlocks their doors. Our advice: always charge your purchase to a credit card. If the store disappears, you can dispute the charge with your credit card company and (most likely) get your money back. Another red flag: stores that ask for payment up front on a special order. The typical deal is half down with the balance due upon delivery. Stores that are desperate for cash might demand the entire purchase price upfront. Be suspicious. Another piece of advice: keep a close eye on what's going on with your furniture maker. How? Read our blog or surf our message boards at BabyBargains.com. Over the years, we've seen it all—strikes, floods, fires, port shutdowns and more. You name it, it can happen to the factory that makes your furniture. When we get a whiff of a problem, we blog about it. That way you can switch to another brand if you've haven't placed an order yet . . . or formulate a plan B if your furniture is caught by a delivery delay.

◆ *Never assume something in a sealed box is undamaged.* Always OPEN boxes and inspect furniture before taking it out of a store. Yes, that is a hassle, but we've had numerous complains about boxed furniture that someone has driven 50 miles home, only to discover a major gash or other damage. Or the wrong color is in the right box. Or a major piece is missing. A word to the wise: inspect it BEFORE going home.

◆ **If it is in stock, BUY IT.** Let's say you see a crib that is in stock, but the matching dresser is on back order. Do you get the crib now and wait on the dresser? Or special order both? Our advice: if an item is sitting there in a store (even if it is a floor sample), it is ALWAYS better to take the in-stock item now.

◆ *Your special order merchandise will be backordered until 2016, despite our promise to get it to you before your baby is born.* Almost all furniture today is imported . . . we are not talking from close-by countries like Canada or Mexico. Nope, odds are your furniture will be made in some far flung locale in Asia. A myriad of problems (backorders, labor unrest, port shutdowns, etc.) can delay orders. Our advice: ORDER EARLY. When a store gives you a 10-14 week delivery estimate, remember that is an *estimate*. It can easily morph to 16, 20 or 24 weeks. Build in a cushion just in case.

◆ *Just because the crib maker has an Italian name doesn't mean your furniture is made in, say, Italy.* Prior to the 1990's, you had domestic makers of cribs (Child Craft, Simmons) and the imports, most of which were from Italy. Those days are long gone—today almost all nursery furniture is imported from Asia (specifically, China).

Here's where it gets confusing: sometimes the very same brand will import furniture from different countries. Sorelle, for example, started out as an Italian importer. Today, Sorelle imports most of its cribs and furniture from China . . . but some of its cribs are made in Eastern Europe. Ditto for Bonavita, which despite the Italian sounding name, imports most of its furniture from China and other factories in Asia.

Bottom line: key on the brand's reputation for quality and customer service, not so much the country the crib is made in. Yes, we realize some folks are nervous about Chinese-made products. To address those concerns, we have a box on later in this chapter that points out the brands not made in China. However, we don't think a crib or dresser made in China is inherently dangerous—again, it is the company's reputation for quality and customer service that is key, not the country of origin.

◆ *That special mattress we insist you buy isn't necessary.* Some baby stores are trying a new tactic to sell their pricey in-house brand of crib mattress: scaring the pants off new parents. We've heard all the stories—only OUR mattress fits OUR crib, a less expensive foam mattress is DANGEROUS for your baby and so on. Please! Government standards require both cribs and mattresses to be within standard measurements. Yes, fancy boutiques might make their mattress a bit larger to give a tighter fit . . . but that doesn't mean a regular mattress won't work just as well (and is just as safe). It's no wonder stores push the in-house mattress—it can cost $300 or more. Our advice: save your money and get a plain crib mattress for half the price at another store.

◆ **Just because we say this item is discontinued does NOT mean you can't find it anywhere else.** This is especially true for chain stores—just because Babies R Us says the crib you've fallen in love with is now discontinued does NOT mean you can't find it from another store. That's because chains discontinue items all the time . . . and not just because the manufacturer is discontinuing it. Chains replace slow moving merchandise or just make way for something new. Meanwhile, the very same furniture (or for that matter, any baby gear) is sold down the street at another store.

◆ **The finish on that expensive special-order dresser may match your crib . . . or not.** Here's something baby stores don't advertise: the finishes on that expensive nursery furniture you special ordered may not match. Why? Many furniture companies use different wood for different pieces—say birch for a crib, but pine for a dresser. The problem: each takes stain differently. As a result, a birch crib in cherry may not match a pine dresser in the same cherry stain. While the difference may be small, it bugs some folks more than others. The take home message: if matching stain is important to you, confirm all the pieces of your furniture are made of the same wood—and try to see a sample of the stain on a real piece of furniture to confirm colors (don't rely on online photos).

 ## Money Saving Secrets

1 **CHECK OUT REGULAR FURNITURE STORES FOR ROCKERS, DRESSERS, ETC.** Think about it—most juvenile furniture looks very similar to regular adult furniture. Rockers, dressers, and bookcases are, well, just rockers, dressers, and bookcases. And don't you wonder if companies slap the word "baby" on an item just to raise the price 20%? To test this theory, we visited a local discount furniture store. The prices were incredibly low. A basic four-drawer pine dresser was $200. Even maple or oak four-drawer dressers were just $350. The same quality dresser at a baby store by a "juvenile furniture" manufacturer would set you back at least $500, if not twice that.

We even saw cribs by such mainstream names as Bassett at decent prices in regular furniture stores. What's the disadvantage to shopping there? Well, if you have to buy the crib and dresser at different places, the colors might not match exactly. But, considering the savings, it might be worth it.

2 **GET SOCIAL.** Social media is more than just status updates and tweets—sign up for "deal of the day sites" like Groupon or Zulily.com. As the name implies, deal of the day sites have one great deal (up to 70% off) available for a limited time. For Groupon, that might be a 50% discount on a local maternity store. Zulily, founded by the folks who started Blue Nile, offers cribs, designer kids clothes and baby gear at deep discounts. Of course, part of the fun with these sites is sharing the deals with your friends on Facebook.

3 **THINK TWICE ABOUT MOD.** Modern furniture is the rage in high-end boutiques, but what do you get for that ultra-mod look? Many "modern" cribs and furniture are made of MDF, particle board and laminates . . . and for this you're supposed to shell out $1000 for a crib and $1600 for a dresser? Can someone explain to us why modern furniture costs TWICE as much as "regular" cribs and dressers that are made of all wood? Sure that mod furniture has a few extra coats of lacquer and looks all shiny. But we still don't get it—especially since nearly all nursery furniture (yes, even the mod stuff) is imported from Asia. Our advice: If you decide to go mod, stick with the more affordable options like IKEA (even Walmart now sells a modern furniture collection at reasonable prices).

4 **COMPARE ONLINE PRICES.** Do you wonder if that local baby store has jacked up the price of nursery furniture? We know some of you live in towns or communities with little or no local competition for nursery items. One solution: hit the web. Now, we realize we listed all sorts of caveats for online orders earlier in the book (high shipping fees, problems with damage, etc)—but let's face it. In some parts of the country, this is really your best option. As always, don't ASSUME local stores will be higher in price than the web. Do your homework first. And always ask local retailers if they will price match what you see online. Many quietly do!

A caveat to online shopping: if you live in Alaska or Hawaii (or are overseas military with an APO address), you may be out of luck. While Walmart and Target will ship some items to Alaska and Hawaii, other sites refuse.

5 **ONE WORD: IKEA.** Sure, it's basic and no frills . . . but it's hard to beat the price! IKEA's ultra affordable cribs and dressers make even Walmart look expensive. Example: the HENSVIK crib for $99 and matching wardrobe for $119. Yes, you will have to assemble it yourself. And no, it won't last through three kids. But hey—it's hard to beat the price. (See the brand reviews later for more on IKEA, including some key things to know before you buy).

6 **GO NAKED.** Naked furniture, that is. An increasing number of stores sell unfinished (or naked) furniture at great prices. Such places even sell the finishing supplies and give you directions (make sure to use a non-toxic finish). The prices are hard to beat. At a local unfinished furniture store, we found a three-drawer pine dresser (23" wide) for $150, while a four-drawer dresser (38" wide) was $225. Compare that to baby store prices, which can top $500 to $700 for a similar size dresser. A reader in California e-mailed us with a great example of this trend in the Bay Area: Hoot Judkins in Redwood City (hootjudkins.com). An unfinished double dresser in solid pine double dresser is $470 from this store—most finished versions of this dresser in a baby store would run twice the price. While unfinished cribs are somewhat rare, unfinished furniture stores often offer affordable alternatives for dressers, bookcases, and more.

7 **SKIP THE SLEIGH CRIB.** Lots of folks fall in love with the look of a sleigh-style crib, which looks like (you guessed it) a sleigh. The only problem? Most sleigh cribs have solid foot and headboards. All that extra wood means higher prices, as much as TWICE that of non-sleigh styles. If you have your heart set on a sleigh style, look for one with slats on the headboard instead of solid wood.

8 **CONSIDER AN AFFORDABLE CONVERTIBLE CRIB.** Before you jump on the bandwagon and consider a convertible crib, there is key question to ask: do you have room in the nursery for the crib to convert to a full-size bed? If the answer is yes, then consider an affordable convertible. At chains stores like Babies R Us convertible cribs run $350 to $500. At specialty stores, brands like Munire and Westwood offer convertibles in the $400 to $600 range. Don't forget to factor in the price of the kit to convert the crib to a twin or full-size bed—this is another $60 to $200. At press time, Costco was selling a convertible crib by CaféKids (including the conversion kit) for a $400. One tip: make sure the design has a true headboard and shorter footboard (many low-end convertible cribs cheat on this point by having the same size head and foot boards). This looks much better when converted to a double bed.

9 **TRY CRAIGSLIST.ORG.** As you probably know, Craigslist's popular online classified site has versions for dozens of cities, with a special "for sale" section for baby/kids stuff. Use Craigslist to find a local family that is unloading unneeded nursery furniture, gear and other items (but do NOT buy a used crib, as we've discussed earlier).

10 **DON'T WAIT ON THE CONVERSION KIT OR NIGHTSTAND.** Many parents like the concept of a convertible crib that can grow with your child from crib to twin or full-size bed. But to make that transition, you often need to buy a separate conversion kit (bedrails and other hardware). We recommend buying the conversion kit (and other matching items like a nightstand) when you first order your nursery furniture, instead of waiting until your child needs the crib converted. Why? Styles and colors can be discontinued at the drop of a hat; some manufacturers disappear altogether. If you wait and the conversion kit is no longer available, you've just spent a fortune on a convertible crib that can't be converted!

Baby Superstore Reviews: The Good, Bad & Ugly

There's good news and bad news when it comes to shopping for baby. Good news: there are an amazing number of stores to shop for baby gear. Bad news: there are an amazing number of stores to shop for baby gear.

And as a first-time parent, you probably have never been in these stores (except for that time you bought a gift for a pregnant co-worker). Walking into a baby superstore for the first time can give even the most levelheaded mom or dad-to-be a case of the willies. It is a blizzard of pacifiers, strollers, cribs and more in a mind-numbing assortment of colors, features and options. So, as a public service, here's our overview of the major players in the baby store biz.

Babies R Us 888-BABYRUS; babiesrus.com. The 800-pound gorilla of baby stores, Babies R Us has 450+ stores nationwide and is the country's leading baby gear retailer. Love 'em or hate 'em, you'll probably find yourself in a BRU at some point—in some towns, BRU is the only baby store around.

FYI: Babies R Us comes in several flavors: there are the 248 standalone stores. Then there are 204 side-by-side stories (where a Toys R Us and Babies R Us are side-by-side). Finally, the chain has a flagship store in New York City's Union Square that is a Babies R Us on steroids.

For the uninitiated, Babies R Us is your typical chain store—big on selection, decent prices . . . but service? That's not the point. Sure, our readers occasionally report they found a knowledgeable sales clerk. But other times, you are lucky to find a person to check you out, much less give advice on a car seat.

To its credit, Babies R Us is trying to fix this by adding registry concierges—specially trained associates whose mission in life is to guide parents-to-be through the registry process. So far, the chain has rolled out this program at three dozen locations.

In recent years, BRU has added more private label and exclusive merchandise to combat online discounting. In some cases, BRU has manufacturers make a special line that is only sold in the chain (example: Baby Cache is made by Munire exclusively for BRU). You'll also see car seats branded as "Babies R Us by Safety 1st."

The Truly Scrumptious by Heidi Klum brand is another BRU creation that you'll see in cribs (made by LaJobi), bedding, strollers (some made by Dorel/Cosco) and other products. We've also seen "Babies R Us" private label products, such as the BRU Baby Sight Video Monitor, which is made by Summer (even though Summer's name doesn't appear on the product).

These private label efforts are clearly muscling out other name brands from BRU's shelves. And if you are looking for luxury brands like UPPAbaby or Bugaboo strollers, this isn't your store.

BRU wins kudos for their web site, which has been upgraded to

How to snag the best deals on Craigslist

Sure there are great deals on Craigslist, but how do you use this online wonder to save the most? Here are a few tips:

◆ **Be patient.** When you first go on Craigslist, you will be amazed at the prices and think you have to snap up deals quickly. But take some time to see what really are the best prices. A reader says she thought she got a good deal when she hastily bought a Baby Bjorn carrier off Craigslist for 50% retail—until she noticed the going rate is more like 75% off.

◆ **Use Craigslist list to find garage sales.** On Friday night or Saturday morning, just do a quick search in the garage sale listings for "baby."

◆ **Deals are even better than they look.** That's because there is no shipping or sales tax. Examples from our readers: a Dutailier rocker and ottoman for $260 (retail $600+), Boppy pillow for $5 (retail $35), cradle swing for $60 (retail: $140).

include a gift-finding tool, store inventory levels and wish lists. The web site features additional brands not sold in BRU's stores.

Babies R Us' ace in the hole is their gift registry, which now has a quick start option and other online tools. While no gift registry is perfect (and BRU's registry has seen its fair share of complaints on our message boards), we have noted that readers lately seem happier with BRU's registry after the company divorced itself from a disastrous partnership with Amazon.

FYI: Watch for high dollar coupon books that Babies R Us distributes in January—ask your local store for details.

So, how to grade Babies R Us? For selection, make it an A-, service gets a C, pricing a B+ and the registry, an A. Overall, let's call it a B. ***Rating: B***

Baby Depot *800-444-COAT; burlingtoncoatfactory.com.* Baby Depot is a store-within-a-store concept. Tucked inside the cavernous Burlington Coat Factory, Baby Depot is a nook stuffed with nursery furniture, strollers and a smattering of other gear.

Even though there as many Baby Depots as Babies R Us stores (370+ at last count), Baby Depot has always played second-fiddle to BRU. Part of the problem has been marketing strategy: Baby Depot could use one. Burlington/Baby Depot operates in a wide range of locations, some in shiny new suburban power centers and others in dingy warehouses.

The selection of brands at Baby Depot is decent, but merchandising isn't exactly Baby Depot's strong suit. The aisles of the stores are often disorganized and cluttered.

The service at Baby Depot makes Babies R Us look like Nordstroms. We get frequent letters from Baby Depot furniture customers, complaining about late orders, botched orders and worse.

On the plus side, Baby Depot has changed their draconian return policy—now you can return items within 30 days and get cash back (as long as you have a receipt and the tags are still attached).

So, here's our advice: if you see something here that is in stock and the price is right, go for it. But forget about special ordering anything such as furniture. ***Rating: C-***

Buy Buy Baby *BuyBuyBaby.com.* Owned by the Bed, Bath & Beyond chain, Buy Buy Baby is our top pick in this category. Yes, they only 80+ locations, but the chain is expanding and may be worth a trip if one is nearby. FYI: In some markets, like Denver, CO, Buy Buy Baby operates combination stores with its parent, Bed Bath & Beyond. Basically, two stores with one entrance.

Service is the strong point here—folks at Buy Buy Baby know their stuff. Now, we realize that this might not be a fair fight—can Babies R Us with its zillion stores ever compete on service with a much smaller rival? It will be interesting to see if Buy Buy Baby can maintain that advantage as it expands into new stores.

Given the urban slant to its locations, the brands and selection skew toward the expensive. Yes, there are Graco travel systems here . . . but also Bugaboo's $900 models. Ditto for the furniture, with Million Dollar Baby sharing floor space with more pricey options from Baby Appleseed and Westwood.

The stores are merchandised a bit like Bed Bath and Beyond—that is crowded, with stacks of merchandise rising to the ceiling. While Babies R Us is a bit easier to navigate, Buy Buy Baby has more selection in several categories.

If we had to pick one point on which Buy Buy could improve, it would have to be their lackluster web site. Poor organization and little in the way of buying advice—Buy Buy Baby's web site might have done the trick five years ago, but now it is among the weakest online entries. Yes, the web site has just added user reviews (what took so long?); overall, Amazon and Babies R Us are light years ahead.

Despite their web site, we still give Buy Buy Baby our top rating among chain stores—if you happen to be near one, this store is a keeper. *Rating: A*

The Discounters: Target, Walmart, Kmart

Any discussion of national stores that sell baby items wouldn't be complete without a mention of the discounters: Target, Walmart, Kmart and their ilk. In recent years, the discounters have realized one sure-fire way to drive store traffic—discount baby supplies! As a result, you'll often see formula, diapers and other baby essentials at rock-bottom prices. And there are even better deals on "in-house" brands. The goal is to have you drop by to pick up some diapers . . . and then walk out with a big-screen TV.

Of all the discounters, we think Target is best (with one big caveat—their ruthless return policy, see below for a discussion). Target's baby department is a notch above Walmart and Kmart when it comes to brand names and selection. Yes, sometimes Walmart has lower prices—but usually that's on lower-quality brands. Target, by contrast, carries Perego high chairs and a wider selection of products like baby monitors. The best bet: Super Targets, which have expanded baby products sections.

One important trend: discounters have bulked up their web sites with brands, products and models that are NOT carried in their stores. Sometimes you'll even find an upscale brand online at discount prices. We'll discuss the discounter web sites specifically below.

Of course, there are some downsides to the discounters. If you're looking for premium brand names, forget it. Most discounters only stock the so-called mass-market brands: Graco strollers, Cosco car seats, Gerber sheets, etc. And the baby departments always seem to be in chaos when we visit, with items strewn about hither and yon. Kmart is probably the worst when it comes to organization, Walmart the best. We like Target's selection (especially of feeding items and baby monitors), but their prices are somewhat higher than Walmart. What about service? Forget it—no matter which store you're in, you're on your own.

While we do recommend Target, we should warn readers about their return policy. Once among the most generous, Target now requires a receipt for just about any return. A raft of new rules and restrictions greet customers (sample: exchanges now must be made for items within the same department). This has understandably ticked off a fair number of our readers, especially those who have unfortunately chosen to register at Target for their baby gifts. Among the biggest roadblocks: Target won't let you exchange duplicate baby gifts if you don't have a gift receipt (and there are numerous other rules/restrictions as well). Of course, your friends may forget to ask for a gift receipt or throw it away. And watch out: gift receipts have expiration dates; be sure to return any item before that date. Target also limits the number of returns you can do in one year.

After receiving a fair amount of consumer complaints about this, Target now allows returns of registry gifts without a gift receipt IF the item is listed on your registry. The rub: you will get the lowest sales price in the last 90 days, not necessarily what your guest paid for it. That's a special gotcha for new parents—many baby products and clothes go on sale frequently, rendering your gift almost worthless on an exchange. This and other concerns with Target have spawned many complaints about their registry and even blogs dedicated to dissing the chain.

Our advice: think twice about registering at Target. While we get complaints about all baby registries (even industry leader Babies R Us), be sure to read the fine print for ANY baby registry before signing up. Ask about returns and exchange policies, including specifically what happens if you have to return/exchange a duplicate item without a gift receipt. And check for limits on the number of returns you can do within a certain time period. Finally, ask about HOW the store integrates your registry with the web site—if someone buys an item online instead of at a store, will this be reflected on your registry? Check our blog and message boards for the latest buzz on baby registries.

Each of the major discounters sells baby products online. Here's an overview of each site:

◆ **WalMart.com** Hit the baby tab and you'll find yourself in Walmart's extensive online baby gear department. We like how the chain has expanded online offerings in recent years—there's much more on the web site than in the stores (particularly strollers). Walmart has steadily improved the site over the last year or so—now you can search by brand, read product reviews and get a product delivered to a nearby store at no charge. And, of course, the prices are excellent.

◆ **Kmart.com** Kmart's online outpost is a winner—we liked the graphics and easy navigation. You can search by brand, price and more. We also liked the Deals tab for the latest specials. The only bummer: unlike Target, Kmart's online selection brand-wise is much the same as the store—heavy on low-end brands like Baby Trend. And the site is confusing in some areas—in car seats, Kmart mixes infant, convertible and booster seats. That's not very helpful.

◆ **Target.com** is our pick as the best discounter web site—their online offerings go way beyond what's in the stores. We also like the user reviews, as well as the ability to sort any category by brand, price or best-sellers. Perhaps the biggest drawback with Target.com (as with other sites) is the sometimes skimpy product descriptions. You can often find more about a product by reading the user reviews than Target's own descriptions.

◆ **Diapers.com** New kid on the block, Diapers.com started off selling diapers online (naturally) and evolved into a baby gear behemoth in recent years. That caught the attention of Amazon, which scooped up the site in 2010. Diapers.com has extensive sections of nursery furniture and décor (along with other baby gear). The product reviews from pulled from Amazon's site. A Green Baby tab highlights eco-friendly diapers, gear and clothing. For bargain hunters, zero in on the Sale tab for the latest discounts and clearance items.

Specialty Chains That Sell Baby Furniture

Inspired by the success of Pottery Barn Kids, several chains have ventured into the nursery business. An example: Room & Board (RoomandBoard.com), an 11 store chain (plus an outlet) with locations in California, Colorado, Illinois, Minnesota, Georgia and the

New York City area. Their well-designed web site has a nursery section with a couple of cribs ($700 to $1000), dressers and accessories. Quality is good, say our readers who've ordered from them.

And that's just the beginning: Land of Nod, a subsidiary of Crate & Barrel, has an extensive website (landofnod.com) with nursery offerings (ten cribs) as well as five stores in Chicago and Seattle. FYI: The Land of Nod is owned by Crate & Barrel—you can use gift cards from one chain at the other.

What's driving this is a boom in babies born to older moms and dads. Tired of the cutesy baby stuff in chain stores, many parents are looking for something more sophisticated and hip. Of course, it remains to be seen what this means for bargain shoppers. On one hand, more competition is always good—having a wide diversity of places to buy nursery furniture and accessories is always a plus. On the downside, most of these chains are chasing that "upscale" customer with outrageously priced cribs and bedding. "As much as parents love the furniture at Pottery Barn Kids, some wince at the prices," said the *Wall Street Journal* in a recent article on this trend. And we agree—while we love the PBK look, our goal in life is to try to find that same look . . . at half the price!

Outlets

There are dozens of outlets that sell kids' clothing, but when it comes to furniture the pickings are slim. In fact, we found just a handful of nursery furniture outlets out there. Here's a round up:

Pottery Barn Kids has nine outlets for their kids catalog, scattered around the country (there's a list on their web site). Readers report some good deals there, including a changing table for $100 (regularly $200) and a rocker for $200 (down from $700). The outlet also carries the PBK bedding line at good discounts. A reader in Georgia said the PBK outlet there features 75% off deals on furniture and you can get a coupon book at the food court for an additional 10% discount. "The best time to shop is during the week—they run more specials then," she said. "And bring a truck—they don't deliver." One final tip: call AHEAD before you go. The selection of nursery furniture can vary widely from outlet to outlet . . . some may have no stock during certain months.

Live in the Northeast? Check out **Baby Boudoir Outlet,** an offshoot of a baby store in New Bedford, MA (babyboudoiroutlet. com, 800-272-2293, 508-998-2166). The store is an authorized dealer for Pali, Baby's Dream, Bonavita, Romina and Munire. The Baby Boudoir Outlet has 1000 cribs in stock at any one time at prices from $250 to $450. The store also carries glider rockers, bedding and other baby products at 30% to 70% off retail. FYI: There

crils

is both a Baby Boudoir store and a warehouse outlet—you want to visit the outlet for the best deals. The outlet is around the corner from the main store.

Readers have been mixed on their opinions of the Baby Boudoir outlet. One described it as a "bare bones warehouse in a bad neighborhood." However, another reader described the outlet as "in an urban area, but safe"; she found the warehouse itself "clean and well-organized."

Don't forget that **JCPenney** has 15 outlet stores nationwide, under the name JC's 5 Star Outlets. (Technically, the outlets are owned by another company that has a contract to sell Penney's overstock merchandise). The stores carry a wide variety of items, including children's and baby products (always call before you go to confirm selection). Check out the web site Outlet Bound (outlet-bound.com) for a current listing of locations.

The Name Game: Reviews of Selected Manufacturers

Here's a look at crib brands sold in the U.S. and Canada. Our focus is on the most common nursery furniture brands you see in chains stores, independents and other furniture outlets. If you've discovered a brand that we didn't review, feel free to share your discovery by calling or emailing us (see our contact info at the end of the book).

How did we evaluate the brands? First, we inspected samples of cribs at stores and industry trade shows. With the help of veteran juvenile furniture retailers, we checked construction, release mechanisms, mattress supports, and overall fit and finish. Yes, we did compare styling among the brands but this was only a minor factor in our ratings (we figure you can decide what looks best for your nursery).

Readers of previous editions have asked us how we assign ratings to these manufacturers—what makes one an "A" vs. "B"? The bottom line is quality *and* value. Sure, anyone can make a high-quality crib for $800. The trick is getting that price down to $400 or less while maintaining high-quality standards. Hence, we give more bonus points to brands that give more value for the dollar.

What about the crib makers who got the lowest ratings? Are their cribs unsafe? No, of course not. ALL new cribs sold in the U.S. and Canada must meet minimum federal safety standards. As we mentioned earlier in this chapter, a $150 crib sold at Walmart is just as safe as a $1500 designer brand sold at a posh boutique. The only difference is styling, features and durability—more expensive cribs have thick wood posts, fancy finishes and durability to last through two or more kids. The best companies have the best customer service, taking care of both their retailers and consumers.

Brands that got our lowest rating have poor quality control and abysmal customer service. Serious safety recalls also impacts a brand's rating.

The Ratings

A **EXCELLENT**—*our top pick!*
B **GOOD**— *above average quality, prices, and creativity.*
C **FAIR**—*could stand some improvement.*
D **POOR**—*yuck! could stand some major improvement.*

ABC *See Million Dollar Baby. Sold exclusively at JCPenney.*

Adele *The Adele furniture collection is made by Simmons in Thailand as an exclusive for Babies R Us.*

AFG Furniture. *This crib brand is reviewed in the bonus section on our web site, BabyBargains.com/cribs*

Angel Line *This crib brand is reviewed in the bonus section on our web site, BabyBargains.com/cribs*

Argington. *argington.com* Argington puts a green spin on their modern furniture: New York-based designers Andrew Thornton and Jenny Argie strive to use only solid wood ("virtually no MDF, particle board other similar engineered wood products.") All Argington's wood is FSC certified as part of its "sustainable manufacturing" (glues are low-emission, etc.). The brand's main crib offering is the two-toned Sahara for $500 with matching dresser for $550.

The Bam Bam Collection is Argington's value offering—it starts as a bassinet that converts to a crib for $450 (conversion kit included). A matching dresser is $550 to $700.

New in the past year, Argington rolled out a bunk bed (the Brookline; $950) that can be purchased first as a twin bed ($470) and later converted to a bunk ($90 for the kit).

Argington also offers a limited selection of organic cotton crib bedding ($185 for a set) that can be bought as separates.

As for quality and customer service, to say Argington's customer reviews on Amazon have been mixed would be charitable. More than one customer has complained of late arriving orders, customer service snafus and more. While backordered items can be a problem with many companies today, Argington needs to improve its customer service to better communicate with customers when a problem happens—especially if Argington continues to sell directly on their web site.

Quality is OK—one reader compared it with IKEA, albeit at a higher price. It's hard to find modern nursery furniture under $1000, so Argington has done a good job with value. We've noticed Argington's prices have actually declined about 10% in the past year, a welcome sign.

Argington is sold in specialty stores and some Buy Buy Baby's, as well as on quite a few online stores. ***Rating: B***

Babee Tenda *See box on page 52-53.*

Baby Appleseed *babyappleseed.com.* Baby Appleseed is actually two separate brands: Baby Appleseed (upper-end pricing, sold in Buy Buy Baby, among other stores) and Nursery Smart (more affordable, sold mostly online).

The company's mojo is to combine eco-friendliness and elegant design. The eco-pitch: when you buy one of their cribs, the company will plant ten trees in your baby's name, thanks to a partnership with the non-profit American Forests. The furniture is also GREENGUARD Gold certified to be low emission.

The best-selling Baby Appleseed collection is the Davenport, a curvey crib with thick rails and back board. All that chunkiness will cost you: the Davenport crib is $700, while a double dresser runs $680, armoire $750, hutch $450 and five-drawer chest $580. Rails to convert the Davenport into a full-size bed run another $120.

Finishes in Baby Appleseed are rather limited: the Davenport comes in just three (espresso, cherry and white). Other collections have just two. If you are looking for colors other than white and brown, this probably isn't your brand.

If the Davenport is too much, Baby Appleseed also sells the Stratford (a Buy Buy Baby exclusive). Prices run $300 for a crib and $390 for a five-drawer dresser.

While most of Baby Appleseed's styles are traditional, the company has recently released a collection that is more art deco (Carlisle).

Baby Appleseed's cribs are made of poplar wood; the dressers are poplar with birch veneers. While the wood is from the U.S., the cribs are produced in Vietnam.

On a recent visit to Buy Buy Baby, we asked the clerk in the crib department to give us her top recommendation—she pointed to the Baby Appleseed Davenport and praised its durable finish, which prevents scratches and nicks. It's clear Buy Buy Baby is this brand's biggest account, although a handful of other independent stores carry Baby Appleseed as well.

While we were generally impressed with Baby Appleseed's quality, we hear Buy Buy Baby often quotes an order time of a 12-16 weeks (and sometimes up to 20 weeks) for Baby Appleseed purchases. That's much longer than other furniture brands and a major drawback if your due date is fast approaching.

Nursery Smart is the company's less expensive, less fancy brand. At the time of this writing, Nursery Smart only had one collection (the Darby), but we also see a handful of mini-cribs sold online under the Nursery Smart moniker for under $200. To keep prices

Baby Gift Registries: Disappointing

We have a plea for tomorrow's computer science college graduates: fix the gift registries at chain stores—please!

Sure, computers can pilot a spaceship to Pluto or solve the most complex microbiology problem . . . but for some reason, such computer smarts elude the baby gift registry programmers at chain stores.

No matter how sweet the promises are about computerized registries ("Look Ma! I'm changing an item on the registry at 2 am!") the reality falls WAY short of utopia. Judging from our reader mail and message boards, folks are steamed when they must deal with registry snafus . . . and who can blame them.

While the process of registering at any chain is relatively straightforward (you can scan items in the store or pick them off a web site), USING the registry is where things start to fall apart. You name it, we've heard it: duplicate gifts, out of stock items (with no notice to the parent), endless backorders and other goofs.

Here are the frustrations:

♦ **Online versus offline.** Many stores carry items online that aren't in stores. And in some cases, items can only be found in stores, not online. So if you register online at a major retailer, your friends who visit the retailer's stores may find a large chunk of your registry can't be purchased in the store. Another frustration: at Babies R Us, online-only items can't be returned to BRU stores—they can only be returned via the mail. And then the gift-giver receives the credit, not you.

♦ **Returns**. Stores have Byzantine return policies that can frustrate the seemingly simple task of returning a duplicate gift (which shouldn't happen with registries, right?). Many stores require a gift receipt for returns—but whoops! Your gift-giver for-low, most Nursery Smart dressers are ready to assemble (Baby Appleseed dressers are fully assembled).

This company's parent reviews have been bi-polar—readers generally like and recommend Baby Appleseed, while folks have been more mixed on Nursery Smart (their ready-to-assemble dressers are difficult to put together). And the finish on the lower end Nursery Smart furniture comes in for criticism: it scratches too easily. While that isn't a problem with the pricey Baby Appleseed cribs, we found it odd the brand offers two starkly different levels of quality. As a result, we'll assign two different ratings for this brand: Baby Appleseed: **Rating: B+** Nursery Smart: **Rating: C**

got to include that. No problem, just print out a copy of your registry from the web site? Whoops! The store deleted your registry 14 days after your baby was born. And so on.

◆ **Discontinued items.** You try to be smart and register early for that baby shower—but now several items are discontinued. Does the registry email you with notice? Are you kidding? Registries expect you to monitor your registry and replace items as needed. And product may disappear from an online registry, but still be available in stores.

Some of the problems with a gift registry only become apparent AFTER you've received a gift. Example: Pottery Barn's policy on gift certificates. If you want to use a gift certificate for an online or telephone purchase at Pottery Barn Kids, you must MAIL the certificate in and cool your heels for a two to three week processing period. How convenient.

Babies R Us runs the country's biggest gift registry—and comes in for a regular barbequing from our readers. To its credit, BRU has fixed many of the glitches that were apparent in recent years . . . but we still hear from readers who have problems with returns, discontinued items and more. FYI: Babies R Us changed their return policy for gift registry purchases in the past year—now you have 90 say from your due date (not when the items where purchased) to return items.

Bottom line: take a second and read the gift registry feedback from recent parents on our web site (hang out in the "Lounge" forum or do a search on the site). Always READ the return policies of any gift registry BEFORE you sign up—is there a time limit for returns? Must you have a gift receipt? Are you limited to X number of returns or exchanges? Know ALL the fine print before you plunge in!

Baby Cache *See Munire.*

Baby Italia *See LaJobi.*

Baby Mod. *See Million Dollar Baby.*

Baby Relax. *See Dorel.*

Baby's Dream *BabysDream.com.* Georgia-based Baby's Dream's claim to fame is convertible cribs. The company was among the first to launch the trend in 1990—yes, Baby's Dream was convertible before convertible was cool.

A family-owned business, Baby's Dream splits its production between China and Chile. The furniture is sold only in specialty stores—no chain stores carry the brand. It also is rarely sold online. This devotion to specialty stores has a downside: Baby's Dream is hard to find in some areas. Example: states with few independent baby retailers like Washington State, Montana and Colorado have nary a single dealer for this brand.

One unusual feature for Baby's Dream: it is one of the few brands that still have cribs with drop-sides. Baby's Dream's fold down rail is one of the few (only) designs that survived the purge of drop-side cribs for safety reasons back in 2010.

Prices for Baby's Dream are in the mid to upper ranges of the market—cribs run $500 to $700 and dressers are similar in price. That makes them more expensive than what you'd find in Babies R Us . . . but in specialty stores that carry $1000 cribs, Baby's Dream might be their opening price point.

Most of Baby's Dream furniture is traditionally styled, although the company has occasionally dabbled in modern designs. A typical example is the Renaissance crib.

Pine is the most common wood in this line, although a few styles are made from birch. Quality for Baby's Dream is good—dressers feature a "soft close" and full extension drawer glides. The fit and finish of Baby's Dream is above average.

There is one major caveat to this brand: delivery times. If items are in stock, delivery only takes six to eight weeks. But that is the rub: items that are not in stock can go on forever backordered—retailers complain that while most items are in stock, there inevitably will be one item in an order that is back ordered for *six months* or more, frustrating retailer and consumer alike. Yes, you read that right: you may have to wait 20-24 weeks for some Baby's Dream furniture.

Another gripe: if your crib has a defective part, there may be a long wait for replacement parts. That's because Baby's Dream doesn't stock replacement rails or headboards—you have to wait until the next boat arrives from Chile (which could be weeks or months

Not made in China

From lead paint in toys to tainted baby formula, China has had its share of, uh, quality control issues. And some of our readers have asked us, not surprisingly, how to furnish a nursery with products NOT made in China. While that sounds simple, it isn't: 90% or more of baby furniture sold in the U.S. is made in China—so avoiding Chinese-made items takes some effort.

But there is good news: there ARE a handful of companies that make their furniture somewhere other than China. And yes, there are still firms that make furniture in the U.S.: Newport Cottages, ducduc, Echelon/Munire USA, El Greco, Lolly & Me and Young America by Stanley. Oak Designs (oakdesigns.com) makes dressers and twin beds domestically. Lolly & Me's "Eco-Friendly" collections are made in the U.S.

Other furniture makers import goods from countries other than China: Romina makes furniture in Romania; Munire imports from Indonesia. Westwood and Bratt Décor have factories in Vietnam. Oeuf imports its furniture from Latvia. Natart is made in Canada and Denmark. Baby's Dream is imported from Chile (except for the Cube, which is made in China).

A few caveats to this advice: first, production often shifts, so before you order, reconfirm with the manufacturer or retailer where the furniture is being made. Second, manufacturers that split production between China and other countries often don't publicize which furniture is made where. You have to ask which furniture is made where. .

of waiting). While this is a problem that plagues many imported furniture lines, Baby's Dream could do a better job at quality control and not ship out defective furniture to begin with.

While we recommend Baby's Dream, there is a caveat: we do NOT recommend the cribs with fold-down rails. As we discussed elsewhere, we aren't fans of this design. We think the fold-down rail's hinge gives a toddler a foothold to climb out of the crib. Fortunately, only a handful of Baby's Dream styles have the fold-down rails.

Finally, readers have asked us about this contradiction: how can we recommend Baby's Dream but warn against buying nursery furniture that is made of pine (and most Baby's Dream furniture is pine)? That's because Baby's Dream furniture is made from South American pine, which is harder (and more durable) than North American pine.

Bottom line: this is a good brand to consider—IF (and that's a big if) the pieces you want are actually in stock at Baby's Dream's warehouse. ***Rating: A-***

babyletto. *See Million Dollar Baby.*

Bassettbaby *bassettbaby.com.* Sold in mostly big box stores, Bassett divides its line into three brands: First Choice, Bassettbaby and private label offerings for Babies R Us and Restoration Hardware.

First Choice is Bassett's most affordable line and features simple cribs and smaller-size, ready-to-be-assemble dressers. The brand offers four crib styles in Walmart and Target, with prices running $200 to $400 (cribs) and $225 to $300 (dressers).

Bassettbaby offers an upgrade in both styling and features: fancier finishes and fully assembled dressers with French dovetail drawer construction. Example: a pine 4-in-1 crib is $300; a matching three-drawer dresser is $350.

Generally, Bassett's strategy is to add a bit more bling to the BRU and Restoration Hardware versions of its furniture to justify prices that are $100 or more than competing imports. (See Restoration Hardware's review later in this section for a discussion of Bassett's cribs made for that chain).

All Bassett furniture is imported from China. How's the quality? We like Bassett's cribs, which we think are a good value. Yes, Bassett had two recalls in 2008 for its Wendy B cribs (one for defective bolts; another for spindles that were too far apart), but overall, Basset has a good quality record.

While we like Bassett's cribs, the case pieces are another story. Compared with Bassett's First Choice line, you can find better ready-to-assemble furniture at a lower price at IKEA. And Bassett's assembled dressers didn't impress us with their overall fit and finish.

Bottom line: Bassett's cribs are a good value, but skip the dressers. **Rating: B+**

Bedford Baby *See Westwood.*

Who Is Jenny Lind?

You can't shop for cribs and not hear the name "Jenny Lind." Here's an important point to remember: Jenny Lind isn't a brand name; it refers to a particular *style* of crib. But how did it get this name? Jenny Lind was a popular Swedish soprano living in the 19th century. During her triumphal U.S. tour, it was said that Lind slept in a "spool bed." Hence, cribs that featured turned spindles (which look like stacked spools of thread) became known as Jenny Lind cribs. All this begs the question—what if today we still named juvenile furniture after famous singers? Would we have Lady Gaga cribs and Beyonce dressers? Nah.

Bellini _bellini.com._ Bellini pitches itself as the antidote to giant baby superstores. Instead of a cavernous building stacked to the ceiling with baby gear and clueless salespeople, Bellini boutiques are about 3,000 square feet and carry their own in-house line of furniture and accessories. The goal is personal service and a narrow focus on better merchandise. Example: some stores stock nursery accessories made by local artists.

This franchised chain had its heyday in the 80's and 90's—during those decades, its business model was selling imported Italian nursery furniture with $700 price tags. Of course, that was long before Buy Buy Baby and Pottery Barn Kids, not to mention the slew of luxury baby web sites.

In the last decade, like many independent retailers, Bellini found itself struggling to compete against chains selling better quality goods and the online world of baby gear discounters. After closing some locations, the chain now has 23 stores most of which are on the East Coast and in the Northeast.

Facing a strong euro, Bellini abandoned its Italian import strategy and now imports its furniture from China. Cribs run $500 to $950, with an average price of $700. A three-drawer dresser is $750; a double dresser is $1000. Delivery takes about ten to 12 weeks on average, although some orders can be filled in just two to three weeks.

New in the past year, Bellini has partnered with Newport Cottages (reviewed separately) to produce exclusives for the chain—their first effort is the Stella, a made in the USA crib the chain describes as "clean, transitional" in style. Bellini has also beefed up their web site in the past year; now you can see each of the available finishes for their furniture.

Quality of the furniture is good (the company has never had a safety recall) . . . but the real question here is: does Bellini's customer service justify the price premium? After all, you can buy similar furniture at a Buy Buy Baby or online for 20% to 30% less. And if you are concerned about Chinese-made furniture, Bellini won't be on your list.

Reviews of Bellini from our readers and posted on sites like Yelp are decidedly mixed (most of the complaints centered around late arriving orders and generally poor customer service). Some locations gets good marks on customer service, while other locations are lacking. Some of this can be chalked up to being a franchised chain, since each store is independently owned. But if Bellini wants to compete against high-end specialty stores and chains like Buy Buy Baby and Pottery Barn Kids, it can't be inconsistent. It shouldn't matter whether you walk in a Bellini in New Jersey or Florida.

What you are paying for here is Bellini's design services—that coordinated look for a nursery (furniture, bedding, decor). If that is important to you, then Bellini might be worth the time to check out.
Rating: B+

Bergamo. *See Dorel.*

Bethany James Collection *See Dorel.*

Bivona & Company *bivonaco.com* Industry veteran Larry Bivona is best known for starting LaJobi (Bonavita) in the early 90's, before selling it to Kid Brands in 2008. After parting ways with Kid Brands in 2011, Bivona launched his own eponymous company in 2013.

Bivona & Co is similar to LaJobi, offering cribs under different

Babee Tenda's "safety" seminar: Anatomy of a Hard Sell

We got an interesting invitation in the mail during our second pregnancy—a company called "Babee Tenda" invited us to a free "Getting Ready For Baby" safety seminar at a local hotel. The seminar was described as "brief, light and enjoyable while handing out information on preventing baby injuries." Our curiosity piqued, we joined a couple dozen other expectant parents on a Saturday afternoon to learn their expert safety tips.

What followed was a good lesson for all parents—beware of companies that want to exploit parents' fears of their children being injured in order to sell their expensive safety "solutions." Sure enough, there was safety information dispensed at the seminar. The speaker started his talk with horrific tales of how many children are injured and killed each year. The culprit? Cheap juvenile equipment products like high chairs and cribs, he claimed. It was quite a performance—the speaker entranced the crowd with endless statistics on kids getting hurt and then demonstrated hazards with sample products from major manufacturers.

The seminar then segued into a thinly veiled pitch for their products: the Babee Tenda high chair/feeding table and crib. The speaker (really a salesperson) spent what seemed like an eternity trying to establish the company's credibility, claiming Babee Tenda has been in business for 60 years and only sells its products to hospitals and other institutions. We can see why—these products are far too ugly and expensive to sell in retail stores.

How expensive? The crib sells for $600+ and the feeding table for about $500.

We found Babee Tenda's sales pitch to be disgusting. They used misleading statistics and outright lies to scare parents into thinking they were putting their children in imminent danger if they used store-bought high chairs or cribs. Many of the statistics and "props" used to demonstrate hazards were as much as 20 years old and brands in a variety of price points: Fisher Price (opening price point), Ti Amo (mid-price cribs in the $300 to $450 range) and Dolce Babi (specialty stores, more expensive). Here is a look at each:

Opening-price point cribs under the Fisher-Price brand run $150 to $300. These cribs are available online on Amazon, Target and Walmart and in major retailers. One unique feature to these cribs: you can raise/lower the height of the crib by adjusting the crib feet (called Just the Right Height). There are eight styles and four finishes in this collection; most cribs convert into a full size bed head-

long since removed from the market! Even more reprehensible were claims that certain popular juvenile products were about to be recalled. Specifically, Babee Tenda's salesperson claimed the Evenflo Exersaucer was "unsafe and will be off the market in six months," an accusation that clearly wasn't true.

The fact that Babee Tenda had to use such bogus assertions raised our suspicions about whether they were telling the truth about their own products. Sadly, the high-pressure sales tactics did win over some parents at the seminar we attended—some forked over nearly $800 for Babee Tenda's items. Since then, we've heard from other parents who've attended Babee Tenda's "safety seminars," purchased the products and then suffered a case of "buyer's remorse." Did they spend too much, they ask?

Yes, in our opinion. While we see nothing wrong per se with Babee Tenda's "feeding table" (besides the fact it's god-awful ugly), you should note it costs nearly four times as much as our top recommended high chair, the very well made Fisher Price Healthy Care. There's nothing wrong with the crib either—and yes, Babee Tenda, throws in a mattress and two sheets. But you can find all this for much less than the $600 or so Babee Tenda asks.

A new twist to the Babee Tenda pitch: invitations sent by a Babee Tenda distributor in Virginia in 2004 carried a line that their seminar is sponsored "in conjunction with the Consumer Product Safety Commission and the National Highway Traffic Safety Administration." Whoa, sounds official! Except it isn't true—neither the CPSC nor NHTSA have anything to do with Babee Tenda's seminars . . . in fact, the federal government successfully sued Babee Tenda to stop the practice. In 2007, a federal judge ruled Babee Tenda committed mail fraud, calling their sales tactics "deceitful and reprehensible."

So, we say watch out for Babee Tenda (and other similar companies like Babyhood, who pitches their "Baby Sitter" in hotel safety seminars). We found their "safety seminar" to be bogus, their high-pressure sales tactics reprehensible and their products grossly overpriced.

board. Four ready-to-assemble dressers round out the collection. New for 2013, Bivona is expanding the finish options in Fisher Price to include a series of pastel colors.

Ti Amo is the latest addition to the Bivona family—a mid-priced line ($300 to $450) with smaller scale furniture designed to fit into urban apartments. "Transitional to contemporary" is the style here with all cribs converting into toddler and then full-size beds.

Dolce Babi is the Bivona brand aimed at specialty stores: cribs run $600 to $800 and dressers $650 to $1000. As you can guess from the pricing, Dolce Babi features fancier styling and finishes than Bivona's other offerings. Dolce Babi dressers also have dove-tailed drawers with ball-bearing glides and some of the cribs convert to platform beds (which is unique). Unlike the ready-to-assemble furniture in Fisher Price, these dressers come fully assembled.

All of Bivona & Co's furniture is imported from Vietnam and features poplar wood construction. This is similar to LaJobi.

So how's the quality? Bivona began shipping in 2013, so feedback has just started trickling in from readers. So far, so good. Folks love the Just the Right Height feature and the Fisher Price cribs are an especially good value for the dollar. We also liked the new Ti Amo cribs that were previewed for the press; the line has yet to ship as of this writing.

As for Dolce Babi, the jury is still out—at $600 to $800, Dolce Babi is competing against Munire, Baby Appleseed and other high-end brands. And frankly, the quality of Dolce Babi (example: the drawer glides on the dressers) don't quite measure up to the competition.

So, bottom line, we will recommend Bivona. Here are the ratings broken down by brand. Fisher Price: **Rating: A** Ti Amo: **Rating: Not Yet** Dolce Babi. **Rating: B-**

Bloom *BloomBaby.com* Known for its modern high chairs and accessories, Bloom's main offering in the crib category is a mini-crib called the Alma. With two mattress heights, the Alma folds for storage and is designed for babies under one year of age.

In spite of its $400 price tag, the Alma earns generally good reviews from parents. Dissenters say the mini-crib is too small for even six month olds—some folks were unhappy they couldn't use it for much longer than a bassinet. Of course, Bloom doesn't pitch the Alma as a full-size crib replacement—it is a MINI crib designed for use up to one year of age. Overall, we can see this as a bassinet alternative for urban parents who are starved for space. For others, a playpen with a bassinet feature (that you'd leave set up in your bedroom) would be a more practical alternative than the Alma.

In the past couple of years, Bloom has expanded the Alma line to include two larger versions: the Alma Papa and the Alma Max.

Certifications:
Do they really matter?

As you shop for cribs and other products for your baby, you'll no doubt run into "JPMA-Certified" products sporting a special seal. But who is the JPMA and what does its certification mean?

The Juvenile Products Manufacturers Association (JPMA) is a group of over 300 companies that make juvenile products, both in the United States and Canada. Over twenty-five years ago, the group started a volunteer testing program to head off government regulation of baby products. The JPMA enlisted the support of the Consumer Products Safety Commission and the American Society of Testing and Materials (ASTM) to develop standards for products in several categories, including cribs, high chairs and more.

Manufacturers must have their product tested in an independent testing lab and, if it passes, they can use the JPMA seal. The JPMA touts its seal as "added assurance the product was built with safety in mind."

So is a product like a crib safer if it has the JPMA seal? No, not in our opinion. In fact, the biggest crib recall in history (one million Simplicity cribs in 2007 after three deaths) involved cribs that were JPMA certified. How did that happen?

Well, the JPMA certification is a MINIMUM set of standards that mostly address adequate warning labels. While detailed warning labels for products are helpful, it doesn't stop defective design or faulty instructions (the problem in the Simplicity recall).

The Simplicity recall tarnished the JPMA's certification program—and the JPMA's actions in the recent past (accusations of misleading the public on the safety of crib bumpers and lobbying against baby bottle regulations) have undermined the association's safety message. See our blog at BabyBargains.com (click on news/updates) for details about these stories on bedding and bottles.

The take-home message: the JPMA seal is no guarantee of safety.

What about other certification programs? GREENGUARD (greenguard.org) certifies nursery furniture and mattress makers who comply with its strict standard on chemical emissions. Since this is done by an independent third party, we think GREENGUARD certification has merit—as of this writing, furniture by A.P. Industries, Boori, BSF Baby, Natart/Tulip, Romina, Young America by Stanley are GREENGUARD certified. Mattresses by Baby Cache, Colgate, Contours (Kolcraft), Naturepedic, Sealy, Simmons, Sopora are certified.

Like the mini, the Papa is not a full-size crib (49" long versus 52" for a typical full-size crib). The Papa fold ups and features casters for mobility. Price: $700. A conversion rail ($140) turns the Papa into a toddler bed. One major caveat to the Papa: since it is three inches shorter (in width and length) than a standard size crib, you'll have to use the special mattress to fit the Papa.

The Alma Max, however, is a standard size crib for $845 with similar features as all the Alma cribs (folding feature, etc), although the Max lacks wheel casters for some reason.

Also new in the past year: the Luxor, a modern crib that can be assembled without tools. Price: $1000 for a crib, with a matching dresser for another $1000.

Bottom line: Bloom's Alma mini crib appeals to a small niche: space-starved, urban parents. But the mini crib will only buy you about a year's worth of time before you'll need a full-size crib. The minimalist, modern design is the star here, but the lack of utility and high price limit Bloom's appeal. ***Rating: B-***

Bonavita *See La Jobi.*

Boori *Boori.com* Australian crib company Boori launched in the U.S. in 2011 with collections of expensive nursery furniture that were heavy on a country-style, blonde wood look that sells well in Australia. Unfortunately, that look and the high price didn't sell at all here in the U.S.

So it was back to the drawing board—the company dropped the "country" look and name (Boori Country is now just Boori) and set off to make the line more eco-friendly and designed to American tastes. Gone (mostly) are the country styles, replaced by cribs in white, espresso and pastel finishes like "Heather" (a light green).

Prices are lower (cribs start in the $500 range now; before $800 was the opening price point). The brand is now GREENGUARD certified to be low emission.

Boori is sold under several slightly different names, depending on the market. Regency by Boori is the moniker used exclusively for Buy Buy Baby; Urbane by Boori is in other big box stores and features more contemporary styling with smaller furniture dimensions for "modern urban living."

Overall, cribs run $500-$800; four-drawer dressers are $500-$700.

Typical of their offerings is the $600 Eton crib, a low profile model with included toddler conversion rail. Dressers run $800 for a four-drawer model. At those prices, you'd expect the furniture should knock your socks off . . . but we were under-whelmed when we viewed the collection recently. While we liked the dressers with their solid wood drawers and dove-tail joints, the use of metal glides and a lack of corner blocks simply won't cut it at this price level. And, oddly, Boori offers several ready-to-assemble pieces in the Urbane Boori line. We realize this is done to lower prices, but it seems out of sync with the rest of the brand.

Boori's exclusive deal with Buy Buy Baby features cribs in the $500-$700 range and dressers for $700 to $850. Most collections have three finish options.

We will tick up Boori's rating this year, reflecting the brand's lower pricing and better styling. At this price point, however, Boori competes against Munire/Baby Cache and Baby Appleseed in Buy Buy Baby. Both of those brands edge Boori in quality and features. ***Rating: B***

Bratt Décor brattdecor.com. At least you have to give this company bonus points for creativity—Bratt Decor made their name with over-the-top offerings like the "Casablanca Plume" crib that was topped with (and we're not making this up) ostrich feathers. That (and the $1050 price tag) enabled Bratt Décor to earn a distinguished place on our list of the most ridiculous baby products in a previous edition of this book.

In the past year, Bratt has expanded their line to include a series of wood cribs in various "vintage" and whimsical looks. The Chelsea Sleigh crib comes in several finishes, including "antique silver." Price: $1300. Overall, prices for Bratt Décor's cribs range from $715 to $1400.

Bratt Décor's wood cribs are made in Vietnam; the metal models are imported from China. New in the past year, Bratt Decor has an oval iron crib that coverts from a cradle to full-size crib ($1250).

What parents seem to like here is the gilded style and princess themes; Bratt Décor is one of the few crib makers out there today that makes wrought iron cribs. They also have matching accessories such as nightstands, mirrors, bookcases and other decorative options. FYI: Bratt Décor sells direct via their web site, in case you can't find a local dealer who carries the line.

How's the quality? Readers say it is very good—one reader said after two years, her Bratt Décor crib "has held up beautifully."

On the down side, this company can be incredibly slow at shipping—one source told us Bratt Décor orders require a wait of 25+ weeks on some items. Yes, that is half a YEAR. The company also discontinues product frequently—at one point in a recent year, they dropped half their line. And the company generally seems disorganized, with reports of unreturned phone calls, etc.

Hence, it is a mixed review for Bratt Décor: kudos for the clever design and overall quality. But concerns over shipping delays and discontinued products temper our rating.

FYI: Bratt Decor holds occasional warehouse outlet sales at their Baltimore, MD company store with savings up to 70%. Check their Facebook page for details. ***Rating: C+***

Broyhill. *See Stork Craft.*

C&T International *See Sorelle.*

CaféKid *Cafekid.com.* Better known for its older kid furniture (bunk beds, etc), CafeKid also sells a crib and dresser at Costco, both online and in the warehouses. The Sydney ($400 in store, $650 online—includes shipping and handling) is your standard convertible crib and features rather conservative styling.

We saw a CafeKid crib in a Costco warehouse and were impressed—made in Thailand, it features a wood slat mattress platform and converts to a full-size bed. The price includes the conversion rails to a full-size bed . . . and that's a great deal.

As for the dresser, it featured dovetail drawers, corner blocks and laminate drawer boxes. The metal glides, however, were cheap. Still, not a bad value at $400, but not as good of a deal as the crib.

Reader feedback on these items has been positive. One reader who posted to our message boards said the quality is excellent and the crib is easy to assemble. Others echoed that review.

Of course, the problem with any deal at Costco is availability. These items will probably only be at the warehouse for a limited time. Meanwhile, you can sometimes order the crib online from Costco for $650 or the crib plus dresser for $1250. While those prices include shipping and handling, you can buy a crib and dresser from many of our top-rated brands for less than $1250.

So it is a split opinion on CafeKid—if you can find it in a Costco warehouse, go for it. Otherwise, unless you live in Montana and the nearest baby store is miles away, these offerings are too pricey. **Rating: B+ (store only)**

Capretti *caprettidesign.com.* If money is no object, Capretti Design has got some nursery furniture for you.

This company got its start in 2007 by Mitchell Schwartz, a veteran of the old Ragazzi brand when it was made in Canada. Capretti has gone through several strategies, first importing cribs from Asia and then switching to made-in-the-USA production.

That's why Capretti's prices are so high—these cribs are made by Amish craftsmen. Capretti features solid maple wood construction (no MDF), dust proofing and high-end drawer glides from Blum (Blumotion) that are under-mounted and self-closing.

So how expensive is Capretti? How about cribs for $1300 to $2500? Or a double dresser for $1500 to $3000?

If you are still with us, you might ask, is Capretti worth it? From a design stand-point, these are nice cribs and dressers, but hardly unique (the Milano is probably Capretti's most unique offering, with its curved base). Eight finishes are available for most collections—

cribs

Organic baby furniture

What makes nursery furniture green? As with many products marketed as organic or natural, there isn't a consensus as to what that means—and that's true with baby furniture as well.

Furniture, by its very nature, isn't the most green product on earth. A toxic brew of chemicals is used to manufacture and finish most items. Example: most furniture isn't made of solid wood but veneers (a thin strip of wood over particle board). Glue is often used to adhere the veneer onto particle board for dresser tops and sides. Some glues contain formaldehyde—as we discussed earlier, some baby furniture makers have been sued by the state of California for unsafe levels of this chemical.

For many folks, green means sustainable. So green baby furniture should be made from sustainable wood. But which wood is more eco-friendly? Some say bamboo is the most green (Natart's new Tulip line of furniture is made from bamboo, but is very pricey). Others say rubber wood (ramin) is green since the tree it comes from (Para rubber tree) is usually cut down anyway after it is used to produce latex.

Given all the confusion, here is our advice for green nursery furniture shoppers:

◆ **Look for solid wood furniture that is certified.** There are a handful of non-profit environmental organizations that certify wood as sustainable: the Forest Stewardship Council (FSC) is among the best known. FSC-certified crib makers include Argington, and Oeuf (both are reviewed in this chapter).

◆ **Consider a water-based paint or stain.** Romina offers a "Bees wax" finish that is about as organic as it gets. Pacific Rim also has a similar option: 100% pure tung oil with a beeswax sealant. Stokke's Sleepi crib features a formaldehyde-free varnish.

◆ **Avoid dressers made entirely of MDF or particle board.** The more solid wood, the better.

◆ **Consider an organic mattress.** We review mattresses later in this chapter.

nice, but again not terribly unique.

Perhaps the best feature of Capretti is the ability to customize the furniture (colors, sizes, dimensions) . . . and when you are paying close to $2000 for a double dresser, that makes sense.

At this price level, Capretti is pretty much on its own—the closest competitor is Romina, who makes excellent solid wood furniture that costs about 20% less than Capretti. But Romina makes its furniture in Romania, not in the U.S. by the Amish. Whether folks see that as enough of a reason to part with the extra cash is hard to say.

Quality-wise, Capretti has had a mixed track record. The company started out strong in 2007 and then was hit by complaints of freight damage and other woes in 2008-9. No doubt this led to Capretti's decision to switch production from Asia to the US in 2012. Since the company switched to domestic production, initial quality reports are positive. We also like the eight week turnaround, which is quicker than most upper-end brands.

One last caveat to Capretti: the company only has a handful of dealers. In some states (Texas), there are none. In others (California), there is just one store that carries the line. So seeing this brand in person may be a challenge unless you are on the East Coast. ***Rating: B+***

Caramia *This crib brand is reviewed in the bonus section on our web site, BabyBargains.com/cribs*

Carter's/Child of Mine *summerinfant.com.* Better known for its video monitors, Summer Infant jumped into the nursery furniture market in 2009 and sells under the Carters brand. Most of these cribs are imported from Asia (Indonesia, China and Vietnam).

Just to make it more confusing, these cribs are marketed several ways: Carters, Child of Mine by Carters, Just One You by Carters and My Nursery by Child of Mine, to name a few. FYI: Summer also markets these cribs under the name Disney Princess and its own name.

Prices range from $150 for a Child of Mine by Carters crib at Walmart to a $350 Carters convertible crib at Bed Bath & Beyond. Dressers are $230 to $280; most are ready-to-assemble.

In a nutshell, most of these cribs are simple in styling with few bells and whistles. The styling echoes Pottery Barn and the dressers have a touch of Shaker design.

New in the past year, the Simple Adjust crib has a unique feature: an easy-to-use mattress height adjuster. While other cribs require you to dissemble the entire crib to change the mattress height, the Simple Adjust cribs has two triggers that enable you to change the height in just ten seconds. An example of this crib is the Summer Infant Bryant Convertible Crib with Simple Adjust at Target for $200.

Parent feedback on the brand has been mostly positive: fans like the sturdy construction, easy assembly and included conversion kit. Detractors point out the mattress support is an MDF board and the ready-to-assemble dressers are nothing special, quality-wise.

And one additional point: while Carters/Summer advertises its convertible cribs as 4-in-1 (crib, day bed, toddler bed, full size bed), all those extra uses beyond a crib require a separate purchase of toddler and conversion rails. Hence, of out of the box, Summer's 4-in-1 cribs are just cribs.

We make this point since we've seen a few reviews where parents felt duped by the 4-in-1 pitch, even though the fine print of all these cribs indicate the separate purchase catch. FYI: Most convertible cribs require a separate purchase for the toddler and conversion rails, although a few will include the kits in the price.

Final note: as we were going to press, Summer announced it was phasing out its Carters and Disney Princess licensed furniture. Hence, you'll see this furniture in the future under the Summer brand. As of this writing, however, we still saw plenty of stock of the Carters furniture, so we'll keep this review under the Carters name for time being. **Rating: B**

Child Craft *childcraftindustries.com.* Here's a sad case study of American business and failure to adapt to changing times.

Child Craft, the Indiana-based crib maker that traces its roots back to 1911, was once among the top brands of nursery furniture. In recent years, however, the company has had a slow, painful slide into obscurity. Some of this has been bad luck (a 2004 flood knocked the company offline for several months) . . . while most of the blame can be laid at the company's leadership, which never fully adapted to the flood of Asian-produced nursery furniture, both on the high and low end of the market.

Adding insult to injury, the company has gone through several changes in ownership. The latest: commercial crib maker Foundations acquired the assets of Child Craft in 2009.

Foundations relaunch of the Child Craft brand has been bumpy. The company has abandoned Child Craft's high-end label (Legacy) and now just sells entry-price point cribs under the Child Craft (blue) label. Example: the low-profile London crib is $180 to $220 and available on sites like Amazon and Target. A limited number of fully assembled dresser styles will also be available for $180 to $300.

That crib gets good reviews from parents who like its low height and overall quality. While most folks were happy with their Child Craft cribs purchased off Amazon and other online sites, there was a small minority of folks who reported freight damage, including parts rolling around loose in boxes. However, on balance, the reviews are positive.

Less enthusiastic are the reviews of Child Craft's dressers, which are made by ready-to-assemble king Sauder. We heard more than one parent complain about freight damage to the dressers; assembly is difficult and time consuming. Given the majority of negative reviews on the dressers, we say still clear.

Style-wise, Child Craft is introducing several two-tone and grey crib styles in the coming year that are, dare we say, hip? This is a change from recent seasons, when the line seemed content to churn out very safe and traditional styles.

So it is a mixed review for Child Craft: a thumbs up for the affordable cribs (especially the London). But skip the dressers. ***Rating: B***

Child of Mine *See Carter's.*

College Woodwork *See Kidz Decoeur.*

Corsican Kids *corsican.com.* Looking for a wrought iron crib? California-based Corsican Kids specializes in iron cribs that have a vintage feel, with detailed headboard and footboard decoration. Before you fall in love with the look, however, be sure to turn over the price tag. Most Corsican Kids iron cribs sell for a whopping $1600 to $6000!

Yes, you can choose from a variety of cool finishes like pewter and antique bronze. So if you just won the lottery and have to have a crib no one else on the block has, here's your brand. ***Rating: C+***

Cosco *See Dorel.*

DaVinci *See Million Dollar Baby.*

Delta *DeltaEnterprise.com* Imported from China and Indonesia, Delta (also known as Delta Luv and Babies Love by Delta) is perhaps best known for their low-price cribs sold in big box stores.

Unfortunately, the company became known for something else in 2008: one the biggest crib recalls in history. Nearly 1.6 million Delta cribs were recalled by the CPSC for defective hardware—two babies suffocated to death in their Delta cribs after the cribs' side rails detached. The 2008 recall came on the heels of two smaller recalls in 2004 (high levels of lead paint) and 2005 (defective slats).

Obviously, this was a big black eye for Delta, which responded by redoubling their safety testing. The company built an extensive testing laboratory in their New Jersey warehouse, which the New York Times described:

"Eight hours a day, five days a week, cribs are beaten and battered by machines, subjected to the kind of malevolence a demonic toddler could only dream of doling out."

Of course, Delta had little choice in setting up this lab—tougher new safety standards for cribs went into effect in 2011 and that forced low-price king Delta to face an unsettling reality: it's low-end cribs wouldn't be allowed to be sold without improving their quality and durability.

So far, Delta has been recall free since the meltdown of the last decade. Prices range from $130 to $500, although most Delta cribs sold in chains like Babies R Us range from $200 to $300. Among Delta's big selling point: the cribs don't require any tools to assemble.

A good example of this line is the Canton 4-in-1 convertible crib. At $250, this crib does include a toddler rail to convert into a toddler bed. But, like many of these 4-in-1 cribs, the conversion rails needed to convert to a full-size bed are an extra $100. And while this crib is a good value, one trade-off is the exposed bolts and screw holes. This doesn't impact the crib's safety, just aesthetics.

Another caveat: many Delta dressers are made of soft pine—and that means they scratch very easily. As one parent posted, "if you looked at the dresser funny, it would scratch."

In our last review, we gave Delta an F. Delta earned that grade after their disastrous run of recalls in the past few years. However, the company has turned over a new leaf. Quality of Delta cribs is now good and we'll give them a recommendation. The most recent reader feedback on Delta cribs is generally positive, although a few readers who bought Delta cribs online complained of freight damage (scratches, dings) and other quality issues. And

Rug Burn:
How to save on nursery rug prices

Yes, it's always exciting to get that new Pottery Barn Kids catalog in the mail here at the home office in Boulder, CO. Among our favorites are those oh-so-cute rugs Pottery Barn finds to match their collections. But the prices? Whoa! $300 for a puny 5′ by 8′ rug! $600 for an 8′ by 10′ design! Time to take out a second mortgage on the house. We figured there had to be a much less expensive alternative out there to the PBK options. To the rescue, we found Fun Rugs by General Industries (funrugs.com; 800-4FUNRUGS). This giant kids' rug maker has literally hundreds of options to choose from in a variety of sizes. Fun Rugs makes matching rugs for such well-known bedding lines as California Kids and Olive Kids. Now, their web site lets you see their entire collection, but you can't order direct from Fun Rugs. Instead, go to one of their dealers like American Blind & Wallpaper (American Blinds.com), RugsUSA (RugsUSA.com) and NetKidsWear (netkidswear.com search for rugs). All of those web sites sell Fun Rugs at prices that are significantly below similar rugs at PBK. In fact, we found most of those web sites sell rugs for 40% less than PBK or posh specialty stores.

customer service at Delta is lacking—the company has to do a better job returning customer emails and phone calls.

FYI: Delta also owns the Simmons brand, reviewed separately.
Rating: B-

Dolce Baby *See Bivona & Co.*

Dorel *djgusa.com* Canadian conglomerate Dorel is best known for their Eddie Bauer car seats and Safety 1st gadgets—but the company is also a big player in the nursery furniture biz. Just don't look for Dorel nursery furniture under the name Dorel.

Dorel's furniture subsidiary Dorel Asia employs a blizzard of aliases in the furniture market: Jardine (Babies R Us), Bella D'Este (Babies R Us), Vintage Estate (Sears), Heritage Collection (K-Mart), Bethany James/Secure Reach, Baby Relax (Walmart) and so on. Baby Gap at one point launched its own Dorel-made crib line (under the moniker Dorel Fine Furnishings).

Why more aliases than a Jason Bourne movie? Perhaps it has to do with the numerous recalls that Dorel endured during the 1990's under their main Cosco label. In fact, Dorel/Cosco was fined nearly $2 million for failure to report product defects to the government at the start of this decade.

So, if you were the marketing whiz at Dorel, what would you do? Start calling your furniture anything but Dorel or Cosco.

Unfortunately, the company's safety woes didn't end with the name change. Jardine suffered one of the biggest crib recalls in history in 2008 when 320,000 cribs were yanked from Babies R Us for defective slats. Readers flooded our blog with complaints about how the recall was handled (Jardine and Babies R Us set up a Byzantine process to replace the defective cribs, with multiple steps and long waits).

And, yes, these cribs are cheap (a Dorel Baby Relax is $140 at Walmart), but here are the trade-offs. Parents tell us the quality is slapdash—the crib arrives with wood that is chipped and damaged. Paint and stain appears to be applied randomly by small marsupials. The soft pine of these cribs easily scratches. If you really want to buy one of these crib despite these warnings, we'd suggest picking it up at a store and inspecting it carefully before purchasing.

Given Dorel's longstanding troubles with safety in this segment, we don't recommend their nursery furniture, no matter what name they use. ***Rating: F***

Dream on Me *DreamOnMe.com.* The portable/folding crib market has been rife with problems in recent years, with major players like Evenflo and Delta recalling their models for safety reasons. Yet small player Dream on Me has a winner with their "2 in 1 Portable mini crib." Sold online for about $150-$200, this crib is a good bet for Grandma's house—it converts from a crib to a playpen and changing table.

Dream on Me also makes full-size cribs that fold for $270.

Overall, quality is good. Negatives include vague directions that make first-time assembly difficult, say some parents. Dream on Me's iffy customer service (unreturned emails, phone calls) is another drag on this brand.

New in the past year, Dream on Me released what it touts as the first "electronic" crib—the Wonder crib has a motor that moves the mattress up or down, to enable easier access to baby. The Wonder Crib is Dream On Me's answer to the ban on drop-side cribs and runs a whopping $700 to $1000 (although we saw it discounted online to $500 or so). The Wonder Crib is also pitched as a combo crib and changing table—the crib mattress can rise high enough to become a changing table. In the real world, however, the crib mattress doesn't adjust high enough to make it useable as a changing table, says one consumer who bought the Wonder crib.

Customer service at Dream on Me is wanting—readers tell us of cribs that arrive with missing parts or broken rails. Calls to a customer service line are either not returned or the company promises to ship out replacement parts . . . but never does. That might be acceptable for a $150 crib, but Dream on Me can't get away with this if they want to sell $600 Wonder cribs. Our advice: if you want to buy a crib from Dream on Me, make sure the web site has a good return policy just in case.

Bottom line: Dream on Me's folding cribs are a good alternative for grandma's house. But the $600 Wonder crib is a stretch for this brand. *Rating: B*

Drexel Heritage See Stork Craft.

ducduc ducducnyc.com. New York-based ducduc was among the first entrants into the modern nursery category with an eco twist: all furniture is made in the U.S. (their plant is in Connecticut), contains no MDF or particleboard and features finishes that are air pollutant-free.

Of course, all this eco-fabulousness is going to cost you: a ducduc crib runs $1300 to $2400; matching dressers are $1700 to $2400. No wonder this company's distribution is limited to pricey boutiques on the coasts (new this year, you can buy ducduc direct from their web site).

ducduc divides its furniture into two groups: modern and classic. We couldn't tell the difference between the two, but the classic furniture is more likely to feature a more traditional color palette. On the modern side, the Parker crib runs $1425—you can customize the end panel color, end frame and rails/interior panels to your hearts content (18 different finishes). Shipping is another $225 if you are on the East Coast; or $300 to the Western US.

Quality is good, but we have blogged about one customer's disappointment with the ducduc's "white glove delivery." Given that experience, perhaps one would be better off buying this brand from a boutique instead of direct from the manufacturer. **Rating: B**

Dutailier *dutailier.com.* Canadian rocker-glider maker Dutailier launched its nursery furniture line in 2004 after acquiring fellow Canadian crib maker EG.

For several years, Dutailier turned out traditional nursery furniture made in China. After China's lead paint scare, Dutailier decided to make some big changes: first, production was moved back to Canada. And then the line got a major design make-over: modern was in, traditional was out. The line features nine collections.

The new designs feature a mix of zebra wood and colored accents, all named for fruits. Example: the Papaya ($1100). The exception is the Apricot, which despite the name, features a dark espresso finish. (Perhaps they meant to call it Apricot Pit?).

Price are in the $1000 to $1500 for most cribs and dressers. For most collections, you can choose from 32 finish choices and Dutailier offers many accessories (computer desks, night stands, etc).

How's the quality? All in all, we like Dutailier. We toured the company's plant outside of Montreal in 2012 and were impressed with their attention to detail.

Examples: the drawer casings are made of solid wood and drawers use French dovetail assembly. Dutailier has recently added dust proofing to the bottom of its drawers. One disappointment: the new modern collection lacks corner blocks in the dresser drawers.

A couple of caveats: waits can be long for some items (up to 18 weeks, reported one reader who ordered a Dutailier crib). And bolts and other hardware are sometimes visible on the cribs—not something we'd expect at this price point.

Despite this, we recommend Dutailier. **Rating: B+**

DwellStudio *DwellStudio.com* Fashionable home designer DwellStudio made a splash with their licensed bedding line in Target a few years ago. Now, the company is debuting a nursery furniture collection—but don't look for it in discount stores.

The first effort is the Mid Century crib, available in three finishes (French White, Natural and Espresso). It is sold on Amazon and Giggle for $980.

The basic crib features an unusual "x-base structure" and tapered cone-shaped legs. The effect is a minimalist, 1950's aesthetic (Dwell dubs it "vintage classic")—but we wonder if it will be darn difficult to vacuum under the thing. Made in Canada, the crib has exposed bolts—which is disappointing at this price level.

To compliment the crib, Dwell sells a matching three-drawer dresser for $1080, which has ball-bearing drawer glides, dove-tail joints and a "soft-close" drawer mechanism. The dresser is also made in Canada and features both solid birch and birch veneer, as well as something Dwell dubs "recovered wood." So for those keeping score at home, a Dwell crib and dresser will run $2060. And, oh, the toddler rail for the crib is another $195. And, no, the crib doesn't convert to a full-size bed.

DwellStudio's nursery furniture joins a crowded modern nursery furniture market, where a sagging economy has seen competitors such as Oeuf roll out less expensive versions of their $1000+ cribs. On the other hand, Dwell has a well-known brand name and good reputation . . . so perhaps it will find success at a price point that is hard to sell in today's economy.

One negative note: we've seen several reports from readers of shipping damage and poor packaging. Making matters worse, customers said they were disappointed with Dwell's customer service in fixing glitches. If you're going to sell folks $1000+ nursery furniture, you've got to do better than that. **Rating: B**

Echelon *See Munire.*

Eden *EdenBaby.com.* This LA-based crib importer sells a small collection of traditional and convertible cribs to a handful of independent stores nationwide. Eden offers five collections with matching dressers, armoires, hutches and combo dressers. The styling is very plain vanilla, with prices running $300 to $550 (convertible cribs are on the higher end of that scale). A three-drawer dresser is about $400. This brand is imported from China and is sold online by Sears and Amazon, among other sites.

In the past year, Eden has expanded their modern and contemporary-styled offerings. Example: the Madison crib is $530 and a matching dresser is the same price.

As for Eden's quality, we are not impressed (some dressers featured stapled drawers that lacked a smooth glide). Given the competition on the market, Eden needs to step up the quality in order to better compete.

That said, the reviews on the modern crib have been positive—folks are understandably happy at finding a decent modern crib for less than $1000! However, we'd probably suggest folks look at Baby Mod (Million Dollar Baby), for a similar look from a brand that has a better quality track record. **Rating: C+**

El Greco *ElGrecoFurniture.com* Here's a rare bird in the nursery furniture business: a company that never moved production overseas.

Based in Jamestown, New York, El Greco has been making furniture since 1975 but largely flies under the radar of the industry.
Why? Because most of El Greco's cribs and dressers are sold as private label offerings by Land of Nod, Room & Board and Relics (El
Greco's web site lists which cribs they make for each chain on their
web site). Yes, the brand is also sold in a handful of furniture stores,
but most are regular furniture stores, not baby retailers.

Quality is excellent—cribs are made of poplar and maple, although
some of the dressers are made of MDF. Dressers have corner blocks,
dovetail joints, metal glides and solid wood drawer faces.

FYI: Readers in upstate NY have told us they have been able to
buy furniture direct from El Greco's Jamestown factory store—one
snagged a crib for $200 under the regular retail price. Most cribs
and dressers sold in the outlet store are factory seconds, with small
finishing defects. El Greco helpfully posts an inventory of what's currently at the outlet on their Facebook page. Note: the factory store
appears to be open only for special periodic sales. Check their
Facebook page for the latest schedule.

As for El Greco's regular prices, be prepared to spend a pretty
penny for a U.S.-made crib: prices range from $650 to $1600 at
Land of Nod. A six drawer double dresser is $800. While those
prices are about twice as much as a Chinese-made crib sold in
Babies R Us, El Greco's prices are in line with other made in the
USA furniture companies such as Young America by Stanley.

Given their overall quality and safety, El Greco earns our highest
rating—for parents who want to avoid Chinese-made furniture and
can afford the price tags, this is an excellent choice. **Rating: A**

Europa Baby *See LaJobi.*

Fisher-Price *See Bivona & Co.*

Franklin & Ben *FranklinandBen.com* In 2012, Million Dollar
Baby rolled out an entire new brand: Franklin & Ben. Described as
"new traditionalist," this furniture takes its cue from Federalist styling
and features American poplar accents and birch veneers over MDF.
The result is sort of an updated vintage feel, complete with antique
walnut and weathered grey finishes.

Cribs run $400 to $700; and a four-drawer dresser is $850.
Double dressers are $870. Conversion rails for cribs are $200.

Franklin & Ben is sold in specialty stores only. That's a departure
for Million Dollar Baby, a company that got its start selling low-price
Jenny Lind cribs to discount stores and then its DaVinci brand via

Bait and Switch with Floor Samples

Readers of our first book, *Bridal Bargains*, may remember all the amazing scams and rip-offs when it came to buying a wedding gown. As you read this book, you'll notice many of the shenanigans that happen in the wedding biz are thankfully absent in the world of baby products.

Of course, that doesn't mean there aren't ANY scams or rip-offs to be concerned about. One problem that does crop up from time to time is the old "bait and switch scheme," this time as it applies to floor samples of baby furniture. A reader in New York sent us this story about a bait and switch they encountered at a local store:

"We ordered our baby furniture in August for November delivery. When it all arrived, the crib was damaged and both the side rails were missing paint. We were suspicious they were trying to pass off floor samples on us—when we opened the drawer on a dresser, we found a price tag from the store. The armoire's top was damaged and loose and the entire piece was dirty. There was even a sticky substance on the door front where a price tag once was placed. Another sign: both the changing table and ottoman were not in their original boxes when they were delivered."

The store's manager was adamant that the items were new, not floor samples. Then the consumer noticed the specific pieces they ordered were no longer on the sales floor. After some more haggling, the store agreed to re-order the furniture from their supplier.

Why would a store do this? In a tough economy, a store's inventory may balloon as sales stall. The temptation among some baby storeowners may be to try to pass off used floor samples as new goods, in order to clear out a backlog at the warehouse. Of course, you'd expect them to be smarter about this than the above story—the least they could have done was clean/repair items and make sure the price tags were removed! But some merchants' dishonesty is only matched by their stupidity.

Obviously, when you buy brand new, special-order furniture that is exactly what you deserve to get. While this is not an everyday occurrence in the baby biz, you should take steps to protect yourself. First, pay for any deposits on furniture with a credit card—if the merchant fails to deliver what they promise, you can dispute the charge. Second, carefully inspect any order when it arrives. Items should arrive in their original boxes and be free of dirt/damage or other telltale signs of wear. If you suspect a special-order item is really a used sample, don't accept delivery and immediately contact the store.

ecommerce during the web's early days.

The web site for Franklin & Ben is impressive, with detailed info on the brand and how it beats industry safety standards. We also liked the explanation of the company's materials, stains and paints. We wish more manufacturers were this transparent. And there are even prices for the cribs and accessories posted online! What a concept.

For 2014, Franklin & Ben rolls out two new collections (Providence and Nelson) which continue the early Americana meets distressed vintage look.

So how's the quality? Good, say readers who've been among the early purchasers of this furniture. At this price range, Franklin & Ben competes with brands like Bonavita, Pali and Baby's Dream.

Perhaps the only complaint might be the styling—while we give Franklin & Ben bonus points for trying something different, these looks might not be everyone's cup of tea. And while the company uses poplar in most designs, there is some birch veneers and MDF (medium density fiberboard) in some pieces. While that isn't unheard of in this price point, some competitors offer more wood and less MDF than Franklin & Ben.

So it is a thumbs up for Franklin & Ben. Good quality, decent pricing and a new spin on design. ***Rating: A-***

Giggle *giggle.com.* Specialty chain Giggle sells cribs from Oeuf, DwellStudio, Bloom and Stokke, but the company also imports a few exclusive models. An example is the new "Better Basics" Harper crib for $600. This crib is actually made by Latvian manufacturer Troll Nursery (troll.lv), which has been in business since 1994 and mostly sells cribs in Europe and Russia. The Harper crib features birch rails and plywood end panels and uses low VOC paint. A matching changing table is $350 and a conversion kit (to a toddler bed) is $125.

The Harper is available in two finishes: natural and walnut. Giggle claims the glue used in the plywood end panels is nontoxic, but the crib is not GREENGUARD certified, so it is hard to verify any emission claims. Reader feedback on Giggle's Harper crib has been positive—quality and durability is good. ***Rating: A-***

Graco *See LaJobi.*

Imagio Baby *See Westwood.*

IKEA *ikea.com.* IKEA is an incredibly affordable option for cribs and other nursery furniture items. For example, their simple Sniglar is just $70. IKEA has four other crib options: Gulliver ($100-$130), Hensvik ($99) and Sundvik ($119). Yes, all these cribs meet U.S. safety standards—they are so inexpensive because they are very simply styled.

IKEA carries much more than just cribs: you can buy dressers ($80 to $300), twin beds ($100), lamps, bedding and more.

So what's the catch? Well, most items require assembly that can drive just about any sane person off a cliff—although we should point out, that assembling an IKEA crib is just as easy as assembling any brand of crib. The assembly challenge usually comes in with IKEA dressers or other storage units.

The quality of IKEA's dressers and other furniture items can best be described as no-frills (example: their crib mattress didn't impress us—too soft, in our opinion). Obviously, IKEA furniture isn't intended to be heirloom quality that will last until your kid goes to college. But this is a great stop gap if you need something affordable (even if you plan to replace it down the line).

Reader feedback on IKEA nursery furniture has been positive. If you can survive the assembly process (especially for the dressers), then this is a good choice. ***Rating: A-***

JCPenney *jcpenney.com.* JCPenney is a big player in the online crib business—their site has 40+ crib styles to choose from, along with a raft of other nursery furniture and accessories.

Penney's takes a different approach to the nursery furniture biz than other chains: it uses aliases of big crib makers to make the furniture look exclusive to the company. Hence, most furniture sold here is made by major manufacturers under assumed names. Example: Bedford Baby is really Westwood, ABC/DaVinci is Million Dollar Baby. Only the Rockland and Savanna furniture are Penney's private label. These are made by Yu Wei, a Taiwan-based furniture company, exclusively for JCPenney.

New in the past year, Penney has added cribs from Ragazzi and Munire in the $500-$700 range.

We review all the above brand names separately in this section. As for Rockland and Savannah, most readers tell us they are happy with the quality. Prices for cribs range from $200 to $760 (most are under $500); most of the dressers are $300 to $600.

In the past year, we've noticed Penney's has added several three-piece nursery collections to their web site, with prices in the $700 to $1400 range for a crib plus changer and four-drawer chest.

On the upside, Penney's has a good reputation for safety. Yes, the company has had recalls for some defective side rails and drop-side cribs in recent years, but overall Penney's has had a good safety track record.

Penney's customer service has been up and down in recent years. Although complaints are generally down compared to five years ago, we still see stories like this posted to our message board: a reader ordered a nursery set and it arrived three weeks early. So far so good, right? Yes, but when the reader opened the box with the dresser, she found it damaged (dropped on the corner and the top had buckled). Interestingly, the box was flawless, so someone had dropped the dresser before it had been packed.

So the customer takes the dresser back to Penney's, which promise to ship a replacement. The replacement arrives a week later . . . but is the wrong color. When the customer calls back Penney's to get this fixed, she finds the entire set has now been discontinued. Bottom line: our reader has to return the entire nursery set and start again.

The moral of this story is that, yes, freight damage can happen with any furniture order. But Penney's compounds the error by shipping the wrong color as a replacement—there's no excuse for that.

Bottom line: we only recommend Penney's if you live in a place with few other retail baby store alternatives. **Rating: C+**

Jenny Lind *This is a generic crib style, not a brand name. We explain what a Jenny Lind crib is in a box earlier in this section.*

Jessica McClintock *See Simmons.*

Just One Year *See Carter's.*

Kathy Ireland *See LaJobi.*

Kidz Décoeur *kidzdecoeur.com.* College Woodwork makes this eco-friendly, made-in-Canada furniture line that is sold in specialty stores.

As a division of College Woodwork, Kidz Decoeur features the same quality finish as the main line (dovetail drawer construction, full-extension slides, solid birch construction, etc). The difference is mostly styling: while College Woodwork is traditional, Kidz Decoeur has a more modern/clean aesthetic. Examples: the Greenwich collection features two-tone finishes, while the Augusta features curved legs on both the crib and dresser. The top-selling crib is the Carson, which features a traditional four-square design.

Sixteen finishes are available, including Toasted Cranberry (we didn't realize you could toast a cranberry, but we digress). New for 2014 is a "storm grey" finish that is available in standard or "weathered" looks.

Prices range from $800-$1300 for cribs; dressers are $700-$1300.

How's the quality? We were generally impressed with the line— the one-inch thick tops on dressers as well as self-closing drawers are good signs. It was odd to not see corner blocks on the drawers, however.

Overall, we would recommend this brand. At these prices, Kidz Décoeur competes with Romina (who probably has them beat when it comes to solid wood construction) and Natart (a fellow Canadian company that offers more high style). But Kidz Décoeur does deserve a look if you are in that price range. **Rating: B**

LA Baby *lababyco.com*. Importer LA Baby's main business is commercial-grade, portable cribs sold to hotels and day care centers. In addition, LA Baby has a line of full-size convertible cribs made in China in the $200 price range. The company also has a line of organic crib mattresses.

In the past year, LA Baby has discontinued many of their upper-end cribs, which sold for up to $400. What remains are their bare bones models with clear end panels for about $200; other models without the clear end panels are $200 to $300 online.

We saw LA Baby's furniture at a recent trade show and weren't impressed. Drawers on the dressers are stapled, not dovetailed. The full-size cribs are okay, but there are better choices at this price level. **Rating: C**

LaJobi *lajobi.com*. LaJobi started as an importer of Italian cribs in the 80's, sold in both chain stores and indie retailers. The company transitioned to Asian imports a decade ago and expanded to include a line of entry-level cribs sold under the Graco name plate. In 2008, La Jobi was sold to Kid Brands, which owns several other baby brands including CoCaLo and Kids Line bedding and Sassy (toys, feeding, bath).

Like most large crib sellers, La Jobi markets its wares under different names depending on the retail channel. LaJobi divides its brands into three price ranges: entry-level (Graco, Nursery 101), mid-price (Babi Italia, Europa Baby) and high-end (Bonavita). (Each brand has its own web site go to LaJobi.com to access these sites)

Large chains like Babies R Us (Babi Italia) and Buy Buy Baby (Europa Baby) have their own exclusive La Jobi cribs.

LaJobi's main market niche is value—and unlike their competitors, they've always been aggressive about marketing their goods in chain stores. While the brand typically is the most expensive price point for chains, the company gives you more style and features for the buck. Look at the $400 Babi Italia convertible crib sold at Babies R Us. Similar cribs from Munire and other brands would probably run 20% to 30% more.

Compared to other brands sold in chain stores, LaJobi not only outdoes these other competitors style-wise, but also with quality touches like fit and finish. A typical Babi Italia crib at BRU is $300 to $400—a good buy for parents who want something better than a $200 Delta crib, but can't afford the $600+ cribs sold in specialty stores.

At the entry price level, LaJobi's Graco brand is sold in chains like Target and Walmart. A simple Graco crib at Walmart is $140 to $200. New for 2014, LaJobi is expanding the Graco crib line to included more choices in the $200 to $300 range.

How's the quality? Good, in our opinion. These are probably the best low-price cribs on the market today, especially compared to similarly priced competitors like Delta and Cosco.

We should note that while the Graco cribs get excellent reviews from our readers, there isn't as much love for the dressers. Complaints about poor quality, difficult assembly, parts that don't fit together correctly and more make these dressers a purchase to avoid.

Also in the opening price point, LaJobi has the Nursery 101 brand. Sold in chain stores like Walmart, Nursery 101 offers affordable packages of furniture: a basic crib plus changing table is $150; a crib plus changing table and dresser is $200.

Europa Baby is a mid-price brand where a crib runs $250-$400 and a double dresser is $500. Babi Italia in Babies R Us runs at similar prices. For 2014, LaJobi is expanding its mid-price furniture by launching cribs and dressers under their sister brand, Sassy. Sassy nursery furniture will feature more "clean lines" (read: contemporary looks), coordinating bedding sets and a crib that converts to a desk or play table. Sassy nursery furniture will launch first online with Babies R Us and other retailers in spring.

On the upper end, Bonavita cribs run $400 to $700. Dressers from this line can be pricey, ranging from $500 for a simple chest to $900 for an armoire.

So is it worth it to shell out the extra bucks on the Bonavita line? No—the difference is just aesthetics. These cribs have more details like scalloped edges on the side rail or fancier finishes (the distressed finish on the Francaise Collection, for example). We'd just save the money and buy a basic Babi Italia or Graco crib.

Dressers are another story, however. When you spend more money on a Bonavita dresser, you get more than fancy styling. Bonavita's dressers are fully assembled, for example, while the lower-end Graco dressers are do-it-yourself. Graco dressers are made of "veneered composites," while Bonavita uses more solid wood.

New in the past year, LaJobi rolled out a new high-end license: Kathy Ireland Baby. This line features dressers with all wood drawer glides, corner blocks and dovetail construction. We liked the little touches such as a hutch that comes with feet so it can convert to a bookcase. Prices are $650 to $700 for a crib, $730 for a five-drawer dresser.

We previewed the Kathy Ireland furniture and thought it was well-designed. Yet compared to similarly priced Munire or Young America, the quality isn't quite up to the same level (Munire), nor does it have the same green pedigree (Young America).

Also new on the high end: Truly Scrumptious by Heidi Klum, a Babies R Us exclusive. Cribs run $400; dressers are $650. These items are similar in quality to LaJobi's other mid-price brand, Europa Baby.

La Jobi had a couple of rocky years in 2012 and 2013, with a management shake-up at parent Kid Brands amid slumping sales. In 2012, LaJobi was rocked by a scandal involving the violation of anti-dumping regulations that ended with the firing of two long-time executives.

All this tumult has taken a toll on the company—retailers tell us they are having trouble getting help on customer service issues from LaJobi. Back orders are stacking up and the lack of communication is making even seasoned LaJobi dealers think twice about carrying the brand. Our advice: check with your retailer about these issues before special ordering any LaJobi furniture.

As a result of these concerns, we've separated LaJobi's rating into three parts: one rating for the low-end Graco and Nursery 101 cribs, a second for the mid-price Babi Italia/Baby Europa lines and a third rating for Bonavita. In short, we will recommend the Graco and Nursery 101 cribs (but not the dressers). We will urge more caution on the Babi Italia and Baby Europa lines, since they have to be special ordered. Finally, Bonavita's upper-end line takes the biggest hit, as it is suffering the most in the LaJobi customer service troubles.

In a recent conversation with LaJobi, the company acknowledged its customer service problems and said it is taking steps to fix the problem. We'll update this review as conditions change.

Ratings: Graco / Nursery 101 (cribs only): ***A*** Babi Italia / Baby Europa: ***B*** Bonavita: ***C***

Land of Nod landofnod.com. An off shoot of the Crate and Barrel chain, the Land of Nod (LON) catalog and web site offers a half dozen cribs and a selection of matching accessories (including bedding, bassinets, and other gear.) It ain't cheap: cribs range from $650 to $1600 (although occasional sales see prices drop to $600 or less). Dressers are similarly priced.

The company has shifted its furniture strategy over the years. For a while, they sold Million Dollar Baby cribs with custom finishes. After a China safety scare (LON recalled 2000+ cribs in 2006 for lead paint), the catalog now offers cribs from El Greco, a U.S.-based manufacturer we reviewed earlier.

As for Land of Nod's customer service and quality, readers give the company high marks. But one reader was upset that her furniture order arrived damaged—twice. Land of Nod was accommodating in shipping out replacement pieces, but getting it right in the first place would be nice for a brand that sells such pricey items.

All in all, we like Land of Nod—the El Greco-made cribs are safe and sturdy. And while the prices aren't a bargain, many readers say the custom finishes and other coordinating accessories make it worth the investment. Style and quality-wise, these cribs aren't much different than what you see on Target.com for a $200 Graco crib. The difference is the made-in-the-U.S. label. If that's important to you and you're willing to pay the premium, the Land of Nod is a good alternative. **Rating: A**

Li'l Angels *This crib brand is reviewed in the bonus section on our web site, BabyBargains.com/cribs*

Little Miss Liberty *This crib brand is reviewed in the bonus section on our web site, BabyBargains.com/cribs*

Lolly & Me *lollyandme.com* Minneapolis-based crib maker Lolly & Me is a new company with a made-in-the-USA focus. Founded in 2012 and sold in Target and Kohl's, Lolly & Me's cribs run $330 to $580. Combo dresser/changers run $270 to $550. The company offers nursery packages (crib plus dresser) for $600.

Co-owner and designer Julie Kinsley has 15 years experience designing cribs for companies like Ragazzi, Graco and College Woodwork. She also has designed exclusives for Target, although not in the nursery furniture area. Lolly & Me was born after the company pitched its designs as a Target exclusive, balancing afford-ability with eco-friendly touches.

To that end, Lolly & Me has two collections (McKinley and Sawyer) designated as "eco-friendly." These collections are made in the USA at a small, family-owned factory in Utica, MI. (The rest of the Lolly & Me's furniture is made in Vietnam).

Lolly & Me's web site is a bit vague when it comes to how their furniture is eco-friendly. The company says the furniture is "100% Earth Smart," but is somewhat vague on what that means (example: the site claims its finishes are non-toxic . . . but so are every other crib maker's).

Lolly & Me also claimed at one point that its collections were GREENGUARD certified—but GREENGUARD doesn't list Lolly & Me among their certified companies.

We asked Lolly & Me's Kinsley about this discrepancy and she said that while the company has designed its cribs to meet GREEN-GUARD's strict requirements, it hasn't fully paid GREENGUARD's cer-tification fee yet and therefore isn't listed on their web site.

While we understand why a start-up furniture company would be cash-strapped to start (GREENGUARD certification costs $30,000—the testing isn't cheap), this excuse doesn't cut it for us. You don't list a cer-tification until your products are, well, certified. GREENGUARD certi-fication assures parents furniture meets strict low chemical emission standards. It is deceptive for Lolly & Me to list this on their web site (and on Target) and not actually hold the designation. (Since we first wrote about this issue, Lolly & Me has quietly dropped the GREEN-GUARD claim from their web site and Target product listings; but there still is a GREENGUARD question on the company's online FAQ).

And the product puffery didn't end with GREENGUARD—Lolly & Me claimed its furniture was also JPMA safety-certified. That also isn't true. Lolly & Me is a member of the JPMA and claims its products meet JPMA's safety standards, but the company is NOT listed as JPMA certified as of this writing. Certification and membership are two different things. Again, that is deceptive.

To that end, Kinsley told us Lolly & Me plans to fully certify all its cribs with GREENGUARD soon (right now, only McKinley and Sawyer meet that standard). And the company promises to be JPMA-certified. As of this writing, that isn't the case.

FYI: Three of Lolly & Me's seven finishes are what the company refers to as "Earth Smart"—Chocolate, Whitewash Driftwood and Natural are apparently water-based, low VOC and made in the USA.

Lolly & Me has had some quality issues as it ramped up for production, admitting they have struggled to fill demand. As a result, some cribs shipped out with incorrectly drilled holes for bolts and other quality glitches. The company pledges to do better going forward. Reviews on Target's web site have generally been positive, however, despite these teething pains.

Bottom line: Lolly & Me makes good furniture that is a decent value. But the bogus claims of GREENGUARD and JPMA certification give us pause, knocking down what otherwise would be a higher rating. **Rating: B**

Lusso *See Sorelle.*

Million Dollar Baby Classic *milliondollarbaby.com.* Million Dollar Baby (MDB) is one of the industry's best survival stories. Among the first to jump on the import bandwagon (the company launched in 1989), MDB has thrived by selling its wares in a large variety of stores under a series of aliases. It also didn't hurt that the company was the first to see the potential of the Internet to sell furniture.

Even though this company got its start selling low-price Jenny Lind cribs to discount stores, you'll now find it everywhere from specialty stores to Walmart. The company's cribs are sold under the aliases ABC in JCPenney and Baby Mod at Walmart.

The company divides its line into four brands: DaVinci, Million Dollar Baby Classic (MDBC), Babyletto and Nurseryworks. DaVinci is the entry-level price point, sold online. MDBC is somewhat more expensive than DaVinci and sold in retail stores. Babyletto is modern, but at an affordable price point. Nurseryworks is on the high end, sold in specialty stores.

Style-wise, MDBC and DaVinci are similar. The difference: DaVinci's dressers are ready-to-assemble (and hence easier to ship), while MDBC are pre-assembled.

Cribs in the DaVinci lines are $150 to $550 (most are $200 to $300); dressers are $260 to $500. Million Dollar Baby Classic cribs are $400 to $500.

Babyletto's modern cribs are $300-$400, although Walmart sells a version called Baby Mod with less fancy detailing for $265. Bundles of furniture including a crib, dressing table and three-drawer dresser run $300.

Nurseryworks, however, is priced at the premium end of the market: their modern Aerial crib is $940; the two-toned Loom crib is $650.

In the past year, Million Dollar Baby rolled out an entire new brand: Franklin & Ben. This brand is reviewed separately.

If that weren't enough, in the past year, Million Dollar Baby launched ubabub. This Australian crib brand is new to the U.S.—ultramodern cribs that combine wood and lucite for a Jetsons-like look. The Pod runs $2000 and features ash and popular wood, while the Nifty Clear is $1500.

So, how's the quality overall for Million Dollar Baby? The cribs are good; the dressers are average. Our biggest beef with MDB: their heavy use of Asian pine, which is softer than other pine on the market and more susceptible to damage. We wish MDB had more hardwood groupings in their line and less pine.

Readers like the Baby Mod and Babyletto modern cribs, but the dressers are made of low-quality materials that scratch easily.

Even MDB's upper-end furniture cuts corners on quality: dressers lack corner blocks and the basic metal glides don't stack up well to the competition.

As you can probably tell, Million Dollar Baby has been moving more upscale in recent years. The ubabub cribs are a major departure and it remains to be seen what kind of market there will be for these ultra-expensive cribs.

How is MDB's customer service? We've heard mixed reports. Retailers seem happy with MDB's customer service and deliveries. Consumers are less enthusiastic, telling us about unreturned emails, poor assembly instructions and overall lackluster customer service.

Bottom line: this is a good brand if you just have to have that modern look but are on a limited budget—Baby Mod and Babyletto are stand-outs. ***Rating: B***

Mira Studios *Kolcraft.com* Kolcraft joins the nursery furniture market in 2014 with Mira Studios, a budget to mid-price line of cribs and dressers. Better known for its strollers and crib mattresses, Kolcraft lured away the former head and designer of Westwood Design to give the line a jump start. As such, there is a similarity between Westwood and Mira, both in style and overall approach to the market.

We previewed Mira's cribs at a trade show and found a variety of different styles, most of which would fall into the traditional furniture category. It seemed to us the folks behind Mira are trying to throw as much as they can at the market and see what sticks—hence the design direction is a bit jumbled. The simple Elan ($200) crib features a very basic style, while the Elise adds bowed head and footboards for $300. Yes, there is a sleigh style crib (Noble) and a $600 panel crib (Bridgehampton) that features a multi-layer finish.

Mira Studios furniture is made in Vietnam and China and features six available finishes, although most styles just have two choices. Most cribs are made from New Zealand pine, although a few models are made of poplar. Dressers included both ready to assemble models and already assembled options. The quality of the dressers was OK—most have ball bearing glides and feature a soft close. That seems appropriate for the lower-priced dressers, but this glide system will struggle to compete against competitor's $600 dressers that feature self-closing drawers and smoother glides.

It's hard to get a handle on exactly what Mira Studios wants to do here—are they an affordable brand that is aiming to compete with the $200 to $300 Delta cribs sold at Babies R Us? Or is Mira a mid-priced entry that will compete with Westwood and even Munire's Baby Cache in the $500 price point? We're not sure the folks at Mira have figured this out, as judged by the hodge-podge of styles they plan to launch in 2014.

Quality is also hard to judge here—while the samples we saw looked fine (as samples always seem to do), the proof will be in the shipments. And while Westwood had a good track record, it is anyone's guess whether Mira will have a smooth launch. We'll keep an eye on it and update this review as we head into 2014.

What we would have liked to see here is more of a consistent design and value statement . . . and it looks like Mira will launch without either. ***Rating: Not Yet.***

Mother Hubbard's Cupboard *This crib brand is reviewed in the bonus section on our web site, BabyBargains.com/cribs*

Munire *munirefurniture.com.* Munire got its start as an importer of nursery furniture in the late 90's, selling its wares under private label for baby stores on the East Coast. Over the last few years, the company added a domestic factory in Indiana.

Munire's niche is adult-looking nursery furniture at prices that are a few notches below the other players on the market. Much of the credit goes to owner and designer, Munir. In a sea of look-alike cribs and dressers, Munire's unique looks help the company stand apart: cribs with swooping arches, detailed base moulding, carved headboards, etc.

A typical offering: the Urban with its clean lines ($600 crib, $750 for a double dresser). While a couple of Munire collections are less expensive (a few styles start at $400), most Munire cribs are in the upper $500's to $700 range; all are imported from Indonesia.

Overall, a three-piece Munire furniture collection (crib, dresser, armoire) runs about $2000. Yes, that's more than some lower-end competitors, but you do get quality touches like dove-tail drawers and architectural details such as bun feet on the dressers. In fact, it is the quality that most impressed us about Munire: drawers feature a double-track, ball-bearing system for smooth glides, center supports, corner blocks and more. Most of Munire's collections are made of solid wood, although a few have painted MDF veneers.

Finish options are a bit limited—most collections come in four or five choices, although a few just have two. Munire's furniture is conservatively styled (lots of dark espresso finishes).

In the past year, Munire debuted a handful of simple, non-convertible cribs dubbed Safeside for $350. With a lower-to-the-ground profile, Safeside addresses a complaint some parents voiced about the height of Munire's regular cribs that makes it tough to lay down a baby when the mattress is in its lowest position. While the Safeside cribs convert into a toddler/day bed with an optional toddler rail, they don't covert into a full-size bed.

New in the past year, Munire upgraded its drawer glides (the result is a smoother glide) and added 20% more drawer space.

If you like the Munire look but can't spend $600 for a crib, check out the brand's sister line at Babies R Us under the name Baby Cache. Basically, this is Munire Lite—similar designs, but less fancy detailing. Baby Cache's five collections at BRU run $330 to $600 for cribs, $400 to $800 for a dresser. Hence, a three-piece Baby Cache nursery is about $1500. The downside? Baby Cache doesn't have the accessories Munire offers (such as night stands) and finishes are limited. New this year is the Baby Cache Elite line ($600 to $700) which is made in Munire's U.S. factory, the same place they make their Echelon line.

Munire is also sold under the name Suite Bebe at Baby Depot, where a simple crib is $300 and a six-drawer dressers is $400. Suite Bebe has its own web site at suitebebe.com—the brand is just like Baby Cache: a scaled back, less fancy version of Munire. Also: Munire recently debuted in Buy Buy Baby with four collections under the Munire name. Cribs sell for $400 to $700.

In 2011, Munire debuted Echelon, a made-in-America brand (most of Munire and Baby Cache are imported from Indonesia). Munire built a $5 million factory in Indiana to make Echelon, which features all wood constructions (no MDF or particle board), self-closing/full extension drawers and other upper-end touches. Prices: $900-$1100 for a crib, $1000 for a dresser.

The Indiana factory has expanded in the past year to turn out furniture made under the Munire USA label. Cribs from this line run $750 to $900. The USA line is 100% wood with no MDF. New for 2014, Echelon will introduce three new collections with lower prices: cribs $720-$750 and dressers $860-$900.

How's the quality for Munire overall? Munire is like the Toyota Camry of nursery furniture brands: well-made, solid value but not top-of-the-line. Yes, other brands might have better quality, but you're going to pay more. Ragazzi's drawer glides are nicer . . . but a comparable dresser is $100 to $200 more than Munire. And Romina uses 100% solid beech wood . . . but its cribs and dressers are 30% to 40% more than Munire. The new Echelon furniture aims for a higher quality mark, but of course, you'll pay for it.

So, what's not to like about Munire? Well, the company suffered

True Colors: Swatches and Samples

What's the difference between oak and pecan? When you order baby furniture, those terms don't refer to a species of wood, but the color of the stain. And many parents have been frustrated when their expensive nursery furniture arrives and it looks nothing like the "cherry" furniture they expected. Here's our advice: when ordering furniture, be sure to see ACTUAL wood samples stained with the hue you want. Don't rely on a web site picture or even a printed catalog. And remember that different types of wood take stain, well, differently. If you order your furniture in a pecan finish, but the crib is made of beech wood and the dresser is pine, they may NOT match. That's because beech and pine would look slightly different even when stained with the exact same finish.

Ordering online makes this more of a challenge. Most sites don't offer wood samples—you have to rely on an online picture (and how that is displayed on your monitor). Bottom line: you'll have to be flexible when it comes to what the final stain looks like. But if you have your heart set on a particular hue for your nursery furniture, it might be best to order off-line . . . and see a stained wood sample first.

a black eye with an embarrassing recall in late 2008 for lead paint in one finish of one collection: 3000 Newport cribs in "rubbed black" had a red paint undercoat that contained lead. While the company vows to toughen its testing of paint, this was still a major lapse.

We've also received a scattered number of complaints about the finish on some Munire collections; readers say it scratches way too easily. One reader who ordered the Essex in cherry said it has been a "headache from the beginning. After a few months of use, the finish is scratched up." We're not sure if this was a quality control issue on a particular batch of cribs since other readers report no problems—but we expect more consistency at this price level.

Despite these issues, we still think Munire/Echelon is a good brand and we recommend it. Whenever our readers have sent us a complaint about the company, Munire has been quick to correct the problem. So while the brand isn't perfect, the customer service and overall value of the brand earns them a top rating in our book.
Rating: A

Natart natartfurniture.com. Quebec-based Natart is one of the few survivors of the shake-out of Canadian nursery furniture makers, most of which succumbed to competition from Asian imports.

While Natart did briefly flirt with makings its cribs and dressers in China in the late 2000's, the company now produces all its furniture in the small hamlet of Princeville, Quebec.

Natart's mojo is high style furniture—designs you won't see elsewhere in the market. Touches like silver paint finishes and sculptured dressers help Natart stand out from the crowd.

We toured their factory in the summer of 2012 and were impressed—Natart's emphasis is on eco-friendly furniture, married with an Italian design influence (founders Tony and Michel De Bonis moved Natart from Rome to Quebec in 1995).

Natart features three division: Natart, Tulip and Leander. While all of Natart's furniture are GREENGUARD certified to be low emission, Natart's Tulip sub-line takes the eco-angle one step further: all its cribs and dressers feature "all engineered recycled wood (MDF) and bamboo components." Tulip cribs run about $1000; by contrast, Natart features all solid-wood construction and runs about $800 for a crib. Dressers are similarly priced.

Newest to the Natart family is the Leander line, which is made in Denmark and features an oval crib that converts to a twin bed (like the Stokke Sleepi). Price: $1300, which includes the conversion rails.

For 2014, Natart is debuted a new collection of modern furniture that includes a round crib ($1300, including mattress) that converts to a double bed without any conversion rails. Also new: Nest, a collection that includes a convertible crib for $800 and a $1000 dresser with self-closing drawers. The dresser is made of solid wood and veneers and runs about 20% less than other Natart furniture. Finally, Natart is coming out with upholstered leather rocking chairs that include a handy shelf for your iPad or other tablet computer. Price: $1400.

Quality-wise, we liked Natart. Their dressers features self-closing glides, center stabilizer bars and other quality touches.

In a nutshell, Natart is an excellent choice if you want to avoid Chinese-made furniture and are willing to pay extra for the eco-focus. ***Rating: A***

Nest *See Natart.*

Newport Cottages *newportcottages.com.* When it comes to over-the-top nursery furniture, Newport Cottages turns the knob to 11.

With their trademark look of two-toned case pieces and neon-bright finishes (23 in all), Newport Cottages is a mix of both vintage and contemporary aesthetics. The company got its start in 1996, when designer Cristina Alvarez was disappointed in the plain offerings on the nursery furniture market.

But all this style will cost you: a simple, colorful crib is $1300 to $1800. A dresser will set you back $1600—or more. Newport also sells various accessories and accent pieces, including toy chests, dresser mirrors and more.

Yep, that is darn pricey . . . but at least the furniture is manufactured in the U.S. (which makes Newport Cottages one of the few remaining domestic makers of nursery furniture).

Quality is a mixed bag—the samples we previewed looked fine (Newport Cottages doesn't use MDF or particle board), but this company has struggled with consistency when it comes to quality and shipping. And at that these prices, we'd expect perfection. Bottom line: what you are paying for here are unique finishes/colors, not top-of-the-line furniture quality. ***Rating: C***

Nursery 101 *See LaJobi.*

Nurseryworks *See Million Dollar Baby.*

Oeuf *Oeufnyc.com.* Oeuf (literally, egg in French and pronounced like the "uff" in stuff) traces its roots to 2003, when French-American designers Sophie Demenge and Michael Ryan launched the company (and a family) in Brooklyn, NY. Their goal: pair eco-consciousness with modernist design elements. The result: the Oeuf crib (now called the Classic), which takes its cues from minimalist Euro styling.

The Oeuf crib's fixed side rails, headboard and footboard remove, converting the whole unit to a toddler bed. Like many modern cribs, the Oeuf Classic has a wood base (in this case, birch) and MDF panels covered in a white lacquer finish. Price: $970. A matching double dresser is $1350. Oeuf also sells a variety of other baby items, including mattresses, clothes and toys.

In recent years, Oeuf debuted a slightly less expensive line of furniture (Sparrow), with cribs at $760. Sparrow features natural birch wood accents—there is no MDF in this crib (although a matching dresser is made of MDF with Baltic birch plywood drawer fronts).

New in the past year, Oeuf debuted the Elephant crib ($675), a grey design which can be assembled in ten minutes without tools. The Elephant, a collaboration between Oeuf and Spanish designer Carlos Tiscar, is made in Europe with what Oeuf calls "eco-MDF."

So where does Oeuf fit in the modern furniture universe? Price-wise, Oeuf is on the more affordable end of the modern crib biz—especially the Elephant and Sparrow. With modern crib prices often topping $1000, it's nice to have an option that doesn't break the bank. On the other hand, Baby Mod (Million Dollar Baby) sells a similar crib without all the eco-goodness for under $300.

What's disappointing with Oeuf is the quality of the dressers—we noticed the drawers lack corner blocks and had low-end metal glides. When you are paying $900+ for a three drawer dresser, you are in the same price range as Munire and other better brands. Compared to the competition on dresser quality, Oeuf pales, in our opinion.

We understand the point here of all the eco-goodness, made-in-Europe pedigree and minimalist design aesthetic. And to its credit, Oeuf has good customer service, according to retailers we've interviewed. Whether the brand is worth the price tag compared to competitors that use more solid wood and better dresser construction is an open question. ***Rating: B+***

Pacific Rim Woodworking *This crib brand is reviewed in the bonus section on our web site, BabyBargains.com/cribs*

Pali *pali-design.com.* Italian furniture maker Pali traces its roots to 1919, when the Pali family started out making chairs in Northern Italy. The company switched its focus to juvenile furniture in 1962 and then rode a wave of popularity in the 90's, when its Italian-made cribs and dressers won fans for their craftsmanship and stylish looks.

Pali has had its ups and downs in the past decade, but lately they've been mounting a comeback. To compete on price, the company switched production to Vietnam (made with wood from Europe) and lowered their prices—cribs now start in the $500's, down from $700 in years past. A double dresser in the mod-looking Trieste collection is $900; other dressers are in the $600 to $800 range.

Pali recently introduced two new collections that use solid beech wood (except for drawer bottoms, which are made of MDF). The Onda features a $900 crib and $1200 double dresser with self-closing drawer glides. The other collection, the Aria, features similar prices and a bead board design.

New in the past year, Pali now sells furniture sets (crib plus dresser) for $1000 to $1400. Also new: cribs can either be ordered with a high or flat headboard. And, in the category of Everything Old is New Again, Pali has re-introduced furniture made in Italy. These cribs run $700 and five-drawer dressers about the same. At the time of this writing, there are five collections made in Italy; the other two dozen collections are made in Vietnam.

New for 2014, Pali is taking a stab at modern with Treviso, a two-toned collection featuring a crib in the $600's.

How's the quality? Better—Pali has improved quality in recent years. Yes, Pali uses birch veneers in some collections instead of solid wood like Romina. Of course, you'll pay much more for a Romina dresser than Pali. FYI: Pali is now using three woods in its collections: poplar, New Zealand pine and rubber wood.

Bottom line: Pali is a good, mid-price brand that offers a dash of European design flair and decent quality. ***Rating: A***

Pottery Barn Kids potterybarnkids.com It's rare that one retailer/catalog can change an entire industry. Pottery Barn Kids (PBK) scored that coup during the 2000's when their contemporary nursery décor (accented by vintage motifs and a bright color palette) literally changed the rules. Out went cutesy baby-ish décor, in came a more modern yet still whimsical look, thanks to PBK.

Pottery Barn Kids sells a mixture of name brand and private label furniture from their site. Prices range from a simple $500 crib to $800 for more ornate designs. Occasional sales knock cribs prices as low as $400.

Matching dressers range from $400 to $1200 and run the gamut from simple three-drawer options to extra-wide double dressers. Of course, PBK has all manner of accessories: nightstands, armoires, bookcases, and more.

Watch out for shipping surcharges—PBK charges "delivery surcharges" of $100 to $150 on certain items like dressers (but not on some cribs). That charge is in addition to shipping fees, making the final price much higher than what you see online. Example: a $620 dresser actually costs $790 with shipping and surcharges.

While most parents are happy with PBK's customer service and delivery, we've had more than one parent tell us about quality woes with PBK furniture: peeling paint on a bookcase, splintering wood on a dresser, etc. While the cribs are fine, it's the other furniture items that draw complaints. To PBK's credit, the web site or store usually takes care of the problem and replaces the defective item. But as one reader, who told us PBK's home delivery service miss-assembled her crib, described it, "it's always a canned apology with a pipe dream solution—we'll send someone out, but they never show up."

Quality-wise, you are paying a premium for the PBK look (many items have custom finishes only available at PBK). But take a look under the hood: that $600 crib is cute, but why pay this much for a crib with exposed bolts? You could spend a $100 less on a similar Baby Cache crib from Babies R Us and get a more finished look. And competitors have long since caught up with PBK on style and design, so we're not sure the price premium is justified anymore.

Bottom line: use PBK for décor items like bedding or lamps and order the furniture elsewhere. **Rating (furniture): C**

Ragazzi *ragazzi.com* Ragazzi is a nursery furniture brand with nine lives. The company started in the 70's as a Quebec-based manufacturer of upper-end baby furniture and had its heyday in the '90's. Ragazzi's long rein at the top of the luxury nursery market ended in 2006, when the company suddenly declared bankruptcy and shuttered its Canadian factory. In the end, Ragazzi fell victim to the same forces that doomed other Canadian furniture makers: high costs, competition from Asian imports and an unfavorable currency exchange rate.

Enter Stork Craft, the Vancouver, Canada-based furniture importer best known for its low-end cribs sold in Walmart. For an undisclosed figure, Stork Craft bought the rights to the Ragazzi name and re-launched the brand as an upper-end line in 2008.

We were skeptical this was going to ever work—and at times, we still have our doubts. The re-launch took a year longer than planned . . . and then a switch of factories in 2010 meant Ragazzi was out stock for much of that year. That's right—Ragazzi was missing in action for most of 2010. Then the company switched factories AGAIN in the summer of 2012.

To say this frustrated both retailers and consumers is an understatement—we heard from more than one reader whose Ragazzi furniture was caught in special-order hell.

The bottom line: Stork Craft never quite got its head around the Ragazzi business—instead of shipping container loads of cribs to Walmart stores, Ragazzi's business requires constant care and feeding. Ragazzi customers order one nightstand in espresso. And then another order comes in for one crib in a special finish. The small volume and high expectations of this market segment probably doomed the Ragazzi/Stork Craft marriage from the start.

FYI: Prices for Ragazzi cribs range from $500 to $900 (most are in the $600 range). As for dresser options, Ragazzi offers the gamut, from three/five drawer chests to armoires, night tables and combo dressers. Most dressers are $850.

Quality is impressive: top drawers feature felt-lining, dove-tail joints, self-closing drawers, corner blocks and more. How does that stack up against its other competitors in the premium segment? Compared to Munire, Ragazzi has nicer drawer hardware. But Ragazzi pales a bit next to Romina, which uses 100% solid beech wood (Ragazzi has some veneers). Of course, Romina charges $1200 for a double dresser . . . almost 50% more than Ragazzi.

Even though quality is good, the company's numerous ups and downs with customer service and deliveries prevent us from recommending this brand with any rating more than a C. If you see a Ragazzi crib or dresser on the floor of a nursery store and can buy it on the spot, then go for it. Otherwise, there are other brands with fewer headaches. ***Rating: C***

Relics Furniture *This crib brand is reviewed in the bonus section on our web site, BabyBargains.com/cribs*

Restoration Hardware *RHBabyandChild.com* Restoration Hardware has joined other chains like Pottery Barn in rolling out a luxe kids line, complete with baby furniture, linens, lighting and more.

Sold online only, Restoration Hardware's neo-classical nursery furniture is arranged in two dozen collections, each with crib, dresser, and (sometimes) a bookcase and armoire. Finish options are limited: two choices in most cases, although new distressed options have been added in recent months.

New to the collection are cribs with upholstered end panels for those of you doing a Louis XV theme for your nursery.

Most of Restoration Hardware cribs are made by Bassettbaby, reviewed separately. Obviously, these are upgraded models compared with what Bassett sells to other chain stores—hidden hardware, distressed finishes, etc. Dressers include English dovetail joints, cedar-lined drawers and tip guards.

So, what's not to like? Well, the prices are in the stratosphere: $700 to $1300 for a crib. And that doesn't include "unlimited delivery" fees ($95-$295, depending on your distance to a RH store) and hotel mini-bar prices for accessories (a $500 bookcase, anyone?).

And here's the kicker: cribs only convert to toddler beds, not twin or full size beds as most convertible cribs. Hard to imagine, but Restoration Hardware has managed to make even the most expensive nursery brands sold in specialty stores look like a bargain. At least if you are spending $1000 for a crib in such stores, most likely you are getting a convertible model that turns into a full-size bed. We guess the point here is you are supposed to go back to

Restoration Hardware and spend another $1000 on a big kid bed.

Reader feedback has been mixed on RH—one reader complained that much of her nursery furniture order was on backorder . . . for months! And the quality? "Many of the things I ordered (the mobile in particular) were sub par in terms of quality or arrived broken, however highly priced."

So it is a mixed review for RH: we liked the coordinated collections and the upgraded Bassett furniture . . . but at these prices, we are hard pressed to give RH anything higher than an average rating. The value just isn't there—you can spend *half* the price of these cribs and dressers and get *better* quality and durability. **Rating: C**

Rockland *See JCPenney.*

Romina *RominaKidsFurniture.com* The collapse of Canadian premium furniture maker Ragazzi back in 2006 produced two surprising results: first, Stork Craft re-launched the brand as an Asian import. And second, Ragazzi's former crib supplier, Romina, decided to enter the U.S. market on their own.

Yes, Romina used to supply Ragazzi with unfinished cribs . . . but could Romania-based Romina successfully launch their own line in the U.S.? As it turns out, the answer is yes.

Romina's success here could be attributed to two factors: first, good timing. Romina launched in the midst of the Chinese recall crisis—with furniture made in Romania, the company was one of the few non-China options out there in the late 2000's.

Second, Romina doesn't cut corners when it comes to quality—the line features 100% solid beech wood construction. No MDF, no rubberwood, no veneers over particle board, etc. Romina dressers feature dove-tail joints, corner blocks and self-closing drawer glides that are smooth "like butter," as one retailer described them.

Of course, this isn't cheap—and if you want Romina, you're going to pay for it. Cribs run $850 to $1300; a double dresser is $1200 to $1400. Yes, that's $400 to $500 more than Munire or Ragazzi charges for a similar dresser—you'll have to decide if avoiding an Asian import is worth that premium.

Romina's other major emphasis is their eco-friendly "Bees Wax" finish, which as the name implies, is all-natural. Romina touts it as the ultimate organic finish. If you prefer a darker stain or painted look, Romina also offers eight other finishes, including a navy, white and brown metallic. Adding to their eco-focus, all Romina cribs are now GREENGUARD certified to be low in chemical emissions.

Realizing those prices are a bit rich for the average nursery shopper, Romina is debuting a new, lower-priced line dubbed Silva in 2014. These cribs retail for $700 or less with a double dresser coming in at $900. We know, $700 is hardly "low price" for a crib—but it is an improvement. The difference between Silva and Romina? Silva dressers have veneers with one-inch solid wood borders (Romina is solid wood). Silva dressers also lack the self-closing drawer glides seen on the regular Romina dressers. And Silva's styling is simpler and less ornate.

Design-wise, Romina furniture is traditionally styled; the Ventianni group is the company's only bow to the modern, two-tone finish look. We liked all the available accessories: each collection features nightstands, armoires, bookcases and the like. Our fave Romina style: an over-the-top crib (Cleopatra) that looks like a handlebar mustache, complete with a footboard that can be carved with your baby's name.

All in all, this is one of the best nursery furniture lines on the market . . . there are many expensive nursery furniture brands on the market that aren't worth the asking price when it comes to quality. Romina is the real deal. ***Rating: A***

Room & Board *This nine-store chain with locations in Chicago, San Francisco and New York is reviewed in the bonus section on our web site, BabyBargains.com/cribs*

Room Magic *This crib brand is reviewed in the bonus section on our web site, BabyBargains.com/cribs*

Sauder *This crib brand is reviewed in the bonus section on our web site, BabyBargains.com/cribs*

Savanna *See JCPenney.*

SB2 *See Sorelle.*

Secure Reach by Bethany James *See Dorel.*

Serena & Lily *serenaandlily.com This web site's cribs are actually made by different manufacturers. The Liberty Crib is made by Franklin & Ben, reviewed earlier. The Soho crib is made by Bratt Décor.*

Silva *See Romina.*

Simmons *simmonskidsfurniture.com. Here's an interesting rags to riches and back again tale of an American company. Simmons Juvenile was once one of the country's biggest nursery furniture makers, selling cribs and dressers to many generations of parents.*

Started in 1917 by Thomas Alva Edison to provide wooden cabinets for one of his recent inventions (the phonograph), Simmons morphed into a furniture company that also made mattresses. The company spun off its juvenile division in the 1980's (just to confuse you, there is still a Simmons company that makes mattresses).

Then the company began its slow decline. Simmons made a couple major mistakes, chief among them never adapting to the changing nursery furniture market, which soon became flooded with low-

8 tips to lower the risk of SIDS

Sudden Infant Death Syndrome (SIDS) is the sudden death of an infant under one of year of age due to unexplained causes. Sadly, SIDS is still the number one killer of infants under age one—over 2500 babies die each year.

So, what causes SIDS? Scientists don't know, despite studying the problem for two decades. We do know that SIDS is a threat during the first year of life, with a peak occurrence between one and six months. SIDS also affects more boys than girls; and the SIDS rate in African American babies is twice that of Caucasians. Despite the mystery surrounding SIDS, researchers have discovered several factors that dramatically lower the risk of SIDS. Here is what you can do:

Put your baby to sleep on her back. Infants should be placed on their back (not side or tummy) each time they go to sleep. Since the campaign to get parents to put baby to sleep on their backs began in 1992, the SIDS rate has fallen by 50%. That's the good news. The bad news: while parents are heeding this message, other care givers (that is, grandma or day care centers) are less vigilant. Be sure to tell all your baby's caregivers that baby is to sleep on his back, never his tummy.

Encourage tummy time. When awake, baby should spend some time on their tummy. This helps prevent flat heads caused by lying on their backs (positional plagiocephaly). Vary your child's head position while sleeping (such as, turning his head to the right during one nap and then the left during the next nap). Minimize time spent in car seats (unless baby is in a car, of course!), swings, bouncer seats or carriers—any place baby is kept in a semi-upright position. A good goal: no more than an hour or two a day. To learn more about plagiocephaly, go online to plagiocephaly.org.

Forget gadgets. Special mattresses, sleep positioners, breathing monitors—none have been able to reduce the risk of SIDS, says the American Academy of Pediatrics. Just put baby to sleep on her back.

Use a pacifier. Consider giving baby a pacifier, which has been shown in studies to reduce the rate of SIDS. Why? Scientists don't know exactly, but some speculate pacifiers help keep the airway open.

price imports from Asia. Simmons stuck to making its cribs and dressers in plants in Wisconsin and Canada.

By 2004, Simmons' deteriorating fortunes prompted the management to sell their crib mattress biz and then shutter the Wisconsin plant. Simmons sold the rights to their name to Delta, which then relaunched Simmons as a separate, upscale division aimed at specialty stores. Ironic, no?

However, the re-launch of Simmons has been bumpy for Delta.

Okay, we should acknowledge that pacifiers are controversial—key concerns include breastfeeding interference, tooth development and ear infections. But if you introduce the pacifier after breast-feeding is well-established (around one month), there are few problems. Stop using the pacifier after one year (when the SIDS risk declines) to prevent any dental problems. While pacifiers do increase the risk of ear infections, ear infections are rare in babies when the risk of SIDS is highest (under six months old). Bottom line: Use pacifiers at the time of sleep starting at one month of life for breastfed babies. If the pacifier falls out once the baby is asleep, don't re-insert it. Stop using pacifiers once the risk of SIDS is over (about a year of life).

Don't smoke or overheat the baby's room. Smoking during pregnancy or after the baby is born has been shown to increase the risk of SIDS. Keep baby's room at a comfortable temperature, but don't overheat (do not exceed 70 degrees in the winter; 78 in the summer). Use a wearable blanket or swaddle baby with a blanket.

Bed sharing: bad. Room sharing: good. Why does bed sharing increase the risk of SIDS? Scientists say the risk of suffocation in adult linens (pillows, etc) or entrapment between bed frame and mattress, or by family members is a major contributor to SIDS. That said, *room sharing* (having baby in the same room as the parents, either in a bassinet or crib) is shown to reduce the rate of SIDS. Again, researchers don't know exactly why, but it's possible parents are more attuned to their baby's breathing when baby is nearby.

No soft bedding. Baby's crib or bassinet should have a firm mattress and no soft bedding (quilts, pillows, stuffed animals, bumpers, etc). We will discuss soft bedding more in depth in the next chapter. Also: consider using a swaddling blanket, footed sleeper or SleepSack instead of a blanket. More on these items in Chapter 3.

Make sure all other caregivers follow these instructions. Again, you might be vigilant about back-sleeping . . . but if another caregiver doesn't follow the rules, your baby could be at risk. Make sure your day care provider, grandma or other caregiver is on board.

Their first collection (imported from China and Vietnam) was a bust—$800 cribs and $700 dressers were met with little enthusiasm from shoppers.

Delta/Simmons went back to the drawing board and decided to change strategies: instead of competing in the upper end of the market, they'd aim for the entry-level price point among specialty stores. Hence, Simmon's recent collections feature cribs that are priced in the $300's and are sold in stores like Babies R Us and Target online. There's even a $200 Simmons crib on Amazon

Simmons other offerings run $400 to $600 for cribs, $500 to $600 for dressers. At the top end, Simmons' Jessica McClintock line of cribs features three collections running $600 to $1000 for a crib, $700 to $1000 for a dresser.

How's the quality? Simmons is all over the board: the upper-end McClintock dressers features self-closing drawers and other quality touches. But the lower end Simmons features drawer glides more at home on a Delta dresser at Walmart than a specialty store. A parent who purchased a $550 five-drawer dresser from Babies R Us said she was returning it after found the dresser to be "very cheaply made and constructed." Simmons customer service also lags: more than one reader said they emailed Simmons with questions and received no response. Bottom line: if Simmons is trying to compete against other upper-end crib brands, they've got to do better than this.

So it is a mixed review for Simmons: kudos for the new lower prices . . . but the scattershot quality drags down their overall marks. It seems Simmons is still a brand in search of an identity. **Rating: C+**

Solutions/Kids R Us *The Solutions/Kids R Us furniture line is manufactured exclusively by Delta for Babies R Us.*

Sorelle *sorellefurniture.com* Sorelle is one of the baby gear industry's survival stories. In business since 1977, the company has constantly changed and morphed over time.

The company first imported Italian cribs. It switched gears in the 2000's to importing furniture from Vietnam and China (today most items are imported from Vietnam). Sorelle has succeeded by pursuing a value niche: its furniture is generally regarded as giving consumers more bang for the buck.

Sorelle has also survived by selling its furniture in a variety of channels: specialty stores (under the Sorelle and Lusso brands), chain stores (under Golden Baby and C&T) and online.

In recent years, Sorelle has divided its brand into three parts: high-end (Lusso), mid-price (Sorelle) and entry-level (SB2).

Lusso is sold just in specialty, brick-and-mortar stores—prices range from $500 to $700 for cribs, which includes the toddler conversion rail. Quality touches here include dovetail drawer construction and poplar wood.

Sorelle is the brand you'll see in chain stores—it is similar to Lusso in quality, but scaled down a bit. Cribs run in the $400's.

SB2 is Sorelle's new entry-price point brand sold online. Cribs run $230 to $350; dressers are ready to assemble. Under the SB2 brand, Sorelle offers entire five-piece nursery sets for $400 to $500—crib, four-drawer dresser, hamper, changing table, toddler conversion rail.

Style-wise, Sorelle is middle-of-the-road traditional furniture; yes there are one or two modern groupings with two-tone finishes, but that is the exception to the rule.

In the last couple of years, this brand looks like they've been treading water, style-wise. The lack of innovation and me-too designs are disappointing.

So, how's the quality? If you take a look at the reviews of Sorelle posted to our message boards, you'll note the opinions are all over the board. For every parent who tells us they are pleased with the quality and finish of their Sorelle furniture, another will write to blast a series of problems—quality woes, "nonexistent and rude" customer service, poor assembly instructions, missing parts and more.

It's the lack of customer service that bothers us most here: the attitude at Sorelle seems to be "you're getting a good price on this furniture, so don't complain if we don't return your call for parts." Sorry, but that doesn't cut it.

In general, the cribs get better marks than the dressers, based on our reader feedback. Complaints about the dressers include stains that don't match cribs, uneven finishes, freight damage and more.

Bottom line: great prices but a mixed quality picture and weak customer service drag down Sorelle's rating. ***Rating: C+***

Spot on Square spotonsquare.com California-based Spot on Square launched its modern nursery furniture in 2007. The company offers five crib styles, all with an eco-angle: low VOC paints and formaldehyde-free glue.

Like most modern furniture companies, Spot on Square uses MDF (which it pitches as a recycled material) along with birch, bamboo and walnut. Prices are moderate, at least for modern: the Eicho crib is $690, while a matching dresser/changer is $790. The hiya crib comes in three color variations, ranging in price from $750 (all white MDF) to $900 for a version with bamboo end panels. The most expensive crib in the collection is the high-end Roh crib, made of walnut for $1800 to $2250.

Overall, we were a bit disappointed in the lack of accessories: at most, cribs have a single matching dresser in one configuration. Spot on Square's cribs do not convert to full size beds. Also, it might be hard seeing this furniture in person, as distribution is limited to a handful of small boutiques (although you can buy pieces direct through their company web site).

How's the quality? Most online reviews of this brand are lukewarm at best. Quality control seems to be an issue—one Amazon reviewer point out that her fully assembled dresser arrived with one door that was a completely different color than the other. How does a company miss that in shipping? Others knocked the furniture for "poor workmanship," "drawers that keep falling out and apart," and more. That's disappointing when you are selling furniture at these prices, to say the least.

Bottom line: the modern vibe and eco-goodness of this line are nice, but the quality and lack of accessories is disappointing. **Rating: C**

Stanley *See Young America.*

Status *storkcraft.com.* Stork Craft's mid-price line is positioned as a step up from Stork Craft's furniture sold in chain stores, yet less expensive than their premium Ragazzi brand. Sold in specialty stores and made in China, Status offers 12 collections. Each feature a static convertible crib and two dresser options (combo or double dresser). Five finishes are available. Cribs run $350 to $600 (most are in the $400 range); a combo dresser is $680; armoires are around $700.

Unlike Stork Craft's ready-to-assemble dressers, Status comes fully assembled and features all hardwood construction (pine). The downside? The drawers lack dovetail construction and feature basic wood-on-wood glides (most upper-end nursery furniture has metal glides). We also noticed visible bolts on the cribs, which is something you'd see on a $250 crib at discount store . . . but not usually at this price.

As for quality, several readers tell us of serious issues with Status' quality control—paint splattered all over the finish of a dresser, cribs shipped without assembly instructions and so on. Several folks commented that their Status furniture had strong fumes when removed from its packaging.

Seeking to shake things up from its plain styling, Status changed its design direction in the past year: several groups debuted with "bold and modern" looks. The Tempo, Sonata and Vivo each have interchangeable panels with bright colors.

We'll give Status bonus points for trying to reinvigorate the brand. At these prices, however, Status competes directly with Munire and Westwood—but the quality and design isn't up to par. **Rating: C**

Stella Baby See Westwood

Stokke/Sleepi stokke.com. Norwegian juvenile gear maker Stokke pitches its ultra-expensive crib as a "system" that grows with your child: the Sleepi morphs from a bassinet to a crib, then a toddler bed and finally two chairs . . . all for a mere $1000. You can buy just the crib for $800 (without the toddler bed conversion kit).

A separate changing table (the Care) converts to a play table and desk for $500. As with all these funky European products, you'll have to buy specially made bedding with limited choices ($40 for a sheet; $320 for a set). Yes, you read that right: $40 for a single sheet.

Fans of the Sleepi love its clever oval shape (fits through narrow doorways) and overall ease of use. The Sleepi is perhaps best suited to urban apartment dwellers with little space for a standard-size crib.

Detractors cite the limited choices of bedding, as mentioned above. Quality issues (as noted in online reviews) also dog the Sleepi—parts that don't fit right, wheel casters that don't lock, misaligned screw holes, etc.

For $1000, we'd expect better quality control than this. Hence, we've lowered Stokke's rating this time around to reflect this disappointment. ***Rating: B-***

Stork Craft storkcraft.com. Stork Craft is probably best known as an entry-level brand that's sold in chain stores from Walmart to Babies R Us.

Stork Craft's cribs start at $79 online at Walmart, although most offerings are in the $150 to $200 range. At the top end, a $350 crib model features sleigh styling and the ability to convert to a full-size bed.

All Stork Craft furniture is imported from China.

Stork Craft also makes a wide array of matching accessories, including dressers, rocker gliders and other items—the dressers are an affordable $180 to $300. All of the furniture is ready-to-assemble; readers report assembly ranges from difficult to frustrating, thanks to minimal directions and a lack of labeling for screws and parts. A significant amount of patience is necessary, say most readers.

New in the past year, Stork Craft began selling fully assembled dressers for $500.

So, let's talk quality. Parents generally give Stork Craft low marks, based on reviews posted to our web site. Fans like the affordable pricing and the fact you can order most of this furniture online. But detractors say items often arrive damaged, with missing parts and worse. One parent who paid $450 for a Stork Craft crib said she was extremely disappointed in the poor finish which looked very cheap—and the under-crib drawer's bottom constantly fell off its track when moved. Another parent who bought a $300 Stork Craft dresser said it arrived severely damaged and "looks as if it were purchased at a garage sale." Customer service also came in for criticism, with delays in fixing defective merchandise and parts among the top gripes.

Finally, Stork Craft has downgraded the quality of its cribs in recent years, in our opinion. Example: gone are the spring mattress supports. Now Stork Craft uses a MDF board to support the mattress, which is not our preferred choice.

Stork Craft competes against Million Dollar Baby (Baby Mod) and Graco (made by LaJobi) in this price range. We'd recommend either of those brands over Stork Craft.

Bottom line: if you have your heart set on this brand, stick with the low-price items (the $100 cribs at Walmart are a good bet). Skip the dressers, glider rockers and anything expensive (those $250+ cribs). And be sure to set your expectations accordingly. **Rating: C-**

Suite Bebe *See Munire.*

Summer *See Carter's.*

Thomasville *See Stork Craft.*

Ti Amo *See Bivona & Co.*

Today's Baby *This crib brand is reviewed in the bonus section on our web site, BabyBargains.com/cribs*

Truly Scrumptious by Heidi Klum This furniture is made by LaJobi and sold exclusively at Babies R Us. See LaJobi's review for details.

Tulip *See Natart.*

Vintage Estate *See Dorel.*

Westwood Design *westwoodbaby.com.* Westwood Design was launched in 2005 by several veteran nursery furniture executives who partnered with an adult furniture company for distribution expertise. The company has found success in a crowded market by offering a good quality product with extra features at affordable prices.

Westwood is sold in a variety of outlets, from specialty stores to chains like Buy Buy Baby and online on Amazon. You'll find the brand under the aliases Bedford Baby at JCPenney and Hart at Baby Depot. At the chains, a Westwood crib runs $450 to $550; dressers are similar in price.

In specialty stores, Westwood tends to be a bit fancier in style and higher in price. Example: a new modern two-tone grouping features a $600 crib; dressers are in the $500 to $700 range.

If that is too rich, Westwood has a new entry-level price brand set to debut in 2014: Imagio Baby. Cribs will run $250 and the dresses will be ready-to-assemble. The line will be sold on Walmart.com.

In other news, Westwood recently added several scaled-down furniture pieces (the company calls them "euro-sized") for folks trying to fit furniture in a small nursery.

In 2014, Westwood is introducing a new alias: Stella Baby, a brand it plans to use in specialty stores. Same furniture, just a different name for indie baby stores. Stella will have three collections with prices that range from $400 to $600 for convertible cribs. The brand will have its own web site (stellababychild.com).

FYI: Westwood cribs now ship with "always there hardware"—pre-installed hardware that doesn't detach from the crib. That makes it safer when you disassemble and reassemble a crib. New in the past year, Westwood introduced a line of "no tools assembly" dressers, which the company is touting as an easy way to assemble chests, combos and bookcases.

All Westwood furniture is made in Vietnam.

Quality-wise, Westwood is a good value. Most of the cribs are made from solid hardwood (pine is most common), although the company does use some cherry veneers with dressers and painted MDF in their modern grouping. You'll see some adult furniture touches here and there (hutches with built-in lights; dressers with height-adjustable feet), which is unusual in the nursery market.

We also like how transparent the company is—Westwood even posts pictures of their Vietnam factory to their company blog. That's unusual: most companies don't like talking about their factories, treating their locations like a national security secret.

The downsides? Well, the company only offers a limited number of finishes. And Westwood probably uses more veneers and MDF than its competitors in this price range. That said, parent feedback on Westwood has been very positive—readers love the sturdy construction, ease of assembly on the cribs and overall finished look. Another plus: customer service at Westwood is excellent. ***Rating: A***

Young America by Stanley *youngamerica.com.* Adult furniture maker Stanley entered the juvenile market in 2003 with "Young America," a collection of nursery furniture with a wide range of accessories.

This brand has gone through several changes over the years. It started out as a high-end brand that was made in the U.S. Then

Stanley switched to imports from Asia to lower prices. In 2010, Stanley made the decision to bring production back to the U.S. and added an eco-focus (all their furniture is now GREENGUARD certified).

Stanley's mojo is their "built to grow" theme—cribs that can turn into full-size beds, added accessories like desks/study areas for older kids, trundle storage options and more. It's the plethora of accessories that sets Stanley's Young America apart from its competitors, where offering a matching nightstand is about as "built to grow" as they get.

Price-wise, Stanley is on the premium end of the market: a crib runs $700 to $900. A double dresser runs $1000 to $1500. Armoires are $1250 to $1700. Heck, a Young America nightstand can set you back $600. FYI: this brand is sold in specialty stores and chains like Buy Buy Baby, where it is known as Baby America.

So, is it worth it? Well, if you want made-in-the-U.S. nursery furniture that is GREENGUARD certified, then Stanley is your brand. Fans love the numerous finishes and accessory items—most crib styles can be purchased in over 30 color finishes. That's right, when other brands limit you to three versions of brown, Stanley lets you customize to your heart's content here.

Critics of this brand point out the plain vanilla styling makes it hard to justify the prices. Compare the styling here to Munire and Romina and you'll see what we are referring to—Young America by Stanley needs a bit more zing to justify their $800 price tags.

Quality-wise, Young America doesn't stack up well against competitors like Romina, which offers solid wood construction (Stanley's dressers are more often veneers) and better drawer glides. Yes, Stanley offers felt-lined top drawers and dove-tail construction. That alone doesn't justify these prices. If you want to charge folks a $1000 for a dresser, we'd like to see self-closing glides and more solid wood construction. We are happy to see that Stanley has recently tried to address the quality gap by adding touches like . . . self-closing drawer glides. Better late than never.

Shipping issues have dogged this brand in 2013—orders have been delayed, shipping times have lengthened, etc. One consumer complaint lodged with the Better Business Bureau claimed a furniture order took over four *months* to arrive, finally showing up some five weeks *after* their daughter was born. The initial quote when the order was placed? Eight weeks.

We spoke with David Peterson, Young America's Vice President for Marketing & Brand Development, about these issues. Peterson said Young America was struggling to replace an aging enterprise computer system, which was failing to keep up with the volume of orders. These computer glitches caused the shipping delays. While

Young America said it was working on solving the problems as we went to press, the shipping problems and delays are frustrating consumers and retailers alike. We've dropped Young America's rating this year as a result.

On a positive note, Young America has started a quick ship program, with a limited number of styles in two finishes (white and cherry) that are available for shipment within three weeks.

Bottom line: it's clear what you are paying for here is the made-in-the-U.S. label and numerous finish colors and accessories. If you care more about solid wood dresser construction or fancier styling, look elsewhere. ***Rating: B-***

Zutano See Stork Craft

See the chart on pages 100 to 101 for a summary of the major crib brands.

Brand Recommendations: Our Picks

Good. Our top pick for the best budget crib goes to two brands: Bivona's Fisher Price and La Jobi's Graco cribs. Specifically, we like the ***Fisher Price Newbury*** ($150-$180; pictured) or the ***Charlotte*** ($160-$180). For Graco, the ***Graco Stanton*** ($150-$160) is an excellent choice. Another option: ***IKEA's Sniglar*** crib is $70. Funky name, good value. The same goes for ***IKEA's Gulliver*** crib ($100 in white; $130 in natural).

Quick FYI on the Graco cribs: yes, they are made of pine. Yes, we usually don't recommend pine as a wood for cribs as it easily scratches. However, the prices on these cribs are so low, we think it is a worthwhile exception to the rule.

Better. Step up to the $400 to $600 range and you'll find more convertible models that turn from a crib to full-size bed. Our favorites here include ***Baby Cache's Heritage*** crib (made by Munire, $500, Babies R Us exclusive; pictured). If you want a plain, non-convertible crib, ***Westwood Design's Waverly Cottage*** crib ($300 at BuyBuyBaby.com) is a good buy. There also is a convertible version of this crib for $430. The ***Truly Scrumptious Sienna Curved Lifetime Crib*** ($500; Babies R Us) is a made by LaJobi.

Best. Who's got the very best quality when it comes to cribs and

Continued on page 102

CRIB RATINGS

Name	Rating	Cost	Where Made?
Argington	B	$$ to $$$	China
Baby Appleseed	B+	$$ to $$$	Vietnam
Babys Dream	A-	$$ to $$$	Chile/China
BassettBaby	B+	$ to $$	China
Bellini	B+	$$$	China
Bivona & Co	A/B-	$ to $$$	Vietnam
Bloom	B-	$$ to $$$	China
Boori	B	$$$	China
Bratt Decor	C+	$$$	Vietnam/China
CafeKid	B+	$$ to $$$	Thailand
Capretti	B+	$$$	USA
Carter's	B	$ to $$	Vietnam/China
Child Craft	B	$	Asia
Corsican Kids	C+	$$$	USA
Delta	B-	$ to $$	Asia
Dream on Me	B	$	China
Ducduc	B	$$$	USA
Dutailier	B+	$$ to $$$	Canada
Dwell	B	$$$	Canada
El Greco	A	$$$	USA
Franklin & Ben	A-	$$ to $$$	Asia
IKEA	A-	$	Asia
JcPenney	C+	$$ to $$$	Asia
Kidz Decoeur	B	$$$	Canada
LaJobi	A/B/C	$ to $$$	Vietnam/China
Land of Nod	A	$$$	USA
Lolly & Me	B	$$ to $$$	USA/Vietnam
Million $ Baby/Da Vinci	B	$ to $$$	Asia
Munire	A	$$$	Indonesia/USA
Natart	A	$$$	Canada
Newport Cottage	C	$$$	USA
Oeuf	B+	$$$	Latvia
Pali	A	$$$	Vietnam/Italy
Pottery Barn Kids	C	$$$	Asia
Ragazzi	C	$$$	China
Restoration Hardware	C	$$$	Asia
Romina	A	$$$	Romania
Simmons	C+	$$ to $$$	China/Vietnam
Sorelle	C+	$ to $$$	China/Vietnam
Stokke/Sleepi	B-	$$$	Slovenia
Stork Craft	C-	$ to $$	China
Westwood	A	$$$	Vietnam
Young America	B-	$$$	USA

Key:
RATING: Our opinion of the manufacturer's quality and value.
COST: $=under $250, $$=$250-500, $$$=over $500.
GREENGUARD: Are these cribs GREENGUARD certified? See p 55.

GREENGUARD?	COMMENTS
	Green spin on modern furniture. FSC certified.
◆	Eco-friendly, traditionally styled. Long order times.
	Still have some folding rails; Chile-made cribs best bet.
	Cribs good, case pieces bad.
	Sold only in namesake pricey boutiques.
	3 brands: Fisher Price, Ti Amo mid-price; Dolce Babi pricey.
	Alma mini crib good bassinet alternative for urbanites.
◆	Designed in Australia, good quality.
	Vintage looks, bright colors. Long lead times.
	Sold in Costco; includes conversion rails. Good value.
	Very pricey, made by Amish. Cribs start at $1300!
	Sells under Carter's/Disney brands. Owned by Summer.
	Affordable, but quality/service has slipped. Skip dressers.
	Very pricey wrought-iron cribs; vintage feel.
	Quality has improved; new safety testing facility.
	Affordable mini crib maker, also sells pricey Wonder crib.
	Retro, modernist furniture; high gloss finish. Expensive.
	Quality has improved; expensive, 32 finishes.
	Pricey. Exposed hardware disappoints.
	Excellent quality, sold at Land of Nod
	Early American, distressed vintage looks.
	Do-it-yourself assembly; low prices; very simple styling.
	Sells furniture under several private label brands.
	Eco-focus. Pricey. 16 finshes.
	Mass market Graco cribs good, but Bonavita has issues.
	Stylish but pricey; good service, Made by El Greco.
	Sold in Target; eco-friendly with some items made in US.
	Da Vinci brand sold online; modern cribs under Baby Letto
	Excellent quality; adult looks. Sold as Baby Cache in BRU.
◆	Innovative storage; whimsical touches but very pricey.
	Two-tone, distressed finishes; quality/service inconsistent.
	Eco-style meets modernism; lowest price of modern group.
	Good quality; traditional design. Recently lowered prices.
	Design leader but overpriced; high shipping charges.
	Many accessories. Adult looks.
	Upgraded line made by Bassett; very pricey.
◆	Pricey, but very well-made furniture. Solid wood.
	Owned by Delta; average quality, plain styling.
	Decent prices; mixed customer service reputation.
	Pricey crib "system" best for those with little space.
	Opening price point cribs sold in chains.
	Traditional looks; high quality. Pricey but worth it.
◆	30 color finishes; many accessories.

dressers? In the $500 to $800 range, we like **Munire** and **Natart**. Each makes excellent cribs and very good dressers. **Pali** is another excellent choice in that price range.

Is someone buying your nursery furniture as a gift? Do you want to avoid Chinese-made nursery furniture? If so, we suggest **Romina** or **El Greco**. Romina/Silva offers solid-wood cribs ($700 to $1300) and dressers imported from Romania. El Greco makes its cribs and dressers in the U.S.; they are sold online at sites like Land of Nod. Prices: $650 and up for a crib.

If space is tight (yes, we are talking to you, New Yorkers), we'd suggest the **Stokke Sleepi**. Ok, it isn't cheap ($800-$1000), but when your urban lifestyle requires a compact crib/bassinet, the Sleepi is the answer.

Short. If you are under 5'5", you may find reaching into a standard-size stationary crib challenging. Since drop-side cribs were phased out in 2011, shorter parents may find it difficult putting baby in a stationary crib when the mattress in its lowest position. For those parents, a lower profile crib may just the ticket. A good bet: **babyletto's Modo 3-in-1** crib is made from New Zealand pine and is relatively affordable at $330.

Green. Romina wins the crown in the green nursery race—their uber-natural "Bees Wax" finish is offered on any of their five furniture collections. Romina also earns green points for their 100% solid beech wood and formaldehyde-free construction (no particle board or MDF). Another plus: all furniture is made in Romania.

A runner-up in the green category is **Young America by Stanley**—with GREENGUARD certification and a made-in-the-U.S. pedigree, Young America is eco-conscious but also about 20% less expensive than Romina. Also worth a look: **Natart's Tulip**, made in Canada from recycled wood (MDF) and bamboo.

Grandma's house. If you need a secondary crib for Grandma's house, consider a portable mini crib from Dream on Me for $120, which folds for easy storage or transport. Delta cribs are also a good bet for Grandma's house—they can be quickly assembled without tools.

Bassinets, Cradles & Mini Cribs

A newborn infant can immediately sleep in a full size crib, but some parents like the convenience of bassinets, mini cribs or cradles to use for the first few weeks/months. Why? These smaller beds can be kept

bassinets

in the parents' bedroom, making for convenient midnight feedings.

What's the difference between a bassinet and a cradle? Although most stores use the terms interchangeably, we think of bassinets as small baskets that are typically put onto a stationery stand (pictured at top right). Cradles, on the other hand, are usually made of wood and rock back and forth (center right).

A third option in this category is "Moses baskets," basically woven baskets (lower right) with handles that you can use to carry a newborn from room to room. (Moses-Baskets.com has a good selection). Moses baskets can only be used for a few weeks, while you can typically use a bassinet or cradle for a couple of months.

Mini cribs are yet another alternative: most are similar in size to a bassinet (40" long by 28" wide). By comparison, a full-size crib is about 52" long and 28" wide. We recommend a specific mini crib in the previous section (see Grandma's house). FYI: mini cribs, like bassinets, are NOT a substitute for a full-size crib, which is the safest place for a baby to sleep after the first few weeks or months. Mini cribs are fine for newborns or at grandma's house for the occasional overnight visit.

Key mini crib makers include Argington, Bloom, Dream on Me, Nursery Smart and Stokke. See reviews earlier in this chapter.

Co-sleepers are similar to bassinets, but attach to the parent's bed. We used to recommend this type of product in a previous edition. However, the American Academy of Pediatrics recently came out against co-sleepers (or any device attached to a parent's bed). Pediatricians cited the risk of a parent unknowingly rolling over and injuring a newborn in a co-sleeper. As a result, we don't recommend these products.

Bassinets go for $100 to $200 and include bedding (sheets, liners, skirts, etc). Cradles run $120 to $400, but only need a mattress and sheet. Moses baskets run $50 to $200 and include all the bedding.

So, which should you buy? We say none of the above. As we mentioned at the beginning of this section, a newborn will do just fine in a full-size crib. If you need the convenience of a bassinet, we'd suggest skipping the ones you see in chain stores. Why? Most are very poorly made (stapled together cardboard, etc) and won't last for more than one child. The bedding is also low-quality. One reader said the sheets with her chain store-bought bassinet "were falling apart at the seams even before it went into the wash" for the first time. And the function of these products is somewhat questionable. For example, the functionality of a Moses basket, while pretty to look at, can be easily duplicated by an infant car seat carrier, which most folks buy any way.

Instead, we suggest you borrow a bassinet or cradle from a friend. . . or buy a portable playpen with a bassinet feature. We'll review specific models of playpens in Chapter 7, but basic choices like the Graco Pack 'N Play start at $60. The bassinet feature in most playpens (basically, an insert that creates a small bed area at the top of the playpen) can be used up to 15 pounds, which is about all most folks would need. Then, you simply remove the bassinet attachment and voila! You have a standard size playpen. Since many parents get a playpen anyway, going for a model that has a bassinet attachment doesn't add much to the cost and eliminates the separate $80 to $200 expense of a bassinet. Another way to save: consider a stroller with a bassinet option. Yes, you can typically add this as an accessory to full-size strollers for $100 to $200—and some companies even sell a bassinet stand for use in your bedroom.

Mattresses

Now that you've just spent several hundred dollars on a crib, you're done, right? Wrong. Despite their hefty price tags, most cribs don't come with mattresses. So, here's our guide to buying the best quality mattress for the lowest price.

 Safe & Sound

The key issue in mattress safety is Sudden Infant Death Syndrome (SIDS), the leading cause of death among infants under one year of age, claiming over 2000 lives per year. We have a detailed discussion of SIDS in our book, *Baby 411* (see back of this book for info), but here is the take-home message when it comes to SIDS and mattresses: buy a FIRM mattress that correctly fits your crib, bassinet or cradle. See the box earlier in this chapter for more tips on preventing SIDS.

 Smart Shopper Tips

Smart Shopper Tip #1
Foam or Coil?
"It seems the choice for a crib mattress comes down to foam or coil? Which is better? Does it matter?"

Yes, it does matter. After researching this issue, we've come down on the foam side of the debate. Why? Foam mattresses are lighter than those with coils, making it easier to change the sheets in the middle of the night when Junior reenacts the Great Flood in his crib. Foam mattresses typically weigh less than eight pounds, while coil mattresses can top 20 or 30 pounds! Another plus: foam mattresses are less expensive, usually $100 to $160. Coil mattresses can be pricey, with some models running $200+.

Sounds easy, right? Just buy a foam mattress? Well, as always, life can be complicated—many baby stores (and even chains like Babies R Us) only sell coil mattresses, claiming that coil is superior to foam.

We've consulted with pediatricians and industry experts on this issue and have come to the conclusion that the best course is to choose a *firm* mattress for baby—it doesn't matter whether it's a firm coil mattress or a firm foam one. What about the claim that foam mattresses need to be replaced constantly? In the 15 years we've been researching this topic, we've never heard from even one parent whose foam mattress had to be replaced!

What's going on here? Many baby stores try to make up for the thin profit margins they make on furniture by pitching parents to buy an ultra-expensive mattress. The latest rage are so-called "2 in 1" mattresses that combine foam *and* coil (foam on one side; coil on the other). These can run $200 or more! While these mattresses are nice, they are totally unnecessary. A $100 foam mattress will do just as well.

So why all the pressure to get the fancy-shmancy double dip mattress? Such mattresses cost stores just $50 at wholesale, yet they sell for $200 or more!

Bottom line: foam mattresses are the best deal, but can be hard to find (they are sold online). As a result, we'll recommend mattresses in both the coil and foam categories just in case the baby stores near you only stock coil.

Smart Shopper Tip #2
Coil Overkill and Cheap Foam Mattresses

"How do you tell a cheap-quality coil mattress from a better one? How about foam mattresses—what makes one better than the next?"

Evaluating different crib mattresses isn't easy. Even the cheap ones claim they are "firm" and comparing apples to apples is difficult. When it comes to coil mattresses, the number of coils seems like a good way to compare them, but even that can be deceiving. For example, is a 150-coil mattress better than an 80-coil mattress?

Well, yes and no. While an 80-coil mattress probably won't be as firm as one with 150 coils, it's important to remember that a large number of coils do not necessarily mean the mattress is superior.

Factors such as the wire gauge, number of turns per coil and the temper of the wire contribute to the firmness, durability and strength of the mattress. Unfortunately, most mattresses only note the coil count (and no other details). Hence, the best bet would be to buy a good brand that has a solid quality reputation (we'll recommend specific choices after this section).

What about foam mattresses? The cheapest foam mattresses are made of low-density foam (about .9 pounds per cubic foot). The better foam mattresses are high-density with 1.5 pounds per cubic foot. Easy for us to say, right? Once again, foam mattresses don't list density on their packaging, leaving consumers to wonder whether they're getting high or low density. As with coil mattresses, you have to rely on a reputable brand name to get a good foam mattress (see the next section for more details).

Smart Shopper Tip #3
New crib mattress = dangerous fumes?

"I read on the 'net that some crib mattresses give off dangerous fumes that can cause SIDS."

This internet myth has its roots in New Zealand. In the mid 90's, a New Zealand chemist launched a web site that claimed Sudden Infant Death Syndrome was caused by toxic gasses given off by crib mattresses. His solution: wrap the mattress in a gas-impenetrable cover, which naturally, was sold on his web site.

This theory has been discredited by SIDS researchers and scientists, who have studied SIDS causes for years and have found no link between mattress chemicals and infant deaths. Yet, there is still much online buzz about this theory, amid general concern over exposure of infants to household chemicals.

It is true that conventional crib mattresses (whether foam or coil) are made from scary-sounding chemicals. Most mattresses have these chemicals to meet fire retardant standards, which are mandated by both federal and state rules. *Bottom line: to date, there is no research that links sleeping on traditional crib mattresses to any disease or illness.*

That said, we can understand why new parents want to limit their newborns exposure to environmental hazards—you can't control all chemical exposure, but one place you do have some say is your child's nursery. In recent years, an entire industry of organic crib mattresses have sprung up to meet this concern.

Here's the take-home message: we think conventional crib mattresses (foam or coil) are safe. If you decide you want to go the organic route, however, we will provide some recommendations in that category later in this section.

Here are a few more shopping tips/myths about crib mattresses:

◆ **What's the best way to test the firmness of a crib mattress?** Test the center of the mattress (not the sides or corners)—place the palm of one hand flat on one side of the mattress and then put your other hand on the opposite side. The greater the pressure needed to press your hands together, the more firm the mattress.

◆ **Are all crib mattresses the same size?** No, they can vary a small amount—both in length/width and thickness. Most coil mattresses are 4″ to 6″ in depth. What's the best thickness? It doesn't matter, but 5″ should be fine. FYI: 5″ mattresses are often less expensive then 6″ mattresses. FYI: some crib sheets won't fit the six-inch thick mattresses; it's unsafe to use a sheet that doesn't snugly fit OVER the corner of a mattress and tuck beneath it.

Remember the safest crib mattress is the one that snugly fits your crib—you shouldn't be able to fit more than two fingers between the headboard/side rails and the mattress. A tip: the mattress should be CENTERED on the crib mattress platform, not jammed up to one side or the other!

FYI: For the curious, full-size cribs sold in the U.S. and Canada must be between 27 5/8″ and 28 5/8″ wide (and 51 3/4″ to 53″ in length). Hence most crib *mattresses* are about 27 1/4″ to 28 5/8″ in width.

◆ **All foam mattresses look alike—what separates the better ones from the cheaper options?** Test for firmness (see above). The more firm, the better. Another clue: weight. A slightly heavier foam mattress usually means they used a better-quality foam to make the product. Finally, look at the cover: three layers of laminated/reinforced vinyl are better than a single or double layer. What about quilted covers? They are a waste of money, in our opinion.

Smart Shopper Tip #4
Mattresses & bacteria
"I saw a study that linked crib mattresses with a lack of water-proofing to SIDS. What should I do to protect my baby?"

In a study published in 2008 in the Journal of Applied Microbiology, scientists from the United Kingdom discovered foam crib mattresses that lacked waterproofing near an infant's head could cause bacteria growth. Some researchers believe this can be linked to Sudden Infant Death Syndrome.

Of course, most mattresses sold in U.S. have water-resistant covers (typically a layer of vinyl). However, a new crop of "organic" mattresses without such waterproofing have come on the market, appealing to parents who don't want any petrochemical-based products in their baby's nursery.

Here's our recommendations:

◆ **Get a mattress with a vinyl cover that is triple-laminated** (this provides better waterproofing).

◆ **Use a waterproof pad** over the mattress. Some "sheet savers" (Ultimate Crib Sheet) have waterproof backing that would provide extra protection to keep liquid out of the mattress. Many organic mattress companies sell mattress protectors as an accessory.

◆ **Don't use a hand-me-down mattress**, since it might not have been water-protected.

◆ **Consider changing out the mattress with each child** (new baby, new mattress) since no matter how hard you try, some leakage might happen.

The Name Game: Reviews of Selected Manufacturers

Colgate *colgatekids.com* Colgate has long been one of our favorite brands for affordable foam crib mattresses. The company offers three types of mattress: foam, innerspring and natural/organic. All of Colgate's foam mattresses (regular or organic) are GREEN-GUARD certified to be low in chemical emissions, which is unique in this segment.

Perhaps the best selling Colgate mattress is their simple Classica 1 ($140-$150) foam mattress with a triple layer nylon reinforced cover. Colgate also sells an "eco" version of this mattress (cleverly called the Eco Classica, $190) that replaces most of the petro-chemical foam with plant-based foam. Of course, Colgate sells more than just two models—they sell several versions of the Classica mattress, some of which have dual firmness zones, memory foam and other upgrades. That's nice, but unnecessary.

In the past year, Colgate expanded their collection of eco-mattresses. The EcoFoam Supreme is made of a unique foam. Instead of soy foam, like many of their competitors, this foam is derived from non-food plants which grow in rocky soil. It has square corners and a damask cover that is coated on the underside to be waterproof. The new Postura mattress has a dual firmness option with one inch thick memory foam and a medical grade water proof cover of PVC3. Again, it has square corners plus inverted seams. Prices are reasonable: $130 for the EcoFoam Supreme and the Postura is $260.

In the memory foam category, Colgate has the Visco Classica Angel. This $250 mattress has dual firmness with memory foam made with cooling gel on one side and the Classica 1 foam on the other. It also has inverted seams and a polyester waterproof cover.

Colgate was a bit late to the eco-mattress trend, but it aims to make up time with the Nuzzle Nest, a new mattress to debut in 2014.

This mattresses mojo? AirWeave, made of recyclable and recycled materials, creates a firm mattress that also allows for airflow through the mattress. Complete with an organic cotton waterproof cover, the Nuzzle Nest is Colgate's most expensive mattress at $400,

Overall, we're impressed with Colgate's wide range of offerings. Quality is very good—all mattresses are made in the USA. **Rating: A-**

Greenbuds Baby GreenBudsBaby.com Looking for an eco crib mattress that costs less than your crib? Greenbuds recently entered the now crowded eco crib mattress market with two offerings: the Primrose and Magnolia crib mattresses.

The Primrose has a three inch core of coconut coir and another inch of natural latex. The cover is made of organic quilted cotton, which is removable and washable. Price: $340. There is also a deluxe version of the Primrose that runs $410 and features an upgraded cover made from organic wool (again, this is removable and washable).

The Magnolia is billed as a 2-in-1 crib mattress with a thicker (four inch) core made of coconut coir and an inch of natural latex. There is a firm side for infants and a softer side for toddlers. Like the Primrose, the Magnolia comes in both regular and deluxe versions (cotton vs. wool covers). Price: $390 to $450.

The company also sells water proof mattress pads made of organic cotton and a food-grade polyethylene waterproof membrane. Price: $60.

Greenbuds seems to be trying to find the middle ground price-wise in the eco-market. It is a bit less than Naturalmat's coconut coir mattress (which clocks in at $400+) but more than Naturepedic's eco mattresses (which don't have coconut coir cores, however).

Early feedback on Greenbuds has been positive, but the company is still too new to assign a rating. **Rating: Not Yet.**

Kolcraft kolcraft.com Baby gear maker Kolcraft is also a big player in crib mattresses and one key reason is price: these are some of the most affordable mattresses on the market. An example is their Kolcraft Pure Sleep Therapeutic coil mattress with 150 coils for $50-$70 online—a good deal if you want to go for coil.

Kolcraft also has had a hit with their soybean foam mattresses, which replace some of the typical petrochemical foam found in other crib mattresses with a soybean foam. Made under Kolcraft's sister brand Sealy, these mattresses are affordable and good quality. Example: the Sealy Soybean Foam-Core mattress for $85, a good deal.

In the past year, Kolcraft added a new brand for eco mattresses called Stearns & Foster, which is a kids' version of the luxury adult mattress line. They're offering two options: the Baby Dynasty Eco Foam 2-Stage Infant-Toddler mattress (foam only, $300), and the Baby Dynasty

Eco-Luxe 2-Stage Infant-Toddler mattress (foam and coil, $220). Both use high density soy foam and include Crypton Green covers. As of this writing, they are being sold in Babies R Us as an exclusive.

The major new addition to the Kolcraft mattress line in the past year are mattresses that feature CoolTex gel—these foam mattresses feature a gel that is cool to the touch. This feature addresses a concern that some memory foam mattresses trap heat. Kolcraft makes two versions of this mattress: the Sealy Signature Cool Beginnings 2-stage mattress is at Babies R Us for $200; the similar Sealy Select 2-Cool 2-State is at Buy Buy Baby for $200. These mattresses are GREENGUARD certified.

For 2014, Kolcraft is expanding their cool gel mattresses with a couple of new options: the Cozy Cool ($200) is a hybrid model—coil (204 coils) on the infant side and gel foam on the toddler side.

Bottom line: we like Kolcraft's crib mattresses and would recommend the brand. While the cool gel and memory foam mattresses are nice, they are overkill—the simple soybean foam or coil mattress for under $100 is what we'd recommend. ***Rating: A***

LA Baby *lababyco.com* This company is probably better known for its mini-crib, but they also sell a line of mattresses that include foam, inner spring and natural. An example is the Organic Cotton 2-in-1 Orthopedic mattress for $140, which the company claims is made from certified organic cotton. This mattress gets generally good reviews from parents, but a few complained about its lack of firmness and fumes when first removed from packaging.

In the past year, LA Baby has expanded their Naturals line of eco-friendly mattresses, made in Southern California. The latest offering is their "Pediatrician's Choice Mattress with Medical Grade Cover" for $83 on Walmart.com.

While we think these mattress are okay, other brands like Colgate and Naturepedic offer better overall quality and durability. LA Baby mattresses lack GREENGUARD certification for low emissions and their claims of organic materials aren't certified by any third party standards group. ***Rating: C***

Lullaby Earth *lullabyearth.com* Lullaby Earth is a new division of Naturepedic (reviewed separately) that is aiming for affordable eco crib mattresses priced under $200. Yes, you read that right—an eco crib mattress priced as low as a conventional mattress.

Lullaby Earth's Super Lightweight mattress is made of polyethylene foam (a non-toxic, food-grade foam that requires no fire retardant chemicals) and weighs just 6.5 lbs. (Most other foam mattresses on the market are made of polyurethane). It features seamless edges and GREENGUARD-certification. Price: $170. A two-stage firmness model is $200.

Early feedback on Lullaby Earth's mattresses has been positive—the quality and durability is good. **Rating: A**

Moonlight Slumber moonlightslumber.com Moonlight Slumber was one of the first entrants into the "premium" crib mattress market when they debuted a few years ago. The mojo: "medical grade" and natural crib mattresses. Moonlight Slumber defines medical grade as PVC/vinyl free, non-toxic, antimicrobial and hypoallergenic.

Of course, to claim something is medical grade is fuzzy, as there is no formal definition. But Moonlight Slumber points to their welded seams and a "medical grade" stretch knit fabric cover as key features.

The company's Starlight Support mattress ($250) comes in both foam and innerspring versions, as well as in various sizes (crib, bassinet, cradle, etc). Readers tell us they love the dual-zone firmness, with a less-firm side for toddlers. They also have a Starlight Support Supreme all foam mattress for $270.

FYI: Moonlight Slumber makes a standard and supreme version of its mattress—the latter ($270) has a layer of memory foam. And the company makes a more affordable version of their foam mattress (the Little Dreamer, $150 for one firmness to $185 for dual firmness), which is five inches thick (the Starlight is 6").

Quality is good and most reviews from parents on Moonlight Slumber are quite positive.

One minor quibble: in the past year, Moonlight Slumber has been touting a Green Safety Shield certification for its products, saying this means Its products meet indoor air quality standards, product performance and material contents standards. So who invented the Green Safety Shield? Answer: Moonlight Slumber. While Moonlight Slumber has never marketed itself as an eco-friendly product, we find this attempt at self-greening to be disingenuous. It would be more impressive if Moonlight Slumber achieved third-party certifications like GREENGUARD's testing for indoor air quality. Making up a pretend Green Safety Shield and slapping it on your products insults the intelligence of your customers.

In the end, however, this is a minor issue. Overall, we recommend Moonlight Slumber and think their quality is excellent **Rating: A**

Naturalmat naturalmatusa.com UK-based Naturalmat offers three organic mattresses made of coir (the husk of a coconut), latex or mohair. The Coco Mat is $400, LatexMat is $500 and the Mohair Mat is $600.

Unfortunately, none of these are water-proof; for that, you need a $70 mattress protector that Naturalmat sells as an add-on.

As for quality, readers generally praise Naturalmat, especially for the coconut mattress (Coco Mat). The few complaints we see center on the latex mattress, which some parents deem too soft. Another complained that the cover shrank on her latex mattress after washing according to the manufacturer instructions.

Of course, the biggest issue here is the sky high retail price—and the additional $70 mattress protector. Even when discounted on Amazon, the Coco Mat is still clocks in at over $300. On the other hand, if you want to splurge, at least you know this is a high quality product. Of Naturalmat's three models, the Coco Mat seems to receive the best overall reviews. **Rating: B+**

Naturepedic *naturepedic.com* Naturepedic's "No-Compromise" Classic coil mattress ($260) features feature 150 coils, organic cotton fabric and filling and a food-grade polyethylene cover that is waterproof. The company also makes this mattress in a seamless version (like Moonlight Slumber's design) for $280 to $300 and a 252-coil version for $300.

The Organic Cotton Lightweight mattress swaps out the coils for closed-cell air pockets made from food-grade polyethylene. As a result, this mattress is half the weight of a traditional coil mattress. This seamless mattress is $260 and is Naturepedic's best-selling model; a dual-firmness model is $300 and an "organic cotton ultra" with Wavesupport Plus is $330.

The Ultra series was added recently and comes with a stronger, more durable cover and more support for $360 to $400.

In specialty stores only, Naturepedic sells the Classic Seamless 2-stage 180 coil mattress for $320.

Quality is good—Naturepedic is GREENGUARD certified. We also liked the company's detailed web site, with extensive FAQ's, articles and a blog about shopping for a natural mattress. **Rating: A**

Nook *nooksleep.com* And now for a crib mattress that costs more than most cribs: the $400 Nook Pebble Pure mattress features an organic coconut core layered with one inch of natural latex foam. The mattress' cover is made of eucalyptus fiber, zinc and organic cotton and is machine washable/dryable.

The company claims the pebbled cover design "creates valleys for airflow on the mattress surface." The obvious implication is that other crib mattresses without said valleys are somehow inferior or dangerous—that claim seems baseless to us.

Made in the U.S., Nook also sells a lighter weight version of the mattress (Pebble Lite, 16 lbs.) that features a non-toxic eco-foam core for $295. While these mattresses are certainly unique (they come in six bright colors), neither has a water-proof cover (they claim the mattress is "water resistant").

Feedback on this mattress is generally positive, but there is one major drawback. One parent noted that since cover isn't waterproof, she had to buy multiple extra covers ($100 each) to make sure the mattress was usable when one cover was in the wash. Wrestling the cover off and on in the middle of the night isn't easy either, in our opinion.

Nook's major competitor in this space is Naturalmat, whose Coco Mat mattress costs about the same as the Pebble Lite. On the plus side, the Pebble's cover is water resistant, while Naturalmat requires a separate $70 cover. But . . . the Pebble's cover is difficult to remove, as we mentioned above. So the advantage there goes to Naturalmat.

It is a mixed review for the Nook—readers like the eco-goodness of the coconut fiber mattress, but the price and practical limitations of this mattress curb the Pebble's appeal. **Rating: B-**

Sealy. *See Kolcraft.*

Serta by La Jobi. *lajobi.com* Crib maker La Jobi licenses the well-known Serta name for its crib mattresses. An example is the best-seller Serta Nightstar Extra Firm crib mattress ($80), a coil mattress with a 25-year warranty. Most readers say this is a good, basic crib mattress, but a few dissenters say it isn't as firm as the competition. That's probably because this mattress only has 117 coils—generally we recommend a mattress with at least 150 coils.

Of course, La Jobi/Serta hasn't ignored the eco trend—the Serta Tranquility Eco Firm Mattress runs $160. We're not sure what makes this coil mattress eco-friendly, save for the layer of organic cotton on the top of the mattress.

Serta crib mattresses generally get good reviews, but more than one review criticized the brand for shipping damage. Fans love the value here—it is hard to beat the Serta Perfect Start Crib mattress for $39. Bottom line: if your budget is very tight, Serta is a good choice. **Rating: B**

Simmons *simmonskids.com* Part of the Delta crib company, these mattresses are sold under several names: Beautyrest, Beautysleep Slumber Time and Simmons Kids. There's also an eco brand: Naturally Refreshing.

Altogether, this brand has a dozen coil mattresses, from 90 to 242 coils. There are also two foam mattresses, including a "soy enhanced" foam option.

A typical example is Simmons Kids Beautyrest Beginnings Sleepy Whispers Ultra Deluxe 2 n 1 Crib and Toddler Mattress for $170. It features 231 coils, "natural cotton" (what cotton isn't natural?) and is GREENGUARD certified.

Feedback on this brand is mixed—the low-end mattresses (under $100) are often knocked for poor quality, but the more expensive models (like the one above) get better marks. Bottom line: there are better bets out there than Simmons. ***Rating: C+***

Sopora *SoporaSleep.com* Furniture maker Munire teamed with Terri Paul, one of the founders of Moonlight Slumber, to launch Sopora in 2012. The new crib mattress company is focused on eco-friendly mattresses with the latest technologies.

Sopora has eight made-in-the-US models that feature Baby Safe "sealed seams" to keep out fluid, bed bugs and dust mites. The mattress covers are medical-grade, with no vinyl or phthalates and the corners are square.

What makes these mattresses even more unique? The use of a new lightweight foam (called CertiPUR), which is made of soy and caster oil. Sopora claims this is healthier and lighter than foam made by competing manufacturers.

The lowest priced model, the Classic, is 5" foam with coated nylon and sells for $165. The Premium, is also 5" with a dual firmness zone for $185. The Deluxe ($230) and the Ultimate ($260) are 6" thick and have stretch knit covers with a waterproof urethane coating. The Ultimate has dual firmness zones for babies and toddlers and is Sopora's best-selling mattress. The prices are very reasonable compared to similar quality mattresses.

New to the line, the Ultimate Select mattress is the same as the Ultimate mattress with a new Celliant fabric cover ($260). Celliant is a stretch-knit, medical grade fabric.

Also new: the Perfect Mattress which uses the same Celliant fabric cover as well as a CoolGel foam layer to help keep your baby from overheating or getting cold. Price: $320. The Perfect also uses an air foam technology called BabysBreath on one side to improve airflow, the company claims. The other side is for toddlers and is more like a conventional toddler mattress.

Finally, Sopora has introduced a new organic mattress cover with a water proof backing that you can use with or without a sheet. Price: $60.

All Sopora mattresses are GREENGUARD certified and made in the U.S. Feedback on these mattresses has been positive and overall quality is excellent. ***Rating: A***

Brand Recommendations: Our Picks

Good. The ***Sealy Soybean Foam-Core*** crib mattress is a good deal at $85. Yes, the foam is made from soybeans. At just 8.3 pounds, this lightweight but firm mattress makes changing sheets easy.

Lullaby Earth's Super Lightweight mattress is made of polyethylene foam (a non-toxic, food-grade foam that requires no fire retardant chemicals) and weighs just 6.5 lbs. Most other foam mattresses on the market are made of polyurethane. It features seamless edges and GREENGUARD-certification. Price: $170.

Better. *Moonlight Slumber's Little Dreamer* foam crib mattress is $150-$185 and features stitched seams and a PVC-free, "hospital-grade" vinyl cover. Bonus: it has two firmness zones (one for baby, another for toddler). We also recommend the *Sopora Classic*, a 5" foam mattress with coated nylon for $165.

Best. *Naturepedic's Organic Cotton Lightweight* mattress, which swaps out coils for closed-cell air pockets made from food-grade polyethylene. As a result, this mattress is half the weight of a traditional coil mattress. It runs $260; a dual-firmness model is $300. If you want a coil mattress, Naturepedic's Organic Cotton Classic 150 coil mattress is a good bet at $260. In a nutshell, Naturepedic balances the best of both worlds: organic cotton filling, a firm foam or coil innerspring AND a waterproof cover. All of Naturepedic's mattresses contain no PVC's, polyurethane foam or chemical fire retardants.

Also in the best pick category: *Sopora's Perfect Mattress* ($320) is loaded with high-tech features including a Celliant fabric cover and a CoolGel foam layer to keep baby from overheating.

Green. *Naturepedic* would be our top pick here—see above for model info. A runner-up best pick in the green category goes to *Naturalmat's Coco Mat* ($400), made from coconut fiber. The only bummer: the cover isn't waterproof (you have to add a $70 mattress protector to get that feature).

Dressers & Changing Tables

Now that you've got a place for the baby to sleep, where are you going to put baby's clothes? The juvenile trade refers to dressers, armoires, and the like as "case pieces" since they are essentially furniture made out of a large case (pretty inventive, huh?).

Of course, a dresser is more than just a place to store clothes and supplies. Let's not forget that all too important activity that will occupy so many of your hours after the baby is born: changing diapers. The other day we calculated that by our baby's first birthday, we had changed over 2300 diapers! Wow! To first-time parents, that may seem like an unreal number, but we're not exaggerating. On average, that is about SEVEN diaper changes a day during the first year . . . but for a newborn, expect up to 15 diaper changes a day. So, where are you going to change all those diapers? Most parents use the dresser top, but we'll also discuss changing tables in this section.

What are You Buying

1 **DRESSERS.** As you shop for baby furniture, you'll note a wide variety of dressers—three drawer, four drawer, armoires, combination dresser/changing tables, and more. No matter which type you choose, we do have three general tips for getting the most for your money.

First, choose a model whose drawers glide easily. Test this in the store—drawers with an easy glide typically have tracks on BOTH sides of the drawer. Cheaper dressers have drawers that simply sit on a track at the bottom center of the drawer. As a result, they don't roll out as smoothly and are prone to coming off the track.

Our second piece of advice: look at the drawer sides—the best furniture makers use "dove-tailed" drawer joints. There are two types of dove-tail drawers: English and French (see pictures at right). Either is OK; the cheapest dressers do not have dove-tailed drawers. Instead, the drawer and drawer front are merely stapled together.

English Dove-tail

A third quality indicator: drawers with corner blocks (pictured below). Pull the drawer out and turn it over to look at the corners—if there is a small block that braces the corner, that's good. Cheaper dressers omit this feature, which adds to the stability of the drawer. Also check the sides of the drawers: are they solid wood? Or particle board?

French Dove-tail

Corner Block

Drawer glides are another key point: some dressers have simple metal glides, while others use more elaborate mechanisms including self-closing glides (you push the drawer nearly closed and it automatically/slowly closes the rest of the way). A few dresser makers use wood-on-wood glides, more commonly seen in adult furniture.

When it comes to drawers, consider how far they extend: fully extending drawers are better than partial.

Step back a moment and look at the entire dresser—do the drawers fit? Are the hinges for an armoire adjustable (like what you'd see in good kitchen cabinets)? Is the back of the dresser a flimsy piece of chipboard that is stapled? We've been amazed to see the quality (or lack thereof) when it comes to dressers in chain stores.

Let's talk about wood for a second. Unlike cribs (most of which are made of solid wood), dressers are usually a compromise—solid wood on the parts you see (drawer fronts, front panels) and wood substitutes for the parts you don't see (basically, everything else).

Most dresser makers use fiberboard (sometimes referred to as MDF, medium density fiberboard) and particleboard as well as veneers (thin strips of wood glued over particleboard).

The key shopping tip: how much solid wood is there in the dresser? The better quality the dresser, the more solid wood. While one furniture maker (Romina) uses all solid wood that is the exception. The better quality furniture makers use solid wood drawer boxes, drawer fronts, tops and sometimes even sides. Or if veneers are used, they are over less expensive solid hardwood instead of MDF (Pali uses birch veneers over rubber wood, for example).

In recent years, we've seen more MDF used in baby furniture. Why? It's cheap, easy to sculpt and smooth (there is no wood grain or knots). Many modern/minimalist furniture designers are using MDF (usually coated with a high-gloss lacquer) as a design statement. While we don't see anything wrong with that, we do object to the sky-high prices for this—paying $1500 for a dresser made of MDF is like spending four-figures for a fake-leather jacket.

What are the concerns with MDF and other wood substitutes? In general, fake wood isn't as durable as solid wood, which means more possible warping in very humid or dry climates. Why? MDF is made by compressing/gluing together wood waste fibers. That compression/gluing can be affected by the moisture content in the air—and hence your expensive MDF dresser can warp.

Another concern with MDF: formaldehyde. This chemical can be found in high concentrations in MDF and particle board, thanks to that glue that binds the fibers together. The more MDF or particle board, the more possible formaldehyde, which can lead to unhealthy indoor air. In high concentrations, formaldehyde can cause a burning sensation and nausea . . . as well as a possible link to cancer.

But there is good news on this front: a new California law that went into effect in 2009 limits the amount of formaldehyde emissions from furniture. Since California is a big furniture market, manufacturers will have to adjust their entire production to limit use of these glues (and substitute them for soy-based glue).

The take-home message: when evaluating a dresser, look beyond the pretty finish. Evaluate drawer construction, glides, corner blocks and the amount of solid wood.

2 **CHANGING AREA.** Basically, you have two options here. You can buy a separate changing table or use your dresser as a changing area. As mentioned earlier, we think a separate changing table is a waste of money (as well as a waste of space).

So most folks look for dressers to do double duty: not only a place to store clothes, but also change diapers. Basically, you need a changing area of the right height to do this—evaluate your and your spouse's heights to see what you'd need.

FYI: We aren't big fans of those combination cribs, where a changing table or dresser is attached to the crib. The reason is safety: attached dressers give older babies a place to climb out of the crib and potentially fall from a higher distance.

In fact, a 2011 study from the Nationwide Children's Hospital found 9,600 babies and toddlers are injured a year in cribs, most from falls. While the study didn't have specific statistics on falls from cribs with attached dressers, we think these items are an obvious hazard.

Where do you keep the diaper changing supplies? Well, you can use a drawer in the dresser. Or, a rolling storage cart is another solution (cost: about $25 in many catalogs and stores such as Container Store (containerstore.com).

Safe & Sound

Safety doesn't stop at the crib—consider these items:

◆ **Anchor dressers to the wall.** Why? When baby starts exploring her nursery, she can tip over dressers, bookcases or shelves—no matter how heavy they are. Some furniture brands include anchor straps; in other cases, you'll need to visit a local hardware store. One solution: the Anti-Tip Kit ($10) from HangmanProducts.com.

◆ **Baby proof the diaper station.** If your diaper changing area has open shelves, you may have to baby proof the bottom shelves. As your baby begins to climb, you must remove any dangerous medicines or supplies from easily accessible shelves.

◆ **Air out all that new nursery paint, furniture and decor.** A University of Maryland study suggests new parents should air out freshly painted or wallpapered rooms before baby arrives. New furniture and mattresses also "out-gas" fumes for a brief time, so consider ventilating the nursery when they arrive as well. How much ventilation? The study suggested four to eight weeks of open window ventilation. Another idea: look for environmentally friendly paints that have lower out-gas emissions. If you install new carpet in the house, leave during the installation and open the windows (and turn on fans) for two days.

Our Picks: Brand Recommendations

Our picks for dressers mirror what we picked for cribs. For contact information on these brands, refer to the reviews earlier in this chapter. Here's a round up:

Good. IKEA's affordable dressers (about $100 to $250) are our top pick if money (or space) is tight. Let's be honest: IKEA's dressers aren't for the long haul and are nothing to fancy to look at. Plus you have to assemble everything yourself, which can be challenging. But if you need something on a temporary basis (and plan to swap out all the nursery furniture as your child grows older), IKEA is the answer.

Better. The dressers from brands like *Babi Italia (La Jobi)* and *Baby Cache (Munire)* are better quality than what you'd see in discount stores like Walmart. A simple four-drawer dresser from Baby Italia is $400 to $600; Baby Cache runs in the $500 to $800 range.

Best. Our top picks for dressers are *Munire* and *Westwood*. Each sells dressers in the $500 to $900 range, although Munire and Westwood sell less-expensive options in the chains under names Baby Cache and Bedford Baby/Hart, respectively.

If you've got more cash to burn, the very best quality in dressers can be found in *Ragazzi* and *Romina*. A double dresser from Ragazzi is $950 and features felt-lined top drawers and top notch construction. Romina is even better, with all solid-wood construction—but a double dresser from this brand runs a whopping $1200.

Changing Table Pads. Changing table pads turn a dresser into a changing table. A couple of shopping tips: look for a pad with elevated sides. This will help keep your baby on the mattress pad. A word of caution: elevated sides don't guarantee your baby won't still roll off the mattress pad, so never walk away when changing your baby.

The best pick: *Simmons Beautyrest Two Sided Contour Changing Table Pad with Non-Skid Bottom* ($30 to $40). Also good: *Summer Infant's Contoured Changing Pad* ($16 to $25). Both pads are available at Amazon.com, Target, Babies R Us and Walmart. If you're looking for an organic or natural changing pad, consider *Naturepedic's Organic Cotton Changing Table Pad* ($100).

NURSERY NECESSITIES

Glider Rockers

More than a mere rocking chair, glider rockers feature a ball-bearing system so they glide with little or no effort. They've earned a place in the nursery to help with those long hours of breastfeeding. Many are then repurposed later into a living room or den.

Here are some shopping tips when looking at rocker gliders:

a) Go for padded armrests. You'll be cradling a newborn and spending many hours here. All in all, the more padding in the chair, the better.

b) Consider a chair with a locking mechanism. Some brands (notably Shermag) have an auto-locking feature; when you stand up, the chair can no longer rock. Very helpful if you have a curious toddler who might end up with pinched fingers.

c) Extra width is always smart. Some of the cheapest glider rockers are quite narrow, which might not seem bad if you are a small person. But remember you will most likely be using a nursing pillow with your newborn . . . and having the extra width to accommodate this pillow is most helpful!

The Name Game: Reviews of Selected Manufacturers

Best Chair besthf.com. This Indiana-based rocking chair maker entered the baby biz in 2002, although they trace their roots to the 1960's. We were very impressed with their quality and offerings. Basically, Best specializes in upholstered chairs with over 100+ fabric choices. They claim their gliders have the longest glide in the industry. They also offer an optional 10-position glide lock that makes it easier to in and out of the chair.

Delivery is four weeks and prices are decent for an all-upholstered look: most are $400 to $700. A matching ottoman is $150 to $300. Best is sold only in specialty stores and on JCPenney.com.

New for 2014, Best is debuting a "bonded leather" chair called Performa for $600. Bonded leather is made of leather scraps and is less expensive than a full leather chair (which top $700).

Feedback from readers has been mostly positive on Best—a few complaints centered on Best models sold on JCPenney.com that had backs that were too short for some taller parents. Most folks had no problem, however and generally loved Best's overall quality and durability. For taller parents, it might be good to try out this chair in person before purchasing. *Rating: A*

Brooks *brooksfurnitureonline.com.* Tennessee-based Brooks sells glider-rockers that are old school—traditional chairs feature basic fabrics and exposed wood. Prices run $300 to $600 for the glider rockers, while the ottomans are $120-$200. One plus: all 75 Brooks fabrics are available on any style chair (over 15 styles and ten finishes). Brooks chairs feature solid base panels (Dutailier has an open base), which the company touts as safer. While we liked Brooks' quality, one baby storeowner told us he found the company very disorganized with poor customer service. *Rating: B*

Dutailier *dutailier.com.* Quebec-based Dutailier is to glider-rockers what Google is to online search. Thanks to superior quality and quick delivery, Dutailier probably sells one out of every two glider rockers purchased in the U.S. and Canada each year.

Dutailier has an incredible selection of 45 models, seven finishes, and 80 different fabrics. The result: over 37,000 possible combinations. All wood is solid maple or oak and features non-toxic finishes. You have to try real hard to avoid seeing Dutailier—the company has 3500 retail dealers, from small specialty stores to major retail chains. In the past year, Dutailier's Montreal designer has added a cool modern style chair ($800 and up) to match its Papaya crib, dresser and nightstand (see cribs for more info).

Prices for Dutailier start at about $390 for their "Ultramotion" line sold at discount stores like Target.com. The Ultramotion gliders are entry-level: you get basic fabric cushions and exposed wood accents. Their Value line ($550 to $600) ships in one box.

Dutailier's mid-price line (about $450 to $530) is sold at chains like Babies R Us and features upgraded fabric and more fabric choices. The good news about Dutailier at chain stores: models are often discontinued and then discounted—BRU often sells these chairs and floor models for prices in the $200's.

Of course, you can spend much more than that—Dutailier's specialty store line lets you customize a glider-rocker to your heart's content . . . add a swivel base, plush cushions or leather fabric and you can spend $600. Or $1000. The latest rage: all upholstered glider rockers run $1000 to $1700 and come in leather or fabric.

If you like the upholstered look but don't have that much coin, Dutailier offers an option: chairs with fully upholstered arms (but open bases) for $600 to $650 with ottoman in six fabrics and five finishes. Basically, much the same look, half the price.

Realizing all these choices can be a bit daunting, Dutailier moved in the past to simply its offerings: now, all fabrics can be used on any chair. Dutailier's web site now divides its wood gliders into two categories: modern and traditional.

Dutailier offers an "auto lock" feature on some chairs—it's always locked when no one is sitting in it and then automatically unlocks when you sit down. Also new: a "nursery chair" for $430 with drop-down nursing pillows.

If we had to criticize Dutailier on something, it would have to be their cushions. Most are not machine washable (the covers can't be zipped off and put into the washing machine). As a result, you'll have to take them to a dry cleaner and pay big bucks to get them looking like new. A few of our readers have solved this problem by sewing slipcovers for their glider-rockers (most fabric stores carry pattern books for such items). Of course, if the cushions are shot, you can always order different ones when you move the glider-rocker into the family room—but that can be expensive, as replacement cushions are $150 to $300.

It can take ten to 12 weeks to order a custom Dutailier rocker (more for leather options), but the company does offer a "Quick Ship" program—a selection of 17 chair styles in two or three different fabric choices that are in stock for shipment in two weeks. We have received occasional complaints about how long it takes to order a Dutailier—one reader special-ordered a Dutailier from Babies R Us, only to find out some weeks later that the fabric was discontinued (Dutailier "forgot" to tell Babies R Us, who, to their credit, tried to fix the problem immediately). Other readers complain about fabric backorders, which cause more delays in delivery. Our advice: make sure the store double checks the order with Dutailier.

Quality here is excellent. We toured Dutailier's Quebec plant recently and were impressed with the high tech wizardry used in production—laser-guided water jets slice huge sheets of top-quality leather, computer-controlled ovens make sure stains are baked on chairs for an even finish and so on. At each step, quality is hand checked by an army of workers to insure consistency of fit and finish.

So, who's got the best deals on Dutailier? At the moment, we'd have to give the crown to Target. At both their Super Target locations and online (target.com), you can get a Dutailier for about $390. Yes, Target only carries one or two styles, so your choices are limited.

An optional accessory for glider rockers is the ottoman that glides too. These start at $150 at discounters like Target, but most cost about $170 to $300. FYI: We've noticed more web sites selling glider and ottoman packages today with prices starting at $500.

One tip on rocking ottomans: we suggest skipping this and ordering an inexpensive "nursing" footstool (about $30). Why? Some moms claim the ottoman's height puts additional strain on their backs while breast-feeding. While the nursing footstool doesn't rock, it's lower height puts less strain on your back. (That said, we should note that some ottoman fans point out that once their mom/baby get the hang of nursing, that gliding ottoman is a nice luxury).

One safety note: don't leave an older child sitting in a glider-rocker. Many can be tipped over by a toddler when they climb out of it. (Safety tip: some glider rockers have a lever that locks it in position when not in use). ***Rating: A***

Little Castle *littlecastleinc.com*. Expensive, but good quality is how we'd describe Little Castle's glider rockers. Little Castle specializes in all-upholstered, swivel gliders. An example: the popular Cottage Chase, a soft, over-stuffed chair for $825. Other styles start at $300 (Walmart) and $450 (Target). Custom styles can easily top $1000, although the opening price for Little Castle in most specialty stores is $600.

As you'd expect for that price level, you get a wide choice of fabrics (all of which are online at Little Castle's web site) and other perks like a hidden release button to recline the chair.

FYI: Little Castle gliders are made in Oxnard, California. Each chair is custom made; delivery is about ten weeks.

New in the past year, Little Castle released a leatherette chair ($700 to $800 in white, brown or black) that can be customized with cushions using fabric from their entire line or your own fabric. These extra cushions run $130 for a set.

To differentiate from the gliders it sells to chains like Walmart, Little Castle is launching a collection of chairs under the "Castle Home Furnishings" brand that will be sold in independent stores only. Prices will be similar to Little Castle's main line. FYI: Little Castle is sold under the alias Enchanted on Walmart.com.

Readers generally like this company, but we heard from more than one that had quality issues with their expensive Little Castle gliders. One had a spring that popped out of the bottom of the chair; another said her Cottage Chase glider developed a hole in the arm after just eight months of use. Worse, Little Castle told these reader there was nothing they could to do help her since the fabric was discontinued (even though the chair comes with a one year warranty). In the case of the spring, Little Castle refused to repair the chair since it was outside of their one year warranty. Maybe we're crazy, but when you spend a $1000 on a custom Little Castle chair, we think the company should stand behind the product for more than 12 months.

Bottom line: most folks are happy with their Little Castle gliders, but if you have a problem, you are probably on your own for the repair bill. ***Rating: B***

Monte Toronto-based Monte's gliders epitomize the modern nursery look—simple lines, tailored fabrics, etc. Monte has four basic styles, but you can customize each chair to your heart's content.

All this doesn't come cheap: most chairs run $1000-$1200; swap the fabric for leather and you can add another $200.

So is it worth it? Well, the samples we recently inspected were impressive: solid walnut bases, high quality fabrics, quality foam for the seats, etc. Yes, all that is nice, but other glider makers (Dutailier, for example) do a similar look and quality for about 25% less. Hence, we get the feeling here you are paying a premium for . . . exactly what, we're not sure.

Delivery is about five to seven weeks and don't look for Monte to be discounted online—it is mostly sold specialty stores and chains like Giggle.

Bottom line: beautiful chairs, but at premium prices. *Rating: B*

Newco Sold online at Walmart and Babies R Us (among others), Newco makes upholstered gliders at discount prices. Walmart currently has a $343 Newco glider that features chenille fabric and matching ottoman for $144. Babies R Us also carries this brand—one of the best selling styles (Rosie) is $400.

Feedback on Newco has been mixed. While a good number of reviews are positive and say the chair is a great value, more than a few parents complained of quality issues (freight damage, bases that broke after three months of use, etc). One reader told us she was a bit surprised at how short the back of the chair was (and she wasn't particularly tall). Another said her Newco glider broke after less than a year. As a result of these durability and quality questions, we have lowered Newco's rating this year. *Rating: C+*

Nursery Classics by Klaussner Klaussner Home Furnishings is a large manufacturer of adult upholstered furniture based in North Carolina. They recently decided to market their upholstered rockers to the nursery biz (dubbed Nursery Classics by Klaussner).

Priced competitively at between $500 and $700, these upholstered rockers are manufactured in the US. The company offers 125 frame styles including glider rockers, regular rockers and recliners. Shipping takes three to four weeks.

Initial reviews of this line are positive, but a few detractors complain of quality issues (squeaks, etc) and the overall small size of these chairs (you might want to try them out in the store before ordering).

So we'll give Klaussner a qualified recommendation for now, as we await more feedback.*Rating: B*

Shermag/Chanderic *shermag.com.* Canada-based Shermag's strategy is to under-price Dutailier. Their gliders (which include an ottoman) are sold online for as little as $250. Shermag's focus is the entry glider market, similar to Dutailier's Ultramotion rockers.

So what's the catch with Shermag's affordable line? First, these styles are a bit smaller in size than other glider-rockers—they fit most moms fine, but those six-foot dads may be uncomfortable. The color choices are also limited (just one or two, in most cases). And you should try to sit in these first to make sure you like the cushions (no, they aren't as super comfy as more expensive options but most parents think they're just fine).

Shermag's pricier options are found at stores like Babies R Us, where $350 (including ottoman) is the average price point. For that extra money, you'll get a bigger chair, more fabric and frame color options.

How's the quality of Shermag gliders? Not great, according to a review of the feedback we've received from parents in the past year. We've noticed a deterioration in the reviews Shermag has received, both from our readers and other online postings. Concerns range from freight damage to squeaking—and long-term durability is another weak spot here. More than one parent told us their Shermag glider broke after less than two months of use.

Shermag's cheapest options often come with very cheap fabric, making this bargain not worth the hassle. And even Shermag's more expensive gliders are dogged by quality issues. Bottom line: there are better choices out there. **Rating: C-**

Stork Craft Like their cribs and dressers, Stork Craft's glider rockers are priced for the entry-level part of the market: Amazon and Walmart sell glider and ottoman packages for just $130.

What's the catch? Well, quality for one. More than one parent told us they loved their Stork Craft glider . . . for about four months. Then the squeaking started. Other complaints center on the cheap cushions. Or that their Stork Craft glider simply fell apart after regular use. Customer support is non-existent.

Bottom line: a bargain glider is no bargain if the chair drives you nuts with squeaking . . . or breaks after a few months. Spend a bit more for one of our better rated glider companies (example: Dutailier) and you'll be happier in the end. **Rating: C**

Tulip/Natart Nursery furniture maker Natart is entering the glider rocker market in 2014 with upholstered chairs that feature memory foam seating, adjustable armrests and a nifty accessory: an optional tray for your iPad.

Made in Quebec, the chairs will run $1250; the extra tablet shelf is $150. Two fabrics and two leather choices will be available.

These chairs weren't out on the market yet as of press time, no rating yet: **Rating: Not Yet.**

The Bottom Line:
A Wrap-Up of Our Best Buy Picks

For cribs, you've got two basic choices: a simple model that is, well, just a crib or a convertible model that eventually morphs into a twin or full size bed.

For a basic crib, the Fisher Price Newbury or Graco Stanton are good choices under $200. Another good bet: IKEA's affordable cribs which are under $150.

When it comes to convertible cribs, look at Munire (Baby Cache) or Westwood. These models run $400 to $600. Yep, it costs more money up-front but you get a crib that converts to a full-size bed.

Whatever crib style you pick, check under the hood to look at the mattress support. We like metal springs or wood slats; avoid cheap boards made of MDF. Choose a crib made of hard wood that will resist scratches and nicks.

The best mattress? We like *Sealy Soybean Foam-Core* crib mattress for $85. If you want a coil mattress, Naturepedic's Organic Cotton Classic 150 coil mattress is a good bet at $280. For organic mattresses, *Naturepedic's Organic Cotton Lightweight* mattress is our top pick at for $260.

The best dressers for your baby's nursery should have dove-tail drawers and smooth glides; the more solid wood, the better. Avoid pine and other soft woods, since these show scratches and other damage. The best dressers are the same as our crib picks: Munire, Westwood or Romina.

For glider rockers, Dutailier earns our top mark. A simple glider rocker runs $350, but fancy all-upholstered styles can push $1000.

So, here's a sample budget for an affordable nursery

Fisher Price Newbury crib	$150
Sealy Soybean Form mattress	$85
Baby Cache (Munire) dresser	$500
Dutailier Ultramotion glider-rocker	$350
Miscellaneous	$200
TOTAL	**$1285**

By contrast, if you bought a designer modern crib ($1500) and paired it with a high-end dresser (plus mattress, glider rocker, etc.), you'd be out $3500 by this point. So by following our budget, you will have a safe yet affordable nursery . . . and saved $2215.

Of course, you don't have any sheets for your baby's crib yet. Nor any clothes for Junior to wear. So, next we'll explore those topics and save more of your money.

CHAPTER 3

Baby Bedding & Decor

Inside this chapter

Where can you find brand new, designer-label bedding for as much as 50% off the retail price? We've got the answer in this chapter, plus you'll find eight smart shopper tips to help get the most for your money. We'll share the best web sites for baby linens. Learn the ten important tips that will keep your baby safe and sound. Finally, we've got a chart of the top bedding manufacturers and a must-read list of seven top money-wasters.

Getting Started: When Do You Need This Stuff?

Begin shopping for your baby's linen pattern in the sixth month of your pregnancy, if not earlier. Why? If you're purchasing these items from a baby specialty store, they usually must be special-ordered—allow at least four to eight weeks for delivery. If you leave a few weeks for shopping, you can order the bedding in your seventh month to be assured it arrives before the baby does.

If you're buying bedding from a store or web site that has the desired pattern in stock, you can wait until your eighth month. It still takes time to comparison shop, and some stores may only have certain pieces you need in stock, while other accessories (like wall hangings, etc.) may need to be special ordered.

No matter where you buy your baby's bedding, make sure you take the time to wash it (perhaps more than once) to make sure it doesn't shrink, pill or fall apart. You'll want to return it as soon as possible if there is a problem with the quality.

Sources

There are five basic sources for baby bedding:

1 **BABY SPECIALTY STORES.** These stores tend to have a limited selection of bedding in stock. Typically, you're expected to choose the bedding by seeing what you like on sample cribs or by looking through manufacturers' catalogs. Then you have to special-order your choices and wait four to eight weeks for arrival. And that's the main disadvantage to buying linens at a specialty store: THE WAIT. On the upside, most specialty stores do carry high-quality brand names you can't find at discounters or baby superstores. But you'll pay for it—most specialty stores mark such items at full retail.

2 **DISCOUNTERS.** The sheer variety of discount stores that carry baby bedding is amazing—you can find it everywhere from Walmart to Target, Marshall's to TJ Maxx. As you'd expect, everything is cash and carry at these stores—most carry a decent selection of items in stock. You pick out what you like and that's it; there are no special orders. The downside? Prices are cheap, but so is the quality. Most discounters only carry low-end brands whose synthetic fabrics and cheap construction may not withstand repeated washings. There are exceptions to this rule, which we'll share later in this chapter.

3 **DEPARTMENT STORES.** The selection of baby bedding at department stores is all over the board. Some chains have great baby departments and others need help. For example, JCPenney carries linen sets by nearly ten such manufacturers like CoCaLo and Carter's while Sears carries lines like Lambs & Ivy and Baby Boom. Prices at department stores vary as widely as selection; however, you can guarantee that department stores will hold occasional sales, making them a better deal.

4 **BABY SUPERSTORES.** The superstores reviewed in the last chapter (Babies R Us, Baby Depot, Buy Buy Baby etc.) combine the best of both worlds: decent prices AND quality brands. Best of all, most items are in stock. Unlike in Walmart or K-Mart stores, you're more likely to see 100% cotton bedding and better construction. Yet, the superstores aren't perfect: they are often beaten on price by online sources (reviewed later in this chapter). And superstores are more likely to sell bedding in sets (rather than a la carte), forcing you to buy frivolous items.

5 **ONLINE.** Most of our readers shop for their bedding online. And if there were a perfect baby product to be sold on-line, crib bedding is it. The web's full-color graphics let you see exactly what you'll get. And bedding is lightweight, which minimizes shipping costs. The only bummer: you can't feel the fabric or inspect the stitching. As a result, we recommend sticking to well-known brand names when ordering online. See the next section on best online sources for baby bedding and don't forget to check out online-only bedding on Walmart and Target's web sites.

Best Online Bargains

Baby Supermall

babysupermall.com. As you'd expect from a site with "mall" in its name, BabySupermall tries to be all things to moms and dads. From safety gear to furniture to toys, this site carries quite a wide selection. In the baby bedding department, they had over 500 different bedding options available. Manufacturers include Lambs & Ivy, Glenna Jean, Bananafish and MiGi. Prices are usually affordable, although frequent sales (up to 50% off) make this site a real bargain. You can even click on a link for a bedding set and BabySupermall will send you an email when that bedding goes on sale in the future.

Perhaps the best part of the site is its baby bedding finder. You can choose categories like gender, price range, color, brand and up to four themes. These themes include flora, bugs and butterflies, frogs and 17 other options. Another plus: free shipping if you spend over $69 and fabric samples are available for a small charge. The site claims to have the fastest delivery because they warehouse "nearly 10,000 nursery bedding sets" at their shipping facility.

Our only complaint: the site is very cluttered. It can be as overwhelming visually as your first visit to a Babies R Us store. ***Rating: A***

Baby Supermarket

babysupermarket.com. This online outlet for a Jackson, MS baby store is a good option to consider for bargain bedding. They carry about ten bedding lines, including some of our top picks (Cotton Tale, Sumersault and Lambs & Ivy) and prices are good. For example they sell a four-piece set from CoCaLo for $170 (regular price $200). Baby Supermarket also has a decent selection of separates including the Ultimate Crib Sheet and bedding for cradles and small cribs. Baby Supermarket has improved the site since our last review with easier drop down menus to get you where you're going. ***Rating: B***

Diapers.com

diapers.com. Diapers.com is really the land of discounts. Everywhere you look when you visit there are coupon codes, cash back offers, free shipping over $49, and free returns. The site is a bit busy with all the free/discount offers, but you can easily narrow your search by gender, theme, brand and price. We were impressed that they offered so many mini crib sets and sheets (87 total on our visit). These can be tough to find, so here's a great resource.

Manufacturers include the usual crowd as well as some different names like Clouds & Stars zip off sheets (see box later in this chapter), Egg by Susan Lazar and Babyletto. The site calls out sale prices and any out of stock items clearly, a nice plus. Overall, Diapers.com is one of our favorites for great selection and price. **Rating: A**

Overstock

overstock.com. Overstock.com is a master at finding closeout deals in all kinds of categories. We always buy our regular bed sheets from these guys in amazing Egyptian cotton with incredibly high thread counts. So we figured they'd have some great deals on baby bedding too. And we weren't disappointed. On a recent visit we saw over 160 baby bedding sets from companies like Trend Lab, My Baby Sam, Cotton Tale and more. Prices are 25% to 50% off. Baby bedding is sold as sets and separates.

But remember, if you see something you want on Overstock.com, don't wait too long! They sell out quick! And some designs do not offer a la carte sheets so you're stuck with what comes in the package. Be sure you check customer reviews before you buy to verify you're really getting a deal. **Rating: A**

What Are You Buying?

Walk into any baby store, announce you're having a baby, and stand back: the eager salespeople will probably pitch you on all types of bedding items that you MUST buy. We call this the "Diaper Stacker Syndrome," named in honor of that useless (but expensive) linen item that allegedly provides a convenient place to store diapers. But what do you really need? Here's our list of the absolute necessities for your baby's linen layette:

◆ **Fitted sheets**—at least three to four. This is the workhorse of your baby's linens. When it comes to crib sheets, you have three choices: woven, knit and flannel. Woven (also called percale) sheets are available in all cotton or cotton blend fabrics, while knit and flannel sheets are almost always all cotton. As to which is best, it's up to you. Some folks like flannel sheets, especially in colder climates. Others find woven or knit sheets work fine. One tip: look for sheets that have elastic all-around the edges (cheaper ones just have elastic on the corners). See the "Safe & Sound" section for more info on crib sheet safety issues.

If you plan to use a bassinet/cradle, you'll need a few of these special-size sheets as well . . . but your choices here are pretty limited. You'll usually find solid color pastels or white. Some specialty linen manufacturers do sell bassinet sheets, but they can get rather pricey. And you may find complete bassinet sets that come with all the linens for your baby. Just be sure to check the fabric content (all cotton is best) and washing instructions. By the way, one mom improvised bassinet sheets by putting the bassinet mattress inside a king size pillowcase. You may want to secure the excess fabric under the mattress so it doesn't un-tuck.

◆ **Mattress Pads/Sheet Protector.** While most baby mattresses have waterproof vinyl covers, many parents use either a mattress pad or sheet protector to protect the mattress or sheet from leaky diapers. A mattress pad is the traditional way of dealing with this problem and is placed between the mattress and the crib sheet. A more recent invention, the sheet protector, goes on top of the crib sheet.

A sheet protector has a waterproof vinyl backing to protect against leaking. And here's the cool part: it Velcro's to the crib's posts, making for easy removal. If the baby's diaper leaks, simply pop off the sheet protector and throw it in the wash (instead of the fitted crib sheets). You can buy sheet protectors in most baby stores or online. See "Email from the Real World" nearby for information on sheet savers.

◆ **Blanket?** Baby stores love to pitch expensive quilts to parents and many bedding sets include them as part of the package. But remember this: *all babies need is a simple, thin cotton blanket.* Not only are thick quilts overkill for most climates, they can also be dangerous. The Consumer Product Safety Commission's report on Sudden Infant Death Syndrome (SIDS) concluded that putting babies face down on such soft bedding may contribute to as many as 30% of SIDS deaths each year in the U.S. (As a side note, there is no explanation for the other 70% of SIDS cases, although environmental factors like smoking near the baby and a too-hot room are suspected). Some baby bedding companies have responded to these concerns by rolling out decorative flannel-backed blankets

BABY BEDDING

E-MAIL FROM THE REAL WORLD
Sheet savers make for easy changes

Baby bedding sure looks cute, but the real work is changing all those sheets. Karen Naide found a solution:

"One of our best buys was 'The Ultimate Crib Sheet.' I bought one regular crib sheet that matched the bedding set, and two Ultimate Crib Sheets. This product is waterproof (vinyl on the bottom, and soft white poly/cotton on the top) and lies on top of your regular crib sheet. It has six elastic straps that snap around the bars of your crib. When it gets dirty or the baby soils it, all you have to do is unsnap the straps, lift it off, put a clean one on, and that's it! No taking the entire crib sheet off (which usually entails wrestling with the mattress). It's really quick and easy! While the white sheet may not exactly match your pattern, it can only be seen from inside the crib, and as you have so often stated, it's not like the baby cares about what it looks like. From the outside of the crib, you can still see the crib sheet that matches your bedding. Anyway, I think it's a wonderful product, and really a must."

There are a couple of options for quick change cribs sheets. The Ultimate Crib Sheet (summerinfant.com) retails for $15 to $21 and is sold online and in store. Another good bet is the Quick Zip crib sheet from Clouds and Stars (cloudsandstars.com).

While the Quick Zip isn't waterproof, it has a sheet base that covers the bottom of the mattress and stays in place. The top of the sheet is secured via a plastic zipper. When you need to change sheets at two in the morning, you zip off the top of the sheet and zip on a spare. No lifting of the mattress (except when you first set it up). The white or ecru sheet sets are $35 to $45 for the starter set (a zipper base plus top sheet) and additional top sheets are $17 to $30.

Between the two, we'd suggest the Quick Zip—even though it is more expensive than the Ultimate Crib Sheet, the quality is better and it is easier to use.

(instead of quilts) in their collections.

But what if you live in a cold climate and think a cotton blanket won't cut it? Consider crib blankets made from fleece (a lightweight 100% polyester fabric brushed to a soft finish) available in most stores and online. For example, **Lands End** sells a micro fleece crib blanket for $24. Of course, polar fleece blankets are also available from mainstream bedding companies like **California Kids**. Or how about a "coverlet," which is lighter than a quilt but more substantial than a blanket? Lightweight quilts (instead of the traditional thick and fluffy version) are another option for as little as $30 online.

Halo Innovations' (halosleep.com) SleepSack was the first of its kind "wearable blanket" that helps baby avoid suffocating. Available in three sizes and fabrics, the SleepSack is $25 to $40. A portion of the sale price goes to First Candle/SIDS Alliance. Swaddling blankets are also now the rage. Examples include the **Miracle Blanket** ($24; miracleblanket.com) and the **Summer Infant Swaddle Me** ($13). See the box nearby for more swaddling blanket picks. Note: Be sure when swaddling your infant, you leave the baby's waist and legs loosely enclosed in the blanket. Recent concerns were raised that tight swaddling could lead to hip dysplasia in some infants.

More Money Buys You . . .

Baby bedding sets vary from as little as $40 in discount stores up to nearly $1000 in specialty stores. The basic difference: fabric quality and construction. The cheapest bedding is typically made of 50/50 cotton-poly blends with low thread counts (120 threads per inch). To mask the low quality, many bedding companies splash cutesy licensed cartoon characters on their offerings. So what does more money buy you? First, better fabric. Usually, you'll find 100% cotton with 200 thread counts or more. Cheap quality crib sheets often lack elastic all the way around and some shrink dangerously when washed (see Safe and Sound next for details), while more money buys you preshrunk or oversized (to allow for shrinkage) sheets with elastic all around the edge.

Beyond the $300 price point, you're most likely paying for a designer name and frilly accessories (coordinating lamp shade, anyone?). At the upper end of the crib bedding market, you find luxury fabrics and finishes—silks, brocades, matte lasse, etc.

Safe & Sound

When it comes to baby safety, most folks think of outlet covers and coffee table bumpers—but your baby's crib bedding should be a key priority. Why? Your baby will be spending more time in the crib than any other place in the house. Here are several safety points to remember:

Swaddling & Wearable Blankets

Swaddling and wearable blankets have become increasingly popular in recent years—they keep baby warm and avoid safety concerns with quilts or regular blankets. Here's an overview:

The original **SleepSack** (made by Halo) started the trend and is available in a variety of fabrics for $25 to $40. They are a bit like a sleeping bag with arms (also available as sleeveless for warm climates).

Halo has expanded their line to include swaddling blankets. The SleepSack Swaddle ($27 to $29) is a SleepSack with added flaps and Velcro closures that fold over to hold baby's arms close to their body.

Of course, there's more than just the Sleep Sack out there. Here are some of our reader favorites for swaddling blankets.

Aden & Anais (AdenandAnais.com) makes two types of swaddling blankets: muslin swaddle wraps and Easy Swaddles. The muslin swaddles are do-it-yourself swaddling blankets, while Easy Swaddles have snaps. Prices are $43 for a pack of four muslin swaddles; Easy Swaddles are $23 each. Double layer blankets, organic and bamboo collections are available. Bonus: Aden & Anais' web site includes helpful how-to videos on swaddling.

Another option: **Swaddle Designs** (swaddledesigns.com) swaddling blankets and wearable blankets are also excellent, say readers. This site offers both a wearable blanket option called the zzZipMe Sack ($32 to $45) with a cool two-way zipper for easy diaper changes plus their Ultimate Receiving blanket ($25) and Marquisette Swaddling blanket ($14 to $27). Both blankets have easy directions on a sewn-on tag.

Finally, a small company out of Connecticut makes a wearable blanket/swaddler called the **Woombie** (thewoombie. com). This option is similar to a SleepSack without the arm holes. You just zip it up and it hugs your baby's arms to his chest. Cost: $28 to $30. Winter weight, summer weight and organic fabrics are available.

One note: the International Hip Dysplasia Institute (hipdysplasia.org) points to the potential for increases in hip dysplasia problems when parents swaddle children too tightly around the hips and legs. The institute has an online pamphlet that explains hip dysplasia and the risks of improper swaddling. FYI: wearable blankets from Halo, Swaddle Designs and Woombie help parents avoid a too-tight fit when swaddling a baby.

◆ **Make sure the crib sheets snugly fit the mattress.**
Let's talk about crib sheets. As you might guess, it is the elastic on
a sheet that helps it fit snugly to a mattress. But not all sheets have
the same amount of elastic.

One quality sign: check to make sure the sheet's elastic extends
around the ENTIRE sheet (cheaper quality crib sheets only have
elastic on the ends, making a good fit more difficult to achieve).

One of our favorite brands with this feature are made by the
American Baby Company (ababycompany.com). Their affordable
sheets ($13 to $20) for both cribs and portable playpens come in
a variety of fabrics (percale, flannel, cotton jersey, etc.).

Another issue to consider with crib sheets: shrinkage. *Never use
a sheet that has shrunk so much it can no longer be completely
pulled over the bottom corners of the mattress.*

Unfortunately, some sheets shrink more than others. Generally, the
cheapest sheets sold in discount stores shrink the most. We will offer
our recommendations of bedding brands later in this chapter. Those
with our highest recommendations typically have sheets that are
pre-shrunk. Others make their sheets larger to allow for shrinkage.

Our advice: for any crib sheet you buy, be sure to wash it several times *according to the directions* and see if it correctly fits your
crib. If not, return it to the store.

◆ **No soft bedding in the crib.** Yes, we've said it before and
here it is again: studies on Sudden Infant Death Syndrome (SIDS, also
known as crib death) have linked SIDS to infants sleeping on fluffy
bedding, lambskins, or pillows. A pocket can form around the baby's
face if she is placed face down in fluffy bedding, and she can slowly suffocate while breathing in her own carbon dioxide. The best
advice: put your infant on her back when she sleeps. And don't put

Sheets with All Around Elastic

Here is a list of manufacturers who make their crib sheets
with elastic all around the sheet:

American Baby	Fleece Baby	Bobble Roos
BB Basics	Garnet Hill	Nava's Designs
Baby Basics	Hoohobbers	Restoration
Baby Gap	Kids Line	Hardware
Carousel	Land of Nod	Sweet Kyla
Circo (Target)	Maddie Boo	

pillows, comforters or other soft bedding or toys inside a crib.

The Consumer Product Safety Commission now recommends that parents not use ANY soft bedding around, on top of, or under baby. If you want to use a blanket, tuck a very thin blanket under the mattress at one end of the crib to keep it from moving around. The blanket should then only come up to baby's chest. Safest of all: avoid using any blankets in a crib and put baby in a blanket sleeper (basically, a thick set of pajamas) and t-shirt for warmth. (More on blanket sleepers in the next chapter). See the picture nearby for an example of the correct way to use a blanket.

One mom wrote to tell us about a scary incident in her nursery. She had left a blanket hanging over the side of the crib when she put her son down for a nap. He managed to pull the blanket down and get wrapped up in it, nearly suffocating. Stories like that convince us that putting any soft bedding in or near a crib is risky.

How much bedding is too much? A new father emailed us this question: "With all the waterproof liners, fitted sheets and ultimate crib sheets we're worried that our firm mattress is now becoming soft and squishy. How many layers are safe?"

Good point. We know that some parents figure it is easier to change crib sheets at 2 am if they simply pile on several layers of sheets on the crib mattress. (This way, you simply remove the top wet layer when changing the sheets). While we admire the creative thinking, we suggest NOT doing this. One sheet over a waterproof liner is enough. Or use an Ultimate Crib Sheet over your sheet—you won't need an additional liner since the Ultimate Crib Sheet is waterproof. The take-home message: any more than TWO layers on top of a mattress is dangerous.

◆ **Beware of ribbons and long fringe.** These are possible choking hazards if they are not attached properly. Remove any questionable decoration.

◆ **We DO NOT recommend crib bumpers.** Do not use bumpers in your baby's crib, cradle or bassinet. They are a risk factor for suffocation.

Yes, in past editions of this book, we tried to discourage people from using bumpers, but did not outright reject them. Why did we change our mind? New evidence shows that bumpers can and do cause suffocation deaths in infants. A recent investigation by the

Chicago Tribune detailed a link between crib bumpers and two dozen infant deaths in the past decade. The article ("Hidden Hazard of Crib Bumpers," December 12, 2010) prompted the CPSC to open a review of the safety of crib bumpers.

An earlier study by a Washington University pediatrician, Dr. Bradley Thach "concluded that 27 babies' deaths were attributed to bumper pads from 1985 to 2005." This study, however, has been largely ignored by both the industry and the CPSC, although the American Academy of Pediatrics discourages parents from using bumpers.

In 2011, Chicago became the first city in the U.S. to outright ban the sale of bumper pads in their jurisdiction. The *Chicago Tribune* story mentioned earlier prompted the ban. The state of Maryland has also weighed in on bumpers, considering either an outright ban on their sale or the adoption of voluntary safety standards. As of press time, they were still studying the issue.

As a side note, Canada has discouraged bumper use for many years. One Canadian reader noted: "We are not supposed to use bumper pads due to the increased risk of SIDS. No one I know uses them. When the health nurse comes to visit you in the home, she checks to make sure you don't have bumper pads." It's time parents in the U.S. followed similar guidelines.

Now we know what you're thinking: "What if my baby hits his head on the hard wood slats?" or "What if she gets her arm or leg stuck between the slats?" First, these issues are rare—few kids are injured by knocking their heads against the slats and even fewer get limbs stuck. The only product we recommend for parents who truly have a problem with babies who get their limbs stuck is the Breathable Baby Crib liner ($30).

A fashion note: for parents who miss the attractive side view of a crib that has bumpers, consider sheets from Skip Hop. They are now printing a design on the sides of their crib sheets that makes them look like bumpers (an enlarged graphical item that coordinates with the bedding design). Expect to see more manufacturers adopt this style now that bumpers are becoming verboten.

◆ **Never use sleep positioners.** A recent recall of sleep positioners lead us to urge parents not to use them. These $10 to $20 blocks of foam are supposed to hold baby in place on their back when sleeping. However, the Consumer Product Safety Commission (CPSC.org) issued a "warning to parents and caregivers to stop using sleep positioners." They have received reports of 12 infants who suffocated when positioners were used. In past editions, we discouraged sleep positioners because they were a waste of money, but now we know they are also a serious hazard. Simply put your baby to sleep on his back—no pillows, no rolled up towels.

◆ **Never use an electric blanket/heating pad.** Babies can dangerously overheat, plus any moisture, such as urine, can cause electric shock.

◆ **Avoid blankets that use nylon thread.** Nylon thread melts in the dryer and then breaks. These loose threads can wrap around your baby's neck, fingers or toes or break off and become a choking hazard. Cotton or cotton/poly thread is best.

◆ **Watch out for chenille.** Its popularity has waned in recent years, but we still see some chenille accents on baby bedding and in luxe items like blankets. The problem? With some chenille, you can actually pull out fibers from the fabric backing with little effort. And that might be a choking hazard for baby.

◆ **Travel.** Now that you've created a safe nursery at home, what about when you travel? Parents who frequently travel are often frustrated by hotels, which not only have unsafe cribs (see previous chapter) but also questionable sheets. At one hotel, we were given queen size bed sheets to use in a crib! A solution: one reader recommended bringing a crib sheet from home. That way you know your baby will be safe and sound. (When you reserve a crib at a hotel, find out if it is a portable crib or a standard crib so you know what size sheet to bring.)

◆ **All linens should have a tag** indicating the manufacturer's name and address. That's the only way you would know if the linens were recalled. You can also contact the manufacturer if you have a problem or question. While this is the law, some stores may sell discounted or imported linens that do not have tags. Our advice: DON'T buy them.

 Smart Shopper Tips

Smart Shopper Tip
Pillow Talk: Looking for Mr. Good Bedding
   "Cartoons or more cartoons—that seems to be the basic choice in crib bedding at our local baby store. Since it all looks alike, is the pattern the only difference?"
   There's more to it than that. And buying baby bedding isn't the same as purchasing linens for your own bed—you'll be washing these pieces much more frequently, so they must be made to withstand the extra abuse. Since baby bedding is more than just another set of sheets, here are several quality points to look for:

1 **RUFFLES SHOULD BE FOLDED OVER FOR DOUBLE THICKNESS—INSTEAD OF A SINGLE THICKNESS RUFFLE WITH HEMMED EDGE.** Double ruffles hold up better in the wash.

2 **COLORED DESIGNS ON THE BEDDING SHOULD BE PRINTED OR WOVEN INTO THE FABRIC, NOT STAMPED** (like you'd see on a screen-printed t-shirt). Stamped designs on sheets can fade with only a few washings. The problem: the pieces you wash less frequently (like dust ruffles and bumpers) will fade at different rates, spoiling the coordinated look you paid big money for. In case you're wondering how to determine whether the design is printed rather than stamped, printed fabrics have color that goes through the fabric to the other side. Stamped patterns are merely applied onto the top of the fabric.

3 **MAKE SURE THE PIECES ARE SEWN WITH COTTON/POLY THREAD, NOT NYLON.** While nylon threads can be a safety problem (see earlier discussion), they also are a quality issue. When nylon threads break in a dryer, the filling can bunch up.

4 **CHECK FOR TIGHT, SMOOTH STITCHING ON APPLIQUÉS.** If you can see the edge of the fabric through the appliqué thread, the work is too skimpy. Poor quality appliqués will probably unravel after only a few washings. We've seen some appliqués that were actually fraying in the store—check before you buy.

5 **HIGH THREAD-COUNT SHEETS.** Unlike adult linens, many packages of baby bedding do not list the thread count. But, if you can count the individual threads when you hold a sheet up to the light, you know the thread count is too low. High thread-count sheets (200 threads per inch or more) are preferred since they are softer and smoother against baby's skin, last longer and wear better. Unfortunately, most affordable baby bedding has low thread counts (80 to 120 thread counts are common)—traditionally, it's the design (not the quality) that sells baby bedding. But there is good news on this front: most mid- to upper-priced brands are at least 200 count.

6 **THE DUST RUFFLE PLATFORM SHOULD BE OF GOOD QUALITY FABRIC**—or else it will tear. Longer, full ruffles are more preferable to shorter ones. As a side note, the dust ruffle is sometimes referred to as a crib skirt.

7 **REMEMBER THAT CRIB SHEETS COME IN DIFFERENT SIZES—** bassinet/cradle, portable crib, and full-size crib. Always use the correct size sheet.

Wastes of Money/Worthless Items

"I have a very limited budget for bedding, and I want to avoid spending money on stuff that I won't need. What are some items I should stay away from?"

It may be tempting to buy every matching bedding accessory. And you'll get a lot of sales pressure at some stores to go for the entire "coordinated" look. Yet many baby-bedding items are a complete waste of money—here's our list of the worst offenders:

1 Diaper Stacker. This is basically a bag (in coordinating fabric, of course) used to store diapers—you hang it on the side of a changing table. Apparently, bedding makers must think stacking diapers on the shelf of your changing table or storing them in a drawer is a major etiquette breach. Take my word for it: babies are not worried if their diapers are out in plain sight. Save the $30 to $50 that bedding makers charge for diaper stackers and stack your own. By the way, we've even seen $100 diaper stackers—these typically coordinate with equally expensive bedding sets. Another note: now that many manufacturers aren't selling sets with coordinating bumper pads, expect to see the diaper stacker substituted in four piece sets.

2 Pillows. Some bedding sets still include pillows or pillowcases. Are the bedding designers nuts, or what? Haven't they heard that it's dangerous to put your baby to sleep on a pillow? What a terrible safety hazard, not to mention a waste of your money. We don't even think a decorative pillow is a good idea—what if another caretaker puts your baby to sleep in her crib and forgets to remove the decorative pillow? Forget the pillow and save $30 to $50.

3 Sets of Linens. Sets may include useless or under-used items like those listed above as well as dust ruffles, bumpers and window valances. Another problem: sets are often a mixed bag when it comes to quality. Some items are good, while others are lacking. Here's an example from Overstock.com: a 13-piece set on sale for $115 included a quilt, two valances, skirt, crib sheet, bumper, diaper stacker, toy bag, two pillows and three wall hangings. No surprise, this set was made of a poly/cotton blend fabric. A better bet: many baby stores or even chains now sell bedding items a la carte. That way you can pick and choose just the items you need—at a substantial savings over the all-inclusive sets.

4 **CANOPIES.** Parents-to-be of girls are often pressured to buy frilly accessories like canopies. The pitch is a feminine look for her nursery. Don't buy into it. The whole set-up for a canopy is going to be more expensive (you'll need a special crib, etc.)—it'll set you back $60 to $175 for the linens alone. And enclosing your baby's crib in a canopy won't do much for her visual stimulation or health (canopies are dust collectors).

5 **ALL-WHITE LINENS.** If you think of babies as pristine and unspoiled, you've never had to change a poopy diaper or clean spit-up from the front of an outfit. We're amazed that anyone would consider all-white bedding, since keeping it clean will probably be a full-time job. Stick with colors, preferably bright ones. If you buy all-white linens and then have to go back to buy colored ones, you'll be out another $100 to $200. (Yes, some folks argue that white linens are easier to bleach clean, but extensive bleaching over time can yellow fabric.)

Money Saving Secrets

1 **IF YOU'RE ON A TIGHT BUDGET, GO FOR A GOOD BLANKET AND A NICE SET OF HIGH THREAD-COUNT SHEETS.** What does that cost? A good cotton or fleece blanket runs $15 to $30, while a decent quality fitted sheet is another $15 to $30. Forget all the fancy items like embroidered comforters, duvet covers, window valances, diaper stackers and dust ruffles. After all, your baby won't care if she doesn't have perfectly coordinated accessories.

2 **DON'T BUY A QUILT.** Sure, they look pretty, but do you really need one? Go for a nice cotton blanket, instead—and save the $50 to $200. Better yet, hint to your friends that you'd like receiving blankets as shower gifts.

3 **SKIP EXPENSIVE WALL HANGINGS—DO DECOR ON THE CHEAP.** One of the best new products we've discovered for this is *Wall Nutz* (wallnutz.com). These innovative transfers let you create paint-by-number masterpieces in your baby's room. Paint a six-by-eight foot mural or just add some decorative borders. Cost: $6 to $120 depending on size and complexity (plus the cost of paints).

A new idea: wall decals. These creative graphic "stickers" can be positioned and repositioned, removed and replaced. Choose from animals, flowers, abstract designs and more. Wall Nutz as well as two other companies offer these cool décor options. *Blik Re-Stik*

BABY BEDDING

(whatisblik.com) sells designs start at $22 while **WallPops!** (wall-pops.com) has decals starting at $15 including Dora the Explorer ($50) and SpongeBob ($90). While these are reusable, take care when removing them as they may fray along the edges. **Wallies** (wallies.com) are similar to decals except that they are pre-pasted shapes. You wet the backing and stick them wherever you like. FYI:

LICENSE TRANSLATOR
Who makes what brand of bedding

A perennial trend in crib bedding is licensed characters—just about every cartoon character imaginable has been licensed to one of the big bedding makers for use in juvenile bedding. But how can tell you tell who makes what? Here is a list of popular licensed characters and their bedding makers:

LICENSE	SEE BEDDING MAKER
BABY LOONEY TUNES	CROWN CRAFTS
CARE BEARS	BABY BOOM
D.C. SUPER FRIENDS	CROWN CRAFTS
DISNEY BABY	PEM AMERICA
DISNEY BABY	KIDSLINE
DR. SEUSS	TREND LAB
DORA THE EXPLORER	BABY BOOM
EDDIE BAUER	CROWN CRAFTS
FISHER-PRICE	CROWN CRAFTS
HELLO KITTY & FRIENDS	LAMBS & IVY
KATHY IRELAND	THANK YOU BABY
LAURA ASHLEY	PEM AMERICA
MAISY	SLEEPING PARTNERS
NAUTICAKIDS	CROWN CRAFTS
NOJO	CROWN CRAFTS
ORGANICALLY GROWN	CROWN CRAFTS
PRECIOUS MOMENTS	BABY BOOM
SESAME STREET	CROWN CRAFTS
SNOOPY	LAMBS & IVY
THOMAS AND FRIENDS	BABY BOOM
TOO GOOD BY JENNY	PEM AMERICA
WAMSUTTA	SPRING
WINNIE THE POOH	CROWN CRAFTS
ZUTANO	KIDSLINE

Some Wallies aren't reusable—you have to strip them off like wall-paper. A pack of Flower Fairies (30 pieces) runs $20. They now offer bigger, mural size Wallies starting at $50.

Of course, crafts stores are another great source for do-it-your-self inspiration. Michaels Arts & Crafts (michaels.com) sells stencils and supplies for nursery decor.

4 **MAKE YOUR OWN SHEETS, DUST RUFFLES AND OTHER LINEN ITEMS.** Think that's too complicated? A mom in Georgia called in this great tip on curtain valances—she bought an extra dust ruffle, sewed a curtain valance from the material and saved $70. All you need to do is remove the ruffle from the fabric platform and sew a pocket along one edge. I managed to do this simple pro-cedure on my sewing machine without killing myself, so it's quite possible you could do it too. A good place for inspiration is your local fabric store—most carry pattern books like Butterick, Simplicity and McCalls, all of which have baby bedding patterns that are under $10. There are other pattern books you can purchase that specialize in baby quilts—some of these books also have patterns for other linen items like valances, crib skirts or wall hangings. Even if you buy good quality fabric at $10 per yard, your total savings will be 75% or more compared to "pre-made" items.

5 **SHOP AT OUTLETS.** Scattered across the country, we found a few outlets that discount linens. Among the better ones: Garnet Hill and Carousel (also known as babybeddingonline.com)—we recommend them as a Best Bet later in the chapter. Another reader praised the Pottery Barn Outlet. They have ten locations at the time of this writing. The discounts start at 50% on bedding and furniture from their web sites and retail stores. Other outlets: Carter's, Baby Gap, and Nautica. Check Outlet Bound (www.out-letbound.com) for locations.

6 **DON'T PICK AN OBSCURE BEDDING THEME.** Sure, that "Exploding Kiwi Fruit" bedding is cute, but where will you find any matching accessories to decorate your baby's room? Chances are they'll only be available "exclusively" from the bed-ding's manufacturer—at exclusively high prices. A better bet is to choose a more common theme with lots of accessories (wall decor, lamps, rugs, etc.). The more plentiful the options, the lower the prices. Winnie the Pooh is a good example, although you'll find quite a few accessories for other common themes like Noah's Ark, teddy bears, rocking horses, etc.

7 **GO FOR SOLID COLOR SHEETS AND USE THEMED ACCESSORIES.**
Just because you want to have a Disney-themed nursery does-
n't mean you have to buy Disney *bedding*. A great money-saving
strategy: use low-cost solid color sheets, blankets and other linen
items in the crib. Get these in colors that match/compliment theme
accessories like a lamp, clock, poster, wallpaper, rugs, etc. (Hint: register for these items, which make nice shower gifts). You still have the
Disney look, but without the hefty tag for Disney bedding. Many of
the online sites we reviewed earlier in this chapter are excellent
sources for affordable, solid-color bedding. Another bonus: solid
color sheets/linens from these web sites we recommend are often
much higher quality (yet at a lower price) than theme bedding.

8 **SURF THE WEB.** Earlier in this chapter, we discussed the best
web sites for baby bedding deals. The savings can be as
much as 50% off retail prices. Even simple items like crib sheets can
be affordably mail ordered.

Tips on green bedding

Like many organic products today, there is no standard for
organic baby bedding. This leaves it up to bedding manufacturers to determine for themselves what's organic. So, let's
review some terms you'll see.

Organic cotton simply means cotton that's been grown with
a minimum amount of toxic pesticides or fertilizers. That's right,
there is no guarantee that organic cotton is completely free of
all pesticides and fertilizers. But it is as close as you can get.

So, you want to go for organic cotton sheets—but what
about the sheet's color? Since conventional sheets are dyed
with synthetic chemicals, can an organic sheet be colored anything than the natural shade of cotton (that is, an off-white)?

Turns out, the answer is yes. Organic cotton can be
grown in a few colors. Yes, that's right, just like you can buy
naturally orange or purple cauliflower, you can buy colored
cotton. Three colors are available: pink, light brown and
green. Another solution: vegetable dyes. Look for manufacturers that sell baby bedding made with low-impact vegetable dyed cotton.

Of course, all this comes for a price: organic crib bedding
is often 20% to 35% more expensive than conventional
bedding.

The Name Game: Our Picks for the Best Brands

Perhaps the biggest challenge with baby bedding is there are so many choices! To help you whittle down the list a bit, we present our Best Bets, Good But Not Great and Skip It list of bedding brands. (Individual reviews of each bedding manufacturer listed below can be found on the subscription side of our web site at BabyBargains.com).

The Best Bets are the brands that have the best quality and durability. Typically, they feature sheets that are 100% cotton. While some of these brands can be pricey, most offer good value for the dollar.

Good But Not Great picks are just that—not our first choices for quality, but a close runner-up. In some cases, these are lines that have good quality but poor overall value. Example: Annette Tatum makes great quality bedding, but the price for a single sheet is a whopping $66. Whoa!

The Skip-It brands are the poorest quality: they shrink in the wash or fall apart. They may be made of poly/cotton blends, which tend to be less comfortable. Poor stitching on appliqués as well as stamped designs lead to bedding that wears out fast so even if it's very affordable, it's a waste of money.

Some of these brands sell direct; others just through retailers.

SAFETY NOTE: We do NOT recommend parents use bumpers in their babies' cribs. See the Safe and Sound section earlier for an in depth explanation. Note that many brands below sell bedding sets that include bumpers.

Affordable Artwork

Framed artwork for baby's room has to be very expensive, right? Nope, not if you buy a framed print from **Creative Images** (www.crimages.com). This Florida-based company sells prints, growth charts, wall hangings and more at very affordable prices—just $30 to $100. Each print is mounted on wood and laminated (no glass frame) so baby can enjoy it at eye-level (just sponge it off if it gets dirty). Best of all, there are hundreds of images in any theme to choose from: Pooh, bunnies, Noah's Ark, plus other collections of animals, sports and pastels. Check out their web site for samples.

Best Bets

Bobble Roos (blankets)	BOBBLEROOS.COM
Caden Lane	CADENLANE.COM
California Kids	CALKIDS.COM
Carousel/Baby Bedding Online	BABYBEDDINGONLINE.COM
CoCalo	COCALO.COM
Cotton Tale	COTTONTALEDESIGNS.COM
Glenna Jean	GLENNAJEAN.COM
Hoohobbers	HOOHOBBERS.COM
Kimberly Grant	KIMBERLYGRANT.COM
Lambs & Ivy	LAMBSIVY.COM
Land of Nod	LANDOFNOD.COM
Living Textiles	LIVINGTEXTILES.COM
Pine Creek Bedding/Over the Moon	PINECREEKBEDDING.COM
Serena & Lily	SERENAANDLILY.COM
Sumersault	SUMERSAULT.COM
Ultimate Crib Sheet	SUMMERINFANT.COM
Sweet Kyla	SWEETKYLA.COM

Good But Not Great

Annette Tatum	ANNETTETATUM.COM
BB Basics Online	BUYBUYBABY.COM
Carter's	CARTERS.KIDSLINEINC.COM
Company Kids	COMPANYKIDS.COM
BananaFish	BANANAFISH.COM
NoJo	NOJO.COM
Dwell	DWELLSTUDIO.COM
Garnet Hill	GARNETHILL.COM
GrahamKracker	GRAHAMKRACKER.COM
Jessica McClintock	PACIFICCOASTHOMEFURNISHINGS.COM
JoJo Designs	JOJODESIGNS.COM
Kidsline	KIDSLINEINC.COM
Koala Baby	BABIESRUS.COM
Maddie Boo	MADDIEBOOBEDDING.COM
My Baby Sam	MYBABYSAM.COM
Nava's Designs	NAVASDESIGNS.COM
Pottery Barn Kids	POTTERYBARNKIDS.COM
Restoration Hardware	RHBABYANDCHILD.COM
Sleeping Partners	SLEEPINGPARTNERS.COM
Summer Infant	SUMMERINFANT.COM
Tadpole Basics	TARGET.COM
Trend Lab Baby	TREND-LAB.COM
Whistle & Wink	WHISTLEANDWINK.COM

Skip It: CROWN CRAFTS (DISNEY BABY, FISHER-PRICE, NAUTICA KIDS, EDDIE BAUER, SESAME STREET, DC SUPER FRIENDS, BABY LOONEY TUNES, PRECIOUS MOMENTS); GERBER; CIRCO (TARGET); TOO GOOD BY JENNY

Brand Recommendations : Our Picks

Bedding Basics (sheets)

Good. Tadpole by Sleeping Partners is a good basic sheet that sells for $30 for a set of two. Parents tell us the quality is good and the sheets are soft. Pottery Barn Kids chamois sheets ($30 for one) are a great option for cold climates. Readers love their softness.

Better. Land of Nod makes stylish bedding, buy you don't have to buy an entire set—they sell 100% cotton fitted sheets separately. Ranging in price from $24 to $29 each, the sheets have all around elastic and wash well.

Best. Crib sheets from the American Baby Company are an affordable $13 to $20, yet are excellent in quality (all cotton, all around elastic, 9" deep pockets). Another top pick is Carousel (babybedding.com)—at $24 to $34 per sheet, they are a bit more pricey, but quality is also excellent. And there are many patterns and choices to customize your nursery's look.

Coordinated Sets

Our favorites hear include Skip Hop, Cottontale, Sumersault, Sweet Kyla and California Kids. Got an uncle named Bill Gates? If Bill is paying, bedding from Nava's sets the standard for top-of-the-line luxury in crib bedding.

Blankets and wearable blankets

Bobble Roos are our top pick for plain blankets. These 100% cotton flannel blankets are great to have around the house or throw in the diaper bag. At $11 to $29, they are a pretty great deal too.

Looking for a wearable blanket? We like the Halo Sleep Sack and the zzZipMe Sack from Swaddle Designs. Also excellent: **Aden & Anais** (AdenandAnais.com)'s muslin cotton wraps (for do-it-your-selfers; $43 for a pack of four) or the Easy Swaddle ($25).

BEDDING RATINGS

Name	Rating	Cost	Organic?
Annette Tatum	B	$$ to $$$	
BB Basics Online	B-	$	
Banana Fish	B	$ to $$$	
Caden Lane	B+	$$ to $$$	
California Kids	A	$$ to $$$	
Carousel	A	$ to $$	
Carter's	B	$	
CoCaLo	B+	$ to $$	◆
Cotton Tale	A-	$ to $$$	
Crown Crafts	C+	$ to $$$	◆
Dwell	B+	$ to $$$	
Gerber	D	$	
Glenna Jean	B+	$$ to $$$	
Hoohobbers	B+	$$$	
Jessica McClintock	B-	$$ to $$$	
JoJo Designs	B	$ to $$	
Kids Line	B	$	◆
Kimberly Grant	A-	$ to $$$	
Koala Baby	C+	$	
Lambs & Ivy	B+	$ to $$	
Land of Nod	B	$ to $$	◆
Lolli Living/Living Textiles	A-	$	
Maddie Boo	B	$$ to $$$	
My Baby Sam	B+	$	
Nava's Designs	B	$$$	
Pine Creek	A-	$$ to $$$	
Pottery Barn	C+	$$	◆
Restoration Hardware	B-	$$	◆
Serena & Lily	B+	$$ to $$$	
Skip Hop	A	$	
Sleeping partners	B	$ to $$	◆
Sumersault	A	$ to $$	
Summer	A/B+	$	◆
Sweet Kyla	A	$$	◆
Target (Circo)	C	$	
Too Good By Jenny	F	$	
Trend Lab	B-	$ to $$	
Truly Scrumptious	D	$	
Whistle & Wink	B+	$$$	

Key *See next page*

A quick look at some top crib bedding brands

Fiber Content	Notes
100% COTTON	Very expensive; markdowns on own web site.
100% COTTON	Buy Buy Baby's private label; quality is mixed.
100% COTTON	MiGi line starts at $145 per set. Adult-like fashions.
100% COTTON	Modern vintage collections; 230 thread ct sheets.
100% COTTON	60+ patterns, most made in California.
100% COTTON	Nursery designer tool online for custom looks
100% COTTON	Baby Basics is mix-and-match separates line.
MIX	Good quality; decent value for the dollar.
100% COTTON	All made in the U.S. Innovative designs.
MIX	Baby-ish designs; sold in major chain stores.
100% COTTON	Dwell Studio line at Target earns kudos.
POLY/COTTON	Cute patterns, but poor quality.
MIX	Made in the U.S.; higher-end fabrics.
100% COTTON	Made in the U.S.; 40 patterns. Many accessories.
100% COTTON	Lacey, Victorian looks. Mid-price.
100% COTTON	9-piece beddings sets offer value; sold online.
MIX	Expanded accessory line; make Tiddliwinks brand.
100% COTTON	Cartoony styles, made by Crown Craft.
100% COTTON	BRU store brand, sold as separates.
POLY/COTTON	Quilts have sewn-on rod pocket for hanging.
100% COTTON	Nice selection of accessories such as lamps.
100% COTTON	Affordable 5-pc sets, designed in Australia.
100% COTTON	Sophisticated looks, accented by silk and linen.
100% COTTON	Affordable, readers love quality and soft fabrics.
100% COTTON	Over the top luxe looks; prices start at $980.
100% COTTON	Custom-made or off-the-shelf designs, pricey.
100% COTTON	Curious George and Dr. Seuss themed sheets.
100% COTTON	600 thread count sheets; customer service issues.
100% COTTON	Embroidery, bold designs. Many accessories.
100% COTTON	Clever no-bumper sheet designs. Wash well.
100% COTTON	Sold as Tadpole Basics in Target.
100% COTTON	10 pc sets sold on Target.com and other sites.
100% COTTON	Maker of Ultimate Crib Sheet; separates line.
100% COTTON	Quality is good; sets can be ordered w/o bumpers
100% COTTON	Low price, low thread counts. Shrinkage issues.
100% COTTON	Reversible bumpers.
MIX	12 to 14 pc sets; readers like sheets.
MIX	Quality issues; cutesy designs. BRU exclusive.
100% COTTON	Vintage looks with embroidery accents.

BABY BEDDING

bedding

BABY
BEDDING

The Bottom Line:
A Wrap-Up of Our Best Buy Picks

All your baby really needs is a set of sheets and a cotton blanket. Web sites like Baby Bedding Online and Land of Nod sell affordable, high-quality basics like sheets ($21 to $30) and blankets ($16 to $60). Instead of spending $300 to $500 on bedding sets with uneeded items like bumpers and diaper stackers, use creative solutions (like wall decals) to decorate the nursery affordably and leave the crib simple.

And if you fall in love with a licensed cartoon character like Pooh, don't shell out big bucks on a fancy character-themed bedding set. Instead, we recommend buying solid color sheets and accessorizing with affordable Pooh items like lamps, posters, rugs, etc.

Who's got the best deals on bedding? Web sites like Amazon (for sheets), BabySuperMall.com, Diapers.com and Overstock.com have the best bargains. If you're lucky to be near a manufacturer's outlet, search these stores for discontinued patterns.

Let's take a look at the savings. Here is a sample bedding budget:

American Baby Co. sheets (three)	$42
Wearable blanket (instead of a blanket)	$30
Miscellaneous (lamp, other decor)	$150
TOTAL	**$222**

By contrast, if you go for a designer brand and buy all those silly extras like diaper stackers, you could be out as much as $800 on bedding alone—add in wall paper, accessories like wall hangings, matching lamps and you'll be out $1200 or more. So, the total savings from following the tips in this chapter could be nearly $1000.

Now that your baby's room is outfitted, what about the baby? Flip to the next chapter to get the lowdown on those little clothes.

CHAPTER 4

REALITY LAYETTE

The Reality Layette:
Little Clothes for Little Prices

Inside this chapter

What the heck is a "Onesie"? How many clothes does your baby need? How come such little clothes have such big price tags? These and other mysteries are unraveled in this chapter as we take you on a guided tour of Baby Clothes Land. We'll reveal our secret sources for finding name brand clothes at half off retail prices. Which brands are best? Check out our picks and our nine tips from smart shoppers on getting the best deals. Next, read about the many outlets for children's apparel that have been popping up all over the country. At the end of this chapter, we'll even show you how to save big bucks on diapers

Getting Started:
When Do You Need This Stuff?

◆ **Baby Clothing.** You'll need basic baby clothing like t-shirts and sleepers as soon as you're ready to leave the hospital. Depending on the weather, you may need a heavy fleece sleeper at that time as well.

You'll probably want to start stocking up on baby clothing around the seventh month of your pregnancy—if you deliver early, you will need some basics. However, you may want to wait to do major shopping until after any baby showers to see what clothing your friends and family give as gifts.

Be sure to keep a running list of your acquisitions so you won't buy too much of one item. Thanks to gifts and our own buying, we had about two thousand teeny, side-snap shirts by the time our baby was born. In the end, our son didn't wear the shirts much (he grew out of the newborn sizes quickly and wasn't really wild about them anyway), and we ended up wasting money.

◆ **Diapers.** How many diapers do you need for starters? Are you sitting down? If you're going with disposables, we recommend 600 diapers for the first six weeks (about 14 diapers a day). Yes, that's six packages of 100 diapers each (purchase them in your eighth month of pregnancy, just in case Junior arrives early). You may think this is a lot, but believe us, we bought that much and we still had to do another diaper run by the time our son was a month old. Newborns go through many more diapers than older infants because they feed more frequently. Also, if you're a first time parent, you'll find yourself taking off diapers that turn out to be dry. Or worse, you may change a diaper three times in a row because baby wasn't really finished.

Now that you know how many diapers you need for the first six weeks, what sizes should you buy? We recommend 100 newborn-size diapers and 500 "size one" (or Step 1) diapers. This assumes an average-size baby (about seven lbs. at birth). But remember to keep the receipts—if your baby is larger, you might have to exchange the newborns for size one's (and some of the one's for two's). Note for parents-to-be of multiples: your babies tend to be smaller at birth, so buy all newborn diapers to start. And double or triple our recommended quantity!

If you plan to use a diaper service to supply cloth diapers, sign up in your eighth month. Some diaper services will give you an initial batch of diapers (so you're ready when baby arrives) and then await your call to start up regular service. If you plan to wash your own cloth diapers, buy two to five dozen diapers about two months before your due date. You'll also probably want to buy diaper covers (six to ten) at that time. We'll discuss cloth diapers in depth later in this chapter.

Even if you plan to use disposable diapers, you should pick up one package of high-quality, flat-fold cloth diapers. Why? You'll need them as spit-up rags, spot cleaners and other assorted uses you'd never imagined before becoming a parent.

Sources

There are nine basic sources for baby clothing and diapers:

1 BABY SPECIALTY STORES. Specialty stores typically carry 100% cotton, high-quality clothes, but you won't usually find them affordably priced. While you may find attractive dressy clothes, play clothes are typically a better deal elsewhere. Because the stores themselves are frequently small, selection is limited. On the upside, you can still find old-fashioned service at specialty stores—and that's helpful when buying items like shoes. In that case, the extra help with sizing may be worth the higher price.

As for diapers, you can forget about it—most specialty baby stores long ago ceded the diaper market to discounters and grocery stores (who sell disposables), as well as mail-order/online companies (who dominate the cloth diaper and supply business). Occasionally, we see specialty stores carry an offbeat product like Seventh Generation, an eco-friendly disposable diaper. And some may have diaper covers, but the selection is typically limited.

2 DEPARTMENT STORES. Clothing is a department store's bread and butter, so it's not surprising to see many of these stores excel at merchandising baby clothes. Everyone from Sears to Nordstrom sells baby clothes and frequent sales often make the selection more affordable.

3 SPECIALTY CHAINS. Our readers love Old Navy (see money-saving tips section) and Gap Kids. Both sell 100% cotton, high-quality clothes that are stylish and durable. Not to mention their price adjustment policies—if you buy an item at Gap/Old Navy and it goes on sale within seven days, you get the new price. Old Navy's selection of baby clothes is somewhat limited compared to Gap Kids. Other chains to check out include Gymboree, and Children's Place. All are reviewed later in this chapter.

4 DISCOUNTERS. Walmart, Target and K-Mart have moved aggressively into baby clothes in the last decade. Instead of cheap, polyester outfits that were once common at these stores, most discounters now emphasize 100% cotton clothing in fashionable styles.

Target has vastly expanded their baby clothes with their in-store brand, Cherokee. Not only have they expanded, but the quality is terrific in most cases. Many of our readers shop Target for all cotton play clothes and day care clothes. Durability is good.

Diapers are another discounter strong suit—you'll find both name brand and generic disposables at most stores; some even carry a selection of cloth diaper supplies like diaper covers (although they are the cheaper brands; see the diaper section later in this book for more details). Discounters seem to be locked into an endless price battle with warehouse clubs on baby items, so you can usually find deals.

5 BABY SUPERSTORES. Babies R Us, Baby Depot and Buy Buy Baby carry a decent selection of name-brand clothing at low prices.

Most of the selection focuses on basics, however. You'll see more Carter's and Little Me than the fancy brands common at department stores. Over the years, Babies R Us has tried to upgrade their clothing options with a bit of embroidery here or an embellishment there.

Diapers are a mixed bag at superstores. Babies R Us carries them, but Baby Depot doesn't. When you find them, though, the prices are comparable to discounters. We've seen diapers priced 20% to 30% lower at Babies R Us than grocery stores.

6 WAREHOUSE CLUBS. Members-only warehouse clubs like Sam's, Costco and BJ's sell diapers at rock-bottom prices. The selection is often hit-or-miss—sometimes you'll see brand names like Huggies and Pampers; other times it is an in-house brand. While you won't find the range of sizes that you'd see in grocery stores, the prices will be hard to beat. The downside? You have to buy them in "bulk," huge cases of multiple diaper packs that might require a forklift to get home.

Check out the clubs' infant and toddler clothing as well. We'll talk later about some of the bargains we've found.

7 WEB SITES. There are a zillion catalogs and web sites that offer clothing for infants. The choices can be quite overwhelming, and the prices can range from reasonable to ridiculous (don't worry, we'll give you the best bets). It's undeniably a great way to shop when you have a newborn and just don't want to drag your baby out to the mall. Another strength of the web: cloth diapers and related supplies. Chains and specialty stores have abandoned these items, so online suppliers have picked up the slack. Check out Best Online Sources next for more information on great web sites.

CPSC Issues Thrift Shop Warning

In a recent report from the Consumer Product Safety Commission (CPSC), the agency reported that in a survey of thrift shops nationwide, "an estimated 69 percent of the stores were selling at least one type of hazardous consumer product. Many of these were children's products." One of the most dangerous items for children are clothes with drawstrings. The CPSC reports 27 deaths and 70 non-fatal accidents involving drawstring between 1985 and 2008. If you buy clothing at a consignment or thrift store or from a garage sale, be sure to avoid clothes with drawstrings. Keep your smart phone handy at resale shops when you're looking gear—that way you can immediately determine if an item was recalled by going to cpsc.gov and searching the site.

Second Hand Shopping Tips & Advice

Experienced moms know: it's a great idea to buy used. Especially when you're talking about infant clothing. After all, infants don't do much damage to their clothes. They aren't playing in puddles, sucking down OtterPops or finger painting yet. So you can bet the wear and tear on used infant clothing is minimal.

Most towns and cities have a variety of resale shops, but not all of them concentrate on baby clothes. The good news: there is now a national chain plus some great online resalers frugal moms can target.

That national chain, Once Upon a Child (onceuponachild. com), is a favorite among our readers. Sheila Bayer of Connecticut wrote: "We have seven locations of Once Upon a Child and I love them! The clothes and toys are of great quality and very affordable." With locations in all but a few states (even Alaska has two locations!), most people should be able to find a store. The company claims their inventory is as much as 70% off retail. If you read the company policy on what items they'll resell, you'll be impressed with their stringent requirements. This weeds out the less desirable items. And finally, if you want to resell items, you can bring them into the stores where they pay cash (30-50% of estimated retail price) for the items they like. No waiting for your money!

How about an online resale option? StorkBrokers.com, an Atlanta-based site specializing in childrens' products, facilitates direct purchases from other moms getting rid of their used items. They charge a 6.5% fee to the seller, so you may find prices slightly higher than a local resale store, but because they draw inventory from all over the country, you have a wider variety of items to choose from. And it's pretty simple to post items for sale on the site, once you're ready to sell.

While we're talking about baby clothing here, many resale shops carry gear as well. One caution about these second hand stores—if you buy an item like a stroller or high chair at a resale shop, you may not be able to get replacement parts. One mom told us she got a great deal on a stroller that was missing a front bar . . . that is, it was a great deal until she discovered the model was discontinued and she couldn't get a replacement bar from the manufacturer.

8 **CONSIGNMENT OR THRIFT STORES.** You might think of these stores as dingy shops with musty smells—purveyors of old, used clothes that aren't in great shape. Think again—many consignment stores today are bright and attractive, with name brand clothes at a fraction of the retail price. Yes, the clothes have been worn before, but most stores only stock high-quality brands that are in excellent condition. And stores that specialize in children's apparel are popping up everywhere, from coast to coast. Later in this

Garage & Yard Sales
Nine Tips to Get The Best Bargains

It's an American bargain institution—the garage sale.

Sure you can save money on baby clothes online or get a deal at a department store sale. But there's no comparing to the steals you can get at your neighbor's garage sale.

We love getting email from readers who've found great deals at garage sales. How about 25¢ onesies, a snowsuit for $1, barely used high chairs for $5? But getting the most out of garage sales requires some pre-planning. Here are the insider tips from our readers:

1 **CHECK CRAIGSLIST FIRST.** Many folks advertise their garage sales online a few days before the event—zero in on the ads/posts that mention kids/baby items to keep from wasting time on sales that won't be fruitful. Church rummage sales and city-wide or neighborhood sales are excellent sources of deals.

2 **A GOOD MAP IS KEY.** Find those obscure streets and cul de sacs. A GPS or smartphone navigation app is a must.

3 **START EARLY.** The professional bargain hunters get going at the crack of dawn—especially if you are looking for something specific. An even better bet: if you know the family, ask if you can drop by the day before the sale. That way you have a first shot before the competition arrives. One trick: if it's a neighbor, offer to help set-up for the sale. That's a great way to get those "early bird" deals.

4 **DO THE "BOX DIVE."** Many garage sale hosts will just dump kids clothes into a big box, all jumbled together in different sizes, styles, etc. Figuring out how to get the best picks while three other moms are digging through the same box is a challenge. The best advice: familiarize yourself with the better name brands in this chapter and pluck out the best bets as fast as possible. Then evaluate the clothes away from the melee.

chapter, we'll tell you how to find a consignment store near you. Look for the box on second-hand shopping tips nearby.

9 GARAGE/YARD SALES. Check out the box nearby for tips on how to shop garage sales like the pros.

clothes

//

5 CONCENTRATE ON "FAMILY AREAS." A mom here in Colorado told us she found garage sales in Boulder (a college town) were mostly students getting rid of electronics, clothes and other junk. A better bet was nearby Louisville, a suburban bedroom community with lots of growing families. Also: leave the kids at home, if you can. And pack snacks and drinks (water/coffee).

6 HAGGLE. Prices on big-ticket items (that is, anything over $5) are usually negotiable. Another great tip we read in the newsletter *Cheapskate Monthly*: to test out products, carry a few "C" and "D" batteries with you to garage sales. Why? Most swings, bouncers and other gear use such batteries. Pop in your test batteries to make sure items are in good working order!

7 SMALL BILLS. Take small bills with you to sales—lots of $1's and a few $5's. Why? When negotiating over price, slowly counting out small bills makes the seller feel like they are getting more money. A wad of 20 $1's for a high chair feels like a more substantial offer than a $20 bill.

8 DON'T BUY A USED CRIB OR CAR SEAT. Old cribs may not meet current safety standards. It's also difficult to get replacement parts for obscure brands. Car seats are also a second-hand no-no - you can't be sure it wasn't in an accident, weakening its safety and effectiveness. And watch out for clothing with drawstrings, loose buttons or other safety hazards.

9 BE CREATIVE. See a great stroller but the fabric is dirty? And non-removable so you can't throw it in the washing machine? Take a cue from one dad we interviewed. He takes dirty second-hand strollers or high chairs to a car wash and blasts them with a high-pressure hose! Voila! Clean and useable items are the result. For a small investment, you can rehabilitate a dingy stroller into a showpiece.

//

Baby Clothing

So you thought all the big-ticket items were taken care of when you bought the crib and other furniture? Ha! It's time to prepare for your baby's "layette," a French word that translated literally means "spending large sums of cash on baby clothes and other such items, as required by Federal Baby Law." But, of course, there are some creative (dare we say, sneaky?) ways of keeping your layette bills down.

At this point, you may be wondering just what does your baby need? Sure you've seen those cute ruffled dresses and sailor suits in department stores—but what does your baby *really* wear everyday?

Meet the layette, a collection of clothes and accessories that your baby will use daily. While your baby's birthday suit was free, outfitting him in something more "traditional" will cost some bucks. In fact, a recent study estimated that parents spend $13,000 on clothes for a child by the time he or she hits 18 years of age—and that sounds like a conservative estimate to us. Baby clothes translate into a $20 *billion* business for children's clothing retailers. Follow our tips, and we estimate that you'll save 20% or more on your baby's wardrobe.

Best Online Sources

Bargain Childrens Clothing

bargainchildrensclothing.com. This site carries lots of "workhorse" brands like Hanes, and OshKosh, as well as character items from Sesame Street, Barbie and Dora the Explorer. The site also carries higher-quality brands such Wes and Willy, Izod or Flapdoodles, at discounts of up to 85%. For example, we found a long sleeve girls jumper dress set by MulberrieBush regularly priced at $48 for only $24.90, a 51% savings. The site is a bit of a mishmash making it difficult to find the good stuff, but take your time and you'll see some really great money saving bargains. ***Rating: A-***

Chez Ami

patsyaiken.com or chezami.com. Once upon a time, independent baby stores carried a much wider selection of adorable outfits for babies. And the brand they all carried was Patsy Aiken. You can't get it from a store anymore, but thankfully Patsy still make their clothes under the name Chez Ami. And the clothes are still as wonderful as we remember. These U.S.-made clothes are all cotton with amazing embroidery and appliqué. You'll find beautiful, bright colors with fun accents. They've cut out a lot of the super dressy designs and seem to be concentrating on fun casual clothes. Prices

clothes

average around $30 to $50 for the typical dress or overall. Not cheap but the quality is terrific. This is a great site for grandmas looking for a cute shower gift.

Besides selling directly online, Chez Ami is also available through distributorships modeled on the old Tupperware parties. You get a group of your friends together and have a Chez Ami clothing party. Check out the web site for more details. **Rating: A**

Forget Me Not Kids

foregetmenotkids.com. Selection at Forget Me Not Kids is amazing. You'll see brand names like Miniman, Pepper Toes, Hartstrings and Klim Babys. We also saw shoes, baby blankets, hair bows, dress-up clothes and accessories, even diaper bags, slings and carriers for parents. While regular prices can be quite stiff, selection is great and they were offering seven pages of sale items when we visited. **Rating: B**

Hanna Andersson

hannaandersson.com Hanna Andersson claim to fame is "Swedish quality" 100% cotton clothes. And our readers agree—they rank HA a top favorite. Unfortunately, Swedish quality is going to set you back some big American bucks. For example, a cute hooded romper was a whopping $39. At that price, it's hard to imagine buying a complete wardrobe here, no matter how cute their clothes are.

These aren't clothes you'd have your baby trash at daycare— Hanna Andersson's outfits are more suitable for weekend wear or going to Grandma's house. One note of caution: while the quality is very high, some items have difficult diaper access (or none at all). Another negative: Hanna Andersson uses "European sizing," which can be confusing. Thankfully, they are now including the age range for each size. On the plus side, we liked their web site especially the sale section—makes them a bit more reasonable. **Rating: B-**

LL Bean

llbean.com Rugged basics are what LL Bean is known for, and that's reflected in their baby collection. Lots of fleece, flannel and fashion are what you'll find on their site. We love the bold floral prints for girls and the lumberjack plaids for boys. While the collection isn't huge, the quality is terrific. No shrink cottons top our list of decent buys at $16.95 for long sleeve t-shirts. Sales prices are about 15-25% off and they sell lots of cold weather items plus some gear like BOB strollers. **Rating: B**

MiniBoden

bodenusa.com Designed in London, MiniBoden is a children's off-shoot of Boden, a terrific women's and men's clothing line. Chock full of fun patterns and great colors, we were thrilled when they added a kids line. Ok, it's not cheap ($20 polo shirt anyone?), but Boden offers many year-round sales and the children's line is sold at Nordstrom.com, where sales are common as well. Our readers think these Brits have great fashion sense and style—they aren't making the same old t-shirts and jeans. Quality is excellent as well. **Rating: B+**

Naartjie

naartjiekids.com Naartjie is a western U.S. chain that originally started in South Africa. In fact, "naartjie" (pronounced nar chee) is an Afrikaans word for a small, sweet citrus fruit. Sounds delish! Anyway, we first heard about this chain from one of our readers and were excited to have a store near us we could visit. We agree with our reader: the quality is comparable to Gymboree and Hanna Andersson. And yes, this line is full of cute stuff. We saw embroidered tunics for $16, corduroy pants for $29 and even some great dress up clothes. We loved the outfit ideas section on their web site with those adorable baby models. Very inspiring if you're just too tired to make decisions. **Rating: A**

The Preemie Store

preemiestore.com Preemie.com is a wonderful oasis for parents of preemies. Sizes start as small as one to three lbs.! If you need clothes for the NICU like IV shirts, open sided shirts, NICU wraps and more, this is the place. But that's not all. Basic gowns and onesies as well as designer baby clothes for preemies are available at super low prices on this site. New items are called out as are christening gowns and even preemie pacifiers! The site is run by the mom of a former preemie and she really knows what parents need. We highly recommend this site for parents of preemies. **Rating: A**

TrendiTikes

trenditikes.com Looking for something really specific for your child? Here's a site that allows you to shop by designer, price, style and size. Organization seems to be their forte. We're impressed with the brands as well: Mimi & Maggie, Junk Food (love their t-shirts), Monkey Bar Buddies, Mim Pi and more. Prices are regular retail, but sales are frequent as are free shipping deals. **Rating: A-**

Wooden Soldier

woodensoldier.com If you really need a formal outfit for your child for a wedding or special occasion, Wooden Soldier has the most expansive selection of children's formalwear we've ever seen. Unfortunately, the prices are quite expensive—a girls' cotton plaid dress with corduroy collar is $54; a boy's corduroy coverall with embroidery and smocking plus shirt is $89. And those are for infant and toddler sized clothes (6 to 24 months)!

On the plus side, the quality is certainly impressive. And you won't find a bigger selection of dressy clothes around. They even offer some matching adult outfits. Wooden Soldier also continues to expand their casual offerings, which now include overalls, jump-suits and cotton sweaters. If you've got the cash and the occasion for these clothes, they're pretty cool. But for most people, these items, even the casual clothes, are way out of range. ***Rating: B-***

What Are You Buying?

Figuring out what your baby should wear is hardly intuitive to first-time parents. We had no earthly idea what types of (and how many) clothes a newborn needed, so we did what we normally do—we went to the bookstore to do research. We found three-dozen books on "childcare and parenting"—with three-dozen different lists of items that you *must* have for your baby and without which you're a very bad parent. Speaking of guilt, we also heard from relatives, who had their own opinions as to what was best for baby.

All of this begs the question: what do you *really* need? And how much? We learned that the answer to that last, age-old question was the age-old answer, "It depends." That's right, nobody really

E-Mail from The Real World
How Much Laundry Will I Do?

Anna B. of Brooklyn, NY had a good question about baby's layette and laundry:

"You have a list of clothes a new baby needs, but you don't say how often I would need to do laundry if I go with the list. I work full time and would like to have enough for a week. Is the list too short for me?"

Our answer: there is no answer. Factors such as whether you use cloth or disposable diapers (cloth can leak more; hence more laundry) and how much your baby spits up will greatly determine the laundry load. Another factor: breast versus bottle-feeding. Bottle-fed babies have fewer poops (and hence, less laundry from possible leaks). An "average" laundry cycle with our layette list would be every two to three days, assuming breast feeding, disposable diapers and an average amount of spit-up.

knows. In fact, we surveyed several department stores, interviewed dozens of parents, and consulted several "experts," only to find no consensus whatsoever. So, in order to better serve humanity, we have developed THE OFFICIAL FIELDS' LIST OF ALMOST EVERY ITEM YOU NEED FOR YOUR BABY IF YOU LIVE ON PLANET EARTH. We hope this clears up the confusion. (For those living on another planet, please consult our *Baby Bargains* edition for Mars and beyond).

Feel free to now ignore those lists of "suggested layette items" provided by retail stores. Many of the "suggestions" are self-serving, to say the least.

Of course, even when you decide what and how much to buy for your baby, you still need to know what *sizes* to buy. Fortunately, we have this covered, too. First, recognize that most baby clothes come in a range of sizes rather than one specific size ("newborn to 3 months" or "3-6 months"). For first time parents buying for a newborn, *we recommend you buy "3-6 month" sizes (instead of newborn sizes).* Why? Because the average size newborn will grow out of "newborn" sizes way too fast. The exception to this rule: preemies and multiples, which tend to be on the small side. (See previous section for a great preemie website).

No matter how big or small your newborn, a smart piece of advice: keep all receipts and tags so you can exchange clothes for larger sizes—you may find you're into six-month sizes by the time your baby hits one month old! (Along the same lines, don't wash all those new baby clothes immediately. Wash just a few items for the initial few weeks. Keep all the other items in their original packaging to make returns easier).

Ever wonder how fast your baby will grow? *Babies double their birth weight by five months . . . and triple it by one year!* On average, babies grow ten inches in their first year of life. (Just an FYI: your child will average four inches of growth in her second year, then three inches a year from ages 3 to 5 and two inches a year until puberty.) Given those stats, you can understand why we don't recommend stocking up on "newborn" size clothes.

Also: remember, you can always buy more later if you need them. In fact, this is a good way to make use of those close friends and relatives who stop by and offer to "help" right after you've suffered through 36 hours of hard labor—send them to the store!

We should point out that this layette list is just to get you started. This supply should last for the first month or two of your baby's life. Also along these lines, we received a question from a mom-to-be who wondered, given these quantities, how often do we assume you'll do laundry. The answer is in the next box.

The "Baby Bargains" Layette

Let's talk quality when it comes to baby clothes.

First, you want clothing that doesn't shrink. Look at the washing instructions. "Cold water wash/low dryer setting" is your clue that this item has NOT been pre-shrunk. Also, do the instructions tell you to wash with "like colors?" This may be a clue that the color will run. Next check the detailing. Are the seams sewn straight? Are they reinforced, particularly on the diaper area?

Go online and check message boards for posts on different brands. On our boards (Babybargains.com), parents comment frequently on whether a brand shrinks, has plenty of diaper room, falls apart after a few washings, etc. Spend a little time online to get some intel on the best brands—and which ones to avoid.

Now, let's get to the list:

◆ **T-Shirts.** Oh sure, a t-shirt is a t-shirt, right? Not when it comes to baby t-shirts. These t-shirts could have side snaps, snaps at the crotch (also known as infant bodysuits, Onesies, creepers) or over-the-head openings. If you have a child who is allergic to metal snaps (they leave a red ring on their skin), you might want to consider over-the-head t-shirts. (FYI: While some folks refer to Onesies as a generic item, the term Onesie is a registered trademark brand by Gerber.)

By the way, is a t-shirt an outfit or an undergarment? Answer: it's both. In the summer, you'll find Onesies with printed patterns that are intended as outfits. In the winter, most stores just sell white or pastel onesies, intended as undergarments.

HOW MANY? T-shirts usually come in packs of three. Our recommendation is to buy two packages of three (or a total of six shirts) of the side-snap variety. We also suggest buying two packs of over-the-head t-shirts. This way, if your baby does have an allergy to the snaps, you have a backup. Later you'll find the snap-at-the-crouch t-shirts to be most convenient since they don't ride up under clothes.

◆ **Gowns.** These are one-piece gowns with elastic at the bottom. They are used as sleeping garments in most cases. (We'll discuss more pros/cons of gowns later in this chapter.)

HOW MANY? This is a toss-up. If you want to experiment, go for one or two of these items. If they work well, you can always go back and get more later.

◆ **Sleepers.** This is the real workhorse of your infant's wardrobe, since babies usually sleep most of the day in the first months. Also known as stretchies, sleepers are most commonly used as pajamas for infants. They have feet, are often made of flame-retardant polyester, and snap up the front. As a side note, we've seen an increase in the numbers of cotton sleepers in recent years. Another related item: cotton long johns for baby. These are similar to sleepers, but don't have feet (and hence, may necessitate the use of socks in winter months).

One parent emailed us asking if she was supposed to dress her baby in pants, shirts, etc. or if it was OK to keep her daughter in sleepers all day long. She noted the baby was quite comfortable and happy. Of course, you can use sleepers exclusively for the first few months. We certainly did. As we've said all along, a comfortable baby is a happy parent!

HOW MANY? Because of their heavy use, we recommend parents buy at least four to eight sleepers.

◆ **Blanket Sleepers/wearable blankets.** These are heavyweight, footed one-piece garments made of polyester. Used often in winter, blanket sleepers usually have a zipper down the front. In recent years, we've also seen quite a few fleece blanket sleepers, their key advantage being a softer fabric and a resistance to pilling.

Another option is a wearable blanket or swaddling blanket. See the previous chapter for a box on "Swaddling and Wearable Blankets." We have a few recommendations for parents who want to try one of these items. You may want to put a t-shirt on baby and then wrap her up in a swaddling blanket or wearable blanket.

HOW MANY? If you live in a cold climate or your baby is born in the winter, you may want to purchase two to four of these items. As an alternative to buying blanket sleepers, you could put a t-shirt on underneath a sleeper or stretchie for extra warmth.

◆ **Coveralls.** One-piece play outfits, coveralls (also known as rompers) are usually cotton or cotton/poly blends. Small sizes (under 6 months) may have feet, while larger sizes don't.

HOW MANY? Since these are really play clothes and small infants don't do a lot of playing, we recommend you only buy two to four coveralls for babies less than four months of age. However, if your child will be going into daycare at an early age, you may need to start with four to six coveralls.

◆ **Booties/socks.** These are necessary for outfits that don't have feet (like gowns and coveralls). As your child gets older (at about six months), look for the kind of socks that have rubber skids on the bottom (they keep baby from slipping when learning to walk).

HOW MANY? Three to four pairs are all you'll need at first, since baby will probably be dressed in footed sleepers most of the time.

◆ **Sweaters.** HOW MANY? Most parents will find one sweater is plenty (they're nice for holiday picture sessions). Avoid all-white sweaters for obvious reasons!

 ◆ **Hats.** Believe it or not, you'll still want a light cap for your baby in the early months of life, even if you live in a hot climate. Babies lose a large amount of heat from their heads, so protecting them with a cap or bonnet is a good

Clothing: What you need, when

If you're new to this baby thing, you may be wondering how to pair the right clothing with your baby's developmental stage (if you're back for another round, think of this as a refresher). Here's a little primer on ages and stages.

◆ **0-3 months:** Newborns aren't even lifting their heads and they aren't able to do much besides eat, sleep and poop. Stick with sleepers, wearable blankets, and nightgowns for these guys. They don't need overalls or shirts and pants. Look for items sized by weight if possible since 0-3 month sizes can be all over the board.

◆ **3-6 months:** By the end of this stage your little one will be rolling over, sitting up and sleeping somewhat less. Still need those sleepers, but you're probably going to expand the wardrobe to include a few more play clothes. Two new items you will need now: bibs and socks. Depending on your baby's growth, you may find that you're buying nine and 12-month sizes.

◆ **6-12 months:** Finally, your baby is crawling, standing, maybe even cruising. At the end of a year she's likely tried those first tentative steps! Play clothes are a layette mainstay during these months. You'll also need good, no-skid socks that stay on (or very flexible shoes). You may find you're buying into the 18-month sizes.

idea. And don't expect to go out for a walk in the park without the baby's sun hat either.

HOW MANY? A couple of hats would be a good idea—sun hats in summer, warmer caps for winter. We like the safari-style hats best (they have flaps to protect the ears and neck).

◆ **Snowsuit/bunting.** Similar to the type of fabric used for blanket sleepers, buntings also have hoods and covers for the hands. Most buntings are like a sack and don't have leg openings, while snowsuits do. Both versions usually have zippered fronts.

FYI: Snowsuits and buntings should NOT be worn by infants when they ride in a car seat. Why? Thick fabric on these items can compress in an accident, compromising the infant's safety in the seat. So how can you keep your baby warm in an infant car seat?

HOW MANY? Only buy one of these if you live in a climate where you need it. Even with a Colorado winter, we got away with layering clothes on our baby, then wrapping him in a blanket for the walk out to a warmed-up car. If you live in a city without a car, you might need two or three snowsuits for those stroller rides to the market.

◆ **Kimonos.** Just like the adult version. Some are zippered sacks with a hood and terry-cloth lining. You use them after a bath.

HOW MANY? Are you kidding? What a joke! These items are one of our "wastes of money." We recommend you pass on the kimonos and instead invest in good quality towels.

◆ **Saque Sets.** Two-piece outfits with a shirt and diaper cover.

HOW MANY? Forget buying these as well.

◆ **Bibs.** These come in two versions, believe it or not. The little, tiny bibs are for the baby that occasionally drools. The larger versions are used when you begin feeding her solid foods (at about six months). Don't expect to be able to use the drool bibs later for feedings, unless you plan to change her carrot-stained outfit frequently.

HOW MANY? Skip the drool bibs (we'll discuss why later in this chapter under Wastes of Money). The exception: if your baby really can't keep dry because he's drooling the equivalent of a bathtub full every day, consider buying a few of these. When baby starts eating solid foods, you'll need at least three or four large bibs. One option: plastic bibs for feeding so you can just sponge them off after a meal.

◆ **Washcloths and Hooded Towels.** OK, so these aren't actually clothes, but baby washcloths and hooded towels are a necessity. Why? Because they are small and easier to use . . . plus they're softer than adult towels and washcloths.

How many? At first, you'll probably need only three sets of towels and washcloths (you get one of each per set). But as baby gets older and dirtier, invest in a few more washcloths to spot clean during the day.

 ◆ **Receiving Blankets.** You'll need these small, cotton blankets for all kinds of uses: to swaddle the baby, as a play quilt, or even for an extra layer of warmth on a cold day.

How many? We believe you can never have too many of these blankets, but since you'll probably get a few as gifts, you'll only need to buy two or three yourself. A total of seven to eight is probably optimal.

What about the future? While our layette list only addresses clothes to buy for a newborn, you will want to plan for your child's future wardrobe as well. For today's baby, clothes come in two categories: play clothes (to be used in daycare situations) and dress-up clothes. Later in this chapter, we'll discuss more money-saving tips and list several recommended brands of play and dress-up clothes.

 ## More Money Buys You . . .

Even the biggest discounters now offer good quality clothing. But with more money you tend to get heavier weight cottons, nicer fasteners, better quality embellishments and more generous sizing. At some point, however, considering how fast your little one is growing, it's a waste to spend top dollar on baby clothes!

Safe & Sound

Should your baby's sleepwear (that is, the items he'll wear almost non-stop for the first several months of life) be flame retardant? What the heck does "flame retardant" mean anyway?

According to the Consumer Product Safety Commission (CPSC), items made of flame retardant fabric will not burn under a direct flame. Huh? Doesn't "flame retardant" mean it won't burn at all? No—that's a common myth among parents who think such clothes

One Size Does Not Fit All

A six month-size t-shirt is a six-month-size t-shirt, right? Wrong. For some reason, baby clothing companies have yet to synchronize their watches when it comes to sizes. Hence, a clothing item that says "six-month size" from one manufacturer can be just the same dimensions as a "twelve-month size" from another. All this begs the question: how can you avoid widespread confusion? First, open packages to check out actual dimensions. Take your baby along and hold items up to her to gauge whether they'd fit. Second, note whether items are pre-shrunk—you'll probably have to ask (if not, allow for shrinkage). Third, don't key on length from head to foot. Instead, focus on the length from neck to crotch—a common problem is items that seem roomy but are too tight in the crotch. Finally, forget age ranges and pay more attention to labels that specify an infant's size in weight and height, which are much more accurate. To show how widely sizing can vary, check out the following chart. We compared "six-month" t-shirts from six major clothing makers (sold at Babies R Us and Amazon.com) plus two popular web sites, Hanna Andersson, and Baby Gap. Here's what these six-month t-shirts really translated to in terms of a baby's weight and height:

What a six month t-shirt really means

MAKER	WEIGHT	HEIGHT
BABY GAP	17-22 LBS.	27-29"
CARTER'S/OSHKOSH	12.5-16.5 LBS.	24-26.5"
GYMBOREE	17-22 LBS.	25-29"
HANNA ANDERSSON	14-21 LBS.	26-30"
GERBER	16-20 LBS.	26-28"
LITTLE ME	12-16 LBS.	24-27"
LUVABLE FRIENDS	16.5-20.5 LBS.	26.5-28.5"
SPASILK	12-18 LBS.	24-26.5"

Here's another secret from the baby clothing trade: the more expensive the brand, the more roomy the clothes. Conversely, cheap items usually have the skimpiest sizing. What about the old wives' tale that you should just double your baby's age to find the right size (that is, buying twelve-month clothes for a six-month old?). That's bogus—as you can see, sizing is so all over the board that this rule just doesn't work.

clothes

are a Superman-style second skin that will protect baby against any and all fire hazards.

Prior to 1996, the CPSC mandated that an item labeled as sleepwear be made of "flame retardant fabric." More often than not, that meant polyester because the alternative (untreated cotton fabric) DOES burn under direct flame. While there are a few companies that make cotton sleepwear that is chemically treated to be fire retardant, the prices of such items were so high that the de facto standard for children's sleepwear for many years was polyester.

Then the government changed its mind. The CPSC noticed that many parents were rebelling against the rules and putting their babies in all-cotton items at bedtime. After an investigation, the CPSC revised the rules to more closely fit reality.

First, pajamas for babies nine months and under were totally exempt from the flame-retardant rules. Why? Since these babies aren't mobile, the odds they'll come in contact with a fire hazard that would catch their clothes on fire is slim. What if the whole house catches fire? Well, the smoke is much more dangerous than the flames—hence, a good smoke detector in the nursery and every other major room of your house is a much better investment than fire-retardant clothes.

What about sleepwear for older babies? Well, the government admits that "close-fitting" all-cotton items don't pose a risk either. Only flowing nightgowns or pajamas that are loose fitting must meet the flame retardant rules today.

If you still want to go with "flame retardant" baby items, there are a couple of options beyond plain polyester. Look for fleece PJ's—Old Navy sells fleece sleepers for $16.50. There use to be a few treated cotton pajama options on the market, but now that the rules have changed to allow close fitting, untreated cotton pajamas, we don't see the treated ones anymore.

Finally, one last myth to dispel on this topic: does washing flame-retardant clothing reduce its ability to retard flames? Nope—fabrics like polyester are *naturally* flame retardant (that is, there is no magic chemical they've been doused with that can wash out in the laundry).

There is one exception to the laundry rule: if you do choose to buy flame-retardant clothing, be sure to avoid washing such clothing in soap flakes. Soap flakes actually add a flammable chemical residue to clothes. And so do dryer sheets and liquid softeners. For more advice on washing baby clothes, see the discussion in the next section.

What about other safety hazards with children's clothing? Here are a few more to consider:

◆ **Check for loose threads.** These could become a choking hazard, or the threads could wrap around fingers or toes, cutting off circulation.

◆ *Be careful about appliqués.* "Heat-welded" plastic appliqués on clothes can come off and cause choking. Poorly sewn appliqués can also be a hazard as the thread can unravel. Look for appliqués that have thick layers of thread attaching them to the clothing.

◆ *Avoid outfits with easy-to-detach, decorative buttons or bows—these may also be a choking hazard.* If you have any doubts, cut the decorations off.

◆ *Watch out for drawstrings.* In recent years, most manufacturers have voluntarily eliminated such drawstrings. But if you get hand-me-downs or buy second-hand clothes, be sure to remove any strings. We're amazed, however, at the continued use of drawstrings by some manufacturers of new children's clothing. We get frequent alerts from the Consumer Product Safety Commission (CPSC) about recalls of new items with drawstrings.

◆ *Lead in jewelry.* Cheap jewelry from China has consistently turned up on the CPSC's recall list. These items are sold in mall stores and from vending machines. Best bet: never purchase jewelry for infants and toddlers. Items like necklaces are likely to end up in their mouths and can be a potential lead and choking hazard. If you choose to pierce your child's ears, stick with high-quality hypoallergenic metals like gold.

Laundry Conundrum: What's Best for Baby's Clothes?

Ever since Dr. Spock's best-selling tome on taking care of baby came out in 1946, most parenting authors have advised washing baby's clothes and linens in mild soap or detergents. The implication is that baby's skin is delicate and could be irritated by harsh chemicals.

So should baby's clothes be washed only in expensive detergents like Dreft? The answer is a definite no. But we do recommend you choose a dye-free, fragrance-free detergent like *All Free & Clear*, which, by the way, is HALF the cost of Dreft.

More advice: do not use fabric softeners on any sleepwear. Most sleepwear is polyester, which is a flame retardant material. However, fabric softeners will leave a residue on polyester and that residue is flammable.

What if your child develops eczema or a reaction to your detergent? Consider cleaning your baby's clothes with a natural pure soap product. One such brand: *Cal-Ben's Seafoam Liquid* laundry soap (CalBenPureSoap.com). Unfortunately, this soap does NOT clean as well as detergent, especially in the laundry, so be prepared. And it's expensive: $29 for one gallon of liquid laundry detergent, about 20% more expensive than Dreft.

Soap flakes are another laundry option. Ivory Snow and Dreft no longer make soap flakes so you have to buy them online. One brand, **Dri-Pak,** is available at Soap-Flakes.com. Soap flakes can also leave a residue on flame retardant clothing—don't use it for sleepwear.

Pure soap products are hard to find and expensive, although some natural food stores carry these brands as well. What about "natural" detergents found in health food stores? Read the labels carefully before you buy since some items contain detergents and others may have allergenic fruit or vegetable ingredients.

 Smart Shopper Tips

Smart Shopper Tip
Tips and Tricks to Get the Best Quality
"I've received several outfits from friends for my daughter, but I'm not sure she'll like all the scratchy lace and the poly/cotton blends. What should she wear, and what can I buy that will last through dozens of washings?"

Generally, we recommend dressing your child for comfort. At the same time, you need clothes that can withstand frequent washings. With this in mind, here are our suggestions for baby clothing:

1 SEE WHAT YOUR BABY LIKES BEFORE INVESTING IN MANY GARMENTS. Don't spend $90 on fancy sweaters, only to find baby prefers cotton Onesies.

2 WE GENERALLY RECOMMEND 100% COTTON CLOTHING. Babies are most comfortable in clothing that breathes.

3 IF YOUR CHILD DEVELOPS A RED, ITCHY RASH, IT COULD BE AN ALLERGY. Culprits could include metal snaps on a t-shirt, zippers or even the ink on tagless labels. One idea: consider alternatives such as shirts that have ties or that pull over the head. Stick with clothes that have plastic snaps and zippers.

4 IN GENERAL, BETTER-MADE CLOTHES WILL HAVE THEIR SNAPS ON A REINFORCED FABRIC BAND. Snaps attached directly to the body of the fabric may tear the garment or rip off.

5 IF YOU'RE BUYING 100% COTTON CLOTHES, MAKE SURE THEY'RE PRE-SHRUNK. Some stores, like Gymboree (see review later in this chapter), pre-wash their clothes to prevent shrinkage. With other brands, it's hard to tell. Our advice: read the label. If it says, "wash in cold water" or " tumble dry low," assume the garment will shrink (and hence buy a larger size). On the other hand, care instructions that advise "wash in warm water and tumble dry" usually indicate that the garment is already preshrunk.

6 **GO FOR OUTFITS WITH SNAPS AND ZIPPERS ON BOTH LEGS, NOT JUST ONE.** Dual-leg snaps or zippers make it much easier to change a diaper. Always check a garment for diaper accessibility—some brands actually have no snaps or zippers, meaning you would have to completely undress your baby for a diaper change! Another pet peeve: garments that have snaps up the back also make diaper changes a big hassle.

7 **BE AWARE THAT EACH COMPANY HAS ITS OWN WARPED IDEA ABOUT HOW TO SIZE BABY CLOTHES.** See the box "One Size Does Not Fit All" earlier in this chapter for more details.

8 **BEWARE OF APPLIQUES.** Some appliqué work can be quite scratchy on the inside of the outfit (it rubs against baby's skin). Feel the inside of the outfit before you buy to make sure it's soft. Some manufacturers will use additional fabric between the appliqué and baby's skin.

9 **KEEP THE TAGS AND RECEIPTS.** A reader emailed us her strategy for dealing with baby clothes that shrink: until she has a chance to wash the item, she keeps all packaging, tags and receipts. If it shrinks, she returns it immediately.

Wastes of Money

Waste of Money #1
Clothing that Leads to Diaper Changing Gymnastics

"My aunt sent me an adorable outfit for my little girl. The only problem: it snaps up the back making diaper changes a real pain. In fact, I don't dress her in it often because it's so inconvenient. Shouldn't clothing like this be outlawed?"

It's pretty obvious that some designers of baby clothing have never had children of their own. What else could explain outfits that snap up the back, have super tiny head, leg and arm openings, and snaps in inconvenient places (or worse, no snaps at all)? One mother we spoke with was furious about outfits that have snaps only down one leg, requiring her baby to be a contortionist to get into and out of the outfit.

Our advice: stay away from outfits that don't have easy access to the diaper. Look instead for snaps or zippers down the front of the outfit or on the crotch. If your baby doesn't like having things pulled over his head, look for shirts with wide, stretchie necklines.

Waste of Money #2
The Fuzz Factor

"My friend's daughter has several outfits that aren't very old but are already pilling and fuzzing. They look awful and my friend is thinking of throwing them out. What causes this?"

Your friend has managed to have a close encounter with that miracle fabric known as polyester. Synthetics such as polyester will often pill or fuzz after washing, making your baby look a little rag-tag. Of course, this is less of a concern with sleepwear—the flame retardancy of polyester fabric outweighs the garment's appearance.

However, when you're talking about a play outfit, we recommend sticking to all-cotton clothes. They wash better, usually last longer, and generally look nicer—not to mention they feel better to your baby. Cotton allergies are rare, unlike sensitivities to the chemicals used to make synthetic fabrics. You will pay more for all-cotton clothing, but in this case, the extra expense is worth it. Remember, just because you find the cheapest price on a polyester outfit doesn't mean you're getting a bargain. The best deal is not wasting money on outfits that you have to throw away after two washings.

If you get polyester outfits as gifts, here's a laundry tip: wash the items inside out. That helps lessen pilling/fuzzing. And some polyester items are better than others—polar fleece sweatshirts and pajamas are still made of polyester, but are softer and more durable.

Waste of Money #3
Do I Really Need These?

"My mother bought me a zillion gowns before my baby was born, and I haven't used a single one. What the heck are they for?"

"The list of layette items recommended by my local department store includes something called a saque set. I've never seen one, and no one seems to know what it is. Do I really need one?"

"A bath robe with matching towel and washcloth seems like a neat baby gift for my pregnant friend. But another friend told me it probably wouldn't get used. What do you think?"

All of these items come under the heading "Do I Really Need These?" Heck, we didn't even know what some of these were when we were shopping for our baby's layette. For example, what in the world is a saque set? Well, it turns out it's just a two-piece outfit with a shirt and diaper cover. Although they sound rather benign, saque sets are a waste of money. Whenever you pick up a baby under the arms, it's a sure bet her clothes will ride up. In order to avoid having to constantly pull down the baby's shirt, most parents find they use one-piece garments much more often than two-piece ones.

As for gowns, the jury is still out on whether these items are useful. We thought they were a waste of money, but a parent we interviewed did mention that she used the gowns when her baby had colic (that persistent crying condition; see our other book *Baby 411* for a discussion). She believed that the extra room in the gown made her baby more comfortable. Still others praise gowns for their easy access to diapers, making changes easy, especially in the middle of the night. Finally, parents in hot climates say gowns keep their infants more comfortable. So, you can see there's a wide range of opinions on this item.

There is no question in our minds about the usefulness of a baby bathrobe, however. Don't buy it. For a baby who will only wear it for a few minutes after a bath, it seems like the quintessential waste of your money (we saw monogrammed options for a whopping $90!). Instead, invest in some good quality towels and washcloths and forget those cute (but useless) kimonos.

Waste of Money #4
Covering Up Those Little Piggies
"I was looking at baby shoes the other day and I saw a $42 pair of Nike Jordan Retro sneakers! This is highway robbery! I can't believe babies' shoes are so expensive. Are they worth it?"

Developmentally, babies don't need shoes until after they become quite proficient at walking. In fact, it's better for their muscle development to go barefoot or wear socks. While those expensive Merrells might look cute, they're really a waste of time and money. Of course, at some point, your baby will need some shoes. See the box nearby for our tips on how to buy babies' first shoes.

Waste of Money #5
To Drool or Not to Drool
"I received a few bibs from my mother-in-law as gifts. I know my baby won't need them until she's at least four to six months old when I start feeding her solids. Plus, they seem so small!"

What you actually received was a supply of *drool* bibs. Drool bibs are tiny bibs intended for small infants who drool all over everything. Or infants who spit-up frequently. Our opinion: they're pretty useless—they're too small to catch much drool or spit-up.

When you do buy bibs, stay away from the ones that tie. Bibs that snap or have Velcro are much easier to get on and off. Another good bet: bibs that go on over the head (and have no snaps or Velcro). Why? Older babies can't pull them off by themselves.

Stay away from the super-size vinyl bibs that cover the arms, since babies who wear them can get too hot and sweaty. However, we do recommend you buy a few regular-style vinyl bibs for trav-

Baby Needs a New Pair of Shoes

As your baby gets older, you may find she's kicking off her socks every five minutes. And at some point she's going to start standing, crawling and even walking. While we suggest waiting to buy shoes until walking is firmly established, there will come a day when you will need to buy that first set of shoes. Here are some suggestions:

First, look for shoes that have the most flexible soles. You'll also want fabrics that breath and stretch, like canvas and leather—stay away from vinyl shoes. The best brands we found were recommended by readers. Reader Teri D. wrote us about Canada's **Robeez** (robeez.com, now a division of Stride Rite). "They are the most AWESOME shoes—I highly recommend them," she said in an email. And Teri wasn't the only one who loves them. Our email has been blitzed by fans. Robeez are made of leather, have soft, skid-resistant soles and are machine washable. They start at $24 for a basic pair. Another reader recommended New Zealand-made **Bobux** shoes ($30, bobuxusa.com). These cute leather soft soles "do the trick by staying on extremely well," according to a reader. Finally, we also like **PediPeds** (pedipeds.com). The soft-soled shoes are hand stitched and made of leather. They are sized from 0 to five years start at $35.

What about shoes for one or two year olds? We've found great deals at Target, where a wide selection of sizes and offerings was impressive. Another good source: Gap Kids/Baby Gap. Their affordable line of sneakers are very good quality. Parents have also told us they've had success with Babies R Us' in-house brand; others like Stride Rite shoes, which are often on sale at department stores. Many of the sites we list in the Best Online Sources earlier in this chapter sell shoes as well.

el. You can wash them off much more easily than the standard terry-
cloth bibs. As for sources of bibs, many of the catalogs we review
in this book carry such items. Readers have also recommended the
long sleeve bib from **A Better Bib** (abetterbib.com). Made of soft,
breathable fabrics, these bibs run $17.

Money Saving Secrets

**1 REMEMBER THESE TWO STORES: OLD NAVY AND THE
CHILDREN'S PLACE.** Old Navy (oldnavy.com) is the hip, discount offshoot of the Gap (gap.com) with 1000+ stores in the U.S.
and Canada. Readers rave about the buys they find at Old Navy
(sample: "adorable" 100% cotton Onesies for just $13-$15 per 3-
pack; gripper socks, $8), although most admit the selection is limit-
ed. The options change rapidly and Old Navy's sales and clearance
racks are "bargain heaven," say our spies. An insider tip to Old
Navy and Gap Kids: the stores change out their merchandise every
six weeks, moving the "old" stuff to the clearance racks rather quickly. Ask your local Old Navy or Gap Kids which day they do their
markdowns (typically it is Tuesday night, effective Wednesday).

Here's another tip for folks who shop Old Navy or the Gap regularly: check to see if your recent purchases have been marked
down. You may be able to get a refund if items you've bought are
marked down even more. One reader emailed us her great deal:
"Last month I found a hooded sweatshirt for baby on clearance. It
was originally $15 marked down to $10.50. The next week, I went
back and the same sweatshirt had been marked down from $10.50
to $1.99. So they refunded me $8.60!" Both Old Navy and the Gap
allow you a price adjustment within 14 days of purchase. You don't
have to bring the clothes back, just your receipt.

A Gap employee emailed us the inside scoop on their markdowns.
She told us that prices ending in $.97 are the lowest price you'll see
on the markdown rack. After 14 days at the $.97 price, the stores
have the authority to cut the price in half to "kill" the item. Finally, if
you have a Gap credit card, you can get an additional 10% off
everything on the first Tuesday of every month. And our source says
don't forget to take the register surveys—they'll save you 10% as well.

The Children's Place (childrensplace.com) has over 900 stores in
the U.S. and Canada. They're about as ubiquitous as Old Navy, and
the prices are just as good. They offer their clothing in sizes newborn to 4T. One reader wrote: "I found that this chain has really
great looking and durable clothes for extremely reasonable prices."
She did note that sizes run a bit small, so buy up a size. An example of their offerings: we saw a striped girl's cardigan for a mere

$19.95. If you order online, the site offers a flat $5 shipping fee plus you can make returns at their stores.

2 **WAIT UNTIL AFTER SHOWERS AND PARTIES TO PURCHASE CLOTHES.** Clothing is a popular gift item—you may not need to buy much yourself.

3 **STICK WITH BASICS—T-SHIRTS, SLEEPERS, CAPS, SOCKS AND BLANKETS.** For the first month or more, that's all you need since you won't be taking Junior to the opera.

4 **SALES!** The baby area in most department stores is definitely SALE LAND. At one chain we researched, the baby section has at least some items that are on sale every week! Big baby sales occur throughout the year, but especially in January. You can often snag bargains at up to 50% off the retail price. Another tip: consider buying for the future during end-of-season sales. If you're pregnant during the fall, for example, shop the end-of-summer sales for next summer's baby clothes. Hint: our research shows the sale prices at department stores are often better deals than the "discounted" prices you see at outlets.

5 **CHOOSE QUALITY OVER LOW PRICE FOR PLAYCLOTHES AND BASICS.** Sure that polyester outfit is 20% cheaper than the cotton alternative. HOWEVER, beware of the revenge of the washing machine! You don't realize how many times you'll be doing laundry—that play outfit may get washed every couple of days. Cheap polyester clothes pill or fuzz up after just a few washings—making you more likely to chuck them. Quality clothes have longer lives, making them less expensive over time.

6 **FOR SLEEPWEAR, TRY THE AFFORDABLE BRANDS.** Let's get real here: babies pee and poop in their sleepers. Hence, fancy designer brands are a money-waster. A friend of ours who lives in Texas uses affordable all-cotton Onesies as sleepwear in the hot summer months. For the winter here in Colorado, we use thermal underwear, which we've found for as little as $15 in Target.

7 **CAN'T RETURN IT?** Did you get gifts of clothing you don't want but can't return? Consign it at a local thrift store. We took a basketful of clothes that we couldn't use or didn't like and placed them on consignment. We turned these duplicates into $40 cash.

8 **SPEAKING OF CONSIGNMENT STORES, HERE IS A WONDERFUL WAY TO SAVE MONEY:** Buy barely used, consigned clothing for your baby. We found outfits ranging from $5 to $7 from high quality designers like Alexis. How can you find a consignment or thrift shop in your area specializing in high-quality children's clothes? Besides a quick Google or Yelp search, check out web sites like the National Association of Resale & Thrift Shops (narts.com, click on the shopping guide icon). Here are two tips for getting the best bargains at second-hand stores: First, shop the resale stores in the richest part of town. Why? They are most likely to stock the best brands with steep discounts off retail prices. Such stores also have clothes with the least wear (we guess rich kids have so many clothes they don't have time to wear them all out)! Second: ask the consignment store which day is best to shop. Some stores accept new consignments on certain days; others tell us that days like Tuesday and Wednesday offer the best selection of newly consigned items.

9 **CHECK OUT DISCOUNTERS.** In the past, discount stores like Target and Walmart typically carried cheap baby clothes that were mostly polyester. Well, there's good news for bargain shoppers: in recent years, these chains have upgraded their offerings, adding more all-cotton clothes and even some brand names.

For basic items like t-shirts and play clothes that will be trashed at day care, these stores are good bets. Walmart sure impressed one of our readers: "I spent $25 for a baby bathing suit in a specialty store, and for a little over twice that (about $60) I bought my daughter's entire summer wardrobe at Walmart—shorts, t-shirts, leggings, Capri pants, overalls and matching socks. Some of the pieces were as low as $2.88." And don't forget other discounters like Marshalls, TJ Maxx and Ross. Bargain tip: ask the manager when they get in new shipments—that's when selection is best.

By the way, Carter's makes Child of Mine brand clothing sold at Walmart and Just One You at Target.

10 **WAREHOUSE CLUBS.** Warehouse clubs like Sam's, BJ's and Costco carry baby clothes at prices far below retail. On a recent visit to Costco we saw Carter's fleece sleepers for only $7.29. All-cotton play clothes were a mere $13 while all-cotton pajamas (2T-10) were $12. Even baby Halloween costumes and kids outerwear (raincoats, fleece jackets) are terrific seasonal deals.

11 **DON'T FORGET ABOUT CHARITY SALES.** Readers tell us they've found great deals on baby clothes and equipment at church-sponsored charity sales. Essentially, these sales are like large garage/yard sales where multiple families donate kids' items as a fund-raiser for a church or other charity.

Outlets

Here's a round up of our favorite outlet stores for baby and kids clothes. Remember: outlet locations open and close frequently—check their web sites or OutletBound.com for up-to-date information on locations.

CARTER'S

Locations: Over 150 outlets.

It shows you how widespread the outlet craze is when you realize that Carter's has over 150 outlets in the U.S. That's right, 150. If you don't have one near you, you probably live in Bolivia.

We visited a Carter's outlet and found a huge selection of infant clothes, bedding, and accessories. Prices were generally marked 50% off retail although sharp-eyed readers noted that department store sale prices are often just as good.

The best deals, however, are at the outlet's yearly clearance sale in January when they knock an additional 25% to 30% off their already discounted prices. A store manager at the Carter's outlet we visited said that they also have two other sales: back-to-school and a "pajama sale." In the past, we noted that all the goods in their outlet stores were first quality. However, they have added a couple "seconds" racks (called "Oops" racks) in most of their stores with flawed merchandise. Our readers report that most seconds have only minor problems and the savings are worth it.

GAP

Locations: Over 130 outlets.

Gap sells such great play clothes, you probably find yourself buying them at full retail sometimes. But now you don't have to. With so many outlet stores, you can buy your baby those cute little mini skinny jeans, Fair Isle sweaters and itty bitty swim trunks at drastically reduced prices. And check out the $1.99 rack. Readers tell us these are amazing deals. Some parents complain that the outlet stores are a bit trashed, but pants for $4 and shirts for a dollar make it worth the mess.

HANNA ANDERSSON

Outlets Stores: Lake Oswego, OR; Michigan City, IN; Kittery, ME; Woodinville, WA; Williamsburg; VA, Wrentham, MA; Clinton, CT

If you like Hanna Anderson's catalog, you'll love their outlet stores, which feature overstocks, returned items and factory seconds. For more information on Hanna Anderson, see Best Online Sources earlier in this chapter.

HARTSTRINGS

Locations: 28 outlets

Hartstrings' 31 outlet stores specialize in first-quality apparel for infants, boys, and girls and even have some mother/child outfits. Infant sizes range from three months to 24 months; savings up to 50%.

JCPENNEY

Locations: 22 outlets

A reader in Columbus, Ohio emailed her high praise for the Penney's outlet there. She snagged one-piece rompers for $5 (regularly $25) and hand-loomed coveralls for $2.99 (compared to $28 in stores). She also found satin christening outfits for both boys and girls for just $5 that regularly sell for as much as $70! The outlet carries everything from layette to play clothes, at discounts of 50% or more. (Hint: the outlet stores also have maternity clothes).

OSHKOSH

Locations: 147 outlets.

OshKosh, the maker of all those cute little overalls worn by just about every kid, sells their clothes direct at over 140 outlet stores. With prices that are 30% to 70% off retail, buying these play clothes staples is even easier on the pocketbook. They split the store up by gender, as well as by size. Infant and toddler clothes are usually in the back of the store.

The outlet also carries OshKosh shoes, socks, hats, and even stuffed bears dressed in overalls and engineer hats. Some clothes are irregulars, so inspect the garments carefully before you buy.

The Name Game: Our Picks for the Best Brands

Walk into any department store and you'll see a blizzard of brand names for baby clothes. Which ones stand up to frequent washings? Which ones have snaps that stay snapped? Which are a good value for the dollar? We asked our readers to divide their favorite clothing brands/stores into three categories: best bets, good but not great and skip it.

The Best Bets tend to be clothes that were not only stylish but also held up in the wash. The fabric was usually softer and pilled less. Customer service also comes into play with the best brands. Hanna Andersson is a great example of a company that bends over backwards for their customers. Gymboree, on the other hand, seems to be less satisfactory for many parents, souring them on the brand. Keep in mind, some brands are pricey, so look for sales and second hand deals. Or just point Grandma to these sites!

Good but not Great clothes were pretty good, just not as soft or as stylish as Best Bets. The Skip-It brands were most likely the poorest quality: they shrunk in the wash, pilled up or fell apart. Inconsistent sizing was also a problem with brands like Babies R Us' Koala Kids.

Some of these brands sell direct; others just through retailers.

Best Bets

BABY GAP	(800) GAP-STYLE	BABYGAP.COM
BABY LULU		BABYLULU.COM
CARTER'S	(770) 961-8722	CARTERS.COM
CHEZ AMI		CHEZAMI.COM
COZY TOES		COZYTOESDESIGNSTUDIO.COM
FIRST IMPRESSIONS		MACYS.COM
FLAP HAPPY	(800) 234-3527	FLAPHAPPY.COM
FLAPDOODLES	(302) 731-9793	FLAPDOODLES.COM
FUNTASIA! TOO	(214) 634-7770	FUNTASIATOO.COM
H & M		HM.COM
HANNA ANDERSSON		HANNAANDERSSON.COM
HARTSTRINGS/KITESTRINGS	(212) 868-0950	HARTSTRINGS.COM
JANIE AND JACK		JANIEANDJACK.COM
KISSY KISSY		KISSYKISSYONLINE.COM
LITTLE ME	(800) 533-5497	LITTLEME.COM
LL BEAN		LLBEAN.COM
MINIBODEN		MINIBODEN.COM
MULBERRIBUSH (TUMBLEWEED TOO)		MULBERRIBUSH.COM
NAARTJIE		NAARTJIE.COM
OLD NAVY		OLDNAVY.COM
OSHKOSH B'GOSH	(800) 692-4674	OSHKOSHBGOSH.COM
PUMPKIN PATCH		PUMPKINPATCHUSA.COM
SARAH'S PRINTS	(888) 477-4687	SARASPRINTS.COM
SWEET POTATOES/SPUDZ	(800) 634-2584	SWEETPOTATOESINC.COM
TEA COLLECTION		TEACOLLECTION.COM
WES & WILLY		WESANDWILLY.COM
ZUTANO		ZUTANO.COM

Good But Not Great

CHILDREN'S PLACE	CHILDRENSPLACE.COM
GOOD LAD OF PHILADELPHIA	GOODLAD.COM
GYMBOREE	GYMBOREE.COM
LANDS END	LANDSEND.COM
LE TOP	LETOP-USA.COM
TARGET (LITTLE ME, CARTER'S JUST ONE YOU, HALO, CIRCO)	TARGET.COM
WALMART (FADED GLORY, CARTER'S CHILD OF MINE)	WALMART.COM

Skip It: GERBER, HANES, KOALA KIDS (BABIES R US), DISNEY, CARTER'S JUST ONE YEAR AT TARGET, GEORGE BY WALMART

Our Picks: Brand Recommendations

What clothing brands are best? Well, there is no one correct answer. An outfit that's perfect for day care (that is, to be trashed in Junior's first painting experiment) is different from an outfit for a weekend outing with friends. And dress-up occasions may require an entirely different set of clothing criteria. Hence, we've divided our clothing brand recommendations into three areas: good (day care), better (weekend wear) and best (special occasions). While some brands make items in two or even three categories, here's how we see it:

Good. For everyday comfort (and day-care situations), basic brands like Carter's, Little Me, and OshKosh are your best bets. We also like the basics (when on sale) at Baby Gap (Gap Kids) for day-care wardrobes. For great price to value, take a look at Old Navy and Target.

Better. What if you have a miniature golf outing planned with friends? Or a visit to Grandma's house? The brands of better-made casual wear we like best include Baby Gap, Flapdoodles, and Gymboree. Also recommended: Jake and Me, MulberriBush, and Wes and Willy. For online sites, we like the clothes in Hanna Andersson and MiniBoden as good brands, especially on sale.

Best. Holidays and other special occasions call for special outfits. We like Chez Ami, and the dressier items at Baby Gap. Of course, department stores are great sources for these outfits, as are consignment shops. As for catalogs, check out Wooden Soldier.

Diapers

The great diaper debate still rages on: should you use cloth or disposable? On one side are environmentalists, who argue cloth is better for the planet. On the other hand, those disposable diapers are darn convenient.

Considering the average baby will go through 2300 diaper changes in the first year of life, this isn't a moot issue—you'll be dealing with diapers until your baby is three or four years old (the average girl potty trains at 35 months; boys at 39 months). Yes, you read that last sentence right . . . you will be diapering for the next 35 to 39 MONTHS.

Now, in this section, we've decided NOT to rehash all the environmental arguments pro or con for cloth versus disposable. Fire up your web browser and you'll find plenty of diaper debate on parenting sites like BabyCenter.com or ParentsPlace.com. Instead, we'll focus here on the FINANCIAL and PRACTICAL impacts of your decision.

Let's look at each option:

Cloth. Prior to the 1960's, this was the only diaper option available to parents. Fans of cloth diapering point to babies that had less diaper rash and toilet trained faster. From a practical point of view, cloth diapers have improved in design over the years, offering more absorbency and fewer leaks. They aren't perfect, but the advent of diaper covers (no more plastic pants) has helped as well.

Another practical point: laundry. You've got to decide if you will use a cloth diaper service or launder at home. Obviously, the latter requires more effort on your part. We'll have laundry tips for cloth diapers later in this chapter. Meanwhile, we'll discuss the financial costs of cloth in general at the end of this section.

Final practical point about cloth: most day care centers don't allow them. This may be a sanitation requirement governed by state day care regulators and not a negotiating point. Check with local day care centers or your state board.

Disposables. Disposable diapers were first introduced in 1961 and now hold an overwhelming lead over cloth—about 95% of all households that have kids in diapers use disposables. Today's diapers have super-absorbent gels that lower the number of needed diaper changes, especially at night (which helps baby sleep through the night sooner). Even many parents who swear cloth diapers are best often use disposables at night. The downside? All that super-absorbency means babies are in no rush to potty train—they simply don't feel as wet or uncomfortable as babies in cloth diapers.

The jury on diaper rash is still out—disposable diaper users generally don't experience any more diaper rash than cloth diaper users.

Besides the eco-arguments about disposables, there is one other disadvantage—higher trash costs. In many communities, the more trash you put out, the higher the bill.

The financial bottom line: Surprisingly, there is no clear winner when you factor financial costs into the diaper equation.

Cloth diapers may seem cheap at first, but consider the hidden costs. Besides the diapers themselves ($100 for the basic varieties; $200 to $300 for the fancy ones), you also have to buy diaper covers. Like everything you buy with baby, there is a wide cost variation. The cheap stuff (like Dappi covers) will set you back $3 to $6 each. And you've got to buy several in different sizes as your child grows, so the total investment could be nearly $100. If you're lucky, you can find diaper covers second-hand for $1 to $3. Of course, some parents find low-cost covers leak and quickly wear out. As a result, they turn to the more expensive covers—a single Mother-Ease (see later for more info on this brand) is $12.25. Invest in a half dozen of those covers (in various sizes, of course) and you've spent another $240 to $480 (if you buy them new).

What about laundry? Well, washing your own cloth diapers at home may be the most economical way to go, but often folks don't have the time or energy. Instead, some parents use a cloth diaper service. In a recent cost survey of such services across the U.S., we found that the average is about $750 a year. While each service does supply you with diapers (relieving you of that expense), you're still on the hook for the diaper covers. Some services also don't provide enough diapers each month. You'll make an average of eight changes a day (more when a baby is newborn, less as they grow older), so be sure you're getting about 60 diapers a week from your service.

Proponents of cloth diapers argue that if you plan to have more than one child, you can reuse those covers, spreading out the cost. You may also not need as many sizes depending on the brands you use and the way your child grows.

So, what's the bottom line cost for cloth diapers? We estimate the total financial damage for cloth diapers (using a cloth diaper service and buying diaper covers) for just the first year is $850 to $1200 (less if you buy used items).

By contrast, let's take a look at disposables. If you buy disposable diapers from the most expensive source in town (typically, a grocery store), you'd spend about $650 to $750 for the first year. Yet, we've found the best deals are buying in bulk from the discount sources we'll discuss shortly. By shopping at these sources, we figure you'd spend $400 to $500 per year (the lowest figure is for private label diapers, the highest is for brand names).

The bottom line: the cheapest way to go is cloth diapers laundered at home. The next best bet is disposables. Finally, cloth diapers from a diaper service are the most expensive.

 ## Best Online Sources: Diapers

Families that use disposable diapers really have it easy. After all, there are only three main manufacturers and a few in-store brands to choose from. Yes, each manufacturer may have a few sub lines with different features, but a disposable is still basically a disposable.

Life's not that easy for cloth diaper aficionados—the choices seem endless. After researching this topic for fifteen years, we realize cloth diaper parents are like snowflakes—no two are exactly alike. Some like pockets, some love prefolds. Others think wool is great while still others like microfiber. And some use one product during the day and another at night. A few of our readers have confessed to being cloth diaper obsessed: they've collected a wide variety of different brands and types. So if you don't find all the answers here, we recommend you check out cloth diapering message boards,

---

Break glass for emergency diaper

In our never-ending quest to discover cool baby products and share them with our readers, we scour trade shows each year, meeting with hundreds of entrepreneurs who are convinced they've invented the next Diaper Genie. While the hype doesn't often match reality, we occasionally unearth a something really amazing.

Exhibit one: Diaper Buds.

Diaper Buds are vacuum-sealed, disposable diapers that you can fit in your jeans pocket. The idea? Diaper Buds are an emergency diaper—when you're fresh out of diapers and something bad happens. And since they are vacuum-packed, they take up little space. Diaper Buds are individually wrapped and when opened expand into a full size diaper. They come in sizes 2 to 5 and sell for $6 to $18, depending on size and quantity. You can purchase a sample from their web site (DiaperBuds.com) for just $1 per bud.

both on our site and others.

Here are a few web sites our readers have recommended for both cloth and disposable diapers (in that order).

ClothDiaper.com

clothdiaper.com. Home of the OsoCozy line of cloth diapers, ClothDiaper.com offers just about everything parents need for cloth diapering: covers, inserts, swim diapers, training pants and more. Package deals are available as well. When we first reviewed these guys, we were impressed by their All-in-One diapers. The system has soft cotton inside against baby's skin (gauze in the bleached version, birdseye weave in the unbleached), a polyurethane waterproof liner, adjustable Velcro-style closures and elastic leg openings. The cost: $15 each with quantity discounts available. The advantage of the all-in-one is pretty obvious, but if you'd rather buy prefolds or flat diapers, they are also available on this site as are organic fabric options. Package options are available on both fitted and prefolds at up to 35% off. Cloth Diaper.com does sell FuzziBunz and GroVia diapers as well as Bummi, Imse Vimse, Whisper Pant and Gerber diaper covers. Finally, we love this sites "all the diapers your baby will need" options. Let's say you want to buy all the fitted diapers your baby will need up to 18 lbs and you don't want to wash too often. That package sells for $465.95. If the items were purchased separately, the cost would be $735. ***Rating: B***

Diapers.com

diapers.com. So you think Walmart and Amazon are aggressive discounters? You ain't seen nothin' till you've shopped at Diapers.com. Deals abound here: on a recent visit they were offering 30% cash back on diapers for three months and 10% off everything else. Impressive. Diapers.com's regular price on Huggies Snug & Dry sizes 1&2: $37.99 for 192 pack. Cost per diaper runs 20¢ each. But. . . you can use a coupon and save $3 per package (now 18¢ each) or that promotion we mention earlier of 30% cash back for three months (this works out to 14¢ per diaper). At that price, Diapers.com is among the cheapest sources for diapers in the U.S.

So why are diapers such a deal here? Because Diapers.com sells diapers as a loss leader, hoping that when you come to their site for diapers, you'll stay to buy a few of their over 25,000 additional products. But the real mojo of the site is their free two-day delivery if you buy at least $49 worth of stuff.

Thanks to those prices and super-fast shipping, Diapers.com has quickly become one of the top sites selling baby gear. The site became such a threat to Amazon that the company acquired them in late 2010. ***Rating: A***

Green Mountain Diapers

greenmountaindiapers.com. Looking for some help figuring out the cloth diapering options out there? Check out Green Mountain Diapers. This site may not look as sophisticated as others, but the info and photos make it a useful resource. Most helpful: photos of real babies wearing the products they sell, which helps new cloth diaper parents get a better idea of what each product is like. Green Mountain Diapers sells a wide variety of products, include preemie cloth diapers. Wool and cotton is the specialty here, with flat-rate shipping. **Rating: A**

Mother-Ease

mother-ease.com. Mother-Ease has been around for over 20 years, manufacturing their own line of cloth diapers. They offer all-in-one diapers, one size diapers (in two levels of absorbency), and two types of diaper covers. Prices start at $12 for the original One Size diaper and range up to $14.75 depending on the type of fabric (choose from unbleached cotton, bleached cotton, bamboo/cotton and organic cotton). Sandy's diapers come in two sizes for a more custom size and are priced the same as the One Size option. All in One diapers run $16 to $18 each. While parents like Mother-Ease diapers, options are limited to their three styles—if one of these does-n't work, you'll have to look elsewhere. **Rating: B+**

Nicki's Diapers

nickisdiapers.com. Nicki's Diapers is a popular site mentioned often on our message boards here at Baby Bargains. And with good reason. They carry a wide range of cloth diapering supplies including their Best Bottom diapers. Best Bottoms are a water-proof, adjustable shell with a snap-in insert inside. Inserts are available in three different sizes and different materials (microfiber or hemp/organic cotton) as well. Shells sell for $17 while inserts range from $4 to $7 each. Nicki's recommends buying eight to ten shells and 18 to 24 inserts per size. But that's not all. Nicki's sells a huge number of brands including FuzziBunz, GroVia, Happy Heiny's, Bumkins, bumGenius and many more. Readers praise their customer service and give this web site a cloth diapering thumbs up. **Rating: A**

Zoolikins.com

zoolikins.com. A reader recommended Zoolikins (formerly Wild Flower Diapers) for their amazing inventory of cloth diapering products as well as their great articles. They carry products from Babykicks, Thirsties, Bummis, Little Beetle, FuzziBunz, bumGenius, and our favorite: Knickernapies. Prices are regular retail, but if you live in Phoenix, you can pick up amazing bargains at their retail location, including used diapers for as little as $1. Zoolikins has a sale section online. **Rating: B**

Our Picks: Brand Recommendations

Disposables. The evolution of disposable diapers is rather amazing. They started out in the 1960's as bulky and ineffective at stopping leaks. In the last 60 years, disposables morphed into ultra-thin, super-absorbent miracle workers that command 95% of the market.

And writing about disposable diaper brands is like trying to nail Jell-O to a wall—every five minutes, the diaper makers come out with new features and new gimmicks as they jostle for a piece of the nearly $27 billion worldwide diaper market. In the 16 years since the first edition of this book came out, the constant innovation in this category is amazing. We used to talk about three types of diapers: basic (thick, tape tabs), ultrathin (with the gel and tape tabs) and supreme (fabric-like outer layer, Velcro tabs). But in recent years, almost all diapers have added Velcro tabs, nicer outer layers and the ubiquitous super absorbent gels. So what separates the good from the bad diapers? *The key is good fit, no leaks and comfort for baby.*

No matter what brand you try, remember that sizing of diapers is all over the board. The "size two" diaper in one brand may be cut totally different from the "medium" of another, even though the weight guidelines on the package are similar. Finding a diaper that fits is critical to you and your baby's happiness.

Now, let's answer some common questions about disposables:

Q. What makes one brand different from another?

A. Surprisingly, the absorbency of diapers varies little from brand to brand. A *Consumer Reports* test of 14 families with infants and toddlers is a case in point. They tested seven types of disposable diapers. Five of them tested "very good" or "excellent" for leak protection. No matter what brand you choose, you'll probably have a diaper that fits well and doesn't leak. Yes, the premium/supreme diapers scored highest in CR's tests, but the difference between them and the cheaper options was minimal (except for the price, of course).

In 2010, Houston, Texas TV station KPRC did a blind test of diapers with local viewers—and the results were similar to what *Consumer Reports* found. KPRC reporter Amy Davis gave two unmarked packages of diapers to viewers, asking them to score them on quality and fit. The station compared both national brands and private label options from Walmart, Target and Babies R Us.

The winner? Parents named the Babies R Us' Supreme Diaper brand (a private label) as their favorite. BRU's diapers are priced below national brands, but a bit more than store brands at Walmart and other discounters.

Q. What about store brands like Babies R Us and others? Is there much difference?

A. Although store diapers used to be less impressive than name brands, as we noted above, they've caught up in terms of cloth like covers, Velcro fasteners and ultra absorbency. And they cost as much as 30% less too.

Q. Do certain brands work better for boys or girls?

A. We used to hear anecdotal evidence from our readers that Huggies were better for boys and Pampers better for girls. In recent years, however, parents tell us there doesn't seem to be a gender difference at all.

Q. How many diapers of each size is a good starting point?

A. Most babies go through 12 to 14 diapers *per day* for the first few months. That translates into about 500 to 600 diapers for the first six weeks. As you read at the beginning of the chapter we recommend buying 100 "newborn" size diapers and 400 to 500 "size one" diapers before baby is born. Caveat: some families have large babies, so keep the receipts just in case you have to exchange some of those newborns for size 1.

So how many do you need of the larger sizes? It's a good idea to start with a case of each size as you transition to larger diapers. There are typically 100 diapers or more in a case. As you near a transition to a larger size, scale back the amount of smaller size diapers you buy so you don't have any half opened packs lying around.

Finally, remember that as your baby grows, she will require fewer diaper changes. Once you add solid foods to her feeding schedule you may only be doing eight to ten changes a day (we know—eight to ten a day still seems like a ton of changes; but it will feel much less than baby's first few weeks). Plus you'll be much more experienced about when a diaper really is wet.

Q. Can disposable diapers cause rashes on my baby?

A. Good question. One look through our message boards at BabyBargains.com and you'll see more than a few threads asking this very question. The answer? We don't know. Anecdotally, parents have seen a rise in rashiness when manufacturers change the makeup of the diaper. But no studies have been done to compare brands either to each other or two new iterations of a brand. However, if you switch brands or a manufacturer changes the way they make their diapers, watch your baby's skin carefully. You may need to switch to another brand, ASAP. So keep the receipt!

Check out our comments on different diaper brands. They are arranged alphabetically. By the way, all their web sites offer coupons of some sort—check them out and sign up for the deals.

◆ **Babies R Us Supreme diapers.** As we mentioned above, BRU's Supreme diapers won a blind test run by a Houston TV station in 2010. Fans of these diapers like their overall quality—the liner is hypoallergenic and contains vitamin E, aloe and zinc. They also have a waterproof cover and stretchy waistband. And the price is decent: size 1's are 18¢ each. But the verdict on these diapers isn't unanimous. Critics say leaks are a problem—and the stretchable grip tabs don't stretch enough.

◆ **Huggies (huggies.com).** Huggies has been a strong brand for years. They now offer five diaper options: Pure & Natural, Little Snugglers, Little Movers, Snug & Dry and Overnight. One of the best features of the line is the pocketed waistbands designed to avoid blowouts. This feature is available on the Pure & Natural and Little Snugglers/Movers lines.

Huggies Pure & Natural have an organic cotton exterior and are hypoallergenic with aloe and vitamin E. The liner is also made of recycled material and they use less ink on the graphics on these diapers. Obviously, this is an attempt to convince parents that these diapers are more eco-friendly. You'll pay for it—on Walmart.com we priced size 1 Pure & Natural at 27¢ per diaper while the size 1 Little Snugglers was 20¢ per diaper. Hence using the more eco-friendly Huggies will run you about $50 extra a year.

Little Snugglers (formally Huggies Supreme) feature a cloth-like outer cover, wetness indicator and pocketed waistband. Huggies Snug & Dry are their less expensive option with Absorb Away (layers to "lock in wetness") and the SnugFit elastic waistband. The Snug & Dry Diapers are about 20% cheaper than Little Snugglers.

Overnights are made to be even more absorbent so babies can actually sleep through the night (and parents too!). And they still have their "Little Swimmers" swim diapers—great for the pool or beach.

As for wipes, Huggies offers five varieties from Sensitive to Natural Care to Soft Skin. Feedback from parents was a thumbs up on the wipes, no matter the type.

Reader feedback on Huggies is positive. Parents note that the pocket waistband (they call it the "poop pocket") really does help avoid up-the-back blowouts.

◆ **Luvs (luvsdiapers.com).** Made by Procter & Gamble (who also makes Pampers), Luvs are marketed as a lower-price brand. They are often less expensive than even store brand diapers.

Thankfully, Luvs doesn't try to be all things to all people with multiple diaper options. They just have one diaper with basic features. Luvs stresses their Ultra Leakguard guarantee that claims Luvs will have fewer leaks that your current brand—or your money back.

So, do they work? Readers were mixed in their appraisal of Luvs. Some said they leaked, but others praised the low price and thought they worked fine. In the blind test in Houston mentioned earlier, parents ranked Luvs in the middle of the pack (in a tie with Huggies). Walmart.com's price for size 2 Luvs was an amazing 13¢ per diaper. Compared to Huggies Little Snugglers at 19¢ per diaper, we'd say try Luvs first!

◆ *Pampers (pampers.com).* Pampers continues to offer an extensive line of diapers including Swaddlers Sensitive, Swaddlers, Cruisers and Baby Dry diapers. In our last edition, we noted that Pampers' Dry Max technology had been a bit controversial. Pampers was stung by parent criticism that claimed their babies got

Who's got the cheapest diapers?

What's the best place to buy disposable diapers? We did a price comparison among several major sources, listed here from least to most expensive:

Store or Web Site	Diaper Type	Count	Price	Per Diaper
Diapers.com***	Huggies #1	234	$40.17	17¢
Costco	Huggies #2	228	$38.99	17¢
Sam's Club	Huggies #1-2	216	$38.98	18¢
BabiesRUs.com**	Huggies #1	216	$43.99	20¢
Amazon.com**	Huggies #1-2	234	$34.50	20¢
Target.com**	Huggies #1	234	$47.19	20¢
Walmart.com**	Huggies #1	160	$34.50	22¢
Grocery Store*	Huggies #2	76	$19.99	26¢

Per Diaper: The cost per diaper.

* Checked at Kroger (King Soopers).

** Free shipping; minimum dollar amount may be required.

*** Diapers.com offers periodic coupons and cash back offers.

Note: Prices check 2013.

a rash from the super absorbing technology, a claim Pampers denies. In fact, Pampers has aggressively countered the bad press with a money-back guarantee and online FAQ's addressing the controversy. An inquiry from the Consumer Product Safety Commission found no evidence the diapers caused rashes. Now they no longer emphasize Dry Max.

Baby Dry diapers are Pampers' lower-priced line. They offer pretty basic features like contoured fit and absorbent core.

Swaddlers Sensitive are Pampers' hypoallergenic option with an absorbent liner like the Baby Dry diapers.

Walmart.com sells the Baby Dry diapers for 19¢ per diaper and Swaddlers (size 1) for 21¢ per diaper; Swaddlers Sensitive (size 1) sell for 33¢ each. Overall, reader feedback on the Pampers line has been positive.

◆ *Parent's Choice by Walmart.* Walmart's private label brand, Parent's Choice, has features similar to name-brand diapers: a cloth-like cover, absorbent core, elastic leg openings and flexible fit waistband. But the price is what's impressive. On their web site, we found a 200 pack of size 1 diapers for only $23.88. The per diaper price: 12¢, among the lowest prices out there. So what do readers think of Parent's Choice? Fans note that Walmart has re-engineered their diapers, changing the tabs and sizing to compare more with Pampers' diapers. Reviews have been generally positive, although in the blind test we mentioned above, Parent's Choice ranked dead last. This is a great brand to consider taking to daycare if you have to provide the diapers.

◆ *Up & Up by Target.* Target's in store brand, Up & Up sells for 16¢ per diaper for a pack of size 1's. These diapers feature leak guards, and the usual contoured shape. They are hypoallergenic, chlorine free and latex free. Parents apparently liked an earlier version of the diapers better—recent reviews complain they now leak and are smaller and thinner. They also scored near the bottom in the Houston test. As a result, we wouldn't recommend this brand.

Eco-friendly Disposables. Are there diapers that combine the convenience of disposables with the ecological benefits of cloth diapers? Yes—here's an overview of so-called eco-friendly disposables:

Seventh Generation (seventhgeneration.com) is one brand of chlorine-free disposable diapers with a thin design. The diapers have a cloth like outer layer, reusable tabs, and are latex and fragrance free. Made of wood pulp, a polyolefin backing and a polyolefin outer cover, Seventh Generation also includes an absorbent polymer gel. They are careful to explain that the gel they use is non-toxic, non-carcinogenic and non-irritating. In fact, you can view material safety data sheets on all the diaper's components on their web site. A reader also recommends the company's wipes saying they are "free of chemicals and full of good stuff for my baby's skin." You can find these diapers online at Amazon or in stores such as Whole Foods and Vitamin Cottage. On Amazon.com, 224 stage 1 Seventh Generation diapers was $49.99 (a pricey 22¢ per diaper). Coupons are available on Seventh Generation's web site.

Another eco-friendly disposable is **Nature Babycare** diapers by Naty (naty.com). These diapers are chlorine free and use no plastics (corn-based materials). They were designed by a Swedish mom and are compostable. At 30¢ per diaper for the small size, they seem out of the range of most people. You'll find them on web sites like Walgreens.com.

Earth's Best, known for its baby food line, has entered the eco friendly diaper arena with their Chlorine Free Disposable Diapers (clever name). These diapers use corn and wheat products as absorbing agents and they use fewer petro-chemicals in the manufacturing process. They are also latex-free. But what if your child has a corn or wheat allergy? We wonder if that would be a problem. And at 29¢ per diaper for size ones, they're still an expensive option.

Here's a popular new diaper that isn't quite a disposable, nor a cloth diaper—**gDiapers** are flushable cloth diapers. Yep, you read it right. Flushable. To be precise, part of a gDiaper is flushable.

A gDiapers newborn starter kit comes with 12 reusable "tiny gPants" (like cloth diaper covers), six small gPants and 80 biodegradable diaper refills for $150 on Diapers.com. Once you are ready to dispose of the diaper refills, you have a choice: flush them, compost the wet ones or throw them in the garbage. GDiapers notes you never compost a poopy diaper, only flush it. But what about throwing them out? Isn't that the same as disposables? Not necessarily since there is no plastic in gDiapers, so they degrade fast (supposedly 50 to 150 days) . . . if you don't put them in a plastic trash bag, of course.

GDiapers' web site has several videos showing their product at work. And we've heard from several moms who love this idea. It is a nice compromise in the cloth versus disposable debate. One caveat: you'll find gDiapers aren't as absorbent as disposables, simply because they use only wood pulp (fluffed for extra absorbency) rather than that super absorbent gel in most diapers. Price is probably the biggest stumbling block with gDiapers. Additional washable "little g" pants range from $14 to $18. Refills start at 35¢ each for 40 of the small size. Ouch! That's more than twice the price of disposables when bought at discount stores! You can also buy reusable snap-in liners, $20 for six.

Ultimately, while these products are promising options for parents looking for a natural alternative to mainstream disposables, the price of all these options severely limits their popularity. And there is still an issue of where these diapers will go. Until recycling centers with composting options become more widely available, there's a question as to whether these diapers won't still end up buried under tons of earth and trash waiting to decompose.

Cloth Diapers. As we noted earlier, if you ask 100 parents for their recommendations on cloth diapers you're likely to get 100 different opinions—it seems everyone has their special system or favorite brand! So what's an aspiring CD'er (cloth diaperer) to do? First let's take you through the basics with Karen F., our CD guru from our message boards:

A cloth diaper has three basic functions. Working from the inside out:

E-MAIL FROM THE REAL WORLD
Cloth diaper laundry tips

Once you make the decision to use cloth diapers, you'll want to research the "art" of cleaning them. Too many harsh chemicals can damage and fade cloth diapers and covers, not enough will leave diapers looking less than pristine. So what's a parent to do? Here's some advice from readers who've experienced lots of diaper cleaning.

Rowan Cerrelli writes:

"I do not like to use chlorine bleach to wash out diapers since they are expensive and the chlorine ruins them. There are some products out there that use natural enzymes to predigest 'stuff' out of the diapers, therefore eliminating the need for bleach. Companies that have these products include Seventh Generation and Ecover. They are also available in natural food grocery stores."

Catherine Advocate-Ross recommends:

"I use BioKleen laundry powder on the diapers. Works great and you need very little."

BioKleen's web site biokleenhome.com explains their products and directs consumers to stores or web sites that carry them. They have an extensive line including liquid as well as powder detergent and stain and odor eliminator. The main ingredient in the line is grapefruit seed and pulp extract.

Kelly Small, from Wallingford, CT emailed us to say:

"I highly recommend OxyClean— it is great on the poop stains!!!"

1. Wick it away. This layer is intended to keep baby from sitting in her pee. This layer lets moisture through in one direction but not back towards the skin. In cloth diapers, this layer is fleece or suede-cloth, but only certain kinds of fleece will do this. Some people just cut rectangles of fleece and lay them inside the diaper. Some diapers are lined with fleece, sewn in place while others are pocket diapers with the fleece next to the skin. And there are some people who skip this layer and change the diaper as soon as baby pees.

2. Soak it up. Typically, the absorbent layer in cloth diapers is made of cotton or hemp and is sewn in layers. There are also some diapers with a micro fiber towel for the absorbent layer. Some people add an extra layer called a "doubler" which is just layers of cloth sewn together. This allows parents to increase absorption when needed (overnight, for example). Options include paper, cotton, microfiber or even silk.

Finally, Rebecca Parish has some practical advice on cloth diapers:
"We (my friends and I) have run across a shortcut that I had not heard about before we attempted cloth diapering. Mainly, we have found it entirely unnecessary to rinse diapers out at all before laundering them. We own a four-day supply of pre-fold diapers and wraps. When our baby poops, we take an extra diaper wipe with us to the toilet, and use it to scrape what easily comes off into the toilet. Then we throw the dirty diaper into our diaper pail, right along with all the other dirty diapers. There's no liquid in the pail for soaking—they just sit in there dry. About every three or four days we throw the entire contents of the diaper pail into the laundry machine, add regular detergent (we use Cheer) and two capfuls of bleach (about 4 teaspoons), and run the machine. The diapers and wraps all come out clean. Just two extra loads of laundry a week (which is nothing compared to the extra loads of clothes we now wash), and no dipping our hands into toilet water. I generally use about five diaper wipes every time I change a messy diaper as it is, so using one extra one for scraping poop into the toilet seems like no big deal.

I think washer technology has improved significantly enough in recent years to allow for this much easier diaper cleaning. We own a fairly new front-loader washer. I don't think the brand name is important; we have a friend who owns a different brand of front-loader, and gets equally good results. However, one of our friends with an older top-loader uses our same system but ends up with stains; she doesn't care but I would."

Bottom line: new technologies (detergents, additives and washers) have led to great improvements in the cleaning of cloth diapers.

3. Keep the rest of the world dry. Remember those awful plastic/rubber pants of yesteryear? Uncomfortable for baby and noisy too! Today's options are much more comfortable to wear and touch. Cloth diaper covers can be polyurethane laminate (PUL) over cotton or polyester, nylon, wool or fleece. Wool is naturally water repellent when it has natural lanolin in it. (Otherwise sheep would bulk up like a sponge in a rainstorm!). The type of fleece that is used as diaper covers is water repellent."

Okay, now that you know the mechanics of cloth diapering, what should you use for your little guy or gal? First, here's the lingo you'll need to master:

1 **PREFOLDS** (CPF for Chinese prefolds or DSQ for diaper-service quality). These are what most parents think of when they envision cloth diapers. They are heavyweight 100% cotton cloths that have been prefolded (so that there is extra padding in the middle) and sewn down. This process leads to a diaper with six to eight layers in the middle and two to four layers on the sides. They can then be pinned onto your baby (not our favorite idea) or folded into a diaper cover. Avoid flat fold diapers—these are really just burp pads and great dust cloths!

2 **FITTED DIAPER:** Sometimes called pre-fitteds, these are prefolded diapers that have elastic sewn in for the leg openings. They don't have snaps or Velcro so they have to be secured with pins or in a cover. You'll get a more snug fit around the leg openings with these.

3 **DOUBLER (ALSO CALLED LINER).** Available in paper, cotton, microfiber or even silk, doublers are used when you need extra absorbency. They are inserted between the diaper and baby's bottom. These would be a great option at night or on a long car trip.

4 **DIAPER COVER/WRAP.** This item is placed over the diaper to stop leaks. One style of diaper cover is called a wrap—think of it as baby origami. You'll wrap your baby up and secure the Velcro tabs to the front strip. Some covers snap in place and there are other pants that can be pulled on (elastic waist).

5 **ALL-IN-ONE.** Just what you'd think, an all-in-one (AIO) is a diaper and cover sewn together. There are pluses and minuses to this design. Yes, the convenience of grabbing one item and snapping or Velcro-ing it on your baby is great, but if your baby makes a mess, you have to wash the whole thing. With a traditional diaper/cover combination, you won't have to wash the cover every time unless baby gets poop on it. So you'll end up buying more all-in-ones to keep yourself from doing laundry constantly.

6 **POCKET DIAPER.** Made famous by Fuzzi Bunz, the pocket diaper is an all-in-one with a pocket sewn into the lining. You can then customize the diaper for more absorbency by adding an insert or a prefolded diaper.

7 **SNAPPI FASTENERS.** Made in South Africa, these cutting-edge diaper fasteners replace the traditional (and potentially painful) diaper pin. Check out their website at snappibaby.com for a look at how they work.

Whew! That's a lot to remember. So anyway, what's the bottom line? What should you buy? Great question. Here's what our cloth diaper guru recommends if you're just starting out and have a new-born: Buy two to three dozen prefold diapers and four to six diaper covers. You may also want to get a few pocket diapers or all-in-ones and a couple Snappis.

Now you probably want to know which brands to buy. So we polled our readers to find out their favorites. Right off the bat, they told us "it depends." Depends on your baby's body type, whether you're looking for nighttime leak protection and many other factors. A couple of the brands readers *could* agree on were Fuzzi Bunz (fuzzibunz.com) and Snap-EZ Fleece Pocket diapers (snap-ez.com). Here is a list of the other brands readers recommend:

◆ *Fitted Diapers:*
Happy Heiney (happyheiny.com)
Kissaluvs (kissaluvs.com)
Monkey Toe Diapers (monkeytoediapers.com)
Nicki's (nikisdiapers.com)

◆ *Diaper Covers:*
Aristocrat (wool) (aristocratsbabyproducts.com)
FLIP (flipdiapers.com)
gDiapers (gdiapers.com)
Imse Vimse Bumpy (imsevimse.us)
Swaddlebees ABC Snap Wraps (swaddlebees.com)

◆ *All-In-Ones:*
Bum Genius (bumgenius.com)
Daisy Doodles (daisy-doodles.com)
DryBees (drybees.com)
Gro Via (gro-via.com)
Lullaby Diapers (lullabydiapers.com)
Swaddlebees Simplex (swaddlebees.com)

diapers

◆ *Pockets:*
bumGenius (bumgenius.com)
Fuzzi Bunz (fuzzibunz.com)
Happy Heiny's (happyheinys.com)
Nicki's (nickisdiapers.com)
Olive Branch Baby Marathon (obbdiapers.com)
Thirsties (thirstiesbaby.com)

◆ *Inserts/Doubler:*
Babykicks Hemparoo Joey Bunz (babykicks.com)
bumGenius Stay Dry Doubler (bumgenius.com)
FLIP (flipdiapers.com)
FuzziBunz Hemp Inserts (fuzzibunz.com)
gDiaper—disposable and reusable (gdiaper.com)
Gro Via Stay Dry Booster (gro-via.com)
Happy Heiney's Stuffins (happyheineys.com)
Imse Vimse Stay Dry Liners (imsevimse.us/)

Need more information? A good book on using cloth diapers is *Diaper Changes* by Theresa Rodriquez (M. Evans and Co., publisher; $15, Amazon.com). A new book, *Changing Diapers: the Hip Mom's Guide to Modern Cloth Diapering* by Kelly Wels (Green Team Enterprises, publisher, $18, Amazon.com) is another book with positive reviews from parents. Also, check out our online message boards on our web site at babybargains.com. They have extensive commentary from cloth diaper parents with tips and recommendations.

Wipes. Like diapers, you have a basic choice with wipes: name brand or generic. Our advice: stick to the name brands. We polled our readers and their top pick was: **Huggies Natural Care**. The reviews were more mixed with Pampers wipes: some parents thought they were too wet and too expensive.

We found most cheap generic wipes to be inferior. With less water and thinner construction, store brand wipes we sampled were losers. There are a couple exceptions to Sensitive baby wipes. One mom emailed: "Kirkland are not as rigid as Huggies or Pampers, have a lighter scent and are stronger than any other wipe we tried." And it's hard to beat the price: $20 for 900 (that's 2.2¢ per wipe). As for Walgreens' brand, a mom emailed saying they "are as good at Huggies in thickness and durability." And they cost about 3¢ a wipe. Another mom really loves BJ's Berkely & Jensen brand of wipes. She thought they were softer than Costco's Kirkland wipes and more like Huggies for less than 2¢ a wipe.

Money Saving Secrets

Here are some tips for saving on disposable diapers (cloth diaper bargain advice is at the end of this section):

1 **THINK PRICE PER DIAPER.** Stores sell diapers in all sorts of package sizes—always compare diaper prices per diaper, not per box.

2 **BUY IN BULK.** Don't buy those little packs of 20 diapers—look for the 80 or 100 count packs instead. You'll find the price per diaper goes down when you buy larger packs. That's why grocery stores are usually the most expensive place to buy diapers—they sell diapers in smaller packages, with the highest per diaper price.

3 **GO FOR WAREHOUSE CLUBS.** Sam's (samsclub.com), BJ's and Costco (costco.com) wholesale clubs sell diapers at incredibly low prices. For example, Costco sells a 228-count package of Huggies stage 2 for just $38.99 or about 17¢ per diaper. We also found great deals on wipes at the wholesale clubs. The downside to these warehouse clubs? You buy a membership to shop at clubs, which runs about $50 a year. And clubs don't stock the usual sizes of diapers—Costco carries "size 1-2" Kirkland diapers, instead of just size 1 or 2. Readers are frustrated with this combined sizing, according to our message boards.

4 **BUY STORE BRANDS.** As mentioned earlier, many parents find store brand diapers to be equal to the name brands. And the prices can't be beat—many are 20% to 30% cheaper. Chains like Target, Walmart and Toys R Us/Babies R Us carry in-house diaper brands, as do many grocery stores. See the reviews earlier on these store brands. Warehouse clubs also carry in store brands: Costco's Kirkland, BJ's Little Bundles and Sam's Club's Member's Mark. Sample price: Costco's Kirkland diapers are just 15¢ each.

5 **FORGET BRAND LOYALTY.** Buy whatever diaper is on sale this week at your favorite store. Ok, some diapers are losers (Target's Up & Up are an example), but if Huggies are on sale this week, go for the Huggies. When Pampers go on sale next week, buy those. Since the name brands and most private label diapers are equivalent in quality, it doesn't pay to be brand loyal.

6 **CONSIDER TOYS R US.** You may not have a wholesale club nearby, but you're bound to be close to a Toys R Us (or their sister division, Babies R Us). And we found them to be a great source for affordable name-brand diapers. The best bet: buy in bulk. You

diapers

can often buy diapers (both name brand and generic) by the case at Toys R Us, saving you about 20% or more over grocery store prices. A recent price check by Houston TV station KPRC found Babies R Us had the lowest prices on diapers in that city—beating out grocery stores, Target and even warehouse clubs (once you factor in the annual membership cost). A year's worth of diapers ran $365.70 at BRU versus $370 at Costco or Sam's, the station reported. Bonus: TRU and BRU often offer in-store coupons for diapers—combine these with manufacturer's coupons for double savings.

7 **ONLINE DEALS MAY BEAT IN-STORE PRICES.** Hard to believe, but sometimes buying diapers online and having them shipped to your house is cheaper than buying at a store. Why? Online sites often sell bigger packages of diapers than stores—and the bigger the package, the lower the cost per diaper. Walmart.com is one example according to our readers. They've seen lower prices (as much as 17% lower) online compared to the stores. With many sites offering free or low-cost shipping, online dealers may be better than shopping in store.

8 **WHEN BABY IS NEARING A TRANSITION POINT, DON'T STOCK UP.** Quick growing babies may move into another size faster than you think, leaving you with an excess supply of too-small diapers.

9 **DON'T BUY DIAPERS IN GROCERY STORES.** We compared prices at grocery stores and usually found them to be sky-high. Most were selling diapers in packages that worked out to over 25¢ per diaper. We should note there are exceptions to this rule, however: some grocery chains (especially in the South) use diapers as a "loss-leader." They'll sell diapers at attractive prices in order to entice shoppers into the store. Also, store brands can be more attractively priced, even at grocery stores. Use coupons (see below) to save even more.

10 **USE COUPONS.** You'll be amazed at how many coupons you receive in the mail, usually for 75¢ off diapers and 50¢ off wipes. One tip: to keep those "introductory" packages of coupons coming, continue signing up to be on the mailing lists of the maternity chain stores (apparently, these chains sell your name to diaper manufacturers, formula companies, etc.) or online at diaper manufacturers' web sites.

11 **IF YOU HAVE TO BUY YOUR DIAPERS FROM A GROCERY STORE OR PHARMACY, SIGN UP FOR A LOYALTY CARD**. Yes, we just said don't buy diapers at the grocery store. But we know—sometimes the grocery store is the most convenient choice for a 2 am diaper run. Our advice: sign up for the store's loyalty card, which often offers discounts on items like diapers and wipes. Combine this with in-store sales and manufacturer's coupons and you might find the price per diaper approaching what you'd pay at a discount store.

12 **ASK FOR GIFT CERTIFICATES.** When friends ask you what you'd like as a shower gift, you can drop hints for gift certificates/cards from stores that sell a wide variety of baby items—including diapers and wipes. That way you can get what you really need, instead of cute accessories of marginal value. You'd be surprised at how many stores offer gift certificate programs.

13 **FOR CLOTH DIAPER USERS, GO FOR "INTRODUCTORY PACKAGES."** Many suppliers have special introductory deals (Mother-Ease offers their One-Size diaper, a liner and cover for 30% off including shipping). Before you invest hundreds of dollars in one brand, give it a test drive first.

14 **BUY USED CLOTH DIAPERS.** Many of the best brands of cloth diapers last and last and last. So you may see them on eBay or cloth-diaper message boards. Buy them—you can get some brands for as little a buck or two. As long as you know the quality and age of the diapers you're buying, this tip can really be a money saver.

15 **REUSE THEM.** Okay, we know this may be obvious, but hang onto your cloth diapers and use them for your next child. Every child is different, so even if you buy a brand and it doesn't fit your baby well, it may work on your next child. And of course, you can always sell them on eBay or Craigslist when you're all finished.

16 **MANUFACTURERS' SECONDS.** Diaper site Kissaluvs.com emailed us this tip: every six to eight weeks, the site offers diaper seconds at a huge discount. The diapers are still perfectly fine, they just have minor flaws that don't affect their quality like a slightly too large waistline, a button a millimeter out of place or stitching in the wrong color. If you have a favorite cloth diaper brand, consider checking directly with the manufacturer to see if they offer any seconds deals as well.

The Bottom Line: A Wrap-Up of Our Best Buy Picks

In summary, we recommend you buy the following layette items for your baby (see chart on next page).

Quantity	Item	Cost
6	T-shirts/onesies (over the head)	$16-$20
6	T-shirts (side snap)	$14
4-6	Sleepers/Sleep Sack	$64-$120
2-4	Coveralls	$50-$100
3-4	Booties/socks	$5-$15
1	Sweater	$16.50
3	Hats (safari and caps)	$13
1	Snowsuit/bunting	$30-$40
4	Large bibs (for feeding)	$26
3 sets	Wash cloths and towels	$36
7-8	Receiving blankets	$30
TOTAL		**$301 to $450**

These prices are from discounters, outlet stores, or sale prices at department stores. What would all these clothes cost at full retail? $550 to $650, at least. The bottom line: follow our tips and you'll save $200 to $300 on your baby's layette alone. (Of course, you may receive some of these items as gifts, so your actual outlay may be less.)

Which brands are best? See "Our Picks: Brand Recommendations" earlier in this chapter. In general, we found that 100% cotton clothes are best. Yes, you'll pay a little more for cotton, but it lasts longer and looks better than clothes made of polyester blends (the exception: fleece outerwear and sleepwear). Other wastes of money for infants include kimonos, saque sets, and shoes.

What about diapers? We found little financial difference between cloth and disposable, especially when you use a cloth diaper service. Cloth does have several hidden costs, however—diaper covers can add hundreds of dollars to the expense of this option although the cost can be spread out among additional children.

For disposables, we found that brand choice was more of a personal preference—all the majors did a good job at stopping leaks. The best way to save money on disposable diapers is to skip the grocery store and buy in bulk (100+ diaper packages) from a warehouse club. Diapers from discount sources run about $400. The same diapers from grocery stores could be $750 or more. Another great money-saver: generic, store-brand diapers from Babies R Us, Walmart, Target and the like. These diapers performed just as well as the name brands at a 20% to 30% discount.

Whew! Now that you have an advanced degree in baby clothing and diaper deals, let's talk about maternity clothes, up next!

CHAPTER 5

Maternity & Nursing

Inside this chapter

Love 'em or hate 'em, every mother-to-be needs maternity clothes at some point in her pregnancy. Still, you don't have to break the bank to get comfortable, and, yes, fashionable maternity items. In this chapter, we tell you which sources sell all-cotton, casual clothes at unbelievably low prices. Then, we'll review the biggest maternity chains and reveal our list of top wastes of money. Finally, you'll learn which nursing clothes moms prefer most.

Maternity & Nursing Clothes

Getting Started:
When Do You Need This Stuff?

It may seem obvious that you'll need to buy maternity clothes when you get pregnant, but the truth is you don't actually need all of them immediately. The first thing you'll notice is the need for a new bra. At least, that was my first clue that my body was changing. Breast changes occur as early as the first month and you may find yourself going through several different bra sizes along the way.

Next, it's time for the bump. Yes, the baby is making its presence known by making you feel a bit bigger around the middle. Skirts and pants feel tight as early as your third month. Maternity clothes at this point may seem like overkill, but some women do begin to "show" enough that they find it necessary to head out to the maternity shop.

If you have decided to breastfeed, you'll need to consider what type of nursing bras you'll want. Buy two or three in your eighth month so you'll be prepared. You may find it necessary to buy more nursing bras after the baby is born, but this will get you started. As for other nursing clothes, you may or may not find these worth the money. Don't go out and buy a whole new wardrobe right off the bat. Some women find nursing shirts and tops to be helpful while others manage quite well with regular clothes. More on this topic later in this chapter.

Sources

1 MATERNITY WEAR CHAINS. Pea in the Pod, Destination Maternity and Motherhood are probably the best known maternity stores—all owned by the same company. More on these chains later in the chapter.

2 MOM AND POP MATERNITY SHOPS. These small, independent stores sell a wide variety of maternity clothes, from affordable weekend wear to high-priced career wear. Some baby specialty stores carry maternity clothes as well. The chief advantage to the smaller stores is personalized service—we usually found salespeople who were knowledgeable about the different brands. In addition, these stores may offer other services. For example, some rent formal wear for special occasions, saving you big bucks. Of course, you may pay for the extra service with higher prices. While you're shopping at the independents look for better quality lines from manufacturers like Meet Me in Miami (meetmeinmiami.com), Juicy Couture Maternity and Olian (olianmaternity.com).

3 CONSIGNMENT STORES. Many consignment or thrift stores that specialize in children's clothing may also have a rack of maternity clothes. In visits to several such stores, we found some incredible bargains (at least 50% off retail) on maternity clothes that were in good to excellent condition. Of course, the selection varies widely, but we strongly advise you to check out any second-hand stores for deals.

4 DISCOUNTERS. When we talk about discounters, we're referring to chains like Target, Walmart and K-Mart. Now, let's be honest here—these discounters probably aren't the first place you'd think of to outfit your maternity wardrobe. Yet, each has a surprisingly nice selection of maternity clothes, especially casual wear. Later, we'll tell you about the incredible prices on these all-cotton clothes.

5 DEPARTMENT STORES. As you might guess, most department stores carry some maternity fashions. The big disadvantage:

the selection is usually rather small. Selection is much greater, however, on store websites. And department stores like Penney's and Sears often have end-of-the-season sales with decent maternity bargains. Look for maternity sections at Kohl's, JCPenney, Sears, Macy's, Nordstrom, Neiman Marcus and Saks Fifth Avenue.

6 **WEBSITES.** Shopping online has a hidden benefit for maternity clothes—many sites offer more generous return policies than retail stores. While maternity chains limit returns to a short period and only for store credit, online sites from the very same chains give you cash back and a longer return window. Another bonus to online shopping: it's easier to find sale items. And sites show what the clothes look like on real people, instead of a hanger.

7 **NON-MATERNITY STORES.** Maternity stores don't have a monopoly on pregnancy clothes—and you can save big bucks by shopping at stores that don't have the word "maternity" in their name. Some of our favorites: Old Navy, the Gap, Ann Taylor Loft. Their maternity clothes are both stylish and affordable.

8 **YOUR HUSBAND'S CLOSET.** Where's a good place for comfy weekend wear? Look no further than the other side of your closet, where your husband's clothes can often double as maternity wear.

9 **OUTLETS.** Yes, there are several outlets that sell maternity clothes and the prices can be a steal. Many of the chain maternity stores we discuss later in this chapter have outlets.

10 **YOUR FRIENDS.** It's a time-honored tradition—handing down "old" maternity clothes to the newly pregnant. Of course, maternity styles don't change that much from year to year and since outfits aren't worn for a long time, they are usually in great shape. Just be sure to pass on the favor when you are through with your pregnancy.

Best Online Bargains and Sources

2 Chix

2Chix.com Check out the sassy maternity t-shirts on 2 Chix. Potato sacks these are not. Form-fitting tank tops as well as short and long sleeved T's are the rule here, many with cutesy sayings like "Does this BABY make my BUTT look big?" These 100% cotton, preshrunk tops are $38 and work great for weekends. The site also sells maternity dresses, pants and even skirts that fit throughout your pregnancy and after with lots of stretch and cute detailing plus a drawstring at the waist. We also chuckled at the dad shirts with sayings like "he shoots, he scores." Not that you'd want him to wear this around your dad, but his friends would be amused. ***Rating: A-***

Ann Taylor LOFT

loft.com Ann Taylor's fashion esthetic seems to be more focused on designs for work than weekend lounging. They offer in house brands and designs by Olian and Cotton Glam. We like their trousers, top-of-the-knee length skirts and corduroys. They work well with cute cardigans, comfy jersey tops and tailored shirts. Our favorite designs are the dresses: a couple sweater dresses and jersey knit dresses in great shapes and colors were affordably priced between $75 and $115. The site's fit guide is helpful with pictures of their three belly-panel options. ***Rating: A***

Due Maternity

duematernity.com Due Maternity is a combo web site: they sell their in house brand as well as a plethora of designer maternity brands like Nuka, Maternal America, Olian and Egg. They have one of the nicest collections of formal wear for pregnant moms, with a wider variety of styles than we've seen on most sites. Prices are up there, but most run less than $200—not bad for formal wear. We like the section of undergarments too: belly bands, slips and camis, Spanx hose and more. They even carry leggings. Nursing clothes are available from Japanese Weekend, Bravado, Majamas and Boob (we're not making that up). Styles are attractive, selection is great but prices are regular retail— check out sale items for better deals. ***Rating: B+***

Expressiva

expressiva.com Wow! That's all we could say when we took a look at Expressiva's designs. You really never would know these are nursing clothes. And they don't make you look like a sack of potatoes. Tops, dresses, casual clothes, bras, swimsuits and sleepwear are available here. Sizes range from extra small to 3X and the site includes hints about sizing for specific outfits. We love the special collection for plus sizes. Eight styles of nursing openings are available and the site shows you exactly how each type works (click on the "why nursing wear" link). Prices are reasonable for the quality. ***Rating: A***

Gap

gap.com You probably already shop the Gap for basics like jeans or t-shirts, but you can also find maternity here. There are some stores with maternity sections, but the best selection is online. You'll find classics like cardigans and jeans as well as stretch shirts, swim suits and more. Check out the Fit & Style Guide with style secrets, size charts and tips. We also like their Starter Styles (lots of basics like classic shirts, tanks and pants) and their Work Essentials section. If you've never been pregnant before, this is a great resource. Sizes range from 00 to 16-18 plus inseams go up to 34". Check frequently for sale items—they seem to offer more sales than most maternity retailers. Readers have been impressed with the quality of Gap maternity, according to our email. Note: the Gap only accepts mailed in returns of maternity clothes bought online—you can't take them back to the store. You also have to pay the return shipping. A few readers report they were able to return online maternity purchases to Gap maternity stores, but not regular Gap outlets. **Rating: A**

Isabella Oliver

isabellaoliver.com This stylish site offers the usual categories like work and casual, but also includes fourth trimester clothes and resort wear. While the designs are very hip, they are expensive. Sale items however, are a great deal. And we like the attitude on this site. The designers have a blog—they offer good fashion advice and interesting "style notes." **Rating: B+**

JCPenney

jcpenney.com JCPenney may not be the source you turn to for everything in your maternity wardrobe, but you might want to take a look at some of their basics. T-shirts, jeans, bras, maternity belts and pajamas are priced reasonably. We found a lot of sale items as well: twill cargo pants marked down from $36 to $13 and more. Yes, the fashion could use a little updating, but the basics are a good value. **Rating: B-**

Motherwear

motherwear.com "This site makes the best clothes for nursing!" gushed one mom in an email to us and we have to agree—this is a great catalog and web site. The quality is excellent with prices in the reasonable range (a special occasion dress for $69, anyone?). They have a clearance section as well, and don't forget to check their weekly specials. Motherwear also has a factory outlet on eBay. The web site has detailed info on how their 12 different nursing openings work, with photos. Motherwear has a satisfaction guarantee and easy return policy. **Rating: A**

Mine For Nine

MineForNine.com If the thought of buying thousands of dollars worth of pregnancy clothes to wear for a mere four or five months makes your head spin, consider renting. Mine for Nine is a new web site that offers designer maternity clothes for rent at up to 75% off the retail price. Dresses, suits, pants, skirts and more from designers like Ripe Maternity, Olian and Maternite can be rented for amazing prices. Example: a beautiful silk floor length gown that sells for $293 can be rented for just $73 for one month. For weddings, New Years and other special events, this is a great deal.

How does it work? You can rent by the month or longer if you want work or casual clothes . . . and more than one item can be rented at a time. Evening clothes can be rented for as little as 14 days. Amazingly, there are no late fees if you keep the clothes longer (you pay for the extra days on a pro-rated basis). Clothes are either new or "like new" which means they have been professionally dry cleaned and inspected. The site has plenty of information on how to get the right fit, plus any order over $75 qualifies for free shipping. To ship your items back, use the return shipping label that comes in the box. Mine for Nine is sort of like Netflix for maternity clothes. You can even buy the clothes if something really impresses you. ***Rating: A***

Old Navy

oldnavy.com Like their parent company the Gap, Old Navy also sells maternity. Yes, the quality is less impressive here, but the prices are a steal. The category selection is similar to Gap—they carry jeans and pants, dresses and skirts, even pajamas and nursing clothes. A short sleeve nursing top in cotton jersey goes for a mere $19.50. At this price, you can try one without investing a huge amount. We like their Favorites categories like "shop by semester" and "wear to work." ***Rating: B***

One Hot Mama

onehotmama.com Nursing clothes are where One Hot Mama got their start, but they have expanded into maternity clothes as well. Their niche: hip styles from manufacturers like Glamourmom and Prego. Fun fabrics and colors are highlighted in the selection on this site. Prices are regular retail and sizing ranges from 2 to 18. ***Rating: B***

 ## What Are You Buying?

What will you need when you get pregnant? There is no shortage of advice on this topic, especially from the folks trying to sell you stuff. But here's what real moms advise you to buy (divided into two topic areas, maternity clothes and then nursing clothes):

Maternity Clothes

◆ **Maternity Bras.** Maternity bras are designed to grow with you as your pregnancy progresses; these bras also offer extra support (you'll need it). Maternity bras are available just about everywhere, from specialty maternity shops to department stores, mail order catalogs and discount chains. More on this topic later in this chapter; look for our recommendations for maternity underwear.

HOW MANY? Two in each size as your bust line expands. I found that I went through three different sizes during my pregnancy, and buying two in each size allowed me to wear one while the other was washed.

◆ **Sleep Bras.** Why a sleep bra, you ask? Well, some women find it more comfortable to have a little extra support at night as their breasts change. Toward the end of pregnancy, some women also start to leak breast milk (to be technical, this is actually colostrum). Sleep bras hold breast pads in place to soak up any leaks. And once the baby arrives, a sleeping bra (about $10-$20) also keeps you from leaking when you inadvertently roll onto your stomach—yes, there will come a day when you can do that again. Some women just need light support, while others find a full-featured bra a necessity.

HOW MANY? Two sleep bras—one to wear while one is in the wash.

◆ **Underpants.** In the past, our recommendation for maternity underpants extolled the virtues of traditional maternity underwear. But time rolls on—and fashion has changed. Most women today are wearing bikini-style underpants as standard gear. And, readers note, you can continue to wear those same styles when you're pregnant. So, save yourself some money and forget the maternity underpants. If you're already wearing bikini styles, stick with them. But now is a good time to consider upgrading your underpants wardrobe in case you've let your skivvies wear out a bit. After all, you'll be going to lots of check ups and eventually the hospital—your mom would be embarrassed if your unmentionables were full of holes!

HOW MANY? If you need new underpants or plan to ignore our advice and buy maternity underpants, we recommend at least eight pairs.

◆ **Maternity belts.** Pregnancy support belts can be critical for some moms. For example, Pam A., one of our readers sent the following email when she was 7 1/2 months along:

"Last week I got the worst pain/cramp that I have ever had in my life. It kept coming and going while I was walking, but it was

Plus-size Maternity Clothing

What's the number one frustration with maternity wear? Finding the right size, particularly if you're looking for plus-size maternity clothes, say our readers. Some maternity clothing manufacturers think only women with supermodel bodies get pregnant. But what to do if you want to look attractive and your dress size starts at 16 or above? Our readers have recommended the following sites:

Baby Becoming	babybecoming.com
JCPenney	jcpenney.com
MomShop	momshop.com
Motherhood	maternitymall.com
Expressiva	expressiva.com
Plus Maternity	plusmaternity.com

so bad that I doubled over in pain when it hit. I went to my doctor and she said that the baby was pushing on a ligament that goes between the abdomen and the leg. She recommended that I get a "Prenatal Cradle" (prenatalcradle.com). I'll tell you what—it is the most wonderful purchase I have ever made in my life. It was about $70, but it works wonders. It does not totally eliminate the pain, but it gives enough support that it drastically reduces the pain and even gives me time to change positions so that it does not get worse. I have even found that wearing it at night helps to alleviate the pain at night rolling over in bed."

In our pregnancy book, *Expecting 411*, obstetrician Michele Hakakha explains the need for maternity belts for some women:

"(During pregnancy) the curvature of your spine changes and so does your center of gravity. The bigger your belly gets, the more you will feel the aching. This usually happens earlier and earlier with each subsequent pregnancy. (Maternity belts) really help lift the belly up and relieve the pressure and discomfort. But you have to wear them correctly to get relief. You need to try on many different styles and decide what fits best before you purchase."

HOW MANY? Kind of obvious, but one or two should be enough.

◆ **Career Clothing.** Our best advice about career clothing for the pregnant mom is to stick with basics. Buy yourself a coordinating outfit with a skirt, jacket, and pair of pants and then accessorize.

Now, we know what you're saying. You'd love to follow this advice, but you don't want to wear the same old thing several times a week—even if it is beautifully accessorized. I don't blame you. So, go for a couple dresses and sweaters too. The good news is you don't have to pay full price. And chances are you know someone who is finished with her pregnancy and will lend you some clothes.

Thanks to casual office wear trends, pregnant woman can spend hundreds of dollars LESS than they might have had to ten or twenty years ago. Today, you can pair a pencil skirt with a sweater set for most office situations.

◆ **Casual Clothes.** Your best bet here is to stick with simple basics, like jeans and cords. You don't necessarily have to buy these from maternity stores. In fact, later in this chapter, we'll talk about less-expensive alternatives. If you're pregnant in the summer, dresses can be a cooler alternative to pants and shorts.

◆ **Dress or Formal Clothes.** Forget them unless you have a full social calendar or have many social engagements associated with your job. Sometimes, you can find a local store that rents maternity formalwear for the one or two occasions when you might need it. Look at sale items on some of our recommended web sites. You may be able to find a nice outfit at a great price, especially right after holidays.

◆ **Spanx.** Spanx has become famous for their "slimming intimates" and their Mama Spanx support hose expand that philosophy to maternity. Made especially for pregnant bellies, these hose will smooth you out, front and back (the part you seldom see and forget about sometimes!). Available in footless and full lengths for $28, they are worth the money. And if you're not interested in hose but still want some reshaping, Power Mama ($32) is a thigh length shaper made to accommodate your pregnant belly, support your back and smooth out the bulges—and it will eliminate panty lines.

Nursing Clothes

◆ **Nursing Bras.** The one piece of advice every nursing mom gives is: buy a well-made, high quality, nursing bra *that fits you*. Easier said than done you say? Maybe. But we can offer some tips we gleaned from a reader poll we took.

Nursing bras have special flaps that fold down to give baby easy access to the breast. Access is usually with a hook or snaps either in the middle or on top of the bra near the straps. So first, our readers insist new moms should look for the easiest access they can find with a nursing bra. You'll need to be able to open your nursing bra quickly and with only one hand in most cases.

Next, avoid under wire bras at all cost. They can cause plugged ducts, a very painful condition. If you sport a large cup size, you'll need a bra that is ultra supportive. Also, in most cases, nursing moms require a sleep bra too—some for support, some just to hold nursing pads.

Mothers living near a locally owned maternity shop or specialized lingerie store recommended going in and having a nursing bra fitted to you. One reader reported that "I was wearing a bra at least three cup sizes too small. The consultant fitted me properly and I couldn't believe how comfortable I was!" In fact this should probably be our first tip: make sure your bra is comfortable! Straps shouldn't dig into your shoulders or chest, cups shouldn't look as if they are "overflowing" (we're talking to you, Kardashian sisters!) If you don't have the luxury of a shop full of specialists, Motherwear (motherwear.com) has good online tips and information (click the link for "how does it work") and Bravado (bravadodesigns.com) offers extensive sizing tips for different bras models.

If you plan to nurse, you should probably buy at least two bras during your eighth month (they cost about $30 to $45 each). Why then? Theoretically, your breast size won't change much once your baby is born and your milk comes in. I'd suggest buying one with a little larger cup size (than your eighth month size) so you can compensate for the engorgement phase. You can always buy more later and, if your size changes once the baby is born, you won't have invested too much in the wrong size. If you want more advice on nursing bras, you can check out Playtex's cool web site at playtex.com. Click on the link to "Expectant Moments," their maternity brand.

How many? Buy one to two bras in your eighth month. After the baby is born, you may want to buy a couple more.

◆ **Nursing Pads.** There are two options with nursing pads: disposable and reusable. Common sense tells you that reusable breast pads make the most economical sense, particularly if you plan to have more children. Still, if you aren't a big leaker, don't plan to breast feed for long or just need something quick and easy when you're on the go, disposables are handy.

When we polled our readers, we were surprised to learn that the majority preferred disposables. Those by Lansinoh (lansinoh.com; $7.50 for 60 at drugstore.com) were by far the favorite followed by Johnson and Johnson ($5.80 per 60), Gerber (60 for $5.69) and Curity (12 for $1.44). What's the secret to these disposables? The same type of super absorbent polymer that makes your baby's diapers so absorbent. That makes them super thin too so you aren't embarrassed by telltale "bulls-eyes" in your bra. Moms also love the individually wrapped pads because they can just grab a couple and throw them in the diaper bag on the way out of the house. Interestingly, moms were divided on whether they like contoured or flat pads or those with adhesive strips or without. New options on the market include NUK ($7 for 60), First Years ($5 for 30), and Evenflo ($7.50 for 48). We don't have feedback yet on the performance of these pads.

While there wasn't one discount source mentioned for disposable breast pads, moms tell us when they see their favorite brands on sale at Walmart, Target or Babies R Us, they snapped up multiple boxes.

For the minority who preferred reusable, washable pads, Medela ($6 per pair), Avent ($6.50 for three pair) and Gerber ($7 for three pair) made the top of the list. Some moms recommend Bravado's (bravadodesigns.com) Cool Max pads ($16 for three pair) for superior absorption. A few parents have raved about Danish Wool pads (danishwool.com). These soft, felted pads contain natural lanolin, a godsend for moms with sore, cracked nipples. They aren't cheap ($21 to $31 per pair) but we thought them worth the mention. Another pad recommended by a reader is LilyPadz by Lilypadz.com. She told us they are streamlined and reusable, can be worn with or without a bra and cost about $23 per pair.

If you have nipple soreness (you have our sympathies!), Jeri from Stoneham, MA recommended a product called Soothies made by Lansinoh. These reusable gel pads can be slipped into your bra to cool and soothe painful nipples. You can find them online or in drugstores for $10 to $12.

How many? With disposable pads, buy the smaller package—don't buy the Costco-sized box. You may not need that many or may not like the brand. As for reusable pads, we recommend starting with three pair. That give you one to wear, one to wash and an extra just in case.

◆ **Nursing Clothes.** You may not think so (especially at 8 1/2 months), but there will come a day when you won't need to wear those maternity clothes. But what if you want to nurse in public after baby is born? Some women swear by nursing clothes as the best way to be discreet, but others do just fine with loose knit tops and button front shirts as well as discrete blanket placement. Bottom line: one obvious way to save money with nursing clothes is not to buy any. If you want to experiment, buy one or two nursing tops and see how they work for you. By the way, parents of twins found it difficult if not impossible to use a nursing top when nursing both babies at the same time. See the box on the next page for more reader feedback on nursing clothes.

Reader Tracy G. suggested that working moms who are nursing or expressing milk might want to check into getting a nursing camisole or tank top. "I wear them under a regular shirt and don't feel so exposed when I pump at work or nurse in public." Her favorite: a Walmart brand camisole. She thought it was softer than Motherhood Maternity options.

Another tip: a reader, Sandra F., came up with an ingenious way to use her breast pumps hands free. While Sandra's sister bought a special hands free bra, Sandra bought a zip-up-the-front sports bra and cut holes in it. She emailed us to say it worked better at holding the pumps phalanges to her breasts than her sister's, which was a tube top style that kept slipping. And Sandra saved some big

Reader Poll: Nursing clothes brands

When we polled our readers about nursing clothes we were immediately chastised by at least half the respondents for even considering recommending them. "A waste of money," "ugly!" and "useless" were a few of the more charitable comments from these readers. As many as one third had never even used a single nursing top. They preferred to wear button up shirts or t-shirts and loose tops that they just pulled up. One mom told us "I got pretty good at being discreet in public with my regular clothes and no one was the wiser."

But other moms loved nursing clothes. And their favorites were those from *Motherwear* (motherwear.com). In our poll over 100 respondents mentioned Motherwear as the best source for well-made, comfortable nursing clothes. The biggest complaint about Motherwear was that their clothes are expensive. Readers suggested buying them used from ebay.com. The next closest company was *One Hot Mama* (onehotmama.com) with 17 votes.

Other sites recommended by parents included *Expressiva* (expressiva.com), and *Birth and Baby* (birthandbaby.com).

Regardless of where nursing clothes were purchased, moms were universal in thinking that the best tops have two vertical openings over the breasts. Forget the single center opening! And no buttons either. Too hard, our moms said, to open with one hand while baby is screaming in your ear. Twin sets and cardigan sweaters were the preferred styles. Readers thought they looked least like nursing clothes. And lots of moms thought just having a few nursing camisoles and t-shirts to wear under a regular shirt was the way to go. Finally, several parents recommended the Super Secret Nursing Shirt from One Hot Mama ($68).

Want to make your own nursing clothes? Creative sewers will find great patterns on *Elizabeth Lee's* web site (elizabethlee.com).

bucks: her sports bra was a $6 sale item while her sister bought a $40 special pumping bra.

◆ *Nursing Pajamas.* Looking for something comfortable to sleep in that allows you to nurse easily? Nursing PJ's are one answer, although only a few moms we interviewed use them. Most hated nursing gowns and found it much simpler to sleep in pajamas with tops they could pull up or unbutton quickly

If you are interested in a specific nursing pajama, check out *Majamas* (majamas.com). One of our product testers tried out their nightgown ($60 online) with her newborn and thought it was great, worthy of a recommendation. It allowed her to sleep without wearing a nursing bra since it had pockets for holding breast pads and had easy nursing access. They have several pajama pant and gown designs and have expanded the line to include maternity clothes.

 ## More Money Buys You . . .

Like any clothing, the more you spend, the better quality fabric and construction you get. Of course, do you really need a cashmere maternity sweater you'll wear for only a few months? Besides fabric, you'll note more designer names as prices go up. For example, Lilly Pulitzer and Juicy Couture are making maternity clothes now.

 ## Smart Shopper Tips

Smart Shopper Tip #1
Battling your wacky thermostat

"It's early in my pregnancy, and I'm finding that the lycra-blend blouses that I wear to work have become very uncomfortable. I'm starting to shop for maternity clothes—what should I look for that will be more comfortable?"

It's a fact of life for us pregnant folks—your body's thermostat has gone berserk. Thanks to those pregnancy hormones, it may be hard to regulate your body's temperature. And those lycra-blend clothes may not be so comfortable anymore.

Our advice: stick with natural fabrics as much as possible, especially cotton, silk, light wools and some high tech fabrics. You need fabrics that breathe. Unfortunately, a lot of lower-priced maternity clothing is made of polyester/cotton blend fabrics.

Smart Shopper Tip #2
Seasons change

"Help! My baby is due in October, but I still need maternity clothes for the hot summer months! How can I buy my maternity wardrobe without investing a fortune?"

Unless you live in a place with endless summer, most women have to buy maternity clothes that will span both warm and cold seasons. The best bets are items that work in BOTH winter or summer—for example, lightweight long-sleeve shirts can be rolled up in the summer. Cropped pants can work in both spring and fall. Another tip: layer clothes to ward off cold. Of course, there's another obvious way to save: borrow items from friends. If you just need a few items to bridge the seasons (a coat, heavy sweater, etc), try to borrow before buying.

Smart Shopper Tip #3
Petites aren't always petite

"I'm only 5 feet 2 inches tall and obviously wear petite sizes. I ordered a pair of pants in a petite size from an online discounter, but they weren't really shorter in the leg. In fact, I'd have to have the pants reconstructed to get the right fit. What gives?"

Many maternity web sites advertise that they carry a wide range of sizes but in truth you may find the choices very limited. And in some cases, "petite" is really just sizes 2 to 4. Translation: these pants aren't really shorter in the leg. How can you tell without ordering and then having to return items? Your best bet is to try on items before you buy. That's not always easy, of course, especially when ordering online. In that case, check the size charts on each site to be sure they offer *real* petites. And if a manufacturer (like the Gap, for example) makes petites that fit you in their regular clothing, chances are their maternity line will be comparable.

Here are our readers recommendations for petite maternity: Kohl's, JCPenney, Old Navy, Gap, Japanese Weekend, Juicy Couture, Rebel jeans and Lands End.

Smart Shopper Tip #4
Tall isn't easy either

"At nearly six feet, I can't find any maternity pants that don't look dorky. Help!"

Just as with petites, we see lots of sites promising a wide range of sizes . . . only to find they have one style that comes in a 31" inseam. And you need a 34." I feel your pain. At 5'9" myself, I recall finding almost nothing in the right length for me. There are more choices today for tall women, but you may find yourself forced to wear more skirts and dresses than pants during your pregnancy.

Here's a partial list of sites that carry tall maternity: Mommy Long Legs (mommylonglegs.com), JC Penney, Isabella Oliver (isabellaoliver.com), Gap, and Old Navy, Long Tall Sally (longtallsally.com), and RG Maternity (rgmaternity.com). If you discover any new sites or stores with tall sizing, email us and we'll add them.

Our Picks: Brand Recommendations for Maternity Undergarments

Here are our readers top picks for maternity undergarments.

God bless Canada—those Maple Leaf-heads make one of the best maternity bras in the world. Toronto-based *Bravado Designs'* (bravadodesigns.com) maternity/nursing bra of the same name is just incredible. "A godsend!" raved one reader. "It's built like a sports bra with no under wire and supports better than any other bra I've tried . . . and this is my third pregnancy!" raved another.

Bravado makes five different styles and one nursing bra tank top. Prices start at $35 for the basic Original Nursing Bra. Other styles include the Body Silk Seamless bra ($49), the Bliss ($54), the Sublime ($49) and the Allure ($54). Sizes range from a B cup to J/K (a few go to I I/I). The nursing tank top option includes a built in full bra (not a shelf bra) and goes up to a G cup for $49.

Another plus: the Bravado reps are knowledgeable and helpful with sizing questions. In the past, some of our readers criticized the Bravado for not providing enough support, but the Supreme should answer those concerns. Our readers have noticed great prices on Bravado Bras at WearstheBaby.com ($32 including shipping).

Playtex Expectant Moments brand was mentioned by our readers as a good choice as well. They offer two nursing bra choices, an underwire and an underwire alternative. Sizes range from B to DDD cups and 34" to 44." A nice touch, they offer sizing advice specifically for maternity and nursing customers on their web site at playtex.com. You'll find these bras at stores like JCPenney. *Medela*, as you'd imagine, also has a big following for their bras. Five options are available: Comfort, Seamless Underwire, Seamless Soft Cup, Sleep Bra and a new Nursing Camisole. Some are also available in extended sizes from 36F to 46H. Prices average around $40 for the nursing bras.

Finally, many readers have recommended Leading Lady maternity and nursing bras (leadinglady.com). They are available widely in many department stores and maternity outlets. Leading Lady has quite a wide assortment of bras in a huge range of sizes.

Looking for maternity shorts/tights for working out? One of the best is **Fit Maternity** (fitmaternity.com; 800-961-9100). They offer an unbelievable assortment of workout clothes including unitards, tights, swimsuits, tennis clothes and more. On the same subject, **Due Maternity** (duematernity.com) offers several yoga and workout pants as well as swimsuits.

Our Picks: Brand Recommendations for Nursing Bras, Pads and Clothes

Nursing pads are a passionate topic for many of our readers with disposables beating out reusables as moms' favorites. They loved both **Lansinoh** and **Johnson & Johnson** disposable by an overwhelming number. **Medela**, **Advent** and **Bravado** make great reusable nursing pads.

Bravado is also quite popular as a nursing bra for all but the largest of cup sizes as are **Playtex** and **Medela**. If you need a size larger than DD, consider **Motherhood Maternity's** brand as well as **Leading Lady**. The web is the best place to find bras on deal including **Decent Exposures** (decentexposures.com) and **Birth and**

Fetal Monitors: Good or Bad Idea?

Can you buy your own Doppler ultrasound monitor to listen to your baby's heartbeat? Sure . . . but is it a good idea? To answer that question, we turned to our favorite obstetrician, Dr. Michele Hakakha. Michele is the co-author of our new book on pregnancy, Expecting 411. Here's why she says pass on these gizmos:

"First of all, home Dopplers are an unnecessary expense (some are under $100 but others are $200+). Secondly, using the Doppler requires the experienced hands of someone who has used one about a thousand times. And even in those experienced hands, it can be hard to find the baby's heartbeat, especially early in the pregnancy.

What ends up happening is that the pregnant couple can't detect the baby's heartbeat at home and they frantically rush into their practitioner's office. Other times, couples listen cheerfully to mom's pulse instead of baby's heartbeat!

You can do a much better job of tracking the health of your unborn baby by following your baby's movements in the womb. So, skip the panic (you'll have your share of that as new parents), save your money (you'll need it for the college fund), and leave the Fun-With-The-Doppler game up to your practitioner."

Baby (birthandbaby.com).

Most moms found that specialized nursing clothes weren't a necessity, but for those who want to try them, nearly everyone recommended *Motherwear* (motherwear.com). *One Hot Mama* (onehotmama.com) and *Expressiva* (expressiva.com) are other stylish sites to consider. Look for discounts on clearance pages or eBay.

 ## Wastes of Money

Waste of Money #1
Maternity Bra Blues

"My old bras are getting very tight. While visiting a store to get a larger size, a salesperson suggested I purchase a maternity bra for more comfort and support. Should I buy a regular bra in a larger size or plunk down the extra money for a maternity bra?

We've heard from quite a few readers who've complained that

As a side note, the FDA says that fetal heart monitors are a medical device and, as such, require a prescription from a doctor to use at home. While some sites will not rent or sell a monitor to a parent without a prescription, others assume you have your doctor's okay.

Why do you need a prescription? After all, isn't a heart monitor just a Doppler ultrasound that checks the heartbeat? What's the big deal?

Doppler ultrasound devices use acoustical energy that is emitted continuously from the unit. It's the "continuous" part that has doctors and the FDA concerned. In your doctor's office, he or she will use a fetal heart monitor for a few minutes. But unsupervised parents at home may decide to use it every day for longer periods of time. The risk: the unit could heat up, causing damage to the fetus.

Our advice: don't bother with a fetal heart monitor.

As for the "entertainment value" of hearing your baby's heartbeat and sharing it with others we'd recommend a simple option—consider buying a good stethoscope. Then have your doctor teach you how to use it to hear your baby's heartbeat. By about 18 weeks you can usually hear a heartbeat with a stethoscope. And you can buy one for as little as $100.

expensive maternity bras were very uncomfortable and/or fell apart after just a few washings. Our best advice: try on the bra before purchase and stick to the better brands. Compared to regular bras, the best maternity bras typically have thicker straps, more give on the sides and more hook and eye closures in back (so the bra can grow with you). Most of all, the bra should be comfortable and have no scratchy lace or detailing. Readers tell us that a good sports bra can also be a fine (and affordable) alternative.

Waste of Money #2
Overexposed Nursing Gowns/Tops

"I refuse to buy those awful nursing tops! Not only are they ugly, but those weird looking panels are like wearing a neon sign that says BREASTFEEDING MOM AHEAD!"

"I plan to nurse my baby and all my friends say I should buy nursing gowns for night feedings. Problem is, I've tried on a few and even though the slits are hidden, I still feel exposed. Not to mention they're the ugliest things I've ever seen. Can't I just wear a regular gown that buttons down the front?"

Of course you can. And considering how expensive some nursing gowns can be ($35 to $50 each), buying a regular button-up nightshirt or gown will certainly save you a few bucks. Every mother we interviewed about nursing gowns had the same complaint. There isn't a delicate way to put this: it's not easy to get a breast out of one of those teenie-weenie slits. Did the person who designed these ever breastfeed a baby? I always felt uncovered whenever I wore a nursing gown, like one gust of wind would have turned me into a centerfold for a nudist magazine.

And can we talk about nursing shirts with those "convenient button flaps for discreet breastfeeding"? Convenient, my fanny. There's so much work involved in lifting the flap up, unbuttoning it, and getting your baby positioned that you might as well forget it. My advice: stick with shirts you can pull up or unbutton down the front. These are just as discreet, easier to work with, and (best of all) you don't have to add some expensive nursing shirts (at $30 to $75 each) to your wardrobe.

Another tip: if possible, try on any nursing clothing BEFORE you buy. See how easy they are to use. You might be surprised how easy (or difficult) an item can be. Imagine as you are doing this that you have an infant that is screaming his head off wanting to eat NOW, not five seconds from now. You can see why buying any nursing clothes sight unseen is a risk.

Waste of Money #3
New shoes
"Help! My feet have swollen and none of my shoes fit!"

Here's a little fact of pregnancy that no one tells you: your feet are going to swell. And, sadly, after the baby is born, those tootsies won't necessarily shrink back to your pre-pregnancy size. A word to the wise: don't buy lots of new shoes at the start of your pregnancy. But no need to despair. After your baby is born, you'll likely have a built-in excuse to go shoe shopping!

Another suggestion from reader Gretchen C. of Rochester, WA: "It is never too early to buy shoes that don't tie! I go to the gym every morning, and it was getting to be a huge ordeal just to get my shoes tied. I bought some slip on shoes at 20 weeks and I still think it's one of the smartest things I've done."

 Money-Saving Secrets

1 CONSIDER BUYING "PLUS" SIZES FROM A REGULAR STORE. Thankfully, fashion continues to be heavy on casual looks . . . even for the office. This makes pregnancy a lot easier since you can buy the same styles in larger ladies' sizes to cover your belly without compromising your fashion sense or investing in expensive and often shoddy maternity clothes. We found the same fashions in plus-size stores for 20% to 35% less than maternity shops (and even more during sales).

One drawback to this strategy: by the end of your pregnancy, your hemlines may start to look a little "high low"—your expanding belly will raise the hemline in front. This may be especially pronounced with dresses. Of course, that's the advantage of buying maternity clothes: the designers compensate with more fabric in front to balance the hemline. Nonetheless, we found that many moms we interviewed were able to get away with plus-size fashions for much (if not all) of their pregnancy. How much can you save? In many cases, from 25% to 50% off those high prices in maternity chains like Pea in the Pod.

2 DON'T OVER-BUY BRAS. As your pregnancy progresses, your bra size is going to change at least a couple times. Running out to buy five new bras when you hit a new cup size is probably foolish—in another month, all those bras may not fit. The best advice: buy the bare minimum (two or three).

3 **TRY BRA EXTENDERS, BELLA BAND.** You may be able to avoid buying lots of maternity bras by purchasing a few bra extenders. Available from fabric stores, OneHanesPlace.com and even Amazon.com among other sites, these little miracles cost as little as $1.50. You simply hook the extender onto the back of your bra and you can add up to two inches around the bust. You may still need to purchase new bras at some point, but with extenders, you can continue to use your pre-pregnancy bra for quite a while.

By the way, Candy from San Diego wrote to us about a similar product for pants called the Bella Band (bellaband.com).: "I bought the Bella Band early on in my pregnancy and love it so much that I recently bought another one. It was perfect for keeping my "normal" clothes on when I couldn't button them anymore. Then it helped me keep maternity pants on when they were still a little too big but I couldn't fit in my regular clothes anymore." Keep in mind the Bella Band is really for use in early pregnancy before you're big enough to buy true maternity pants and skirts. It will allow you to wear your regular pants during that stage where you're just not ready for maternity. Another, similar product called the Baby Be Mine Belly Band (Amazon.com) was only $16 for one while a three pack of BellaBands was $74.

4 **BUT DON'T SKIMP ON QUALITY WHEN IT COMES TO MATERNITY BRAS.** Take some of the money you save from other parts of this book and invest in good maternity underwear. Yes, you can find cheap bras for $20 at discount stores, but don't be penny-wise and pound-foolish. We found the cheap stuff is very uncomfortable and falls apart, forcing you to go back and buy more. Invest in better-quality bras if you plan to have more than one child—you can actually wear it again for subsequent pregnancies. No need to purchase special maternity underpants—use your own and save money.

5 **CONSIDER DISCOUNTERS FOR CASUAL CLOTHES.** Okay, I admit that I don't normally shop at K-Mart or Target for my clothes. But I was surprised to discover these chains (and even department stores like Sears) carry casual maternity clothes in 100% cotton at very affordable prices. Let's repeat that—they have 100% cotton t-shirts, shorts, pants, and more at prices you won't believe. Most of these clothes are in basic solid colors—sorry, no fancy prints. At Target, for example, I found a cotton/spandex maternity shirt (long sleeves) for $15. Jeans were only $30. Even a rayon jersey dress was a mere $30. The best part: Liz Lange designs a big part of the Target line. Our readers say the quality is a bit less than Liz's regular, specialty store version, but the style is good and the prices can't be beat. Don't forget to check Target's sale rack too. One reader found items for as little as $4 on sale.

While the discounters don't carry much in the way of career wear, you'll save so much on casual/weekend clothes that you'll be ecstatic anyway. Witness this example: at A Pea in the Pod, we found a striped cotton-knit, short-sleeved top and ponte knit pants. The price for the two pieces: a heart-stopping $245. A similar all-cotton tank top/pants outfit from Target was $50. Whip out a calculator, and you'll note the savings is an amazing 80%. Need we say more?

By the way, don't forget to check out stores like Kohl's, Marshall's, Ross and TJ MAXX. One reader told us she found maternity clothes at 60% off at TJ MAXX. Of course, as we've mentioned, readers like Old Navy and the Gap as well. Corrie, a reader from Chicago, did all her maternity shopping on line at Old Navy. She spent a total of $365 for eight pairs of pants, one pair of jeans, eleven sweaters, eight long sleeve tops, three button-down shirts, five sleeveless tops and two cardigans. This works out to less than $10 per piece!

For fans of the hip discounter H&M, there's great news: the chain has a maternity section in 20 of their stores! Granted most of them (11) are in New York, but if you live in a major metropolitan area and have an H & M, check to see if yours has a maternity section. Dubbed "Mama," our readers report these departments are selling tops for $12 to $16, camisoles for $8 and more. They carry pretty much everything except underwear. Prices are fantastic.

6 **RENT EVENING WEAR—DON'T BUY.** We found that some indie maternity stores rent eveningwear. For example, a local shop we visited had an entire rack of rental formalwear. An off-white lace dress (perfect for attending a wedding) rented for just $50. Compare that with the purchase price of $200+. Sadly, places that rent maternity wear are few and far between, but it might be worth a look-see in your local community. Another idea: try RentMaternityWear.com as an online source for rentals! Pregnant moms can rent the company's dresses for $39 to $79. Rent Maternity Wear also allows moms to rent two sizes of an item to make sure it really fits well. Shipping is a flat $8 and you can specify the exact date you want a dress. Such a deal!

7 **CHECK OUT CONSIGNMENT STORES.** You can find "gently worn" career and casual maternity clothes for 40% to 70% off the original retail! Many consignment or second-hand stores carry only designer-label clothing in good to excellent condition. If you don't want to buy used garments, consider recouping some of your investment in maternity clothes by consigning them after the baby is born. You can usually find listings for these stores in a quick Yelp or Google search. (Don't forget to look for listings of children's consignment stores as well. Some stores that carry second-hand baby gear and clothes also have a significant stock of maternity wear.) One web source to find consignment shops is narts.org.

8 **FIND AN OUTLET.** Go to OutletBound.com to find a maternity outlet near you.

9 **BE CREATIVE.** Raid your husband's closet for over-sized shirts and pants.

10 **SEW IT YOURSELF.** A reader in California emailed in this recommendation: she loved the patterns for nursing clothes by Elizabeth Lee Designs (elizabethlee.com). "I would think anyone with a bit of sewing experience could handle any of the patterns, which don't LOOK like nursing dresses or tops." In addition to patterns, Elizabeth Lee also sells ready-made dresses and tops. Another bonus: the company has one of the largest selections of nursing bras we've seen, including Bravado Bras.

Pattern companies like Simplicity (simplicity.com) and McCall (mccall.com includes Butterick and Vogue as well) sell their patterns online and in fabric stores. You'll find a limited selection of designs, but if you're a sewing maven, here's a way to avoid the high prices and frustrating return policies of retail maternity stores.

11 **BEG AND BORROW.** Unless you're the first of your friends to get pregnant you know someone who's already been through this. Check around to see if you can borrow old maternity clothes from other moms. In fact, we loaned out a big box after our second baby was born and it has made the rounds of the whole neighborhood. And don't forget to be generous after your baby making days are over too.

12 **CHECK OUT CLEARANCE AREAS IN CATALOGS AND ONLINE.** Many of our most devoted discount shopping readers have scored big deals on their favorite web sites' clearance pages.

13 **WHEN ORDERING MATERNITY CLOTHES FROM WEB SITES, POOL YOUR ORDERS!** Most web sites offer a free shipping option on orders of $75 to $100 or more (especially after holidays and during end of season sales). Check to see what deals they're offering when you visit. Also, some chain stores will let you return items to your local store, saving you the return-shipping fee.

The Name Game:
Reviews of Selected Maternity Stores

Usually this section is intended to acquaint you with the clothing name brands you'll see in local stores. But now there is only one giant chain of maternity wear in North America—Destination Maternity Corp., which operates stores under three brand names. This company is the 800 pound gorilla of maternity clothes with over 1700 locations, many of which are leased departments in chains like Babies R Us, Macy's, Sears, Kohl's and other stores. Destination Maternity has over a 40% share of the $1.2 billion maternity clothing market in the U.S. There are also 36 Motherhood stores in Canada.

FYI: keep in mind that these chains often offer a larger selection of maternity clothing online than what you see in the stores. This is, of course, frustrating since you can't try them on. On the upside, the draconian return policies of the bricks and mortar stores don't apply to online purchases. So you'll be able to return online purchases more easily.

So let's take a look at these three divisions, a new concept they've added, and their web site.

◆ **Motherhood.** Motherhood is the biggest sister in the chain with 567 locations. While most stores are located in malls and power centers, 232 are also leased departments within Kohl's

Watch out for return policies!

Have you bought a maternity dress you don't like or that doesn't fit? Too bad—most maternity stores have draconian return policies that essentially say "tough!"

Motherhood Maternity stores (including their sister chain A Pea in the Pod) only allow returns to their stores if you have the receipt, the item is unworn, unopened and with all the tags. The item also must have been purchased within 10 days. These returns are only for store credit or exchange—no money back. Independent maternity stores may have a similar returns policy.

Online return policies are a bit more generous from Motherhood.com: you can get cash back, given you returned the item within 30 days and have all the tags attached. Unfortunately, returning an online purchase to a Motherhood or Pea in the Pod store only gets you store credit, no cash.

The take-home message: if you are unsure about an item, consider buying it online and then return it by mail.

(called Oh! Baby by Motherhood). Motherhood carries maternity clothes in the lowest price points. As an example, dresses at Motherhood range from $20 to $50.

◆ **A Pea in the Pod.** A Pea in the Pod (APIP) is Destination Maternity's most expensive division. With dress prices ranging from $59 to $325, A Pea in the Pod's 56 stores are positioned as designer boutiques. They even have a line designed by Heidi Klum called "lavish."

◆ **Destination Maternity Superstore.** These stores combine A Pea in the Pod and Motherhood Maternity under one roof. More than just a clothing store, some of these locations also boast a spa and classes in yoga, financial planning and scrapbooking. As of this writing, there are 75 Destination Maternity Superstores.

All these stores carry merchandise designed in house, exclusively for the different divisions, as well as well known brands like Spanx, C&C California, Lucky Brand and Lilly Pulitzer.

Now that you know the basics, what do real moms think of Destination Maternity's stores? First and foremost, moms dislike, no, hate their return policy. The policy is pretty basic: once you've bought an item, you have ten days to return it for store credit or exchange only (you must have the tags and receipt too). No refunds. What if it falls apart in the wash on day 11? Too bad for you. By the way, if you order an item online from Mother Works web site, you'll find a more generous return policy: *Items can be returned for refund or exchange and you have 30 days to return the clothing.* You cannot return items bought online to the store or vice versa, but at least you get extra time and even the money back with an online return. Our advice, if you see it in the store, try it on. If you like it, go home and order it online.

And don't forget that Motherhood has in-store "boutiques" in Kohl's department stores as well as other department stores. In these cases, the leased stores have to comply with the same generous return policy of the department store where they lease space.

As for individual chains, most moms agreed that the quality at Motherhood is poor. Although some readers have praised their maternity and nursing bras, in general, most agree with this reader's sum-up: "I have found the quality to be inconsistent. I've bought shirts that have unraveled within a few months. . . trashy!" The consensus seems to be that if you buy at Motherhood, you should stick to the sale rack and don't expect high quality except for their bras. However, a recent reader took issue with our review of Motherhood's quality. She told us: "Motherhood clothes are just as well made, if not better made, than Old Navy maternity."

A Pea in the Pod is just way too expensive. That's the general feeling among our readers about this store. Most moms don't think the style of clothing at this chain is anything special. Certainly not to spend $60 for a cotton t-shirt. Considering how short a time a pregnancy is it's a huge waste of money to spend over $245 on a Pea in the Pod pants outfit. And what about their "legendary" service, as Pea in the Pod likes to tout? It's a joke, say our readers. One mom summed it up best by saying: "For the price that one is paying, one expects a certain degree of customer service and satisfaction, both of which are lacking in this over-priced store. What a complete and utter disappointment!"

Consumer alert: one new mom warned us about giving personal info to a maternity chain when you make a purchase (clerks may ask you if you want to receive sales notices). The problem: you often end up on junk mailing lists. In the case of our reader, even though she specifically requested the chain not sell her information to third parties, they did so. Once on those lists, it's tough to stop the junk from arriving in your mailbox.

E-MAIL FROM THE REAL WORLD
Stay fit with pregnancy workout videos

Sure, there are plenty of workout DVDs targeted at the preggo crowd. But which are the best? Readers give their top picks, starting with Margaret Griffin:

"As a former certified aerobics instructor, I have been trying out the DVD workouts for pregnancy. I have only found three DVDs available in my local stores, but I wanted to rate them for your readers.

"**Buns of Steel: Pregnancy & Post-Pregnancy Workouts** with Madeleine Lewis ($13) gets my top rating. Madeleine Lewis has excellent cueing, so the workout is easy to follow. Your heart rate and perceived exertion are both used to monitor your exertion. There is an informative introduction. And I really like the fact that the toning segment utilizes a chair to help you keep your balance, which can be off a little during pregnancy. Most of the toning segment is done standing. This is a safe, effective workout led by a very capable instructor and I highly recommend it."

"A middle rating goes to **Denise Austin's: Fit & Firm Pregnancy** ($15). Denise has a good information segment during which she actually interviews a physician. She also provides heart rate checks during the workout. However, there are a couple of things about this workout that I don't particularly like. First, during the workout, there are times when safety information is provided regarding a particular move. This is fine and good, but instead of telling you to continue the movement and/or providing a picture-in-a-picture format, they actually change the screen to show the safety information and then cut back into the workout in progress. Surprise! You were supposed to keep doing the movement. Second, Denise Austin is a popular instructor, but I personally find that her cueing is not as sharp as I prefer and sometimes she seems to be a little off-beat with the music. My suggestion is get this DVD to use in addition to other DVDs if you are the type who gets easily bored with one workout."

Reader Laura McDowell recommended a few different workout DVDs. **Leisa Hart's FitMama** ($4) workout DVD was a favorite. "I loved it! Leisa has great energy and her peppy attitude made me smile through the whole workout. It has about 20 minutes of salsa dancing and then modified yoga." Laura also enjoyed **Kathy Smith's Pregnancy Workout** (discontinued by manufacturer, but still available used on Amazon). It was "a total

80's throwback; fun and energizing. She moves through the steps fast at times, but is always clear about offering ways to slow down if you need to. The hair, outfits and music are highly entertaining so the workout goes fast and feels great."

Another reader recommended **The Perfect Pregnancy Workout** DVD ($25). "It's by a former Cirque du Soleil acrobat, who leads the exercises with a French accent. It also offers beginner, intermediate and advanced options for each exercise."

Yoga is a terrific low impact exercise that does a wonderful job of stretching muscles you'll use while carrying and delivering your child. It's a terrific option for pregnant moms. And it's definitely become one of the most popular exercise options in North America. So it was only a matter of time before our readers began reviewing yoga DVDs. Here are some of their comments:

Reader Sheri Gomez recommended Yoga Zone's DVD **Postures for Pregnancy** ($15), calling it "wonderful for stretching and preventing back problems. It's beginner friendly and not too out there with the yoga thing." Her only complaint: there is no accompanying music, so she played her own DVDs along with the tape.

Reader Eufemia Campagna recommended Yoga Journal's **Prenatal Yoga** with Shiva Rea ($20). She noted that each segment of the tape is done using three women at different stages of pregnancy. "The segments are all accompanied by lovely, relaxing music and the instructor's directions are so clear that you don't even have to look at the TV to know what you need to do!" Another reader, Carolyn Oliner, also complimented this DVD: "It's not so much of a traditional yoga workout but a great series of poses and stretches that work for pregnant women and leave you feeling warm and stretched and (more gently) exercised." Finally, another reader noted that this workout is "really gentle (pretty easy for experienced yogini)."

Finally, we should note that Pilates has also been adapted for pregnancy exercise. You'll find several options on DVD including **Pilates During Pregnancy, Jennifer Gianni's Fusion Pilates for Pregnancy**, and **Prenatal Pilates** as well as many others.

Note: Amazon.com is a great source to find these DVDs. If you have any favorite DVDs, email us your review of them and we'll add them to our collection. And NetFlix (netflix.com) has a huge assortment of pregnancy DVDs for rent, so you can try before you buy.

The Bottom Line:
A Wrap-Up of Our Best Buy Picks

For career and casual maternity clothes, we thought the best deals were from the Old Navy, the Gap and H&M stores. Compared to retail maternity chains (where one outfit can run $200), you can buy your entire wardrobe from these places for a song.

If your place of work allows more casual dress, check out the prices at plus-size stores or alternatives like Old Navy. A simple pair of jeans that could cost $140 at a maternity shop are only $36 or less at Old Navy. And if you prefer the style at maternity shops, only hit them during sales, where you can find decent bargains. Another good idea: borrow from your husband's closet—many items can do double-duty as maternity clothes.

For weekend wear, we couldn't find a better deal than the 100% cotton shirts and shorts at discounters like Target, Walmart and K-Mart. Prices are as little as $10 per shirt—compare that to the $34 price tag at maternity chain stores for a simple cotton shirt.

Invited to a wedding? Rent that dress from a maternity store and save $100 or more. Don't forget to borrow all you can from friends who've already had babies. In fact, if you follow all our tips on maternity wear, bras, and underwear, you'll save $700 or more. Here's the breakdown:

1. Career Wear: $300.

2. Casual Clothes: $100.

3. Underwear: $150 to $200.

Total damage: $550 to $650. If you think that's too much money for clothes you'll only wear for a few months, consider the cost if you outfit yourself at full-price maternity shops. The same selection of outfits would run $1300 to $1700.

CHAPTER 6

FEEDING

Feeding Baby

Inside this chapter

H ow much money can you save by breastfeeding? What are the best options for pumps? Which bottles are best? We'll discuss these topics as well as ways to get discount formula, including details on which places have the best deals. And of course, we'll have tips and reviews on the next step in feeding: solid food. Finally, let's talk about high chairs—who's got the best value? Durability? Looks?

Breastfeeding

As readers of past editions of this book know, we are big proponents of breastfeeding. The medical benefits of breast milk are well documented, but obviously the decision to breast or bottle-feed is a personal call for each new mom. In the past, we spent time in this chapter encouraging breast-feeding . . . but we realize now we are preaching to the choir. Our time is better spent discussing how to save on feeding your baby, no matter which way you go. So, we'll leave the discussion of breast versus bottle to our other book *Baby 411* (as well your doctor and family). Let's talk about the monetary impact of the decision, however.

Breastfeed Your Baby and Save $900

Since this is a book on bargains, we'd be remiss in not mentioning the tremendous amount of money you can save if you breast-feed. Just think about it: no bottles, no expensive formula to prepare, no special insulated carriers to keep bottles warm/cold, etc.

So, how much money would you save? Obviously, NOT buying formula would be the biggest money-saver. Even if you were to use the less-expensive powdered formula, you would still have to spend nearly $24 per 23.4-ounce can of powdered formula. Since each can makes about 150 ounces of formula, the cost per ounce of formula is about 16¢. And, by the way, the American Academy of Pediatrics and the American Dental Association now say that parents who use powdered formula should use bottled water when they make up a bottle for baby. What kind of bottled water? Purified, demineralize, deionized, distilled or reverse osmosis filtered water. So that's going to cost you too—about a penny per ounce.

That doesn't sound too bad, does it? Unless you factor in that a baby will down 32 ounces of formula per day by 12 weeks of age. Your cost per day would be $5.12. Assuming you breastfeed for at least the first six months, you would save a grand total of $934.40 just *on formula alone*. The American Academy of Pediatrics recommends breastfeeding for 12 months (with solid foods added to the mix at six months), so in that case your savings could be as much as $1869! That doesn't include the expense of bottles, nipples and accessories! By the way, statistically speaking, nearly 74% of American moms breastfeed their babies at birth. By six months, however, the number of breastfeeding moms drops to nearly 43% (although this is an improvement up from 33% in 2007).

To be fair, there are some additional expenses that might go along with breastfeeding too. The biggest dollar item: you might decide to buy a breast pump. Costs for this item range from $50 for a manual pump to $300+ for a professional-grade breast pump. Or you can rent a pump for $45 a month (plus a kit—one time cost of about $50 to $60). On the plus side, the new heath care law requires health insurance companies to pay for breast pumps, so your out-of-pocket expense may vary.

And of course, you'll also need some bottles—but arguably fewer than if you formula-feed.

If $934.50 doesn't sound like a lot of money, consider the savings if you had to buy formula in the concentrated liquid form instead of the cheaper powder. A 32-ounce can of Enfamil ready-to-eat liquid costs about $7.29 at a grocery store and makes up only eight 4-ounce bottles. The bottom line: you could spend over $1300 on formula for your baby in the first six months alone!

Of course, we realize that some moms will decide to use formula because of a personal, medical or work situation—to help out, we have a section later in this chapter on how to save on formula, bottle systems and other necessary accessories.

Sources: Where to Find Breast Feeding Help

The basis of breastfeeding is attachment. Getting your new little one to latch onto your breast properly is not a matter of instinct. Some babies have no trouble figuring it out, while many others need your help and guidance. In fact, problems with attachment can lead to sore nipples and painful engorgement. Of course, you should be able to turn to your pediatrician or the nurses at the hospital for breastfeeding advice. However, if you find that they do not offer you the support you need, consider the following sources for breastfeeding help:

1 **LA LECHE LEAGUE** (llli.org). Started in 1956 by a group of moms in Chicago, La Leche League has traditionally been the most vocal supporter of breastfeeding in this country. You've got to imagine the amount of chutzpah these women had to have to buck the bottle trend and promote breastfeeding at a time when it wasn't fashionable (to say the least).

In recent years, La Leche has established branches in many communities around the world, providing support groups for nursing moms. Their web site also offers reviews and recommendations of books and videotapes on nursing, as well as other child care topics.

2 **NURSING MOTHERS' COUNCIL** (nursingmothers.org). Similar in mission to La Leche League, the Nursing Mothers' Council differs on one point: the group emphasizes working moms and their unique needs and problems.

3 **LACTATION CONSULTANTS**. Lactation consultants are usually nurses who specialize in breastfeeding education and problem solving. You can find them through your pediatrician, hospital, or the International Lactation Consultants Association (iblce.org). New eligibility requirements for members of this group in 2012 will include "90 contact hours of re-exam education in human lactation and breastfeeding and either be a registered/licensed/recognize health professional in their country or have completed high education in 14 subjects" before they can take the licensing exam.

At some hospitals, resident lactation consultants are available to answer questions by phone at no charge. If a problem persists, you can set up an in-person consultation for a minimal fee (about $65 to $200 per session, although your health insurance provider may pick up the tab).

Unfortunately, the availability and cost of lactation consultants seems to vary from region to region. Our advice: call area hospitals before you give birth to determine the availability of breastfeeding support. Another good source for a referral to a lactation consultant is your pediatrician.

4 **HOSPITALS.** Look for a hospital in your area that has breastfeeding-friendly policies. These include 24-hour rooming in (where your baby can stay with you instead of in a nursery) and breastfeeding on demand. Pro-nursing hospitals do not supplement babies with a bottle and don't push free formula samples.

5 **BOOKS.** Although they aren't a substitute for support from your doctor, hospital, and family, many books provide plenty of info and encouragement. Check the La Leche League web site for titles.

6 **THE WEB.** Our message board (BabyBargains.com, click on Talk) include a special forum on feeding, Kid Food. Discuss breastfeeding, formula feeding, bottle questions, first foods and more. With 42,000+ members and 1000 new posts a day, you can query other moms about their breast pump experiences, ask a question about food allergies and more.

7 **HEALTH INSURANCE PROVIDERS.** The new healthcare law mandates certain breastfeeding supplies and assistance—check with your provider for benefits.

Best Online Sources

Medela
medela.com Medela's web site offers useful info, tips and advice on breastfeeding. "Tips and Solutions" is an excellent FAQ for nursing moms. You can even submit questions to online lactation consultants. **Rating: A**

Nursing Mother Supplies
nursingmothersupplies.com Not only does this site carry breast pumps and supplies from Medela and Ameda Egnell, they also offer support to customers after they buy. We liked the extensive FAQ and breast pump comparison charts. Nursing pillows, storage options, Medela bottles and pads are also available. This site isn't too preachy—we like their low-key approach to encouraging breastfeeding. **Rating: A**

Breast Pumps Direct

breastpumpsdirect.com Breast Pumps Direct is an online discounter of breast pumps. They carry the major brands (Medela, Avent), as well as accessories and other items. Overall, we found their prices about 5% to 10% below other discounters. The advice section includes pump reviews, comparison charts and more. **Rating: A**

◆ *Other web sites:* The major baby gear sites (Diapers.com, BabiesRUs.com and of course, Amazon.com) have extensive offerings of breast pumps and supplies.

What Are You Buying?

Even if you exclusively breastfeed, you probably will find yourself needing to pump an occasional bottle. After all, you might want to go out to dinner without the baby. Maybe you'll have an overnight trip for your job or just need to get back to work full or part time. Your spouse might even be interested in relieving you of a night feeding. The solution? Pumping milk. Whether you want to pump occasionally or every day, you have a wide range of options. Here's an overview:

◆ **Manual Expression:** OK, technically, this isn't a breast pump in the sense we're talking about. But it is an option. There are several good breastfeeding books that describe how to express milk manually. Most women find that the amount of milk expressed, compared to the time and trouble involved, hardly makes it worth using this method. A few women (we think they are modern miracle workers) can manage to express enough for an occasional bottle; for the majority of women, however, using a breast pump is a more practical alternative. Manual expression is typically used only to relieve engorgement.

◆ **Manual Pumps:** Non-electric, hand-held pumps are operated by squeezing on a handle. While the most affordable option, manual pumps are generally also the least efficient—you simply can't duplicate your baby's sucking action by hand. Therefore, these pumps are best for moms who only need an occasional bottle or who need to relieve engorgement.

◆ **Mini-Electrics:** These breast pumps (most work either with batteries or an A/C adapter) are designed to express an occasional bottle. Unfortunately, the sucking action is so weak that it often takes twenty minutes per side to express a significant amount of milk. And doing so is not very comfortable. Why is it so slow? Most models only cycle nine to fifteen times per minute—compare that to a baby who sucks the equivalent of 50 cycles per minute!

◆ **High-End Double Pumps:** The Mercedes of breast pumps—we can't sing the praises of these work horses enough. In just ten to twenty minutes, you can pump both breasts. And high-end double pumps are much more comfortable than mini-electrics. In fact, at first I didn't think a high-end pump I rented was working well because it was so comfortable. The bottom line: there is no better option for a working woman who wants to provide her baby with breast milk.

Today, you have two options when it comes to these pumps: rent a hospital-grade pump (which often is called a piston-electric) or buy a high-end consumer grade double-pump.

Rental Pumps. These are what the industry refers to as hospital-grade or piston electric pumps. They are built to withstand continuous use of up to eight to ten times a day for many years. Often they are much heavier than personal use pumps like the Medela Pump-In-Style. And all the interior parts are sealed to prevent contamination from one renter to the next. *In fact, the Food and Drug Administration (FDA) certifies rental pumps for multiple use.* The only item each renter must buy is a new collection kit.

WHERE TO FIND: Pediatricians, lactation consultants, doulas, midwives, hospitals, maternity stores and home medical care companies are sources to find rental pumps. You can also call La Leche League (800-LALECHE; web: lalecheleague.org) or other lactation support groups for a referral to a rental company in your area.

HOW MUCH: Prices generally average about $65 to $90 per month to rent a breast pump. Common brands of hospital-grade pumps include Hygeia and White River Concepts, although consumer brands Medela and Ameda also have hospital versions. Collection kits cost about $32 to $60 for the bottles, shields and tubes.

Professional-Grade Electric Pumps. These electric pumps are available for sale to consumers and are intended to be used no more than three or four times a day. Unlike rental pumps, they are lighter weight and easier to carry around (to work or elsewhere). Examples of these pumps include the Medela Pump-In-Style and the Ameda Purely Yours.

These pumps have an open system without sealed parts and are therefore only recommended as a single-use item. *The FDA, lactation consultants, pediatricians and manufacturers DO NOT recommend using a second-hand personal pump.* Even if you change the tubes and shields, there is a possibility of cross contamination. (The exception is the Bailey Nurture III breast pump, which is one of the very

Breast Pumps

Which pump works best in which situation?

	Manual	Mini-Elec.	Professional	Rental*
Do you need a pump for:				
A missed feeding?	■	◆		
Evening out from baby?	■	◆		
Working part-time.	■	◆		
Occasional use, a few times a week.	■	◆		
Daily use; full-time work			●	●
Premature or hospitalized baby?			●	●
Low milk supply?			●	●
Sore nipples/engorgement?	■		●	●
Latch-on problems or breast infection?			■	●
Drawing out flat or inverted nipples?	■	◆	●	●

Key: ■ = Good ◆ = Better ● = Best
*Rental refers to renting a hospital-grade pump. These can usually be rented on a monthly basis.
Source: Medela.

pumps

few consumer-grade pumps certified by the FDA for multiple users).

WHERE TO FIND: Online is a primary source. Also most independent baby stores and Babies R Us carry a selection of electric breast pumps. See earlier in the chapter for some of our favorite sources.

HOW MUCH: Prices range from about $120 to $400 depending on the brand and accessories included. We will review pumps later in this chapter.

Safe and Sound

As we mentioned in the last section, we don't recommend buying a used breast pump. Models like Medela's Pump In Style can actually collect milk in the pump mechanism. So, let's state it clearly: DO NOT PURCHASE A USED BREAST PUMP. The risk of exposing your baby to any pathogens isn't worth the savings.

Of course, it is fine to re-use your own breast pump for another child down the road. Just replace the tubing and collection bottles to make sure there are no bacteria left over from previous uses.

One more safety tip: if it hurts stop. No kidding! Pumping to express milk for your baby should not be a painful experience.

Smart Shopper Tip

Smart Shopper Tip #1
When to buy that pump.

"I don't know how long I want to breastfeed. And I'll be going back to work soon after my baby is born. When should I get a pump?"

We'd suggest waiting a bit before you invest in a breast pump or even nursing clothes. Many moms start with breast-feeding, but can't or don't want to continue it after a few weeks. For them investing in a pump would be a waste of money. If you aren't sure how long you want to breast feed, but you'd like to pump some extra bottles of milk anyway, consider renting a hospital grade pump first and trying it out before you invest a couple hundred dollars. You can often rent for as little as one month, which will be much cheaper than buying a pump that can run $200 to $350.

The best milk storage options

Once you've decided to express breast milk for your child, you'll need to consider how to store it. Freezer bags are the most common method and most major pump manufactures and bottle makers sell bags. So, who's got the best storage bags? **Lansinoh** (sold in Target; 50 pack for $10) is the hands-down winner. "They are sturdy, stand on their own and have an excellent double lock seal closure," said one mom. Others echoed that recommendation. Lansinoh also sells BPA-free storage bottles that fit most breast pumps ($10 for four at Target.com).

Another good choice is **Medela**, the king of breast pumps. Their bags attach to any Medela pump and feature a zipper-top. Amazon.com sells a box of 50 for $17. Medela also sells 80 ml. breast milk containers and lids (12-pack is $15.40) and plastic collection bottles ($4 each). Both options are compatible with Medela breast pumps and are BPA free.

A completely different alternative is **Mothers Milk Mate**

Waste of Money

Even Cows Opt for the Electric Kind

"I'm going back to work a couple of months after my baby is born. My co-worker who breastfeeds her baby thinks manual and mini-electrics pumps are a waste of money. Your thoughts?

While they may be useful to relieve engorgement, manual pumps aren't very practical for long-term pumping when you're at work. They are very slow, which makes it hard to get much milk. Mini-electric breast pumps are better but are really best only for occasional use—for example, expressing a small amount of milk to mix with cereal for a baby who's learning to eat solids. The problem with mini-electrics: some are painful and most are too slow.

Your best bet if you plan to do some serious pumping is to rent a hospital-grade pump. These monsters maintain a high rate of extraction with amazing comfort. A lactation consultant we interviewed said these pumps can empty both breasts in about ten to 15 minutes—contrast that with 20 to 30 minutes for mini-electrics and 45 minutes to an hour for manual pumps.

We note later in our reviews of pumps that the manual pump that received top rating from our readers is the Avent Isis—and even

(mothersmilkmate.com). For $29, you get a ten-bottle storage system with rack. The 5 oz. bottles are BPA free and the set comes with freshness dating labels.

Speaking of labels, it's pretty important to know when milk has been expressed so you don't your feed baby milk that is past its freshness date. Be sure to label bottles with expressed dates. Medela's labeling lids run $12.25 for six.

Yet another great option for freezer storage: **Milk Trays** by Sensible Lines (SensibleLines.com). It's hard to believe no one has thought of this before—Milk Trays are like old-fashioned ice cube trays but with a twist. The tray's 16 one-ounce capacity cubes are shaped like skinny cylinders, small enough to fit into any baby bottle. They come with lids to block freezer burn and are made from BPA-free, phthalate-free plastic. The trays sell for $22 for two.

Don't forget there are numerous apps for your smart phone that can help you keep track of your frozen or refrigerated expressed milk, baby feedings, diapers changes and more. Baby logs range in price from free up to $5.

though it is a vast improvement over previous options, it still is a MANUAL pump. It may not work well for moms who plan to work part or full-time and still nurse their baby. That said, one solution is to use two pumps—a mom we interviewed uses a Medela Pump In Style when she's tired (during the evening or night-time) and an Avent Isis at work (it's much quieter; doesn't need electricity, etc).

Affordable Care Act & Breast Pumps

In case you've been living off the planet since 2010 and just got back, the Affordable Care Act (ACA, Obamacare) has rolled out . . . and it includes a special benefit for new moms: a "free" breast pump.

Before you get too excited, though, there are "a few, uh, provisos. Ah, a couple of quid pro quos," as the Genie in *Aladdin* would say. The biggest catch: the ACA doesn't specify which pump you get. Not even what kind (manual, mini electric, dual electric, rental). But, you say, you'd like a top of the line Medela or Ameda personal use pump? Well, the answer is: maybe yes, maybe no.

Turns out insurance companies (and some state insurance rules) determine what pump you can get. And in most cases, you also won't be able to stop by your favorite retailer to purchase your pump. Why? Many insurance companies require customers to purchase pumps from the company's designated durable medical equipment company (DME). These DME's distribute medical equipment (like oxygen bottles and nebulizers).

Yep, that means you'll have to track down one of your insurance company's DME's and then call to see what pumps they might have in stock. Parents have complained on message boards and blogs that they called their insurance providers' designated DME's and discovered they didn't even have breast pumps available. Others noted that their provider only offers a manual pump—not very helpful if you plan to pump at work!

What if you want a more powerful pump like a hospital grade option? Again, this option may or may not be covered by your insurance. Some insurers will allow you to rent a hospital grade pump but only if you have a "medical necessity." Translation: your doctor will have to fill out even more paperwork to "prescribe" a rental pump.

Bottom line in all this: you'll need to talk to your insurance provider. See our blog at BabyBargains.com for questions to ask your provider (search for Affordable Care Act and Breastpumps).

Breast Pumps (model by model reviews)

Manual Pumps

AVENT COMFORT MANUAL (SCF310/20)
Web: AventAmerica.com
Price: $40-$45.
Type: Manual.
Comments: Our readers love this pump, which Avent claims is as efficient as a mini-electric (it takes about eight to ten minutes to empty a breast). Mom feedback is very positive and at this price, it's a real winner **Rating: A**

DR. BROWN'S MANUAL BREAST PUMP BY SIMPLISSE
Web: Simplisse.com
Price: $25-$50.
Type: Manual.
Comments: In 2012, Dr. Brown's merged with Simplisse. The Simplesse pumps have since been renamed Dr. Brown's, including this one. The company claims this pump mimics Mother Nature better than other manual pumps, which have a suck-and-release action. Fans love the soft breast cup; dissenters say it isn't as good as the Medela or Avent models. One online reviewer chimed in, saying "the Simplisse must be French for many ridiculous steps for assembly and disassembly and miserable to clean." **Rating: C+**

EVENFLO MANUAL
Web: Evenflo.com
Price: $16-$20.
Type: Manual.
Comments: The SimplyGo Manual features a lightweight design, "Advance MemoryFlex" fastener for better milk expression and silicone inserts for different size nipples. The unit comes with one 5 oz. collection bottle and a carry case. Reader feedback on this one has been split. Fans say it works okay for that occasional bottle. Critics, on the other hand, complain about lack of suction and pain while pumping. **Rating: C+**

LANSINOH MANUAL
Web: Lansinoh.com
Price: $30-$35.
Type: Manual.

Comments: Readers think this pump is a good runner up to Medela or Avent—Lansinoh's manual pump is easy to use and has few parts to clean. A few dissenters say it doesn't quite have the suction of the Medela, however. That was confirmed by our lactation consultant, who said her measurements showed the Lansinoh pump had about 20% less suction compared to the Avent or Medela. FYI: Lansinoh has revised the pump with a new ComfortSeal cushion for a better seal to make it more efficient. **Rating: B**

MEDELA HARMONY
Web: Medela.com
Price: $30-$35.
Type: Manual.
Comments: The Harmony is a winner. Similar to the Avent Comfort Manual, it has fewer parts to wash than the Avent and is easier to assemble. Medela notes the Harmony offers a 2-phase expression technology that is supposed to stimulate let down, then slows down to mimic slower, deeper sucking action. One mom with larger breasts found this pump worked better for her than the Avent. The Harmony is more affordable than the Avent. **Rating: A**

Mini Electric Pumps

EVENFLO DUAL ELECTRIC
Web: Evenflo.com
Price: $40 single, $55-$60 dual.
Type: Mini-electric.
Comments: Evenflo has completely revamped its line of breast pumps. The Dual Electric breast pump is a double pump mini electric which sells for an affordable $60. The pump features an adjustable vacuum which Evenflo claims allows moms to customize the comfort level. It also has a silicone insert to "accommodate different nipple sizes" and comes with a cooler bag and two ice packs, an AC adapter and 5 oz. bottle. This pump is also available as a single for $40.

Evenflo only recommends this pump for occasional use. In fact, they note on their web site that moms should not use it more than two times per day. So far, feedback is not very positive. Critics complain about defective units, the suction that stopped working and an overall lack of power. **Rating: C**

FIRST YEARS MIPUMP
Web: learningcurve.com
Price: $45-$50 single; $70-$80 double.
Type: Mini-electric.

Comments: With both a single and double mini-electric version (pictured), the First Years MiPump is affordable and quiet—but the suction is inadequate. They claim the pumps offer eight levels of suction but some readers were disappointed. And more than one reader criticized the overall quality of the MiPump. Several reports of the pump breaking within a month or so of purchase make this one a loser. ***Rating: D***

MEDELA SWING BREAST PUMP
Web: Medela.com
Price: $150-$170
Type: Mini electric.
Comments: This single electric pump offers Medela's 2-Phase Expression (the same system as Medela's more expensive pumps), which is supposed to copy baby's natural sucking rhythm. The pump has two different modes: first to stimulate letdown and then to simulate baby's normal sucking pattern. Moms applaud this pump's ease of use and comfort. The only negative: it's a single pump and hence is best for occasional use. In fact, some moms wish it came as a double version. Despite that, we will give it our highest rating. ***Rating: A***

PLAYTEX PETITE DOUBLE ELECTRIC
Web: playtex.com
Price: $80-$124
Type: Mini electric.
Comments: The Playtex Petite has soft silicone breast shields, a closed system design and air cushioned opening. It's smaller than most electric pumps (as the name implies) which might make it a lot easier to carry and use. Another plus: it works directly with the Playtex wide bottle system.

The downsides? Parents complained that suction didn't work well at emptying both breasts compared to Medela pumps and Purely Yours. The motor even burned out on several readers!

The weak suction and poor quality is a deal-killer—we don't recommend this pump. ***Rating: F***

More mini-electrics: You'll see several other brands of mini-electric breast pumps on the market today. With the exception of the Medela Swing, most of these pumps fare poorly according to our reader feedback. For occasional use, you are better off getting a sim-

pumps

ple manual pump. Or if you need a serious pump for daily pumping, the professional-grade options (reviewed below) are the best bets.

Professional-Grade Pumps

AMEDA PURELY YOURS

Web: Ameda.com

Price: $140 for the pump only; $200 for the Carry All version; $205-$240 for the Backpack; $300 Ultra.

Type: Professional.

Comments: It's smaller! It's lighter! And its less expensive—the Ameda Purely Yours has won a legion of fans for its Purely Yours Pump, which comes in four versions: pump only (use your own bag), Carry All and Backpack. A new "Ultra" version throws in an extra tote bag, cooler bag and six bottles. The pump weighs about five pounds and has eight suction settings and nine speeds. The backpack includes a car adapter. The Ameda has a built-in AA battery pack, versus the Medela, which has a separate battery pack. Best of all, the Ameda is easy to maintain (milk can't get into the tubes, which means less cleaning than the Medela). The downside? Medela is sold in many more retail outlets than Ameda meaning you can get spare parts and supplies easier (although to its credit, Ameda has great customer service). FYI: We previously reported that Evenflo purchased Ameda in 2009. Evenflo recently spun off Ameda as an independent company. **Rating: A**

AVENT COMFORT SINGLE/TWIN ELECTRIC

Web: AventAmerica.com

Price: $140 single, $170-$200 pictured.

Type: Professional.

Comments: New this year, Avent adjusted it's single and double pumps so moms no longer have to lean forward to use them. Hence, the "comfort" name of these pumps. Moms say it does save your back since you no longer have to hunch over. They've also improved the assembly with easy to follow graphical instructions.

The pumps work with a massage cushion that is supposed to stimulate a more natural let down. Then you can choose one of three pump settings. Included in the pack is one bottle with nipple, 40 breast pads, travel pouch and bra clip.

So what's the downside to the Avent electric pumps? Well, there are a lot of parts to assemble, but with practice it gets easier. Some parents complain that the Avent is louder than other pumps. Moms who remember the IQ (Avent's previous model), note that it only offers three pumping settings.

And finally, the price is a big stumbling block. Although you can find it discounted online to $92 for the single version, the price in some stores is closer to $200 . . . that is quite a bit more than the Ameda Purely Yours online. At least Avent doesn't skimp on what comes with the pump: besides the pump itself, you get two Avent 4 oz. bottles, four bottle stand/funnel covers, two sealing discs, two nipple travel packs and two newborn nipples, a spare part and an electric adapter in a microfiber bag. But compared to the old Isis IQ, that's a bit skimpy. The Isis came with a insulated carry bag and eight gel packs for cold storage. It's comparable to the top-of-the-line Medela Pump In Style Advanced without the nice bag.

Our readers are generally split into two camps when it comes to pumps: Medela vs. Avent. Medela fans like the wide availability of parts and Medela's excellent customer service. Avent fans love the pump's overall quality and compatibility with Avent's very popular bottles—the pump connects directly to the bottles, etc. Moms criticized the cost of the Avent Electric, but it appears they lowered the price a bit making it more competitive with the Ameda.

Moms thought it was quiet, comfortable and easy to clean. And it does the job. *Rating: A*

BAILEY MEDICAL NURTURE III
Web: BaileyMed.com
Price: $130 basic, $160 deluxe.
Type: Professional
Comments: This pump comes in two versions—basic ($130) and deluxe ($160). It's claim to fame: the Nurture III is one of the few small pump approved for multiple users by the FDA. Hence you can buy this pump and hand it down to a friend or sell it online. The Nurture III features fully adjustable suction and manual cycling, where mom can control the cycling pattern. This fea-

Pumps: Have a Plan B

If you plan to return to work and will rely on pumping to feed your baby, make sure you have a Plan B in case your breast pump breaks. Yes, pumps are just machines and sometimes they break down—that means tracking down replacement parts at a store across town. Or waiting for parts to arrive by mail. The best advice: have a Plan B, like a back-up manual or mini-electric pump on hand. This is especially important if you choose a brand (like Ameda) that is mostly sold online—the only way to get replacement parts for such pumps is through the mail!

Nursing Pillows

Many nursing moms find a nursing pillow makes breastfeeding easier and more comfortable. Our readers have emailed us positive comments for *My Brest Friend* by Zenoff Products (zenoffproducts.com). Okay, it probably qualifies as the Most Stupid Name for a Baby Product Ever award, but it really works—it wraps around your waist and is secured with Velcro. It comes in original, deluxe, professional, travel and twins models. The original retails for about $40.

An old favorite is the *Boppy* pillow. Sold for $30 to $40 online, this perennial favorite doesn't have a waist strap, but many moms swear by it as a simple, affordable nursing pillow.

Got twins? Check out Double Blessing's *EZ-2-NURSE's* pillow (we found it on Amazon.com) A mom told us this was the "absolute best" for her twins, adding, "I could not successfully nurse my girls together without this pillow. It was wonderful." Cost: $70.

If you're not sold in the idea of a big, bulky nursing pillow, we did find an alternative. *Utterly Yours* (utterlyyours.com) makes a small, hand-sized pillow that you position directly under the breast. Cost: $25 (including pillow cover).

ture takes some practice, say our readers—and isn't a plus for sleep-deprived moms. Fans say it does a great job at expressing milk, but others have a problem letting-down with the Nurture III. The deluxe version includes an insulated carry bag with ice pack, four extra bottles and an instructional DVD (pictured). Bottom line: this is a good pump, but hard to find in stores. It is mostly sold online. *Rating: B+*

DR. BROWN'S DOUBLE ELECTRIC BY SIMPLISSE
Web: Simplisse.com
Price: $195-$250.

Type: Professional.
Comments: The Dr. Brown's Double Electric breast pump features "gentle compression technology to gently elicit milk expression." The pump also has flexible breast cups for better fit and adjustable pump pressure settings, as well as a purse-like tote bag that includes a cooler pack and four milk collection bottles. Moms seem a lot more impressed with the electric version than with Dr. Brown's manual pump. They tell us the pump is very comfortable and easy to use. On the other hand, we've heard a few complaints that the compression wasn't enough to get much milk. FYI: In 2012, Simplisse merged with Dr. Brown's and rebranded all Simplisse

products with the Dr. Brown's name. ***Rating: B***

HYGEIA ENJOYE
Web: Hygeiababy.com
Price: $190-$340
Type: Professional
Comments: A reader recommended this
brand to us—she loved her EnJoye pump, which is comparable in
suction to hospital-grade pumps. It comes in three versions: a
rechargeable battery version ($299), one with an external power
supply ($240) or a deluxe tote ($340, pictured). Retail prices online
are less.

Unique features include a "CARE button" that "records your
baby's cry or other sounds for playback during pumping." This is
ostensibly to help with let down. It also has independently adjustable
speed and suction controls. Finally, like the Nurture III, this pump is
sealed and can be used by more than one person—you can lend or
sell it when you're done.

The pumps have a three year warranty. After three years, return
your pump to the company and they offer to recycle or refurbish
your pumps so you don't have to throw it away.

The only bummer: Hygeia doesn't make smaller size flanges.
Hygeia isn't as well known as Medela or Avent, but a worthy alternative to consider. ***Rating: A***

LANSINOH AFFINITY
Web: Lansinoh.com
Price: $120-$130.
Type: Professional.
Comments: The Affinity is an affordable
pump that is lightweight and has the same stimulation model (one-
touch let-down) that Medela offers. We liked the improved white
membrane, which should make it less likely to tear and need
replacement. The filter in the model is much like Medela's Freestyle.
Also good: eight suction and six cycle settings let you customize
pumping plus the company guarantees milk will not back up into
the tubing or motor.

On the downside, the suction isn't as strong as Medela's pumps
(about 10% less, based on our measurements). And readers say the
Affinity is rather loud and not as comfortable as other pumps. Also:
there is just one size flange (24 mm), so it won't be as accommodating for smaller or larger breasts. Finally, we aren't wild about that
purple lip around the flange—like the manual pump, we worry it
would stiffen over time after you sterilize the pump (making it
uncomfortable). So it's a mixed review for the Lansinoh Affinity—

good price and decent features make it a better bet than other low-price models like Evenflo and First Years. But it still can't hold a candle to our top rated picks in this category (Ameda and Medela).

FYI: Lansinoh has revised this model with a new pump called the Affinity Pro (see below) and are phasing our this model. However, we still see it for sale online at this time. **Rating: B-**

LANSINOH AFFINITY PRO

Web: Lansinoh.com
Price: $130
Type: Professional.
Comments: What makes this pump different from the Affinity? It has three customizable suction rhythms, an LCD screen for keeping track of pumping time, and the system is closed so milk won't collect in the tubes or motor.

The pump is also affordably priced at $130 retail and includes a carry tote, two milk storage bags, two nursing pads and a lanolin sample. This new model replaces the Affinity.

Now that the Pro has been on the market for a bit, we have considerable parent feedback, which was mixed. Some parents are disappointed in the suction power of the pump and others complain their pumps stopped working. What did moms like? The Pro is very light weight, has the easy-to-read LCD screen with time and is a whole lot cheaper. With these mixed reviews, we'll give the Pro an average rating. **Rating: C**

MEDELA FREESTYLE BREAST PUMP

Web: Medela.com
Price: $340-$380
Type: Professional
Comments: The Freestyle is Medela's latest pump and they pulled out all the stops: hands-free option, LED display, pumping session timer, memory function and more.

How does it differ from the Pump in Style (PIS)? Well, the Freestyle can be removed from its bag (unlike the PIS backpack or shoulder bag) and it features a rechargeable battery for three hours of pumping (the PIS can use AA batteries or a wall outlet). Most moms only have to charge it once a week. No, it doesn't have the PIS's "2-Phase Expression technology" but it does have the one touch let-down button. It's also missing the ability to independently control the speed and suction.

Yet it is the hands-free option that is the killer app here: fans call it "life changing," especially for moms with another toddler at home.

Of course, at $380, this pump better be darn impressive. And it's amazing that all this comes from a pump that basically fits in the palm of your hand (ok, if you have big hands).

So why buy the Freestyle instead of the Pump In Style? Fans of the Freestyle say it is easier to use and clean than the PIS. Even the breast shields are softer and more comfortable. The downside? The Freestyle isn't exactly quiet, although no louder than the Pump In Style. And if you don't keep the bottles at the right angle, milk can spill out. Also the Freestyle can be a bit fussy to assemble—if you don't assemble the parts just so, you can get less suction. Finally, moms complain that the battery is not as powerful as the corded Pump In Style Advance meaning you won't get as much milk or it will take longer. Those cons aside, we still think this is an good pump. The Freestyle is highly recommended. ***Rating: A***

MEDELA PUMP IN STYLE ADVANCED

Web: Medela.com
Price: $225-$300.
Type: Professional

Comments: It's the 800-pound gorilla of the breast pump category: the Medela Pump In Style Advance (PIS).

So what's all the fuss about? If you are serious about pumping every day, the Pump In Style allows you to carry a high quality pump to work. You can empty both breasts in a short amount of time with great comfort. As a nursing mom, I remember using the Original version and found it pretty comparable to a hospital-grade pump.

The PIS has evolved over the years—gone is the basic "Original" version and now we have the Advanced, which comes in three flavors: backpack, on-the-go tote bag and metro bag.

In general, the Advanced features Medela's new "2-Phase Expression" technology that mimics the way infants nurse at the breast. At first, infants apparently nurse quickly to simulate let down. Then they settle into a deeper, slower sucking action—the Pump In Style Advance simulates this pattern.

The three versions are similar: all have the same motor, just a different bag. The Metro has a removable pump motor, storage bags and two breast shield sizes.

So what's the disadvantage of the Pump In Styles? Cost is a biggie: the PIS is $100 or so more than the Ameda Purely Yours, which is smaller, lighter and has several other attractive features. Medela's higher price is no doubt attributable to their "minimum advertised price" policy, which prevents Internet discounters from selling their pumps below a certain price. Hence, you'll see Medela priced about the same on most sites.

Fans of Medela love the availability of parts (sold in many retail stores) and Medela's excellent customer service. So, all in all, we will recommend the Pump in Style—it is an excellent pump. **Rating: A**

Our Picks: Brand Recommendations

◆ **Manual Pump:** The best manual pumps are the *Avent Comfort Manual* (SCF310/20; $40-$45) and *Medela Harmony* ($30-$35). Between the two, the Medela Harmony has the edge, given its lower price and easier-to-clean design.

◆ **Mini Electric Pump:** The *Medela Swing* mini-electric is pricey ($150-$170) but very good quality. Yes, you may be tempted by other mini-electric pumps in discount stores for under $50, but we have one word of advice: don't. They simply don't work well.

◆ **Professional Grade Pump:** You can't go wrong with either, so we'll make it a tie: the *Medela Pump In Style* ($225 to $300) and *Ameda Purely Yours* ($140 to $300) are the co-champs. For daily pumping, they are the standard. If hands-free operation is important, then consider the excellent Medela Freestyle ($340-$380).

Before you buy a pump, we suggest RENTING a hospital-grade pump first for a week or two (or a month). After you decide you're committed to pumping and you're comfortable with how double pumps work, then consider buying one of your own. Given the hefty retail prices, it makes sense to buy only if you plan to pump for several months or have a second child.

Formula

Is there any nutritional difference between brands of formula? No, the federal government mandates that all formula have the same nutritional value (the amount of protein, etc). That's right—the "generic" formula sold at a discounter is nutritionally no different than pricey name brands. How pricey? A 23.4-ounce can of name brand powdered formula runs $24 today. Yep, 24 bucks a can. At these prices, you can see how buying formula can take a bite out of your baby budget in a hurry. As we mentioned earlier, the American Academy of Pediatrics and the American Dental Association now say that parents who use powdered or concentrated formula should use bottled water when they make up a bottle for baby. What kind of bottled water? Purified, demineralize, deionized, distilled or reverse osmosis filtered water. So that's going to cost you too—add about a penny per ounce to the cost of powdered formula. Let's talk formula!

FEEDING

The most popular formula brands

Market share by brand, 2013

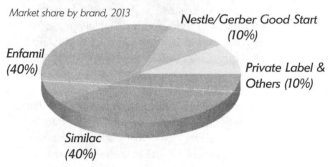

Nestle/Gerber Good Start (10%)

Enfamil (40%)

Private Label & Others (10%)

Similac (40%)

formula

What Are You Buying?

Baby formula is just baby formula, right? Nope, it is more complicated that—formula comes in several versions (powdered, liquid concentrate, ready-to-drink) as well as types (cow's milk, soy, etc). Not to mention organic, specialty formulas and more. Here's a quick overview:

◆ **Versions.** Formula comes in three different versions: powder, liquid concentrate and ready-to-drink. Powder is least expensive, followed by liquid concentrate—you add water to both these. Ready-to-drink is the priciest. A recent online price survey revealed the lowest cost per ounce of powdered formula is 11¢ (we include the cost of bottled water per oz of 1¢). Compare that to liquid concentrate at 21¢ (also includes 1¢ per oz. bottled water expense), and ready to drink at 28¢ to 50¢ per ounce.

◆ **Infant stages.** Manufacturers are now making different formulas for different ages and stages of infancy. For example, Enfamil makes a formula for newborns to three month olds with additional vitamin D. Meanwhile, Enfamil's regular formula (for newborns up to 12 months) has added prebiotics to aid in the growth of good bacteria in the gut. "Enfagrow" formula is intended for older babies and toddlers (nine-24 months).

◆ **Toddler formula.** First created by Carnation ("Good Start 2" formula, now marketed under the Gerber name), then copied by other formula manufacturers, "toddler" formulas are intended to be used for older children (typically nine months old and up) instead of regular cows milk or soymilk. Typically, parents move to whole milk or soymilk when their child reaches one year of age. In order to hang on to consumers longer, formula manufacturers have developed these toddler formulas. So what's the big difference between baby formula and toddler formula? All these toddler formulas add calcium and iron as well as a variety of vitamins (E, C, D) depending on the brand.

◆ *Types.* Beside cow's milk-based formula, there is also soy-based formula. Which is best? Cow's milk formula with iron—this formula is tolerated best by the most babies and recommended first by most doctors. Of course, there are many specialty formulas for babies with special problems—we call these the "gourmet" formulas, described in more detail below. Our advice in a nutshell: buy the cheapest cow's milk based formula you can find to start with.

◆ *Organic.* These formulas are certified "antibiotic, pesticide and growth hormone free." Organic formula is almost always more expensive than regular formulas, just like organic foods typically cost more. Whole Foods and other natural grocery stores carry organic formula as well as many regular grocery chains. Other options are available online. These are the brands we've found in our research:

Baby's Only Organic (for toddlers only; naturesone.com)
Earth's Best Infant Formula (earthsbest.com)
Kroger Private Selection Organic Formula
O Organic Formula (safeway.com)
Parents Choice (parentschoiceformula.com)
Similac Advance Organic (similac.com)

◆ *Gourmet formula.* Formula makers have been busy rolling out additional formula to accommodate a range of baby needs. For example, there is formula for babies with stomach viruses called Isomil DF, Nutramigen with Enflora LGG for colic due to milk allergy, Similac Sensitive for lactose insensitivity, Enfamil AR for babies with gastro esophageal reflux and more. We discuss these formulas in greater detail in our other book, *Baby 411* (see our web site for more information).

◆ *Packaging.* Concerns about Bisphenol-A (we've discussed this issue on our blog) have prompted formula makers to change their packaging in recent years. Newer plastic tubs and bottles are BPA-free. Other manufacturers like Nature's One have never lined their cans with BPA.

That's just a brief overview of formula—we have an in-depth discussion of formula in our *Baby 411* book. Co-written with a pediatrician, Dr. Ari Brown, the book extensively discusses breastfeeding, formula and feeding challenges for all infants. It's all in a fun-filled chapter called "Liquids." Check our web site (Baby411.com) for Dr. Brown's blog, which covers breaking news items on infant feeding.

Safe and Sound

Formula is one of the most closely regulated food items in the U.S. The Food and Drug Administration has strict guidelines about what can and cannot go into baby formula. The FDA requires expiration dates, warning labels and so on. So what are the safety hazards you might run up against? Here are a few:

1 **ASK YOUR DOC FIRST.** Never switch formula types or brands without discussing it with your pediatrician first. While our recommendation is to buy the cheapest cow's milk you can find, some babies have health problems that require special formula.

2 **CONFUSING CANS CONFRONT SOY FORMULA USERS.** Soy formula now accounts for 25% of the infant formula market. Yet, a case of mistaken identity has caused problems. Some parents mistakenly thought they were feeding their babies soy formula, when in fact they were using soymilk. The problem: soymilk is missing important nutrients and vitamins found in soy formula. As a result, babies fed soymilk were malnourished and some required hospitalization. Adding to the confusion, soymilk is often sold in cans that look very similar to soy formula. The government has asked soymilk makers to put warning labels on their products, so most should be labeled. If you use soy formula, be careful to choose the right can.

3 **IRON.** Another concern: low iron formula. A myth among some parents is that the iron in standard formula causes constipation—it does not, says pediatrician Dr. Ari Brown, co-author of Baby 411. Yes, constipation can be a problem with ALL formulas. But babies should NEVER be on low-iron formula unless instructed by a pediatrician.

4 **EXPIRED FORMULA.** While formula comes in sealed cans and tubs that look like they have an infinite shelf life, they do have expiration dates. And many of our readers have written to tell us that stores don't always remove expired formula from the shelves in a timely manner. That includes grocery stores, discounters and even warehouse clubs. So read the label carefully and check your own supply of formula before you open a tub or bottle. Also, watch out for formula sold on auction sites. Be sure to ask about expiration dates.

5 **DON'T BUY OFF BRAND FORMULA IN ETHNIC GROCERY STORES.** While the 2008 melamine scare mainly affected families in China, a few cans did make it into the U.S. through ethnic grocery stores. Federal law bans such black market imports, but that doesn't mean they don't happen. Stick to name brand formula bought in mainstream stores.

6 **DON'T FORGET THE BOTTLED WATER.** Factor in the cost of bottled water, as you'll need to mix your powdered or concentrated formula with special water. What kind? Purified, demineralize, deionized, distilled or reverse osmosis filtered water. The American Academy of Pediatrics and the American Dental Association recommend this to help avoid consuming too much fluoride which causes tooth discoloration. You can use tap water if it contains less than .3 ppm of fluoride or if you have a reverse osmosis filter. For everyone else, there will be an extra expense. Be sure to buy your water in bulk—gallon jugs are the most economical. A reasonable price per ounce will be about 1¢. For more details on fluoride and your baby, check out our other book, *Baby 411* (see back of this book for info).

Money Saving Tips

Here are our tips on saving money when purchasing baby formula:

1 **STAY AWAY FROM PRE-MIXED FORMULA.** Liquid concentrate formula and ready-to-drink formula are 50% to 200% more expensive than powdered formula. Yes, it is more convenient but you pay big time for that. We priced name brand, ready to drink formula at a whopping 22¢ to 60¢ per ounce. Guess what type of formula is given out as freebies in doctors' offices and hospitals? Yes, it's often the ready-to-drink liquid formula. These companies know babies get hooked on the particular texture of the expensive stuff, making it hard (if not impossible) to switch to the powdered formula later. Sneaky, eh? What's the most popular type of formula in the U.S.? Powder. Over 60% of the formula sold in the U.S. is powdered while liquid concentrate accounts for only 27% of formula sales.

2 **CONSIDER GENERIC FORMULA.** Most grocery stores and discounters sell "private" label formula at considerable savings, at least 30% to 40%. At one grocery store chain, their generic powdered formula worked out to just 7¢ per fluid ounce, a 50% savings. The largest maker of generic formula is Perrigo Nutritionals/PBM Products (known as Store Brand Formula; PBMProducts.com). This company makes generic formula under several different brand names including Bright Beginnings (BrightBeginnings.com), Member's Mark (sold at Sam's Club) and Parent's Choice (sold at Walmart). Generic formula has come a long way in recent years—now you can buy generic organic formula as well as several other special varieties. We should note that some pediatricians are concerned about recommending generic formula—doctors fret that such low-cost formula might discourage breastfeeding. On PBM's web site you'll find a link to coupons as well.

3 **BUY IT ONLINE.** Yep, you can buy formula online from eBay. You can save big but watch out—some unscrupulous sellers try to pawn off expired formula on unsuspecting buyers. Be sure to confirm the expiration date before buying formula online. And watch out for shipping charges—formula is heavy and shipping can outweigh any deal, depending on the price you pay.

4 **BUY IN BULK.** We found wholesale clubs had the best prices on name brand formula. For example, Costco (Costco.com) sells a 34 oz. can of Similac Advance for $31.99 (12¢ per oz. of mixed formula). That is 27% less than grocery stores. And generic formula at wholesale clubs is an even bigger bargain. Costco's Kirkland brand formula was $18.33 for a 36 oz can (7¢ per oz. of mixed formula). Don't forget to pick up bottled water to mix with formula at the wholesale club as well.

5 **ASK YOUR PEDIATRICIAN FOR FREE SAMPLES.** Just make sure you get the powdered formula (not the liquid concentrate or ready to pour). One reader in Arizona said she got several free cases from her doctor, who simply requested more from the formula makers.

6 **SHOP AROUND.** Yes, powdered formula at a grocery store can run $20 to $25 for a 25-ounce can (approximately)—but there's no federal law that says you must buy it at full retail. Readers of our book have noticed that formula prices vary widely, sometimes even at different locations of the same chain. In Chicago, a reader said they found one Toys R Us charged over a dollar less per can for the same ready-to-feed formula than another TRU across town. "They actually have a price check book at the registers with the codes for each store in the Chicagoland area," the reader said. "At our last visit, we saved $13.20 for two cases (about 30% of the cost), just by mentioning we wanted to pay the lower price."

Another reader noticed a similar price discrepancy at Walmart stores in Florida. When she priced Carnation Good Start powdered formula, she found one Walmart that marked it at $6.61 per can. Another Walmart (about 20 miles from the first location) sells the same can for $3.68! When the reader inquired about the price discrepancy, a customer service clerk admitted that each store independently sets the price for such items, based on nearby competition. That's a good lesson—many chains in more rural or poorer locations (with no nearby competition) often mark prices higher than suburban stores.

7 FORGET TODDLER FORMULA. When your child is ready for whole milk (usually at one year of age, according to most pediatricians), you can switch from formula (about 15¢ per ounce) to milk (about 4¢ per ounce). Yep, that is a savings of over 70%! No, you don't need toddler formula. What about the claim that toddler formulas have extra calcium, iron and vitamins? Nutritionists point out that toddlers should be getting most of their nutrition from solid foods, not formula. Toddlers should only be drinking about two cups a day of whole milk. Additional calcium can be found in foods as diverse as yogurt and broccoli; iron in red meat and spinach; vitamins in a wide variety of foods.

But what if you don't think your child is getting enough of those nutrients? Adding a vitamin and mineral supplement to your child's diet would still be less expensive than blowing your money on toddler formulas.

You may be wondering, in the day of increasing concern about obesity, why whole milk is recommended. Pediatricians tell us toddlers between 12 and 24 months of age need the fat in whole milk to foster brain development. At age two, you should switch to skim milk or 1%. For more on toddler development and nutrition, check out our Toddler 411 book (toddler411.com).

8 CHECK OUT AMAZON. Yep, Amazon sells formula (and even diapers) in their health and personal care store. Prices for formula were about 10% to 15% cheaper than full retail and if you order more than $25 (which is pretty easy), you may qualify for free shipping. Sign up for Amazon Mom—a free membership program that gives you free two-day shipping with Amazon Prime and 30% off items like diapers and wipes. You get additional months of free two-day shipping the more you buy from Amazon's baby store.

9 JOIN A FORMULA CLUB. Several formula makers have frequent buyer clubs. Example: Enfamil's Family Beginnings offers checks for purchasing formula, a free diaper bag, and more. It's free (sign up at Enfamil.com) but be prepared to fill out lots of forms asking for information on where you live, when your baby is due and your attitudes toward breast and formula feeding. Bonus savings idea: Sam's Club accepts Enfamil's checks, which lets you stretch those freebies even farther! And you can find lots of checks for sale on eBay.com at great prices.

Bottles/Nipples

What are you buying?

What's the best bottle for baby? Actually, it's more than just the bottle. The nipple (how the milk is delivered to baby) is just as important as the container.

When it comes to nipples, there are a myriad of choices. Your first decision will be the shape of the nipple. They come in orthodontic (bulb shaped), flat-topped or original (bell shaped). See graphics at right. Experts tell us that the bell shaped nipple seems to work best for breast fed babies who are either taking an occasional bottle or permanently transitioning from breast to bottle.

Orthodontic

Most nipples are made of latex or silicone. We recommend silicone. They last longer, don't have any flavor, are heat resistant and may resist bacteria better than latex. Latex can be allergenic as well.

Flat-topped

Finally, nipples have different flow levels. If you are starting immediately with bottle feeding, begin with a low flow nipple so your baby doesn't become overwhelmed with formula and gag. This is also a good idea for parents who are giving an occasional bottle to a breast fed baby—it forces your baby to work hard-

Bell shaped

er, more like when breastfeeding. As baby grows, you may need to buy a faster flow nipple.

What about the bottle itself? After the government issued a report in 2008 that questioned the safety of a chemical (Bisphenol-A or BPA) used in polycarbonate bottles, manufacturers began making BPA-free bottles. So, pretty much all the new bottles on the shelves today are BPA-free. (We've posted a Q&A about BPA on our web site BabyBargains.com, click on Bonus Material). Some parents prefer glass bottles since they have always been a safe, chemical free option.

Of course, there may be older baby bottles still on the back of some store shelves—a word to the wise: make sure the package says BPA-free before buying any bottle, breast pump or sippy cup. And if a friend offers you her old baby bottles, we say politely decline. You likely wouldn't be able to tell if they had BPA or not.

Smart Shopper Tips

Smart Shopper Tip #1
Bottle confusion?

"How many bottles will I need if I formula feed? What nipple sizes do I need? Do I need a bottle sterilizer?"

Yes, the questions about bottles and feeding baby can be rather endless! To help, on our web site, we've posted a great email from a mom who's been there, done that. This email actually appeared first as a thread on our message boards, but we thought it was the most comprehensive discussion of bottle-feeding we've ever seen. Since it is eight pages long, however, we didn't have room to reprint it here. Go to Babybargains.com/Bonus to read it.

Smart Shopper Tip #2
Getting started

"I think I'm going to bottle feed for at least some of the time, but I don't want to spend a fortune on bottles. What should I buy?"

Consider getting a starter kit from one or two of our top recommended bottle makers (see Our Picks below). Starter kits usually include a selection of bottle sizes, slow flow nipples and bottle caps. They may also have accessories like a bottle brush included. Prices range from $15 to $60 depending on brand and number of items included.

Our Picks: Brand Recommendations

Good. First Years offers an interesting option to parents looking for a good bottle to help with the transition between bottle and breast. Their **Breastflow** bottles have a unique double nipple that forces baby to use both suction and compression—just like at mother's breast. Price: about $5 per 5 oz. bottle. While feedback from parents is mostly positive, some thought the double nipple design was hard to clean and using them required practice.

Better. MAM bottles may be popular for their soft silicone nipples and attractive design, but we just love the way they clean. You can unscrew the bottom of the bottle as well as the top, making it so easy to really get the bottle clean. The bottles are also microwave safe and BPA free. MAM makes an anti-colic bottle and a regular bottle ($15 for a 3-pack of regular MAM bottles).

Best. Tied for first place in the bottle battle are *Avent* and *Dr. Brown's*. It's a real toss up as to which is best. Our readers seem to be split evenly. Avent gets a nod for its well-designed nipple, which is clinically proven to reduce colic (uncontrollable, extended crying that starts in some babies around one month of age). Ditto for Dr. Brown's Natural Flow bottle (handi-craft.com), which has a patented vent system that eliminates bubbles and nipple collapse. Avent and Dr. Brown's are pricey, however—they cost about $5 to $8 a bottle. That compares to $2 to $4 for other bottles from makers like Evenflo and Playtex.

Best Glass Bottle. Nobody beats *Evenflo's* glass bottles. They are very affordable, available in several sizes and quantities and the best choice for folks who don't want plastic. Prices range from $2 to $3.50 per bottle. The more expensive versions have elasticized plastic sleeve to help avoid breakage if dropped.

One quick note: in most cases, bottles and nipples aren't interchangeable. You can't use an Avent nipple on a Gerber bottle and so on. The exception: Dr. Brown's nipples DO fit on Evenflo's glass bottles (see above), report our readers—a bit of trimming on the vent tube is required.

Bottle Warmers & Sterilizers

Do you need to sterilize bottles every time you use them? Or boil water for formula? Or use bottled water?

The answers are no, no and yes.

There's no need to sterilize baby bottles every time you use them—yes, run them through the dishwasher when you first open the package. But you can clean bottles with warm, soapy water thereafter (or use the dishwasher again).

There's also no need to boil water for formula. That's because most tap water in the U.S. is treated and is safe to drink. However, the standard recommendation today is to use bottled water to mix with formula.

As for the temperature of a bottle of formula, room temperature is fine—bottles neither need to be heated nor cooled.

The take-home message: bottle warmers and sterilizers are purely optional. Since we realize some readers still want to purchase these items, here are our recommendations:

Avent seems to win the sterilizer war with their Express II Microwave

bottles

Pacifiers: Good or Bad?

Should your baby use a pacifier? Surprisingly, this is a controversial topic.

Some experts argue that early use of pacifiers may interfere with breastfeeding. But new studies show that pacifier use in children actually reduces the risk of Sudden Infant Death Syndrome (SIDS). It's unclear why pacifiers work, but studies clearly show a lowered risk of SIDS.

So, here are our recommendations for pacifier use: wait to give your child a pacifier until breastfeeding is well established (about a month of age). Discontinue pacifier use by six months of age. Why? Ninety percent of SIDS deaths occur between one month and six months of age.

So, now that you know what's good about a pacifier, which type of pacifier is best? There are two types—regular pacifiers have round nipples, while "orthodontic" pacifiers have flat nipples. Either is fine—but consult with your pediatrician if you have concerns on this topic. Our resident pediatrician, Dr. Ari Brown recommends "Soothies" (soothie-pacifiers.com) brand to her patients.

Steam Sterilizer. This model holds up to six Avent bottles or two Avent Breast Pumps and two bottles for $32. If you prefer a plug in sterilizer, the Digital Steam Sterilizer sterilizes six bottles in six minutes and keeps bottles sterile for up to 24 hours. Like the microwave version, it can also sterilize up to two breast pumps. Cost: about $75.

While Avent makes a good sterilizer, we would suggest getting the matching sterilizer for your bottle brand. For example, if you decide to use Born Free bottles, then the **Born Free sterilizer** ($45) is a good bet. Why? Sterilizers for one brand can sometimes damage other brand's bottles—for example, we did receive a report that **Medela's Quick Clean Micro-Steam** bags can melt Born Free bottles.

What about bottle warmers? Avent makes a good one: the Electric Bottle and Baby Food Warmer ($46), which warms a room temperature bottle in about four minutes. It fits baby food jars and all types of baby bottles (not just Avent).

New to the bottle warmer market is the **Kiinde Kozii Breast Milk & Bottle Warmer** ($70). This warmer accepts frozen breast milk storage bags, liner bottles, plastic bottles, glass bottles and even food containers—any type, any brand. Kiinde's SAFEHeat technology consists of a "circulating bath of warm water" to heat a bottle. Since the water is about room temperature, Kiinde claims to prevents hot spots and allays concerns that boiling water can cause chemicals like BPA to leach out of older bottles. A timer and automatic shutoff means it won't overheat and the water reservoir does not require parents to add water each time it's used.

The Kiinde is new to the market (it debuted in early 2012) and so far, feedback is positive. Most folks like the warmer, despite the price tag. A few dissenters note the Kiinde requires regular maintenance (you have to clean the water scale out periodically). And we heard one or two reports of the warmer breaking after just 8 or 10 weeks. We'd like to see the company step up its customer service on these issues—more than one parent who had a problem said the company wasn't helpful in solving the issue.

Baby Food

At the tender age of four to six months, you and your baby will depart on a magical journey to a new place filled with exciting adventures and never-before-seen wonders. Yes, you've entered the SOLID FOOD ZONE.

 ### Best Online Sources

Looking for a schedule of what foods to introduce when? Earth's Best's web site has a comprehensive chart with suggestions (earthsbest.com, click on Resource Center, then Doctor's Corner, then Guides and Tools). Gerber's slick web site (gerber.com) also has lots of information. Unfortunately, you'll have to sign up on the site to get to information like recommended feeding schedules. Consider using a special Gmail address to sign up for sites like this, to prevent your main email account from being spammed.

We also liked Beechnut's site (beechnut.com), which includes suggested menus and feeding tips. Although it is designed for Canadian parents, Heinz's baby food web site, heinzbaby.com contains extensive nutritional advice and menu planners among other information. Canadians can take advantage of rebate offers and other deals on this site (hopefully, they'll add the rest of North America to the coupon deals soon).

 ### Safe & Sound

1 **FEED FROM A BOWL, NOT FROM THE JAR.** Why? If you feed from a jar, bacteria from baby's mouth can find its way back to the jar, spoiling the food much more quickly. Also, saliva enzymes begin to break down the food's nutrients. The best strategy: pour the amount of baby food you need into a bowl and feed from there (unless it's the last serving from the jar). And be sure to refrigerate any unused portions.

2 **DON'T STORE FOOD IN PLASTIC BAGS.** If you leave plastic bags on the baby's high chair, they can be a suffocation hazard. A better solution: store leftover food in small, Tupperware-type containers.

3 **DO A TASTE TEST.** Make sure it isn't too hot, too cold, or spoiled. We know you aren't dying to taste the Creamed Ham Surprise from Gerber, but it is a necessary task.

Another tip: a dental hygienist wrote to remind us that parents should taste baby's food with a different spoon than the one baby will be using. Why? "The bacteria from your mouth can be transferred to the baby's mouth when you use the same spoon."

4 **CHECK FOR EXPIRATION DATES.** Gerber's jarred food looks like it would last through the next Ice Age, but check that expiration date. Most unopened baby food is only good for a year or two. Use opened jars within one to two days.

5 **AVOID UNPASTEURIZED MILK, MILK PRODUCTS AND JUICES.** Babies don't have the ability to fight off serious bacterium like e. coli. Avoid these hazards by feeding your child only pasteurized dairy and juice products.

Also steer clear of feeding honey to children less than one year of age. Botulism spores can be found in honey—while not harmful to adults and older kids, these spores can be fatal to infants.

6 **WHAT ABOUT INTRODUCING HIGH ALLERGENIC FOODS?** When can you introduce nuts like peanuts and tree nuts to your baby? The advice on this has changed over the years. Until 2008, the American Academy of Pediatrics (AAP) recommended waiting on introducing peanuts and other highly allergenic foods (like shellfish) until age 3 to prevent lifelong allergies. However, the latest studies indicate there is no benefit to waiting—and even the AAP now says there is no need to wait. Our advice: consult with your pediatrician on this one, especially if you have a family history of food allergies.

Smart Shopper Tips

Smart Shopper Tip #1
Tracking Down UFFOs (Unidentifiable Flying Food Objects)
"We fed our baby rice cereal for the first time. It was really cute, except when baby knocked the bowl to the floor . . . multiple times! Should we have bought some special stuff for this occasion?"

Well, unless you want your kitchen to be redecorated in Early Baby Food, we do have a few suggestions. First, a bowl with a bottom that suctions to the table is a great way to avoid flying saucers. Plastic spoons that have a round handle are nice, so baby can't stick the spoon handle in her eye (yes, that does happen—babies do try to feed themselves even at a young age). Spoons with rubber coatings are also recommended; they don't transfer the heat or cold of the food to the baby's mouth and are easier on the gums. One clever spoon is Munchkin's White Hot Safety Spoon (web: munchkin.com, four for $6). This spoon uses a special coating that changes color when baby's food is too hot (over 110°).

Smart Shopper Tip #2
Avoiding Mealtime Baths
"Our baby loves to drink from a cup, except for one small problem. Most of the liquid ends up on her, instead of in her. Any tips?"

Congratulations! You have a child who is ready to join the rest of the world and give up the bottle or breast. You may have mixed feelings about this, especially when you have to wash all those additional bibs, the floor and yourself more frequently. But this is a cool milestone. Babies are developmentally able to use a cup between ten and 16 months.

So what's the solution to the inevitable mess your baby will make when learning to drink from a cup? Most parents turn to sippy cups. But we don't recommend them. Why? Sippy cups aren't exactly beloved by doctors and dentists. Turns out babies use the same sucking action to get milk from a sippy cup as they do when sucking from a baby bottle. Hence they are not learning how to drink from a cup. Plus, sippy cups direct the flow of liquid straight at the back of baby's top front teeth—this promotes tooth decay.

Is there an answer to this dilemma? When being clean and pristine aren't that important (say when eating at home in the kitchen with lots of clean up gear handy) let your baby practice with a regular plastic cup. But also try to teach her to use a straw. That way, when you're out at a restaurant, she won't be taking a bath in public.

Money-Saving Tips

1 **MAKE YOUR OWN.** Let's be honest: baby foods like mashed bananas are really just . . . mashed bananas. You can easily whip up this stuff with that common kitchen helper, the food processor. Many parents skip baby food altogether and make their own. How much can you save? Mint.com estimates homemade

organic baby food runs 38 cents per serving, compared with 69 cents for store bought—a 44% percent savings. There's even bigger savings for non-organic baby food—it's 30 cents per saving cheaper for making it at home versus store bought. One tip: make up a big batch at one time and freeze the leftovers in ice cube trays. Check the library for cookbooks that provide tips on making baby food at home. A reader suggestion: "Top 100 Baby Purees" by Annabel Karmel ($17, Atria). This 128-page book is a best-selling guide to making your own baby food.

2 **FYI: TOYS R US AND BABIES R US SELL BABY FOOD.** If you think your grocery store is gouging you on the price of baby food, you might want to check out the prices at Babies R Us. We found Gerber 1st Foods in a two-pack of 3.5-ounce jars for $1.29— that works out to about 18¢ per ounce or about 15% less than grocery store prices. Toys R Us also sells four-packs of assorted dinners from Gerber's 2nd and 3rd Food collections.

3 **COUPONS! COUPONS! COUPONS!** Yes, we've seen quite a few cents-off and buy-one-get-one-free coupons on baby food and formula—not just in the Sunday paper but also through the mail. Our advice: don't toss that junk mail until you've made sure you're not trashing valuable baby food coupons. Another coupon trick: look for "bounce-back" coupons. Those are the coupons put in packages of baby food to encourage you to bounce back to the store and buy more.

4 **SKIP ORGANIC.** Organic baby food in a grocery store costs 23% more than conventional baby food. A 2012 report by the American Academy of Pediatrics states there is no nutritional difference between organic and conventional baby foods. "In the long term, there is currently no direct evidence that consuming an organic diet leads to improved health or lower risk of disease," AAP officials said in a statement.

5 **SUBSTITUTE COMPARABLE ADULT FOODS.** What's the difference between adult applesauce and baby applesauce? Not much, except for the fact that applesauce in a jar with a cute baby on it costs several times more than the adult version. (One caveat: make sure the regular applesauce is NOT loaded with extra sugar). Another rip-off: "next step" foods for older babies. Gerber loves to tout its special toddler meals in its "Graduates" line. What's the point? When baby is ready to eat pasta, just serve him small bites of the adult stuff. Bottom line: babies should learn to eat the same (hopefully healthy) foods you are eating, with the same spices and flavors. Toddler or graduate foods are a waste of time and money.

The Name Game: Reviews of Selected Manufacturers

Here's a round up of some of the best-known names in baby food. Unlike our brand name ratings for clothing or other baby products, food is a much trickier rating proposition. We rated the following brand names based on how healthy they are and how much they approximate real food (aroma, appearance, and, yes, taste). Our subjective opinions reflect our experience and those of our readers—always consult with your pediatrician or family doctor if you have any questions about feeding your baby. (Special thanks to Ben and Jack for their help in researching this topic.)

The Ratings

  A **EXCELLENT**—our top pick!
  B **GOOD**— above average quality, prices, and creativity.
  C **FAIR**—could stand some improvement.
  D **POOR**—yuck! could stand some major improvement.

Beech-Nut beechnut.com. Beech-Nut was one of the first baby food companies to eliminate fillers (starches, sugar, salt) or artificial colors/flavors in its 120 flavors. While Beech-Nut is not organic, the company claims to be made of "all-natural ingredients." Our readers generally give Beech-Nut good marks (some like it better than Gerber). Beechnut is affordable: we've seen it on sale for as little as 13¢ per oz. New this year: toddler snack pouches. These are similar to the pouches organic baby food producers like Ella's Kitchen are using.

The only bummer about Beech-Nut baby food: it can be hard to find (not every state has stores that carry it). You can use their "where to buy" function to find a store that carries it. ***Rating: B+***

Bella Baby Foods Bella Baby Food is one of a few baby food manufacturers who doesn't "can" their foods; they freeze their organic (and Kosher) ingredients. The company (named after the founders' daughter Bella) offers typical flavors like apple as well as some fun ones like mango, pumpkin and even spinach. They don't offer combinations, but encourage parents to mix and match on their own for greater flexibility. You can order directly from their site with a minimum of six packages for a flat price of $7.33 per item (includes shipping). Each package includes ten 1.5 oz. packets. That works out to 77¢ per ounce making it more affordable than other frozen food options but still twice the cost of Earth's Best. Parents report that the taste is impressive. ***Rating: A***

Earth's Best *earthsbest.com.* Earth's Best started the organic baby food trend 25 years ago in (where else?) Vermont. Since those early beginnings Earth's Best has gone through several owners before landing in the lap of natural foods conglomerate Hain Celestial (parent of Celestial Seasonings Tea). Despite all the changes in ownership, Earth's Best has maintained its focus, with one of the largest lines of "natural" baby foods on the market—all vegetables and grains are certified organically grown (no pesticides are used), and meats are raised without antibiotics or steroids. Another advantage: Earth's Best never adds any salt, sugar or modified starches to its food. And the foods are only made from whole grains, fruits and vegetables (instead of concentrates). Yes, Earth's Best is more expensive (32¢ per oz.; or 15% more than conventional baby food) but as we pointed out earlier, that's works out to only about $90 more per

---

E-Mail from The Real World
Making your own baby food isn't time consuming

A mom in New Mexico told us she found making her own baby food isn't as difficult as it sounds:

"My husband and I watch what we eat, so we definitely watch what our baby eats. One of the things I do is buy organic carrots, quick boil them, throw them in a blender and then freeze them in an ice cube tray. Once they are frozen, I separate the cubes into freezer baggies (they would get freezer burn if left in the ice tray). When mealtime arrives, I just throw them in the microwave. Organic carrots taste great! This whole process might sound complicated, but it only takes me about 20 minutes to do, and then another five to ten minutes to put the cubes in baggies."

year and ready to print coupons are easy to find on their web site.

Reader feedback on Earth's Best has been positive—fans like the extensive choice and commitment to organic principals. All in all, Earth's Best is a much-needed natural alternative to the standard fare that babies have been fed for far too many years. *Rating: A*

Ella's Kitchen Organics When Ella's Kitchen first debuted, their initial products were designed for older kids. The brand still offers smoothies for older kids but has since added three stages of baby foods and snacks. All their foods include just organic fruits, vegetables or grains and a bit of lemon juice to keep them from spoiling. That's it! At 54¢ per oz., Ella's is pricey. And there have been consumer complaints that accuse the company of incorrectly labeling nutritional content, overstating iron content, for example. Ella's acknowledged these errors and told us they since corrected the packaging—but this leaves a sour taste in our mouth for this brand. *Rating: C*

Gerber gerber.com. Dominating the baby food business with a whopping 83% market share (that's right, three out of every four baby food containers sold sport that familiar label), Gerber sure has come a long way from its humble beginnings. Back in 1907, Joseph Gerber (whose trade was canning) mashed up peas for his daughter, following the suggestion of a family doctor. Today Gerber sells over $2.4 billion in baby food a year.

Over the years, Gerber has tried to expand beyond jarred baby food. It launched microwavable toddler meals in 2002 and has licensed its name out for a variety of baby products, including cups, infant toys and even baby skincare items. Yet controversy has constantly dogged Gerber—in the 90's, consumer pressure forced the company to stop adding sugar and starch to its baby foods. The Federal Trade Commission has accused the company of deceptive advertising when it claimed a survey showed that four out of five pediatricians recommended the brand (the actual number was 16%).

On the upside, Gerber offers parents two key advantages: choice and availability. The line boasts an amazing 200 different flavors. And Gerber is sold in just about every grocery store on Earth at around 25¢ per oz. We have to give Gerber credit: bowing to consumer interest in all things organic, they rolled out "Gerber Organic" to compete with Earth's Best. The new line is made with "whole grains and certified organic fruits and vegetables" and costs around 30¢ per oz. (note that Gerber's regular line still uses some fruit and vegetable concentrates). They now make the organic line in squeeze pouches similar to other brands. Finally, we noticed that Gerber is now packing its first foods in plastic rather than glass. While we like the changes Gerber has made, we still have problems with the brand: we think

baby food

their "Graduates" line of "toddler" foods is a waste of money. And their juice line is overpriced compared to others on the market. Quality-wise, we will give Gerber an average rating. ***Rating: C***

HappyBaby *happyfamilybrands.com* How do you differentiate yourself from the competition in the baby food market? After all, even Gerber has an organic line of baby food now. Happy Baby's mojo is food with prebiotics and probiotics, vegan DHA, and Choline. They also use Salba, a "super grain" along with amaranth, quinoa, man-gosteen and yumberry. Wow, sounds like a Whole Foods grocery store in a BPA-free pouch. If you want to know more about Salba, check the FAQ on HappyBaby's web site.

If you have an allergy prone child, you'll like the fact that HappyBaby foods are processed in a nut-free facility with no soy (only some refined soybean oil–no protein allergens), no gluten and no dairy products. If you don't like the non-recyclable pouches, HappyBaby also makes a frozen line of food. Pouches run a reason-able 32¢; frozen foods aren't available online. Overall, reader feed-back has been quite positive on this brand. ***Rating: A***

Healthy Times *healthytimes.com.* Healthy Times got its start selling one of the first health-food baby products back in 1980: a teething biscuit. Since then, the company has expanded their baby food offer-ings to include 22 jarred baby foods, baby cereal, snacks and toiletry items. The baby food line is certified organic and contains no soy, flour or other fillers. You'll find single fruits and vegetables (stage 1), fruit and veggie blends (stage 2) and dinners (combos of several veggies, and meat and veggies). You can buy Healthy Times online on the compa-ny's web site for 25¢ per oz. jar for stage one foods. We also saw Healthy Times foods on Amazon.com. ***Rating: A-***

Plum Organics *plumorganics.com* Plum Organics was one of the first baby foods packaged in those cute little re-sealable pouches. Plums' JUST fruits are made without any additives . . . just fruit. Second Blends include yummy sounding combinations like blueberry, pear and purple carrot (expect some heavy duty staining on your bibs with this one!). Parents seem to like the single fruit and Second Blends best; the training meals (Stage 3) were less popular. We saw Plum priced between 40¢ and 50¢ per ounce online and in stores. ***Rating: A-***

Yummy Spoonfuls *yummyspoonfuls.com* Like almost every baby food story, Yummy Spoonfuls has a committed mom behind the creation of its organic baby food line. Founder Agatha Achindu was inspired by her love of cooking and her disgust at jarred baby foods. As she notes on her web site: "none of the (commercially jarred baby) foods was recognizable; peas were brownish green, and carrots were dull brown." Flash freezing baby food helps it keep the color and flavor of the ingredients. All the ingredients used in Yummy Spoonfuls are certified by the USDA to be grown organically. Flavors include carrots, broccoli, butternut squash, apples, green beans, pears and peas as well as variety packs.

The brand offers three stages of baby food: Creamy, Mushy and Chunky Yummy. Parent feedback on this brand has been quite positive. The biggest gripe with this brand: price. At 94¢ per oz., these foods are three times as expensive as Earth's Best! ***Rating: A-***

High Chairs

As soon as Junior starts to eat solid food, you'll need this quintessential piece of baby furniture—the high chair. Surprisingly, this seemingly innocuous product generates over 11,300 injuries each year. So, what are the safest high chairs? And how do you use them properly? We'll share these insights, as well as some money-saving tips and brand reviews in this section.

Safe and Sound

1 **STRAP ME IN.** *Most high chair injuries occur when babies are not strapped into their chairs.* Sadly, one to two deaths occur each year when babies "submarine" under the tray. To address these types of accidents, new high chairs now feature a "passive restraint" (a plastic post) under the tray to prevent this. Note: some high chair makers attach this submarine protection to the tray; others have it on the seat. We prefer the seat. Why? If it is on the tray and the tray is removed, there is a risk a child might be able to squirm out of the safety belts (which is all that would hold them in the chair). As a side note, some wooden high chairs only seem to have a crotch strap— no plastic post. Again, not much is keeping baby safely in the chair.

FYI: Even if the high chair has a passive restraint, you STILL must strap in baby with the safety harness with EACH use. This prevents them from climbing out or otherwise hurting themselves.

2 **THE SAFETY STANDARDS FOR HIGH CHAIRS ARE VOLUNTARY.** Unlike the mandatory safety rules for cribs or car seats, high chair makers only have a series of voluntary standards. This will change shortly, when the government issues mandatory safety standards for high chairs as part of the 2008 Consumer Product Safety Improvement Act. But . . . as of press time, high chair safety standards are purely voluntary.

3 **INSPECT THE SEAT PAD.** Make sure it won't tear or puncture easily.

4 **LOOK FOR STABILITY.** It's basic physics: the wider the base, the more stable the chair. Another tip: never put the high chair near a wall—babies have been injured in the past when they pushed off a wall or object, tipping over the chair. This problem is rare with the newest high chairs (as they have wide, stable bases), but you still can tip over older, hand-me-down models.

5 **CAREFULLY INSPECT THE RESTRAINING SYSTEM.** We prefer a five-point harness (straps that go over the baby's shoulders and around the waist); some high chairs only have three-point harnesses (just a waist belt).

6 **DOES THE SEAT RECLINE?** Many high chairs have a reclining seat function that makes it easier to feed a young infant. The problem? Feeding a baby solid foods in a reclining position is a choking hazard. If you want to use the reclining feature, it should be exclusively for bottle-feeding. We do think the recline feature is a plus for another reason, however: it is easier to move baby in and out of the high chair when it is reclined. And when babies start out with solid foods, they may go back and forth between the bottle and solid food during meals. Hence, the recline feature is helpful when they need to take a bottle break.

More Money Buys You

Whether you spend $30 or $500, most high chairs do one simple thing—provide you with a place to safely ensconce your baby while he eats. The more money you spend, however, the more comforts there are for both you and baby. As you go up in price, you find chairs with various height positions, reclining seats, larger trays, more padding, casters for mobility and more. From a safety point of view, some of the more expensive high chairs feature five-point restraint harnesses (instead of just a waist belt). As for usability, some high chairs are easier to clean than others, but that doesn't necessary correspond to price. Look for removable vinyl seat covers that are machine-washable (cloth covers are harder to clean). And watch out for crevices in seats, pads and trays—these are food magnets. Models with seamless trays, seats and pads may cost more but will be easier to keep clean.

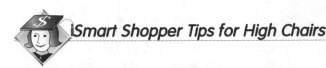

Smart Shopper Tips for High Chairs

Smart Shopper Tip #1
High Chair Basics 101

"What's the difference between a $50 high chair and one that's $400? And does it matter what color you got? I like white best."

The high chair market is basically divided into four camps:

♦ **Low-end chairs** sold in discount stores aimed at Grandma. These cost around $50 and are bare bones, without many features.

♦ **Multi-function chairs.** These range from $100 to $250 and feature seat recline, adjustable height positions, footrests and upgraded pads. The more expensive models have toys, designer fabrics and other upgrades.

♦ **Modern high chairs.** Pricey at $300 to $450, these chairs are sold mostly on aesthetics—their ultra-modern looks appeal to parents who want to make a style statement.

♦ **Wood high chairs.** Either all wood or a hybrid of wood and plastic (wood base, plastic tray), these high chairs run $150 to $200. Wood high chairs appeal to traditionalists who are turned off by the plastic-y look of most high chairs. The trade-off is a lack of features or adjustments.

As you can see, high chairs are often sold more on aesthetics than function—and that's a classic first-time parent mistake. A pretty high chair that is impossible to clean is a big headache. And while we understand that a high chair that sits in middle of your kitchen shouldn't be an eyesore, consider these practical features before falling in love with a high chair:

♦ **Tray release.** The best high chairs have a one-hand tray release that enables you to easily remove the tray with a quick motion. Of course, some are easier to use than others. Our advice: take a second in the store and remove the tray a few times from sample models. You'll note some trays are sticky; other "one-hand" tray releases really require two hands.

♦ **Dishwasher-safe trays—NOT!** Most high chairs today come with a dishwasher-safe tray insert. This cover snaps off the main tray and pops in the dishwasher for clean-up . . . or does it? In the reviews in this section, we'll note some models whose dishwasher-safe trays are too big to fit in an actual dishwasher. A word of advice: measure the bottom rack of your dishwasher and take that dimension with you when high chair shopping.

♦ **Tray height.** Some parents complain the tray height of certain high chairs is too high—making it hard for smaller babies to use.

A smart tip: take your baby with you when you go high chair shopping and actually sit them in the different options. You can evaluate the tray heights in person to make sure the chair will work for both you and baby. We'll note which chairs have the best/worst tray heights later in our reviews. Generally, a chair with a tray height of less than 8" should work for most babies. A few models have tray heights over 8"—those can be a major problem since a child can't reach the food on the tray. Why is this important? Some day (we know it seems light years away), your baby will feed himself . . . and being able to see and reach the food is important!

◆ **Seat depth.** Most chairs have multiple tray positions and reclining seats. But what is the distance between the seat back when it is upright and the tray in its closest position? A distance of 5" to 7" is acceptable. Over 7" and you run the risk that there will be a large gap between your baby and the tray—and all their food will end up in their lap. Again, take your baby with you when shopping for a chair, as smaller babies may be harder to fit.

◆ **Cleanability.** Here's an obvious tip some first-time parents seem to miss: make sure the high chair you buy has a removable, washable seat cover OR a seat that easily sponges clean. In the latter category, chairs with VINYL trump those made of cloth—vinyl can be wiped clean, while cloth typically has to be washed. This might be one of those first-time parent traps—seats with cloth covers sure look nicer than those made of vinyl. But the extra effort to machine wash a cloth cover is a pain . . and some cloth covers can't be thrown in the dryer! That means waiting a day or more for a cover to line dry.

Watch out for seat pads that have ruffles or numerous crevices—these are food magnets and a bear to keep clean.

What color cover should you get? Answer: anything but white. Sure, that fancy white "leatherette" high chair looks all shiny and new at the baby store, but it will forever be a cleaning nightmare once you start using it. Darker colors and patterns are better.

Of course, keeping a chair clean involves more than just the pad—look at the seat and tray itself. Avoid models with numerous crevices and cracks. Seamless seats and trays are best.

FYI: Many high chair trays claim they are dishwasher safe. But some have cracks that let water collect inside the tray—this can be a mold hazard, as it is hard to get the tray to dry properly. We will note these models in our reviews later in this section.

Smart Shopper Tip #2
Tray Chic and Other Restaurant Tips

"We have a great high chair at home, but we're always appalled at the lack of safe high chairs at restaurants. Our favorite cafe has a high chair that must date back to 1952—no straps, a

metal tray with sharp edges, and a hard seat with no cushion. Have restaurateurs lost their minds?

Some folks who run restaurants must search obscure foreign countries to find the world's most hazardous high chairs. The biggest problem? No straps, enabling babies to slide out of the chair, submarine-style. The solution? When the baby is young, keep her in her infant car seat; the safe harness keeps baby secure. When your baby is older (and if you eat out a lot), you may want to invest in a portable booster seat. We'll discuss and recommend hook on chairs and booster seats later in this chapter.

If you decide to use the restaurant high chair, you may want to do a quick clean with baby wipes just to make sure. Nothing grosser than a dirty restaurant high chair. In fact, there are some grocery cart covers (reviewed in the stroller section) can also be used in restaurant high chairs.

The Name Game: Reviews of High Chair Makers

Here's a round up of the best high chairs on the market today:

The Ratings

A EXCELLENT—*our top pick!*
B GOOD— *above average quality, prices, and creativity.*
C FAIR—*could stand some improvement*
D POOR—*yuck! could stand some major improvement.*

Baby Bjorn babybjorn.com Best known for its iconic baby carrier, Baby Bjorn has been slowly expanding into other categories in recent years. First there was the Bjorn potty, then a bouncer, and a playpen last year. And given their recent debut of kitchen ware (bowls, spoons, bibs), it's not too

surprising to see Bjorn debut its first high chair, cleverly dubbed the Baby Bjorn High Chair.

The Bjorn high chair has all the Swedish minimalist design you'd expect from a Bjorn—the white/black color motif, seamless seat design and so on. It is also available in red and black. Of course, Bjorn hasn't forgotten about safety: the high chair features a "Smart Safety Lock," which is a two-stage lock that Bjorn says "ensures that children cannot open or close the safety table on their own." This is probably the Bjorn's most unique feature: the tray pivots down to enable a parent to put a child in or out of the chair. That differs from other high chairs, where the entire tray is removable—or the tray slides forward to let you move a child in or out.

So what's not to love? Well, first of all, the price: at $300 (we've seen it as low as $220), the chair is seriously overpriced. At this lofty price point, the Bjorn high chair is competing against both modern high chairs such as the Bloom Fresco and Boon Flair (both beat the Bjorn on style) and multi-function models like the Perego Tatamia, which transforms into a baby swing and recliner. The Bjorn doesn't transform into anything. And considering Bjorn's emphasis on safety, we were disappointed to see the chair lacks a five-point harness (instead it has a three-point harness).

Real world feedback on the Bjorn high chair has been positive overall. Parents like the seamless design (easy to clean) and easy assembly. The compact fold (a mere 10" wide when folded) also is a plus. But the small size of the seat had more than one parent grumbling that, despite Bjorn's claim the chair will work up to three years of age, it is too small for bigger toddlers. The chair is light weight and the footprint is small making it easy to move around the kitchen. Finally, parents praise the tray mechanism saying their clever toddlers haven't been able to figure out how to get out of the seat.

A few negatives: while the tray has a three-position adjustment (to allow more room for growing babies), there is no height adjustment for the chair. While we understand that Bjorn's intention is to have the high chair fit most kitchen tables, this seems like a major oversight. Ditto for the lack of casters to make the chair more mobile. Finally, we should note the seat doesn't recline—as a result, you won't be able to use this chair with newborns who don't have any head control. Add in the lack of a five-point harness and we are left scratching our heads at how this chair ever got out of Bjorn's R&D lab.

Bottom line: this is a pricey but good high chair if (and only if) you have a small baby. ***Rating: B+***

Baby Trend *babytrend.com* Baby Trend's high chair was one of our top picks in a previous edition of this book, but our rating of this chair continues to drift down as complaints from readers stack up. Yes, it is a credible knock-off of the Perego and Chicco chairs, yet sells for 40% less ($80 to $100 in most stores). You get all the standard features you'd expect: five-point harness, three-position reclining seat, three-position tray with one hand release, six height positions, compact fold and casters. Some models have a separate dishwasher-safe tray. And, yes, the Baby Trend high chair is generally easier to use than competitors (it requires little assembly and the seat recline is easy to adjust, for example).

Baby Trend sells a $60 version of their high chair at Walmart and a $70 to $100 version elsewhere. The more expensive model has a fully reclining seat and is fully assembled (the cheaper one has a partial seat recline and requires assembly). All in all, Baby Trend churns out 24 different versions of the Trend, most of which are just variations in fashion.

In the past year, Baby Trend has rolled out versions of this high chair with new names (Mylift, Tempo, Trend2). It is unclear how these chairs are different from Baby Trend's main high chair offering—they pretty much look the same to us.

Given Baby Trend high chairs' numerous features, why all the complaints? The pad is this chair's Achilles' heel. We've received several reports that the cloth pad (which has a reversible vinyl side) fell apart or bunched up after machine washing. Even Baby Trend, in an email to us, admitted the pad "responds best to hand washing." Gee, that's nice—too bad the instructions for the chair say to machine wash the pad on the gentle cycle . . . with no mention of hand washing. Add that to the fact the pad has to be line dried and you have a deal-breaker here.

Another major complaint centers on the tray height, which is way too high for average-size babies. And finally, the crotch bar is attached to the tray making it frustrating to set down and removing any safety advantage. Of course, not all the reviews are negative: some parents have had success with this high chair. And we give Baby Trend bonus points for improving the chair over the years. But Baby Trend's customer service stumbles and the pad washing issue have convinced us that this chair isn't worthy of a recommendation. **Rating: C+**

Bloom *BloomBaby.com* Bloom's Fresco high chair is the latest entrant in the space-age, Jetsons-style high chair category. Its egg-shaped, seamless seat and circular base echo the Boon Flair with one big exception: the Bloom Fresco can recline, making it suitable for infants. The Fresco comes with microsuede seat upholstery (14 colors) and pneumatic-assist height adjustment. But the price? $450 is too high, in our opinion.

In the past year, Bloom debuted a chrome version of the Fresco, dubbed the Fresco Chrome. Same chair, chrome base and seat. Price: $450-$550. In case you don't like shiny silver, the Fresco Chrome also comes in black, white and a grey color called Mercury.

Feedback on the Bloom Fresco has been mixed. For every fan who loves the chair's Jetsons' look and function, others say it just isn't worth the money (the chair is very heavy, making it hard to move; assembly is a challenge; the color fades after a year or two, etc). Quality is a major complaint area: one reader said the chair's lift feature worked well for a week . . . and then broke. The Bloom Fresco is also so hard to clean, some parents have just given up and junked the chair.

Bloom has a second high chair model: the Nano, which is tagged as an "iconic minimalist" model with a flat fold and "micro leather" seat in six colors. Price: $180—that's about three times the price of other simple high chairs that don't recline, lack wheels and fold up flat. In the past year, Bloom modified the Nano so it has a smaller footprint.

Feedback on the Nano is similar to the Fresco: for every parent who likes the Nano, we found another who knocked its difficulty to clean and fold.

As a result of the mixed feedback on this brand, we've decided to lower Bloom's rating this time. Prices are too high and the quality is too low. Yes, these chairs are cool to look at, but that's about it. *Rating: D*

Boon booninc.com Boon's Flair high chair debuted in 2007, part of the modernist wave sweeping the baby products biz at the time.

At least this chair features something unique: a pneumatic lift, which gives the chair "effortless height adjustment." Basically, a button on the base will automatically lower the chair.

We do like the seamless seat, which is easier to clean than other high chairs (where food finds its way into every last crack and crevice). The pad and harness remove for cleaning and a dishwasher-safe tray within a tray is easy to use. The Flair retails for $200 to $250. (We can't help but wonder if the folks at Boon were watching a DVD of Office Space when they named this chair).

There haven't been many changes to the Flair in the past year, except for a few new colors—currently the chair comes in white with an orange pad or grey with a green pad.

One negative for the Flair: the seat doesn't recline, making this chair inappropriate for smaller infants who are bottle-feeding. A reclining seat is a standard feature on almost all high chairs, so we wonder why Boon left this out.

Reader feedback on the Flair is mostly positive: fans love how easy it is to clean and the small footprint. Their only complaint: the straps should tighten a bit more for smaller babies. And the lack of a chest buckle means the harness can slide off the shoulders of some kids. While most folks say the Boon Flair is easy to clean, a few dissenters say there are parts of the chair that can be trouble-some—the underside of the tray and the harness buckle (which can't be removed) are two magnets for grime.

Overall, however, most folks love this chair, whose sleek look is the big draw. *Rating: A*

Chicco chiccousa.com Chicco's Polly high chair is the successor to the Mamma, a high chair we only gave a C in a previous edition of this book. So is the Polly an improvement? Yes, but only slightly.

Retailing for $130 to $150, the Polly features an adjustable footrest, compact fold, three-position seat recline, seven height positions and removable dishwasher-safe tray. You also get two pads—one can be on the chair while the other is being cleaned. An SE model of the Polly is identical to the regular version, just different fabric patterns. FYI: The Polly has either cloth or vinyl seat pads, usually noted online.

Fans of the Chicco Polly like the tray, which can be removed with one-hand and hung off pegs on the back of the frame. The compact fold is nice, but the chair doesn't stand well by itself. Readers who like the Polly love the stylish look—it comes in one of 12 snazzy color combinations.

As for negatives, the Polly's pad is not machine-washable, which is a bummer. You can only spot clean it. Cleanability is a major negative to the Polly: the chair and tray have numerous seams, cracks and crevices that are food magnets. Also: the submarine protection is attached to the tray and not the seat, as we prefer for safety reasons. To top it off, the harness can be difficult to adjust.

FYI: a few older Polly's still have cloth pads—we'd avoid these and stick with the newer, vinyl seat versions (much easier to clean).

There is also an upgraded version of the Polly available, dubbed the Polly Magic. It is similar to the regular Polly, but adds an upgraded leatherette pad, toys and a storage basket. The frame is slightly different and includes a "CradleRecline" seat and infant pad. Where's the magic? That's the price, which magically rises to $160. As of this writing, the Polly Magic is a Babies R Us exclusive. Parent feedback on the Polly Magic has been divided, with quite a few critics knocking the cleanability.

So it's a mixed review for the Chicco Polly: fans like the stylish design and easy fold—and when the chair is discounted like it is on Walmart for $116, it is a good deal. But the negative reviews outweigh the positives in our research, so the Chicco Polly only earns an average rating. There are better options out there than this. **Rating: C+**

Combi combi-intl.com Best known for its strollers, Combi has been trying to crack the high chair category but its efforts have met with little success.

Giving the category another try, Combi rolled out a new high chair in 2013, cleverly called the Combi High Chair. This $125 chair has all the usual features you'd expect: five-position height adjustment, three-position seat recline, removable dishwasher tray insert, etc. Unlike other chairs on the market, the fabric pad covers the entire chair, which theoretically should make it easier to keep clean. One negative: the tray has to be removed to fold the chair.

This chair was new as of this writing, so no parent feedback yet. When we previewed the chair at a trade show, we were a bit underwhelmed. While the feature set is on par with other high chairs offering, the plain jane looks of this chair will probably turn off some folks. It feels like Combi phoned in the fashion on this product—and since a high chair sits in the middle of the kitchen, that could be a handicap. ***Rating: Not Yet.***

Cosco *djgusa.com* Like most things Cosco makes, their high chairs define the entry-level price point in this market. The Cosco Flat Fold high chair (pictured) is a bare bones model for $31 at Walmart. This would do the trick for grandma's house—this simple chair has a three-position seat recline plus, as the name implies, a flat fold for storage. Nothing too fancy to look at, but how many bells and whistles does Grandma need?

While these high chairs are fine for occasional use at Grandma's house, we aren't keen on these offerings as a primary high chair. Why? A lack of safety features (example: three-point harnesses instead of a five-point) make these chairs better for occasional use. And the pad doesn't remove from the chair, making it harder to clean after repeated use.

Oddly, the seat in this chair doesn't sit up right, so baby is always reclined—hence this may not be a good choice until your baby can sit up unassisted. We saw more than one complaint about the seat angle. Again, all these negatives would be negated if you only used it occasionally at Grandma's house; but not as a primary high-chair. ***Rating: C+***

Eddie Bauer *djgusa.com* Cosco/Eddie Bauer offers a mash-up here: a hybrid wood chair with plastic tray. Yep, in the category of "everything old is new again," the Eddie Bauer Classic high chair ($130-$150; this chair is also called the Newport) combines the look of wood with the convenience of plastic.

So, what are the trade-offs? Well, you can forget about many of the features you'll find in plastic chairs—Eddie Bauer's chair lacks wheels, height adjustments, seat recline and more.

Reader feedback on this chair has turned sharply negative over the past year. When it first debuted, the Eddie Bauer wood high chair had a full pad that covered the entire seat; subsequently, the pad design changed to a smaller size, showing more wood. We speculated in the last edition this would make it harder to clean

(more food would get on the wood) and we were right—the negative reviews shot up after the design change.

"It's pretty out of the box, but impossible to keep that way," said
one reader, who summed up the frustrations of many parents. Food
sticks to the dark wood finish, the slats on the side of the seat, just
about anywhere—and it is impossible to clean. The finish also comes
off, say others, indicating Cosco cut some corners here. Most wor-
risome are recent quality complaints that include screws that fall out;
miss-aligned screw holes, and other woes.

FYI: Babies R Us has an exclusive version of this chair, sold under
the name Safety 1st Decor Wood high chair. It is basically the same
as the Eddie Bauer model, but with a less fancy base. Price: $96.

Bottom line: the Eddie Bauer wood high chair is not recommended. ***Rating: F***

Evenflo *evenflo.com* Evenflo has always been an
also-ran in the high chair market, thanks to quality
woes and designs that lack pizzazz.

Evenflo seems to be trying to address its so-so
high chair offerings with the new Modern 200
chair. With a machine washable seat pad, dish-
washer safe tray insert, 5-point harness, three-position recline, six
height adjustments, four position tray and one-hand tray release,
the Modern 200 is trying to compete against the full feature Peg
Perego and Chicco chairs. At a mere $90, however, the price is
substantially less than those premium high chairs.

What do parents think? Most reviews have been good. Readers
like the cleanability, the t-bar attached to the seat not the tray, and
the fold. And the price is a definite plus. Dissenters note the lack of
wheels on the back of the chair make it hard to move (why Evenflo
didn't go with wheels on all four legs is a mystery). And others
noted little details can be frustrating, such as the lack of a locking
mechanism when the chair is folded.

FYI: Target has a version of the Modern high chair called the
ModTot for $100. It is basically the same as the Modern 200.

The Evenflo Convertible high chair is another recent effort by the
company to innovate in this category. As the name suggests, this
simple chair converts from high chair to table and chair for about
$45 to $50. No bells and whistles here: just a removable tray and
five point harness. FYI: This chair is also called the Mini-Meal.

In the entry price point level, Evenflo offers the Compact Fold
high chair. As you might guess from the name, it's main feature is
the compact fold. This chair gets good reviews from parents, but
there is one major flaw: the chair pad can't be removed for cleaning. Hence, you can only spot clean the pad with a sponge. While
most folks seem happy enough with this chair even without that

limitation, we'd only recommend the Compact Fold for occasional use at Grandma's house because of the cleaning issues.

Overall, Evenflo has had a bumpy track record in the high chair category. The low point came in 2008 when the company recalled nearly 100,000 high chairs because "plastic caps and metal screws can loosen and fall out, posing both a fall and choking hazards to children," reported the CPSC.

That said, the company's more recent offerings have earned better parent reviews as quality has improved. So we will tick up Evenflo's rating this time around. Evenflo's high chairs aren't among our top picks in this category, but the company is closing the gap. *Rating: B-*

Fisher-Price *fisher-price.com* Folks, we have a winner! Fisher-Price has hit a home run with its well-designed line-up of high chairs, including the best-sellers, Healthy Care and Space Saver.

In fact, Fisher Price now has six high chair models: the Healthy Care, Space Saver, Zen Collection, EZ Clean, Home & Away and Grow with Me. Here's an overview:

The Healthy Care high chair features a three-position seat recline, five-point restraint, one-hand tray removal, dishwasher-safe tray liner, and various height adjustments. FYI: The Healthy Care comes in three versions: a basic model (Healthy Care) that starts at $100 in Walmart and then fancier versions (dubbed Ocean Wonders, Adorable Animals or Precious Planet Sky Blue, pictured) for $110 to $130. Basically, these are the same high chair, but the more expensive versions include a fancier pad and more toys.

Parents universally praise the Healthy Care for its ease of use and cleanability (yep, those harness straps and toys can be thrown into the dishwasher). The major negative to this chair is the fashion—that cutesy color scheme turns some folks off. We know, you are putting it in the middle of your kitchen, so the fashion can be an issue.

Other negatives? Some complain the chair tends to collect food in crevices of the seat pad. And the Healthy Care requires quite a bit of assembly. The Healthy Care hasn't changed much in recent years either. Despite that, this is a best bet in the high chair market and we give the Healthy Care our highest rating.

The second best-selling Fisher Price high chair is the Space Saver ($50 to $60), the first high chair that sits on a dining chair (sort of a souped-up booster). This model features a full-size tray and three-position recline—plus it converts to a toddler booster. If you are short of space (think New York City apartment), this is a great choice. Detractors point out that once you strap this thing to a chair, you can't push the chair under the table—hence defeating the space saving concept. We see that point, but still think this is a great solution for urban condos with little space to store a bulky high chair. Reader feedback on the Space Saver is very positive—we recommend it.

Fisher Price's first wood hybrid chair, the Zen, is an attempt to address the complaints that the fashion for the Healthy Care is too baby-ish. This $120 to $150 high chair features a plastic seat with three-position recline, a tray with dishwasher-safe insert and three-position height adjustment. The Zen is actually a combination of plastic, wood and metal—the chair is plastic (with a vinyl cover), the legs are metal and the footrest and support bars are wood.

The Zen is quite a departure for Fisher Price—this company is not exactly known for its design aesthetic. Most folks have to hide their Fisher Price chairs when guests come over; this one you can leave out and it will fit in most contemporary kitchens.

Reader feedback on the Zen is mixed, especially considering the glowing reviews for the Healthy Care or Space Saver. Critics of the Zen say the lack of a compact fold is a negative, as is the dishwasher safe tray, which is too easy for baby to remove. Although the main tray is dishwasher safe, water can get into it and that can create a mold problem if not properly drained. Bottom line: save the $50 and get a regular Healthy Care instead. FYI: Even though the Zen has an official retail of $150, we see it discounted online on many sites.

The E7 Clean is a $90 high chair that has as its main focus, if you hadn't guessed by the name, cleanability: it features a seamless pad (no crevices for food to stick), coated straps and a seamless dishwasher-safe tray. Of course, you also get the standard high chair features like four position seat recline, one-hand tray release and more. Reader feedback on this model has been quite positive (folks love the seamless pad), but a few dissenters knock the lack of wheels on the back of the chair (there are only wheels upfront). This makes it difficult to move around the kitchen. A few parents with bigger toddlers also found the seat too snug. Overall, however, we would recommend the EZ Clean.

The Home & Away 3-in-1 high chair ($105 to $120) converts from a high chair to a booster for use at restaurants as an alternative to grimy high chairs. Our only complaint: they claim it folds but it still looks big and bulky when folded, so it may not be convenient to take to restaurants. The Home & Away is probably the least popular chair in the Fisher Price line-up; feedback on it has been sparse.

Rounding out the high chair line-up is the Grow With Me, an entry-price point model for $60. This bare-bones chair features two height adjustments and machine washable pad . . . but it lacks wheels and doesn't recline, so it isn't suitable for newborns who can't sit up on their own. This chair is aimed at Grandma, but she'd probably do better with the Cosco Flat Fold, which is half the price.

Bottom line: Fisher Price is our top pick for high chairs. We like the Healthy Care, Space Saver and EZ Clean the best; skip the Zen. ***Rating: A***

Graco *gracobaby.com* Graco is the second-biggest selling brand in the high chair category, behind Fisher Price. The company has had a hit with their flagship Blossom high chair, as well as their compact-folding Contempo.

At the same time, safety recalls have hit the brand in recent years, tarnishing Graco's reputation. The biggest recall (1.2 million high chairs in 2010) targeted construction defects (screws that held the chair's front legs loosened, causing the chair to tip over unexpectedly). This hazard injured 24 babies. Then in 2012, Graco recalled all its wood high chairs (now discontinued) for defective seats that detached from the base (injuring nine children).

Graco offers eight high chair models, divided into three categories: all-in-one models in a group called Grow With Me (Blossom, pictured, Duo Diner, SimpleSwitch), "classic" high chairs (Meal Time, Contempo, Slim Spaces, TableFit) and travel models (Toddler Booster). Gone are the wood high chairs of years past, after a 2012 recall mentioned above.

Graco's flagship "all-in-one" high chair is the Blossom, which strikes a much more modern pose than most Graco models. It has all the standard features you expect from today's chairs (three-position recline, six position height adjustment, dishwasher safe tray insert) plus a few surprises: an adjustable footrest and a parent tray under the chair. The Blossom's key feature: it converts to a toddler booster with a seat back insert that adjusts in size. Price: $135 to $180. Feedback for this chair has been positive, with fans citing its cleanability and ease of use. One negative: the t-bar is attached to the tray, not the seat (as we prefer for safety reasons). And the Blossom lacks a fold feature, which means you can't store it away. Despite those negatives, most reader feedback on the Blossom is positive.

Graco's Duo Diner is similar to the Blossom—it also converts to a booster seat for use with older children. But it is 20% cheaper ($116 to $140) and can be folded for storage. Readers are generally happy with the Duo Diner, with a caveat that the dishwasher-safe tray is too big to fit in some dishwashers (you may want to confirm yours will fit before purchasing).

If you need a compact fold, consider the Graco Contempo ($89 to $140). Feedback on this model has been quite positive, with folks loving the ultra compact fold and extra seat pad. You also get six-position height adjustment, three-position recline and a dishwasher-safe tray insert. Very similar to the Contempo is the newer Slim Spaces ($130), which has a compact fold to just 8.5." The Slim Spaces high chair comes pre-assembled, has six height adjustments, three position recline plus extra padding and body support for smaller infants. FYI: the Slim Spaces was a Babies R Us exclusive in 2013, but should see wider distribution shortly.

On the more affordable price spectrum (the "classic" high chair category), the Graco Meal Time high chair ($70 to $80) features a one-hand, three-position recline, dishwasher-safe tray, four height adjustments, casters and one-hand tray release. Readers like the Meal Time, but the praise isn't as positive compared to the Contempo. Fans like the vinyl seat cover and smaller seat dimensions, but critics say this chair is rather bulky and the tray insert and even the tray itself can easily be removed by baby (which of course, is not good!).

Finally, we have the Graco SimpleSwitch, which converts from a high chair to a booster seat. At $60 to $70, the SimpleSwitch features a three position recline, five position height adjustment and washable pad. Reader feedback on the SimpleSwitch has been positive. One negative to the SimpleSwitch: the safety T-bar is attached to the tray instead of the seat, as we'd prefer to prevent babies from sliding out of the chair when the tray is removed.

New to the line-up in the past year is the TableFit. As the name implies, the TableFit is sized so it can slide right up to a dining room table. Eight height adjustments enable it to fit various tables, plus you also get a snack tray that fits over the larger tray and three position recline with infant support. One unique touch: the TableFit will have a no rethread harness (you can adjust the height of the harness without rethreading it), which is seen on some car seats but this is a first for high chairs. We also like the machine washable pad. Price: $100.

Feedback on the TableFit has generally been positive, but a few vocal critics knock the tray design, which requires multiple hands to remove, hold your baby, etc. To fold the chair, you have to remove the tray . . . which then has no storage place. While most folks are happy with the TableFit, the concerns over the tray would lead us to pass on recommending this model.

So to sum up, Graco high chairs generally earn positive reviews from readers, especially the Blossom and Contempo. However, the company's safety record in this category tempers our enthusiasm. **Rating: B+**

IKEA *ikea.com* IKEA has three minimalistic high chairs offerings. The Antilop ($20; pictured) is a plastic chair with metal legs . . . but doesn't include a tray (that's $5 extra) and doesn't fold up. The Blames ($60) is a wood high chair with plastic tray.

Finally, the Spoling is a $40 high chair without tray (but with a safety belt) that folds for storage. These chairs are clearly designed for older kids, but the lack of five-point harness (the "safety belt" doesn't quite cut it) or other adjustments make these a hard sell. That said, readers have generally given good reviews to the Antilop—one mom said it was incredibly easy to clean and just the ticket for her twins. ***Rating: C+***

Inglesina *inglesina.com* Inglesina is probably best known for its strollers, but the company has recently expanded its high chair offerings. The flagship is the pricey Zuma, which attempts to be both high style and practical. The rounded seat echoes modern seats by Bloom and Boon, but the more traditional base echoes a bit of Pali.

The Zuma has eight height positions, three-position seat recline and a hefty price tag: $300 (although we've seen it online for as little as $238). As a relative newcomer to the high chair market, Inglesina made a few rookie mistakes: the tray requires two hands to remove. An earlier version also had a dishwasher-safe tray that didn't cover the entire main tray. We're happy to note they enlarged the tray so it now covers the under-tray. And Inglesina fixed the distance between baby and tray—they've brought the tray closer to baby, so less food ends up in his lap.

Reader feedback on the Zuma is mixed—some laud the design, while others find its negatives too much for the price (food sticks to the Velcro that attaches the seat pad, making it hard to clean). We continue to see complaints about the cleanability on line, but it's unclear whether they are referring to the new version with the closer tray or older versions. We will give them a slightly higher rating due to the improvements.

Inglesina also has a second, simpler high chair: the Club ($113 to $120). This chair doesn't really do anything but look pretty. The Club is probably best for toddlers who aren't ready for a booster seat yet. The feedback on the Club is more positive than the Zuma, although critics claim it takes up too much floor space and the seat is too shallow. The safety harness on the Cub is oddly anchored to the bottom of the chair, not the back, which is a safety concern in our opinion.

New for 2014, Inglesina is adding a third high chair to their line-up, the Gusto ($150). The bar to keep a child from sliding out of the chair is attached to the tray, not the chair. That isn't our preference for safety reasons. The Gusto wasn't out as of this writing, so no feedback yet.

Bottom line: Inglesina's high chair offerings look pretty, but their drawbacks outweigh the positives. ***Rating: C+***

Joovy *joovy.com* Joovy is best known for its strollers, but its Nook high chair ($120 to 130) is worth a look. It features a swing-open tray, plush seat cushion (fabric or leatherette), dishwasher-safe insert and compact fold. We liked the five-point harness and most reader feedback on the chair has been positive. Critics note the large gap between the tray and seat means too much food ends up in baby's lap. The sleek look has its fans, but note there are no wheels. This chair is relatively easy to clean and that super-compact fold makes this one a winner. We liked the $130 price, which is below that of similar simple high chair offerings from Inglesina, Bloom and Valco.

New as of this writing, Joovy has added the HiLo, a convertible chair (baby to toddler) with a unique flipable seat. The plastic seat sits in a solid beech frame with dishwasher safe tray, five-point harness and wheels. Price? A ridiculous $500. So far, it's only available on Joovy's web site. ***Rating: A-***

Mamas and Papas *mamasandpapas.com* British manufacturer Mamas and Papas is like the Graco of the UK. Now the company has landed on this side of the Atlantic, with a collection of strollers, bouncers and two high chair models.

Mamas & Papas most popular high chair is the Juice ($150, pictured), which has a 2-in-1 pitch: the high chair's legs pop off and it becomes a little chair for toddlers. The seat pad is molded foam and the design is sleek and modern.

A second offering, the Pixi ($120) features a compact fold, removable tray and storage for the tray. It's low height means you can pull this high chair up to the table.

Feedback on the Juice is mostly quite positive although slim babies have a hard time keeping the harness straps on, while parents complain a bit about the cleanability of both chairs. The Pixi has lots of nooks and crannies for food to get stuck and the pad on the Juice allows food to get stuck underneath the seat.

We're raising the rating for Mamas and Papas as they've discontinued some of their more disappointing high priced high chairs (the Go Eat and the Loop) and feedback on the Juice and Pixi is overall very positive. ***Rating: A-***

Nuna *nuna.eu* Dutch-based Nuna has launched a full scale U.S. invasion in the past year, leading the way with their strollers that marry Euro minimalism with modern aesthetics. That design element continues with Nuna's first high chair effort, the Zaaz ($250).

The "grow with me" Zaaz strikes a modern pose

with its chunky, anodized aluminum legs. It converts into a chair for older kids when the tray and footrest are removed. Nuna touts the Zaaz's "crumb free" design which includes a smooth air-filled foam seat that is crevice-free, for easier cleaning.

Nuna did their homework for the Zaaz: the tray is dishwasher safe, the seat is height adjustable, etc. What's missing? Well, there is no seat recline, so this might not be the best choice for infants who can't sit up unassisted. And the tray doesn't adjust, so there is a large space between baby and the tray—which means most of the food will end up in baby's lap.

Parent feedback has been sparse, as the Zaaz is rather new and distribution is limited to specialty stores and sites like Giggle. We'll wait to assign a rating until we get more reader response here. But the Zaaz looks promising. ***Rating: Not Yet.***

OXO Tot oxotot.com Kitchen gadget maker OXO's first high chair, the Sprout, strikes an über modern pose, with its wooden legs and plastic seat. We liked the overall design, with its two height positions, adjustable footrest and more. But at $250, we'd expect to see a dishwasher-safe insert tray (it lacks this), compact fold (the Sprout doesn't fold) and reclining seat (again, missing). The Sprout comes in two base colors, a light birch and dark walnut. The birch comes with either an orange or taupe pad; the dark walnut has green, pink or taupe pads.

The Sprout garners mostly positive reviews, with folks liking the chair's small footprint and easy assembly. Unfortunately, the pads are surface clean only and more than one parent noted that water can easily get trapped in the tray when cleaning. This then rusts out the springs in the tray's attachment mechanism. Other folks said this chair (especially the straps and Velcro) is hard to keep clean and stains easily. Several others complained about the durability of the seat pad.

We gave the OXO Tot Sprout a B+ in our last edition, since the reviews were mostly positive even though the chair was relatively new at the time (it debuted in 2011). But now that we see more long-term concerns about how durable and cleanable the chair is, we are lowering the rating. The Sprout seems to fall into that classic trap with high chairs: it looks pretty, but in real life, the usage experience falls short . . . that might be somewhat forgivable at $100, but not at $250.

New for 2014, OXO Tot has debuted a lower-price chair, the $150 Seedling High Chair. This all-plastic chair features five height adjustments, a safety bar attached to the chair, dishwasher safe tray, one-hand adjustments, reclining seat (three positions) and even machine washable cushions.

FYI: OXO Tot recently debuted its first booster seat: the Seedling Youth Booster is $40 and folds up for easy transport.

So it looks like OXO has learned some of the lessons from the Sprout's shortcomings . . . but as an all plastic chair, the Seedling looks like something Graco would sell for $100 (or 30% less than OXO Tot's pricing). Hence, it remains to be seen whether this will be a success. The Sprout was brand new as of this writing, so no parent feedback yet. **Rating: B-**

Peg Perego perego.com The Peg Perego Prima Pappa high chair had been a best selling high chair for years, but its day has come and gone. Sure, it looks stylish and features a four-position reclining seat, seven height adjustments, a dishwasher-safe dinner tray, five-point restraint and compact fold. And the fabrics! Tre chic!

But let's look at the chair's key flaw: the tray. It sits a whopping 8.5" above the seat, making it too tall except perhaps for Shaq's kids. Another problem: the tray sits 7" from the back of the seat, creating a gap the size of the Grand Canyon between your baby and her food. (There is some good news on this front: in the past year, Peg added a newborn cushion to one model of the Prima Pappa to address this issue).

Then let's talk about this chair's cleanability—it's notorious for collecting food in every little nook and cranny. And the dishwasher-safe tray insert is too big to fit in most dishwashers. All this for $200+! Wow, what a deal.

Perego makes three versions of the Prima Pappa: Best, Diner and Zero 3. The Best ($250, pictured) features an upgraded, tailored seat cushion. The Diner ($200) has a seat pad made of microfiber.

The Zero 3 ($200) is the newest version of the Prima Pappa. This chair features a reclining seat (four positions), vinyl pad, simple wheels, easy fold, adjustable footrest, and the ability to store the tray on the back.

Perhaps the best thing about the Pappa high chair is how it looks—the fabrics are gorgeous. And this chair is made in Italy (and your only option if you want to avoid Chinese-made high chairs, which is basically everything else on the market). But when you actually use the chair, the design flaws (it lacks a compact fold, the tray is sticky and tough to remove with one hand, lack of cleanability, etc.) quickly outweigh how pretty it looks. As one mom summed it up in an online review: "this chair should only be sold together with a 2000 psi power washer!"

Besides Pappa, Perego has two other high chair offerings: The Tatamia and the Siesta.

The pricey Tatamia ($350) is billed as a "multi-purpose baby seat" since it also functions as a swing and bouncer. Given the high price, reader feedback on this model has been thin, but in general, the few who have it, like it. In contrast to the Prima Pappa, the Tatamia is easy to clean. And fans like the multi-function swing/bouncer plus the compact fold. On the other hand, critics say this chair has a steep learning curve—the directions to convert functions are complicated, etc. Other negatives: the Tatamia's large base takes up a lot of space and the swing motion can trap a baby's arm, creating a safety hazard.

The newest Perego high chair is the Siesta. Billed as a "multi function, ultra-compact" model, the Siesta has nine height positions and a full recline. We liked the hi-tech "eco-leather" covering, which should be easy to clean. The Siesta also includes a dishwasher safe tray, wheels that have a unique "stop and go" break system and a storage net on the back. When folded it measures just 11.8." That is a bit wider than the 9" depth of the Graco Contempo when folded, but overall, impressive.

At $240 to $300, the Siesta is no bargain, but reader feedback has been mostly positive. Fans love the overall design and ease of use, but critics say the overly complicated wheels aren't user-friendly. Since the front wheels are fixed, the Siesta only pushes in a straight line. That sort of defeats the point of having wheels in the first place.

Other parents complained about the Siesta's tray (it is hard to release with one hand; it can get stuck); others say the chair is hard to adjust. Bottom line: while the Siesta has its fans, the drawbacks are too much for this pricey model.

To sum up, Peg's Italian tailored high chairs are pretty to look at— but high prices and design flaws prevent us from recommending them. If you have the space and a rich uncle, the Tatamia is probably the best of the bunch here. **Rating: C+**

Phil & Teds *philandteds.com* Stroller maker Phil & Teds offers two high chair options, the HighPod, which features a modern look and five height adjustments as well as a three position infant recline and the stripped down Poppy.

Good news about the HighPod: it's selling now for only $200 (although that's hardly cheap) down from $300 when it originally came out. Fans like the seamless chair/pad (no crevices for food to hide) and deep seat recline for infants although critics note the seat is small and bigger babies will outgrow it quickly.

More negatives: a very small tray that takes two hands to remove. Plus, it is too easy for babies to remove the dishwasher safe insert, in our opinion. Add in the fact that the safety bar is attached to the tray and not the seat (for safety reasons, we like it the other way around) and the lack of wheels, and you've got a mixed review for the HighPod. This high chair feels like a version 1.0 product . . . it needs some work. Reader feedback on the HighPod is more positive now that the price has dropped significantly. The biggest complaints are about the tray (too small, hard to remove, clips break).

Phil & Teds Poppy is a more scaled down high chair design for $120. The lightweight chair (8 lbs.) doesn't recline or feature much in the way of adjustments but does have a relatively large tray (unlike the HighPod). It's biggest trick: after your child outgrows the high chair, the Poppy converts to a kids chair by removing the legs, similar to the Juice from Mamas & Papas. The Poppy comes in four rather bright patterns and features an "Aerocore" foam seat which is both dishwasher safe and comfortable.

The Poppy is still relatively new, but initial reviews are mixed. Readers like the tray size, but complain it's hard to remove. The harness also appears to be difficult to adjust and the shoulder straps don't stay on the child. On the other hand, the Poppy is very easy to keep clean with it's seamless seat pad. It's also very light weight.

Finally, more than one reader mentioned the leg design on the Poppy (the legs stick straight out from the chair in every direction) means you might end up tripping over it if you have limited room in your kitchen.

Bottom line: the HighPod is a much better bet at $200, and the Poppy is an interesting chair, but Phil & Teds needs to go back to the design room and fix tray issues on both chairs and the harness on the Poppy. ***Rating: B-***

Safety 1st *Safety1st.com* While parent Cosco sells bare-bones high chairs to the discount chains, Safety 1st focuses on a slightly more upscale market. Example: Safety 1st's AdapTable High Chair ($60 to $80, pictured) has all the standard features you expect in a high chair (machine-washable cushion, three position recline, six height adjust- ments, one-hand tray release with dishwasher safe insert) plus an ultra-compact, standing fold. The Disney version is called the Serve n' Store; basically it is the same as the AdapTable.

The AdapTable is probably the best rated Safety 1st model, given parent feedback.

The Safety 1st Nourish high chair is an upgraded version of the AdapTable with fancier fabric and an extra infant cushion to better fit smaller newborns. Price: $120.

Safety 1st next high chair model: the Comfy Seat, which comes in both regular and Disney versions. The Comfy Seat has seven height positions, one-hand tray release, three-position recline, five point harness and a machine washable cloth seat with infant insert. This model is sold mostly in Babies R Us stores for $110.

New in the past year, Safety 1st debuted a wood high chair: the Decor, a Babies R Us exclusive for $120. Safety 1st parent Dorel has had a mixed track record in this category, with several Eddie Bauer wood high chairs earning less than stellar parent reviews. The Decor was too new as of this writing for parent feedback.

Overall, the quality of Safety 1st's high chairs is only average—the AdapTable is the best of the litter.

If you want a bare bones chair for Grandma, you're better off with one of Cosco's offerings for $30 less. If you want a full feature high chair, you're better off with Fisher Price or Graco, which are priced about the same as Safety 1st, yet offer enhanced features and better quality. **Rating: C+**

Stokke *stokkeUSA.com* The Stokke Tripp Trapp is reviewed on the free side of our web site at BabyBargains.com/?p=973

Summer *summerinfant.com* Better known for their video monitors, Summer has three high chairs: the Carters Newborn to Toddler, the Classic Comfort Wood and the Bentwood high chair.

As of this writing, Summer was phasing out the Carter's license, so we'll focus on the two active models: the Classic Comfort and Bentwood.

Like the Eddie Bauer wood high chairs, the Classic Comfort ($130) is a hybrid with wood base and plastic tray. One unique feature: the seat has a three position recline; most wood high chairs don't have this.

The Bentwood ($170; pictured) looks similar to the OXO Tot Sprout, with its wooden legs and plastic tray (key differences: the Bentwood is height adjustable, has a wood seat and folds up). There has been little parent feedback on this model since it is new as of this writing, but early reports are mixed. One reader told us the snack tray on the Bentwood is fixed, meaning you have to wrestle a toddler over it each time you use the chair. The chair cushion is also quite thin.

Feedback on the Classic high chair is similarly mixed. More than one reader complained about the difficulty in assembling the Classic Comfort.

Bottom line: Summer is only a bit player in the high chair market and it shows. While models like the Bentwood show promise, Summer needs to establish more of a track record here for quality and durability before we can recommend them. **Rating: D+**

Svan of Sweden *scichild.com* Svan high chairs are reviewed on the free side of our web site at BabyBargains.com/?p=979

Valco *valcobaby.com* Stroller maker Valco debuted its first high chair in the past year. The simple $80 to $130 Astro is a basic high chair that folds flat (and comes with a travel bag). Reader feedback on the

Astro has been quite positive—the impressive feature here is its compact fold and light weight (about 15 lbs.), which makes it a good bet for travel.

On the downside, the tray is now dishwasher safe but requires two hands to remove. We also don't like how far it sits away from the child, although the deep lip is nice. Bottom line: this is probably a better bet for older babies and for parents with a small kitchen that need a high chair with a compact fold. **Rating: B**

◆ **Other Brands.** Kettler is a brand better known in this country for their tricycles, but their Tipp Topp high chair has won fans for its simple design. We found it for $73 on BabiesRUs.com.

If you like those wood high chairs at restaurants, you can buy a similar model online: the Lipper wood high chair is $58 on Amazon.com.

high chairs

Our Picks: Brand Recommendations

Here is our round up of the best high chair bets.

Good. Is space tight in your kitchen? *The Fisher-Price Space Saver* ($50-$60) lives up to its name—it straps to a regular chair and provides most of the features of a full-feature high chair, yet costs half as much. Another good option: the *Graco Contempo* ($89 to $140), which has the most compact fold of any high chair on the market and positive feedback. Also good in the compact fold, simple high chair category: *Joovy's Nook* ($120-$130), which has a swing-out tray and a sleek, modern look.

Better. *Graco's Blossom* takes second place with its more modern design and a slew of features. Among its best tricks: it converts to a toddler booster chair that straps to a regular kitchen chair for older babies. Yes, the Blossom is pricey at $135-$180, but worth it. One bummer: the Blossom doesn't fold away for storage.

Best. The *Fisher-Price Healthy Care* has got it all—great safety features, ease of use, cleanability and more. We like the snap-off dishwasher-safe tray, good design and easy-to-clean vinyl pad. At $100 to $130, it is about 30% to 50% cheaper than the Graco Blossom depending on the version. FYI: This high chair goes under several names, including Ocean Wonders, Rainforest and Precious Planet Blue Sky. The more expensive versions include an upgraded pad and toys. If you find the Fisher Price patterns too cutesy, the

Continued on page 294

HIGH CHAIRS

High chairs, compared

NAME	RATING	PRICE	TRAY HEIGHT	TRAY DEPTH
BABY BJORN	B+	$220-$300	5.5"	5.5"
BABY TREND	C+	$60-$100	8.5	8
BLOOM FRESCO	D	$450-$550	10	8
BOON FLAIR	A	$200-$250	5.5	7
CHICCO POLLY	C+	$130-$150	7.5	7
COSCO FLAT FOLD	C+	$31	*	*
EDDIE BAUER CLASSIC	F	$130-$150	8	5
EVENFLO MODERN 200	B-	$90-$100	*	*
FISHER PRICE HEALTHY CARE	A	$100-$130	7.5	6
FISHER PRICE SPACE SAVER	A	$50-$60	7.5	5
GRACO BLOSSOM	B+	$135-$180	6	6
GRACO CONTEMPO	B+	$89-$140	7.5	6
IKEA ANTILOP	C+	$20	*	*
IKEA BLAMES	C+	$60	*	*
INGLESINA CLUB	C+	$113-$120	5.5	8
INGLESINA ZUMA	C+	$238-$300	7.5	7.25
JOVVY NOOK	A-	$120-$130	*	*
MAMAS & PAPAS JUICE	A-	$150	7	9.5
OXO TOT SPROUT	B-	$250	7	7
OXO TOT SEEDLING	B-	$150	6	7
PEG PEREGO PRIMA PAPPA	C+	$200-$250	8.5	7
PEG PEREGO SIESTA	C+	$240-$300	7.5	9
PHIL & TEDS HIGHPOD	B-	$200-$300	*	*
SAFETY 1ST ADAPTABLE	C+	$60-$80	*	*
STOKKE TRIPP TRAPP	A-	$250	*	*
SUMMER BENTWOOD	D+	$170	7	6.5
VALCO ASTRO	B	$80-$130	8	9

KEY

TRAY HEIGHT: Distance from the seat to the top of the tray. Any measurement under 8" is acceptable. Above 8" is too tall.

DEPTH (tray to seat): Distance from the back of the seat to the tray. 5" to 7" is acceptable.

SUB?: Most high chairs have a special guard to prevent a child from submarining under the tray. Some models attach this to the chair; others to the tray. A better bet: those that attach to the seat. See discussion earlier in this chapter.

Sub?	Pad	Comment
Seat	None	No 5-pt. harness, easy clean, small seat
Seat	Cloth	Pad should be hand-washed, line dried.
Seat	Cloth	Seamless seat, auto height, seat reclines
Seat	Vinyl	Seamless seat; automatic height adjust.
Tray	Vinyl	Hard to clean, difficult to adjust harness
Seat	Vinyl	Lowest price, good for grandma's house.
Tray	Both	Wood with plastic tray; hard to clean.
Seat	Foam	Machine-washable seat pad.
Seat	Vinyl	Top rated pick; comes in 3 versions.
Seat	Vinyl	Attaches to chair; great for small spaces.
Tray	Vinyl	Converts to toddler booster.
Seat	Vinyl	Among narrowest fold on market.
Seat	None	Tray is $5 extra; better for older toddlers.
None	None	No harness; better for older toddlers.
Seat	Vinyl	Best for toddlers not ready for booster.
Seat	Cloth	Seamless seat, mod look, very pricey.
Seat	Vinyl	Easy fold, like a beach chair.
Seat	Vinyl	Legs pop off to convert to a chair.
Tray	Vinyl	Doesn't fold; wood hybrid.
Seat	Vinyl	New, plastic/metal, dishwasher safe tray.
Seat	Vinyl	3 versions; many colors, hard to clean.
Seat	Vinyl	9 height positions, compact fold.
Tray	Vinyl	Seamless pad, but small tray.
Tray	Cloth	Ultra compact, standing fold.
Seat	Cloth	Baby rail is $70 extra; no tray.
Tray	Vinyl	Hybrid wood/plastic, fixed snack tray.
Seat	Vinyl	Folds flat, comes with carry bag.

Pad: Is the seat made of cloth or vinyl? We prefer vinyl for easier clean up. Cloth seats must be laundered and some can't be thrown in the drier (requiring a long wait for it to line dry). Of course, this feature isn't black and white—some vinyl seats have cloth edging/piping.

* Not applicable or not available. Some of these models were new as of press time, so we didn't have these specs yet.

Graco Duo Diner LX ($116-$140) offers many of the same features as the Healthy Care, but in more subtle fashions.

Grandma's house. For grandma's house, a simple *Cosco Flat Fold* ($34) should do the trick. No, it doesn't have casters or other fancy features, but Grandma doesn't need all that.

Hook-on Chairs and Boosters

Your toddler has outgrown his high chair, but doesn't quite fit into the adult chairs at the kitchen table. What to do? Consider a booster. There are three types of kitchen booster seats on the market today:

1 **Hook-on chairs.** As the name implies, these seats hook on to a table, instead of attaching to a chair. Pros: Lightweight; yet most can hold toddlers up to 35 to 40 lbs. Very portable—many parents use these chairs as a sanitary alternative when they dine out since many restaurants seemed to have last cleaned their high chairs during the Carter administration. Cons: May not work with certain tables, like those with pedestal bases. Fear of tipping an unstable table leads some restaurants to prohibit these chairs. Hook-on chairs do not recline, a feature you see on regular boosters.

2 **Booster seats with trays.** These boosters strap to a chair and usually have a tray. Pros: Most fold flat for travel. Some have multiple seat levels. Can use with or without a tray. Cons: Child may not be sitting up at table height. Some brands have too-small trays and difficult to adjust straps make for a loose fit.

3 **Plain boosters (no tray).** These chairs are just boosters— nothing fancy, no trays. Pros: Better bet for older toddlers (age four or five) who want to eat at the table. Cons: No restraint system or belt, so this isn't a choice for younger toddlers.

Our Picks: Brand Recommendations

◆ **Hook-on chair. Top pick:** Chicco's two entrants in this category are excellent. The *Caddy* ($40) has a compact fold, three point harness and "quick grip" table clamps. The seat pad is removable and
machine washable. FYI: Chicco makes a version of this hook-on chair with a seat that rotates, dubbed the 360 Hook On ($75).

Either one is a good bet.

◆ **Kitchen booster seat with tray. Top pick:** *Fisher Price Healthy Care Booster Seat* (fisher-price.com). Fisher Price has a win-

ner here: we liked the snap-off feeding tray that can go into the dishwasher, easy fold and shoulder strap for road trips plus three different height settings. When your child gets older, the tray removes so the seat becomes a basic booster. The only caveat: the back does not recline, so your baby must be able to sit up on his own to use it safely. (No biggie for most toddlers, but we know some folks consider these boosters as high-chair replacements—not a good idea unless your child can sit upright). Price: $24, making this a good value.

Runner Up: *Summer Infant Deluxe Comfort Booster* (summerinfant.com). This affordable ($20) booster is similar to our top pick, but adds one

nice bonus: it features a compact fold for easy transport. No snack tray, but the full-size tray is dishwasher-safe. Be aware: this seat has a 33-pound limit—as a result this one won't work for larger toddlers. (FYI: The Fisher Price Healthy Care booster is good up to 45 lbs.).

◆ **Kitchen booster seat without tray.**
The *Soft Gear My Booster* is our pick for kids who've outgrown their highchairs, but still need a boost in a regular chair. Designed for

kids three and up, the foam seat includes a rub-berized, slip-resistant grip. Price: $33.

A brief warning: The *Bumbo Seat* ($36) is a popular seat designed for younger infants to sit upright. The problem? Babies have fallen out of the seat and been injured, especially when

the Bumbo is used on elevated surfaces (which is contrary to the manufacturer's instructions that it only be used on a floor). There have also been reports of injuries to children when the Bumbo has been on the floor. As a result, the seat has been the subject of several safety recalls. We suggest passing on the Bumbo.

The Bottom Line:
A Wrap-Up of Our Best Buy Picks

What's the most affordable way to feed baby? Breastfeeding, by a mile. We estimate you can save $900 in just the first six months alone by choosing to breast-feed instead of bottle-feed.

Of course, that's easy for us to say—breastfeeding takes some practice, for both you and baby. One product that can help: a breast pump, to relieve engorgement or provide a long-term solution to baby's feeding if you go back to work. Which pumps are best? For manual pumps, we like the Avent Comfort Manual ($40-$45) and the Medela's Harmony ($30-$35) for that occasional bottle. If you plan to pump so you can go back to work, a professional-grade pump works best. Tip: rent one first before you buy. If you like it and decide you are serious about pumping, we liked the Medela Pump In Style ($225-$300) or Ameda Purely Yours (about $140 to $300).

If you decide to bottle feed or need to wean your baby off breast milk, the most affordable formulas are the generic brands sold in discount stores under various private-label names. You'll save up to 40% by choosing generic over name brands, but your baby gets the exact same nutrition.

Who makes the best bottles? Our readers say Avent and Dr. Brown's are tops, but others find cheaper options like Playtex work just was well at half the price.

Let's talk baby food—besides the ubiquitous Gerber, there are several other brands that are good alternatives. One of the best is Earth's Best, although it is more pricey than affordable brands like Beechnut. How can you save? Make your own baby food for pennies or buy jarred baby food in bulk at discount stores. And skip the toddler meals, which are a waste of money.

Finally, consider that quintessential piece of baby gear—the high chair. We felt the best bets were those that were easiest to clean (go for a vinyl, not cloth pad) and had snap-off dishwasher-safe trays. Our top pick is the Fisher Price Healthy Care ($100 to $130), although the Graco Blossom ($135-$180) is a stylish alternative, albeit at a higher price.

Now that you've got the food and kitchen covered, what about the rest of your house? We'll explore all the other baby gear you might need for your home next.

CHAPTER 7

Around the House: Monitors, Diaper Pails, Safety

Inside this chapter

What's the best bathtub for baby? Which baby monitor can save you $40 a year in batteries? What's the best—and least stinky—diaper pail? In this chapter, we explore everything for baby that's around the house. From bouncer seats to safety gates, we'll give you tricks and tips to saving money. You'll learn about play yards and swings. Finally, let's talk safety—we'll give you advice on affordable baby proofing.

Getting Started: When Do You Need This Stuff?

The good news is you don't need all this stuff right away. While you'll probably purchase a monitor before the baby is born, other items like bouncer seats and even bath-time products aren't necessary immediately (you'll give the baby sponge baths for the first few weeks, until the belly button area heals). Of course, you still might want to register for these items before baby is born. In each section of this chapter, we'll be more specific about when you need certain items.

What Are You Buying?

Let's take a tour around the house to see what items you might consider for baby. Of course, these ideas are merely suggestions—none of these items are "mandatory." We've divided them into two categories: bath-time and the baby's room.

Bath

1 TOYS/BOOKS. What fun is taking a bath without toys? Many stores sell inexpensive plastic tub toys, but you can use other items like stacking cups in the tub as well. And don't forget about tub safety items, which can also double as toys. For example, Safety 1st (800) 739-7233 (safety1st.com) makes a **TempGuard Rubber Ducky**, a yellow duck with attached thermometer (to make sure the water isn't too hot) for $3. **Tubbly Bubbly** by Kel-Gar (972) 250-3838 (kelgar.com) is a $12 elephant or hippo spout cover that protects against scalding, bumps and bruises. But it doesn't fit on some spouts that have a shower diverter.

2 TOILETRIES. Basic baby shampoo like the famous brand made by Johnson & Johnson works just fine, and you'll probably need some lotion as well. The best tip: first try lotion that is unscented in case your baby has any allergies. Also, never use talcum powder on your baby—it's a health hazard. If you need to use an absorbent powder, good old cornstarch will do the trick.

What about those natural baby products that are all the rage, like Mustela or Calidou? We got a gift basket of an expensive boutique's natural baby potions and didn't see what the big deal was. Worse yet, the $20-a-bottle shampoo dried out our baby's scalp so much he had scratching fits. We suppose the biggest advantage of these products is that they don't contain extraneous chemicals or petroleum by-products. Also, most don't have perfumes, but then, many low-price products now come in unscented versions as well. The bottom line: it's your comfort level. If you want to try them out without making a big investment, register for them as a shower gift.

If you have a history of allergies or skin problems in your family, consider washing baby's skin and hair with Dove or Cetaphil bar soap.

Moms clubs great way to share, save

Mom's clubs today are a great way to meet other moms, learn about new products and save money. In Dallas, Metro Moms (metroplexbaby.com) holds monthly events that include dinner and numerous product giveaways. Some events feature a guest speaker (usually a parenting expert), guided museum tours, book signings and other seasonal events. In Chicago, the BumpClubChicago.com is aimed at both moms and moms-to-be with girl's night out, lunch and dinner seminars, shopping events and more. Many of these new moms' clubs spread the word via social media (Facebook, Twitter, Foursquare).

These do not contain detergents that you find in even the most basic baby shampoo. And remember, just because a product is "organic" or "all-natural" doesn't mean it's non-allergic. In fact, ingredients like shea butter (made from a tree nut), calendula and chamomile all have potential for reactions including rashes, breathing problems (anaphylaxis) and eye irritation. See our other book, *Baby 411* for more on alternative ingredients and their potential side effects.

3 **BABY BATHTUB.** While not a necessity, a baby bathtub is a nice convenience (especially if you are bathing baby solo). See later in this chapter for more info on bathtubs.

Safe & Sound

◆ **BATH SEATS SHOULD NOT BE USED.** It looks innocuous—the baby bath seat—but it can be a disaster waiting to happen. These seats suction to the bottom of a tub, holding baby in place while she takes a bath. The problem? Parents get a false sense of security from such items and often leave the bathroom to answer the phone, etc. We've seen several tragic reports of babies who've drowned when they fell out of the seats (or the seats became unsuctioned from the tub). The best advice: AVOID these seats and NEVER leave baby alone in the tub, even for just a few seconds.

◆ **TURN DOWN YOUR WATER HEATER.** Ideally, your water heater should be set at no more than 120° F. At 140° F it poses a safety hazard. You can also consider installing anti-scalding devices on your showers and faucets. One such device is called *ScaldShield* and sells at hardware stores for about $50.

◆ **NO SKID RUGS IN THE BATHROOM.** Invest in rugs that have rubberized, no skid bottoms. You don't want to slip carrying your baby, and you don't want your new walking toddler to bang his head on the toilet or tub.

◆ **LOCK IT UP.** Install cabinet and toilet locks. This is just as important as safeguarding baby from dangers in the kitchen. And now is a great time to retrain your husband to put the lid down on the toilet seat. Locks don't work unless you actually use them.

Baby Bathtubs

Sometimes, it is the simplest products that are the best. Take baby bathtubs—if you look at the offerings in this category, you'll note some baby bathtubs convert to step stools and then, small compact cars. Okay, just kidding on the car, but these products are a good example of brand manager overkill—companies think the way to success with baby bath tubs is to make them work from birth to college.

So, it shouldn't be a surprise that our top picks for baby bathtub are, well, just bathtubs. Here's an overview

Best (full size tub). The *EuroBath by Primo* ($44; primobaby.com; pictured right) is a sturdy tub for babies, age birth to two. It weighs less than two pounds and is easy to use—just add baby, water and poof! Clean baby. The EuroBath is well designed, although it is big—almost three feet from end to end. It may be a tight fit if you have a small bathroom.

Another good choice is the *First Year's Infant to Toddler Tub with Sling* ($17). This simple tub includes a sling and foam pads to better fit a newborn.

Best (folding tub). The *Puj Tub* ($45) is a soft, foldable tub designed to fit in a sink. Made of foam, it unfolds when not in use and can hang on the back of a door—perfect if you live in a tiny urban apartment. The only caveat: it doesn't work with all sinks or faucets (an oval sink with a 6.5" depth is best). And it is designed for infants to six month-olds, so this won't work for older babies and toddlers. Safety 1st makes a similar design called the *Sink Snuggler* for less: $20.

Boon has introduced a cool new tub for the space deprived (and fashion forward) parent. The *Naked* baby bathtub is collapsible with a hook to hang it in the shower and can be placed in a reclining position. The simple, colorful design makes it a pleasure to look at and use. Cost: $60. It comes in bright teal blue and traffic cone orange.

What about tubs with bells and whistles like built-in thermometers? A waste of money, say our readers, who complain the thermometers often don't work.

A baby bathtub is a great item to pick up second-hand or at a garage sale. Or borrow from a friend. Readers say they've snagged baby bath tubs for $2 or so at garage sales—with a little cleaning, they are just fine. What if you want to give baby a bath in a regular tub or kitchen sink? A bath pad like *Leacho Safer Bather Infant Bath Pad* ($19) will do the trick.

Now let's talk about that big milestone, potty training.

Potty Seats

Potty seats come in two flavors: floor models and inserts. Inserts are molded (and sometimes padded) seats made for smaller bottoms. They are installed on top of the regular toilet seat. Floor models are traditional self-contained units with a base and seat.

Some potty seats start out as floor models and then the seat can be removed and used as an insert on the regular toilet. Our advice: go for the insert only. Yes, you'll need a step stool for your little one to climb up, but it's much easier to transition to a regular toilet if your child is already using one. And think about how excited your child will be to use the same toilet as his parents (trust us, it is a big deal).

Our Picks: Brand Recommendations

Best (Seat Insert). The *Baby Bjorn Toilet Trainer* ($32) has an adjustment dial to fit most toilet seats and an angled splashguard. The contoured seat works well, say readers.

Best (Potty Chair). The *Fisher Price Precious Planet Froggie Potty* ($10) is shaped like a frog and is very simple. Does the trick at an affordable price. A closer runner-up is *Baby Bjorn's Potty Chair* at $25. Very good as well.

Ceiling Fans & White Noise

Many parents swear they'd never survive without the ceiling fan in their baby's room—the "white noise" made by a whirling fan soothed their fussy baby (and quieted sounds from the rest of the house).

Interestingly, a study in the *Archives of Pediatrics and Adolescent Medicine* published in 2008, showed that babies who sleep in a room with a ceiling fan have a much lower risk of dying of Sudden Infant Death Syndrome (SIDS). Why would a ceiling fan make a difference, you ask? Turns out that by circulating the air in your baby's room, you lower the chances that he or she will "re-breathe" exhaled carbon dioxide. This re-breathing has been suggested as one cause of SIDS. So we definitely recommend a ceiling fan, both for that low hum in the background and the recirculation of the room's air.

What about other white noise generators that play rain forest or ocean sounds? Our advice is to skip them. In a 2003 study published in the journal *Science*, researchers say using white noise can be dangerous to your child's developing hearing. Our advice now is to avoid those white noise generators, although a ceiling fan is fine.

Diaper Pails

Pop quiz! Remember our discussion of how many diapers you will change in your baby's first year? What was the amount?

Pencils down—yes, it is 2300 diapers! A staggering figure . . . only made more staggering by figuring out what do with the dirty ones once you've changed baby. Yes, we can hear first-time parents raising their hands right now and saying "Duh! They go in the trash!"

Oh, not so fast, new parental one. Stick a dirty diaper in a regular trashcan and you may quickly perfume your entire home—not to mention draw a curious pet and we won't even go there.

So, most parents use a diaper pail, that specialized trashcan designed by trained scientists to limit stink and keep out babies, pets and stray relatives. But which diaper pail? Here's our Diaper Pail 411:

Diaper pails fall into two camps: those that use refill cartridges to wrap diapers in deodorized plastic and pails that use regular kitchen trash bags.

As you'd guess, pails that use special refills are more expensive (the refills cost about $6 each) and wrap about 140 or so diapers. The pail can hold 20-25 diapers at a time, which is about three days worth of diapers. Bottom line: you'll about need to buy 16 refill cartridges per year—which means $100. And that's on top of the $30 to $40 that the pails cost.

So, should you just get a diaper pail that uses regular kitchen trash bags? Yes, they are less expensive to use—but there is sometimes a major trade-off. Stink. These pails tend to stink more and hence, have to be emptied more frequently (perhaps daily or every other day) than the diaper pails that use special deodorized plastic.

Obviously, the decision on which diaper pail is right for you and your baby's nursery depends on several factors. What is the distance to the trash? If you live in a house with easy access to an outside trashcan, it might be easier to go with the lower-cost alternatives and just take out the diapers more frequently. If you live in an apartment where the nearest dumpster is down three flights of stairs

Wipe Warmers: Not Recommended

These $20 gizmos warm wipes to a comfy 90 degrees, so baby isn't surprised by a cold wipe at 2am. While this sounds like a good idea, there have been a series of safety recalls for these devices, which have caused fires, electric shock and other problems. Besides, you can just warm the wipes up in your hands for a few seconds—voila! Warm wipe without spending $20.

and a long walk across a parking lot, well, it might make sense to go with an option that requires less work.

Another factor: how sensitive are you to the smell? Some folks don't have a major problem with this, while moms who are pregnant again with a second child may need an industrial strength diaper pail to keep from losing it when walking into baby's nursery. A great tip from our readers: dump the poop. Before tossing the diaper, dump the poop into the toilet.

Whatever your decision, remember you'll live with this diaper pail for three or more YEARS (that's how long before most children potty train).

And it's a fact of life: diapers get stinkier as your baby gets older . . . so the diaper removal strategy that works for a newborn may have to be chucked for a toddler. Yes, you may be able to use a plain trashcan with liner when your newborn is breastfeeding . . . but after you start solid foods, it will be time to buy a more stink-free diaper pail.

Given those caveats, here is an overview of what's out there:

CLEAN AIR ODOR FREE DIAPER DISPOSAL BY FIRST YEARS

Type: Kitchen trash bag.
Price: $40-$50. Extra carbon filters $10 for two.
Web: learningcurve.com
Pros: Uses a fan and carbon filter to trap odors. Holds 40 diapers. Uses standard kitchen trash bags.
Cons: LOUD! Requires four D batteries. Smell escapes.
Comments: First Years decided they couldn't just design a regular diaper pail. They needed a gimmick! Voila! They came up with the first diaper pail with a fan plus carbon filter! Readers have one universal complaint: it is too LOUD! When you put a diaper in, the pail cranks up the decibels like a 747 (okay, an exaggeration, but you get the idea). Other readers report diapers that jam and a general lack of stink control. **Bottom line:** A loser. *Rating: F*

DIAPER CHAMP BY BABY TREND

Type: Kitchen trash bag.
Price: $35.
Pros: Did we mention no expensive refills? The Diaper Champ uses regular ol' kitchen bags, yet the contraption works to seal out odor by using a flip handle design. Easy to use. Taller design means it holds more diapers than the Genie.
Cons: Not as stink-free as the Genie or Dekor, especially when

diaper pails

baby starts solid foods. Bigger footprint than other pails.

Comments: When you redesign a best-selling product, you're supposed to improve it, right? Yes, unless you are Baby Trend, a brand that seems to botch even the simplest task. Fans loved the original Diaper Champ, which started the concept of using regular kitchen trash bags (and hence, saved hundreds of dollars in refill cartridges). The most recent version of Diaper Champ, unfortunately, is a step backwards: yes it has a wider opening, but parents tell us it doesn't work as well (diapers get stuck, the smell can be atrocious, etc). And the diaper removal process may require an EPA HazMat Rapid Response team, given the stink level. Fans of this diaper pail seem to like it . . . until their baby starts solid foods. Then the smell can be overwhelming, forcing folks to buy a Dekor or Genie. One tip: if you go with the Champ, put a fabric softener sheet in the pail with each load (this cuts down on the smell). And be prepared to scrub it every month or two with bleach, leaving it outside to air out. Also the Champ probably isn't the best bet if you have an older toddler, who can put toys into the slot (trust us, not a pretty sight). New this year, Baby Trend is offering Odor Grabber refills that can be used in any diaper pail on the market: Diaper Genie, Diaper Dekor and more.

Bottom line: A mixed review: good for the first few months, not so good after baby starts solid food. A bargain—but beware the stink trade-offs. *Rating: C+*

DIAPER DEKOR

Type: Refill canister.

Price: $40-$80. Refill packs are $5-$7.50 each and wrap 480 newborn diapers.

Pros: Hands free operation—you hit the foot pedal and drop in a diaper. Comes in three sizes, largest can holds 5+ days of diapers. Converts to a regular trashcan after baby is done with diapers. Parents say it is much easier to use than the Diaper Genie, reviewed below.

Cons: New "biodegradable" refills are terrible at containing stink, readers report. Hinges on the "trap door" seem prone to breakage, as does the foot pedal.

Comments: The only serious competition for the Diaper Genie, the Diaper Dekor comes in three sizes: regular ($40, holds 40 newborn diapers), Plus ($45, 60 newborn diapers) and XL ($90, 105 newborn diapers). The classic Diaper Dekor is best for newborns; the Plus is pitched for larger families (where more than one child is in diapers) and the XL is best for multiple births or a daycare center . . . or the Octomom. As of this writing, we saw more Plus versions for sale than the XL or Classic. Be careful which size inserts you buy: the classic size won't fit in a Plus can.

The Dekor was one of our top picks for diaper pails in our last edition—but then the company re-designed the refills . . . the result is a disaster. The worst part is a change in the plastic: the new refills are now "biodegradable." And in case you missed the eco-friendly message, the plastic is now green. The problem? The new refills are horrible at blocking odor, the main reason why you'd part with the big bucks to buy one of these pails.

While we are all for saving the environment, ruining the effectiveness of a product in order to make it more green is a colossal mistake.

Some good news: the stink about the new refills was so great, Regal Lager has brought back the original refills, which work great. So we will recommend this diaper pail, as long as you use the original refills. **Bottom line:** Re-designed refills are a disaster; stick with the original ones (which are white). *Rating: A* (original refills only)

Diaper Genie Essentials / Elite by Playtex

Type: Refill canister.

Price: Essentials: $20-$30; Elite: $30-$40 (both are a lot less online depending on the web site). Refill cartridges ($8) hold 180 diapers.

Pros: Wraps each diaper in deodorized plastic. One-hand operation. Easy to remove diapers. Some say better at stink control than Diaper Champ.

Cons: Expensive, since you have to keep buying those refills.

Comments: Diaper Genie was the original "odor free" diaper pail with plastic refills. The pail has been through a few iterations over the years with most recent being the Diaper Genie Essentials. Basically, diapers go in the top, past a clamp which keeps the diapers (and the smell) inside the container (called the AIR TITE system). A plus over past Genies: Playtex actually designed a cutter that, well, cuts the plastic liner so you can easily remove the dirty diapers.

The Diaper Genie Elite features a foot pedal, is taller and has anti-microbial coated plastic (to control odor). Both versions use the same refills (in case you find an old Twistaway Genie at a garage sale, it uses different refills that are still sold in some stores).

There used to be a three-way competition in diaper pails between the Genie, the Dekor and Baby Trend's Diaper Champ. But after Baby Trend muffed the re-design of the Champ, the Dekor changed the plastic on it's refills and Munchkin released its Arm & Hammer diaper pail, it looks to be a two way race for odor control between the Arm & Hammer and the Genie.

That doesn't mean the Genie doesn't have its detractors, many of whom cite the cost of refill cartridges as a major negative. Those parents think a steel trashcan with tight fitting lid (with frequent emptying) is just as effective as the Genie. That is debatable, but others object to the process of putting a diaper in the Genie, which requires pushing it below a clamp (ew, we know).

FYI: Between the two pails, the Genie Essentials gets slightly better marks than the Elite—but the feedback on both is similar. **Bottom line:** The Genie is among the best in its field—but that doesn't mean its perfect. There is probably no such thing as a stink-free diaper pail, especially when baby starts solid foods. *Rating: A*

MUNCHKIN ARM & HAMMER DIAPER PAIL
Type: Refill canister.
Price: $35 ($25 on Target.com); refills $13.
Pros: Baking soda + diapers = less stink.
Cons: Requires two hands to open the lid.
Comments: This diaper pail's secret weapon is baking soda—once you put a diaper in, a built-in dispenser sprinkles the diaper with baking soda to control odor. Yes, you still have to push in the diaper (like the Diaper Genie), but the self-sealing system is a bit easier to use and does what it supposed to do: control the stink.

Reader feedback on this has been trending more positive on this pail than in the past. Parents praise the lack of odor saying it seals better than other brands. And the little shot of baking soda from the refillable cartridge can't hurt. It's also easy to replace the bag and remove the dirty diapers.

Perhaps the biggest complaint we hear from readers is what's called the "squish factor." You have to really push the diaper down to get it into the pail—not fun when it's a really full diaper. And some enterprising toddlers have easily figured out how to get the door open in the base. Finally, it does take two hands to open the lid making for tough going if you have your baby in one hand. **Bottom line:** Even with all its faults, Munchkin's Arm & Hammer diaper pail is a great option for odor control. *Rating: A*

UBBI DIAPER PAIL
Web site: ubbiworld.com
Type: Kitchen trash bag or their own liners.
Price: $70 to $90.
Comments: This steel diaper pail has a sliding top lid with a rubber seal to keep odors in. The reason for the slide? Ubbi told us they think this keeps the smell from wafting out like other diaper pails. And the steel doesn't absorb odors like plastic. Best of all, it uses regular trash bags. The Ubbi has received overall positive reviews from readers, although the slide lid has its critics. We tried it ourselves and thought the slide

was a bit sticky so you may not be able to use it one-handed. **Bottom line:** The Ubbi a lot less expensive than a VIPP, comes in a lot of different colors and you can really use this as a trash can after baby is out of diapers. ***Rating: A-***

VIPP DIAPER PAIL

Type: Refill canister.

Price: $320 for four gallon capacity. Plastic liners: $75 for 800 liners.

Pros: Uh . . . it's from Denmark?

Cons: Yes, the world's first $300+ diaper pail!

Comments: We'll let one of our readers describe her experience with the Vipp: "So I gave in and bought the VIPP diaper pail from Giggle. I thought that despite the obscene price this would be a worthwhile investment that would fight smell, not take up too much space, and look attractive in my Manhattan apartment. I saw that it is made in Denmark, used in doctor's offices and has a steel liner. Basically no plastic to absorb smell. And despite the many debates about Dekor/Genie, it seemed that neither one is quite ideal.

"Well this story does not end well. For $320, I also wanted ease of use (special bags are needed)—but even their special VIPP bag is rather difficult to get in and out. Sadly, I took my 39-week pregnant self to return the trashcan and the woman at Giggle confirmed that although it is great at keeping the smell at bay, it is difficult to change the bag. I really was shocked to find that this 80-year-old Danish company did not have this down to more of a science. While this is not an official 'diaper pail' I think this is aggravating even if using this for regular trash." **Bottom line:** You don't need to spend $320 on a trashcan. ***Rating: F***

◆ ***More pails:*** There are several other basic diaper pails on the market today, such as the $20 Safety 1st Simple Step Diaper Pail. Most are simple plastic trashcans with lids. Our suggestion: if you go this route, just get a stainless steel step-on trashcan ($40 to $100 at stores like Bed Bath & Beyond). Why steel? They are easier to clean—and less likely to stink like plastic. And you are getting a real trashcan you can repurpose to another part of the house after baby is done with diapers.

Humidifiers

We always know when its wintertime here at the ranch in Colorado—the furnace kicks in and everyone's skin dries out quicker than you can say Palm Desert. Hence, humidifiers are a way of life here. But even if you live in a moist climate, running a humidifier in your baby's room in the winter can keep throats, nasal passages and skin from drying out—and make everyone happier.

Here's the 411 on buying a humidifier. First, there are two basic types of humidifiers:

1 **EVAPORATIVE HUMIDIFIERS.** Water is soaked into a wick and then a fan blows the moisture out. While these are affordable, they can be rather noisy (the fan) and you have to replace the filters regularly.

2 **ULTRASONIC HUMIDIFIERS.** Sound waves disperse the moisture, so there's no fan—hence these humidifiers are quieter. The downside: sometime these humidifiers leave a coating of white dust on furniture.

There's also one more choice to make when it comes to humidifiers: warm or cool mist. Like the name implies, warm mist humidifiers use a heating element to warm the water. While that might sound appealing if you live in a cold climate, we do NOT recommend these humidifiers for baby's room. That's because warm mist humidifiers can overheat the room—and that is a risk factor for Sudden Infant Death Syndrome. Also: the warm mist coming out of the humidifier can cause a scalding injury if touched by a wayward toddler.

Some quick additional points:

◆ **CONSIDER ROOM SIZE.** Humidifiers are rated by gallon output and most will tell you the size room they cover—match this to the size room your baby is in. You don't need a giant humidifier for most bedrooms.

Tracking Online Coupon Codes

If you've earned your black belt in online shopping, you know discount codes are a common way for web sites to lure customers or reward customer loyalty. And while there are sites that list coupon deals across the web (FatWallet.com, eDealFinder.com), how do you find the best coupon codes just for baby stuff? Check out our message boards (BabyBargains.com, click on Message Boards). On the Bargain Alert board, we keep a pinned thread with all the latest coupon deals, all submitted by our readers (spam isn't allowed). Updated regularly, this thread has all the best deals. (And there's even a separate pinned thread for freebies.)

◆ **CLEAN IT REGULARLY.** Humidifiers have detailed cleaning instructions—follow these! If not, you risk mold or mildew build-up in the unit or shortening the life of the humidifier.

◆ **ADJUSTABLE HUMIDISTAT.** A humidistat works like a thermostat, setting the humidity at a certain level and turning on or off the humidifier until it reaches that level. This is a nice feature, but not completely necessary.

◆ **REMODELING? CONSIDER A WHOLE-HOUSE HUMIDIFIER.** If you are planning to do any HVAC work on your home, consider installing a whole-house humidifier. These automatically kick in when your furnace runs (or can be controlled by a thermostat). Since they are permanently installed and plumbed to a water line, you never have to refill the humidifier. You do have to change the filter and clean out the unit, but that's just once a year.

◆ **SKIP THE VAPORIZER.** A vaporizer is a humidifier that lets you disperse medication in your child's room. Generally, this is NOT recommended—that's because pediatricians rarely prescribe medication that needs to be vaporized these days.

Brand Recommendations: Our Picks

Good. The *Crane EE-5301* is a $45 cool mist humidifier with a 2.3 gallon output and automatic shut-off feature. But it lacks a humidistat—you adjust the amount of output with a knob on the front. This is a very good model that is quiet. FYI: Crane also makes the same humidifier in a series of animal shapes—basically the same model, but these units are smaller and only hold one gallon of water.

Best. The *Air-O-Swiss 7135 Ultrasonic Humidifier* is pricey ($180) but features a built-in humidistat and a replaceable demineralization cartridge to cut down on white dust. Offers either warm or cool mist (when used in a baby's room, always use cool mist). A sleep mode turns the unit

off after eight hours. Very quiet, 3.5 gallon tank. But the anti-microbial features of this unit come at a price: regular maintenance is a must—and that requires about $100 per year in supplies (demineralization cartridges and other parts). FYI: The *Air-O-Swiss 7147* has the same features/price as the 7135, but is a bit more compact in size.

Bouncer Seat/Activity Gyms

◆ **ACTIVITY GYM.** Among our favorites is the *Gymini by Tiny Love* (tinylove.com). The Gymini is a three-foot square blanket that has two criss-cross arches. You clip rattles, mirrors and other toys onto the arches, providing endless fun for baby as she lies on her back and reaches for the toys. The Gymini comes in several versions that range from $35 to $60. The *Gymini Super Deluxe Lights & Music* is a good bet at $60. A runner-up: the *Fisher Price Rainforest Melodies and Lights Deluxe Gym* is $46. Both of these activity gyms fold up for travel.

◆ **ACTIVITY SEAT/BOUNCER WITH TOY BAR.** An activity seat (also called a bouncer) provides a comfy place for baby to hang out while you eat dinner, and the toy bar adds some mild amusement. The latest twist to these products is a "Magic Fingers" vibration feature—the bouncer basically vibrates, simulating a car ride. Parents who have these bouncers tell us they'd rather have a kidney removed than give up their vibrating bouncer, as it appears the last line of defense in soothing a fussy baby, short of checking into a mental institution.

What features should you look for in a bouncer? Readers say a carrying handle is a big plus. Also: get a neutral fabric pattern, says another parent, since you'll probably be taking lots of photos of baby and a garish pattern may grate on your nerves.

What is the best brand for bouncers? Fisher Price (fisher-price.com) makes the most popular one in the category; most are about $35 to $75, depending on the version. A good choice: the *Fisher Price RainForest bouncer* ($60). Although some of the sounds were a little loud, the toys and waterfall got high marks. Yes, other companies make similar products (KIDS II is a good runner-up), but the feedback we get from parents is that Fisher-Price is the best.

Readers also give kudos to the *Fisher Price Newborn Rock 'n Play Sleeper* ($45) which doubles as both a place to sleep and a rocker.

One caveat: most bouncer seats have a 25-pound weight limit. If you want something that will last longer, consider the *Baby Bjorn Balance*. Yes, it is more pricey than the Fisher-Price (about $150, depending on the store) and lacks a vibrating feature . . . but you can use it up to 29 lbs. Fisher-Price does have a bouncer that can even be used up to 40 lbs.—the *Infant-to-Toddler* rocker ($40). Parent feedback on that model is very positive.

Graco has added a new sub-category to bouncers: a "soothing center." The *Graco Sweet Peace* ($180; pictured) provides four cradling motions, six speeds and the removable carrier doubles as a floor rocker (or you can use it with a Graco infant car seat). Feedback on the Sweet Peace has been mostly positive with only a few complaints that the motor is a bit loud. Parents really like that it plugs into the wall (battery-operation is optional) and is easy to put together.

Along the same lines, we like the **4Moms MamaRoo.** Pricey at $200, the MamaRoo's fans love the five unique motions (including car ride, ocean wave, etc) as well as the built-in nature sounds and the relative compact footprint. One negative: it only has a three-point safety harness (we prefer a five-point).

What about those $100+ bouncers from Oeuf or Svan? Pretty to look at but not practical, say our readers. The lack of vibration or just about any other feature you find on a $50 bouncer makes these bouncers not worth the extra investment.

◆ **TOY BARS FOR YOUR CAR SEAT.** Here's another money-saving tip: turn your infant car seat into an activity center with an attachable toy bar. Manhattan Toy makes a **Whoozit Activity Spiral** with dangling toys that wraps around carrier handles for $20. Another plus: your baby is safer in an infant car seat carrier than in other activity seats, thanks to that industrial-strength harness safety system. Safety warning: only use these toy bars when the car seat is NOT inside a vehicle (that is, at home, etc.). Toy bars are not safe in a vehicle as they can be a hazard/projectile in an accident.

One caveat: some parents and pediatricians believe that leaving an infant in a car seat for extended periods of time can contribute to breathing problems in very young infants. For older babies, excessive time in an infant seat could lead to flat head syndrome (plagiocephaly). Unfortunately, doctors don't agree on how much time in an infant seat is too much. Use your common sense and move your child out of the seat frequently.

Play Yards

The portable play yard has been so popular in recent years that many parents consider it a necessity. Compared to rickety playpens of old, today's play yards fold compactly for portability and offer such handy features as bassinets, wheels and more. Some shopping tips:

◆ **Don't buy a second-hand play yard or use a hand-me-down.** Many models have been the subject of recalls in recent years. Why? Those same features that make them convenient (the collapsibility to make the play yards "portable") worked too well in the past—some play yards collapsed with babies inside. Others had protruding rivets that caught some babies who wore pacifiers on a string (a BIG no-no, never have your baby wear a pacifier on a string). A slew of injuries and deaths have prompted the recall of ten million playpens over the years. Yes, you can search government recall lists (cpsc.gov) to see if that hand-me-down is recalled, but we'd skip the hassle and just buy new.

◆ *Go for the bassinet feature.* Some play yards feature bassinet inserts, which can be used for babies under three months of age (always check the weight guidelines). This is a handy feature that we recommend. Other worthwhile features: wheels for mobility, side-rail storage compartments and a canopy (if you plan to take the play yard outside or to the beach). If you want a play yard with canopy, look for those models that have "aluminized fabric" canopies—they reflect the sun's heat and UV rays to keep baby cooler.

◆ *Skip the "newborn napper."* Graco has recently added a new-born napper feature to some of its playpens. This is a separate sleep area designed to "cuddle your baby." You are supposed to use this napper before you use the bassinet feature. Our concern: the nap-per includes plush fabrics and a head pillow—we consider this an unsafe sleep environment. As we discussed in Chapter 2, Nursery, your baby should always be put down to sleep on his back on a flat surface with no soft bedding. Graco also makes a model (the Chadwick) that has non-removeable bumpers on the bassinet. We do not recommend this model play yard for the same reason we don't recommend you use bumpers in a crib.

◆ *Check the weight limits.* Play yards have two weight limits: one for the bassinet and one for the entire play yard (without the bassinet). Graco and most other play yard versions have an overall weight limit of 30 lbs. and height limit of 35" The exception is the Arms Reach Co-Sleeper which tops out at 50 lbs. However, there is more variation in the weight limits for the bassinet attachments. Here are the weight limits for the *bassinet attachments* on various play yards:

Arms Reach Co-Sleeper	30 lbs.
Graco Pack N Play	15 lbs.
Chicco Lullaby	15 lbs.
Compass Aluminum	18 lbs.
Combi Play Yard	15 lbs.

Our Picks: Brand Recommendations

Good. Joovy's Room2 Portable
Play Yard ($150) has ten square feet
of area—twice the size of most standard playpens, giving baby more
room to play. No, it doesn't include
many other features you see in other
playpens (there is no bassinet, diaper changing area, etc). However, it

does what it does well—provide a large, safe area for baby to play.
Readers love the easy set-up and heavy weight canvas fabric.

Better. Chicco's Lullaby LX Play
Yard ($190) is loaded with all the bells
and whistles: bassinet, changing station, toys, storage areas, remote control electronics and more. Readers
love the quality and ease of set-up for
the Chicco playpen, but a few critics

knocked the hefty 30-pound weight (which we admit stretches the
definition of a *portable* play yard). And the two gimmicky features (a
vibrating mattress that doesn't really vibrate) and a somewhat useless
mobile had more than one reader scratching their heads. Overall,
however, folks are generally happy with this unit.

Best (for home). Graco is the market
leader in this category—and given the
value and features they offer, that's no
surprise. The company offers a dozen
models of playpens and each is well
designed. A good example is the
Graco Pack N Play On the Go ($70),

which lacks all the whiz-bang electronics and toys of the Chicco
playpen, but then again, is that really needed? It features a bassinet,
toy bar and wheels. Of course, if you want all the toys and gizmos,
Graco has models with those features too—but you'll pay $100 to
$200 for those versions. A couple final caveats: skip the Graco mod-
els with "newborn nappers." As we explained in the Buying Advice,
we don't recommend these for safety reasons.

Best (for travel). Baby Bjorn's Travel Crib Light 2 ($240 to
$300). Not cheap, but this ultra-light play yard folds up like an
umbrella and fits in a smaller size carry case. Parent feedback has
been universally positive. At 11 pounds, it is half the weight of a

AROUND THE HOUSE

Playpen Bassinets: Naps vs. Sleeping?

As you may remember from Chapter 2, we recommend the bassinet feature of playpens as an alternative to a stand-alone bassinet for newborns.

However, some readers note that manufacturers like Graco advise the product is "intended for naps and play" and question whether a newborn should sleep full time in the bassinet.

We understand the confusion, but here's our advice: when it comes to newborns, there isn't much of a distinction between "naps" and nighttime sleep—day or night, most newborns are sleeping only four hours at a stretch (they need to feed at roughly that interval). Hence, we interpret Graco's advice to only use the Pack N Play for "naps or play" applies more to older babies—the product shouldn't take the place of a full-size crib (but is fine for occasional use at Grandma's house or a hotel room). The bottom line: we believe the bassinet feature is fine for full-time use for newborns who are under the weight limits (typically 15 pounds).

FYI: Be sure to check out some of our recommendations for play yard sheets in Chapter 3. While most parents love their play yards, the cheap-o sheets that come with most are a pain (they slip off the mattress too easily, etc). We discuss alternatives in Chapter 3 that solve this problem.

standard Graco Pack N Play. Parents did complain that the legs on the Travel Crib Light were wonky. Good news: a Travel Crib Light 2 will be available soon with stronger leg mechanisms.

Swings

You can't talk to new parents without hearing the heated debate on swings, those battery-operated surrogate parents. Some think they're a godsend, soothing a fussy baby when nothing else seems to work. Cynics refer to them as "neglect-o-matics," sinister devices that can become far too addictive for a society that thinks parenting is like a microwave meal—the quicker, the better.

Whatever side you come down on, we do have a few shopping tips. First, ALWAYS try a swing before you buy. Give it a whirl in the store or borrow one from a friend. Why? Some babies love swings. Others hate 'em. Don't spend $120 on a fancy swing only to discover your little one is a swing-hater.

When we last wrote on the topic of swings, you still had a choice between wind-up swings and battery-operated models. While you may still find some wind-up models at garage sales or on eBay, most swings sold in stores are battery-operated. On Craigslist, we've seen wind-up swings for as little as $20. Of course, check with the CPSC (cpsc.gov) to make sure a used swing hasn't been recalled.

If you are in the market for a new swing, remember this rule: swings eat batteries faster than toddlers can scarf M&M's. Look for swings that use fewer batteries—some use as little as two or three (others up to four). Good news: many swings now also include an AC adapter so you can plug the swing into a wall outlet. This saves tremendously on batteries. Fisher-Price has several options with adapters.

Swings range in price from $50 to $140. The more money you spend the more bells and whistles you get—toys, music, etc.

Remember to observe safety warnings about swings, which are close to the top ten most dangerous products, as far as injuries go. You must always stay with your baby, use the safety belt, and stop using the swing once your baby reaches the weight limit (about 25 lbs. in most cases). Always remember that a swing is not a baby-sitter.

Our picks: Brand recommendations

Swings today come in three flavors: full-size, compact or travel. As you might guess, the latter category folds up for easy transport. Each work fine—if you have the space, go for a full-size model. If not, try a compact or travel version.

Who makes the best swings? Here are our picks:

Good. *Kids II's InGenuity Portable Swing* is a very affordable swing ($53) with TrueSpeed technology to keep baby swinging even when she gets heavier.

Better. Graco's top-selling swing is the *Sweetpeace Infant Soothing Swing*, ($170) which we discussed earlier in the bouncer section of this chapter. This one is a hybrid between a swing and bouncer and gets very good review from readers.

Best. Fisher-Price has the cradle swing down to a science. The *Fisher Price My Little Lamb Cradle 'n Swing* ($150) allows for both side-to-side and front-back motion, three seat positions and a plush seat. There are six speeds, eight musical tunes and two-position seat recline. FYI:

Fisher Price makes many different versions of its cradle swing in prices that range from $100 to $160—the difference is typically fashion and toys. For example, the **Papasan Cradle Swing** ($110) is a reader favorite.

Portable. How about a swing for Grandma's house? We like the **Fisher Price Space Saver Swing and Seat**. This cool swing folds up for portability, making it a good bet for $60.

Monitors

For her first nine months, your baby is tethered to you via the umbilical cord. After that, it's the baby monitor that becomes your surrogate umbilical cord—enabling you to work in the garden, wander about the house, and do many things that other, childless human beings do, while still keeping tabs on a sleeping baby. Hence, this is a pretty important piece of equipment you'll use every day—a good one will make your life easier . . . and a bad one will be a never-ending source of irritation.

 Smart Shopper Tips for Monitors

Smart Shopper Tip #1
Bugging your house
"I saw a TV report where a reporter was able to drive around a neighborhood and peer in on folks' video baby monitors. Are these monitors secure?"

Let's consider what a baby monitor really is: the base unit is the transmitter and the receiver is, well, a receiver. So anyone with another baby monitor on the same frequency can often pick up your monitor—not just the sound of your baby crying, but also *any* conversations you have with your mate in the nursery.

Ditto for video monitors—most work at the same frequency. If you get another receiver and drive around the neighborhood, you'll probably be able to pick up other video signals.

The take home message: most audio and video monitors are not encrypted. Therefore the best advice is to remember that your house (or at least, your baby's room) is bugged. If you want to protect your privacy, don't have any sensitive conversations within earshot of the baby monitor. You never know who might be listening. It is wise to turn OFF the baby monitor when baby isn't in the room.

So are there any monitors that are private? Until just recently, the answer was no. But there is good news: several models feature "digital" (DECT) technology—their signals can't be intercepted, unlike older analog monitors. We'll discuss DECT later in this section and point out which models feature this technology in our product reviews.

As for baby video monitors, most are analog, not digital (and hence, not secure). However, there are a few digital models. We'll note such monitors in the reviews later in this chapter.

Side note: you can use a network webcam as a baby monitor—and several of these cameras can be password protected (so not just anyone can look in on the signal). But setting up a network webcam to view online is rather geeky and beyond the scope of this book!

Smart Shopper Tip #2
Battery woes

"Boy, we should have bought stock in Duracell when our baby was born! We go through dozens of batteries each month to feed our very hungry baby monitor."

Most baby monitors have the option of running on batteries or regular current (by plugging it into a wall outlet). Our advice: use the wall outlet as often as possible. Batteries don't last long—as little as eight to ten hours with continual use. Another idea: you can buy another AC adapter from a source like Radio Shack for $10 or less—you can leave one AC adapter in your bedroom and have another one available in a different part of the house. (Warning: make sure you get the correct AC adapter for your monitor, in terms of voltage and polarity. Take your existing AC adapter to Radio Shack and ask for help to make sure you are getting the correct unit. If not, you can fry your monitor).

Another solution: several baby monitors (reviewed later in this chapter) feature rechargeable receivers! You'll never buy a set of batteries for these units—you just plug them into an outlet to recharge.

Smart Shopper Tip #3
Interference issues

"We have a cordless phone and a baby monitor. Boy, it took us two weeks to figure out how to use both without having a nervous breakdown."

If we could take a rocket launcher and zap one person in this world, it would have to be the idiot who decided that baby monitors and cordless phones should share the same radio frequency. What were they thinking? Gee, let's take two people who are already dangerously short of sleep and mess with their phone and baby monitor.

So, here are our tips to avoid frustration:

First, the higher the frequency, the longer the range of the monitor. Basic baby monitors work on the 49 MHz frequency—these will work for a few hundred feet. Step up to a 900 MHz monitor and you can double the distance the monitor will work (some makers claim up to 1000 feet). Finally, there are baby monitors that work on the 2.4 GHz frequency, where you can pick up your baby in Brazil. Okay, not that far, but you get the idea. Of course, "range" estimates are just that—your real-life range will probably be much less than what's touted on the box.

Now here's the rub: cordless phones and WiFi networks can often interfere with your baby monitor. Old cordless phones worked on the 49 MHz frequency, but modern models are more likely to be found in the 900 MHz or the 2.4 GHz (or even 5.8 GHz) bands. If you've got a baby monitor at 900 MHz and a cordless phone on the same frequency, expect trouble. Ironically, as more and more devices use the higher frequency, the old 49 MHz for baby monitors now seems to be the most trouble free when it comes to interference.

WiFi networks work on the 2.4 GHz band—yep, the same frequency used by some baby monitors. The same advice as above: don't get a baby monitor on the same frequency as your WiFi network. FYI: Baby VIDEO monitors work on either the 900 MHz or 2.4 GHz frequencies and can have the same interference issues as audio monitors.

New to the market are digital or DECT monitors, which work in the 1.9 GHz range. Since very few other electronics operate on this band, DECT monitors are virtually interference-free and work at even longer range than 2.4 GHz monitors. Another plus: DECT monitors can't be monitored by noisy neighbors. Bottom line: if your house is buzzing with electronics, consider a DECT monitor (we'll suggest specific models later in the reviews section).

So, to sum up, here is our advice: first, try to buy a baby monitor on a different frequency than your cordless phone or WiFi network. Second, always keep the receipt. Baby monitors have one of the biggest complaint rates of all products we review. We suspect all the electronic equipment in people's homes today (cell phones, WiFi routers, fax machines, large-screen TVs the size of a Sony Jumbotron), not to mention all the interference sources near your home (cell phone towers, etc.) must account for some of the problems folks have with baby monitors. Common complaints include static, lack of range, buzzing and worse—and those problems can happen with a baby monitor in any price range.

So, read our monitor recommendations later with a grain of salt. ANY monitor (even those we rate the highest) can still run into static and interference problems, based on your home's electronics.

Again, the best advice: always keep the receipt for any baby monitor you buy—you may have to take it back and exchange it for another brand if problems develop.

Smart Shopper Tip #4
The one-way dilemma

"Our baby monitor is nice, but it would be great to be able to buzz my husband so he could bring me something to drink while I'm feeding the baby. Are there any monitors out there that let you communicate two ways?"

Yep, Philips has models that do just that (see review later in this chapter). Of course, there is another alternative: you can always go to Radio Shack and buy a basic intercom for about $50. Most also have a "lock" feature that you can leave on to listen to the baby when he's sleeping. Another advantage to intercoms: you can always deploy the unit to another part of your house after you're done monitoring the baby. Of course, the only disadvantage to intercoms is that they aren't portable—most must be plugged into a wall outlet.

Here are other features to consider when shopping for monitors:

◆ *Out of range indicators*. If you plan to wander from the house and visit your garden, you may want to go for a monitor that warns you when you've strayed too far from its transmitter. Some models have a visual out of range indicator, while others beep at you. Of course, even if your monitor doesn't offer this feature, you'll probably realize when you're out of range—the background noise you hear in your home will disappear from the receiver.

◆ *Low battery indicator.* Considering how quickly monitors can eat batteries, you'd think this would be a standard feature for monitors. Nope—very few current models actually warn you when you're running out of juice. Most units will just die. If you plan to heavily use your monitor on battery power (out in the garden, for example), look for this feature.

◆ *What's the frequency?* As we discussed above, the right or wrong frequency can make a world of difference. Before selecting a monitor, think about the wireless gadgets you have in your home (particularly cordless phones). Then look carefully at packages . . . not all monitors put that info up front.

◆ *Extra receivers.* It is convenient to leave one receiver in your bedroom and then tote around another receiver in your home.

◆ **Digital technology.** New models use digital technology to prevent eavesdropping by your neighbors. Digital monitors also avoid static and interference from other electronics in your home.

◆ **Great, but not necessary.** Some monitors have a temperature display, which might help you spot a nursery that's too warm. Others have a base with nightlight or play lullabies to sooth baby. Nice, but most folks don't need this.

Smart Shopper Tip #5
The cordless phone trick

"A techie friend of mind mentioned that some of the new cordless phones can double as baby monitors. Which phone does that?

Here's a clever way to avoid spending $50 on a baby monitor. Simply use your cordless phone to monitor the baby's room. Uniden (uniden.com), for example, sells not one but 55 cordless phone models with a room monitor feature. A typical package includes two handsets for about $40—then you can buy extra handsets for about $20. FYI: Panasonic also has several models with this feature as well.

Basically, you put one handset in the baby's room, turn on the room monitor feature and you can listen in on a second handset. One caveat: with some models you can't both monitor a room and receive a phone call at the same time. Make sure your model can receive a call when in monitor mode.

The bottom line: if you need a new cordless phone for your house, consider buying one with a room-monitoring feature.

Smart Shopper Tip #6
Video monitor shopping advice

"We want a video baby monitor. What are the key features to consider?

Video baby monitors have become increasingly popular in recent years, thanks to improved technology and lower prices, starting at just $100. Here are some key features to look for:

◆ **Fixed . . . or not.** There are three basic types of video monitors out there: fixed, PTZ and streaming. Fixed monitors have a camera that is, well, fixed and is the most economical choice. PTZ stands for point/tilt/zoom, where a camera can move and tilt: some parents prefer PTZ monitors since they can scan a room for a wayward baby or toddler. Finally, streaming baby monitors can send a video signal over the internet, so grandparents and relatives can see the baby's nursery. Each type has its trade-offs—most streaming monitors are fixed. And most PTZ monitors can be pricey.

◆ *Zero Dark Nursery.* One of the key times you use a monitor is at night—or to see in a darkened room, while baby is sleeping. To help make visible pictures, cameras use night vision—basically a series of LED lights that bathe a nursery in infrared light. While some cameras have better night vision than others (we'll note this in reviews), realize that baby monitor night vision is rather rudimentary. The goal isn't to have a super-crisp picture to see your baby's facial expressions. You just want to see if baby is sleeping. Or playing. Or standing up crying, etc. Of course, weak night vision that doesn't let you even see if your baby is sleeping or sitting up is a problem. And night vision is often limited in distance—you can't put the camera ten feet away from the crib and expect to see clearly in the dark.

◆ *Battery life.* In a word, it sucks for most video monitors. That's because portable video screens are power hogs. Expect to plug in the monitor for over-night monitoring—that's because most monitors only last two to four hours on battery power.

◆ *Resolution.* Don't expect HDTV-quality pictures from most baby monitors. Remember, you are viewing most monitors on a small (2.4" to 3.5") screen. The resolution should enable you to get a clear view of your baby's crib or nursery, not to count the freckles on his cute little face (no matter how tempting). The best video monitors have a resolution of 640 x 280 pixels. HDTV, by contrast, is 1920 x 1080 pixels.

◆ *VOX.* Voice-on-exchange mode is an optional setting on many monitors that only turns on the screen when baby makes a sound above a preset level. This is helpful to conserve battery. Folks either love or hate VOX—fans love not having to hear every peep or squeak from baby. Critics say VOX mode can falsely trigger, awakening sleep-deprived parents when there isn't a problem in the nursery.

◆ *Zoom.* The Z in PTZ cameras stands for zoom. And some cameras offer this feature to let you zoom in on a particular area in the nursery. Be aware that most cameras have a digital zoom. This means the pixels in the camera are enlarged when you zoom. As a result, the picture becomes grainy. Hence, the zoom feature is less helpful than you'd think.

◆ *Stream.* The latest trend in baby monitors are those that can stream a picture online—so you can check baby while you are at work. Or a grandparent can see the nursery. This type of monitor can be tricky to set up, as it requires a secure connection to the internet. Depending on your internet router, these monitors can work fabulously . . . or not at all. We'll discuss the options in detail in the reviews.

More Money Buys You

Basic baby monitors are just that—an audio monitor and transmitter. No-frills monitors start at $20 or $25. More money buys you a sound/light display (helpful in noisy environments, since the lights indicate if your baby is crying) and rechargeable batteries (you can go through $50 a year in 9-volts with regular monitors). More expensive monitors even have transmitters that also work on batteries (so you could take it outside if you wish) or dual receivers (helpful if you want to leave the main unit inside the house and take the second one outside if you need to work in the garage, etc.). Finally, the top-end monitors either have digital technology or intercom features, where you can use the receiver to talk to your baby as you walk back to the room. The most expensive monitor on the market, Philips' $200 Digital Monitor, adds a room temperature thermometer, adjustable sound sensitivity, music and a night light.

For video monitors, more money buys you a color viewing screen (the cheaper ones are just black and white). Some more expensive models have point-tilt-zoom capability (PTZ) as well as extra monitors (Summer's "complete" coverage video monitor comes with a 7" LCD screen and 1.8" handheld unit).

Audio Baby Monitors

The Name Game: Audio Baby Monitors

Here's a look at the best audio baby monitors (video monitor reviews start on page 330).

Major caveat to these reviews: ANY baby monitor, even those that earn our highest ratings, can have problems with static, poor reception or interference (see earlier discussion). The best advice: keep your receipt and buy a monitor from a store with a good return policy. It might be trial and error to find one that works for you.

A quick safety tip for monitors: always keep the cord away from your baby's crib. Cords from cameras/monitors are a strangulation hazard.

The Ratings

A EXCELLENT—*our top pick!*
B GOOD— *above average quality, prices, and creativity.*
C FAIR—*could stand some improvement.*
D POOR—*yuck! could stand some major improvement.*

Angelcare *angelcare-monitor.com* The Angelcare monitor launched in 1997 after engineer Maurice Pinsonnault bought the patent rights to a breathing monitor sold in the UK. In a nutshell, Angelcare has two functions: first, it is a regular audio baby monitor. Second, it measures baby's "breathing movements" through a sensor placed under the crib mattress. If baby stops moving for 20 seconds, an alarm sounds on the parent unit.

Here's our problem with this concept: Angelcare clearly preys on parents' fears of Sudden Infant Death Syndrome. However, experts such as the American Academy of Pediatrics say monitors like Angelcare don't work in preventing SIDS. And Angelcare is very careful to steer clear of such promises (its website doesn't refer to SIDS, only the "anxiety which all new parents face").

Bottom line: if your baby has a medical condition that requires a breathing monitor, you need to get a medical grade monitor from your pediatrician.

In Angelcare's defense, folks who have this monitor generally praise it for the "piece of mind." But you can generally get the same piece of mind from any audio monitor that costs half as much as the Angelcare ($74 for a single, $110 for a double receiver).

As a side note, we should mention that Angelcare does make an audio-only model (the AC420, $48 to $58). This model omits the breathing sensor and generally gets very good marks from parents. But it is rather pricey (by comparison, the Sony monitor we recommend is about 25% cheaper). And there is no dual receiver version of the Angelcare audio only monitor, limiting its appeal. They have expanded the line with other options as well: a color video monitor with movement sensor ($300; online for as little as $190), a movement only monitor ($54 to $65) and a couple analog models.

So we will give Angelcare a failing grade: if experts say it doesn't prevent SIDS, what is the point? ***Rating: F***

BabySense The BabySense V Movement Monitor ($130) is similar to the Angelcare—using sensor pads, it detects baby's movements to prevent SIDS. If she stops breathing, the parent unit sounds an alarm. But it isn't an audio monitor so you won't hear your baby crying. Regardless, we don't recommend monitors like the

BabySense; see the Angelcare review for our reasoning. ***Rating: F***

Belkin (WeMo Baby) *belkin.com* The pitch for the Belkin WeMo Baby monitor goes like this: if you've got an iPhone, iPad or iPod Touch that you carry around, why do you need a separate audio baby monitor receiver? Why not just use your smartphone to monitor baby?

That's Belkin's idea behind what it calls the iPhone Baby Monitor: a device that streams audio from your baby's nursery direct to your iPhone, via an easy-to-use free app. The $53 gadget creates its own WiFi network. You log in to the network on your iPhone with the app—and then select the WiFi home network you want the device to connect to. Easy, no?

Well . . . like too many tech gadgets, that's where the Belkin WeMo baby monitor falls down. Parent feedback on this product has been mostly negative: folks have a problem setting it up (getting it to connect), the app crashes and more woes. On Belkin's support message boards, we noticed quite a few complaints about monitors that frequently disconnected and others that worked 50% of the time. Unfortunately for Belkin, you want your baby monitor to work 100% of the time.

So perhaps this is a classic example of a 1.0 tech product that is not ready for prime time. While the Belkin WeMo Baby has promise, we say skip it until Belkin can figure out the bugs. ***Rating: F***

First Years *thefirstyears.com* First Years sells one audio monitor, the Crisp & Clear ($20 single, $30 double) at Target.

This bare-bones analog monitor (using the 49 MHz range) has sound, lights, low battery and out of range alerts.

In the past, several of First Years older digital audio monitors were discontinued (but still for sale online).

Generally, First Years monitors get very poor reviews. Quality woes dog these monitors with static, connection drops, clicking and other complaints. There are better choices in this category. **Rating: D**

Fisher Price *fisher-price.com*. Fisher Price has exited the baby monitor category, discontinuing all monitors. We still see some of their old models for sale online; given parent feedback, we'd suggest passing on this brand. ***Rating: C***

Graco *gracobaby.com* Graco has been in the monitor market for several years, but they've run into stiff competition from tech brands. Here's an overview of their current offerings:

At the opening price point for audio monitors, the Sound Select analog monitor is a bare bones 49 MHz monitor that just has audio (no lights or other features) for $17 in Walmart.

A more deluxe version of this model (Sound Select LX) features sound lights and vibration. It runs $30 at Walmart for a single, $40 double.

For digital monitors, Graco has three offerings: the Secure Coverage, Direct Connect and imonitor.

Secure Coverage ($44 single, $54 double) is a 900 MHz monitor with vibration, sound/lights and a low battery alarm. Direct Connect ($48 single, $90 double) is similar, but adds an intercom feature as well as a display of the baby's room temperature on the parent unit.

The imonitor Vibe ($60 single, $90 double) is a simple digital monitor with 900 MHz frequency and vibration. This model will be discontinued shortly, although we notice it is still for sale on quite a few sites.

So how's the quality? Graco says its "static filter technology" on its analog monitors allows you to hear only baby's cry, not background noise. Readers give a thumbs down on the static filter, saying it just doesn't work. It's hard to know whether it is the 49 MHz technology that is the failure here or the numerous interference points that most folks have in their homes.

Graco's digital monitors fared even worse in reader feedback. The imonitor, for example, is often criticized for its lack of range and short battery life. Sound clarity is good, but more than one parent complained about lack of long-term durability (the monitor won't hold a charge after a year, etc.). No surprise that the imonitor is headed for the discontinued bin.

Similar complaints about quality and lack of range dog the Secure Coverage and Direct Connect monitors—Graco clearly over-promises (a 2000 foot range?) and under-performs (readers say it is more like 30 feet line of sight).

Overall, Graco falls short in this category. **Rating: D**

Motorola binatonetelecom.com Electronics maker Binatone has licensed the Motorola name for a line of baby monitors that are mostly sold online.

The lowest cost Motorola model is the MBP8, which features DECT transmission for a range of 165 feet—the transmitter plugs directly into a wall outlet. There is an out of range alert, sound/lights and a night-light on the baby's unit. Price: $30 at Target.

Next, the simple MBP11($40) has a basic sound/light display, out of range indicator, rechargeable batteries on the parent unit only and . . . that's about it. The main difference between this model and the 10: the 10 has a transmitter that will also work on a battery (for five hours of wireless monitoring). The 11 lacks that feature (of course, it is also $10 cheaper).

The MBP16 ($60) adds a night light, two-way intercom, lullaby player and room temperature display (see below).

FYI: There several older, discontinued models by Motorola still being sold online.

So how's the quality? Motorola monitors get mixed reviews at best. The lowest price model (MBP8) gets the best marks, but that isn't saying much. The biggest complaints center on quality—units that quit working after five days, transmission that cuts out, etc.

The reviews turn even more negative for the more expensive Motorola models.

Previously, we recommended the entry-level monitors from this brand with a B+; however, as the feedback has turned more sharply negative in recent months, we are dropping Motorola's grade. ***Rating: D***

Philips Avent *Consumer.Philips.com* Consumer products giant Philips Avent makes an excellent line of baby monitors.

Key to the quality: DECT transmission technology that not only maintains privacy but allows for a good connection distance.

The SCD560 ($80) features sound/light display, intercom, temperature sensor/display, rechargeable batteries and an ECO mode that saves power consumption when the monitor isn't in use.

The SCD570 ($110) adds a vibration alert feature, but is other wise the same as the 560.

Reader feedback has been positive on these new models—parents like the ability to adjust the microphone sensitivity to screen out background noise in baby's room. Fans also laud the interference-free reception and long battery life (about 24 hours on a charge).

The few complaints we get on these monitors center on the display unit's screen—it's hard to read the display in certain light conditions. The screen contrast frustrates some users.

Bottom line: while these audio monitors are pricey, the quality is excellent. ***Rating: A***

Safety 1st *safety1st.com* Safety 1st offers a dozen audio baby monitors, most of which are affordably priced.

Example: a bare bones 49 MHz model with no sound and light display (Crystal Clear, $16). The Glow & Go adds sound/lights and a temperature display (on base) and comes in both single ($25) and dual ($40) versions. The baby's unit has a glow light with a 15 minute auto shut-off.

Sound Moments is a newer 49 MHz monitor available with one ($45) or two parent units ($60). It also features a quick mute button, sound and lights, power and low battery indicators and an audio jack for headphones. Sure Glow ($25 for single version, $25 to $44 for double) is similar to Sound Moments but has only the sound and lights and audio jack.

Safety 1st has brought back their digital monitor, the High Def Monitor. This simple monitor features DECT technology, sound/light display, rechargeable battery, out of range and low battery indicators. This monitor sells for about $50—one of the more affordable digital monitors on the market.

So, how's the quality for Safety 1st's monitors? The simple Crystal Clear monitor gets semi-decent reviews here—perhaps after spending just $16, folks don't have high expectations. While it worked for most parents, the Crystal Clear occasionally suffers from being less than crystal clear (static is the biggest issue for some parents).

Reviews for the High Def have been mixed, with quite a few reports of defective units cropping up in recent months. This mars the model's otherwise positive reader reports

Bottom line: Safety 1st monitors earn only average marks from our readers—makers like Philips Avent have much better quality. While Safety 1st's monitors (especially the lower priced ones) perform somewhat better than those by other juvenile product makers like Graco . . . that isn't saying very much. ***Rating: C***

Sony *sonystyle.com* Sony keeps it simple with one audio baby monitor model: the Sony BabyCall NTM-910 is a 27-channel model with rechargeable batteries for $30 to $50 single, $55 to $70 dual. Yes, you read that right—the BabyCall has 27 channels (most monitors have at most one or two). The result is less chance for interference.

The downside? Well, the receiver is rather bulky. And since this monitor isn't digital, it is possible to eavesdrop on the signal. And the 900 MHz frequency has less range than 2.4 GHz or DECT. But this model does have an out-of-range indicator and an optional sound-activated mode that silences the receiver until sufficient noise activates it.

This Sony BabyCall monitor was one of our top picks in a previous edition of our book, but now it is showing its age. DECT monitors from competitors like Philips Avent outscore Sony, say readers. In the past year, we see more reports of interference and static. We're not sure what is turning the reviews more negative, but we can't help but wonder if the thicket of electronic gear in homes today is to blame. That's why DECT audio monitors seem to make folks happier.

As we were going to press, we noticed Sony has released a new baby monitor, the NTM-DA1 ($70). This digital monitor works on the 2.4 GHz range and features an out of range indicator and low battery light. This model was too new for any parent feedback yet.

Bottom line: we are dropping our rating of the Sony BabyCall NTM-910. It still works for some folks, but increasingly it looks like it is now past its prime. **Rating: B**

Summer *summerinfant.com* Summer is probably best known for its video monitors, but the company does have a couple of offerings in the audio space. Both models offer digital transmission for privacy.

The Baby Wave Digital Audio monitor ($45) is a basic model with digital transmission and sound/lights. A deluxe version of this monitor ($55) adds temperature monitoring of the nursery (with an on-screen read out on the parent unit), as well as an intercom and nightlight feature. These monitors were too new as of press time for parent feedback.

The Slim & Secure Digital Audio Monitor ($50 single, $80 dual, less online; pictured) is a 2.4 GHz monitor with sound/lights and rechargeable batteries. Reader feedback on this new model has been mixed: folks like the audio clarity, but the bright blue LED on the parent unit makes this one a pain to use a night (one reviewer said it was like a blue strobe light). FYI: This model is also called the Slim & Clear.

Bottom line: Summer's audio monitors are only average performers. For every reader who says it works great for them, another reports the monitor was a bust—static, interference, durability issues, etc. **Ratings: C-**

VTech *babymonitors.vtech.com* VTech is probably best-known for their cordless phones and interactive toys. They have successfully entered the baby monitor market in the past year with both audio and video units.

The Safe & Sound Digital Audio monitor comes in both single ($30) and double ($50) receiver versions and boasts 6.0 DECT technology for a secure transmission that is free from most interference. There is also an intercom feature, sound/light display, vibrating sound alert, night light and rechargeable batteries with 18 hour life. Range is rated to 1000 feet.

Parent feedback has been very positive—it's clear VTech's successful track record in cordless phones is a major help here with the technology. The few criticisms centered on the range being less than the stated 1000 feet (that's probably a given for most monitors, sorry to say). We like the fact that the manufacturer comments on their negative Amazon reviews, either offering to swap out a defective unit or giving suggestions on how to adjust the monitor to address the complaint.

While we will recommend this monitor, we should note we have received occasional reports from readers about defective VTech units. One reader said the quality of the monitor was excellent, but the battery on his unit would not hold a charge. Others report monitors that don't link properly. As with all monitors, we'd recommend purchasing this unit from a store or site that has a decent return policy just in case.

FYI: VTech has one other audio monitor on its web site, the DM111 ($20). This monitor is simpler, with no LCD display but still offers DECT transmission and sound/light indicators. This model doesn't seem to be sold in stores yet, so no parent feedback at this writing.

Bottom line: this is an excellent choice for those who want a reliable, affordable audio-only baby monitor. **Rating: A**

Our Picks: Brand Recommendations

Here are our picks for audio baby monitors, with one BIG caveat: how well a monitor will work in your house depends on interference sources (like cordless phones, wireless internet routers), the presence of other monitors in the neighborhood, etc. Since we get so many complaints about this category, it is imperative you buy a monitor from a place with a good return policy. Keep the receipts in case you have to make an exchange.

You'll note that we just have two recommendations in this category: good and best. In the past, we included a recommendation for an analog monitor like the Sony BabyCall N1M-910. While we still think this is a decent monitor, the fact is that ANY analog monitor is likely to disappoint these days, thanks to all the electronic gizmos in a typical home that can interfere with analog monitors. Hence, we now only recommend DECT (digital) monitors, such as the two below:

Good. The *Philips Avent SCD560* ($80) features DECT digital technology to stop interference and eavesdropping. The SCD510 also has rechargeable batteries, out-of-range indicator and intercom feature. The only bummer: it doesn't have a double receiver option. Quality is very good.

Best. VTech's affordable *Safe & Sound Digital Audio Monitor* ($30 single, $50 double) has 6.0 DECT technology for a secure, interference-free signal. This monitor is loaded with features (intercom, vibrating sound alert, rechargeable batteries and more). It is the best of the audio bunch.

Video Baby Monitors

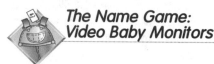

The Name Game: Video Baby Monitors

Axis *axis.com* Most baby video monitors come with both a camera and monitor you can view baby via a handheld or small TV monitor. But what if you want to watch baby's nursery from your computer or iPhone? Axis makes excellent network cameras—small video cameras that connect to your home Internet network either via a wired or wireless connection. The M10 series are among the smallest wireless network cameras on the market today. Yes, they are expensive (about $200 to $300, sold on Amazon) but they work much better than other so-called baby video monitors.

FYI: There are eight different models in the Axis M10 series—wired and wireless—with different resolutions. One good model is the Axis 1034-W, which is wireless and runs about $300 online.

Most Axis cameras work with Axis Camera Companion software—this free software (Windows only) has viewing apps for iPhone, iPad and Android and records footage to a SD card installed in the camera. This software makes viewing the camera over the Internet much easier than past solutions.

One caveat: The M10 series Axis cameras do not have night vision (they work down to 1 lux)—so if your baby's room is completely dark, you won't see anything on this camera. That's obviously a major negative; however, if your nursery has some ambient light or you want to use this camera for daytime monitoring, the Axis M10 series is a good choice.

So are these cameras worth the extra expense? Yes, in our opinion. The quality of Axis cameras greatly exceeds other baby video monitors. Example: the new M1034-W streams video in high definition at 720p. By contrast, other baby monitors have cameras that work at a much lower resolution. And you can repurpose an Axis camera later to be a security camera at your front door or another part of your home. ***Rating: A***

Dropcam *dropcam.com* The last couple of years have seen a convergence of the baby video monitor market and home security cameras. Many parents are realizing that affordable home security cameras can be used to securely stream video from a baby's nursery with quality that surpasses so-called baby monitors . . . at a cheaper price to boot.

A good example of this trend is Dropcam, an affordable ($150) WiFi security camera that lets you view your baby's nursery on a computer or smartphone (there is no parent handheld unit). Quick and easy set-up is Dropcam's secret sauce—they promise a 60 second set-up. No special software is needed and the Dropcam works on a Mac or PC. Apps are available for iPhone and Android devices—there's even a Kindle Fire app.

New in this past year is the Dropcam Pro ($200), which looks almost identical to the original Dropcam but adds a wider field of view (130° vs 107°), better zoom (8x vs 4x) and improved night vision and audio quality.

Dropcam can send you a mobile alert if it detects movement or sound in your baby's nursery. You can also record video to Dropcam's cloud web site—but this incurs a monthly fee ($9.95 a month or $99 a year for seven days of recording, $29.95 for 30 days or $299 a year) Of course, you don't have to record the video (it's free to monitor the feed online or via a smartphone. And email/mobile alerts are also free).

Dropcam uses a special low bandwidth technology (H.264) to avoid hogging your WiFi bandwidth—but a Dropcam can easily use up to 60 GB of internet bandwidth during a month's time especially when used in HD mode (that's because it streams video 24/7). That could be a problem if you are on a metered internet plan (which is more common in Canada than the U.S.).

Parent feedback on the Dropcam is excellent—it does live up to the promise of easy set-up. Of course, there are a always a few trade-offs: depending on your router speed, there can be a 3-5 second delay between the sound in your baby's nursery and what you hear on your smartphone. Hence, there might be an echo-like effect. And of course if you plan to use a Dropcam for night-time monitoring, you'll need to dedicate a device to keep the app open (a retired iPhone or iPod touch would be a good bet). Finally, we saw a few reports of Dropcams that dropped their connection (and needed to be manually reset every week or so).

We purchased a Dropcam to demo here at the home office and are generally impressed—it probably is the easiest to set up webcam we've seen. A few thoughts: the cloud storage feature is nice but expensive (adding another $100 a year if you want to store the last seven days worth of videos). And the aforementioned few second delay irks some users, understandably. Also: a few users report that the Dropcam occasionally drops/disconnects, especially if they have a weak WiFi where the cameras is located—which is a good point. If your WiFi router is a long distance from the Dropcam, you may need to get a WiFi repeater to boost the signal near the camera.

Those issues aside, we'd recommend Dropcam. We noticed as we were going to press that Dropcam is now the best-selling baby monitor on Amazon—so clearly, they are doing something right.

Of course, a Dropcam isn't for everyone (Blackberry and

Windows phone users—you are out of luck, no app for you). And if you have a slow internet connection (say, 2 mbps), this probably isn't the best choice. But if you are looking for a simple streaming solution to viewing your baby's nursery from an iPhone or Android device (as well as computer at work), Dropcam is a worthy choice. **Rating: A**

First Years thefirstyears.com Baby gear and toy maker First Years is a relative newcomer to the video baby monitor market, launching their first offering in 2012.

The Home & Away Portable ($150 to $190) features a 3.5″ monitor, 650 foot range, night vision, rechargeable batteries and the ability to expand up to four cameras. The camera is Skype-compatible, letting you view the camera from Windows-based PC's. It also has an intercom feature and can take snapshots.

Reviews of the monitor are mixed. Parents complain that the range wasn't anywhere near 650 feet—some users complain the signal drops just a few feet away from their baby's room. Other complaints: the Skype feature is cumbersome (you have to tether the parent unit to a PC via USB) and is not Mac compatible. Others complained about the battery life, which sharply deteriorates over the course of a year.

New in the past year, the Talk & Soothe Video Monitor ($100) features a two-way intercom and lullabies. But the screen on the parent unit is a tiny 2.4″. This model was new as of press time, no parent feedback yet. Coming soon: the See & Share Monitor ($200) will have a 3.5″ screen and Skype compatibility (PC only, not Mac).

Bottom line: the First Years is struggling in this category with quality and usability issues. There are better choices out there than this. **Rating: D+**

Foscam Foscam.com Like our review of Axis cameras in this category, Foscam offers an easy-to-set-up network camera (the FI8910W, $70-90) with an impressive list of features: remote pan/tilt, night vision (you can turn this remotely on or off), two-way audio monitoring and a sharp picture. Built-in Wi-Fi means you don't have to run an Ethernet cord to the camera. The one downside: there is no monitor to view the camera—you do that from your computer or smart phone (apps are available for iPhone, iPad, Blackberry and Android).

Readers on our message boards have been quite happy with Foscam (most of this discussion was focused on an earlier, similar model). Fair warning: like many network cams, it does take a fair amount of tech skill to set it up. The Foscam Surveillance Pro app for iPhone ($5) is an easy to use app for live streaming of any Foscam camera.

Of course, Foscam has many other camera options, including the FI9821W which has a higher resolution (720p) HD picture but otherwise looks the same as the model above. It runs $130.

Bottom line: considering the affordable price and good quality, Foscam is a decent alternative to "baby" monitors, if you have the tech chops to set it up! **Rating: A-**

Graco *gracobaby.com* Graco has struggled to get traction in this category. Their last effort (the ill-fated imonitor) suffered from range, battery life and quality complaints. It is now discontinued.

Taking another swing at the category, Graco has launched the True Focus video monitor with 1000-foot range and pan and tilt feature. It also has night vision and rechargeable batteries. Price: $130-$150.

Parent feedback on this model is much more positive then Graco's previous efforts. Fans like the True Focus's overall value, since many other baby video monitors can top $200. Other positives include the night vision (noted as good), decent range and lack of interference.

Critics don't like the fact you can't turn off the sound (and just watch the video). And mounting this camera to a wall isn't easy (Graco intends it to be on a dresser top, apparently). While the range is good, it isn't anywhere close to the 1000 feet Graco claims. Also note the zoom feature is digital(not optical) zoom—which means you lose some resolution as you zoom in. And some parents say the True Focus drops its signal frequently and its quality degrades over just a few months (range worsens, buttons stop working, etc).

Finally, we should note the Graco True Focus is not a streaming monitor (you can't view it on a TV, computer or smart phone). But not everyone needs or wants that feature . . . and the price of the True Focus reflects its stand-alone capabilities. You can't add on additional cameras to this unit—it is a solo deal.

Bottom line: Graco's monitor is good, but not great. Long term durability and reliability issues mar this model, leading us to drop its rating this time. **Rating: C+**

iBaby *ibabylabs.com* iBaby is the latest streaming baby video monitor to hit the market. The company offers two models: the M2 and M3.

The M2 ($150) is a fixed camera with a magnetic base that allows you to rotate it for the best view. The camera can be operated on battery only, if you want to move it to another room. iBaby has an app (Apple only) that allows four users at once to see the feed. The M2 connects via WiFi or Ethernet to your router.

The monitor has a two-way intercom feature and the ability to capture snapshots.

The M3 is much like the M2, but adds a point/tilt/zoom feature. Price: $160-$200.

iBaby's cams were relatively new to the market as we went to press, so parent feedback has been limited. Some folks report connectivity issues and others are disappointed in the video quality (it is far from HD). Unstable connections were a common gripe, with the monitor dropping its signal from some users. Lack of volume is another complaint, as is a five second delay in transmitted images. iBaby's iPhone app also gets a huge share of unlove on the iTunes store—the app has a weak 2.5 rating with 242 one-star reviews.

One of the challenges of WiFi cameras is getting them to connect to your router and then to broadcast video to the 'net. Troubleshooting connectivity issues can be a challenge unless you have serious tech chops—you know there is a challenge when iBaby's web site has an entire section on Port Forwarding. If you don't know what that is, don't buy this camera.

That said, fans of iBaby say when it is working, it is an excellent baby monitor. Unfortunately for iBaby, there is another company that has perfected the WiFi camera—Dropcam. No, it doesn't have PTZ, but Dropcam runs circles around this monitor for less money. Bottom line: iBaby needs to polish its cameras and apps before it is ready for prime time. **Rating: D**

Infant Optics *infantoptics.com* Infant Optics is a good example of how online shopping has reshaped the baby gear world. This small company (part of San Francisco-based importer Genexus) has landed its DXR-5 video baby monitor on the top of Amazon's best-seller chart for video monitors. Yes, tiny Infant Optics is out-selling baby gear heavyweights like Summer and Graco and tech giants like Samsung in this category—with little more than a web site, a single product . . . and the reach of Amazon.

The DXR-5 boasts an impressive list of features: digital and secure transmission with 800-foot range (2.4 GHz with FHSS technology to avoid interference), 2.4" display, voice-triggered (VOX) or manual operation, night vision, camera that can be wall mounted, and four hours of battery life. And the unit is expandable with up to four additional cameras.

Of course, what is more amazing about this is the price: $99. No, you don't get point/tilt/zoom—but then again, most cameras with that feature are 50% more than the DXR-5. Additional cameras are just $79.

Feedback on this monitor has been largely positive: folks like the clear audio (no static), simple set-up and VOX mode. For $99, the DXR-5 is a great value.

Of course, there are a few criticisms: quality control seems to be an issue here, with scattered reports of defective units or units that broke after a week (fortunately, the company offers a one-year warranty). Some folks found the audio to be too quiet; others said it was just fine. And some said their Infant Optics monitor interfered with their WiFi router (the company has troubleshooting suggestions if this happens to you).

One suggested improvement to this monitor could be a low battery warning for the parent unit—unfortunately, it just shuts off when it runs out of juice. And it would be nice to have an option to turn the screen off and just listen to the audio at night.

Bottom line: this is an excellent video monitor for the price.

FYI: Infant Optics debuted a new model as we were going to press, the DXR-8—this $230 unit has pan/tilt/zoom and interchangeable lenses (normal, zoom and wide angle, which are sold separately).The DXR-8 also has an intercom feature and temperature sensor. The screen is larger (3.5) and you can link up to four cameras to a single display, which will then cycle through the additional cameras every 12 seconds. We're not sure we see the point of the interchangeable lenses, which would easily just get lost in our house. Early feedback on this model has been positive. ***Rating: A***

Levana mylevana.com Canadian-based Levana is the baby monitor division of Svat, which makes security cameras. Levana has an affordable line of video monitors (mostly sold online), as well as two audio-only monitors.

Levana's first effort in this category is the BabyView20 (aka the Interference-Free Digital Wireless Video Baby Monitor), a $100 monitor featuring rechargeable batteries, a magnetic base and hardware to mount the camera and a 2.3" color LCD screen. This digital video monitor works on the 2.4 GHz frequency and provides a secure connection. Range is about a 100 feet. Like many monitors, the Levana BabyView20 has a standby mode that mutes the audio and turns off the screen until baby cries. The base also doubles as a nightlight and has a lullaby feature.

FYI: The BabyView20 has been discontinued, but we still see it for sale online.

Levana offers eight other video models, ranging from the $100 Jena to the $300 Ovia.

Levana's flagship (and newest) model is the Astra, a $220 model with pan/tilt/zoom, sound-sensitive LED display, 3.5" screen, 720p resolution, 2.64 GHz frequency, invisible LEDS on the camera for night vision, and eight hour battery life (48 hours on a special energy-saving mode, which activates when baby cries). You can mount the Astra on the ceiling or wall, which is a nice touch. We played with a prototype of the Astra at a trade show and thought it was well designed, much more polished than Levana's previous efforts. Example: the pan/tilt feature is silent in the Astra.

Similar to the Astra is the Jena ($180), which is also new and features an eight hour battery, talk to baby intercom feature, 500-foot range and temperature reading. Jena lacks the pan/tilt/zoom of the Astra, but is otherwise similar.

The Lila ($140) has a fixed camera with 72-hour battery, intercom and invisible night vision. Feedback on this monitor is mostly positive.

The Stella ($260) is a PTZ camera with "smart LED" indicator ring, which gives you a visual read-out of noise in the nursery (blue for low volume; red for wailing). The Stella also has a large 4.3" screen and intercom feature and a 36 hour battery life in "peep" mode (power-on/off, energy efficient picture). Price: $260. Feedback on the Stella has been positive, although more than one parent commented about the relatively low resolution for the parent unit (don't expect HD quality).

The Ovia ($300) is Levana's kitchen sink monitor; they throw in just about every possible feature: 24 hour battery life, PTZ, intercom, 4.3" screen with touch screen controls, SD photo and video recording and more.

So how's the quality? Mixed is the best way to describe Levana's overall track record. Folks like the affordable prices and extensive feature list of these monitors. But more than one parent told us the range was nowhere close to the promises Levana makes in its marketing. Battery life is another gripe. And perhaps the biggest problem is long-term reliability—we saw more than one report of Levana monitors that just stopped working after a few months (in some cases, a few weeks).

On the plus side, we should note that Levana's reviews are trending more positive in the last year—the newer models (Jena, Stella, Lila) are garnering better marks then the older ones. Levana still needs to pay attention to quality control: we saw more than one review that claimed their Levana unit was DOA (dead on arrival). Yes, Levana has decent customer service and they will replace these units, but the best advice would be not to ship them in the first place.

Bottom line: Levana's video baby monitors are in the middle of the pack. On the plus side, we like the affordable prices and extensive features (intercom, temperature monitoring). Quality-wise, Levana ranks above competitors like First Years and Safety 1st . . . but that isn't saying much. The company needs to improve long-term reliability of its monitors to be a player. We'll tick up Levana's rating this year to reflect the more positive reviews and improved newer models. We'd stick with their newest models, especially the Jena and Lila. ***Rating: B***

Lorex *lorextechnology.com* Like Levana, Lorex is a security camera maker that has branched out into baby monitors. The company has rapidly released and discontinued models over the last couple of years.

The current flagship Lorex model is the Sweet Peek video monitor (BB2411, $85). It features a 2.4" screen on the parent unit, eight hours of battery life, intercom feature and lullabies.

The Care 'n' Share comes in two flavors: the BB3521 ($110) has a fixed camera, while the BB3525 ($130) adds point/tilt/zoom. These cameras have a snapshot feature that lets you save pics with one click of a button on the parent unit. The Care 'n' Share also has an intercom feature and lullabies. FYI: there is also a version of this monitor with a larger 4.3" screen for $200 (the BB4325X).

For 2014, Lorex is debuting its first WiFi camera, the Little Link (LBN511, $180). This HD 720p camera connects to your WiFi network and works a bit like the Dropcam.

The reviews of Lorex baby monitors are mixed at best. Fans say the picture quality is good and set up is easy, but more than one reader complained that the cheap plastic camera broke after a few months of use. The newer Lorex models seem to be earning better marks then the older models, however.

Bottom line: Lorex is improving, but other brands outshine these offerings quality-wise. ***Rating: C***

Mobicam getmobi.com Mobicam was among the first affordable video baby monitors (under $100) with an LCD screen to score widespread distribution. You'd think after being first to the market with video baby monitors, Mobicam would have the video monitor thing down to a science. You'd think . . . but you'd be wrong.

Numerous quality woes have dogged Mobicam for years, including broken on/off switches, broken power cords, etc. Interference and static were other major issues for users—some of this is caused by the 2.4 GHz frequency that Mobicam uses . . . the same as WiFi Internet routers.

Mobicam attempted to address these problems with an updated version dubbed Mobicam Ultra. The updated camera sports a larger display, voice activation and "new technology for clear sound and picture" (it now works on the 900 MHz frequency). And the verdict from consumers? Numerous gripes about constant static, poor night vision and poor customer service.

To their credit, Mobicam has steadily released new models with updated technology. Their latest: the Mobicam DL Digital Monitoring system for $150 retail ($107 on Amazon). This model features a high-resolution 2.4 inch TFT LCD monitor and camera as well as voice-activated audio and video alerts. The DL has a digital transmission that prevents eavesdropping—the company claims a 300-foot range. You can expand the system with up to three additional cameras. The Digital DL can work on regular batteries and AC power (but no rechargeable battery).

At the high end, Mobicam now offers the Digital DXR ($229 retail, $140 Amazon). This model features a larger LCD screen (3.5" versus the 2.4 for the DL), longer transmission range and a built-in rechargeable battery. Similar to the DL, the DXR features voice activation and an audio-only mode. But the DXR adds two-way audio communication and a SD card slot for recording. You can also watch up to four cameras at the same time on the parent's unit, which is unique.

New in the past year, the Secure Start ($100) is a bare bones, fixed camera model with intercom feature and an audio-only mode.

Feedback on Mobicam's new models (such as the DXR) has been mixed. Glitches with volume control and multi-camera set-up are two common complaints. Fans like their Mobicam—as long as it's working. Which, sad to say in some cases, is a matter of just a few weeks or months before it conks out. Mobicam just can't quite seem to get quality control right, even for its more pricey monitors.

Bottom line: Mobicam may have been first to the market here, but competitors have out-classed it in recent years. **Rating: D**

Motorola binatonetelecom.com Electronic gadget maker Binatone licensed the Motorola name for a line of baby monitors that debuted in 2011.

Binatone has been expanding their video offerings in recent months and now have 12 models. All feature infrared night vision, lullabies, sound/light display, room temperature monitor and a two-way intercom feature. The main difference is the size of the screen.

The basic MBP20 ($130) has a 1.5" color LCD screen, while the MBP33 ($160) has a 2.8" screen.

The MBP36 ($200) is probably Binatone's most popular monitor: it has a 3.5 screen and adds a camera that can pan, tilt and zoom (plus there is two way communication). If you want two cameras, the MBP28 ($100) offers that option.

FYI: Motorola has a WiFi camera called the Blink1 ($200), which is similar to Dropcam since it has no parent viewer (it is compatible with smartphones, tablets, etc).

Parent feedback on Motorola video monitors has been mostly positive, with few reports of static or interference. Much of that credit probably goes to the monitor's 2.4 GHz FHSS technology—FHSS stands for frequency-hopping spread spectrum—which enables strong, secure reception. Both the MBP33 and MBP36 have FHSS, while the simpler MBP20 works on DECT.

Perhaps the biggest complaint about these cameras is their weak night vision—compared to other brands, the Motorola night vision pictures are not very clear. That means the camera will have to be very close to the crib to get a clear picture . . . that can be an issue since cords aren't supposed to be within arm's length of a crib for safety reasons.

And want to quickly adjust the volume in the middle of the night? Too bad if you have the MBP36—you have to navigate through menus to make the change. Binatone could also beef up their customer service . . . we heard many complaints of slow response, slow replacement of defective units, etc.

These complaints aside, we will recommend this brand. Motorola's video baby monitors are a good choice in a flawed field. **Rating: B+**

Philips *usa.philips.com* After debuting well received audio monitors, Philips has tip toed into the video category with a digital offering, appropriately named the Digital Video Monitor. While the official retail is $220, we've seen it discounted to $150 online, making it one of the more affordable digital video monitors on the market.

The unit features a private/secure connection (DECT signal helps avoid interference), night vision and 2.4" viewing screen. Overall quality is good—while the picture is hardly high definition, it is good enough. The rechargeable batteries last about five to six hours. Range is decent (about 400 feet) and set-up is easy enough.

So what are the negatives? Well, the screen automatically activates when noise is detected in the baby's room—that sounds good in theory (it saves battery), but is lousy in practice. That's because the monitor doesn't transmit any audio while in this rest mode. Unfortunately, it takes a very loud noise for the monitor to trigger on and that bugged more than one reader—it would make more sense for the audio to be on 24/7 and the video screen to activate when sound reaches a certain level you could set.

Another negative: Philips clearly intends you to set the camera on a dresser that is eye-level with baby. There are no mounting options for a wall or ceiling. And placing the camera on a shelf above the crib is difficult, since the base can block the camera's view when it is rotated down. (As a reminder, make sure monitor cords are at least three feet from a crib—if not, they can become a strangulation hazard).

Philips addressed this issue in a recent update for the monitor (confusingly, still named the Digital Video Monitor. The updated model is SCD603; the old one is SCD600). It features a camera base that allows more rotation of the camera in a downward position. The new base can also be wall mountable.

Those negatives aside, the majority of parents who have this monitor like it. Yes, at this price point ($220 retail), you might expect a pan/tilt/zoom function like you see on the Motorola monitors—but Phillips lacks that. And Philips doesn't have a monitor that streams to the internet. So if you can live without those features, this isn't a bad choice. FYI: We recommend the updated SCD603 model over the previous version. **Rating: B**

Safety 1st *safety1st.com* Part of the Dorel Baby Industrial Complex, Safety 1st has had limited success in the video monitor category. Like other mass market baby gear brands (Graco, First Years), Safety 1st's weak offerings here have struggled to compete against tech and security company brands (Samsung, Motorola, Levana, etc).

Safety 1st's current offering in this space is the Genesis Digital Color Video monitor, a pricey ($200) PTZ model with a 2.4" LCD screen, intercom feature, temperature display and the ability to add up to four more cameras. The base of the baby's unit features a nightlight and can be wall mounted.

The Genesis was too new as of press time for any parent feedback, but if the past is any guide, this model will disappoint. Parent feedback on Safety 1st's video monitors has been mostly negative. Brutal to be exact. You name it, folks are unhappy about it—static, battery woes, poor range, unit dies after a few months . . .

Bottom line: Safety 1st's video monitors are a pass. **_Rating: F_**

Samsung *Samsung.com* Samsung has SEVEN video monitors, all with confusingly similar sounding names (RemoteVIEW, SmartVIEW, etc). And if that weren't enough Amazon also sells a Samsung video monitor (model SEW3030, $110) that is pitched as a security system, not a baby monitor—and costs less than most baby video monitors. Interesting—add "baby" to the name and the price goes up!

This monitor features a 3.5" LCD, 2.4 GHZ camera with night vision and the ability to monitor the camera remotely via Skype. The Samsung Wireless Video Security Monitoring System also monitors the temperature in baby's room. And it has digital zoom and two-way intercom.

Parent reviews on this monitor are mixed, with most saying the picture quality is better than other video monitors they've tried. Detractors say the "sound sensitivity sensor" (which beeps at you if it detects baby moving) is a hassle, constantly beeping at you—you can turn this down via a sensitivity setting. And the temp sensor is about five to ten degrees above the actual room temperature.

As for Samsung's other monitors, the EzVIEW and SmartVIEW are sold at Target for $179 and $199 respectively (although they are less on Amazon.com). The EzVIEW is the entry-level model with a 2.4" monitor, 2x digital zoom, built-in temperature sensor and remotely activated night light. The SmartVIEW is basically the same, but adds a 3.5" monitor and two-way talk feature.

Samsung's other two models offer slight variations on the theme. The RemoteVIEW ($200 to $220) has the smaller 2.4" screen but adds four remote-activated lullabies. The SecureVIEW ($175 to $250) is similar to the SmartVIEW.

All Samsung video monitors feature a digital signal with 350 feet of promised range. You can also add up to three additional cameras. Two models (the RemoteVIEW and SecureVIEW) allow you to view the baby video via Skype or MSN. All the monitors offer a SD card slot so you can record videos.

New in the past year, Samsung has rolled out the SafeVIEW, a $230 unit with point/tilt/zoom, remotely activate nightlight, voice activated mode, and a 3.5" screen (with 320 x 240 resolution). A similar unit dubbed BabyVIEW has all the same features of the SafeVIEW but has a stationary camera (not PTZ).

If you are looking for a camera that streams online, Samsung has one model: the SmartCam ($150) can stream to a smartphone or PC (with a free app). A supposedly simple push-button setup and free account on SamsungSmartCam.com enables remote viewing (note: there is no parent or handheld unit for this camera).

So how does that work in the real world? Not so good, say parents. The SmartCam can be difficult to set-up (depending on your Internet router) and the streamed video is choppy at best. Wonky iPhone and Android apps frequently time out, making the remote viewing dicey at best.

As for Samsung's other models, the reviews are mixed. It appears the best-rated model is the new SafeVIEW (SEW-3037W) or its fixed companion, BabyVIEW (SEW-3036WN). Folks say the night vision is superior to Motorola's offerings and generally is more user-friendly than Samsung's earlier offerings. Screen resolution (640 x 480) is also better. Negatives include poor battery life (you'll need to keep it plugged for overnight use) and an annoyingly loud start-up jingle. FYI: These models feature a digital signal that is secure.

Bottom line: the SafeVIEW or BabyVIEW are recommended for overall quality and ease of use—we'd skip the other models (including the buggy SmartCam). **Rating: A**

Summer summerinfant.com Summer's video monitors are this brand's key mojo—the company offers a mind-numbing assortment of 20+ models, from simple fixed camera models and tiny screens to PTZ models with larger displays.

While you'll see many of the older models still sold online, we'll focus on two new flagship models Summer is promoting both online and in stores: The BabyTouch Digital Video Monitor and the Peek Plus Internet Baby Monitor System.

The BabyTouch Digital Video Monitor ($180) has a touch-screen parent unit with special docking station that charges the camera. This PTZ camera has a 3.5" color display and a 400-foot range (secure digital transmission). The model also has an intercom feature and you can add multiple cameras to monitor more than one child or room (both audio and video).

Parent feedback on this monitor has generally been positive. The few negatives include lack of a belt-clip for the parent unit and battery life is about half the stated ten hours. A few folks reported interference with their WiFi router.

The Peek Plus Internet Baby Monitor System ($235, a Babies R Us exclusive) is a streaming monitor that has a parent handheld unit with 2.5" screen as well. The camera works on 2.4 GHz frequency with digital transmission and a 400-foot range. A "plug and play" Internet gateway connects to your wireless router and enables remote viewing (free apps for iPhone, Android, Blackberry) via a secure web site that is password protected.

So what's not to like about the Peek Plus? Well, the camera lacks a pan/tilt/zoom function—for $235, you'd think Summer could have thrown that in. And while the phone apps allow for remote viewing, you can't use a smartphone for regular monitoring since the app times out after five minutes. Night vision is only okay. While Summer has done an admirable job in making this monitor easy to set up, there were still some parents who couldn't get it to work with their router.

New for 2013, Summer has two Babies R Us exclusive models: the Privacy Plus Series Touch and Baby Touch 2.0 ($200 either model). These models are very similar to the BabyTouch Digital Video Monitor reviewed above, but add a couple more bells and whistles. Example: the Baby Touch 2.0 has "motion-tracking" technology that follows baby's movements. We're not exactly sure of the point to this—so what if your baby scoots three inches across her crib?

Reviews on these models are lukewarm at best, with several complaints about lack of range (hard to tell if this is a quality problem with an initial batch of models or not). All things considered, it would probably be a better bet at this time to stick with the BabyTouch Digital Video Monitor until Summer works out the kinks in these BRU exclusives.

New for 2014, Summer is rolling out the Baby Zoom WiFi monitor, which has a 2.5" parent monitor PLUS it works with smartphones and tablets. The Baby Zoom has PTZ, two way intercom, the ability to add extra cameras and more. Price: $260. If you want to skip the parent unit, you can buy the camera only for $170. And Summer plans a Babies R Us version of the WiFi monitor (called the Baby Touch WiFi) for $300 with much the same features.

Perhaps our biggest gripe with Summer is their monitors' long-term reliability. "Awesome—while it worked" is a common review complaint, with parent after parent reporting units dying after several months, cameras fizzing out after a year, etc. We realize baby monitors get intense use (on 24 hours a day, batteries that are charged frequently), but Summer can't charge premium prices and get away with such lousy reliability. If Summer wants to charge the same amount of money that Samsung, Motorola and Dropcam charge, they must achieve similar reliability. Right now, Summer is not quite measuring up.

So while we recommend Summer, we'll do it with a caveat: be aware that your shiny new Summer video monitor may not make it to your baby's first birthday. **Rating: A-**

VTech babymonitors.vtech.com Cordless phone and educational toy maker VTech joined the baby video market craze in the past year with their affordable Safe & Sound Full Color Video and Audio monitor (the company also makes an audio-only monitor).

This $110 model features a vibrating sound alert when there is sound in baby's room, intercom feature, temperature sensor, digital zoom, night vision, 2.8" LCD that features a 320×240 color display. The Safe & Sound (VM321) camera can be wall mounted and has 1000 foot range, which is digital and secure. You can expand the system with up to four cameras (additional cameras are $42 each), although you can't hear audio from secondary cameras (only a display alert and vibration of the parent unit notes sound detected from a secondary camera).

The voice activated sound feature (VOX) is a pro and con—this turns on the parent unit's speaker when it detects sound in the nursery (instead of continuously playing the audio). While this is a plus since it saves on battery, some found it frustrating because it can't be turned off and causes the monitor to turn off and on when the slightest sound is detected.

This camera features a digital zoom option, but it has one setting (zoom in or not).

FYI: VTech also makes a PTZ version of this camera, the VM333 for $170.

Overall, feedback on this monitor has been positive, with folks generally happy with the video quality and lack of interference. Yes, there are a few glitches—the parent unit lacks a belt clip, you can't remotely trigger the lullabies that the camera plays, etc. And the VOX feature is hit or miss, as far as parent feedback goes. While this probably isn't the best choice to monitor multiple rooms, for a single camera set-up, the VTech Safe & Sound is a good bet. **Rating: A-**

Withing withings.com Gadget maker Withings was among the first to market a streaming baby video monitor, the Smart Baby Monitor.

Unlike many other baby monitors, this unit is just a camera with built-in night vision—there is no monitor or receiver. Your baby's image is streamed to an iPhone or Android device over your home network. You can remotely view the image/audio over cellular networks or your work WiFi. The camera unit also monitors temperature and humidity in the baby's nursery, allowing you to set up personal alarms if these exceed a certain threshold. Price is $230 to $250.

Parent feedback on Withings has been all over the board. When it works, fans like the overall quality (good video images, etc.). The monitor includes such extras as temperature and humidity–the latter is unusual for this category. There is also a music and lights feature. A clever graph tracks your baby's recent movement and noise for the last 15 minutes. There also is no limit to the number of devices you can use to monitor your Smart Monitor (but you can only have three devices simultaneously viewing the feed).

Critics point out the way the camera is situated on the base, it is hard to see most of the crib without also seeing the base. You can't view the video on a desktop computer either, which is unfortunate.

Night vision was weak in the first version of this monitor, but that has been fixed. Yet there still is no point/tilt/zoom function, which you'd expect at this price level. On the plus side, Withings has made small improvements to the monitor to address complaints. Example: now streaming is unlimited, even over 3G or 4G networks (there use to be a 15 minute limit a day over cell phone networks; then a charge after that).

In a previous edition of our book, we gave this monitor an A-rating. But we are downgrading Withings this time out. Why? First, the company hasn't significantly upgraded this unit for while . . . and competitors like Dropcam have surpassed Withings in quality, ease of use, etc. We also see reports of app crashes, especially for Android. Withings' app for iOS7 is also very glitchy, judging from the feedback on the iTunes store. That's a major bummer, since the only way this model works is with an app.

One final gripe: Withings has a picture of this monitor attached to a crib on its web site—that is a major no-no. Cords from baby monitors are a major safety hazard. Monitors should always be mounted at least three feet from a crib, never on a crib.

Bottom line: Withings monitor was once a winner, but now competitors like Dropcam have surpassed it. Glitches with its apps are a crippling blow. **Rating: C**

Our Picks: Brand Recommendations

There are three types of baby video monitors: fixed, PTZ and streaming. Fixed monitors have a camera that is, well, fixed and is the most economical choice. PTZ stands for point/tilt/zoom, where a camera can move and tilt: some parents prefer PTZ monitors since they can scan a room for a wayward baby or toddler. Finally, streaming baby monitors can send a video signal over the internet, so grandparents and relatives can see the baby's nursery.

Best Bet: Fixed camera. The *Infant Optics DXR-5* is an excellent, yet affordable fixed baby monitor at just $99. FHSS technology helps avoid interference and a 2.4″ display provides a crisp picture. Simple set-up and voice-activated mode are two key features.

Runner-up: Samsung's BabyVIEW (SEW-3036WN) is more expensive ($180), but does have a bigger viewing screen (3.5″), as well as time display and intercom. FYI: While the BabyVIEW is a fixed camera it does have a zoom feature.

Best Bet: PTZ camera. The *Samsung SafeVIEW (SEW-3037W, $230)* is the best of the PTZ (point/tilt/zoom) cameras—it features a voice-activated option, remote nightlight and a crisp 3.5″ screen. Night vision is very good.

Runner-up: The Summer BabyTouch Digital Monitor ($190-$260) features a unique touch-screen parent unit and 3.5″ color display, as well as intercom feature. Another runner-up is the Motorola MBP36 ($200) which is similar to the Summer unit, but has a more clunky inter-face to navigate when changing settings. And the night vision on the Motorola camera is poor compared to Summer or Samsung.

Best Bet: Streaming camera. You'd like grandma or an aunt to be able to see your baby? Then you need a camera that can stream an image over the internet. While that sounds simple, this category of camera can be tricky to set up. The best bet here is the *Summer Peek Plus Internet Baby Monitor System* ($235). Yes it is pricey and only has a fixed camera with 2.5″ parent screen. But it comes with a "plug and play" internet router that enables viewing online or via free apps for iPhone, Android and Blackberry via secure site that is password protected.

Runner-up: Dropcam is a simple, fixed $150 camera with a 60 second set-up. You can view your baby's nursery via the Dropcam web site or via an iPhone or Android app. The down-side: there is no parent dis- play unit, so you'll have to re-purpose an old iPhone or iPod Touch to be a viewer. Dropcam recently debuted a new version of its camera (Dropam Pro) for $200 that has a wider field of view and improved night vision and audio.

BABY MONITORS

A quick look at baby video monitor features

BRAND	MODEL	PRICE
AXIS	M1034W	$300
DROPCAM	DROPCAM	$150
	DROPCAM PRO	$200
FIRST YEARS	HOME & AWAY	$150-$190
FOSCOM	F18910W	$70-$90
GRACO	TRUE FOCUS	$130-$150
IBABY	M2	$150
INFANT OPTICS	DXR-5	$99
LEVANA	JENA	$100
	ASTRA	$220
	LILA	$140
LOREX	SWEET PEEK	$85
MOBICAM	DXR	$140-$230
MOTOROLA	MBP36	$200
PHILIPS	DIGITAL VIDEO MONITOR	$150-$220
SAFETY 1ST	GENESIS	$200
SAMSUNG	SAFEVIEW	$230
	BABYVIEW	$180
SUMMER	BABYTOUCH DIGITAL	$180
	PEEK PLUS	$235
VTECH	SAFE & SOUND VM321	$110
	SAFE & SOUND WM333	$170
WITHINGS	SMART BABY MONITOR	$230-$250

Baby Proofing

All parents want to create a safe environment for their baby. And safety begins at the place where baby spends the most time—your home.

✔ = Yes
PTZ: Point/tilt/zoom feature.
MONITOR: Included display monitor. Models without a monitor are
intended to stream to a smartphone or tablet.
STREAM: Can the monitor stream video online?

PTZ	MONITOR	STREAM	OUR RATING
		✔	A
		✔	A
		✔	A
	✔		D+
✔		✔	A-
ZOOM ONLY	✔		C+
		✔	D
	✔		A
✔	✔		B
✔	✔		B
	✔		B
	✔		C
	✔	✔	D
✔	✔		B+
	✔		B
✔	✔		F
✔	✔		A
	✔		A
✔	✔		A-
	✔	✔	A-
	✔		A-
✔	✔		A-
		✔	C

Getting Started:
When Do You Need This Stuff?

Whatever you do, start early. It's never too soon to think about
baby proofing your house. Many parents we interviewed admitted
they waited until their baby "almost did something" (like playing
with extension cords or dipping into the dog's dish) before they
panicked and began childproofing.

Remember Murphy's Law of Baby Proofing: your baby will be instantly attracted to any object that can cause harm. The more harm it will cause, the more attractive it will be to him or her. A word to the wise: start baby proofing as soon as your child begins to roll over.

Safe & Sound: Smart Baby Proofing Tips

The statistics are alarming—each year, over 100 children die and millions more are injured in avoidable household accidents. Obviously, no parent wants their child to be injured by a preventable accident, yet many folks are not aware of common dangers. Others think if they load up their house with safety gadgets, their baby will be safe. Yet, there is one basic truth about child safety: *safety devices are no substitute for adult supervision.* While this section is packed with safety must-haves like gates, you still have to watch your baby at all times.

Where do you start? Get down on your hands and knees and look at the house from your baby's point of view. Be sure to go room by room throughout the entire house. On our web site, BabyBargains.com (click on bonus material), we have room-by-room advice on how to baby proof on a shoestring.

Top 10 Baby Products That Should Be Banned

We asked Dr. Ari Brown, a pediatrician in Austin, TX and co-author of our book *Baby411* for a list of baby products that should be banned. Some are dangerous, others simply foolish and unnecessary. Here is her take:

1 **BABY WALKERS: NO!** There are so many cases of serious injury associated with these death traps on wheels that some countries (including Canada) completely ban baby walkers.

2 **DON'T GET YOUR KIDS HOOKED ON BABY EINSTEIN.** TV and electronic media of any type, even "educational videos" designed for babies, are bad for developing brains. Babies need active, not passive learning, and getting them used to watching TV is a bad habit.

3 **THROW AWAY THE PACIFIER AT SIX MONTHS.** As we discussed in the feeding chapter, pacifiers are now recommended after breastfeeding is well established (about one month). But . . . remember to STOP the pacifier at six months! Your baby needs to learn to fall asleep and/or comfort herself without a crutch.

4 **AVOID EAR THERMOMETERS.** They are notoriously unreliable, and since fever in infants (over 100.3 degrees) could be serious, an inaccurate reading might give parents a false sense of security. Rectal thermometers are the most accurate.

5 **DON'T FALL FOR THE BABY TOOTHPASTE HYPE.** The best way to clean your baby's teeth is to wipe them with a wet washcloth, twice daily. The sweet taste of baby toothpaste encourages

The Most Dangerous Baby Products

The Consumer Product Safety Commission releases yearly figures for injuries and deaths for children under five years old related to juvenile products. The latest figures from the CPSC are for 2011 and show a 9.3% decrease in the number of injuries. The following chart details the statistics:

PRODUCT CATEGORY	INJURIES	DEATHS
INFANT CARRIES/CAR SEATS*	13,200	12
STROLLERS/CARRIAGES	12,900	1
CRIBS, MATTRESSES	12,200	49
HIGH CHAIRS	11,300	1
BOUNCER SEATS	4,200	2
CHANGING TABLES	3,900	1
WALKERS/JUMPERS	3,300	1
BABY GATES/BARRIERS	2,800	1
PLAY YARDS/ PLAYPENS	2,200	12
PORTABLE BABY SWINGS	2,100	1
BOTTLES/WARMERS/STERILIZERS	1,800	0
BATH SEATS	**	7
BASSINETS/CRADLES	**	20
OTHER	4,600	3
TOTAL	**74,100**	**114**

Key:
Deaths: This figure is an annual average from 2009-11, the latest figures available.
* Excludes motor vehicle incidents
** In the CPSC's latest report bath seat and bassinets/cradle injuries were not tabulated due to a low sample size.

safety

your baby to suck on the toothbrush once in his mouth and you can't maneuver it around well.

6 **BEWARE OF NATURAL BABY SKIN-CARE PRODUCTS.** Over 25% of "natural" infant skin-care items contain common allergens including peanuts.

7 **NATURAL TEETHING TABLETS.** Some of these contain *caffeine* as an ingredient! Save the espresso for kindergarten! In 2010, the Food & Drug Administration recalled Hyland's Teething tablets because they contained belladonna, a potentially toxic substance that can cause serious harm at high doses. Specifically, the FDA found Hyland's Teething tablets contained "inconsistent amounts of belladonna" and has received reports of "serious adverse events in children taking this product."

8 **FORGET SIPPY CUPS.** They promote tooth decay because the flow of liquid heads straight to the back of the top front teeth. If your baby hasn't quite mastered drinking from a cup yet, offer her a straw instead.

9 **HANGING MOBILES ARE ONLY FOR NEWBORNS.** Remove all toys and decorations hanging over your baby's crib by the time he or she is five months old. They become hazardous when babies start to pull themselves up and grab for them.

10 **ENJOY THOSE BEAUTIFUL QUILTS AS WALL HANGINGS**, not in the crib.

Safety Gates: Our Picks

Safety gates are needed in four key areas:

◆ **STAIRS**. Gates should be permanently mounted at the top and bottom of stairs.

◆ **NO BABY ZONES.** You may want to gate off the dining room or other areas baby isn't allowed.

◆ **PLAY AREAS.** Some gates can be linked together to form playards—a space where baby can play, but not escape.

◆ **WINDOWS/FIREPLACES**. Unless you plan to leave your windows closed and locked, safety gates are needed when a window is opened. Fireplaces hearths are another area that need gating.

Gates come in two flavors: hardware or pressure mounted. Hardware-mounted gates are permanently affixed to walls or door openings. Pressure-mounted gates use a spring to create pressure, holding the gate in place. In general, we recommend hardware-mounted gates at the top and bottom of stairs. Pressure-mounted gates are fine for no baby zones.

When it comes to hardware-mounted gates, it is always best to mount the gate's brackets into solid wood (not drywall). Use a "stud finder" (sold in hardware stores) to find wood studs in walls.

Here are specific recommendations by use:

Best stair gate. *KidCo's Safeway Gate* ($43-$50) comes in different versions: a steel gate (G2000) for straight stair openings and a model that can be mounted on angled stairways (G2100). The latter is available in white, black or wood. The basic gate fits openings 24.75" to 43.5" and can be used for either stairs or windows. Reader feedback on this gate is very positive, with fans loving the ease of installation and small footprint (when open, it doesn't restrict

---

E-MAIL FROM THE REAL WORLD
A solution for those coffee tables

Reader Jennifer K. came up with this affordable solution to expensive coffee table bumpers.

"When our son started to walk we were very worried about his head crashing into the glass top tables in our living room. We checked into the safety catalogs and found those fitted bumpers for about $60 just for the coffee table. Well, I guess being the selfish person that I am, and already removing everything else dangerous from my living room, I just didn't want to give up my tables! Where do we put the lamps, and where do I fold the laundry?

"My mother-in-law had the perfect solution. FOAM PIPE WRAPPING!!! We bought it at a home improvement store for $3. You can cut it to fit any table. It is already sliced down the middle and has adhesive, (the gummy kind that rolls right off the glass if you need to replace it). The only disadvantage that we've come across is that our son has learned to pull it off. But at $3 a bag we keep extras in the closet for 'touch-ups.'

"Now the novelty has worn off, so I have NOT had to replace it as often. And I'm happy to report that we've had plenty of collisions, but not one stitch!"

---

the stairway). Got a wider opening? Kidco sells an 24" extension of the Safeway for $20 to $40.

Best soft gate. *Evenflo's Crosstown Pressure Mounted Soft Gate* ($34) is 20" tall and expands from 38" to 60" wide—perfect for funky openings you need to gate. Mesh lets baby see through the gate. However, this gate isn't designed to be set-up and removed frequently—it is better to set it up and have the adults walk over it to access the non-baby zone.

Best play yard gate. Want to cre- ate a safe place for an infant to play in the living room? *The North States Superyard XT Gate Play Yard* ($70 to $120) is an expandable panel system that is 26" high and provides a play area of 18.5 square feet. A two-panel extension

kit ($30) nearly doubles the area. Some readers use this to protect a Christmas tree from toddlers. Yes, it is all-plastic, but it is durable enough to corral toddlers. A few parents say it is hard to open and close the gate (the hinges are tight), but overall, readers give this play yard solution the thumbs up.

Best fireplace hearth gate. A fireplace is an obvious place baby doesn't need to visit—but how do you protect it? *KidCo's HearthGate* ($160) is pricey but does the trick. It is 29.95" tall and works on hearths six feet wide by

two feet deep; extensions are available for bigger openings. The HearthGate also includes a walk-through gate.

Best window guard. *Guardian Angel* (angleguards.com) sells affordable metal window guards that fit just about any type of win- dow. A gate that works on windows 23" to 35" runs about $75 and is hardware mounted. A must for low windows your toddler can access or if you live in a high-rise condo building. Remember babies can climb furniture and access windows you think are safe— keep them locked or install a window guard. Runner-up: Kidco sells a *Mesh Window Guard* ($37) in case you don't want metal bars over your windows. Another idea: the *Super Stopper* from Parent Units ($10; parentunits.com) is a simple device that suctions on a window, preventing it from opening too far to let a toddler out.

Top 11 Safety Must Haves

To sum up, here's our list of top safety items to have for your home (in no particular order).

◆ **Fire extinguishers** rated "ABC," which means they are appropriate for any type of fire.

◆ **Outlet covers.**

◆ **Baby monitor**—unless your house or apartment is very small, and you don't think it will be useful.

◆ **Smoke alarms.** The best smoke alarms have two systems for detecting fires—a photoelectric sensor for early detection of smoldering fires and a dual chamber ionization sensor for early detection of flaming fires. An example of this is the First Alert "Double Sensor" ($25 to $60). We'd recommend one smoke alarm for every bedroom, plus main hallways, basement and living rooms. And don't forget to replace the batteries twice a year. Both smoke alarms and carbon monoxide detectors can be found in warehouse clubs like Sam's and Costco at low prices.

◆ **Carbon monoxide detectors.** These special detectors sniff out dangerous carbon monoxide (CO) gas, which can result from a malfunctioning furnace. Put one CO detector in your baby's room and another in the main hallway of your home.

◆ **Cabinet and drawer locks.** For cabinets and drawers containing harmful cleaning supplies or utensils like knives, these are an essential investment. For playtime, designate at least one unsecured cabinet or drawer as "safe" and stock it with pots and pans for baby.

◆ **Spout cover for tub.**

◆ **Bath thermometer or anti-scald device.**

◆ **Toilet locks**—so your baby doesn't visit the Tidy Bowl Man. One of the best we've seen in years is KidCo's toilet lock ($17), an award-winning gizmo that does the trick. Check their web site at kidco-inc.com for a store that carries it.

◆ **Baby gates.** See the section earlier for recommendations.

◆ **Furniture wall straps.** Since 2000, over 100 deaths have been caused by TV's and furniture tipping over onto kids. We recommend you anchor all your large furniture to the wall, especially shelves and dressers in baby's room. Once your child becomes a climber, she'll climb anything so be prepared.

The Bottom Line:
A Wrap-Up of Our Best Buy Picks

For baby bathtubs, we like the simple EuroBath by Primo ($44) or the Puj Tub folding tub for $45.

When it comes to potty seats, a seat insert like the Baby Bjorn Toilet Trainer ($32) when paired with a step stool is the best bet for most toddlers. For potty chairs, the Fisher Price Precious Planet Potty ($10) should do the trick.

What's the best diaper pail? We like the Diaper Dekor, Diaper Genie and Munchkin Arm & Hammer diaper pails best, although they require costly refill packages.

Many find a simple can with regular kitchen trash bags will do the trick.

Stay away from wipe warmers, which have safety concerns.

An activity/bouncer seat with a toy bar is a good idea, with prices ranging from $30 to $75—we like the Fisher Price bouncers best. An affordable alternative: adding a $10 toy bar to an infant seat.

For baby monitors, our top pick for an audio baby monitor is VTech's Safe & Sound digital audio monitor for $30 single, $50 double. For video monitors, we like the Infant Optics DXR-5 for $99 for a fixed camera and the Samsung SafeVIEW ($230) as a PTZ model.

Play yards are a great way to keep baby safe, but also provide a place to sleep (bassinet) for newborns. The Graco Pack N Play On the Go is $70 and does the trick.

Our top pick for swings is the Fisher Price My Little Lamb Cradle Swing ($150), although the Graco SweetPeace Newborn Soothing Center combines both a swing and bouncer/soother for $170.

Chapter 8

Car Seats: Picking the right child safety seat

Inside this chapter

What's the best car seat for your baby? What is the difference between an infant, convertible or booster seat? We'll discuss these issues and more in this chapter. You'll find complete reviews and ratings of the major car seat brands as well as informative charts that compare the best choices.

Here's a sobering figure: in the most recent year's statistics, motor vehicle crashes killed 1,320 children under age 14 and injured another 171,000. And 59 infants under age one were killed in traffic accidents in 2010.

According to government research, child safety seats reduce fatal injury by 71% for infants and by 54% for toddlers. And of course, child safety seats are required in every state in the U.S. and province in Canada. So this is one of the few products every parent must purchase. In fact you may find yourself buying multiple car seats as your baby grows older—and for secondary cars, grandma's car, a caregiver's vehicle and more.

So, which seat is the safest? Easiest to use? One thing you'll learn in this chapter is that there is not one "safest" or "best" seat. Yes, we will review and rate the various car seat brands and examine their recall/safety history. BUT, *remember the best seat for your child is the one that correctly fits your child's weight and size—and can be correctly installed in your vehicle.*

And that's the rub: roadside safety checks reveal 80% to 90% of child safety seats are NOT installed or used properly. Although the exact figure isn't known, a large number of child fatalities and injuries from crashes are caused by improper use or installation of seats.

Realizing that many of today's child safety seats are a failure due to complex installation and other hurdles, the federal government has rolled out a safety standard (called LATCH) for child seats and vows to fix loopholes in current crash testing. The results so far are mixed—we'll discuss these issues later in this chapter.

Getting Started: When Do You Need This Stuff?

You can't leave the hospital without a car seat. By law, all states require children to be restrained in a child safety seat. You'll want to get this item early (in your sixth to eighth month of pregnancy) so you can install it in your car before baby arrives.

Sources to Find Car Seats

1 **DISCOUNTERS**. Car seats have become a loss leader for many discount stores. Chains like Target and Walmart sell these items at small mark-ups in hopes you'll spend money elsewhere in the store. The only caveat: most discounters only carry a limited selection of seats, typically of the no-frills models.

2 **BABY SPECIALTY STORES.** Independent juvenile retailers carry car seats, but the selection is often limited by the size of the

---

E-MAIL FROM THE REAL WORLD
Car seats save lives

"When I was expecting my first child, I used your book extensively. I followed your recommendation for a car seat for my baby. I'm so glad I did because we recently were involved in a potentially deadly accident. My car's left back-side (where my ten-month-old baby was sitting), hit a lamppost. To give you an idea how serious it was, the car door was pushed in nearly a foot and a half.

"My son was riding in his Graco SnugRide infant seat, installed rear facing and attached to its base. He was actually injured by the collision when the door was damaged and the air bag deployed. We rushed him to the hospital where he was found to have superficial skull fractures and minor bruises. Good news: he recovered quickly without any permanent damage. Later, when we showed the hospital staff the photos of the vehicle, they were amazed that our son survived the accident."

---

store (small boutiques may just have one or two brands).

3 **THE SUPERSTORES.** Chains like Babies R Us, Buy Buy Baby and Burlington Coat Factory's Baby Depot dominate the car seat business, thanks to a wider selection of models than discounters. Prices can be a few dollars higher than the discounters, but sales often bring better deals.

4 **ONLINE.** We'll discuss our favorite sites to buy a car seat online shortly, but remember this caveat: Prices are usually discounted, but watch out for shipping—the cost of shipping bulky items like car seats can outweigh the discount in some cases. Use an online coupon (sites like RetailMeNot.com catalog current discount codes) to save and look for free shipping specials.

Best Online Sources

The web is teeming with both information and bargains on car seats. Here's the best of what's out there.

car seats

◆ **NHTSA.** The National Highway Traffic Safety Administration site (nhtsa.gov) is a treasure trove of car seat info—you can read about recalls, the latest news on changing standards and installation tips. Confused about how to use your LATCH car seat? The web site offers instructional videos for both rear and forward facing seats. You can also contact the government's Auto Safety Hotline at 800-424-9393 to ask car seat related questions. Even better: NHTSA now ranks car seats on their *ease of use* (assembly, instructions, securing a child, etc). The most recent report covers over 90 seats, from infant to booster. Note: these ratings do NOT cover how well a seat does in crash tests or compatibility with different vehicles.

◆ *The American Academy of Pediatrics* (HealthyChildrebn.org, go to Safety & Prevention then On the Go) is an excellent resource for buying tips.

◆ *The National Safe Kids Campaign* (safekids.org) has a helpful interactive "safety seat guide" that helps you determine which seat is right for the age and weight of the child.

◆ *Safety Belt Safe USA* (carseat.org) has a good site with tips on picking the best seat for your child, as well as the latest recalls and info on child safety seats.

◆ *Our web site* has a message board dedicated to car seats. Plus: we have a brochure called "Buying a Better Car Seat Restraint" produced by a Canadian auto insurance company. This publication (downloadable as a PDF) has excellent advice on buying a seat. For a link to the brochure and the ratings web page, go to BabyBargains.com and click on the "Bonus Material" section.

◆ *Insurance Institute for Highway Safety* booster seat report is linked from our site at BabyBargains.com/boosters.

◆ *Where to buy online.* Our readers' favorite sites to buy car seats at a discount include Amazon, Babies R Us and Bed Bath & Beyond (owners of Buy Buy Baby). As always, look for a coupon code for additional savings, free shipping and the like. Check out the Bargain Alert message board on our site (BabyBargains.com/coupons) for a regularly updated list of coupon deals and discounts.

More Money Buys You . . .

As you'll read later in this chapter, all child safety seats are regulated by the federal government to meet minimum safety standards. So whether you buy a $50 seat from Walmart or a $400 brand from a specialty store, your baby is safe. When you pay extra money, however, there are some perks. First, on the safety front, the more expensive seats often have shock-absorbing foam that better protects a child from side-impact collisions. The more expensive seats are also easier to use and adjust . . . and clearly that is a major safety benefit. For infant seats, when you spend more money, you get an adjustable base (which enables a better fit in vehicles), a canopy to block the sun and plush padding.

Speaking of padding, the more money you spend, the cushier the seat—some makers throw in infant head pillows, body cushions and more . . . all of which raises the price. These are not marketed as a safety benefit, but more for the baby's "comfort." The problem? Newborns and infants don't really care. They are just fine in a seat with basic padding (versus the deluxe version). Of course, if you have a super long commute or an older child (say over two years), padding and comfort becomes more of a relevant issue. But for most babies, basic padding is just fine.

Smart Shopper Tips

Smart Shopper Tip #1
So many seats, so much confusion

"I'm so confused by all the car seat options out there. For example, are infant car seats a waste of money? Should I go with a convertible seat? Or one of those models that is good from birth to college?"

Children's car seats come in four flavors: "infant," "convertible," "booster" and "hybrid." Let's break it down:

◆ **Infant** car seats are just that—these rear facing seats are designed for infants up to 35 lbs. or so and 33″ in height (weight/height limits will vary; some models only works up to 22 lbs. and 29″). On average, parents get about six months of use out of an infant seat (of course, that varies with the size/height of the child). Infant car seats have an internal harness (usually five-point) that holds the infant to the carrier, which is then snapped into a base. The base is secured to the car. Why the snap-in base? That way you can release the seat and use the carrier to tote your baby around.

◆ **Convertible** car seats (see left) can be used for both infants *and* older children (most seats go up to 40 lbs., but newer models top out at 65, 70 and even 80 lbs.) infants ride rear facing; older kids over two years of age ride facing forward. Convertible seats have different harness options (more on this later); unlike infant seats, however, they do not have snap-in bases.

◆ **Booster** seats come in three types: hybrid/combo seats, high back and backless boosters. We'll discuss each in-depth in a special section on boosters later in this chapter. In a nutshell, here's how they work: after your child outgrows his convertible seat, the booster correctly positions the safety belt. Most states have laws that require booster seat use until 60 or 80 lbs. (or up to age eight).

◆ **Hybrid** seats. Of course, real life doesn't always fit neatly into

car seats

these categories—some seats pitch their use from birth to 100 lbs. The most well known is the Safety 1st Alpha Omega (also called the Eddie Bauer Three in One)—the pitch here is one seat that can be used for an infant, toddler and then older child. The Alpha Omega is used rear facing from 5 to 35 lbs., then forward facing 22 lbs. to 40 lbs. From 40 lbs. to 100 lbs. the Alpha Omega converts to a booster seat that uses the auto safety belt to restrain an older child. We'll review this seat later in this chapter. (There will be a quiz on this later as well).

So, does it make more sense to buy one car seat (that is a convertible model) and just skip the infant car seat? There is considerable debate on this subject. Some safety advocates think convertible car seats are safer, pointing to recalls of infant car seats. Others deride infant car seats for their overuse *outside* of a car (as a place for baby to nap), speculating that such babies are at risk for SIDS (Sudden Infant Death Syndrome, discussed in Chapter 2). Fuel was added to this fire in 2006, when a *British Medical Journal* study generated headlines, saying that babies in infant car seats are at risk for breathing problems.

But . . . we analyzed that study and found the researchers examined only nine babies in New Zealand to come up with that conclusion (see our *Baby 411* blog for a detailed discussion). And while babies born prematurely (less than 37 weeks in gestation) are at an increased risk for breathing problems while in a car seat, full term infants ARE NOT. Sure, you should always supervise a newborn in an infant seat (have someone ride in the back seat if possible). And limit your baby's time in an infant seat. But that doesn't mean infant seats are UNSAFE or dangerous for sleeping infants.

On the other side of the debate are advocates who say infant car seats fit newborns better—most are designed to accommodate a smaller body and baby travels in a semi-reclined position, which supports an infant's head and neck. Yes, some convertible seats recline—but the degree of recline can be affected by the angle of your vehicle's seat back.

Furthermore, most babies don't outgrow their infant car seats until six months (and some as late as 12 months, depending the baby's weight and seat's limits)—and that can be a very long period of time if you don't have an infant car seat.

Why? First, it's helpful to understand that an infant car seat is more than just a car seat—it's also an infant carrier when detached from its base. Big deal, you might say? Well, since infants spend much of their time sleeping (and often fall asleep in the car), this *is* a big deal. By detaching the carrier from the auto base, you don't have to wake the baby when you leave the car. Buy a convertible car seat, and you'll have to unbuckle the baby and move her into another type of carrier or stroller (and most likely wake her in the process). Take it from us: let sleeping babies lie and spend the additional $100 for an infant car seat, even if you use it for just six months.

Remember: babies should be REAR FACING until they reach two years of age, regardless of weight. If your child outgrows his infant car seat before one year of age, be sure to use a convertible seat in rear facing mode for as long as possible. Most convertible seats can be used rear facing until baby is 30 to 35 lbs. (depending on the model).

Smart Shopper Tip #2
New standards, new problems?

"I hear there are problems with LATCH. What is LATCH anyway?"

Stop any ten cars on the road with child safety seats and we'll bet eight or nine are not installed or used correctly. That's what road-side checks by local law enforcement in many states have uncovered: a recent study by the National Highway Traffic Safety Administration stopped 4000 drivers in four states and found a whopping 80% made mistakes in installing or securing a child safety seat.

What's causing all the problems?

Many child safety seats have failed parents, in our opinion. Installation of a car seat is an exercise in frustration—even parents who spend hours with the instructions still made mistakes. The number one culprit: the auto seat belt—it is great at restraining adults, but not so good at child safety seats. And those seats simply won't work well if they aren't attached to a car correctly   that's the crux of the problem. Simply put, thanks to the quirkiness of auto safety belts (different auto makers have different systems), putting a child safety seat in a car is still like trying to fit a square peg into a round hole. Some seats wobble too much; others can't be secured tightly to the back seat.

The bottom line: some child safety seats simply DON'T FIT in some vehicles. Which cars? Which seats? There is no easy answer. Often, parents find it's trial and error to see what works.

So, that's where LATCH comes in. The federal government rolled out a mandated "uniform" attachment (called LATCH or ISOFIX), required for all vehicles and safety seats made after 2002. LATCH stands for "Lower Anchors and Tethers for Children." ISOFIX stands for International Standards Organization FIX, which is the international version of LATCH.

What is LATCH? Instead of using the auto's seat belt, car seats attach to two anchor bars in the lower seatback. The result: fewer confusing installations, no more locking clips or other apparatus needed to make sure the seat is correctly attached. (Another part of the new standard: tether straps, which are discussed later in this section.) See picture of a LATCH-installed car seat.

Here is a sum up of frequent questions we get on LATCH seats:

Located in rear filler panel of passenger cars.

Located in cargo floor of station wagons/vans.

◆ **Which manufacturers sell LATCH seats?** Answer: all. Every infant and convertible car seat sold now includes LATCH. However, booster car seats aren't required to us LATCH (although a few do).

◆ **Will I have to junk my old car seat?** Yes, car seat safety advocates do NOT recommend using a seat that is over five years old. Why? Belts, clips and interior parts in car seats wear out over time . . . hence, seats over five years old may no longer be safe to use.

◆ **My car does not have LATCH. What is the safest seat I can buy?** All LATCH seats are backward compatible—that is, they can be safely installed and used in older vehicles that do NOT have LATCH anchors. Remember the safest seat is the one that best fits your car *and* your child. There is no one "safest" seat. Get the best seat you can afford (we'll have recommendations later in this chapter) and use it with a tether strap. And get your car seat safety checked to make sure you have the best installation and fit.

◆ **I need to move my LATCH seat to a second car that doesn't have the new attachments. Will it work?** Yes, see above.

◆ **I know the safest place for a baby is in the middle of the back seat. But my car doesn't have LATCH anchors there, just in the outboard positions! Where should I put the seat?** Our advice: use the LATCH positions, even if they are only on the side. Some car seat and vehicle makers say it is okay to use a LATCH seat in the middle of the back seat if you use the LATCH anchors in the outboard positions—check with your car seat and vehicle owner's manual to see if this is permissible.

◆ **I got a LATCH seat that doesn't fit in my vehicle! I thought this was supposed to be universal.** LATCH has been sold to the public as some kind of magic pill that will instantly make all seats fit all vehicles. Hardly. Because of the wide variety of vehicles and seats (a SUV versus a compact, minivan versus pickup), it is unreasonable to expect any system would make this happen. While LATCH helps, it is not the cure-all.

◆ **I find LATCH hard to use.** You're not alone: a recent survey showed that 40% of parents aren't using LATCH. Problems with LATCH include hard-to-reach anchors that are buried in the seat back, making installation a challenge. Some LATCH clips are also easier to use than others. Car seat makers are trying to respond to these issues. Example: Evenflo's new Symphony car seat has an improved LATCH clip that is easier to install.

Smart Shopper Tip #3
Strap Me In

"What is a tether strap? Do I want one?"

Way back in 1999, the federal government mandated that all convertible child safety seats be sold with a tether strap—these prevent a car seat from moving forward in the event of a crash. How? One end of the tether strap attaches to the top of the car seat; the other is hooked to an "anchor bolt" that is permanently installed on the back of the rear seat or on the floor in your vehicle.

Most newer vehicles already have anchor bolts, making the use of a tether strap a snap. (Hint: check your vehicle's owner's manual to find instructions on using tether straps). Older vehicles may have pre-drilled anchorage points—just ask your car dealer for the "anchor bolt installation kit" (a part number that's listed in your owner's manual in the section on installing child safety seats). You can install the bolt or have the dealer do it.

Of course, really old cars are trickier since they lack anchor bolts or even pre-drilled holes—to install the anchor bolt, you may need to drill through your car's sub floor (a job for the car dealer, as you can guess). And just finding out the part number for the anchor bolt can be a challenge; some car dealers are clueless about this issue.

A side note: most seats can only use tether straps when FORWARD FACING. Few models (examples include the Britax Roundabout, Marathon and Boulevard and the Diono Radian) have a tether that can be used in either rear or forward facing positions. Note: tether straps are typically not used with infant seats or booster seats (but always consult your seat's directions for specific advice on this).

So, is the tether strap worth all the hassle? Yes—crash tests show car seats are SAFER when used with a tether strap. The strap keeps the car seat (and hence, your baby's head) from moving forward in a crash, lowering the chance of injury. Unfortunately, parents don't seem to be getting this message: a 2006 survey from the NHTSA revealed that only 55% of parents are using a top tether.

Are seats used *without* tethers unsafe? No, the federal government requires seats to be safe even when a tether is not in use. Of course, the tether adds that extra measure of safety and is always preferable to a tether-less installation.

Smart Shopper Tip #4
One Size Does Not Fit All

"My friend has a car seat that just doesn't fit very well into her car. Does anyone put out a rating system that says which seats are most compatible? Easiest to use? Safest?"

The National Highway Traffic Safety Administration rates car seats on their ease of use and posts the results on the web at nhtsa.gov or call 888-327-4236. Note these are not crash test results. NHTSA rates seats on how a seat assembles, installs and secures a child. In the latest report, over 90 seats were rated. The government updates the report every year.

Smart Shopper Tip #5
Recalls

"I saw online that a particular car seat is being recalled. Should I be skeptical of other seats by that manufacturer?"

Here's a sobering fact of car seat shopping: most major brands of car seats have had a recall over the past five years. We've seen recalls on cheap seats sold in Walmart and $300 car seats sold in specialty stores, making recalls a reality no matter what brand you consider. So if all major brands have had recalls, how do you shop for the best seat?

First, understand that some recalls are more serious than others. Some car seats are recalled for minor problems, like incorrect warning labels. Other companies do voluntary recalls when their own testing reveals a problem. The key issue: look to see if there are any injuries associated with the defective product. Obviously, car seats that are so defective as to cause injury to babies are much more serious than minor labeling recalls.

Another issue: how does a company handle a recall? Do they fight the government, forcing regulators to order a recall? Or do they voluntarily recall the item and set up an efficient process to get replacements or retrofit kits to consumers? In the past, we have lowered our ratings for car seat manufacturers who bungled a recall effort.

When a company announces a recall, the product is typically removed from store shelves (if the recall is for the current production run). If the recall is for a product's previous production, you may still see it on store shelves (since the defect may have been corrected months before). That's why it is key to see WHEN the recalled product was manufactured. Of course, different car seats in the same manufacturer's line may be totally unaffected by a recall.

Another tip: make sure to fill out the registration card that comes with any car seat you buy . . . and send it in! In theory, this will get you expedited recall information and repair kits. Also: sign up for a recall email list on Recalls.gov.

Unfortunately, with some car seat makers, even if you fill out a registration card you may not get a recall notice.

Smart Shopper Tip #6
Watch the height limit

"My son isn't anywhere near the 26 lb. limit for his infant seat, but he's so tall I don't think it is safe anymore—he has to bend his legs when we put him in!"

Here's a little known fact about most infant seats: in addition to WEIGHT limits, all infant car seats also have HEIGHT limits. And like everything in the car seat world, each seat has different limits (check the sticker on the side of the carrier—by law, the manufacturer must list both height and weight limits). Once your baby exceeds EITHER the height or weight limit, you should move him to a convertible seat.

One note on this: while the weight limit is important, do one other test if your child is approaching the height limit—is there less than an inch of seat left above baby's head? If so, then move your baby to a convertible seat (facing the rear of the vehicle until they pass one year of age).

With the bigger babies everyone seems to be having these days, this isn't a moot point. A large infant might exceed the height limit BEFORE he or she passes the weight limit. And of course, different seats have different limits (see the seat reviews for specs).

Later in this section, we'll have a chart that lists the height and weight limits of all major infant car seats. Also, individual reviews of seats later in this chapter also list weight and height limits.

Smart Shopper Tip #7
Do I have to buy THREE seats?

"My baby has outgrown his infant seat. Can I buy a combo seat that converts to a booster?"

The short answer: yes. Do we recommend it? No. Why? We think the safest place for an infant who has outgrown an infant seat is in a CONVERTIBLE seat in rear facing mode. Leave them there until they are AT LEAST two years of age—longer if they still are under the weight limit. Note: nearly all "combo" seats with five-point harnesses that convert to a belt-positioning booster are FORWARD FACING only seats.

So, what is best? When your child outgrows her convertible seat, THEN we recommend a booster seat (combo or belt-positioning). Now, we realize what you are thinking: have we lost our minds? We are recommending you buy THREE seats for your child: infant, convertible, and then a booster. Wouldn't it be cheaper to get one of those all-in-one seats or at least one that combines the convertible/booster function? No, not in our opinion. The all-in-one-seats (like the Safety 1st Alpha Omega) are generally a poor choice.

And while those combo boosters are a good choice for a three or four year old child who has outgrown his convertible seat but is not mature enough to sit in a belt-positioning booster, combo seats are NOT good for infants—they often don't recline and have less sleeping support than convertibles.

Smart Shopper Tip #8
European seats
"I saw a cool European car seat online—is that safe or legal to use in the U.S.?"

Short answer: no.

Thanks to the web, you can order a car seat from Switzerland . . . or South Africa. Making this more tempting: the belief among some safety advocates that Europe has better car seats than the U.S. or Canada.

But let's do a reality check: European standards are DIFFERENT than the U.S. or Canada. Different does not necessarily mean better, however. European seats are designed to work in European cars, which have different safety features compared to vehicles sold in North America.

Bottom line: it is ILLEGAL (and foolish) to use a seat from overseas here in the U.S. (Ditto for you Canadians—seats must be certified to meet Canadian standards before they can be sold or used in Canada. So if you are a Canadian reading this book, you can't buy a seat in the U.S. and use it legally in Canada.)

Smart Shopper Tip #9
Holding Your Baby Back: Safety Harness Advice
"Which seats are easiest to adjust?"

You will adjust your baby's car seat's harness two ways: first, you will tighten or loosen it as they grow. And then you will adjust the HEIGHT of the harness as she gets taller.

The best car seats have upfront adjusters to tighten or loosen a harness. Unfortunately, some seats require you to do this from the back of the seat—that is a major pain. We'll note which seats have this feature in the review section of the book.

As for adjusting the height, the best seats have a harness that can be raised without having to re-thread the harness (which requires disassembling the seat to a certain degree). Again, we'll note this feature later in this chapter.

FYI: do not put your child in a bulky coat or snowsuit when sitting in a safety seat. In the case of an accident, the bulky coat might compress, compromising the safety of the seat. At most, only put a child in a thin coat (like a fleece) when they are riding in a child safety seat. (To keep an infant warm, you can purchase an infant car seat that comes with a boot. Or purchase one as an accessory—Graco has an infant car seat boot accessory for $8).

Here are nine more shopping tips for car seats:

◆ *How easily does it recline?* Many convertible seats have a recline feature to make sure baby is at a proper angle. Of course, how easily the seat reclines varies from model to model—and reaching that lever in a rear facing seat may be a challenge. Check it out in the store before you buy.

◆ *No-twist straps.* Better car seats have thicker straps that don't twist. The result: it is easier to get a child in and out of a seat. Cheaper seats have cheaper webbing that can be a nightmare— "twisty straps" are a key reason why parents hate their car seats. Later when we review specific car seat models, we'll note which ones have twisty straps.

◆ *Look at the chest clip.* The chest clip or harness tie holds the two belts in place. Lower-quality seats have a simple "slide-in" clip—you slip the belt under a tab. That's OK, but some older toddlers can slip out from this type of chest clip. A better bet: a chest clip that SNAPS the two belts together like a seat belt. This is more kid-proof.

◆ *Are the instructions in Greek?* Before you buy the car seat, take a minute to look at the set-up and use instructions. Make sure you can make sense of the seat's documentation. Another tip: if possible, ask the store for any installation tips and advice.

◆ *Is the pad cover machine-washable?* You'd think this would be a no-brainer, but a surprising number of seats (both convertible

car seats

and infant) have covers that aren't removable or machine washable. Considering how grimy these covers can get, it's smart to look for this feature. Also check to see if you can wash the harness.

◆ *Will the seat be a sauna in the summer?* Speaking of the seat pad, check the material. Plush, velvet-like covers might seem nice in the store, but think about next August. Will your baby be sitting in a mini-sauna? Light weight, light colored fabric pads are better than heavier weight, dark fabrics.

◆ *Does the seat need to be installed with each use?* The best car seats are "permanently" installed in your car. When you put baby in, all you do is buckle them into the seat's harness system. Yet a few models need to be installed with each use—that means you have to belt the thing into your car every time you use it. Suffice it to say, that's a major drawback.

◆ *Watch out for hot buckles.* Some inexpensive car seats have exposed metal buckles and hardware. In the hot sun, these buckles can get toasty and possibly burn a child. Yes, you can cover these buckles with a blanket when you leave the car, but that's a hassle. A better bet is to buy a seat with a buckle cover or no exposed metal.

◆ *How heavy is it?* This is a critical factor for infant car seats, but also important for convertibles. Why? First, remember you are lugging that infant seat WITH a baby that will weigh seven to ten lbs. *to start.* When your baby outgrows the infant seat, she will weigh 22 to 35 lbs. *in addition to the seat weight!* To help you shop, we list the weights for major infant car seat brands later in this chapter. What about convertible seats? If you buy one seat and plan to move it from car to car, weight may be a factor here as well.

◆ *Buying a new car?* Consider getting a built-in (also called integrated) child safety seat, which is a $200 to $400 option on vehicles like minivans. This is an option for parents who have a child who is older than one year of age and heavier than 20 lbs. The only caveat: most integrated seats lack side-impact protection and may not fit small children well. Of course, offerings vary by maker. For example, Volvo offers an integrated booster seat ($500 for two seats) that has won kudos for its innovative design.

Safe & Sound

1 **NEVER BUY A USED CAR SEAT.** If the seat has been in an accident, it may be damaged and no longer safe to use. Bottom line: used seats are a big risk unless you know their history. And the technology of car seats improves every year; a seat that is just five years old may lack important safety features compared to today's models. (And, as we discussed earlier, seats older than five years also have parts that may wear out and fail . . . a big reason not to use an old seat). Another tip: make sure the seat has not been recalled (search the National Highway Traffic Safety Administration's recall database at Recalls.gov). Safety seats made before 2000 may not meet current safety standards (unfortunately, most seats aren't stamped with their year of manufacture, so this may be difficult to determine). The bottom line: risky hand-me-downs aren't worth it. Brand new car seats (which start at $50) aren't that huge of an investment to ensure your child's safety.

2 **GET YOUR SEAT SAFETY CHECKED.** No matter how hard you try to buy and install the best seat for your child, mistakes with installation can still occur. There's nothing like the added peace of mind of having your car seat safety checked by an expert. Such checks are free and widely available. The National Highway Traffic Safety Administration's web site (nhtsa.dot.gov) has a national listing of fitting/inspection stations.

3 **DON'T TRUST THE LEVEL INDICATOR.** Yes, many infant car seats come with "level indicators" and instructions to make sure the seat is installed so the indicator is in the "green" area. When in the green, the seat is supposedly at the correct

angle to protect your baby in case of a crash. Nice idea, but thanks to the myriad of back seat designs in dozens of cars, the seat may be incorrectly installed even if the indicator says it is fine. At car seat safety checks, many techs ignore the level indicator and instead use this test: They take a piece of paper and fold one corner to form a 45-degree angle. Then they place the side of the paper against the back of the infant car seat where the baby's back would lie. When the folded corner is level with the horizon, the seat is at the correct angle—even if the indicator says it ain't so. If you aren't sure your seat is installed to the correct angle, take it to a car seat safety check.

4 **FORGET CAR SEAT ADD-ONS.** We've seen all manner of travel "accessories" for kids in car seats, including bottle holders, activity trays and so on. The problem: all these objects are potential hazards in an accident, flying around the car and possibly striking you (the adult) or your child.

5 **HOW TALL IS TOO TALL?** You'll notice that most child safety seats utilize two types of limits: weight and height. It's the latter limit that creates some confusion among parents. Convertible seats have both a rear and forward facing height limit—this is required by federal law (for those inquiring minds, the standards are FMVSS 208, 213, 225). Most safety techs say the maximum height for a child is when their head is one inch below the top of the shell (the 1" rule) or if your child's shoulders exceed the height of the top harness slot. The problem: some car seat makers have more strict height limits than the 1" rule. Here's the frustrating part: kids often outgrow the seat's stated height limit *before* they reach that 1" rule or their shoulders are taller than the top harness slot, leaving some parents to wonder if they should continue using the seat. The problem is one of interpretation: while the federal law requires every seat to have height limits, car seat makers are free to interpret this rule (and usage of the seat). Some seat makers just interpret the rules more strictly than others. Bottom line: while we understand seat makers might have their own take on federal safety standards, it is generally safe to use a seat until your child's head is 1" below the top of the seat or their shoulders exceed the top harness slot—even if their height is slightly above the stated limit for the seat.

6 **READ THE DIRECTIONS VERY CAREFULLY.** Many car accidents end in tragedy because a car seat was installed improperly. If you have any questions about the directions, call the company or return the car seat for a model that is easier to use. Another tip: read your vehicle's owner's manual for any special installation instructions. Consult with your auto dealer if you have any additional questions.

What's the number-one problem with car seat installation? Getting a tight fit, say safety techs. Make sure the safety seat is held firmly against the back of the car seat and doesn't wobble from side to side (or front to back). One tip: put your knee in the seat and push down with your full weight while you tighten the seat belt or LATCH strap. This eliminates belt slack and ensures a snug installation.

7 **KEEP YOUR CHILD REAR FACING AS LONG AS POSSIBLE.** Safety experts agree that the longer a child is rear facing, the safer the child is in an accident. Why? Newborns and even young toddlers have undeveloped neck muscles—this can lead to an injury, especially if a child is forward facing in an accident. Good news: more and more seats have higher rear facing limits. Several infant car seats now work to 30 or 32 lbs. rear facing. And many convertibles also work up to 33 lbs. or even 40 lbs. rear facing. The take home message: keep your child rear facing as long as possible (to age two or three if you can).

8 **PUT THE CAR SEAT IN THE BACK SEAT.** Air bags and car seats don't mix—several reports of injuries and deaths have been attributed to passenger side air bags that deployed when a car seat was in the front seat. As a result, the safest place for kids is the back seat. In fact, whether the car has an air bag or not, the back is always safer—federal government statistics say putting a child in the back seat instead of the front reduces the risk of death by 27%.

And where is the safest part of the back seat? Safety experts say it's the middle—it is the furthest away from side-impact risks. The only problem with that advice is that some cars have a raised hump in the middle of the back seat that makes it difficult/impossible to safely install a car seat. Another problem: safety seats are best held against the car's back seat by a three-point belt—and some middle seats just have a two-point belt. Finally, consider the LATCH problem we noted above (where many vehicles have no LATCH anchors in the middle of the back seat, only the sides). Bottom line: while the middle of the back seat is the safest spot, sometimes you just can't install a seat there. The next best place is in an outboard position of the back seat with a lap/shoulder belt.

What about side curtain air bags you see in the back seats of some cars? Many new cars come equipped with side-impact air bags or curtains. These air bags are NOT as dangerous as front air bags, as they deploy with much less force in the event of a side impact crash. Therefore, putting a car seat next to a door that has a side curtain air bag is not a danger.

9 **REGISTER YOUR SEAT.** Don't forget to send the registration card back to the manufacturer. Yes, earlier we discussed how some manufacturers fail to send notices to registered users when a car seat is recalled (instead, relying on a media announcement) . . . but register your seat anyway just in case.

10 **PICKUP TRUCKS ARE OFTEN NOT SAFE FOR CAR SEATS.** "A pickup truck should not be considered a family vehicle," concluded an article by the Children's Hospital of Philadelphia on car seat safety—and we agree. Why? "Children in the rear seat of

car seats

compact extended-cab pickups are nearly five times as likely to be injured as children seated in the back seat of other vehicles," according to a study by Partners for Child Passenger Safety, sponsored by the same hospital.

Of course, not all pickup trucks are alike. Some larger pickup trucks with full-size rear seats do allow car seats (check your vehicle manual for advice). Depending on the vehicle maker, pickup trucks with these seats are called SuperCrew, Double Cab, Crew Cab or Quad Cab. However, pickup trucks with jump seats should NEVER be used with car seats—these are often referred to as Extended Cab or SuperCab trucks. If your pickup truck does not have a rear seat and you must use the front seat (again, not recommended), you must disable the passenger-side air bag.

Even if your pickup truck has a full-size rear seat that allows for car seat installations, think twice about using this vehicle with car seats. Again, studies show that all passenger cars are generally safer in an accident (for kids in a car seat) compared to pickup trucks.

11 CONSIDER SEATS WITH SIDE IMPACT PROTECTION. About 25% of all vehicle accidents are side-impact collisions. Over the last few years, more and more seats have been adding side-impact protection. This would be especially important if your vehicle does not have rear-curtain airbags to protect rear occupants. Yes, these seats tend to cost a bit more than those without side-impact protection, but we think it is a wise investment.

Recalls

The National Highway Traffic Safety Administration (NHTSA) posts recalls online (nhtsa.dot.gov) and has a toll-free hot line to check for recalls or to report a safety problem. Call (800) 424-9393 or (202) 366-0123. You can have a list of recalled car seats automatically faxed to you at no charge (in case you don't have online access). Note that this is a different governmental agency than the Consumer Product Safety Commission, which regulates and recalls other juvenile products.

 Money-Saving Secrets

1 TRACK AMAZON PRICES. Baby gear prices on Amazon often rise or fall with little notice. Tracking web sites like CamelCamelCamel.com will send you free email alerts when prices drop. You can also look up historical price charts (a Firefox plug-in lets you see this even while looking at the Amazon pages). We tracked the Britax Marathon and noticed the prices ranged between $192 and $290 in the past six months. And we saw Amazon drop the price on a Combi infant car seat by 31% in the past month.

2 GET A FREE SEAT! A reader emailed in this great tip—her health insurance carrier provides free infant car seats to parents who complete a parenting class. No specific class is required . . . you just provide proof of completion. And health insurance providers aren't the only ones with car seat deals—check with your auto insurance provider or employer as well. Some companies sell discounted car seats as a family-friendly perk, so check that too.

3 IF YOU HAVE TWO CARS, YOU DON'T NEED TO BUY TWO INFANT SEATS. Instead, just buy one seat and then get an extra stay-in-the-car base. Major infant seat makers sell their auto bases separately for $30 to $100. Retail stores rarely carry these bases; you'll probably have to buy an extra base online.

4 COUPONS! Find the latest coupons and discounts by popping over to our Bargain Alert message boards (BabyBargains. com/coupons). Right at the top, we keep a pinned thread with a list of the best online coupon codes, discounts and deals. The thread is updated regularly, so come back to visit when you need a code.

5 EXPENSIVE MODELS AREN'T NECESSARILY BETTER. If you spend $200 on a car seat, are you getting one that's twice as safe as a seat that's $100? Not necessarily. All car seats must meet federal minimum safety standards. In fact, we will recommend a simple Cosco Scenera, which costs $40 to $70 as a good bet for your second car or Grandma's vehicle.

So what do you get when you spend more? First, plusher fabric and padding. That doesn't have anything to do with safety—it's more comfort. Based on our research, extra padding isn't worth the extra money for infant car seats; however, for convertible seats or boosters, we can see the point (especially for longer trips). That's because older infants and toddlers are more likely to notice skimpy padding than newborns.

Also when you spend more you get a car seat that is easier to adjust (and that is a major plus and safety advantage). And some of the most expensive seats have added side-impact crash protection, again worthy of the extra investment.

6 LAST YEAR'S FASHION. Car seat makers frequently discontinue fashions (not the seat, just the fabric). Look for closeouts and save. Example: we saw a closeout pattern for a Britax seat for 40% off on Amazon.

The Name Game: Reviews of Selected Manufacturers

Here are our reviews of the major car seat brands. FYI: many of the infant seats reviewed here are sold as travel systems that combine a car seat and stroller; the strollers are reviewed separately in the next chapter. Of course, you don't have to buy a travel system—nearly all infant seats are sold separately.

Special note: this section gives you an overview of each brand; we review each model seat separately later in this chapter!

The Ratings

A **EXCELLENT**—*our top pick!*
B **GOOD**— *above average quality, prices, and creativity.*
C **FAIR**—*could stand some improvement.*
D **POOR**—*yuck! could stand some major improvement.*

4Moms Best known for their mamaRoo bouncer, 4Moms plans to launch an infant car seat in 2014. Details were sketchy at press time, but the key feature will be a seat that installs itself (tightening belt, leveling the base, etc.).

Baby Trend babytrend.com. Baby Trend sells both infant car seats and booster seats. Unfortunately Baby Trend, the company, has been dogged by poor customer service and other glitches. Example: the availability of Baby Trend's car seats has been inconsistent in recent years. And Baby Trend recently had to declare bankruptcy after losing a multi-million dollar jury verdict in a patent dispute. The big news for Baby Trend in the past year was their release of a new infant car seat, the Inertia.

Safety Track Record. Baby Trend has been relatively free of recalls, with the exception of the 2008 recall of 6000 infant car seats for a defective latch.

Britax britax.com. European-car seat maker Britax came to the U.S. car seat market in 1996 and changed the rules of the game: the company introduced several premium car seats that were packed with extra safety features . . . and sold at premium prices. Britax was the first seat maker to cross the $200 price level (and some of its seats now top $300).

Britax's success is due to both its innovation (side impact crash protection, a tether can that can be used in rear or forward facing position) and ease of use. On that latter score, Britax's seats are easy to install (they are a favorite of safety techs) and simple for parents to use (the harness adjustments, etc).

While a leader in convertible car seats, Britax has been weak with infant car seats until recently. New models with lower prices have helped in recent years. Meanwhile, Britax's booster seats (anchored by the Frontier) have been best-sellers.

Side impact protection is a key feature for the Britax line, although their offerings (True Side impact versus side impact cushions) can be confusing to parse.

Safety track record: Despite its emphasis on safety, Britax hasn't been immune to recalls for production defects and other snafus—the company has had several major recalls in the past ten years (including a recall in 2010 for the Chaperone infant car seat). In 2012, Britax recalled a slew of convertible seats for defective chest pads.

Chicco chiccousa.com Chicco makes an infant car seat (KeyFit) and a booster (Strada). While well known in Europe, Chicco took a while to get traction in North America. But their KeyFit infant car seat has been a smashing success in recent years. The big news in the past year was the debut of a new convertible seat (NextFit).

Safety track record: In 2008, Chicco recalled 18,000 infant car seats for defective bases.

Combi combi-intl.com. While better known for its strollers, Combi is also a small player in the car seat market. The main emphasis here is on infant seats that pair with Combi strollers to form travel systems, although Combi does have one offering in both the convertible and booster categories. Among the highlights is the Coccoro, a compact convertible that can fit three seats across in most vehicles.

Safety track record. Combi recalled 33,000 convertible seats in 2014 for defective harnesses. The brand's biggest recall was back in 2008, when all its infant seats were recalled for defective bases—this was a big black eye that the brand has struggled to overcome.

Cosco djgusa.com. Owned by Canadian conglomerate Dorel Industries, Cosco is a big player in the car seat market with over six million seats sold each year. As one blogger once put it, Dorel/Cosco puts the industrial in the Baby Industrial Complex.

Dorel/Cosco sells its seats under a variety of brand names: Eddie Bauer, Alpha Elite, Alpha Sport, Safety 1st and Maxi Cosi, which is a European division.

In previous years, Cosco would take the same basic seat, change the fabric pad and sell it under various brand names, depending on the outlet. Hence, you'd see the same seat sold in Walmart under the Cosco brand, an upgraded version with fancier fabric in Target sold under the Safety 1st nameplate and then a top-of-the-line model sold

car seats

under the Eddie Bauer moniker at chains like Babies R Us.

Realizing parents aren't likely to be fooled by such small distinctions, Cosco recently moved to make each brand more unique. So, you now see basic seats under the Cosco name in discount stores . . . but Safety 1st car seats will now have brand-specific technology like "Air Protect" (side-impact technology).

Perhaps Cosco's most unique brand is the Maxi Cosi line of car seats—since these are imported (and designed) by Cosco's European division, these seats aren't simply rehashes of Cosco's domestic seats. The Maxi Cosi car seats pair with a line of strollers under the Quinny brand (another Dorel Euro import).

Safety track record: Cosco's safety track record has been marred by recalls—20+ at last count since 1990. On the plus side, the number of major recalls has slowed in recent years.

Yes, you could point out that since Cosco is the largest seller of car seats in North America, it follows the company would have more recalls than a smaller competitor. True, but it is the *type* of safety lapses that bother us.

Example: Cosco allegedly sold hundreds of thousands of Touriva convertible seats AFTER the company knew a plastic notch in the seat caused skull fractures in low-speed crashes. That allegation came to light in a 2007 investigation by the *Chicago Tribune* (July 14, 2007, "When car-seat safety, commerce collide"). Despite Dorel's own engineers labeling the notch a "child safety concern," Dorel continued to make Tourivas with the notch for three years. Why? The *Tribune* alleges that Cosco didn't want to shut down its production lines (losing roughly $4 million in Touriva sales) to switch molds to a notch-less seat.

For the record, Dorel maintains it did investigate the notch allegation and its own testing confirmed "these recesses will not injure a child." When asked point blank if it delayed fixing the Touriva to rack up extra sales, the company replied: "The suggestion that Dorel would sacrifice the safety of children for a few extra dollars of profit is insulting and not worthy of further comment."

Cybex *cybexonline.com*. Based in Germany, Cybex's Aton infant car seat is their major U.S. offering. Despite winning kudos for its overall design, the Aton hasn't had much traction sales-wise.

Safety track record: No recalls as of this writing.

Diono *diono.com*. Formerly Sunshine Kids. Diono's key entry in this category is a combination convertible seat plus booster called the Radian. Available in versions that work up to 100 or 120 lbs., the Radian is the only folding car seat on the market. Diono accomplishes this by omitting the typical base you see on a convertible seat—this clever design trick makes the Radian perfect for car pools. In a recent update, Diono rolled out upgraded versions of the Radian, with a version that now adds side impact protection (the Radian RXT).

New for 2014, Diono is rolling out a new generation of convertibles, under the names Olympia, Pacifica and Rainer. The headline is improved side impact protection and upgraded fabrics.

In addition to their convertible seats, Diono also has two entries in the booster category: the Monterey, which features a deep seat with width adjustment and a backless booster called the Santa Fe. New for 2014 is the Diono Cambria, which is priced lower than the Monterey.

Safety track record: No recalls as of this writing.

Eddie Bauer. *See Cosco.*

Evenflo *evenflo.com.* Evenflo has struggled in this category, thanks to a string of disastrous recalls (eight since 2003) and other snafus. Yes, Evenflo has tried to add innovative features (mostly to their convertible seats), but the company has had a tough time overcoming its poor reputation in the marketplace. All in all, Evenflo often seems outflanked in the car seat market; Britax trumps them on safety features and Graco outguns them in infant seats and travel systems. Even downscale Cosco has a hotter license (Eddie Bauer).

Judging from parent reviews posted to our web site, Evenflo has a ways to go to win the hearts of car seat buyers. Ease of use (or lack thereof) is a common gripe, with seats that have difficult-to-adjust belts and other frustrations.

In recent years, Evenflo has been rolling out seats with side-impact technology, dubbed e3. As the name implies, e3 has three layers of foam and is seen on Evenflo's high-price seats.

Safety track record: Evenflo's safety track record is mixed, with many recalls of their infant car seats during the past 15 years. Example: the 2008 recall of one million Discovery infant seats that separated from their bases in a crash. This followed a 2006 recall of the Embrace infant seat for defective handles that unexpectedly released, causing some infants to tumble out of the seat. If that sounds familiar, you may remember the huge recalls of Evenflo infant car seats from the 1990's for a similar issue.

In 2010, Evenflo recalled Maestro combination toddler booster seats after *Consumer Reports* said the seat failed their crash tests. On the plus side, since 2010, Evenflo has not had a major safety recall.

First Years *thefirstyears.com.* First Years entered the car seat market when they acquired Compass in 2007. Compass was most famous for their folding booster seat, but struggled to compete against bigger car seat makers.

This brand has a schizophrenic personality when it comes to brand names. Some seats still retain the Compass brand, while others are marketed as First Years and Lamaze (a licensed brand sold at Babies R Us stores). FYI: First Years parent is toy maker Learning Curve/Tomy—sometimes you'll even see these brands listed along with First Years.

There's been very little innovation here with car seats in recent years, as First Years seems content to sell Compass old models with little or no improvements. The exception is the True Fit iAlert, which is a clumsy attempt to marry the world of smartphone apps and car seats.

The biggest issue with these car seats: trying to see them in person. Few stores carry them, as First Years mostly relies on online sales.

Safety track record. First Years/Compass recalled the 1420 infant car seat in 2006 because of a defective harness strap.

Graco *gracobaby.com.* Graco's success in the car seat market boils down to one model: its best-selling infant seat, the SnugRide. That gave Graco a major leg-up in the travel system market (travel systems combine both an infant car seat and stroller). As a result, when you walk into chain stores, you'll see many Graco car seats.

Graco has had less success with its convertible seat line, which has struggled to compete against Britax. To amp up the competition, Graco has focused on higher-weight limit seats in recent years. In the past year, Graco released several new seats with enhanced side impact protection called Safety Surround.

In the booster seat category, Graco has had a home run with its TurboBooster and Nautilus seats.

Safety track record: Compared to brands like Dorel/Cosco and Evenflo, Graco's safety record is good. Graco's last major recall was back in 2008.

Harmony *harmonyjuvenile.com* Montreal, Canada-based Harmony is a small manufacturer of booster car seats. In the past year, Harmony has tried to branch out into convertible seats.

Safety track record. No recalls as of this writing.

Kiddy *kiddy.de* German juvenile product company Kiddy recently launched a couple of booster seats in the U.S. Their unique feature: an energy absorbing shield that the company claims offers the best impact protection in a head-on collision.

Safety track record. No recalls as of this writing.

Orbit *orbitbaby.com* Orbit aims to the Apple of baby gear—their conversation-starting travel system marries a funky-looking infant car seat to a high-tech stroller. All this design goodness doesn't come cheap, however—the travel system weighs in at $1170.

For 2014, Orbit is updating its car seats with small tweaks. These seats are called G3. There is also a toddler car seat ($360) that "docks" with its car base and fits on the stroller frame.

Safety track record: Orbit got into a spat with *Consumer Reports* in 2009, after the magazine deemed its infant seat unsafe. Orbit disputed the findings and the government (that is, the NHTSA) declared the seat safe. CR then pulled this report off its web site, but still says the seat is a safety risk. A detailed report about this is archived on our blog. In 2013, Orbit had a recall for defective car seat bases.

Peg Perego perego.com. Peg's key entry in this category is an infant car seat, the Primo Viaggio. Launched to stop the loss of stroller sales to cheaper "travel systems," the Viaggio has gone on to be quite a hit, despite its relatively high price tag (about $100 more than Graco's popular seat). Chalk that up to Peg's sense of style (the Viaggio features luxury Italian fabrics) and pairing with Peg's strollers. This year sees a major update to the seat, now dubbed Primo Viaggio 4.35.

Peg has expanded to convertible seats and boosters in recent years. Confusingly, Peg calls all its car seats the Primo Viaggio. So there will be a Primo Viaggio infant seat and a Primo Viaggio convertible seat, for those scoring along at home. And the booster seat is called, wait for it, the Viaggio High Back Booster.

Safety track record: Peg had a 2009 recall on its infant seat for sharp plastic edges that cut some babies. Other than that, the company has had a good safety track record.

Phil & Teds Stroller maker Phil & Teds will give the infant car seat market a spin with their first offering in 2014. See a preview of this seat later in this chapter.

Radian See Diono.

Recaro recaro.com. Recaro is a 100-year old German-based company well known in Europe for their racing seats and other safety gear. After watching Britax's success on this side of the Atlantic, Recaro decided to give the U.S. market a try. Their main entries are in the convertible and booster seat category, with prices about that of Britax. Recaro's distribution is a bit thin in retail stores; seeing it in person can be a challenge. New for 2014, Recaro will launch its first infant car seat.

Safety track record: Recaro had a recall on its convertible seats in 2007 for defective harnesses. This recall was extended in 2009 to cover more seats.

Safety 1st See Cosco.

Summer summerinfant.com. Summer Infant is probably best known for its video monitors, but it has been slowly expanding into other gear categories. The latest: infant car seats. The Summer Prodigy features a slew of new technologies, including a harness than automatically adjusts for the height of your child. Also new: SmartScreen tells you whether you have installed the seat correctly. The seat has struggled to get traction, however, as Summer's mediocre stroller offerings have weighed negatively on the Prodigy.

Safety track record. No recalls as of this writing.

Infant Car Seats (model by model reviews)

4MOMS

Comments: 4Moms had a hit with their futuristic (if pricey) bouncer seat, the mamaRoo. They hope to bring some of that magic to their first infant car seat offering.

The seat's key feature: the 4Moms is the "the world's first self-installing car seat." Yep, you read that right—plop the base in your back seat, attach LATCH anchors, push the button on the side of the seat and voila! The seat automatically tightens the straps and levels the seat.

Snap in the infant carrier and the seat provides a check to make sure it is correctly attached—and the belts are tightened, the level is correct, etc. Dual LCD screens give you a thumbs up that all is correct.

Other details about this seat were up in the air as of press time— the price is undetermined. The launch date is a vague "late 2014." The weight limits? Side impact protection? Unknown. There isn't even a formal name yet.

So we'll report more on this seat later in 2014 as we get more details. **Rating: Not Yet.**

BABY TREND FLEX-LOC

Price: $80 to $130. Extra bases $40.
Type: Infant seat, five-point harness.
Limits: 30 lbs. and 30"
NHTSA ease of use rating: ★★★★☆
Pros: Top rated seat in recent crash test— back in 2007.

Cons: Carrier is quite heavy; hard to find in some stores—mostly sold as part of a travel system with an inferior stroller.

Comments: Baby Trend's Flex-Loc features a four-position height adjustable base and EPS foam for head protection. Some models come with a boot for extra warmth.

The downsides? Well, the carrier is quite heavy at 9.4 lbs. And, confusingly, Baby Trend markets two versions of this seat, one that works to 22 lbs. and one to 30 . . . yet they go by the same name (Flex-Loc).

More criticism: the handle release button can be hard to reach and stiff to release. And the strange triangle handle takes a bit of getting used to.

Baby Trend advertises this as the #1 rated infant car seat—we assume they are referring to a 2007 report from *Consumer Reports* that named the seat a "Best Buy." But that was 2007 . . . in CR's most recent report, the Flex Loc dropped to 15th out of 18 infant car seats. While crash protection in CR's tests was very good, others have better ease of use and fit to vehicle in CR's opinion, which we would agree with based on our reader feedback. As a result, we've lowered our rating on this seat this year.

Another negative for this seat: it hasn't been updated in years and is showing its age.

Finally, we should note that Baby Trend is a company with a checkered history. As of press time, the company is still languishing in bankruptcy after it lost a multi-million dollar verdict in a patent dispute. Baby Trend's customer service, or lack thereof, is also disappointing. Unanswered emails, un-returned phone calls and a general "we don't care" attitude mar Baby Trend's brand.

Baby Trend is also selling a similar seat called the EZ Flex-Loc (some sites just call it the Flex-Loc so check the weight limit to make sure which seat you're getting). Same latch straps, but the weight is lower (5 to 22 lbs.) and some don't have a height adjustable base. *Rating: C-*

BABY TREND INERTIA
Price: $180 to $240.
Type: Infant seat, five-point harness.
Limits: 5 32 lbs.
NHTSA ease of use rating: ★★★★★
Pros: Anti-rebound bar.
Cons: Rigid latch may not work in some vehicles.

Comments: The Baby Trend Inertia car seat debuted in 2013 and

EPP vs. EPS foam

When you take the fancy fabric cover off a car seat, you'll notice that many car seats are lined with foam for crash protection. Car seat makers use two types of foam: EPS and EPP. EPS (expanded polystyrene foam) is the hard yet lightweight foam used in bicycle helmets. EPP (expanded polypropylene foam) is similar to EPS but softer (and hence more comfortable) for older toddlers. The take-home message: either foam is fine, but more makers are using EPP foam as an upgrade.

features a "controlled motion base" that moves the seat up and at an angle in a crash. There is also an anti-rebound bar, a first for a Baby Trend seat. The straps on this seat are easy to adjust with a knob on the back of the seat. Rounding out the features is an ergonomic handle and 32 lb. weight limit (Baby Trend's previous infant seat only went to 30 lbs).

The Inertia includes a rigid latch connector—and that could mean some trouble fitting in vehicles. Most infant seats have flexible latch straps instead of rigid for that reason. A big negative for the Inertia: you can't buy extra bases. So you'll have to move the seat and the base from car to car if you need to switch vehicles, which is a big pain.

At $180, Baby Trend is pricing this seat at almost twice as much as the company's other infant car seat (Flex Loc)—and at about the same price as the highest-rated Chicco or Britax seats.

Initially, we rated this seat an A- minus when early field reports on the seat were positive. However, now that we see more real world feedback, we are dropping the grade. Why? We've seen multiple reports that the recline feature on the seat doesn't work. We're not sure if there was a defective batch of seats or what, but that is very disappointing for such an expensive car seat. Adding insult to injury, folks had to navigate Baby Trend's notoriously lackluster customer service (40 minute waits on hold, etc) to get replacement seats. As a result, we can't recommend the Inertia. ***Rating: C-***

BRITAX B-SAFE
Price: $135-$180
Type: Infant seat, five-point harness.
Limits: 4-30 lbs., 32"
NHTSA ease of use rating: ★★★★☆
Pros: Under $200, lighter carrier. Side-impact protection, tangle-free harness.

Cons: Omits rebound bar and no-rethread harness found on Britax Chaperone, not compatible with many strollers.

Comments: Britax has always finished back in the pack for infant car seats, thanks to its slow-selling models. One big reason: price. The brand's flagship model (the Chaperone) is $230 at retail (though often discounted below $200 online).

We gave the Chaperone an A- in our ratings—we liked the innovative features (anti-rebound bar, no-rethread harness), but the heavy carrier weight (11.2 pounds), lack of compatible strollers and high retail price are drawbacks.

Britax recently decided to scale back the Chaperone and lower the price. The result: the B-SAFE, a less-expensive version of the Chaperone that clocks in $135-$180 (which is similar to the price of the Chicco KeyFit 30), or about $50 less than the Chaperone.

So what are the trade-offs? The B-SAFE omits the anti-rebound bar and no-thread harness of the Chaperone—those were key features that impressed us. The anti-rebound bar is an excellent safety feature, but most seats with this feature haven't really caught on in the U.S. On the plus side, the B-SAFE is lighter than the Chaperone (9.6 lbs) and the base is shorter, so those of you with small cars should find it easier to fit compared with the bulky Chaperone.

Another negative: while the B-SAFE has basic side-impact protection, the Chaperone features adjustable, "true" side impact protection wings.

Real world feedback on the B-SAFE has been generally positive. A mom's in-depth review_posted on Amazon compared the B-SAFE to the similarly priced Chicco KeyFit and we agree with this assessment. She gave the Chicco higher marks for ease of install, but the Britax had better fabric (albeit only two choices) and a superior canopy. As for fit, it is probably a tie. While most parents give the B-SAFE high marks, a few detractors say the infant insert is difficult to use and the straps on the seat are too twisty.

Consumer Reports judged the B-SAFE "excellent" in crash protection, but gave the Chicco KeyFit better marks for ease of use and install (fit to vehicle). Overall, the B-SAFE scored five out of 18 models, which of course isn't too shabby.

One major consideration for this seat: stroller compatibility. If you are getting a Britax stroller, then this infant seat or the Chaperone would be a no-brainer. As for compatibility with other strollers, well, that's going to be hit and miss (mostly miss). Fewer strollers are compatible with Britax's infant seat, compared with Graco and Chicco.

FYI: With Britax's recent purchase of BOB strollers, Britax has rolled out a version of this car seat that matches the fabric on the BOB strollers: the BOB B-SAFE is exactly the same as the Britax B-SAFE, just different fabrics. And as you might guess, BOB's car seat adapter now works with Britax infant car seats.

So it's a mixed review for the B-SAFE: we like the lower price and weight. But if you are getting a Britax stroller, it might be worth the extra $50 to splurge on the Chaperone for the anti-rebound bar and no-rethread harness. **Rating: A-**

BRITAX CHAPERONE
Price: $160-$230
Type: Infant seat, five-point harness.
Limits: 4-30 lbs., 32"
NHTSA ease of use rating: ★★★★☆
Pros: Anti-rebound bar, side-impact protec-

infant seats

tion, EPS foam.

Cons: Price, not compatible with most strollers.

Comments: Britax's infant car seats haven't been as successful as its convertible seats for a couple of reasons. First, high prices: while Britax's reputation for safety features and enhancements is good, folks balked at the $200+ price tags. The Britax Chaperone, the company's flagship model, follows that trend with an official $230 retail (although we seen it discounted online to $160 or so).

Secondly, Britax infant seats, until recently, lacked many companion strollers. Britax has addressed that shortcoming in the past year or so with a stronger line up of strollers.

And to address the price issue, Britax debuted a scaled down infant seat (the B-Safe), which runs $50 to $70 less than the Chaperone. We like the B-Safe—so is the Chaperone worth the extra money? Here's an overview.

Both the Chaperone and B-Safe work to 30 lbs. The key difference: the Chaperone has an anti-rebound bar (for more crash protection—this keeps the seat from moving forward in a collision). And the Chaperone has an no thread-harness; the B-Safe requires you to rethread the harness to adjust the harness height.

The Chaperone's biggest weakness: it is too darn big too fit in many vehicles. The long base may make it a no go, even in a mid-size car. And with the carrier clocking in at 11.2 lbs. empty, it is sig-

What is the lightest infant car seat carrier?

Here at *Baby Bargains*, we have Ivy League-trained scientists who help us determine important stuff like which infant car seat weighs the least (and hence, is easiest to lug around).

Oh, we're just kidding. Actually, we the authors just went to our local baby store and stood there in the aisles lifting each infant seat and saying things like "Yep, this one is lighter!" For this edition, we actually employed a scale to get accurate readings (and you thought only the folks in lab coats at *Consumer Reports* got to play with such toys). Our official results: the lightest seat is the Cosco Light 'N Comfy (6.3 lbs.) followed by the Safety 1st onBoard Air (9.4 lbs.). The heaviest seats? That crown goes to the Orbit at 12 lbs. and Britax Chaperone (11.2 lbs). The Combi Shuttle and Peg Perego Primo Viaggio were close behind at 11.1 lbs.

We list the weights for infant car seat carriers in a chart later in this chapter (pages 434-435). Of course, the weight of an infant seat isn't the only factor we used to decide which was best, but it certainly is important.

nificantly heavier than most infant seats. Another negative: few strollers (except Britax) have adapters for the Chaperone.

Consumer Reports gave this seat an excellent mark for crash protection—but overall the Chaperone scored only in the middle of the pack, as it had a less-than-average score for fit to vehicle compared to other seats (again, the large size here is a factor in our opinion).

Bottom line: for parents who have a big enough vehicle, this seat is a winner—the anti-rebound bar and no re-thread harness make the Chaperone an excellent choice. Parent feedback is mostly positive . . . if you can get past the heavy carrier issue (this might not be the best choice for smaller moms or grandparents). **Rating: A-**

CHICCO KEYFIT 30

Price: $190 to $260, extra base $85.
Type: Infant seat, five-point harness.
Limits: 4-30 lbs., 30"
NHTSA ease of use rating: ★★★★☆
Pros: EPS foam, newborn insert, adapters available to work with other strollers.

Cons: Skimpy canopy. Large base may be tight fit for smaller vehicles. Pricey.

Comments: The Chicco KeyFit scored at the top of *Consumer Reports* latest car seat report and that has helped propel the sales of this already popular seat into best-seller status. It is well deserved.

The Chicco KeyFit boasts a nice list of features: a seat lined with EPS foam for improved side impact protection, thick seat padding, multi-position canopy and comfort grip handle. Chicco hired a former Graco engineer who worked on the SnugRide to design the KeyFit and it shows in the details . . . the base has a "single-pull" LATCH adjustment, a leveling foot to account for uneven back seats and even a smooth underside to keep from damaging your back seat upholstery. As you'd expect from Chicco, the fashion of this seat boasts Italian flair and there is even a newborn insert for a better fit.

Our readers have been very positive about the KeyFit's ease of use, lauding the no-twist, easy-to-adjust straps, the ability to leave the handle in the up position when driving (most seats require it to be lowered), and overall ease of installation. Quibbles? The KeyFit carrier weighs 9.4 lbs., a tad heavier than other similar seats. It takes two hands to release the handle on the seat. And the sunshade is too small (even with the extended visor). A few readers also report the fabric doesn't breathe, so the seat can get hot.

Perhaps the biggest drawback to the Chicco KeyFit 30 is the large base, which may not fit in smaller vehicles. And removing the cover for cleaning can be challenging. And yes, this seat clocks in at nearly $200, so it might be a stretch for those on tighter budgets. But

infant seats

this seat's ease of use and overall excellent design make it worth the extra cash, in our opinion.

FYI: Chicco makes three versions of the KeyFit—one that works to 22 lbs. (called the KeyFit) and one to 30 lbs. (the KeyFit 30) and the KeyFit 30 Magic with upgraded fabrics and infant insert. Between them, we'd suggest the plain KeyFit 30 version. And also note: the same base works with either the 22 lb. or the 30 lb. carriers.

In recent years, more stroller companies have rolled out adapters for the KeyFit and that's great news. Of course, you can also use it in Chicco's strollers, which are generally well regarded.

Overall, an excellent seat that is highly recommended. ***Rating: A***

COMBI SHUTTLE
Price: $160-$180. Extra base: $70.
Type: Infant seat, five-point harness.
Limits: 35 lbs., 33″
NHTSA ease of use rating: ★★★★★
Pros: EPS foam, one-pull harness adjustment, nice padding. Works to 35 lbs.
Cons: Complex belt path and puzzle buckle. Large seat.
Comments: The newest version of the Combi Shuttle works to 35 lbs. and features EPS foam for crash protection, comfort pads on the harness and one pull harness adjustment. The seat has an anti-rebound bar, which keeps the seat more stable in the case of a crash. Babies R Us is selling an exclusive version, the Shuttle 33, with a weight limit of 33 lbs. It's virtually the same seat, and sells for $180. The Shuttle's base is smaller and easier to use, thanks to its new built-in lock-off design. But the belt path on the Shuttle base had us scratching our heads: it is way too complex compared to other seats. Four position height adjustment rounds out the features. All of Combi's strollers work with the Shuttle infant seat.

Reader and expert feedback on the Shuttle 35 has been mixed. *Consumer Reports* ranked it second in a recent survey of seats, giving it above average remarks for ease of use and crash protection. Our readers weren't so generous, with numerous complaints about difficulty fitting the seat into the base. The carrier is also heavy at 10.1 lbs.

Fans of the seat like that the handle can be left in the upright position when in a vehicle. But be forewarned: the Shuttle is a large seat that won't fit into some smaller vehicles (and even mid-size sedans).

Overall, readers gave the Shuttle merely good marks—but for the same money, folks felt the Chicco KeyFit was better made and easier to use. Regarding safety, Combi's track record has been mixed, with several major recalls. Example: a 2008 recall for 67,000 Shuttle and Centre seats after testing revealed the seats could separate from the base in a crash. ***Rating: B-***

Cosco Comfy Carry

Price: $75 to $90; extra base $35.
Type: Infant seat, five-point harness.
Limits: 22 lbs., 29″
NHTSA ease of use rating: ★★★☆☆
Pros: Low price.
Cons: Base isn't adjustable; no level indicator. Very basic seat.

Comments: This is Cosco's low-price infant seat. The Comfy Carry features a 22 lb. weight and 29″ height limit. And that's about it: the base isn't adjustable, nor is there a level indicator.

As usual, Dorel makes different versions of this seat, marketed under their Cosco and Safety 1st brands. Here's an overview:

◆ The Cosco Comfy Carry: $75. As we mentioned above, it is rather bare bones: no head support insert, the harness adjusts from the rear and the base is non adjustable. Sold at Walmart and online.

◆ The Safety 1st Comfy Carry Elite: $80. This version adds a head support insert and front harness adjuster. Available in chain stores like Sears, Toys R Us, etc.

◆ The Safety 1st Comfy Carry Elite Plus (pictured): $90. All the features of the Elite plus an adjustable base and infant insert and upgraded fabrics. Of all the versions of the seat, this is probably the best bet as we prefer the adjustable base and front harness adjuster.

Parent reviews on this seat have been mixed. Yes, this seat is affordable and is easy to install. But . . . it only works with a handful of Safety 1st or Cosco strollers—few stroller makers bother to make an adapter for this seat, given its low sales. Another complaint: some parents had to return their seats because they weren't snapping into the base properly. They were able to dislodge the seats quite easily by just wiggling it out. Twisty straps are another complaint parents have.

As for *Consumer Reports*, CR says crash protection of this seat is excellent—the Elite Plus model has better ease of use (the adjustable base makes a difference here).

Bottom line: it's basic. We'd say it's "good enough" as long as it's installed correctly **Rating: C**

Cosco Light 'N Comfy

Price: $60-$70.
Type: Infant seat, five-point
Limits: 4 to 22 lbs., 29″.
NHTSA Ease of Use Rating: Not yet.
Pros: Very lightweight carrier, affordable.
Cons: No side impact protection, rear harness adjustment on base model.
Comments: The Cosco Light 'N Comfy is new for 2014 and fea-

infant seats

tures the lightest weight carrier on the market: 6.3 lbs. When you consider other carriers can top ten pounds, this might be a big plus for smaller moms or grandparents.

The Cosco Light 'N Comfy is clearly aimed at the entry price point ($60-$80)—it works to just 22 lbs. and lacks extra safety and ease of use features you'd see in more expensive seats (no side impact protection, etc). So this might be a good bet for occasional use by grandparents or other caregivers.

Like the similar Comfy Carry, the Light 'N Comfy will come in both a basic model and "elite" versions. The latter features upgraded details such as a front harness adjuster (the basic model will have a rear adjust) with a price point only about $10 to $20 more.

Given Cosco's track record for the similar Comfy Carry (which earned excellent crash protection ratings from *Consumer Reports*), we expect the Light and Comfy to perform similarly. This seat was not out as of this writing, so no parent feedback yet. **Rating: Not Yet.**

CYBEX ATON 1/2/Q
Price: $250-$300.
Type: Infant seat, five-point
Limits: 4 to 32 lbs., 30".
NHTSA ease of use rating: ★★★☆☆
Pros: Light carrier weight, easy to install. Short shell might fit compact cars better than others.
Cons: Funky canopy has skimpy coverage. Steep price tag. Hard to get the cover back on if you wash it.
Comments: German baby gear maker Cybex's innovative car seat, the Aton is worth checking out, despite its relatively limited distribution.

Launched in 2011, the Aton has a striking, Euro-minimal look, but its key features are impressive: a secure belt-tightening system and sleek hidden canopy. Safety-wise, the Aton's steel base-to-car seat connectors provide a rock solid installation. You also get infant inserts (a newborn inlay for babies up to 11 lbs. and an insert for babies up to 22 lbs.) and a padded harness. Of course, the Aton snaps into most Cybex strollers to form a travel system. A key fact to note: you can use Maxi Cosi adapters made for other strollers with the Aton.

What's not to like? Well, the seat shell is rather short—about 17" for the seatback. That compares to 20" for most other seats (like the Britax Chaperone, Graco SnugRide, etc). So some larger babies might out grow the seat before they reach 32 lbs. On the plus side, the shorter shell might work better for small, compact vehicles.

So is it worth the steep, nearly $300 price tag? Well, yes, in our opinion. We like the carrier's overall safety, ease of use and light weight (8.8 lbs). Reports from parents say the seat is very easy to install—it is very compact and a good fit for smaller vehicles. One negative: a few readers report it is difficult to reattach the Aton's padding after washing. And the large chest clip is too, well, large for smaller newborns, in our evaluation.

The Aton's canopy gets mixed reviews. Folks like how it hides away and its fabric quality. But the coverage is rather skimpy compared to other brands. And we worry the giant piece of plastic that borders the canopy might break after extended use. When the canopy is hidden away, it interferes with the carry handle.

Parent reviews for the Aton are mostly positive. *Consumer Reports*, however, was not so wild about the Aton, ranking it 12 out of 18 seats. While the crash protection was very good, other seats were easier to use, judged CR. The NHTSA gives the Aton three out of five stars for ease of use.

FYI: There are actually three versions of the Aton on the market: the Aton 1, Aton 2 and the new Aton Q.

The Aton 1 is the original, described above. The Aton 2 ($300) adds an anti-rebound load leg that reduces forward motion in a crash. The Aton 2 also has added side impact protection—a small bar that flips up from the handle that helps cushion side impacts. That's different from most other infant seats that have side impact protection built into the carrier or headrest. Confusingly, the Aton 2 is sometimes referred to online as the Aton 2013.

New for 2014, the Aton Q (named in homage to the famed James Bond gadget scientist, or at least that's how we see it) includes a new, bigger canopy and top-of-the-line fabrics and padding. The Q works from 4 to 35 pounds.

The Aton Q features an enhancement to the Linear Side Impact Protection first introduced on the Aton 2. The Q now has a telescoping side impact bar for additional crash protection—yes, that is a Cybex first. The bar telescopes off the top of the carrier in whichever direction protection is needed. The Aton Q also has a no rethread harness (not available on the Aton 1 or 2) and will fit any Aton base. Price: $350. The weight of Aton Q will be slightly more than the Aton 2, but final numbers weren't available as of press time.

So to sum up, the Aton 1 is about $250; the Aton 2 is $300 and the Aton Q is $350. Bottom line: the Aton is a great seat if you have a compact car and would like a lighter carrier. The Aton 1 and 2 are recommended; the Q wasn't out as of this writing. ***Rating: A-***

EDDIE BAUER SUREFIT *See the Safety 1st OnBoard.*

EVENFLO DISCOVERY / NURTURE
Price: $50 to $60; extra base $25.
Type: Infant car seat, five-point harness.
Limits: 5 to 22 lbs., 26″
NHTSA ease of use rating: ★★☆☆☆

Pros: Lightweight carrier, low price. Z-shaped handle is easy to carry.
Cons: Not easy to use.
Comments: This bare-bones seat is sold in discount stores like Walmart. The carrier (at 6.5 lbs.) is one of the lightest on the market. And yes, Evenflo has added EPS foam to the seat (a few years after the competition). But . . . you don't get many features with this seat—the base doesn't adjust, there is just one crotch strap position and so on. Want to adjust the straps? You'll have to do that from the back of the seat, a major pain.

And the list of negatives goes on: the handle must be in the down position when travelling in a car, an extra step that takes up extra space. Amazingly, a version of this seat first debuted in 1998, yet it is still on the market (albeit, in an updated form). Using a car seat with 90's technology is hard to imagine, considering all the advances in child passenger safety since then.

That probably explains why the Evenflo Discovery scored at the very bottom of *Consumer Reports* most recent report on infant car seats—that report weighed ease of use heavily in their rankings. And our feedback from parents is similar: yes, this seat is cheap, but in this case, you get what you pay for.

FYI: Evenflo is selling a similar version called the Evenflo Nurture ($50). It features a new handle design. Otherwise, it is the same as the Discovery (same weight limits, very similar base, etc). ***Rating: F***

EVENFLO EMBRACE (35/LX)
Price: $80; extra base $45.
Type: Infant car seat, five-point harness.
Limits: 4 to 35 lbs.
NHTSA ease of use rating: ★★★☆☆
Pros: Three-position adjustable base, easier to release base and handle.
Cons: Recalled in 2007 for faulty handle.
Comments: Here, in a nutshell, is why Evenflo is in last place in the car seat biz: the Embrace infant seat was supposed to be a fresh start for Evenflo, after their last major car seat (the PortAbout) was recalled for failing a crash test back in 2005. The Embrace features a new, easier release mechanism for the carrier (this was a gripe for past models). The seat also has a three-position adjustable base and an ergonomic handle that releases with one hand.

Yet, Evenflo had to recall 450,000 Embrace infant seats in 2007 after 679 reports of the handle of the carrier unexpectedly releasing, causing 160 injuries to children. (As a side note, 679 reports? 160 injuries? At what point did Evenflo think it was time to pull the plug?). Thankfully, there haven't been any more recalls of this seat since then.

As for ease of use, the Embrace scored second to last in

Consumer Reports most recent infant car seat rankings; Evenflo's Discovery 5 was in last place. The Embrace was judged better for crash protections than the Discovery 5, but otherwise ranked far behind the competition. The seat only scores three out of five stars on the NHTSA ease of use ratings.

FYI: The original Embrace only worked to 20 lbs; the latest model (the Embrace 35/LX) works to 35 pounds.

About the best we can say for this seat is it is a bit easier to install and use than the Evenflo Discovery . . . but that's not saying much. Given the past safety issues with this seat and Evenflo's track record, we say pass. ***Rating: D+***

EVENFLO SECURERIDE 35 E3/SERENADE
Price: $120 to $180.
Type: Infant car seat, five-point harness.
Limits: 35 lbs.; 29"
NHTSA ease of use rating: ★★★★★
Pros: Include infinite slide harness for easier

The NYC Taxi Dilemma

Here's a common email we get from parents in New York and other urban areas: are there any portable car seats that can be used in taxis? Something that is lightweight, easy to install and collapses to fit inside a small purse when not in use? Well, the answer is no—there's no perfect solution. But we have a few ideas. Let's break out our advice for New Yorkers by age:

♦ ***Infant (birth to six months).*** The safest way for an infant to ride in a taxi is in an infant car seat. Most (but not all) can be strapped in without the stay-in-the-car base. However, always check the manual BEFORE buying any seat to confirm this feature.

♦ ***Babies/toddlers (six months to four years).*** Many infant car seats can be used up to 30 or 32 lbs. use the seat as long as you can. For older babies, there aren't many good options. If you use a car service to go to or from an airport, you can usually request a car seat in advance. Otherwise, using public transport is probably the safest option.

♦ ***Older kids.*** A booster seat is the safest way to go—and a simple backless booster such as the Graco TurboBooster (backless version) is lightweight and portable.

adjustments plus better side impact protection.

Cons: $180 for an Evenflo seat? Heavy at 10 lbs. and awkward.

Comments: Evenflo's SecureRide 35 e3 is based on an earlier seat, the Serenade (which it will eventually replace). Evenflo added its e3 triple layer foam to this seat which it claims "reduces side impact forces by 50%."

The seat also includes SureLATCH, an infinite slide harness so you don't have to rethread it as baby grows, a base with three positions and angle indicators, and full coverage canopy.

Reader feedback on the SecureRide has been mixed. People complain that it is very heavy and the handle is awkward to use. It's also pretty big, making it a tight fit in smaller cars. But it is easy to install and adjust with the infinite slide harness.

Bottom line: this seat is much better than Evenflo's other offerings and we like the e3 side impact padding. If you can find it for around $120 to $130 it may be a good choice. *Rating: B*

First Years Via/Contigo

Price: $150-$180

Type: Infant seat, five-point harness.

Limits: 5-35 lbs.

NHTSA ease of use rating: ★★★★★

Pros: Carrier is completely lined with foam. Widest, deepest carrier.

Cons: Must use carrier with base. Doesn't fit into shopping carts or stroller frames.

Comments: The First Years Via makes two infant seats, the Via and the Contigo. They are very similar to each other so we have combined them into this review. Both models are decent infant seats . . . but they are difficult to find in most retail stores.

That, in a nutshell, is what is wrong with The First Years and their efforts in this category. When the company bought out Compass in 2007, we had high hopes they'd expand distribution of Compass' innovative (yet under-marketed) seats. But several years later, the seats languish in no man's land.

Take the Via, which features a carrier entirely lined in EPS foam, a padded handle, side impact protection, washable pad, height adjustable base and more. We liked the built-in belt lock-off for non-LATCH installations and steel-on-steel construction for latching the carrier to the base (some cheaper seats use plastic hooks, which can break and have led to past recalls).

The negatives? Well, *Consumer Reports* only gave the Via average marks for crash protection (that's down from "very good" in a previous test). Overall, the seat ranked 10th out of 18 seats.

Feedback from parents has turned more negative in the past

year—several folks complained that the seat stuck in the base. And other quality issues seem to be dragging down this seat, which is now showing its age (it hasn't been updated in quite a few years).

Another downside: The First Years Via doesn't work without its base (hence this isn't the best choice for urban dwellers who want to use it on the go in a taxi), nor is it compatible with most stroller frames.

FYI: This seat is the same as the JJ Cole Newport infant car seat. First Years makes a version of this seat for JJ Cole—same as the 1470, except a slightly different handle design. Also: this seat is marketed as the Lamaze Via Seat at Babies R Us.

The Contigo version of the seat has a different handle which functions as an anti-rebound bar in the down position. This extra feature raises the price about $10 compared to the Via.

Bottom line: the Via/Contigo are good infant car seats—but they are showing their age. And the lack of compatible strollers makes First Years a niche player at best. ***Rating: B-***

GRACO SNUGRIDE

Price: $70-$220; extra base $50-$75.
Type: Infant seat.
Limits: SnugRide Classic Connect: 22 lbs., 29"; SnugRide Classic Connect 30: 30 lbs., 30"; SnugRide Classic Connect 35: 35 lbs., 32"; Snug Ride Click Connect 35: 35 lbs., 37". SnugRide Click Connect 40: 40 lbs, 35".

NHTSA ease of use rating: Three out of five stars for all models, except Click Connect versions, which earned four out of five stars.
Pros: Lightweight carrier (for the base model), level indicator, canopy, easy to use. Front belt adjuster on some models. Works with many strollers.
Cons: Only one crotch position for some models. Other seats have better side-impact protection.
Comments: Here is the country's top-selling infant car seat—and it deserves the crown. The Graco SnugRide is an affordable infant seat with excellent features: good crash protection, EPS foam lining, adjustable base and good fit in most vehicles.

Graco has had such success with the SnugRide that they've rolled out several different versions of the seat over the last few years, keeping the SnugRide name. And that's where it gets confusing: there are now *seven* different SnugRides. With so many versions, be sure to carefully check the box or online description before buying.

Before we wade knee deep into the SnugRide specific models, we should note there are two general families of SnugRide seats: Click Connect and Classic Connect.

Click Connect refers to a new stroller attachment system Graco has rolled out, requiring one step to connect the car seat to a stroller. The old system required two steps and now is called Classic Connect. Graco's older stroller models work with Classic Connect car seats; the newer models work with Click Connect.

Here's a quick overview of the versions:

◆ **SnugRide Classic Connect.** This seats work to 22 lbs., 29". This is the least expensive SnugRide ($70 to $100) and it works only to 22 pounds. Many of these models lack a front harness adjuster (requiring you to adjust the harness from the back, a major pain).

◆ **SnugRide Classic Connect 30.** This one is our pick of the litter among the Classic Connect series: it works to 30 lbs., 30" and scored the best among all SnugRide's for crash protection in *Consumer Reports* lab tests. It runs $120 to $140, but is sometimes discounted to just $100 online.

◆ **SnugRide Classic Connect 35.** Retailing at $150, the SnugRide 35 works to 35 lbs., 32." This model has a base with belt lock-offs; the other Classic Connect SnugRides don't have this feature.

◆ **SnugRide Click Connect 30** works to 30 lbs., 30" and is typically sold as part of travel system. It has a front harness adjuster. As a stand-alone model, it retails for $130.

◆ **SnugRide Click Connect 35** works to 35 lbs., 32" and runs $150 to $180—some of these models add "GracoPedic" foam to the seat. That's a nice extra, but unnecessary (it isn't for crash protection but for baby's comfort). This model would be our pick if you want an infant seat in the Click Connect family. FYI: there is also a SnugRide Click Connect 35 LX that includes a no-rethread harness and base with seat belt lock-offs and upgrade fabric. That model is recommended as well.

◆ **SnugRide Click Connect 40.** This is the newest SnugRide and is a Babies R Us exclusive ($220) as of this writing. As the name implies, it is the first SnugRide to work to 40 lbs. This top-of-the-line model features a no-rethread harness and an adjustable base that slides back to give 8" of additional legroom—allowing babies to use the seat up to age two. That's nice . . . but the downside is the seat and base are much larger/longer than other SnugRides, making fit in smaller cars a challenge.

The overall reader verdict on the SnugRide: thumbs up. For ease of use, the SnugRide earns good marks.

Bottom line: here are our favorites—in the CLASSIC connect family, we like the SnugRide Classic Connect 30, combines good features and an affordable price (about $100). In the CLICK connect family, we like the SnugRide Click Connect 35 (retail: $150-$180; discounted to $120 online). FYI: be aware that the SnugRide 35 and 40 are heavier carriers (9.5 lbs. versus 8 lbs. for the 22 and 30 versions).

Another word of advice: we suggest a CLASSIC connect version of the SnugRide, versus the Click Connect, especially if you are planning to use a non-Graco stroller. Why? While many stroller companies make car seat adapters that are Graco SnugRide compatible, they are mostly compatible with the CLASSIC connect SnugRides.

Is the SnugRide perfect? No. The few complaints centered on the "annoying" handle, which takes two hands to lower. And again, choose a SnugRide with a front harness adjuster—you'll be happier. More than one reader complained about the crotch position on the less-expensive SnugRides— with only one position it is harder for larger, older babies to fit. On the other hand, one big advantage to getting the ever-popular SnugRide: it is compatible with a wide range of strollers and stroller frames, many more than other brands.

Are there trade-offs between the SnugRide and more expensive seats? Well, the SnugRide does lack extra side-impact protection like you see on the Peg Perego and Britax seats. And the seat lacks an anti-rebound bar, seen on the Britax Chaperone and Combi Shuttle seats. As a result, you'll note that other seats (especially Chicco and Britax) score better in crash protection than the SnugRide in *Consumer Reports* crash testing. Does that mean the SnugRide is unsafe? No—the SnugRide is safe. It just means that other seats (especially with anti-rebound bars) would move less in a crash. And that is safer. More expensive seats also have premium LATCH connectors, which are easier to use than the ones that come with the SnugRide (making install easier). Of course, these seats also cost almost $100 more than a SnugRide, so there's your trade-off.

It would be nice if Graco beefed up the side-impact protection in the SnugRide. If this concerns you, make sure your car has rear-curtain airbags if you use a SnugRide. If not, consider a seat with additional side impact protection (Britax, Chicco or Peg Perego).

Despite those points, overall, this seat is a winner—good crash protections, excellent ease of use and features. Add in the affordable price and we have a winner. ***Rating: A***

JJ COLE NEWPORT INFANT SEAT

This seat is the same as the *First Years Via*, except with a slightly different handle design. It sells for $200 and JJ Cole offers canopies in additional colors to swap out for a different look ($25).

MAXI COSI MICO AP/ORIGINAL (NEXT)
Price: $140 to $200.
Limits: 22 lbs., 29"
NHTSA ease of use rating: ★★★★☆
Pros: Works with Quinny strollers, Air Protect foam, four harness heights, deep side wings.
Cons: Canopy doesn't stay up, pricey.
Comments: Cosco imports these seats from their European subsidiary, adapted for the US market and designed to work with

its Quinny strollers.

There are two Micos now on the market: The original Mico (now rebranded as the Mico Next) and the Mico AP, its more plush cousin.

The AP is slightly different from the Next with a new seat pad, visor and air protect technology (hence the AP). Both seats are among the lighter infant seats on the market. The AP is 8.7 lbs while the Next is slightly less. In the past year, Maxi Cosi improved the carrier release on the Mico's base, both for the original and AP models.

Reader feedback has been mixed: fans say it is easy to use and install, plus the EPP foam is softer than the EPS foam you see on most other seats.

Parents universally hate the canopy (which does not stay in place) and others note it's expensive for a low maximum weight seat.

In the past year, the feedback on this seat has trended in a more positive direction. Fans point out that even though the weight limit is 22 lbs., it is one of the biggest seats (the shell is longer) compared to other 22 lb. seats. And at eight pounds, the carrier is among the lighter weight options out there. The Maxi Cosi scored second in *Consumer Reports* latest infant seat crash tests; and the government gives this seat a four star rating for ease of use.

So we'll tick up the rating a bit this year—but at $200, the Mico is rather pricey considering our top picks (like the Chicco KeyFit or Britax B-SAFE) cost less and work to 30 lbs. ***Rating: B***

MAXI COSI PREZI INFANT SEAT
Price: $290.

Limits: 30 lbs., 29"

NHTSA ease of use rating: ★★★★☆

Pros: Anti-rebound bar, easy-out no-rethread harness, extra side-impact protection.

Cons: Very pricey, heavy carrier, stroller adapters may not work.

Comments: The Prezi is Maxi Cosi's latest infant car seat: it features a 30 lb. weight limit, five-position adjustable base, anti-rebound bar and no-rethread, "easy out" harness. The last feature is unique: Maxi Cosi claims this is a quicker way for parents to buckle in or out a child.

Maxi Cosi has borrowed the "Air Protect" technology from their sister-line, Safety 1st, for the Prezi's side impact protection.

So, what's not to like? Well, the Prezi carrier weighs in at a hefty 11.7 lbs. empty. Add an average-size newborn and you've got 20+ pounds to haul around—hope you've been doing your pregnancy bicep workouts.

Another negative: stroller adapters that work for the Maxi Cosi Mico don't necessarily work for the Prezi—that's because the Prezi has a completely different base and attachment system. Since the Prezi is still new, we expect stroller makers will eventually catch up with cor-

Chocolate donuts with sprinkles?

Here's a confusing thing about car seat shopping: most car seat makers offer their models in a plethora of versions. At one point a couple of years ago, one infant seat maker had FIVE different versions of the same seat: the Classic, Plus, Elite, Supreme and the Extra Crispy. Okay, there wasn't an Extra Crispy, but you get the point. The key thing to remember: the seat was basically the very same seat in each configuration, just with minor cosmetic variations (an extra bit of padding here, a pillow there, etc). Yes, sometimes there are more significant variations like a front versus rear harness adjuster or an adjustable base. But often there isn't much differ- ence. Think of it this way: car seat makers produce a chocolate donut and top it with different color sprinkles—the rainbow sprin- kle version goes to Walmart, the green sprinkle donut goes to Target, etc. That way the companies can offer "exclusives" on cer- tain models to large retailers, so the chains don't have the same exact offerings. But remember this: basically, it's the same donut. Bottom line: don't get caught up in all the version stuff. If the basic seat has the features you want, it doesn't really matter whether you buy the Plus or the Elite. Or the Extra Crispy.

rect adapters. But, meanwhile, just because a stroller maker says they make adapters for Maxi Cosi seats, don't assume the Prezi will work.

And the $290 price tag is steep—about a third more than other top-rated car seats. We're not sure if the seat's features justify that pre- mium. At that price, it should have five out of five stars for ease of use!

Real world feedback has been limited so far and mixed overall. Fans like the overall sleek design and high-tech plush fabric—with special kudos to the fancy canopy. Detractors say the fabric is very hot and the carrier weight is a major negative. Several wish the neato canopy extended further over the seat. Others complained that the seat interior was too small. While we expect the anti- rebound bar will mean this seat will crash test very well, we don't have any real world data yet.

So it is a mixed review for the Prezi—we'll give it a qualified thumbs up. Good overall safety features are marred by a too-high price. ***Rating: B***

NUNA PIPA
Price: $300, extra base $85.
Type: Infant seat, five-point harness.
Limits: 4-32 lbs., 32".
NHTSA ease of use rating: Not yet.

infant seats

Pros: Sleek look, anti-rebound leg for additional crash protection, cool canopy, lightweight.

Cons: $300? Limited stroller compatibility. Few retail stores carry it.

Comments: Dutch baby gear maker Nuna landed in the US in 2013 with a handful of products, including the Pipa infant seat. Nuna's mojo is "simple, smart, chic" design, with a green spin (fabrics are Oeko-Tex certified for sustainability, etc).

The big headline for the Pipa infant seat is the "true lock" installation, with indicators that turn green when correctly installed. Also somewhat unique: an anti-rebound leg that is common in Europe, but somewhat rare here in the US.

The Pipa's "dream drape" is a car seat cover that uses hidden magnets to stay in place and then stores away in a hidden compartment.

Overall, we were impressed with the carrier's lightweight design (7.7 lbs) and overall design. So what's not to like? Well, the $300 price for one. Yes, this car seat has a cool design . . . but we aren't sure that alone justifies the price tag. We realize some parents want to have a unique seat that no one else has. So the Pipa will certainly fit that bill.

The Pipa has rigid LATCH connectors—this is both a plus and a minus. While rigid LATCH in theory gives a tight fit without having to tighten any straps, most US car seat makers use flexible LATCH straps. The reason: flexible LATCH works better with most US vehicles. And you must have a relatively flat backseat (not sloped) to use rigid LATCH, otherwise the seat will install an incorrect angle. So the jury is out on how Pipa's rigid LATCH will work in the real world.

And which strollers is the Pipa compatible with? Well, Nuna sells adapters for the Uppa Baby Vista and Bugaboo Cameleon. And the company says the Pipa works with Maxi Cosi stroller adapters made for other strollers—but we don't have any independent confirmation of this as of press time. Nuna itself has one stroller offering (the Pepp) that will accommodate the Pipa as a travel system. So the limited number of "official" Nuna adapters means you'll have to take the chance it will work with a Maxi Cosi adapter if you want a travel system with another stroller brand.

Based on initial parent feedback, we'll give the Nuna Pipa a qualified thumbs up—the seat's innovative design and features are impressive, but two key drawbacks hold it back: the rigid LATCH may make install tricky. Second, the high price certainly limits the Pipa's appeal. Finally, the Pipa may be hard to see in the real world, as it is sold only in a handful of specialty stores. ***Rating: B+***

ORBIT

Price: $1170, as part of a travel system with stroller frame. $440 sold as a stand-alone seat.

Limits: 4-30 lbs., 32"

NHTSA ease of use rating: ★★★★☆

Pros: Well, it is stylish.

Cons: Did we mention it is sold as part of a travel system for $1170?

Comments: Orbit aims to be the Apple of juvenile gear—a company whose innovative products set the bar for everyone else. Do they succeed? Let's discuss.

Orbit's flagship is the Orbit Baby Infant System, includes an infant car seat, in-car base and stroller frame that attempts a Bugaboo-like chic vibe. The infant car seat is a bit strange looking (one parenting blog compared it to a crock pot), with an innovative soft-strap handle and rotating base. We liked Orbit's "SmartHub" base technology, that lets you "dock" the seat at any angle. The base also has a front knob that ensures a tight fit to the vehicle.

The feedback on the Orbit has been mixed. Fans love the Orbit's technology and ergonomic design. Tall parents particularly love the stroller's tall handles; others love how it is a conversation starter with other parents.

But . . . detractors point out the bulky 12 lb. carrier is beyond HEAVY, providing a serious upper body workout as baby gets bigger. The bulk of the Orbit seat makes for a tight fit in even mid-size cars.

And let's get real for a second: does anyone really need to spend $900+ on an infant car seat and stroller frame? Most babies will outgrow the Orbit infant car seat at or before their first birthday. Then you have to pony up another $280 for a toddler stroller seat. So that means you are now spending a total of $1200+. (A bassinet cradle that docks to the stroller frame is another $280).

In the past year, Orbit began offering the infant car seat separately, for an eye-popping $400 retail.

As for crash testing, *Consumer Reports* ranked the Orbit only 14th out of 18 seats, giving it only an average mark for crash protection. Other seats did better and had better ease of us and fit to vehicle.

New for 2014, Orbit is rolling out the third generation (G3) versions of its car seat and stroller. The new travel system will have more customization options and a raft of improvements to the stroller (bigger storage basket, faster fold, better steering). The Orbit G3 will be sold a la carte—the stroller plus car seat will now retail near $1200. While we mostly saw improvements to the stroller during a preview of the new G3 system, we assume there will be small tweaks to the infant car seat as well.

So, it's a mixed review for the Orbit. Kudos to the company for their innovative features and design. But does Orbit reach the Apple level of cutting edge tech *and* accessible pricing? No. Let's do the math. You could buy an Orbit system for a grand. . . or buy a Graco SnugRide for $150 plus a stroller frame for $50 and take the $800+ savings and start a college fund for your child. ***Rating: B***

PEG PEREGO PRIMO VIAGGIO 4.35

Price: $280. extra base: $100.
Limits: 4-35 lbs., 30"
NHTSA ease of use rating: Not yet.
Pros: Newest version of best-selling Primo Viaggio infant seat, now works to 35 lbs. Also accommodates newborns down to 4 lbs.
Cons: Price.
Comments: Peg Perego has made slow but steady improvements to their best selling Primo Viaggio seat. The latest version (dubbed 4.35) works up to 35 lbs. (the previous version worked only to 30 lbs.) and features a series of other improvements: a no-rethread harness adjustable from the rear of the seat, anti-rebound bar, and a canopy that now boasts UV sun protection.

The 4.35 also has two inserts for smaller newborns, adjustable base, and a tensioning system to tighten the belt or LATCH installation. Another nice new improvement: the handle can be left up or down when travelling in a vehicle. The base of the 4.35 is also compact enough to fit in smaller vehicles (it is similar to the Chicco KeyFit, based on our initial measurements).

A pre-production carrier sample weighed in at 9.1 lbs., which is almost 20% lighter than the previous version (although this was a prototype and the final weight wasn't available as of this writing).

The Primo Viaggio 4.35 is scheduled to be released in March. As usual, however, Peg Perego follows Italian Standard Time for product rollouts. That means the 4.35 could be released anywhere between March and late 2015. We'll keep you posted. ***Rating: Not Yet.***

PEG PEREGO PRIMO VIAGGIO SIP 30-30

Price: $200 to $270. extra base: $80-100.
Limits: 5-30 lbs., 30"
NHTSA ease of use rating: ★★★★☆
Pros: Matches Perego's hot-selling strollers. Side impact protection, auto harness adjustment, improved canopy, luxe fabrics.
Cons: Price.
Comments: Peg Perego has had much success in this category, despite the seat's high price tag. Some of that success can be chalked up to Peg's slow but steady improvements to the Primo Viaggio. In recent years, the company has added side impact protection, an automatic adjustable harness and a better canopy to the seat, which now works up to 30 lbs. and can be used with or without the base.

Of course, a big part of Peg's mojo here is their Italian fabrics and style—plus the fact this seat mates with many of Peg's fashionable strollers. The luxe Italian fabrics are sharp, but most of Peg's competitors have caught up in the looks department in recent years.

As for ease of use, most of our readers give the Viaggio good marks, although not quite as high as the Graco SnugRide. Negatives include a bulky, heavy carrier that clocks in at 11.1 lbs. That said, the majority of the reader feedback on this seat is very positive.

Obviously, the price of the Viaggio is its biggest drawback—Peg has let the retail price of this seat creep dangerously close to $300. Seriously, $300 for an infant car seat? While it is a well made, safe infant car seat, it's hard to justify the nearly 50% price premium over similar seats from Chicco and Graco.

That said, we should note that we occasionally see the Primo Viaggio SIP 30-30 discounted online under $200. And there are many bargain Primo Viaggio seats from past years sold online in the $170 to $200 range. Be aware, however, that many earlier models only work to 22 lbs. and omit the side impact protection.

As for the latest crash tests, the Primo Viaggio scores in the middle of the pack in *Consumer Reports* latest tests—above average crash protection but only fair fit to vehicle using a safety belt. The government gave this seat a four-star rating for ease of use.

FYI: In spring 2014, Peg Perego will roll out a new version of the Primo Viaggio, dubbed the 4.35. It will then discontinue this version (SIP 30-30). However, given past experience, we'd guess the SIP 30-30 will live on for quite a few months thereafter. It may also drop in price, as retailers clear out older stock. ***Rating: A-***

PHIL & TEDS ALPHA PROTECT

Comments: Stroller maker Phil & Teds plans to enter the infant car seat market in spring 2014 with a new seat dubbed the Alpha Protect.

Details were still not firm as of press time, but it appears the seat will have a base with an anti-rebound load leg for stability in a crash, similar to the Cybex Aton 2. We saw a prototype of the Alpha Protect and thought it was nicely designed with EPS foam, a cushioned liner for newborns and a projected price tag of $200. The carrier prototype weighed in at about 7.8 lbs. Phil & Teds projects a spring launch for the Alpha Protect. ***Rating: Not Yet.***

RECARO GUARDIA

Comments: Recaro is best known for their convertible and booster seats and now they are adding an infant car seat to their catalog—the unfortunately named Guardia, which sounds rather too close to an intestinal illness for comfort. The seat will work from four to 35 lbs. and is set to debut in mid 2014. Recaro plans to load up the Guardia with goodies—memory foam, side impact protection, their HERO harness system (no rethread), full canopy and more. The innovative base for the Guardia will have numerous adjustments. The final price isn't set, but we'd expect this to be in the $250 range. ***Rating: Not Yet.***

SAFETY 1st onBoard 35/Air/Air Plus

Price: onBoard 35 is $90 to $119. onBoard 35 Air is $110 to $160. onBoard 35 Air Plus is $190. Extra base: $35-$70.

Limits: 35 lbs., 32"

NHTSA ease of use rating: ★★★☆☆

Pros: One of the few seats designed to work with preemies.

Cons: Have to pay an extra $60 to get the version with additional side impact protection.

Comments: This seat features a special insert for preemies (you can use the onBoard for babies from four lbs. and up). You also get EPP foam, four harness height positions and an adjustable base. Otherwise, the onBoard is a plain Jane infant seat without any special bells or whistles.

The Safety 1st OnBoard is only sold in a handful of stores, which probably explains why we've had very little feedback on it.

FYI: Safety 1st sells an upgraded version of this seat, the onBoard 35 Air. This is the infant car seat version of the brand's successful Complete Air convertible seat. It features the same Air Protect side impact protection. Newly released is the onBoard Air Plus with additional crash protecting foam called g-cell on top of the Air Protect technology. This seat was not yet available at press time but should retail for $190.

Reader feedback on the Air version of this car seat has been positive. As for crash tests, both the onBoard and onBoard Air versions scored an excellent rating for crash protection by *Consumer Reports*. CR gave the edge to the plain OnBoard 35, saying it was easier to use than the onBoard Air 35.

The government gives both onBoard versions a three star rating for ease of use—not the worst, and better than Dorel's Designer 22 seat. ***Rating: B***

SUMMER PRODIGY

This infant car seat is reviewed on the free side of web site, BabyBargains.com/?p=4358

UPPA BABY MESA

Price: $280.

Limits: 35 lbs., 32"

NHTSA ease of use rating: Not yet.

Pros: No-rethread harness, side impact protection, adjustable headrest, hideaway canopy with stretch fabric, innovative base with self-retracting LATCH system.

Cons: Pricey, version 1.0 seat. Uppa's first effort in this category. No anti-rebound bar.

Comments: The biggest news in infant car seats las year was Uppa

Baby's launch of their first infant car seat, the Mesa.

Uppa's effort here is nothing but ambitious—the Mesa is loaded with top-end features. Examples: a no-rethread harness, side-impact protection with an adjustable headrest, a canopy made of lightweight stretch material (similar to the Maxi Cosi Prezi) and a base that has a self-retracting LATCH system. Innovations include a tension indicator (Smartsecure) on the base that shows when you've tightened the belts correctly.

They've even thought of the little things, like a base with a smooth bottom surface, so it won't mar your auto's back seat (parents are tempted to use seat protectors with other seats, which are not recommended by safety techs). And the canopy (which disappears when folded) has a 50 SPF protection rating.

Since the Mesa came out after the Vista (Uppa Baby's flagship stroller) was designed, the Mesa doesn't quite integrate smoothly with the Vista. It requires a separate two-piece adapter (which Uppa Baby includes). This is more unwieldy than the built in adapters on the Uppa Baby Cruz stroller. The Mesa works seamlessly with the Cruz.

What's missing? Well, there is no anti-rebound bar as you see on the Britax Chaperone. And at 10.5 lbs, the Mesa's carrier is HEAVY. Parents using the seat in the real world noted that the extra three pounds (compared to Graco, for example) really made a difference.

And one last thing: the Mesa runs $280, among the most expensive infant car seats on the market.

Overall, the Mesa boasts an impressive design and feature list. Whether folks will pony up nearly $300 for it is an open question, however. After all, if you want an Uppa Baby stroller, you can use just about any major brand car seat with it, thanks to Uppa's extensive adapter accessory list. ***Rating: B***

Convertible and Forward Facing-Only Car Seats (model by model reviews)

ALPHA OMEGA THREE IN ONE *See Eddie Bauer Three In One convertible seat.*

BRITAX ADVOCATE G4
Price: $265 to $320.
Type: Convertible seat.
Limits: 5 to 40 lbs. rear facing, 20 to 65 lbs. forward facing, 49" tall.
NHTSA ease of use rating:
★★★★☆ Rear-facing.
★★★★☆ Foward-facing.

Rating is for previous version.

convertible seats

Pros: Same as Boulevard but with added side impact protection.

Cons: Price. Big seat—may not fit into smaller vehicles.

Comments: This seat is the same as the Britax Boulevard, with one major difference: the Advocate has added side impact protection cushions that compress to protect the child during a crash. Yep, think of these as side-impact air bags for your car seat. The CS in the seat's model name stands for Click and Safe—when the harness is correctly adjusted, you hear a click . . . a nice feature.

Two major caveats to this seat: it is much heavier and bigger than other Britax seats (21.2 lbs), which will make it less convenient to switch between vehicles. The Advocate's huge footprint will make it a tough fit in smaller vehicles. Also, the height of this seat is short— and since you have to stop using it when your child's ears reach the top of the shell (in forward facing mode), you're child will probably outgrow it by height long before he hits the 70 pound limit.

One nice feature can also be a negative: the cover is easy to remove for washing. But we noted more than a few readers said it came off way too easily when in the car.

As with all Britax convertible seats, SafeCell technology minimizes seat movement in a crash, integrated steel bars for strength and an energy-absorbing Versa-Tether that can be used forward or rear facing.

The Advocate G4 is shipping as of this writing. However, you will probably still see the third generation seats (known as 70-G3) on the market during the transition. What's the difference between G3 and G4? To meet new federal safety standards, the new G4 seats will work only to 65 lbs. Second, Britax is improving the HUGS harness system with a new scallop design to better position the chest clip and keep kids from pushing it down. The G4s also come with new infant inserts that must be used up to 22 lbs. And the G4s have a new sewn in label to indicate the maximum shoulder height. Finally, the lock-offs and belt paths are now color coded.

Reader feedback on this seat has been very positive. It scored well in *Consumer Reports'* most recent report on convertible seats. Perhaps the only knock to this seat is ease of use—the government only gives it a three-star rating, with "installation features" coming in for criticism. And we heard from more than one reader who was stumped by the instruction manual, which is heavy on illustrations and light on text.

Overall, this is an excellent seat—the rating only falls short of an A because of the high price and seat shell's shortness.***Rating: B+***

BRITAX BOULEVARD G4

Price: $230 to $270.

Type: Convertible seat.

Limits: 5 to 40 lbs. rear facing, 20 to 65 lbs. forward facing, 49" tall.

NHTSA ease of use rating:

⭐⭐⭐⭐☆ Rear facing
⭐⭐⭐⭐☆ Forward facing:
(Rating is for previous version.)
Pros: Same as the Marathon, but seat adds height-adjuster knob. Additional side impact protection with headrest.
Cons: Price. Big seat—may not fit into smaller vehicles. EPS foam only in headrest.

Comments: This seat is virtually the same as the *Marathon*, with two significant differences.

First, you get a height adjuster knob that lets you make numerous adjustments to the harness heights (instead of being stuck with the four positions you see in the Marathon). Hence, you don't have to re-thread the belts every time your child grows.

The second difference is what Britax calls "true impact protection." Basically, this is a reinforced headrest lined with EPS foam that protects your child in a side-impact collision. Like all of Britax's current seats, the Boulevard comes with SafeCell, integrated steel bars and the Versa-Tether (see review of Advocate above for details).

The Boulevard G4 (G4 stands for fourth generation) is shipping as of this writing. However, you will probably still see third generation seats (known as 70-G3) on the market during the transition. What's the difference between G3 and G4? See our review of the Advocate on the previous page for details.

The Boulevard gets very good crash test marks from *Consumer Reports*; the government's ease of use rating indicates the Boulevard is easier to install forward facing than rear facing.

Reader feedback on this seat has been very positive—perhaps the only complaint we heard is about the crotch strap, which isn't adjustable. ***Rating: A-***

BRITAX HIGHWAY

Comments: The Britax Highway is a stripped down Marathon (reviewed nearby), sold as an exclusive at Buy Buy Baby. The Highway omits the Marathon's no-rethread harness but adds a cup holder and storage pouch as accessories.

FYI: The Britax Highway is referred to as the Britax Highway 65 XE on Buy Buy Baby's web site.

Last we looked, Buy Buy Baby was selling this seat for $190. But you can find the regular Marathon for $187 from Target, $197 at Amazon and a bit more in stores like Babies R Us ($220).

Given that the Highway offers little or no savings over a Marathon, we'd suggest the Marathon. The Marathon's no-rethread harness is worth it.

convertible seats

BRITAX MARATHON G4

Price: $200-$260 online.

Type: Convertible seat.

Limits: 5 to 40 lbs. rear facing, 20 to 65 lbs. forward facing, 49" tall.

NHTSA ease of use rating:

★★★★☆ Rear facing

★★★★☆ Forward facing

(Rating is for previous version.)

Pros: Up to 70 lbs. with a five-point harness. Plush pad, EPS foam, same pros as Roundabout.

Cons: HUGS harness system gets mixed reviews.

Comments: The Marathon is Britax's best-selling seat and it's no wonder: this model was one of the first to work to 65 lbs. with a harness. Since its release, Britax has done a series of Marathon spin-offs that add side impact protection (Boulevard, Advocate). Despite being more old school, the Marathon is still worthy of consideration.

The Marathon has four harness heights (the top is 18"), Britax's "Versa-Tether" (which means the seat can be tethered rear or forward facing) and EPS foam.

Thanks to its wide distribution, you can find the Marathon sold in many stores and online. That means you can often snag one on sale: as of this writing. One tip: watch for discontinued patterns, which can sell for 20% to 30% less.

So, what's not to like about the Marathon? Well, first, this is a big seat. At 26" tall (the seat back), the Britax is a few inches taller than other convertible seats. That means it may not fit into smaller cars, especially when in rear facing mode.

The HUGS harness system on the Marathon has its share of mixed reviews. Britax says this harness system is designed to "better distribute webbing loads to reduce head movement and minimize the chance for webbing edge loading on the child's neck in the case of an impact. In addition, it is designed to reduce the chance of improper positioning of the chest clip. "But some folks (a small minority, to be sure) find HUGS hard to use. Britax has tried to improve HUGS over the years, but it still frustrates some parents.

The Marathon G4 (G4 stands for fourth generation) is shipping as of this writing. However, you will probably still see third generation seats (known as 70-G3) on the market during the transition. What's the difference between G3 and G4?

The newest Marathons (G4 and 70-G3) have a no re-thread harness, making it easier to adjust harness height.

The Marathon does have side impact protection (deep side walls), but Britax's other models (Boulevard, Advocate) go a step further with additional head cushions. Those cushions have both fans and detractors—the safety benefit is obvious, but some kids don't like the wings/cushions around their heads, limiting vision and movement.

Reader feedback on this seat has been very positive, with fans citing its ease of use and installation. All in all, we recommend the Marathon—IF you have a vehicle in which it can fit! *Rating: A*

BRITAX PAVILION G4
Price: $340 retail, $221 online
Type: Convertible seat.
Limits: 5 to 40 lbs. rear facing, 20 to 65 lbs. forward facing, 49" tall.

This seat is the same as the Britax Boulevard, with one additional feature: the Click & Safe Snug Harness Indicator. Basically, this is an audible click to indicate you have tightened the harness correctly. See our review of the Boulevard for more details about this seat in general.

The Pavilion G4 (G4 stands for fourth generation) is shipping as of this writing. However, you will probably still see third generation seats (known as 70-G3) on the market during the transition. What's the difference between G3 and G4? See our review of the Britax Advocate (p. 403-4) for details. Bottom line: the Pavilion is an excellent seat, if you can afford it. *Rating: A-*

BRITAX ROUNDABOUT (G4, 55, 50 CLASSIC)
Price: $120 to $180.
Type: Convertible seat.
Limits: 5 to 40 lbs. rear facing, 20 to 55 lbs. forward facing (Roundabout 50 works to 50 lbs). 40" tall.
NHTSA ease of use rating:
★★★☆☆ Rear facing
★★★☆☆ Forward facing
(Rating is for previous version.)
Pros: Excellent features—EPS foam, no-twist straps, can be tethered rear or forward facing, easy to adjust harness, double-strap LATCH.
Cons: Pricey; harness not as easy to adjust as Marathon.
Comments: The Roundabout was Britax's first convertible to be sold in the US and has been a best-seller thanks to its rock-solid installation—the lock-off clips provide snug belt install and Britax's double-strap LATCH connectors are among the best in the business. We also found Britax's harness to be easy to use and the straps don't twist. Finally, we should mention that you can tether the Roundabout either rear or forward facing, a key safety advantage.

Britax has revised the Roundabout over the years with the same technological improvements it rolled out across its entire line, including the SafeCell feature that keeps the seat from rebounding in a crash.

Confusing, Britax now has three different versions of the

Roundabout: the Roundabout 50 Classic is the basic model that works to 50 lbs. The Roundabout 55 works to 55 lbs and features deeper sidewalls for side impact protection and a new, lower first harness height (8"). That addresses a complaint we had about previous Roundabouts, whose lowest harness height was too tall for the smallest infants. Finally, there is a Roundabout G4, described below.

What's not to like? Well, the Roundabout is the same height as the Marathon (26"), which as we pointed out in that review, makes it a snug fit when rear facing in smaller vehicles. And, again like the Marathon, the Roundabout is old school: you have to manually rethread the harness to change the harness height. As we were going to press, we had a reader email us with a concern that the harness Roundabout 55 was much harder to adjust than on her previous Roundabout. And that seemed to be confirmed by another car seat tech we consulted on this issue—for some reason, the new Roundabout has a harness that requires much more effort to adjust.

The Roundabout G4 (G4 stands for fourth generation) is shipping as of this writing. However, you will probably still see third generation seats (55) on the market during the transition. What's the difference between G3 and G4? The G4's come with a new infant insert that must be used up to 22 lbs. And the G4's have a new sewn in label to indicate the maximum shoulder height. Finally, the lock-offs and belt paths are now color coded.

In the past, we recommended the Roundabout, giving it a slight edge over the Marathon since it had a smaller shell (both in back height and width)—that made it a better fit in smaller vehicles. However, now that the Marathon and Roundabout share the same dimensions, we'd suggest the Marathon. That's because you can use it longer with bigger toddlers (thanks to the higher top harness slot)—for kids up to 49" in height, versus 46" for the Roundabout. The Marathon also has a cover that much more easily removes for cleaning, a feature the Roundabout lacks. Hence, it might be worth it to spend the extra $20-$60 for a Marathon, since the street price of the Marathon (on Amazon, for example) is $200 to the Roundabout's $140-$180 retail.

That said, the Roundabout is still an excellent seat—and if that is all your budget will allow, this is a good compromise. Go for the G4 version if you can. **Rating: A**

Chicco NextFit
Price: $280
Type: Convertible seat.
Limits: 5-40 lbs. rear-facing, 22-65 lbs. forward facing. 50" or less.
NHTSA ease of use rating:
★★★★☆ Rear facing
★★★★☆ Front Facing

Pros: Nine recline positions. Side impact protection with deep side wings. Easy to install. Premium LATCH connectors. No rethread harness. Belt lock offs for seatbelt installs. Cover can be machine washed.

Cons: Can't tether this seat rear-facing. Early version had harness pads that were too close to a baby's neck, generating some complaints from users. Also the harness was hard to adjust. This was fixed in a revised version. Large seat may not work in smaller vehicles.

Comments: After successfully topping the infant car seat charts with their KeyFit infant seat, Chicco's NextFit launched in 2013 as the brand's first effort on the convertible car seat market.

The seat features nine (!) recline positions, dual level indicators and a harness rated for 65 lbs. forward-facing (40 lbs. rear-facing). The NextFit has a small footprint (to work well with smaller cars) as well as an infant insert cushion.

The NextFit features "Super Cinch" LATCH technology, which Chicco says will make it easier to install than competing seats. Also innovative: the seat's harness widens to accommodate larger toddlers. The no rethread harness is a major plus. And yes, the NextFit has side impact protection.

What does all this Chicco car seat goodness cost? $280, which makes this seat quite competitive with Britax's offerings. We were surprised the price for this seat is under $300, considering the KeyFit infant seat runs a bit more than most other infant seats.

Feedback on this seat has been positive, although some parents have complained about the strap adjustment–they find the straps get twisted and have to be "dug out" from underneath the child. The high harness height (17.5" for the NextFit; for comparison, the Advocate is 17) is a plus.

It's clear Chicco has done its homework with the NextFit: the seat is very easy to install, either with LATCH or vehicle belt. We like the harness adjuster and recline, which are as easy to use as any Britax seat. The attention to detail is obvious: note the storage compartment for the LATCH and tether straps; the fabric is also excellent and soft to the touch. Many parents say their kids prefer the Chicco NextFit to other convertibles when it comes to comfort.

As with any version 1.0 seat, there are always bugs to work out. Example: unlike the Britax Advocate, there is no Velcro on the sides of the NextFit to hold the harness when the seat isn't in use. As a result, once a child is put in the seat, the parent has to fish around under the child to find the harness. Ditto for the crotch strap.

Other negatives include the seat's large bulk (yes the base is narrow, but the rest of the seat is huge) and weight (you won't want to haul this on an airplane).

And a few folks complained about the NextFit's deep side walls (which are there for side impact protection)—getting a squirmy toddler in and out of the seat can be a challenge, thanks to these walls.

convertible seats

Seats like the Diono Radian are easier to use for toddlers, since they have lower side walls. So even though the NextFit expands to better fit toddlers, the deep side walls somewhat defeat the innovation when it comes to ease of use.

Another minor negative: we also see reports that the rear-facing harness position is too small/tight, positioning the straps too close together.

Perhaps the biggest initial complaint area for the NextFit is the harness. The harness pads are universally panned by readers—too bulky/rough, they cut into a baby's neck, etc. Others complained the harness is hard to tighten. And the chest clip is way too easy to unbuckle (for enterprising toddlers).

Chicco quietly moved to address the harness issues in late 2013—now the hated harness pads are removable (if you choose), the revised crotch strap is now longer and the harness is easier to adjust.

Unfortunately, Chicco hasn't changed the model name to reflect these refinements to the NextFit. The models made after November 2013 have the tweaks. So if you decide this is the convertible seat for you, make sure you are getting a seat made after that time. (One clue: see if the harness pads are removeable. Initial NextFits did not allow for the harness pads to be removed. Revised NextFits have removable harness pads).

Bottom line: this is a excellent seat that we will recommend. Installation is a snap and the overall safety features are excellent. ***Rating: A-***

CLEK FOONF
Price: $379-$500.
Type: Convertible seat.
Limits: 14 to 50 lbs. rear facing, 20 to 65 lbs. forward facing, 49" tall.
NHTSA ease of use:
★★☆☆☆ Rear-facing
★★★☆☆ Front facing

Pros: Premium seat that can fit three across in a backseat. Rigid LATCH for front-facing mode. Unique crumple zone for crash protection. Anti-rebound bar.

Cons: $500? And it doesn't work with infants under 14 lbs.?

Comments: Clek is the Canadian company known for its popular booster seats with rigid LATCH connectors and funky names. The Foonf is their first effort in the convertible seat category and started shipping in late 2012.

The Foonf is ground-breaking. It features a narrow base that allows three-across seating, an aluminum "crumple zone" in the seat for energy absorption, anti-rebound bar more and more. There are also little interesting touches like magnets that hold open the harness when putting baby in or out of the seat.

So is it worth the nearly $500 price tag? Well, you do get quite a few premium features, such as the IMMI flexible LATCH attachments for rear facing and rigid LATCH for forward-facing mode. Like Clek's Oobr, there is also an integrated headrest. And there is a recline feature when the seat is rear-facing. The Foonf's weight limits are 40 lbs. rear-facing and 65 forward-facing.

And while the official retail is $500, many online sites sell the Foonf for $400. Hence, the Foonf is about $100 to $150 more than the upper-end Britax seats.

The biggest negative: the Foonf is not rated for infant use—a child must be at least 14 lbs. and be able to sit up alone to use the seat, which is practically unheard of for a seat that can be used rear-facing. And in case your wondering, the average age a child can sit up unassisted ranges from five to eight months.

Clek continues to tweak the Foonf with improvements. In the past year, Clek has made some minor tweaks to the Foonf: the crotch buckle is now adjustable, with a longer length for bigger kids. Clek has also refined the anti-rebound bar, so it is easier to use and install. For 2014, Clek will add an adjustable crotch strap (two lengths).

Feedback from parents is mostly very positive, although the seat does have its critics. The negatives we've heard include stiff straps, a poorly written manual and a lack of seat padding. Another concern: the lack of recline when the seat is in its forward-facing position frustrates parents of napping toddlers. And the Foonf is very heavy.

Of all the complaints, the lack of seat padding is the Foonf's biggest flaw, in our opinion. For nearly $500, you'd think Clek would have lined the seat with expensive memory foam imported from Sweden . . . making the Foonf the most comfortable, cushiest car seat on the market. Yet, the Foonf is as hard as a gym bleacher, as one parent put it.

Bottom line: is the Foonf really worth the hefty price tag? We will recommend it, as long as you don't plan to do any long road trips or commutes, thanks to the lack of seat padding. Fans love this seat's construction and relatively narrow footprint. Ease of installation is another plus. ***Rating: A-***

COMBI COCCORO

Price: $160-$200
Type: Convertible seat.
Limits: 3 to 33 lbs. rear facing, 20 to 40 lbs. forward facing, 40" tall.
NHTSA ease of use rating:
★★★☆☆ Rear-facing
★★★☆☆ Foward facing
Pros: Small size = good fit for compact vehicles.

convertible seats

Cons: Can be hard to install rear facing.

Comments: The Coccoro is a compact car seat (it weighs just 11 lbs.), pitched for parents with small cars. Thanks to its small base size, Combi pitches this seat as a solution for parents who need to fit three car seats across the backseat. The top harness slot is 15," which is impressive for a compact seat. Another plus: the Coccoro has built-in lock off clips, a nice safety feature. And the Coccoro comes in a series of bright colors.

Parent feedback on this seat has been positive, although a few have complained that it is hard to install rear facing. *Consumer Reports* echoed that view, with a "poor" rating for the Coccoro's fit to vehicle, rear facing. That dragged down CR's overall opinion of the seat, which scored LAST overall, even though crash protection was judged very good. The NHTSA gives the Coccoro an overall three-star rating for ease of use, although again installation in rear facing mode comes in for criticism.

So it is a mixed review for the Coccoro—this is a good seat if you have a smaller child (and only need a seat with a 40 lb. limit) and/or you have a smaller car. The Coccoro's biggest fans are those with the smallest vehicles, such as a VW Beetle or Honda Civic. Overall parent feedback on the Coccoro is quite positive. But be aware of the poor fit and installation issues when in rear facing mode. ***Rating: B***

Cosco Apt 40 RF

Price: $55 to $70

Type: Convertible seat.

NHTSA ease of use rating:

★★★☆☆ Forward facing

★★☆☆☆ Rear facing

Limits: 5 to 40 lbs. rear facing, 22 to 40 lbs. front-facing.

Pros: Budget friendly seat that works to 40 lbs rear-facing. Five harness slots; three crotch positions.

Cons: Built-in cup holders make seat wider than others. Top harness slot is only 13", meaning older toddlers will outgrow this seat quickly.

Comments: The Apt debuted in 2012 and is basically an updated Scenera, Cosco's popular and affordable convertible seat. The differences? The Apt has deep side walls for side impact protection and two integrated cup holders.

Feedback on the Apt has been positive—the seat is easy to install and is one of the more affordable options on the market for rear-facing use up to 40 lbs. On the other hand, critics note the low top harness slot (13") means bigger kids will outgrow this seat by height more quickly than the 40 lb. weight limit.

Another issue: the built-in cup holders make the seat wider than the Cosco Scenera—and that makes the Apt a tight fit in some back seats where space is an issue (or when trying to fit three seats across). Finally, in order to clean the cover (which features all-over elastic), you must first remove the harness, which is a pain.

So it is a mixed review for the Apt. We know kids love cup holders, but that design features makes the Apt much wider than the similarly priced, entry-level Cosco Scenera. And that could be a deal-killer if you have a narrow back seat. **Rating: B**

COSCO SCENERA
Price: $39 to $60
Type: Convertible seat.
NHTSA ease of use rating:
★★☆☆☆ Rear facing
★★☆☆☆ Forward facing
Limits: 5 to 35 lbs. rear facing, 22 to 40 lbs. front-facing.

Pros: Affordable car seat for a second car. Good for airplane travel.
Cons: No side impact protection or EPS foam. Basic fabric, padding.
Comments: This simple seat is our top pick for that occasionally-used second car or Grandma's vehicle. The Scenera isn't fancy: you get a five-point harness with four height positions and three crotch slots. The padding is very simple and there isn't any EPS foam, side-impact protection or other goodies. But then again, this seat starts at just $40—perfect when you need an affordable seat that is easy to install and use.

Consumer Reports picked this seat as a best buy in their most recent rankings, giving it an "excellent" in crash protection. As for ease of use, the Scenera earned just two stars from the NHTSA, with rear facing installation holding the seat's rating down. Nonetheless, we think this is a good, basic seat for secondary use.

Most reader feedback on this seat has been positive, with most parents finding it easy to install and use. The only hitch: the Scenera has a kick-stand that has to be flipped out when forward facing. Some folks forget to do this and complain about difficulty of installation. FYI: Cosco has eliminated this feature from the new, similarly priced Apt seat, (which is somewhat wider).

Critics note the lack of padding or fancy fabric; the Scenera also lacks a body or head pillow, which means the smallest infants may not fit well in the seat. But that's the trade-off for getting the price so low—again, we think this seat is best for that little-used second car or Grandma's car. Fans love the light weight, which is especially nice for airplane travel.

FYI: The Cosco Scenera is a Walmart exclusive, although we occasionally see this seat pop up on other web sites. There used to be a version of the Scenera that worked to 40 lbs. rear-facing (called the Scenera 40RF) . . . but that seat was discontinued, as the Cosco Apt basically fills that niche. **Rating: B+**

Diono Radian RXT/GTX/R120/R100

Price: RXT $255 to $270, GTX $300, R120 $250 to $300, R100 $208

Type: Convertible (RXT converts to belt-positioning booster)

Limits: to 80, 100 or 120 lbs. Height up to 57".

NHTSA ease of use rating:

R100: Rear-facing: 3 out of 5 stars. Forward-facing: 2 out of 5 stars. Booster mode: 2 out of 5 stars.

R120: Rear-facing 2 out of 5 stars. Forward-facing: 2 out of 5 stars. Booster mode: 2 out of 5 stars.

RXT: Rear-facing 2 out of 5 stars. Forward-facing: 2 out of 5 stars. Booster mode: 1 out of 5 stars.

GTX: Same as RXT.

Pros: Folds up! Works to 80/100/120 lbs, depending on the model. EPS foam. RXT has added side impact protection. Narrow base lets you fit three across.

Cons: Heavy weight. Biggest kids may find crotch strap too tight. Not as ideal for kids under one year of age riding rear facing. Low ratings on ease of use.

Comments: Diono, formerly known as Sunshine Kids, is a small company that focuses on car seats and travel accessories. Their claim to fame is their Radian car seat line, which was among the first to have extended use harnesses (most convertible seats used to stop at 40 lbs). And the seats are car pool friendly—yes, they fold up!

The Radian accomplishes its folding trick by omitting the base you see on so many convertible seats—the seat actually sits along the back of the vehicle's seat. One plus to this: the Radian's narrow base allows for a three-across install in the back of a vehicle.

The Radian has recently been refreshed and now comes in four versions: RXT, GTX, R120 and R100. All the seats feature a steel alloy frames. And you can use LATCH up to 80 lbs., much higher than other seats on the market.

The RXT is the flagship and features a new trick: the harness removes so the seat can become a belt positioning booster (up to 120 lbs). The pitch: you can use this from birth (starting at 5 pounds), rear-facing for infants, forward-facing for toddlers with a harness that works to 80 lbs. . . . and then in belt-positioning mode to 120 lbs. The RXT also features memory foam and side impact protection (wings that are near the top of the seat).

The GTX is an upgraded version of the RXT with upgraded fabrics and padding, two cup holders, and bonus waterproof undermat. It runs about $30 more than the RTX.

The R120 omits the side impact protection wings, but otherwise is much like the RXT (example: you still get the memory foam, etc) and has the same weight limits.

The entry level R100 is more bare bones: no memory foam and the booster mode is only rated to 100 lbs.

Reader feedback on the Diono Radian has generally been very positive. Folks love the narrow, low profile of the seats and their overall quality. Yes, you can fit three of these across in a back seat in most vehicles, which is difficult with most other seats.

What's not to like? Well, these seats are rather tall and that can make the fit rear-facing difficult in smaller vehicles. And even though these seats fold up, they are rather heavy (20+ pounds)—so lugging them around is no picnic. And for some reason, Diono bombed on the government's ease of use ratings, earning very low scores. That's odd because most parents tell us these seats are easy to use and install (except the previously noted rear-facing install in smaller vehicles).

Bottom line: the Diono Radian line is an excellent choice, especially for those who car pool or frequently travel. ***Rating: A***

Diono Rainier

Price: $359

Type: Convertible to belt-positioning booster

Limits: 50 lbs. rear-facing, 90 lbs. front-facing, 80 lbs. with Super LATCH, 120 lbs. as a booster.

NHTSA ease of use rating: Not yet.

Comments: The Diono Rainer is the new, improved version of the Radian RXT set to debut in spring 2014.

The Rainier has a few enhancements over the RXT, chief among these are higher weight limits (90 lbs. forward facing with harness for the Rainer vs. 80 lbs. in the harness for the RXT).

Like all the revised Diono models, the Rainier has added side impact protection (compression walls at the head area, a rigid double wall structure on the sides) and upgraded fabrics (called Silk Tech) that are wipeable and wick for comfort in hotter temperatures. The added side impact protection to the Rainer doesn't add to the seat's width, a plus.

This model also includes new, deluxe infant body support cushions.

What's not to like? Well, the Rainier is a few inches taller than the RXT, which itself is already a tall seat. And at an official retail of $360, the Diono Rainer may end up with a street price over $300. ***Rating: Not Yet.***

Diono Pacifica

Price: $319

Type: Convertible to belt-positioning booster

Limits: 50 lbs. rear-facing, 90 lbs. front-facing, 80 lbs. with Super LATCH, 120 lbs. as a booster.

convertible seats

NHTSA ease of use rating: Not yet.

Comments: The Diono Pacifica is the revised version of the Radian R120, a convertible seat that converts to a belt-positioning booster. This seat is the same as the new Diono *Rainier,* but omits the Rainier's headrest. Like all the revised Diono models, the Pacifica has added side impact protection (compression walls at the head area, a rigid double wall structure on the sides) and upgraded fabrics (called Silk Tech) that are wipeable and wick for comfort in hotter temperatures. The added side impact protection to the Pacifica doesn't add to the seat's width, a definite plus.

The Pacifica does have the infant support cushions, same as the Rainier. The Pacifica is set to debut in spring 2014. ***Rating: Not Yet.***

DIONO OLYMPIA

Price: $280

Type: Convertible to belt-positioning booster

Limits: 50 lbs. rear-facing, 90 lbs. front-facing, 80 lbs. with Super LATCH, 120 lbs. as a booster.

NHTSA ease of use rating: Not yet.

Comments: The new Diono Olympia is based on the Radian R100. It has the same enhanced weight limits as the Diono Pacifica and Rainier, but is more basic.

The Olympia omits the infant body support pillow, cup holder and protective headrest seen on the Rainier. Hence, the Olympia might be best for older babies that don't need the infant support pillow.

Like all the revised Diono models, the Olympia has added side impact protection (compression walls at the head area, a rigid double wall structure on the sides) and upgraded fabrics (called Silk Tech) that are wipeable and wick for comfort in hotter temperatures. The added side impact protection to the Olympia doesn't expand the seat's width, which is rather impressive. Like all the new Diono seats, the Olympia is set to debut in spring 2014. **Rating: Not Yet.**

EDDIE BAUER COMFORT 65

Price: $150-$170.

Comments: This seat is very similar to the *Safety 1st Alpha Omega Elite,* with one major difference: the Comfort 65 only works as a convertible seat. It does NOT morph into a belt-positioning booster like the Safety 1st Alpha Omega Elite. Other than that, the seats are virtually identical. Hence, we'll give it the same rating. ***Rating: D***

EDDIE BAUER SPORT
Price: $80 to $110

Limits: 5-40 lbs. rear-facing, 22-40 forward-facing.

Comments: This seat is nearly identical to the *Cosco Scenera*. The only difference is the Scenera works to 35 lbs. (32") rear-facing. The Eddie Bauer Sport works to 40 pounds rear-facing and 40". Another difference: The Eddie Bauer Sport includes an infant body pillow, which would better accommodate newborns.

Since this seat is so close to the Scenera, we will give it the same rating. However, you do pay for that extra weight rating and body pillow: the Eddie Bauer Sport is priced at almost DOUBLE a basic Scenera. If you don't need the infant body pillow, then the less expensive Scenera would be a better value. **Rating: B+**

EDDIE BAUER XRS 65
Price: $130

Limits: 5-40 lbs. rear-facing, 22-65 lbs. forward facing.

Comments: This seat is identical to the *Safety 1st Easy Fit*, which is a Babies R Us Exclusive. The Eddie Bauer XRS 65, however, is sold on many sites/stores. Our rating for the Safety 1st Easy Fit applies here, since the seat is the same. One caveat: you can find this exact seat minus the infant body pillow sold as the Safety 1st Guide 65 for just $78 at Walmart. If you don't need the infant pillow, save yourself $50 can go for the very similar Safety 1st Guide 65. **Rating: A-**

EVENFLO MOMENTUM 65

This seat is reviewed on the free side of our web site at BabyBargains.com/?p=5529

EVENFLO SURERIDE 65
Price: $100

Limits: Rear-facing to 40 lbs. Forward-facing to 65 lbs.

Pros: One of the least expensive seats that works to 65 lbs. forward-facing.

Cons: Short harness means kids will outgrow the seat too soon.

Comments: The Evenflo SureRide is one of Evenflo's more recent efforts in this category. This convertible seat is similar to the Titan, but works to 65 pounds forward-facing (40 lbs. rear-facing). The Titan tops out at 50 lbs. forward-facing.

The biggest flaw for this seat seems to be the harness—we heard from more than one parent who bought the SureRide 65 and was disappointed with how short the harness is, especially for older kids. Yes, the seat shell and harness slots are big enough for kids up to 65 pounds, but the short harness is a deal killer.

FYI: The most current version of this seat is called the Evenflo SureRide DLX. **Rating: D**

EVENFLO SYMPHONY 65
Price: $165 to $230
Type: All in one: convertible seat and booster.
Limits: 5 to 40 lbs. rear-facing, 22 to 65 lbs. forward-facing with five-point harness, 40 to 110 lbs. as a belt-positioning booster.
NHTSA ease of use rating:
★★★☆☆ Rear Facing
★★★☆☆ Forward Facing
★★★☆☆ Booster.

IIHS rating for booster mode: Base model: Good bet.
e3 version: Best bet.
Comments: The Symphony is Evenflo's answer to the Safety 1st Alpha Omega seat . . . it aims to work with newborns to older kids up to 100 lbs.

SureLATCH is the headline here: Evenflo's new LATCH connectors that tout a "super-fast, tight and safe installation." SureLATCH features built-in retractors that eliminate belt slack—this makes the Symphony one of the easier seats to install with LATCH.

Parent feedback on the seat has been positive. Fans like the removable padding for infants and excellent harness adjuster.

In the past year, Evenflo increased the size of the Symphony's head wings. Also new: an aluminum bar inside the shell for stability, Evenflo's new e3 side impact protection and a new feature called TruTether, which indicates whether the tether strap has been correctly tightened. This version is dubbed the Symphony 65 e3.

New for 2014, Evenflo is redesigning the headrest on the Symphony LX and DLX models for additional side impact protection. Also new: integrated cup holders. The price will remain the same.

As for ease of use, the Symphony earned three out of five stars— not the best, not the worst. *Consumer Reports* puts the Symphony in the middle of the pack, with a fair rear fit-to-vehicle rating holding down its overall score.

We found the Symphony's booster mode better designed than Eddie Bauer's—it's easy to adjust and will provide a good fit for older kids. BUT, the Symphony is not a very tall booster . . . that means kids will probably outgrow it by height long before the stated 100 lb. limit.

Bottom line: this seat is probably one of the better attempts at an "all in one" seat. If you have your heart set on buying just one seat that works from birth to 100 pounds, skip the Safety 1st option and go with this one.

FYI: Evenflo sells a version of this seat under their Snugli brand, dubbed the Snugli All-in-One seat. It is the same as the Symphony, but adds memory foam and upgraded "Outlast Technology" fabric which is supposed to keep a child from overheating. **Rating: B+**

EVENFLO TRIBUTE

This seat is reviewed on the free side of our web site at BabyBargains.com/?p=11915

EVENFLO TRIUMPH 65 LX/SELECT

Price: $140 to $190.

Type: Convertible seat.

Limits: 5 to 35 lbs. rear facing, 20 to 65 lbs. forward facing.

NHTSA ease of use rating:

⭐⭐☆☆☆ Rear facing
⭐⭐☆☆☆ Forward facing

Pros: Special harness "remembers" last setting, EPP foam, up-front five-position recline and harness adjustment (no re-threading). Half the price of Britax.

Cons: Tension knob is hard to adjust when seat is in rear facing mode. Wide base may not fit in smaller cars. Can only use the top harness slot when forward facing, making the seat difficult to use for larger (but young) infants.

Comments: Evenflo has made steady improvements to this seat over the years and that's a good thing. Older versions of the Triumph garnered a large number of reader complaints about ease of use.

The latest Triumph works to 65 lbs. (older Triumphs only work to 40 or 50 lbs.) and comes in two trim levels: LX and DLX. The difference in the trim levels is just fabric and a bit more padding with the DLX version. Walmart has their own version called the Triumph Select with more basic padding for $105.

The Triumph's key features are the TensionRight knob that tightens the harness from the side of the seat and the infinite slide harness adjustment system (no rethreading). All the knobs on the Evenflo seat have both fans and detractors—give it a try in the store to see if you find it easy to adjust.

Parent feedback on the Triumph has been positive, although the flimsy cup holder comes in for universal scorn.

In some ways, the Triumph is showing its age. Take ease of use, for example. The Triumph scores just two out of five stars for ease of use

convertible seats

in the NHTSA's evaluation. *Consumer Reports* echoed that view, with average ease of use ratings weighing down the seat's overall score (14th out of 17 seats ranked). That's probably due to the difficulty in adjusting the TensionRight knob when the seat is rear facing. Another negative: the wide base (19.5") may make it a tight fit in smaller vehicles.

New for 2014, Evenflo is tweaking the Triumph with an upgraded, sliding headrest to increase side impact protection. Also new: integrated cup holders. The price will remain the same.

Bottom line: the Triumph is a good seat, but at this price level, competitors like Britax outshine Evenflo's efforts here. ***Rating: B***

FIRST YEARS/LAMAZE TRUE FIT (SI, IALERT)
Price: $140-$350.
Type: Convertible seat.
Limits: 5 to 35 lbs. rear facing, 20 to 65 lbs. forward facing
NHTSA ease of use rating:
★★★★★ Rear facing
★★★★★ Forward facing
Pros: Headrest pops off for easier rear facing installation. EPP foam, easy-off pad for hand-washing, affordable price.

Cons: Harness can be hard to adjust when rear facing.

Comments: Here's a great alternative to the Britax Marathon that costs about 20% less: the First Years True Fit is an excellent seat that works up to 65 lbs. This seat's most amazing feature is a headrest that pops off. That makes the True Fit easier to install rear facing in smaller vehicles (you won't need the headrest for newborns riding rear facing). We also like the automatic harness adjustments (no rethreading), side-impact wings, a seat entirely lined with EPP foam and three crotch positions to adjust for growing babies. Add in the 65 lb. top weight and an affordable under $200 and we have a winner!

We should point there are *five* different True Fit models. The first three True Fits include the basic model (C680) for $220, the Premier (C670, $200-$250, pictured) and the Recline (C650, $150-$200). The Premier features a reclining seat and an anti-rebound bar, making it the only convertible seat on the market with that feature. The bar helps stop the seat from moving in an accident. The True Fit Recline omits the anti-rebound bar, but otherwise is similar to the Premier. Also First Years makes a Lamaze version of the True Fit sold exclusively at Babies R Us.

The First Years recently added two new models to the True Fit line: The True Fit SI has improved side impact protection (redesigned head wings) and an anti-rebound bar for $229. Also new: the True Fit IAlert. Similar in features to the SI, this is the first car seat with its own iPhone app—the IAlert system monitors the seat and sends your iPhone an alert if the child is left unattended in the vehicle (and the vehicle isn't running). There are also alerts if the temperature in the car rises beyond a certain point and if the seat's harness isn't secure.

Early reports on the IAlert seat and app have been mixed—tech glitches (dropped Bluetooth connections, crashing apps) have marred what otherwise is a good concept. Is the IAlert really necessary? While it sounds gimmicky, we do see occasional stories in the news about parents who forgot their baby was sleeping in a car seat and then went inside a store—usually there is some terrible ending to the story. So if this app can help, then more power to First Years. Unfortunately, the price for this seat and the monitor app is steep: the IAlert is $350-$400, which is about twice as expensive as the same seat without the monitoring capability.

Overall, feedback on the True Fit in general (not just the IAlert) has been very positive: fans love the roomy seat, the "easy off" pad that enables quick cleaning and the overall ease of installation (belt lock-offs are a plus). Like the Diono Radian seats, the True Fit does not have a base—this enables the seat to be deeper on the inside without increasing its overall dimensions.

The downsides? The True Fit doesn't have wide distribution, which can make seeing it in person a challenge. And the harness can be hard to adjust when the seat is in the rear facing position.

The True Fit Premier has earned a unique distinction: it was the first seat to earn a five-star ease of use rating from the government, which is impressive. (Both the SI and IAlert earned the top ranking). *Consumer Reports* crash tests indicated the True Fit has "very good" protection and its overall score is in the middle of the pack (rear facing fit-to-vehicle was a concern).

One caveat to the True Fit: in rear facing mode with the headrest removed, the weight limit is just 22 lbs. With the headrest on, it is 35 lbs. ***Rating: A***

GRACO COMFORTSPORT

This seat is reviewed on the free side of our web site at BabyBargains.com/?p=1109

GRACO HEAD WISE

Comments: This seat is the same as the Graco My Size, but adds side impact protection in the form of Graco's "Safety Surround" headrest. The Head Wise 70 retails for $200 at Target. See the review of the Graco My Size (page 422) for specs and a rating.

GRACO MY RIDE 65 / 70

Price: $150 to $180

Type: Convertible seat.

Limits: 4 to 40 lbs., rear facing, up to 65/70 lbs. forward facing

NHTSA ease of use rating:

⭐⭐⭐⭐☆ Rear facing

⭐⭐⭐⭐☆ Forward facing

Pros: Affordable seat that works to 40 lbs. rear-facing and up to 70 lbs. forward. One version has enhanced side impact protection.

Cons: Difficult LATCH installation, strap adjustments.

Comments: This is Graco's effort at an affordable convertible seat that works to 65 pounds. Reaction from readers, however, is mixed and mostly negative. Yes, folks love the 40 lb. rear-facing limit, but the complicated LATCH installation (Graco uses a single strap that runs under the seat in rear facing mode) makes a tight fit difficult in some vehicles. The recessed cup holders are now built into the seat (in earlier versions of the My Ride, they weren't—and that generated quite a few complaints). Adjusting the straps is also quite difficult, especially when compared to Britax's seats.

Despite the mixed reader feedback, this seat earned four out of five stars in the government's ease of use ratings. And *Consumer Reports* picked this seat as a best buy, even though it ended up scoring in the middle of the pack in their most recent report on convertible car seats. We can see their point on affordability: $150 to $180 for a seat that works to 65 lbs. is a value.

Given the split opinion, we'll side with our readers on this seat and only give it an average rating. Bottom line: while we salute Graco's effort to make an affordable 65 lb. limit seat, the trade-offs in ease of use and design drag down the My Ride's rating.

In the past year, Graco added enhanced side impact protection to the My Ride. Dubbed "Safety Surround," this feature adds an optional/removable head cushion for infants and built-in side impact protection for older kids. The head cushion for infants adjusts up or down to accommodate a growing child. The My Ride 65 with Safety Surround is $180 at Buy Buy Baby.

FYI: Some versions of the My Ride 65 feature special newborn insert cushions that enable the seat to fit infants as small as four pounds (parents of preemies, take note). And we should also note there is a My Ride 70 sold at Target for $160. It is basically the same as the My Ride 65 but works to 70 lbs. forward-facing. ***Rating: C***

GRACO MY SIZE 70

Price: $160-$180

Type: Convertible seat.

Limits: 4-40 lbs. rear facing, 20 to 70 lbs. forward facing. In 2014, this seat will work to 65 lbs. forward facing.

NHTSA ease of use rating: Not yet.

Pros: No rethread harness, adjustable headrest, seat recline, extended rear-facing use. Integrated cup holder.

Cons: Harness can be difficult to tighten; buckle hard to release.

Comments: The My Size 70 features an adjustable headrest, no-rethread harness, three-position recline and upgraded LATCH connectors (called Right LATCH). There's also a removable head/body support for newborns.

Parent feedback on this seat has been mixed—while fans laud the extended rear-facing weight limit and easy to clean fabric, several complaints have centered around difficulty in adjusting the harness. Others complain the five-point buckle is difficult to release.

Other negatives include a lack of padding on the seat bottom.

FYI: For 2014, Graco will change the upper weight limit on this seat to 65 from 70 lbs. This is to conform with new federal safety standards. Hence, the seat will be referred to as the Graco My Size 65.

So it is a mixed review for this seat: kudos to Graco for coming out with an affordable seat that can be used rear-facing to 40 lbs. AND forward-facing with harness to 65/70. But the negatives of the harness and buckle temper our enthusiasm for this seat. **_Rating C_**

GRACO SIZE 4 ME 70

This seat is the same as the *Graco My Size 70*. The only differences are fabric and a slightly different way the LATCH strap releases.

GRACO SMART SEAT

Price: $240 to $300.

Type: Convertible seat.

Limits: 5 to 40 lbs., rear facing, 20 to 65 lbs. forward facing, up to 100 lbs. as a belt-positioning booster.

NHTSA ease of use rating:

⭐⭐⭐⭐⭐ Rear facing
⭐⭐⭐⭐⭐ Front facing
⭐⭐⭐⭐⭐ Booster

IIHS rating for booster mode: Check fit.

Pros: First seat with stay in car base, side impact protection, no rethread harness. Converts to booster.

Cons: $300 for a Graco car seat? Big, hefty seat may not fit in smaller vehicles.

Comments: And now for something totally different: Graco's Smart

Seat aims to be one of the first convertible seat with a stay in the car base (like infant car seats). Yes, you install this base once and then snap in the seat, either front or rear facing. Add in a no rethread harness, six position headrest, seat recline, integrated cup holder and the ability to work as a booster (the base and five-point harness are removed) to 100 lbs. and you have one impressive seat. We also liked how the Smart Seat features side impact protection.

So what's not to love? Well, at nearly $300, customer expectations will be very high— this seat better be as easy to use as Britax's most expensive models. And on that score, Graco has a less than stellar track record. As you can read in the reviews for Graco's other convertible seats, this brand struggles to earn over a C for most of its convertible seat offerings.

Reader feedback on the seat has been mostly positive, with fans citing its sturdy construction and overall ease of use (one parent joked in an Amazon review the hefty seat was "apocalypse worthy—our son could survive a nuclear attack in this thing"). And that brings up one disadvantage to the Smart Seat: it is a beast, so heavy it can't be easily moved from vehicle to vehicle. And the large seat size will make rear-facing installations difficult in small or even mid-size cars.

As for crash protection, *Consumer Reports* testing of the Smart Seat put it in the "good" category—other all-in-one seats like the Evenflo Symphony 65 scored better in crash protection and ease of use. And of course, the Symphony costs a $100 less than the Smart Seat. And the IIHS's evaluation of the Smart Seat in booster mode was a "Check Fit"—which means the seat may not fit all kids well in booster mode. Other seats were judged better (good or best bet). On the other hand, the Smart Seat earned a perfect five-star rating for ease of use from the NHTSA. So you can see the opinions on this seat are somewhat all over the board.

Bottom line: the Graco Smart is a good bet IF you have a big enough vehicle to install it in. And like all All-in-One seats, this seat sometimes promises more than it delivers. *Rating: B*

GRACO TRANZITIONS 65

Comments: Based on the Size 4 Me platform, the Tranzitions 65 is a lower-priced version of that model. What's missing? Gone is the fancy sliding recline feature, replaced by a simple two-position bar recline. There's also a single LATCH strap instead of two in the Size 4 Me. Other than that, you basically get the same seat as the Size 4 Me.

Official retail for the Tranzitions convertibles will be $160, but we assume they will be discounted under that. That would make them about $20 to $40 less than the Size 4 Me seats. Our only caveat to Tranzitions would be the single LATCH strap—we've seen complaints about installation of other Graco seats that have this set-up . . . so the jury is out on that until they hit the market. Tranzitions 65 is set to debut in the first quarter of 2014. ***Rating: Not Yet.***

Maxi Cosi Pria 70
Price: $250 to $290.
Type: Convertible seat.
Limits: 4 to 40 lbs. rear facing, 22 to 70 lbs. forward facing.
NHTSA ease of use rating:
★★☆☆☆ Rear-facing
★★★★☆ Forward facing

Pros: TinyFit infant insert good for preemies (starting at 4 lbs.). Side impact protection. Small footprint means seat will fit into smaller vehicles. Nice fabric, padding.

Cons: Can only use tether in forward-facing position. TinyFit makes install rear-facing somewhat challenging. Must rethread harness when changing height.

Comments: Maxi Cosi is Dorel's European subsidiary that has been imported to the U.S. to help shore up Dorel's car seat offerings on the high end.

The Pria 70 replaces the Priori and aims to solve two problems: car seats that don't fit small infants well—and seats that don't fit small cars.

On the first score, the Pria 70 features a "TinyFit" seat—basically a car seat within a car seat for newborns as small as four pounds. It even has a smaller chest clip for newborns. (FYI: There are two Pria models: a basic model without the Tiny Fit insert for $250 and one with the TinyFit for $290).

Unlike the Priori, the Pria 70 has higher rear-facing limit (40 lbs) and a 70 lbs. forward facing limit. And the Pria 70 has the Air Protect feature for side impact protection (seen on Safety 1st seats). The seat also has three recline positions.

So is it worth $250? At this price, Dorel/Maxi Cosi is competing against Britax and Diono . . . and as such, our expectations are high. On some scores (padding, crash protection) the Pria 70 is equal to Britax. And the TinyFit seat does Britax one better (the Pria 70 starts at four pounds; Britax at five) . . . so if you know you're going to have a small newborn (parents of twins, take note), then the Pria is an excellent choice.

More than one parent we spoke with said they preferred the fabric on the Pria over Britax—the Pria's smooth fabric might be a better choice in hot/humid climates than the current crop of Britax seats, which features a less impressive fabric. Another plus for the Pria 70: its relatively small footprint means it will fit nicely in a compact vehicle. Most parent feedback on the Pria is quite positive.

The downsides? The Pria can only be tethered only in a forward-

convertible seats

facing position (Britax can be tether either in forward or rear facing, which gives an extra measure of protection). Another negative: the cover for the headrest isn't removable.

And while the TinyFit seat is innovative, it makes the installation of this seat more complex than others (especially rear-facing). That probably explains the low (two star) rating the Pria earned in rear-facing mode on the NHTSA's ease of use ranking. Finally, the Pria 70 lacks the no rethread harness feature you get on a Britax Boulevard, which is selling for the same price as the Pria 70 online.

Overall, we'll give this seat a B+. While not perfect, the Pria 70 is a good option, especially if you know you will be having a new-born on the small side. **Rating: B+**

ORBIT TODDLER CAR SEAT

This seat is reviewed on the free side of our web site at BabyBargains.com/?p=1115

PEG PEREGO
PRIMO VIAGGIO SIP CONVERTIBLE
Price: $329-$380

Type: Convertible seat.

Limits: Rear facing 5-45 lbs., forward facing 22 to 70 lbs.

NHTSA ease of use:

★★★★☆ Rear-facing
★★★★☆ Forward-facing

Pros: 70 lb. harness limit; adjustable side impact protection. Made in Italy (not China).

Cons: Pricey. Must manually rethread the harness to change harness height. No cup holders.

Comments: Stroller maker Peg Perego has long been a player in the infant car seat market, but this seat is their first shot at the convertible market.

The Primo Viaggio SIP Convertible works to 70 lbs. with a five-point harness and features an adjustable headrest, three recline positions and a newborn insert. The winged headrest provides a measure of side impact protection and shock absorbing foam in the base will add to crash protection.

Perego offers two options for the cover: fabric for $329 and leatherette $380.

This seat first debuted in 2012 and reader feedback has been very positive. Folks say the seat is easy to install and use, plus the fabric is excellent. And of course, the seat is one of the very few not made in China (all Perego products are made in Italy).

Critics point out the lack of a no rethread harness at this price point is a disappointment. And there are no amenities like cup holders for this seat. But those are minor quibbles, considering the vast majority of the feedback here is positive. So we'll recommend this one, despite the stiff price tag. *Rating: A*

RECARO PRORIDE/PERFORMANCERIDE

Price: $210 to $300.

Type: Convertible seat.

Limits: Rear facing 5-35 lbs., forward facing 20-70 lbs.

NHTSA ease of use rating:

★★★★☆ Rear facing
★★★★☆ Forward-facing

Pros: Works to 70 lbs., adjustable headrest, EPP foam, side-impact protection wings. Higher harness slots than the Marathon.

Cons: May not fit rear facing in smaller vehicles. Hard to find in stores.

Comments: German car seat maker Recaro is probably Britax's biggest competitor on the upper-end of the convertible car seat market. And Recaro's flagship seat, the ProRIDE, is a winner.

Among the ProRIDE's unique features: side-impact protection wings made of cushy EPP foam. Similar to the Britax Boulevard, these wings provide both crash protection and head support for napping toddlers. The seat has many seat adjustments and the plush, microfiber fabric is impressive.

The negatives? Well, like the Britax Marathon, this is a big seat—it may not fit rear facing into smaller vehicles. A few parents told us they found the ProRIDE's head pillows to be too restrictive for their older toddlers. And Recaro's thinner distribution (as of this writing, Recaro isn't in as many stores as Britax) means you may have to search for a local store that carries it to see this seat in person.

In the past year, Recaro rolled out a new version of this seat, dubbed the PerformanceRIDE. It features an integrated harness and headrest (called HERO), built in cup holders, memory foam and other upgrades. This model works to 40 lbs. rear-facing (five more pounds than the ProRIDE), 70 lbs. forward-facing. Price: $230 to $300.

In general, parent feedback on both versions of this seat is quite positive—most folks say they are easy to use, although more than one noted the seats' large size makes it a tight fit in smaller vehicles. Compared to the similar Britax seats, readers like the head cushions (side-impact protection) somewhat better. Overall, these are excellent seats that may be hard to find in stores. *Rating: A*

SAFETY 1ST ABLE 65

Price: $150-$200

Comments: This seat has the same features as the Safety 1st Easy

convertible seats

Fit 65, but includes a no-rethread harness. This adds about $30 to $50 to the price. Another small difference: the Able 65 lacks the infant body pillow seen on the Easy Fit 65. **Rating: A-**

SAFETY 1ST ADVANCE 70 AIR+

Price: $190

Limits: 5-40 lbs. rear-facing, 22-70 lbs. forward-facing.

NHTSA ease of use rating: Not yet.

Pros: Side-impact protection, yet priced at only $190.

Cons: Large, bulky seat. Fabric may be hot in summer.

Comments: The Safety 1st Advance 70 Air+ is the brand's first seat to feature both the Air Protect side impact cushions and GCell HX. What is that? Well, it is patented foam with hexagonal shapes that Safety 1st says was inspired from Indy race-car protection technology—the claim is more full body protection, not just the head, in side impacts.

Unfortunately, there are no federal side impact crash tests or standards, so it is hard to evaluate this claim—or even how this seat would compare with competitor's seats that are lined with basic foam.

The Advance 70 also has a few other impressive features: a deep, four-position recline feature, plus color-coded belt bath for easier install. Plus a no-rethread harness. And of course, there is a nice cup holder built-in to the arm rest.

The down side to the Advance 70: it is a BIG, bulky seat. Unless you have a large SUV, this one will be a tight fit. We also saw a few complaints from readers that the seat's velvety fabric, while plush, can be hot in the summer.

These complaints aside, most folks are happy with the Advance 70—readers said it is easy to install and adjust. Yes, it is a large seat, but as long as you have a big enough vehicle and don't see yourself moving it from car to car, this would be a good seat to consider.

FYI: The Advance 70 is a Target-exclusive. So that means you won't be able to price shop it (although we have to say the $190 retail price is affordable). In early 2014, Safety 1st will come out with a version of this seat that will be in more stores: the Advance 70 SE. It will be very similar to the Advance 70 Air+, but now will have a one-hand headrest adjustment. Same price. **Rating: A-**

SAFETY 1ST ALL IN ONE (AKA EDDIE BAUER DELUXE 3-IN-1, SAFETY 1ST ALPHA OMEGA ELITE, ALPHA ELITE 65

This seat is reviewed on the free side of our web site at BabyBargains.com/?p=1097

SAFETY 1ST CHART AIR 65

Price: $118-$140
Limits: 5-40 lbs. rear-facing, 22-65 lbs. forward-facing.
NHTSA ease of use rating:
⭐⭐⭐☆☆ Rear facing
⭐⭐☆☆☆ Forward facing

Pros: Side-impact protection, yet priced under $200.

Cons: Large seat can be difficult to install rear facing in smaller vehicles.

Comments: This newest addition to the "Air" family from Safety 1st features a 65 lb. weight limit and a headrest that adjusts separately from the back of the seat.

The headline here is the Air Protect side impact protection cushions–this is one of the lowest price seats with this enhanced crash protection and a 65-lb. rated harness.

Feedback on this seat has been sparse. So far, reviews seem mixed. While folks like the head cushions, more than a few parents commented on how difficult the seat is to install rear-facing in smaller vehicles, thanks to its large size. ***Rating: B-***

SAFETY 1ST COMPLETE AIR 65

Price: $155 to $200
Type: Convertible seat.
Limits: 5 to 40 lbs. (19" to 40") rear facing, 22 to 65 lbs. (and 34" to 45") forward facing.
NHTSA ease of use rating:
⭐⭐☆☆☆ Rear facing
⭐⭐⭐⭐☆ Forward facing

Pros: 40 lbs. rear facing! Side impact protection.

Cons: Huge seat makes for a tough fit in small or mid-size cars.

Comments: "Revolutionary side impact technology" is how Safety 1st describes the S1 Complete Air, a convertible seat that works to 40 lbs. rear facing, one of the first seats to reach that limit (others have since caught up). The side impact shields inflate during a crash, providing more protection for baby in case of a crash.

The Complete Air also features a "QuickFit" harness system that adjusts the harness height without rethreading.

FYI: Safety 1st sells three versions of the Complete Air: the base model at $180, a LX and SE. The LX adds a three-position recline for $200 and the SE or special edition, has upgraded fabric for $240 (although we've seen it online for closer to $200).

Parent feedback on this seat has been mixed: more than one reader mentioned the seat's large size makes it a tough fit even in mid-size sedans, especially in rear facing mode. We were struck by the large number of reports of this seat not fitting in vehicles as

convertible seats

large as the Honda Pilot, among others.

That said, folks who do like this seat cite its overall quality—the no-rethread harness particularly wins praise for ease of use. No, this seat isn't as polished as other premium brands like Britax and Recaro. Example: the base on the seat is unfinished plastic with rough edges. Upper-end seats have rubberized plastic bases, which better protect an auto's seats. Of course, the Complete Air is $100 less than those seats, so there's your trade-off.

Bottom line: this is a good seat. But you better have a large vehicle to make it work. ***Rating: B***

SAFETY 1ST EASY FIT 65

Price: $85 to $100

Type: Convertible seat.

NHTSA ease of use rating: Not yet.

Limits: 5 to 40 lbs. rear facing, 22 to 65 lbs. front-facing.

Pros: 40 lb. rear facing; compact seat. EPP foam. Easy to install.

Cons: No recline. Must rethread harness to adjust height.

Comments: This seat is a Babies R Us exclusive—the Easy Fit 65 features a 40 lb. rear-facing limit, four harness slots, three crotch positions and a relatively compact size. We liked the multi-position headrest, although the clunky cup holder might make installation near a door problematic (the cup holder is removable).

The key downside to the Easy Fit 65: you have to rethread the harness to adjust the harness height, which of course is common on lower price convertibles. And there are no recline positions for the seat.

Feedback on this seat has been sparse, but mostly positive. Folks like the overall fit and easy install plus the EPP foam is a nice feature at this price point. Critics say it is hard to install rear-facing . . . and the seat lacks many amenities (the harness is a pain to rethread). Of course, the Easy Fit 65 is only $90, so that's the trade-off.

FYI: This seat is also sold as the Eddie Bauer XRS 65 at Target for $130. Same seat, just upgraded fabric. And if you used to own a old Safety 1st Uptown or Avenue and think this seat looks familiar, it is—the Easy Fit 65 has the same shell as those seats (but adds the headrest).

Finally, if lack of a rethread harness on this seat is a deal killer for you, Safety 1st sells a version of this seat with a no-rethread harness, dubbed the Able 65. Unfortunately that seat sells for $100 more than the East Fit. ***Rating: A***

SAFETY 1ST ELITE 80 AIR+

This seat is reviewed on the free side of our web site at BabyBargains.com?p=15915

SAFETY 1ST GUIDE 65

This seat is the same as the Safety 1st Easy Fit (and Eddie Bauer XRS 65). See review on the opposite page.

SAFETY 1ST ONSIDE AIR
Price: $80
Type: Convertible seat.
Limits: 5 to 40 lbs. rear facing, 22 to 40 lbs. forward facing.
NHTSA ease of use rating:
★★★☆☆ Rear Facing
★★★★☆ Front Facing

Pros: 40 lbs. rear facing! Side impact protection.
Cons: Only works to 40 lbs. front facing.
Comments: Safety 1st debuted this seat back in 2010 as a more affordable alternative in its Air Protect line. While it works to the same amazing 40 lbs. rear facing as the $180 Complete Air, the onSide Air tops out at the same 40 lbs. forward facing. That's odd, but we suppose the attraction here is the price: a seat that can be used rear facing to 40 lbs. AND costs under $100. Plus you get the Air Protect side impact technology, which deploys in a crash to better protect a baby's head.

Parent reviews on this seat have been positive—this seat works well in smaller vehicles, which can be a challenge for other car seats. And given the value here with a price under $100, we'll recommend it. **Rating: B+**

As you can imagine, the child safety seat world changes quickly—read our blog (BabyBargains.com) for the latest news, recalls and more with car seats.

Our Picks: Brand Recommendations

Here are our top picks for infant and convertible seats. Are these seats safer than others? No—all child safety seats sold in the U.S. and Canada must meet minimum safety standards. These seats are our top picks because they combine the best features, usability (including ease of installation) and value. Remember the safest and best seat for your baby is the one that best fits your child and vehicle. Finding the right car seat can be a bit of trial and error; you may find a seat CANNOT be installed safely in your vehicle because of the quirks of the seat or your vehicle's safety belt system. All seats do NOT fit all cars. Hence it is always wise to buy a seat from a store or web site with a good return policy.

FYI: See the chart on pages 434-435 for a comparison of features for both infant and convertible/front-facing car seats.

convertible seats

CAR
SEATS

Best Bets: Infant Car Seats

Good. The *Graco SnugRide 30* is one of the most affordable ($100-$140) seats that works to 30 lbs. This best-seller features a front harness adjuster and compatibility with a wide variety of strollers (beyond just Graco). Heads up: The SnugRide comes in several different versions, so make sure you are getting the right one. The other versions are fine, but the SnugRide 30 performed a bit better in crash testing, so that's why we picked that model.

Final note: in our last edition, we picked the Graco SnugRide as our best bet; this year it drops two notches to the good pick. That's because the next two seats now slightly edge out the SnugRide on crash protection and ease of use, based on reader feedback and the latest crash test reports.

Better. The *Britax B-SAFE* gets top marks for crash protection and generally good marks from our readers for ease of us. At $135-$180, the B-SAFE has additional side impact protection compared to the Graco SnugRide. If you shell out another $50 for the B-SAFE's sister model (the Chaperone), you get an anti-rebound bar and additional side impact protection—but that makes the carrier heavier by a couple of pounds. The B-SAFE's narrow base makes it an easier install in more vehicles than the Chaperone. Stroller compatibility is good but not as extensive as the Graco SnugRide—besides Britax strollers, the B-SAFE now works with Britax's BOB brand.

Best. The *Chicco KeyFit 30* is our top overall pick. Crash protection is excellent, with added side impact protection making a difference. The KeyFit gets high scores from our readers on ease of use (somewhat higher than the Graco or Britax seats)—installation is a snap and adjusting the harness is easy. The seat also features EPS foam and a newborn insert. The downsides? The seat is pricey at $190-$260 and doesn't work with as many strollers as the competition.

Best Bets: Convertible Car Seats

Good. For a decent, no-frills car seat, we recommend the *Cosco Scenera*. Yes, we realize Cosco's safety track record has been rocky, but this seat is still worth considering for that little-used second car or Grandma's vehicle. The Scenera is a basic, bare-bones convertible that works to 40 lbs., is easy to install and costs $39-$60—no, that's not a typo. With the prices of some car seats pushing $300, it's nice to know you can find a decent seat for well under $100.

Better. The *Diono Radian RXT* is pricey ($255-$270) but has some amazing stats: it can work rear-facing to 5 to 45 lbs., forward-facing to 80 lbs. in a five-point harness . . . and then to 120 lbs. as a belt-positioning booster. Add in memory foam, side-impact protection and the ability to fold flat for storage and you've got a winner!

If you have a compact car, the *First Years True Fit* ($140-$350) is an excellent seat that works to 65 lbs. but adds this nifty trick: its headrest pops off to make it easier to install rear facing in compact cars. FYI: This seat is sold under the Lamaze brand in Babies R Us.

Best. So, what is our top recommendation for convertible car seats? The *Britax Marathon G4* takes the crown this year. The Marathon ($200-$260) enables you to keep your child rear facing to 40 lbs. and forward facing to 70 with the five-point harness. The seat features EPS foam, side-impact protection, steel bar construction and can be tethered forward or rear facing. Britax has improved the seat in the last year with new technology that absorbs energy in a crash (SafeCell) and a harness that can be height adjusted without re-threading. All in all, an excellent seat worth the extra price.

If Grandma is buying. What if money isn't an issue when buying a seat? One obvious seat that we'd suggest is the top-of-the-line *Britax Advocate G4* ($265-$320), which is much like the Marathon, but adds additional side-impact protection. Similar to the Marathon, the Advocate has a height-adjuster knob for the harness—hence no need to rethread the harness as baby grows. The only negative: It is a large, bulky seat that may not fit into some smaller vehicles.

Another excellent seat if Grandma is buying would be the *Recaro ProRIDE* at $210-$300. Recaro has many of the same features as Britax seats, but is priced about 20% lower.

CAR SEATS

INFANT SEATS

The following is a selection of better known infant car seats and how they compare on features:

MAKER	MODEL	PRICE	WEIGHT/ HEIGHT LIMITS
BABY TREND	FLEX-LOC	$80-$130	30 LBS./30" *
BRITAX	B-SAFE	$135-$180	30 LBS./32"
	CHAPERONE	$160-$230	30 LBS./32"
CHICCO	KEYFIT 30	$190-$260	30 LBS./30"
COMBI	SHUTTLE	$160-$180	35 LBS./33"
COSCO	COMFY CARRY	$75-$90	22 LBS./29"
CYBEX	ATON 1/2/Q	$250-$300	32 LBS./30"
EVENFLO	DISCOVERY/NUTURE	$50-$60	22 LBS./26"
	EMBRACE	$80	35 LBS./30"
	SECURERIDE 35	$120-$180	35 LBS./29"
FIRST YEARS	VIA/I140	$150-$180	35 LBS./30"
GRACO	SNUGRIDE 35	$150-$180	35 LBS./32"
MAXI COSI	PREZI	$290	30 LBS./29"
ORBIT	ORBIT	$440	30 LBS./32"
PEG PEREGO	PRIMO VIAGGIO 4.35	$280	35 LBS./30"
SAFETY 1ST	ONBOARD 35 AIR	$110-$10	35 LBS./32"
UPPA BABY	MESA	$280	35 LBS./32"

CONVERTIBLE SEATS

The following is a selection of popular convertible car seats and how they compare on features:

MAKER	MODEL	PRICE	WEIGHT LIMITS (IN LBS.) REAR	FORWARD
BRITAX	BOULEVARD G4	$230-$270	40 LBS.	65 LBS.
	MARATHON G4	$200-$260	40	65
	ROUNDABOUT 55	$120-$180	40	55
CHICCO	NEXTFIT	$280	40	65
COSCO	SCENERA	$39-$60	35	40
DIONO	RADIAN	$200-$300	40/45	80/100/12(
EVENFLO	SYMPHONY 65	$165-$230	40	65/100
	TRIUMPH 65 LX	$140-$190	35	65
FIRST YEARS	TRUE FIT	$140-$350	35	65
MAXI COSI	PRIA 70	$250-$290	40	70
PEG PEREGO	PRIMO VIAGGIO SIP	$329-$380	45	70
RECARO	PRORIDE	$210-$300	35	70
SAFETY 1ST	COMPLETE AIR 65	$155-$200	40	65

CAR SEATS

KEY
SIDE IMPACT: Does the seat have side-impact protection?
FOAM TYPE: Does the seat have a EPS or EPP foam (or none at all)? This is for crash protection; EPP foam is softer (more comfortable) than EPS.
LEVEL IND.: Does the seat have a level indicator for easier installation?
CARRIER WEIGHT: This is the weight of the carrier only (not the base).

SIDE IMPACT	LEVEL IND.	FOAM TYPE	BASE WIDTH	CARRIER WEIGHT	OUR RATING
◆	◆	EPS	16.5″	9.7 LBS.	C-
◆	◆	EPS	17.5	9.8	A-
◆		EPS	18.3	11.2	A-
◆	◆	EPS	17	9.4	A
	◆	EPS	17	11.1	B-
		NONE	17	6.6	C
◆	◆	EPS	15	8.8	A-
		EPS	17.5	5.5	F
	◆	EPS	18	7.0	D+
◆	◆	EPS	18.25	10.0	B
◆	◆	EPS	18.5	8.4	B-
	◆	EPS	19	9.5	A
◆		EPP	17	11.6	B
	◆	EPP	15.25	12	B
◆	◆	EPS	15.5	11.1	NOT YET
◆	◆	FPP	15	9	B
◆	◆	FPS	14.25	10.5	B

RATING	COMMENT
A-	AUTO HARNESS HEIGHT ADJUSTMENT.
A	MUST RETHREAD BELTS TO ADJUST HARNESS HEIGHT.
A	EPS FOAM, NO-TWIST STRAPS, TETHER REAR OR FORWARD.
A-	NO RETHREAD HARNESS WIDENS FOR LARGER BABIES.
B+	SIMPLE SEAT, GREAT FOR AIR TRAVEL OR GRANDPARENTS.
A	ONLY SEAT THAT FOLDS UP; CAN USE TETHER REAR-FACING.
B+	NEW LATCH SYSTEM MAKES IT EASIER TO INSTALL.
B	MEMORY HARNESS; CAN ADJUST BELTS WITHOUT RETHREAD.
A	EPP FOAM; HEADREST POPS OFF FOR EASIER INSTALL.
B+	INFANT INSERT LETS SEAT START AT 4 LBS.
A	SIDE IMPACT PROTECTION, ADJUSTABLE HEADREST.
A	ADJUSTABLE HEADREST, EPP FOAM, SIDE IMPACT WINGS.
B	SIDE IMPACT WINGS, QUICK FIT HARNESS BUT LARGE SEAT.

car seats compared

Booster Seats

So what is a booster? Simply put, this seat boosts a child to correctly sit in an auto safety belt. Yes, some boosters have five-point harnesses (more on this later), but most boosters work with your vehicle's safety belt.

Most parents know they have to put an infant or toddler into a car seat. What some folks don't realize, however, is that child passenger safety doesn't end when baby outgrows that convertible car seat—any child from 40 to 80 lbs. and less than 4'9" (generally, kids age four to eight) should be restrained in a booster seat (or one of the new harnessed seats that work up to 80 lbs.). And in most states, booster seat use is mandated by law. Numerous states have passed laws requiring the use of booster seats. And more states are following their lead.

Getting Started: When do you need a booster?

Your child needs a booster seat when he outgrows his convertible seat. This happens when he exceeds the weight limit or when he is too tall for the harness (his shoulders are taller than the top slots in the seat). For most children, this happens around ages three to five.

Booster seats use the vehicle's safety belt and hence require your child to be mature enough to stay in the seat. The seat belt is all that is holding your child in the seat—unlike the escape-proof five-point harness of a convertible seat.

What if your child has outgrown a convertible seat but isn't mature enough to stay in a booster? Then consider a hybrid seat that uses a five-point harness up to 65 or 85 lbs.

Best Online Sources

◆ *SafetyBeltSafeUSA* (carseat.org) has three good reports on booster seats (click on the button, Booster Seats) that explain proper installation and offer other tips.

◆ *The National Highway Traffic Safety Administration* (nhtsa.gov) has excellent videos showing proper booster seat installation and use. Click on Driving Safety, then Child Safety, then on Installation Tips. Also cool: the NHTSA now rates and reviews booster seats for ease of use and other factors.

Smart Shopping Tips

Smart Shopper Tip #1
Booster Laws

"My daughter just turned four, and my state doesn't require her to use a car seat anymore. Does she really need a booster?"

A number of states have recently enacted stiffer car seat laws, usually requiring children to use "appropriate restraints" until age six or 60 lbs. (some state laws are now up to age eight or nine and 80 lbs). But other states still only require a car seat until a child turns four (some even just two) years old. So why should you continue to hassle with a car seat or booster after this time?

We like to remind parents that there is the law . . . and then there is the law of physics. Car seat belts are made for adults, and children (as well as some short adults) just don't fit well, and don't get good protection from those belts. Lap belts used with four- to eight-year old children routinely cause such severe injuries and paralysis that the injuries even have their own name: "lap belt syndrome." Children using lap/shoulder belts often put the shoulder belt behind their back (since it is so darn uncomfortable), giving them no more protection than a lap belt alone. Ejections are another common problem with young children in adult belts, even if they are using both the lap and shoulder belt.

Booster seats (and of course regular car seats) work very simply to eliminate this problem. Boosters properly position the lap part of the belt on a child's hip bone, not their soft internal organs. They elevate the child and include a special adjuster so that the lap shoulder belt fits right on the strong shoulder bones. Booster seats should be used until a child fits the adult belts like an adult. Try out the Five Step Test (later in this section) to see if your child is ready.

See our web page for pictures of good and bad fit for a booster (BabyBargains.com, click on Bonus Material).

Smart Shopper Tip #2
Different seats, lots of confusion?

"When I was shopping for a booster seat, I was confused with all the types of seats out there. Why isn't there just one type of booster?"

Good question. We've noticed that buying a booster seat can be a bit more complex than buying another car seat. For example, an infant car seat is, well, an infant car seat. But a booster can come in several versions: high back boosters, backless boosters, combination seat/boosters, and more.

In this chapter, we'll try to simplify things a bit. Any time we refer to a *belt-positioning booster*, we mean a seat that uses the lap/shoulder belt to secure the child. Most other car seats (like convertible seats) use an internal harness to hold the child, while the seat itself is attached to the car with the seat belt or the LATCH system.

What's made this so confusing is that car seat makers have blurred the lines between convertible seats and boosters in recent years by coming out with hybrid models that use a five-point harness up to 65 (or 80) lbs. and then convert to a belt-positioning booster. The Britax Frontier and Graco Nautilus are two examples.

Confusing, yes we know. But we want this section to cover all the options for older children who've outgrown their traditional convertible seat . . . so you'll see a variety of options in this section. Let's break down what's out there:

◆ **High back boosters (HBB):** Belt-positioning boosters come in two flavors: high back boosters and backless boosters. High back boosters have often been called "kid's captain's chairs," which they kind of resemble. They are designed to be simple, but provide vital safety features for children who've outgrown a harnessed seats. These boosters properly position the lap belt on a child's strong hip bones, rather than letting it ride up on the soft internal organs. And they provide correct positioning of the shoulder belt, so the child can comfortably wear it and get critical upper body support. The high back also protects the child's head from whiplash if there are no head restraints in the vehicle, and the high back may also give some side sleeping support. ALL of these boosters require a lap and shoulder belt. FYI: Some high back boosters convert into backless boosters for older kids.

◆ **Backless boosters:** These belt-positioning boosters work the same way as high back boosters—they just don't have a back. Safety-wise, these can be a bit better than a high back booster, since the child sits against the vehicle seat. They do the same job positioning the lap belt, and usually include some sort of strap to adjust the shoulder belt. But they don't provide head support if you have low seat backs, and they don't give any side or sleeping support. On the other hand, they are often popular with older kids, since they can be quite inconspicuous.

◆ **Hybrid/Combo seats:** These are probably the most confusing "booster" seats because sometimes they are a booster, and sometimes they aren't. They come with a five-point harness, which can generally be used up to 40 lbs. (some seats now to 65 and even 80 lbs.). Then the harness comes off, and the seat can be used as a belt-positioning booster, usually to 80 or 100 lbs. They get the name "combination," or "combo" for short, from the two jobs they do.

A recent report by the Insurance Institute for Highway Safety criticized many older combo seats, saying they poorly fit kids when in booster mode. We factored this report into our ratings.

Newer combo seats (namely the Britax Frontier, Graco Nautilus, among others) now work to 65 or 80 lbs. These combo seats do a better job at fitting older kids, whether in harness or booster mode.

The take-home message: hybrid/combo boosters are great for children that have outgrown their convertible seats but aren't mature enough to sit in a belt-positioning booster (the types described earlier). The five-point harness provides that extra measure of safety and security while they are still young (typically, a child has to be three or older to be mature enough to handle the belt-positioners).

◆ **Special Needs Seats:** There are a few seats on the market now that don't really fit into any category. One is the Britax Traveler Plus, which is designed for special needs kids up to 105 lbs.

Smart Shopper Tip #3
Avoid Seat Belt Adjusters

"The shoulder belt was bugging my son's neck, so I bought a little adjuster thing. Is that as good as a booster?"

Several companies make inexpensive belt adjusters ($10 or so), which help to properly position the shoulder belt on your child. Sounds good, right? Wrong. Look closely at the pictures on the box. In order to pull the shoulder belt down, and make it more comfortable for a short passenger, virtually all of these devices also pull the lap part of the belt UP, right back onto the tummy. Marketed to kids 50 lbs. and up, these devices are also packed with statements that confuse even the most safety conscious parents, like "designed to meet FMVSS 213," a reference to a federal safety standard in crash testing. What's wrong with that picture? That federal standard doesn't even apply to items marketed for children 50 lbs. and up! Worse yet, government crash tests show that a three-year-old dummy is less protected when using one of these adjusters compared to using the regular vehicle safety belt. When tested with a six-year-old dummy, same result. Bottom line: forget these adjusters and use a booster seat.

boosters

Smart Shopper Tip #4
Cars with only lap belts
   "What if my car has only lap belts in the back seat?"

While lap belts are just fine with infant and convertible seats, they are a no-no when it comes to boosters. If your vehicle doesn't have shoulder belts, check with your vehicle's manufacturer to see if they offer a retrofit kit. If that doesn't work, consider buying a newer vehicle with lap/shoulder belts in the back seat. In the meantime, there are a few seats that can be used with a lap belt for kids over 40 lbs. See the convertible seat reviews earlier in this chapter for details.

Smart Shopper Tip #5
LATCH system and boosters
   "My car has LATCH attachments. Do booster seats work with this?"
   "My car does NOT have LATCH. Do boosters require LATCH?

We discussed LATCH earlier in this chapter; in short, most booster seats do NOT work with LATCH—you secure them with the regular seat belt. There are a couple of exceptions: see reviews of Clek, Diono, and Graco (Affix) boosters.

If your vehicle does NOT have LATCH, no worries—the vast majority of booster seats don't require LATCH. One exception: Safety 1st's Go Hybrid does require LATCH.

Smart Shopper Tip #6
Back Harness Adjuster
   "I loved our combo seat—until the day I discovered its fatal flaw. When it was cold, my daughter's thick coat required me to loosen the belts on her five-point harness. I discovered this could only be done from the BACK of the seat! What a pain!"

More booster seats are adding five-point harnesses so they can be used at younger ages/weights (some seats start as little as 20 lbs.). The problem? The cheapest combo boosters do NOT have up-front belt adjustments. You must adjust the belts from the back of the seat, which is a pain especially in cold weather. A word to the wise: if you get a combo seat, make sure the belt adjustments are UP FRONT and easy to access. The question of coats/snowsuits and car seats comes up frequently—we should stress that most safety advocates suggest that a child in a safety seat wear a coat that is no thicker than a polar fleece. Big bulky coats are a hazard. Why? In the event of a crash, the coat will compress, creating a gap between the child and the restraint (and possibly ejecting the child from the seat).

Smart Shopper Tip #7
Too Tall for a Convertible

"My daughter is too tall for her convertible car seat but is only 32 lbs. Now what?"

Many children outgrow their convertibles by height before weight. Most convertibles say that they are good from 40″ to 49″ tall, but a better measure is to make sure the child's shoulders are no higher than the top harness slot. Another guideline: when a child's ears reach the top of the car seat shell, he's outgrown the seat.

Remember that while weight limits are set in stone, height rules are more like guidelines. Example: two children could both be 48″ tall, but one still fits in her convertible car seat while the other clearly needs to be a booster. Why? Because a child could be 48″ tall, but have a long torso—and if a child's ears are at the top of the car seat shell, it's time to move to a booster. Yet the other child who is 48″ tall may be shorter in the torso (but have longer legs) and may still fit in the convertible.

Smart Shopper Tip #8
Who crash tests booster seats?

"Are there independent sources to find boost seat crash test ratings?"

There are three sources for booster seat ratings: *Consumer Reports,* The National Highway Traffic and Safety Administration (NHTSA) and the Insurance Institute for Highway Safety (IIHS).

Consumer Reports magazine independently crash tests and evaluates boosters for ease of use. The NHTSA assigns ease of use ratings (on a one to five star scale) for booster seats—these are based on "vehicle installation features" and how well the seat secures a child. In the review section later in this chapter, we list this as the NHTSA ease of use rating.

The Insurance Institute for Highway Safety (IIHS) evaluates how well a booster seat fits the lap and shoulder belt on a four to eight year old child. The IIHS doesn't crash test seats, just evaluates belt fit. Seats are judged best bets, good bets or not recommended. In the review section, we list the IIHS rating for each booster. FYI: In some cases, the IIHS says a booster is rated "check fit." That means these seats may work in *some* vehicles; you need to check the fit.

At *Baby Bargains*, we look at tests and information from these three sources and combine that with parent feedback to come up with our booster seat ratings.

Safe & Sound

1 **CHECK YOUR VEHICLE'S OWNERS MANUAL.** We're amazed at the detailed info on installing child safety seats you can find in your vehicle's owners manual, especially for newer vehicles. Car seats also include detailed installation instructions.

2 **ALWAYS USE THE LAP/SHOULDER BELT WITH THE BOOSTER**—this provides crucial upper body protection in the case of an accident. NEVER use just the lap belt.

3 **DON'T EXPECT TO USE THAT BOOSTER ON AN AIRPLANE.** FAA rules prohibit the use of booster seats on airlines. Why? Booster seats must be used with a shoulder belt to be effective—and airplanes only have lap belts. Our advice: if you travel a lot, consider a harnessed seat that works to 65+ lbs. that is certified to work on airplanes—the Diono Radian is an example.

4 **BE CAREFUL OF HAND-ME-DOWN AND SECOND-HAND BARGAINS.** Most old booster seats don't meet current safety standards. If you do find a newer used booster, make sure you ask the original owner if it has been in a crash, and then check the seat for recalls (Safety Belt Safe has a great recall list at carseat.org). And if your seat has been in a crash, is over six years old or missing its proper labels, stick it in a black garbage bag and throw it away.

5 **ONLY USE CARDBOARD CUPS IN BOOSTER SEAT CUP HOLDERS.** You'll note that some seats now come with cup or juice box holders. These are a great convenience, but most manufacturers only recommend cardboard cups (like to-go cups) or juice boxes be used. Anything harder could become a dangerous projectile in a crash.

6 **WHEN IS A CHILD BIG ENOUGH TO USE JUST THE AUTO'S SAFETY BELT?** When a child is over 4'9" and can sit with his or her back straight against the back seat cushion (with knees bent over the seat's edge), then he or she can go with just the auto's safety belt. Still have doubts? Try this Five-Step Test from Safety Belt Safe, USA:

◆ Does the child sit all the way back against the auto seat?
◆ Does the belt cross the shoulder between neck and arm?
◆ Is the lap belt as low as possible, touching the thighs?
◆ Can the child stay seated like this for the whole trip?
◆ Do the child's knees bend comfortably at the edge of the seat?

If you answered no to any of these questions, your child needs a booster seat, and will probably be more comfortable in one too.

7 **DON'T USE A BOOSTER TOO SOON.** Most safety techs say a child should stay in a harnessed seat as long as possible—many seats can now keep a kid harnessed until 65, 70 or even 80 lbs. Some parents try to switch a too-young toddler to a booster . . . but kids that are under four are often not mature enough to correctly sit in a belt-positioning booster.

Booster Car Seats (model by model reviews)

BABY TREND TRENDZ FASTBACK 3-IN-1
Booster type: Combo
Weight: up to 120 lbs.; 22 to 70 lbs. with harness, belt-positioning booster for 30 to 100 lbs. Backless 40-120 lbs.
Price: $154-$180
IIHS rating: Not yet.

NHTSA ease of use rating:

★★★★☆ Harness mode
★★☆☆☆ Booster mode

Pros: Harnessed works to 70 lbs. Rigid LATCH. EPP foam.
Cons: Top harness slot of 17" means taller toddlers may outgrow the harness too quickly.
Comments: The Baby Trend FastBack is a harnessed booster that works up to 70 lbs. with a harness and then as a belt-positioning booster to 100 lbs. Finally, pop off the back and you'll have a backless booster to 120 lbs. Hence the 3-in-1 moniker. This seat is similar to the Graco Nautilus.

The FastBack features rigid LATCH built into the steel frame and EPS foam lining on the side and head wings of the seat. The "snug sides" are what Baby Trend calls to the seat's head wings. The FastBack has eight harness positions and two crotch buckle positions, plus cup holders (naturally). Unfortunately, the top slot is just 17"—The Graco Nautilus is 18.5" and the Britax Frontier is 20". Why is that important? The higher the harness slot, the longer a toddler can use the harness. So it doesn't matter that Baby Trend promises a 70 lb. weight limit for the five-point harness if the low top harness slot means taller toddlers will outgrow it too soon.

Feedback on this seat has been mostly negative—yes, the rigid LATCH makes the seat a snap to install in most vehicles. But more than one parent complained about the difficult in adjusting the harness and releasing the buckle. Quality woes dog this seat (parts that break, LATCH connectors that get stuck, etc). And Baby Trend's mediocre customer service (calls/emails often go unreturned) tips the recommendation against this booster. *Rating: C-*

BRITAX FRONTIER 90

Booster type: Combo

Weight: 20-90 lbs. with harness, 40 to 120 lbs. as a belt-positioning booster. For kids at least two years old, 25 lbs. and 30-57" for the harness, 42" to 65" in height for belt-positioning booster.

Price: $241-$330.

IIHS rating: Check fit.

NHTSA ease of use rating:

★★★☆☆ Booster mode
★★★★☆ Harness mode

Pros: Works to 90 lbs. with five-point harness. A bit wider, deeper than the Graco Nautilus.

Cons: Large seat, expensive.

Comments: The Frontier aims for a market similar to the *Graco Nautilus*—it is a harnessed seat that works to a whopping 90 lbs. and then a belt-positioning booster to 120 lbs. after that. The Frontier is targeted at kids at least two years old who have outgrown their convertible seats but aren't mature enough to sit in a belt-positioning booster.

Britax has steadily improved this seat over the years. Overall weight and height limits have moved higher and there are a series of small enhancements (example: the cup holders are inset in the seat, rather than stick out from the side, etc.). Compared to the past version of this seat, the Frontier 90 has:

◆ *A new ClickTight seatbelt installation system.* This system automatically tightens and tensions the seat belt—no more locking clips or concerns about LATCH seat limits.

◆ *SafeCell* crash protection in base. Seen in Britax's other models, this system absorbs energy in a crash.

◆ *Higher top harness adjustment.* The top harness slot is now be 20.5", which is the tallest in the industry. That will help kids from outgrowing the seat in harness mode too soon. Other small improvements to the seat include a better recline feature and now the harness hides away when you convert the seat to booster mode (before it had to be removed).

Are there any negatives to this seat? Well, just as before, this is a big, bulky seat. Carrying it through an airport isn't going to be fun (the Frontier is certified for use in an airplane, but only with its five-point harness—not as a booster).

The Frontier is 19.5" wide—that means fitting it three across in a carpool won't be easy for most vehicles. Also: the Frontier has limited recline settings and that might be a negative for some.

In the most recent ratings from the Insurance Institute for Highway Safety (IIHS), the Frontier lost its best bet rating—it is now "check fit." A couple of points about this: this rating is for the booster mode only (not the harness mode). And the IIHS test was done without using the Britax SecureGuard clip (an accessory offered free to Britax booster seat owners if needed), which helps better position the lap belt.

Of course, the price of the Frontier 90 is perhaps its biggest drawback—the similar Graco Nautilus is about HALF the price. And the Graco Nautilus has an extra use as a backless booster (the Frontier only works as a belt-positioning, high back booster). That said, the Britax Frontier 90 is an excellent seat and is highly recommended.

FYI: If you want additional side impact protection, there is a special version of the new Frontier 90 with Side Impact Cushion Technology (SICT). This model is called the Pinnacle 90, $240-$330.
Rating: A

BRITAX PARKWAY SG / SGL
Booster type: High back
Weight: 40 to 120 lbs., 38-63" in height, as a belt-positioning booster.
Price: $95 to $160
IIHS rating: Parkway SG backless: Check fit. Parkway SG high back: Best bet.
Parkway SGL backless: Check fit.
Parkway SGL high back: Best bet.
NHTSA ease of use rating: ★★★☆☆
Three out of five stars.
Pros: Side-impact protection, plush cover.
Cons: Pricey, narrow seat, skimpy armrests.
Comments: The Britax Parkway is Britax's entry-price point booster, competing against the Graco TurboBooster. The SG in the model name refers to the seat's Slide Guard (SG) feature—this keeps a child from submarining out of the seat in a crash. Like other models in this category, the Parkway converts from a high back to a backless booster for older kids (hence the separate ratings from IIHS for each mode).

There are two versions of this seat: SG and SGL. The Parkway SGL includes LATCH connectors (SGL model), which keep the seat anchored when it is unoccupied. It runs $120-$160. Otherwise, the SGL is the same as the SG.

Comparing the Parkway to the Graco TurboBooster, we'd give Britax the advantage when it comes to seat covers—the fabric Britax uses is much nicer than Graco's. That said, the Graco TurboBooster's armrests are bigger than the Parkway's, which are not adjustable. And the Parkway has a somewhat narrower seat than the TurboBooster, which might mean a tight fit for larger toddlers. As for crash protection, *Consumer Reports* rated the TurboBooster as better than the Parkway. And the TurboBooster is about $50-$75 less expensive than the Parkway.

FYI: Britax refreshed the Parkway with a few enhancements in the past year. The 2013 Parkway SGL boasts enhanced side impact protection with deeper head wings and adds the SafeCell technology (seen in Britax's convertible seats) in the base. The 2013 Parkway models also add SecureGuard, which is an anti-submarining technology.

Bottom line: this is a good seat, but at a price that is double the Graco TurboBooster, we'd give the Graco seat the edge in overall value. **Rating: A-**

Britax Pinnacle 90
Booster type: Combo
Weight: 90 lbs. with harness, up to 120 lbs. as a belt-positioning booster. For kids at least two years old, 25 lbs. and 30-58" for the harness, 45" to 62" in height for belt-positioning booster.
Price: $244 to $330.
NHTSA ease of use rating:

★★★★☆ Booster mode
★★★★★ Harness mode
IIHS rating: Check fit.
Comments: This seat is the same as the new *Britax Frontier 90*, but adds Side Impact Cushion Technology (SICT). This gives additional protection if the vehicle is in a side-impact crash.

The Britax Pinnacle 90 debuted in mid 2013 and has received mostly positive parent reviews, according to our research. Readers say it is very easy to install and overall quality is excellent.

As you might expect, one negative here is the seat's large bulk—those side impact cushions add significantly to the seat's width, which might be a concern for fit in smaller vehicles. That said, since this is basically a Frontier with a new feature, we'll recommend it with the same rating we do for the Frontier. **Rating: A**

Britax Pioneer 70
Booster type: Combo
Weight: 25-70 lbs. with harness, 40 to 110 pounds as a belt-positioning booster. For kids 2 years old and 25 pounds and up. Height limit: 30-59" for harness mode; 45-59" in booster mode.
Price: $165 to $200.
IIHS rating: Check fit.
NHTSA ease of use rating: Not yet.
Comments: This is a less expensive version of the Britax Frontier 90 and Pinnacle 90. At $200 retail, the Pioneer is about $50 less than a Frontier.

What are the trade-offs? As you can probably tell from the model name, the Pioneer only works to 70 lbs. (and has a lower height limit as well—59" versus 65" for the Frontier 90). The top seated shoulder height is 18.5", about 2" in less than the Frontier. The Pioneer has less fancy fabric and padding—noticeably lower quality than Britax's other seats.

The Pioneer does have SafeCell technology in its base for energy absorption in a crash, as well as True Side Impact Protection. But you miss the ClickTight belt system found on the Pinnacle and Frontier 90 (the Pioneer does have a no-rethread harness, however).

Our take: unless you have a small child who won't be hitting the Frontier/Pinnacle's higher weight/height limits, we don't see the point of the Pioneer 70. We'd spend the extra $50 and get the Frontier 90. The ClickTight belt system is worth the upgrade. And we've often seen the Frontier (which has wider distribution) discounted online to just about the same price as the Pioneer 70.

Parent feedback on the Pioneer 70 has been mostly positive, but a few dissenters knock the single LATCH strap on the Pioneer (versus dual straps on the Frontier and Pinnacle). That made LATCH harder to install for some parents. The downgraded fabric and pad is too much of a compromise for some folks (compared to other Britax seats).

Bottom line: given the trade-offs of this seat, we'd suggest a Frontier instead if you want a Britax booster. We understand that some folks simply can't afford a Frontier (at least at its official retail price). But Britax made too many quality trade-offs with this seat to earn our top rating. ***Rating: B***

BubbleBum

Booster type: Backless
Weight: 40 lbs. to 100 lbs. (kids over age 4)
Price: $40.
IIHS rating: Best Bet
NHTSA ease of use: ★★★★☆

Pros: Small and lightweight. Deflates and rolls up into carry bag for travel. Good for three-across situation.

Cons: Unstable, wobbly to sit on. Not comfortable for a long car ride.

Comments: BubbleBum is an inflatable, backless booster seat invented by a certified car seat tech from Northern Ireland (it's been available in the UK for quite a while). The idea was to have an easy-to-carry booster seat option for travel, rental cars, etc. But it's also a great option if you live in a place like New York and need a portable option for taxis.

Another plus: it's cheap ($40). But does it work well? Car seat techs report that the BubbleBum does provide good lap and shoulder belt fit (the IIHS gave it a "Best Bet" rating). The seat belt is threaded through a lap belt positioner, which keeps the belt in the proper position.

Critics note it can be confusing to use the positioner at first. Techs recommend threading the seat belt through the positioner after you have buckled your child into the seat to get a tighter fit. Also, it's a small seat and doesn't provide much thigh support. So the BumbleBum isn't going to be comfortable for long-term use. On the plus side, however, the small size of the seat makes it possible to use it in a three-across situation. Most readers are happy with the Bumblebum, although a few noted quality issues with a BumbleBum that developed a slow leak (the company provided replacements).

We like the BumbleBum for it's portability, price and safety. When used for short-term situations and travel, it's a great option. ***Rating: A***

CHICCO KEYFIT STRADA
Booster type: High back
Weight: 33 to 100 lbs.
Price: $150.
IIHS rating:
High back: Best Bet.
Backless: Check fit.

NHTSA ease of use rating: ★★★★☆

Comments: The KeyFit Strada is the belt-positioning booster from Chicco, a brand better known for its infant car seat and strollers. The KeyFit Strada's unique features include a headrest and side wings that adjust up and out, and more EPS foam than other seats. The seat converts to a backless booster for kids up to 100 lbs. and features an adjustable, clip-on cup holder.

The price seems high: $150 is a bit much, when you consider the similar Graco TurboBooster can be had for under $50. It's hard to image how an adjustable headrest and side wings would justify such a price premium. On the plus side, the fabric and padding are nicer than the TurboBooster—so some readers have justified the expense based on comfort. FYI: The Strada is a Babies R Us exclusive as of this writing.

Parent feedback on the Strada has been rather thin—it looks like this is a rare miss for Chicco, which has been on a roll as of late. The few folks who do have the Strada tend to like it, however. The Strada earned a Best Bet from the IIHS for belt fit. A few critics note some kids found the little hump on the seat base uncomfortable, especially for longer trips. And Chicco says the seat cover can only be sponged off for cleaning, instead of hand washing—that's a problem if there's a serious stain that needs to be cleaned.

Other than that, we will recommend the Strada—it is a well designed, if pricey booster. ***Rating: B***

Clek Olli/Ozzi

Booster type: Backless booster
Weight: 40 to 120 lbs., 57" tall.
Price: $100 Olli; $60 to $80 Ozzi
IIHS rating: Check fit.
NHTSA ease of use rating: Not rated.
Pros: Only LATCH backless booster.
Removable, washable seat cover.

Cons: High price. Only scored "fair" in latest crash tests by *Consumer Reports*.

Comments: Canadian car seat maker Magna's (magnaclek.com) backless booster is unique: it is one of only a few backless boosters that use LATCH for a secure fit to the car. Your child then buckles in with the auto safety belt. The main advantage of the Clek is that the LATCH connectors hold the seat in place when it is unoccupied. Nice, but is it worth $100 when most other (LATCH-less) backless boosters run $20?

Reader feedback on the Clek Olli (pictured) has been positive—readers love how easy it is to install and use. One past gripe (a lack of cup holders) has been remedied. There are still older, cup holder-less versions of the Olli on the market, so double check your order if you value this feature.

FYI: Clek makes a scaled down version of the Olli called the Ozzi: it omits the quick release strap, mesh side storage pocket, carry bag, cup holder and armrest padding. The Olli comes in several colors and is made of a micro fiber; the Ozzi comes in one color (black) and has less expensive fabric (accessory color covers run $25 to $35). FYI: The Ozzi is about $20 or so cheaper than the Olli.

Consumer Reports latest crash tests put the Olli at the bottom of the pack, rating it only "fair" for crash protection. As a result, we've dropped our rating of this seat this time out. ***Rating: B-***

Clek Oobr

Booster type: High back and backless booster
Weight: 33 to 100 lbs., 57" tall.
Price: $200-$300
IIHS rating:
Backless: Check fit.
High back: Best Bet.

NHTSA ease of use rating: Not rated.

Comments: The Clek Oobr is a high back booster that has a removable back. As with the Clek Olli/Ozzi, the Oobr features LATCH for a secure fit to the car. The Oobr's other main point is that the seat reclines up to 12 degrees and has an adjustable head restraint. At prices topping $200, however, this is a tough sell for most parents. With the top-selling high back booster (the Graco TurboBooster) selling for less than $50, it is unclear whether these features make it worth the investment.

Despite the price, reader feedback on this seat has been very positive, with folks saying the overall ease of use (the NHTSA gives it five stars) and LATCH feature outweigh the cost issue. Quality and safety-wise, this seat would earn an A if it wasn't priced so high.

Critics knock the skimpy padding of the seat, especially when compared to the similarly priced Britax Frontier (which has a five-point harness). On the plus side, the Clek Oobr scored "very good" in crash protection in *Consumer Reports* latest tests. ***Rating: B***

COMBI KOBUCK

Booster type: High back and backless booster.
Weight: 33 to 125 lbs.; 33" to 57" in height.
Price: $60 to $90
IIHS rating: Good Bet.
NHTSA ease of use rating: ★★★★☆
Four out of five stars.

Pros: Side impact protection; can be used as a backless booster. Picked as a "good bet" by IIHS.

Cons: Funky cup holder; not sold in many stores so it may be hard to see in person.

Comments: Want side impact protection but turned off by the restrictive wings of other booster seats? Combi's Kobuk aims to fill this niche with a protective headrest, minus the tight-fitting wings. We liked the padding of this seat (even the armrests are padded), but the cheesy cup holder that sticks straight out of the seat and relatively high price (twice the price of a Graco TurboBooster) are negatives.

On the plus side, the entire seat is lined with EPS and "egg shock" (comfort) foam. Combi's pitch for the Kobuk includes a claim that its front air vents allow for "healthy ventilation." Well, given parent feedback, we don't think this seat is any cooler than other boosters, but it's hard to measure that claim. In the past year, Combi hasn't made many changes to this seat but it is now rated to 125 lbs. (up from 100 lbs.).

Parent feedback on this seat has been positive. The Kobuk scored as a good bet on the latest IIHS rating and four out of five stars in the government's ease of use tests.

Unfortunately, like many Combi products, this seat may be hard to find at retail. That is more of a problem for a booster seat, as it is best to sit your child in the seat before purchasing. ***Rating: B+***

COSCO AMBASSADOR/HIGH RISE

Booster type: Backless booster
Weight: 30-100 lbs. Kids must be 52" or less.
Price: $15.50 to $26.
IIHS rating: Check fit.
NHTSA ease of use rating: Not rated.
Pros: Cheap backless booster. Cup holder.
Cons: None.
Comments: Very simple and affordable backless boosters. Both versions have padded armrests and a fold-down cup holder. Most parent feedback is positive, but quite a few parents noted the padding on the seat is rather skimpy when compared to similar boosters made by Graco.

FYI: This seat is sold as the Ambassador in Walmart and the High Rise on other sites; it is basically the same seat. *Rating: B*

COSCO HIGH BACK BOOSTER/COMPLETE VOYAGER

This seat is reviewed on the free side of our web site at BabyBargains.com/?p=1146

COSCO PRONTO

Booster type: High back and backless booster
Weight: 30-100 lbs. as belt positioning booster, 40-100 lbs. as backless booster.
Price: $33-$50.
IIHS rating:
Backless mode: Check fit.
High back mode: Best Bet.
NHTSA ease of use rating: ★★★★☆

Pros: Low price, machine washable pad, cup holder.
Cons: None.
Comments: This booster has a roomy seat and adjusts for taller kids. We also like the machine washable pad. And you can't beat the price. This might be a good booster for Grandma's car.

Unlike Cosco's High Back Booster, this seat earns a better rating from the government for ease of use (four out of five stars) and a Best Bet from the IIHS in high back mode. Reader feedback has also been positive—no, the fabric and padding isn't as nice as the Graco TurboBooster. And Evenflo's similar model has armrests that move up (the Pronto has fixed armrests, which makes climbing in and out of the seat a bit more challenging). But the Pronto is less expensive than those options, so there's your trade-off. *Rating: B*

Cosco Rightway

Booster type: High back booster.
Weight: 30-100 lbs. with back; 40-100 lbs. backless.
Price: $33-$50.
IIHS rating: Not rated.
NHTSA ease of use rating: Not yet.
Pros: Cheap backless booster. Two cup holders.
Cons: Only sold at Walmart.
Comments: This model pairs the base of the Stack It booster with the back of the Pronto. Hence, the main difference between the Rightway and Pronto is the Pronto has only one cup holder that slides out from the base. The Rightway has two integrated cup holders that don't slide. FYI: This seat is a Walmart exclusive.

Parent feedback on the Rightway has been positive—most fans say if you check your expectations, this is a good budget pick for a booster. We will give it the same grade as the Cosco Pronto, which is very similar. *Rating: B*

Cosco Stack It

Booster type: Backless booster
Weight: 40-100 lbs.
Price: $16-$29.
IIHS rating: Check fit.
NHTSA ease of use rating: Not yet.
Pros: Cheap backless booster. Two cup holders.
Cons: None.
Comments: This simple backless booster is sold for under $20 and features two cup holders and a removable/machine-washable pad. Parent feedback on this seat has been positive. We will recommend it. *Rating: A*

Cosco Top Side / No Back

Booster type: Backless booster
Weight: 40-100 lbs. Kids must be 57" or less.
Price: $13 to $20.
IIHS rating: Check fit.
NHTSA ease of use rating: ★★★★☆
Pros: Affordable, simple backless booster.
Cons: No cup holders.
Comments: This very simple booster is just, well, a booster. No cup holders, rotating armrests, etc. FYI: This seat is sold in Target as the "No Back" booster (clever, eh?) for $13 and on other sites as the Top Side. Parent feedback on this one has been positive. *Rating: B*

CYBEX SOLUTION X-FIX / Q-FIX
Booster type: High back
Weight: 33-80 lbs.
Price: $200-$250
IIHS rating: Best Bet (previews version).
NHTSA ease of use rating: ★★★★☆
Pros: Rigid LATCH, side impact protection.
Cons: Pricey, doesn't convert into backless booster.

Comments: This LATCH-compatible booster is coming back from the grave. After being discontinued in 2012, Cybex has decided to give it a second chance.

The X-Fix's main feature is a rigid LATCH connector, much like the Clek Oobr. We like the Solution X-Fix's adjustable back and side impact protection. One unique feature: the headrest reclines in three positions.

Reader feedback on this seat was positive before and the IIHS gave the last version a Best Bet rating. We assume it will perform similarly, since it isn't changing in its reincarnation.

Also new for 2014, Cybex is releasing a beefed up version of this seat called the Q-Fix, with extensive side impact protection. As you raise up the headrest, the Q-Fix's sides expand, giving a bigger toddler more room in the seat. Like the X-Fix, the Q-Fix has rigid LATCH. Price: $250. Cybex plans to release this in the first quarter of 2014.

Reader feedback on this seat has been sparse, probably due to Cybex's thin distribution in stores and its relatively recent debut. However, the IIHS picked it as a Best Bet and the government scored it as four out of five stars in ease of use. So we'll recommend this one, even though it is pricey.

Our rating is for the X-Fix; we'll wait for more details and parent feedback on the Q-Fix when it hits the market. ***Rating: B+***

DIONO CAMBRIA
Booster type: High back.
Weight: 40 to 120 lbs.
Price: $100.
IIHS rating: Not yet.
NHTSA ease of use rating: Not yet.
Pros: LATCH connectors, adjustable deep head wings for side impact protection. Seat lined with EPS foam. Affordable.

Cons: Fewer height adjustments than Diono Monterey. Sides aren't adjustable. No five-point harness.

Comments: Diono's newest high back booster will debut in early 2014—the Cambria is designed to be more of an entry-price point seat than Diono's other high back offering (Monterey). The

Cambria features LATCH connectors, swing-out cup holders and deep head wings for side impact protection.

The trade-offs include fewer height adjustments (six for the Cambria) and no adjustable seat width. But you do get a seat that works to 120 lbs., same as the more expensive Diono booster.

The Cambria is priced at about $100, which is competitive with other LATCH-compatible seats like the Graco Affix.

A backless version of the Cambria will be marketed as the Solana; it will work from 30 to 120 pounds and run $40. It will have the same features as the Cambria (LATCH connectors; dual swing-out cup holders, etc.). **Rating: Not Yet.**

DIONO MONTEREY BOOSTER
Booster type: High back
Weight: 30 to 120 lbs., 63" in height.
Price: $120-$150.
IIHS rating:
Backless mode: Check fit.
High back mode: Best bet.
NHTSA ease of use rating: ★★★☆☆
Pros: Works with LATCH, height adjustable, EPS foam, retractable cup holder, seat recline.
Cons: Short LATCH connectors make it hard to install, difficult to remove. Heavy. Complaints about defective belt guides.
Comments: A high back booster that converts to backless mode, the Monterey features a dial-adjustable seat width, EPS foam, a deep seat, retractable cup holders, two recline positions and a cushy foam seat. The Monterey also works with LATCH, one of the few boosters on the market with this feature. But . . . the LATCH connectors are very short and hard to attach. And the seat is quite heavy. Hence, moving this seat from car to car would be a chore.

Feedback on the Monterey had been positive up until 2012, when Diono redesigned the belt guides for the seat. Then we began to see complaints about belts falling out of the guide. To its credit, Diono sent replacement headrests free of charge . . . and Diono told us they started shipping an updated version of the Monterey in early 2013 with revised belt guides. Unfortunately, this has tarnished the Monterey's overall reputation—and we've lowered its rating this time out as a result.

On the plus side, folks like the roomy seat and easy adjustments. Critics note it is a nightmare to clean—small black pins must be removed to take off the cover and the mesh fabric is a hassle to hand wash.

The Monterey is marketed as a backless booster under the name Sante Fe ($49-$66). **Rating: B-**

EDDIE BAUER DELUXE HIGHBACK BOOSTER

This seat is reviewed on the free side of our web site at BabyBagains.com/?p=1154

EVENFLO AMP HIGH BACK BOOSTER

Booster type: High back booster, converts to backless
Weight: 30 to 100 lbs.
Price: $35-$68
IIHS rating:
Amp High Back: Check fit.
Amp High Backless: Best bet.
NHTSA ease of use rating: Not yet.

Pros: Affordable. Deeper side wings for more side impact protection. Comfort touch padding.

Cons: None.

Comments: The Amp High Back Booster is similar to the Evenflo Big Kid with a couple of differences: the Amp has a bigger headrest for more side impact protection. And the Amp has two integrated cup holders (the Big Kid's cup holders can retract into the base). Price-wise, they are about the same. Both seats convert into backless boosters for older children.

As with Evenflo's other Amp seats, the emphasis here is on bright, neon color accents. And just to confuse you, there is also a backless Amp booster (that's how the Amp line started). And for a while, Evenflo even marketed a version of the Big Kid called the Big Kid Amp(it's still for sale on some sites). In the past year, Evenflo has tried to separate the Big Kid and Amp boosters into separate lines.

Parent feedback on this seat has been positive. We'd still give the Graco TurboBooster a slight edge in how well kids fit in the seat, but the Amp High Back is a close second. FYI: Evenflo sells a backless version of the Amp for $25-$37. ***Rating: A-***

EVENFLO BIG KID

Booster type: High back booster
Weight: 30 to 100 lbs.
Price: $30-$60.
IIHS rating:
Big Kid LX: Check fit.
Big Kid LX No Back: Best Bet.
Big Kid Sport No Back: Best bet.
Big Kid Sport high back: Check fit.
NHTSA ease of use rating: ★★★★★
Pros: Low price, extras like reading lights, EPS foam.

Cons: Skimpy padding in low-end version.

Comments: Evenflo's answer to Graco's TurboBooster, the Big Kid adds a few bells and whistles that Graco doesn't have. The Big Kid is adjustable in both height and lap depth (most boosters are just height adjustable). One version of the Big Kid actually comes with reading lights. Like the TurboBooster, the back removes as kids grow bigger, adding a discreet boost to older kids without looking "uncool."

On the plus side, the Big Kid is less expensive than the Graco Turbo Booster (a $40 version called the Big Kid Amp at Babies R Us is especially affordable). On the downside, the padding is a bit skimpier than the Graco, making this seat less comfy for longer trips. And the Big Kid has less side impact protection than other seats. As usual, it is the little things about Evenflo that drive you crazy: the reading lights are nice, but lack an auto shut-off feature (and hence, will consume batteries fast if left on).

Like most Evenflo products, the Big Kid comes in several different versions, including an Advanced, LX and DLX (Deluxe; pictured). The more expensive Deluxe includes upgraded fabric and padding. A Walmart exclusive version of the Big Kid (called the Big Kid Sport) is $30. The Sport omits the activity lights, the one-hand adjustment, energy-absorbing foam liner and pivoting armrests.

Reader feedback on this seat has been positive, with parents lauding the many features and adjustments. And the government awarded this seat its top rating for ease of use. However, the Insurance Institute for Highway Safety only gave this seat a "check fit" rating (a backless version of the this seat did earn a best bet).

Between the two seats, we'd give the Graco TurboBooster the edge in overall quality—it tends to fit kids better than the Evenflo Big Kid. On the other hand, you can often find this seat for a lower price than the TurboBooster. **Rating: B**

EVENFLO CHASE (LX & DLX) / MAESTRO
These older model Evenflo boosters are reviewed on the free side of our web site at BabyBargains.com/bonus.

EVENFLO RIGHTFIT
Booster type: High back booster
Weight: 30 to 110 lbs.; 38"-57" in height. At least four years of age.
Price: $70. Babies R Us exclusive.
IIHS rating: Best Bet.
NHTSA ease of use rating: Not yet.
Pros: Affordable, multiple seat and headrest adjustments. Side impact protection.
Cons: Top harness height of 19" means taller kids may outgrow the seat too soon. Pricey.

Comments: This booster is a Babies R Us exclusive and features some refinements over Evenflo's other booster seats. The headline here is adjustability: the back rest has four adjustments. When combined with three headrest adjustments, you have 12 possible positions. That's more than just about any other seat on the market.

The RightFit also has Evenflo's e3 side impact protection and improved lights (four LED lights on each side wing). Like most Evenflo boosters, the RightFit converts to a backless booster for older kiddos. Two built-in cup holders on the arms are well designed.

The negatives: the top belt height is only 19"—that is much shorter than the Britax Parkway (21.5") or Recaro's ProBooster (21"). Hence this may not be the right booster if you have a tall toddler, as they may grow out of the seat too soon. We also found this seat's $70 price tag a bit high, since you can buy a comparable Graco TurboBooster for $50.

Parent feedback on the RightFit has been mixed, with several folks criticizing the narrow shoulder belt guide (making it difficult to slide a seat belt through). Others report no problem with the guide, so we're not sure if this is a vehicle model specific issue or not. Given some of the mixed reviews, we've downgraded the rating. If you get this seat, make sure you keep the receipt so you can return it if the shoulder belt guide turns out to be an issue in your vehicle. ***Rating: B-***

EVENFLO SECUREKID
Booster type: Combo booster
Weight: 20-65 lbs. with harness; 30 to 110 lbs. as a booster
Price: $93-$150.
IIHS rating: Best Bet.
NHTSA ease of use rating:

⭐⭐⭐☆☆ Harness mode
⭐⭐⭐⭐☆ Booster mode

Pros: Side impact protection plus 65 lb. harness. Best bet by IIHS. LATCH connectors to keep seat in place.

Cons: No harness pads; white accents might get grimy quick.

Comments: The SecureKid is Evenflo's latest booster seat—and the first to have enhanced side impact protection and a 65 lb. weight limit harness. Built on the Maestro platform, the SecureKid comes in two versions: the LX (aka the 300) has basic LATCH connectors and sells for $129. The DLX (aka the 400) adds SureLATCH self-ratcheting connectors and e3 side impact protection for $149. Both models have integrated cup holders and an adjustable headrest.

Reader feedback on this seat has been quite positive, although a few critics note the lack of harness pads means the tightened harness sometimes can cut into a child's neck. And a few found buckling this seat to be somewhat difficult compared to other seats. Another minor quibble: we wonder if those white accents on some models of this seat would become grimy in short order (only a couple of styles have this issue). Overall, however, this is a good seat and worthy of consideration for those who need a combo booster. **Rating: A-**

FIRST YEARS PATHWAY B570
Also sold under Learning Curve, Compass brands
Booster type: High back booster
Weight: 30-100 lbs.
Price: $76 to $110.
IIHS rating: Best Bet (B570 only). Other models are rated Check fit.
NHTSA ease of use rating: Pros: Folds up, nicely padded, flip-up arm- ★★★★★
rests, extra wide seat, good price.

Cons: Earlier models not recommended in previous IIHS report.

Comments: This seat started life as the Compass Folding booster and is still sold that way, even though Compass was acquired by Tomy's The First Years brand a couple of years ago. As you might have guessed from the name, this seat's key selling feature is the ability to fold, unique in the market. That's a boon for carpoolers or anyone who has to shuttle a booster between vehicles. The Folding Booster features excellent padding, side impact protection (EPS foam) and extras like two cup holders, flip-up armrests and six- position height adjustment.

Over the years, The First Years has come out with several different versions of this seat—the Deluxe, Ultra, Premiere, etc. Each is very similar, with the plushness of the fabric being the main difference. The basic model is $76, while the fanciest model tops $110. The most current model numbers for this seat are the B540 and B570—the higher the number, the newer the model (and generally the more plush the fabric). You'll probably see older models online (with lower model numbers).

The latest version of this seat is the B570 Pathway. It adds color-coded belt paths and LATCH attachments. The seat also features three position adjustable shoulder belt and side impact protection. That last feature is unique for First Years and is similar to the Clek Oobr booster, which also features LATCH. Of course, the Pathway folds up like all the other Compass boosters.

Overall, reader feedback has been very positive (parents find it very easy to use, excellent adjustments and overall quality). Plus the government gave this booster its top rating for ease of use.

The Insurance Institute for Highway Safety said the B570 is a Best Bet. Bottom line: we recommend the First years Pathway B570 (skip the older versions that have model numbers below 570). **Rating: B+**

GRACO AFFIX YOUTH BOOSTER
Booster type: High back and backless booster
Weight: 30 to 100 lbs. as high back booster (backless, it is 40 to 100 lbs).
Price: $70 to $100 (high back); $35 (backless)
IIHS rating: Best Bet.
NHTSA ease of use rating: ★★★★☆
Pros: LATCH connectors keep seat in place when unoccupied. Side impact protection.
Cons: Pricey if you don't want to use LATCH.
Comments: The Graco Affix Youth Booster is similar to the Graco TurboBooster with Safety Surround with one main difference: the Affix has LATCH connectors to secure it to the vehicle. This keeps the seat secure if it is unoccupied. An upfront adjuster lets you tighten the LATCH connectors.

Like the TurboBooster, you also get an integrated cup holder.

The downside to this seat: a basic Graco booster like the TurboBooster can be found for 40% less than this model.

What about the LATCH connectors? Well, we can certainly see why parents would want to secure a booster to the vehicle (if unoccupied and there is a crash, an unsecured booster seat could fly about in the vehicle). Graco also pitches the LATCH connection as easier for kids to buckle the seat in (since it can't move around). As far as safety of the seat itself, however, LATCH doesn't necessarily make the seat safer—a booster without LATCH connectors is just as safe for a toddler as one with LATCH.

The Affix earned a Best Bet from the IIHS and four out of five stars in ease of use. FYI: A backless version of the Affix is $35. And a version of the backless Affix is sold at Walmart for $18 that omits the front LATCH adjustment (this model is dubbed the Connext). Buy Buy Baby has an exclusive version of the Affix that has "Safety Surround" side impact protection for $100.

Bottom line: the Affix is a good seat. If LATCH connection is important, then this is a worthy seat to consider. Given Graco's track record in this category, we will give it our recommendation. Parent feedback has been positive. *Rating: A*

GRACO ARGOS 70/80
Price: $170-$200.
Type: Combo.
Limits: 20 to 70 lbs. with harness, up to 100 lbs. has a belt-positioning booster, up to 120 lbs. as a backless booster.
NHTSA ease of use rating:

★★★☆☆ Harness mode
★★★★☆ Booster mode

boosters

★★★☆☆ Elite model

IIHS rating:

High back mode: Best bet.

Backless mode: Check fit.

Comments: The big headline here is a no-rethread harness. Graco is also promoting this seat's side-impact testing and EPS foam. The Argos also has a three-position recline.

Basically, the Argos is like the Nautilus, but works to 70 lbs. with a five-point harness (the Nautilus works to 65 lbs.). Then the Argos becomes a backless booster to 120 lbs. (the Nautilus stops as 100 lbs.). And the no-rethread harness is a big pro over the Nautilus.

So what's not to like? Well, the harness slots are the same height as the Nautilus. You'd think if they are promoting the higher weight, Graco would throw you a harness height an inch or so above the Nautilus. And the price premium is another issue: the Argos is close to $200, while the Nautilus can be found online for as little as $140 on Walmart as we speak. FYI: an "Elite" version of the Argos 70 features belt lock-offs and an adjustable headrest.

New for 2014, Graco is coming out with an Argos 80, which as you might guess, works up to 80 lbs. with harness. This version will be exclusive to Babies R Us and Buy Buy Baby (in different fashions), retail : $220. The Argos 80 will be out in the second quarter of 2014.

Feedback on the Argos is positive—fans generally laud the seat's quality and design. A few critics said the Argos was hard to buckle/unbuckle—Graco is moving to a better buckle system in 2014 (IMMI buckles), which should help this issue. While it is overshadowed by its better-selling sister model (the Nautilus), the Argos is worthy of consideration as well. *Rating: B+*

GRACO NAUTILUS 3-IN-1

Booster type: Combo

Weight: 20-65 lbs. with harness, 30 to 100 lbs. as high back booster.

Backless booster from 40 to 100 lbs.

Price: $150-$200.

IIHS rating:

High back mode: Best Bet.

Backless mode: Check fit.

Elite model: Check fit (both modes).

NHTSA ease of use rating: ★★★☆☆

(all modes, versions).

Pros: Works to 65 lbs. with a five-point harness.

Cons: Harness must be re-threaded to adjust height. No LATCH connectors to keep seat in place when unoccupied.

Comments: Here's the best-selling combo booster seat in the market—the Graco's Nautilus is a combo booster that works with a five-point harness to 65 lbs. and then converts to high back booster (100 lbs.) and even a backless booster for older kids. The harness is a big plus if you have a toddler who has outgrown his convertible seat, but wish to keep him in the harness for a while longer (the 65 lb. limit should fit most five year olds).

The Nautilus' other features include over molded armrests (with side storage), three-position recline and decent padding. The seat is lined with EPS foam. Like most Graco seats, Graco makes a few different versions of the Nautilus, which boils down to fabric plushness. The basic one is $140; Babies R Us sells slightly upgraded versions that run $180.

The Nautilus's biggest competitor is the Britax Frontier, so let's look how they compare. The Britax Frontier is bigger and wider than the Nautilus—and the Britax seat works up to 85 lbs. with the five-point harness. Folks generally give the Frontier better marks for padding, although the more expensive Nautilus models offer similar padding.

In the past, we gave the Nautilus the edge over the Frontier for its ease of install; however, Britax redesigned the Frontier in 2010 and caught up to the Nautilus.

There are a couple of key differences: to adjust the harness height with the Graco Nautilus, you have to rethread the harness. The Frontier harness doesn't require rethreading, which makes it much easier to use. The Frontier has three crotch strap adjustments; the Graco only two. On the other hand, the mesh fabric on the Britax Frontier is much more prone to wear and show stains compared to the Nautilus, which doesn't have this problem.

So it now basically comes down to price: the basic Nautilus is HALF the cost of the Britax Frontier . . . and we know that's nothing to sneeze at.

As for reader feedback, the Graco Nautilus earns positive marks from readers for its overall ease of use. The IIHS ranks the Nautilus as a Best Bet when used in high back mode; the Britax Frontier earns the same rating.

FYI: There are two other versions of the Nautilus on the market. The Nautilus Elite adds an adjustable headrest and belt lock-offs (to ease installation in that mode). The Elite also has enhanced side impact protection (EPS foam lining the headrest). As you'd expect from the Elite name, this model includes upgraded pad and fabric. Oddly, the Elite scored lower on ease of use and the IIHS ratings than the regular model. And you'd think the Elite model would have premium push-button LATCH connectors, right? Nope, the Nautilus Elite uses the same run of the mill LATCH connectors as on the basic model.

The Nautilus Elite sells for $173 on Amazon; since the regular Nautilus runs $150, the Elite might be worth the upgrade.

The second, alternative version of the Nautilus is the Nautilus

Plus. It features a reversible body support pillow and seat protector. Price: $190. The Nautilus Plus is a Buy Buy Baby exclusive. Between the Plus and Elite, the Elite is better in our opinion.

Bottom line: we like the Nautilus—it is among our top picks in this category. ***Rating: A***

GRACO TURBOBOOSTER
Booster type: High back and backless booster
Weight: 30 to 100 lbs. as high back booster (backless, it is 40 to 100 lbs).
Price: $45-$80. Backless version is $18-$35.
IIHS rating:
High back mode: Best Bet.
Backless mode: Best Bet.

NHTSA ease of use rating: ★★★☆☆

★★★★☆ Elite version

★★★☆☆ Elite version with Safety Surround:

Pros: Top choice in booster market—both affordable and well designed.

Cons: No five-point harness; little side impact protection.

Comments: This is our top pick as a great, affordable belt-positioning booster seat (no harness). The TurboBooster features padded armrests that are height adjustable, EPS foam, hide-away cup holders and a one-hand adjustment for the headrest. The seat pad removes for cleaning; the TurboBooster converts into a backless booster for older kids.

As usual, Graco makes this seat in more than a dozen colors and styles. Hence, you'll find a basic version for $45 at Walmart and upgraded models for $90 in specialty stores. What's the difference? Just the fabric pad. More money, fancier pad.

So what are the drawbacks to the Graco TurboBooster? Well, unlike the Graco Nautilus or Britax Frontier, this seat lacks a five-point harness. Hence you must have an older toddler who is mature enough to sit in a regular seat belt. Finally, the TurboBooster requires quite a bit of assembly with various screws (that's the reason this seat only earned three out of five stars in the government's ease of use rating).

One flaw for the TurboBooster, the lack of side impact protection, was addressed in the past year: Graco is adding their "Safety Surround" side impact protection to one version of the TurboBooster (dubbed the Highback TurboBooster with Safety Surround, $80). See our review of the Graco My Ride 65 for details on Safety Surround.

Bottom line: this is a good option for older toddlers who no longer need a seat with a five-point harness. If you can spare the extra cash, go for the version with the Safety Surround padding. ***Rating: A***

HARMONY

These booster seats are reviewed on the free side of our web site at BabyBargains.com/bonus.

KIDDY WORLD CRUISERFIX PRO
Booster type: High back.
Weight: 33 to 100 lbs. as high back booster.
Price: $200 too $260.
IIHS rating: Best Bet.
NHTSA ease of use rating: ★★★★☆

Pros: Side impact protection (wings are adjustable), extendable leg extension. LATCH connectors.
Cons: No backless mode. Hard to find at retail.
Comments: Kiddy is a German car seat maker that is the latest European import to the U.S. Their CruiserFix Pro is a $220 belt-positioning booster that works up to 100 lbs. Among the CruiserFix Pro's unique features is its extendable seat depth (to nearly 17"), as well as being both height and width adjustable. Unlike Kiddy's other model (the World Plus), the CruiserFix Pro lacks a top tether or lap shield. But this seat does have rigid LATCH connectors that pop out of the seat.

If there is one downside to this seat, it would be Kiddy's rather thin distribution—this seat is hard to find in stores to see first hand. Hence, most folks have had to take the plunge and buy it online, sign unseen. Yet, so far, reader feedback has been very positive. Yes, it is pricey, but we like all the adjustments and the detailed side impact protection. One negative: the rigid LATCH may not work in some vehicles, especially if the anchor points don't line up with those on the seat.

Bottom line: we'll give the CruiserFix Pro a thumbs up. **Rating: A**

KIDDY WORLD PLUS

This booster seats is reviewed on the free side of our web site at BabyBargains.com/?p=5667

KIDSEMBRACE CHARACTER TODDLER SEAT
Type: Combo booster
Weight: 22lbs. to 65lbs. with harness; booster 30lbs. to 100 lbs.
Price: $100-$150.
IIHS: Best Bet.
NHTSA ease of use: ★★★★☆

Pros: One hand harness adjustment; 2-position crotch strap; wrap around headrest. Cartoon themes = toddler happiness.
Cons: Cup holders have no bottom. Straps can be twisty.
Comments: As parents of a toddler know, getting their "buy in" to a new situation is crucial to everyone's happiness. Hence, we can see

the point of the KIDSEmbrace themed car eats, featuring the likes of Sponge Bob, Dora the Explorer, Batman and Dale Earnhardt Jr.

Even though they look jokey, these are actually well-designed boosters. Sold on Walmart.com for $118 and in Babies R Us stores for up to $150, KIDSEmbrace's boosters are well priced and may be the solution to toddlers who balk at sitting in a "baby seat." The booster has a one-hand harness adjustment, two-position crotch strap and side impact headrest. Parent feedback is relatively positive—it's easy to install and use. Best bet is how the IIHS rated these seats, which also scored decent ease of use ratings from the NHTSA.

In our last review, we criticized one big negative for these seats: a low top harness slot. Well, Kids Embrace has addressed this problem—their new models have a 17" top harness slot. The similar Graco Nautilus has an 18" top slot, so Kids Embrace is now in the ballpark.

As for the cartoon characters, we realize some folks turn up their nose at the commercialism. But if a Ninja Turtles car seat (new for 2014) gets your kid excited about that long road trip, where's the harm? These seats are safe and generally well reviewed by parents. Are the Kids Embrace as cushy as other more expensive seats? No. is there extensive side impact protection? No. But you do get a decent seat that your toddler will (probably) never argue about sitting in.

So we'll raise the rating on these seats this time out. **Rating: B**

LITTLE TIKES

Comments: These boosters are made by Diono and are similar to the Diono Cambria. Pricing will range from $20 to $60. Little Tikes boosters seats are set to debut in 2014.

MAXI COSI RODI XR/AP/FIX
Booster type: High back booster
Weight: 30 to 100 lbs.
Price: $170-$190.
IIHS rating:
High back mode: Best Bet.
Backless mode: Check fit.
NHTSA ease of use rating: ★★★★☆

Pros: Extra large side wings provide sleep support, adjustable headrest. Seat recline.

Cons: Requires vehicles with rear headrests.

Comments: Maxi Cosi is a European subsidiary of Dorel, the juvenile products giant home to the Cosco, Eddie Bauer and Safety 1st brands.

The Rodi first debuted as a $100 booster with deep side wings for side impact protection and sleeping support. The Rodi also had a recline feature, yet lacked an adjustable headrest. And at $100, it was hard to justify the extra 50% price premium over seats like the Graco TurboBooster, which basically do the same thing.

The new Rodi XR adds an adjustable headrest but is still similar to the old Rodi (seat recline, etc.). At $180 retail, it's overpriced when compared to similar booster seats. Another major negative: like most Dorel boosters, the Rodi requires the rear seat in your vehicle have headrest support—something lacking in many cars.

New for 2014, Maxi Cosi is coming out with two new spin-offs to the Rodi: the Rodi AP ($160) features Dorel's "Air Protect" side impact cushions. Also new: the RodiFix—this will feature the rigid LATCH connectors known as ISOFIX. The RodiFix ($250) also has the Air Protect side impact protection and adjustable headrest feature that also adjusts the seat width at the same time. The new Rodi's also feature a reclining seat and no armrests—this makes it easier to belt in a toddler. The older Rodi and Rodi XR had armrests.

Despite the high price, reader feedback on this seat has been positive. And it earned a Best Bet (in high back mode) from the Insurance Institute for Highway Safety. So we'll tick up the Rodi's rating this year. However, the lack of value keeps this seat from earning a top grade. *Rating: B-*

PEG PEREGO VIAGGIO HBB 120

Booster type: High back and backless booster
Weight: 40 to 120 lbs. as high back booster or backless.
Price: $200.
IIHS rating: Not yet.
NHTSA ease of use rating: ★★★★☆

Pros: EPS foam, side impact protection head wings, use to 120 pounds, converts to backless. LATCH connectors, two recessed cup holders. Made in Italy.

Cons: $200? Similar seats can be had for $50.

Comments: Peg Perego continues to expand its car seat line—after debuting a convertible seat in 2011, the company added a belt-positioning booster in 2012. The Viaggio HBB 120 booster seat works from 40 to 120 lbs. (Confusingly, Perego refers to all its car seats as Viaggio, which is Italian for trip).

The booster features side impact head cushions and integrated cup holders. It comes in both fabric and leatherette versions, the latter of which looked like a poor choice for parents in hot climates. Price $200.

Our first impression of this seat was that it looked like an overpriced knock-off of the Graco TurboBooster. And since you can pick up that seat for just $50, we're not sure what justifies the big price premium here (okay, the Viaggio HBB will work to 120 lbs. versus the TurboBooster's 100 lbs.). And the Viaggio has LATCH attachments to keep the seat secure when unoccupied, another feature the

TurboBooster lacks. But most of the specs of this seat are similar to the TurboBooster, down to the two hide away cup holders in the base.

We wish Perego had come out with some new technology or incredible adjustments (like Kiddy's seats that have amazing adjustments for the seat depth and head rests). Otherwise, this is just another me-too seat with Italian fashion that, unfortunately, is symbolic of Perego's malaise in recent years.

Parent feedback on this seat has been mostly positive. They love the latch system which makes it easy to install. One negative: readers note that if the seat can't be placed flush to the back of the seat because of protruding headrests, you can't use the seat with the high back. It did receive a 4 out of 5 rating from the NHTSA for ease of use. And this seat is made in Italy, not China.

We are ticking down the rating of this seat this time out. Competitors like Britax and Graco have set the bar very high in this category. And the $200 Perego booster just doesn't quite measure up, in our opinion. ***Rating: B***

RECARO PROBOOSTER

Booster type: High back booster
Weight: 30 to 120 lbs., 37" to 61" tall.
Price: $75 to $130.
IIHS rating: Best Bet.
NHTSA ease of use rating: ★★★☆☆
Pros: Side impact protection, works to 120 lbs.
Cons: Hard to find in retail stores, no LATCH. No cup holders. Can be tippy. Criticized by environmental group for chemicals used in fabric.

Comments: Side impact protection is the headline here—the ProBOOSTER works to 120 lbs. and has a wide seat. This model has "cool mesh" air ventilation and a recline feature to better fit the slope of a vehicle's back seat.

The ProBOOSTER earned a Best Bet rating from the IIHS. Price and feature-wise, this seat's closest competitor is probably the Britax Parkway. Comparing the two, the ProBOOSTER lacks the LATCH feature on the Parkway SGL, which keeps the seat in place when unoccupied. That said, the ProBOOSTER gets better marks on comfort and fabric quality, compared to the Parkway, which is similarly priced.

Reader feedback on this seat is mostly positive with one caveat: this seat seems to work best in vehicles with bucket seats (thanks to the narrow base). Without bucket seats, the ProBOOSTER can become tippy, which has generated a fair number of complaints among parents with vehicles that have flat or bench backseats in their vehicle.

FYI: In 2013, Recaro came out with a new version of this seat that attempted to address the tipping concern. The ProBOOSTER 2013 has a wider/deeper seat with integrated cup holders and LATCH. Confusingly, it appears both this revised version and the older ProBOOSTERs are still being sold online.

Another area of concern: the ProBOOSTER came in for criticism from HeathyStuff.org in their chemical car seat tests. The environmental group blasted Recaro for high levels of bromine and chlorine in this seat's fabric. Those criticisms aside, most readers are happy with the ProBOOSTER. We will recommend it. **Rating: A-**

RECARO PROSPORT
Booster type: Combo
Weight: 20 to 120 lbs.; five-point harness to 90 lbs. Up to 59″
Price: $180 to $280.
IIHS rating: Best Bet.
NHTSA ease of use rating:
★★★☆☆ Harness mode
★☆☆☆☆ Booster mode

Pros: Very comfortable, EPS foam, side impact protection. Highest harness rating in class—90 lbs!
Cons: Price. Hard to find in retail stores. Tools required to disassemble the seat for cleaning.
Comments: The ProSPORT features a five-point harness that works up to 90 pounds—yep, you read that right. That is the highest harness weight on the market, equaled only by the Britax Frontier. After your child outgrows the harness, the ProSPORT works as a booster up to 120 pounds.

Like the Recaro ProBOOSTER, side impact protection is the star here. You also get a harness height adjustment that works without re-threading, EPS foam for crash protection, and extra seat padding. The ProSPORT also features LATCH connectors, which is handy to keep the seat in position when not occupied.

In the past year, Recaro gave this seat some minor tweaks: new mesh pockets that can fit cups, additional memory foam in the seat and Recaro's new HERO system (headrest optimization system).

Reader feedback on this seat has been very positive and it earned a Best Bet from the Insurance Institute for Highway Safety. On the downside, we heard a few complaints that the side wings can get protest votes from toddlers who think they are too confining, block their vision, etc. (you may want to sit your child in this seat first before buying). And the NHTSA gave this seat only one-star in booster mode for ease of use, criticizing Recaro for not labeling the belt path. The NHTSA also said conversion of this seat from harness to booster mode is difficult and hand tools are needed to disassemble the seat for cleaning.

While we respect the NHTSA's ratings, we note the real world feedback from parents who've used the ProBOOSTER is much more positive. Priced at about same level as the Britax Frontier, we give the Recaro ProSPORT our top rating. **Rating: A**

SAFETY 1ST BOOST AIR PROTECT

Booster type: High back booster
Weight: 30 to 100 lbs.
Price: $60 to $70.
IIHS rating:
High back mode: Best Bet.
Backless mode: Check fit.

NHTSA ease of use rating: ★★★☆☆

Pros: Affordable. Side impact protection. Two cup holders.
Cons: EPS foam only lines headrest.
Comments: Safety 1st's "Air Protect" feature is the headline here—air cushions that release air if the seat is in a crash. This same technology is used on Safety 1st's infant and convertible seats.

The Boost Air Protect converts to a backless booster and has an adjustable headrest and slide-out cup holders.

Reader feedback on this seat has been mixed; we saw a sample at a local chain store and weren't that impressed. EPS foam only lines the headrest, not the rest of the seat. Parents who've used this seat knock it for quality issues—arm rest pads that keep slipping off, a headrest that doesn't stay put, a cloth cover too easily comes off, etc. The overall feel of this seat is flimsy.

While we like the Air Protect feature, this seat looks like Safety 1st rushed it out without much thought. If you want side impact protection but only have $100 or so to spend on a booster, the First Years Pathways is a better bet. Even though it earns a Best Bet from the Insurance Institute for Highway Safety, we think there are better bets on the market that have side impact protection. **Rating: C**

SAFETY 1ST BOOSTAPAK

Booster type: Backless
Weight: 40-80 lbs. 57"
Price: $70
IIHS rating: Best Bet.
NHTSA ease of use rating: Not Yet.
Pros: It's a backpack! It's a booster
Cons: Pricey

Comments: Yes, this backless booster does its best Transformer imitation, starting out as a backless booster and then morphing into a backpack. The BoostAPak is great for carpoolers and air travel—and it earned a Best Bet rating from the IIHS.

The only negative? It is rather pricey at $70. Considering you can get a good backless booster for $20 to $30, the BoostAPak seems overpriced to us. But you also get a storage compartment in the back, so we can see how some parents would find this a major plus especially for frequent travelers. See pictures below for detail on the seat's modes. FYI: This seat is sold at Buy Buy Baby.

Parent feedback on this seat has been positive. We will recommend it. **Rating: A**

Safety 1st Store 'n Go
Booster type: High back.
Weight: 40-100 lbs. 57"
Price: $60 high back; $25 backless booster.
IIHS rating: Not Yet.
NHTSA ease of use rating: Not Yet.
Pros: Storage drawer. Two cup holders.
Cons: No side impact protection.
Comments: As you might have guessed from the name, the Store 'n Go's claim to fame is its under seat storage drawer. This backless booster also has a side pocket/cup holder. The Store 'n Go comes both as a high back ($60 and backless booster ($25). FYI: Walmart has a Disney version of this seat.

The Store 'n Go looks like Safety 1st's attempt to knock off the Graco TurboBooster, which is similarly priced. Unfortunately, this seat omits Safety 1st's Air Protect side impact protection feature seen on the company's Boost Air Protect model. Considering that the seat is roughly the same price as the Store 'n Go, we think the side impact protection is a better bet than a storage drawer.

The Store 'n Go just debuted as we were going to press, so no parent feedback yet. We'll revise this review once we get more feedback. **Rating: Not Yet.**

Safety 1st Go Hybrid, Summit, Vantage
The Safety 1st Go Hybrid, Summit and Vantage seats are reviewed on the free side of our web site at BabyBargains.com/bonus

Best Bets: Booster Seats

◆ **Best Bets: Harness Seats.** Our top pick is the **Graco Nautilus**—this combo seat has a five-point harness that can be used up to 65 lbs. The Nautilus also converts to a belt-positioning booster and even a backless booster to 100 lbs. Starting at $150, the Nautilus is half the price of our other best bet in this category: the Britax Frontier.

Despite costing twice as much as a Nautilus, we think the **Britax**

Frontier 90 ($240-$330) is also worth a look. Yes, it works up to 90 lbs. with a five-point harness—and that is impressive. Reader feedback on this seat has been very positive.

◆ **Best Bets: Belt-Positioning Booster.** We have one clear winner here and several other strong runners-ups.

The *Graco TurboBooster* ($45 to $80) is the best belt-positioning booster on the market today. It packs a good number of features into an affordable package: height-adjustable headrest, open belt loop design, armrests, back recline, cup holders and more. Note it comes in two versions: a high-back version and backless (the latter is about $25).

Runner up: *Recaro ProBooster* features side impact protection and sleep support, plus EPS foam and Recaro's overall strong reputation for quality. At $75 to $130, it is worth a look compared to the TurboBooster. One advantage: the Recaro seat works to 120 lbs., versus 100 for the TurboBooster.

◆ **Best Bets: Booster for Carpools.** *First Years/Compass Pathway B570* ($76-$110) is an excellent booster seat that has a killer feature for carpools: it folds up. Add in side impact protection and six-position height adjustment and you have the perfect pick for parents who need to shuffle a seat between daycare and home.

◆ **Best Bets: Booster for Taxis.** If you live in a big city and don't own a car, you'll be relying on taxi cabs to get to the airport, the zoo and other special trips. In that case, we recommend the *Safety 1st Go Hybrid*. This excellent seat ($165 to $200) works with a five-point harness up to 60 lbs., yet installs in just one minute. Weighing only 11 lbs., the Go Hybrid also folds down to a compact size and fits in a travel bag—perfect for taxis! One caveat: this seat can only be used with its five-point harness if the vehicle has LATCH and a top tether. Most modern vehicles have these features, but it is an important caveat!

◆ **Best Bets: Backless Booster.** The best backless boosters on the market are the *Graco TurboBooster* backless ($18-$35) and the *Evenflo Big Kid Amp* ($20-$30). Both are affordable and easy to use boosters for older kids who don't need a high back booster.

Whew! You made it through the car seat chapter. Yes, we know—it was slightly shorter than Moby-Dick. Next up: strollers: which brands are best? How can you pick the best stroller for what you need? We've got it covered, starting on the next page.

CHAPTER 9

Strollers, Diaper Bags & Other Gear To Go

Inside this chapter

What are the best strollers? Which brands are the most durable AND affordable? We'll discuss this plus other tips on how to make your baby portable— from diaper bags to bike trailers and more. And what do you put in that diaper bag anyway? We've got nine suggestions, plus advice on the best baby carriers.

Getting Started: When Do You Need This Stuff?

While you don't need a stroller or diaper bag immediately after baby is born, most parents purchase them before baby arrives anyway. And some of the best deals for strollers and other to-go gear are found online, which necessitates leaving time for shipping.

Sources to Find Strollers

As with other baby products, discounters like Target and Walmart tend to specialize in just a handful of models from mass-market companies like Cosco, Kolcraft, Graco and so on (lately, they've been adding premium brands to their web sites although they aren't available in their stores). The baby superstores like Babies R Us and Buy Buy Baby have a wider selection and (sometimes) better brands. Meanwhile, juvenile specialty stores almost always carry the more exclusive brands.

Yet perhaps the best deals for strollers and diaper bags are found online—for some reason, this seems to be one area the web covers very well. This is because strollers are relatively easy to ship (compared to other more bulky juvenile items). Of course, more competition often means lower prices, so you'll see many deals online. Another plus: the web may be the only way to find certain premium-brand strollers if you live in less-populous parts of the U.S. and Canada.

Beware of shipping costs when ordering online or from a catalog—many strollers may run 20 or 30 lbs., which can translate into hefty shipping fees. Use an online coupon (see Chapter 7 for coupon sites) to save and look for free shipping specials.

Strollers

Baby stores offer a bewildering array of strollers for parents. Do you want the model that converts from a car seat to a stroller? What about a stroller that would work for a quick trip to the mall? Or do you want a stroller for jogging? Hiking trails? The urban jungle of New York City or beaches near LA?

And what about all the different brand names? Will a basic brand found at a discount store work? Or do you pine after one of the stylish Euro-designed imports? What about strollers with anti-lock brakes and air bags? (Just kidding on that last one).

The $332 million dollar stroller industry is not dominated by one or two players, like you might see in car seats or high chairs. Instead, you'll find a couple *dozen* stroller makers offering just about anything on wheels, ranging from $30 for a bare-bones model to $900 for a Dutch-designed über stroller. A recent hot trend: all-terrain strollers with three wheels, where the front wheel swivels.

We hope this section takes some of the mystery out of the stroller buying process. First, we'll look at the six different types of strollers on the market today. Next, we'll zero in on features and help you decided what's important and what's not. Then, it's brand ratings and our picks as the best recommendations for different lifestyles. Finally, we'll go over several safety tips, money saving hints, and more.

Whew! Take a deep breath and let's go.

What Are You Buying?

There are six types of strollers you can buy:

◆ **Umbrella Strollers.** The name comes from the appearance of the stroller when it's folded, similar to an umbrella.

WHAT'S COOL: They're lightweight and generally

cheap—that is, low in price (about $20 to $40). We should note that a handful of premium stroller makers (Maclaren and Peg Perego) also offer pricey umbrella strollers that sell for $150 to $300—we discuss them in the next category. Pictured is a no-frills Kolcraft umbrella stroller.

WHAT'S NOT: They're cheap—that is, low in quality. You typically don't get any fancy features like canopies, storage baskets, reclining seats, and so on. Another problem: most umbrella strollers have hammock-style seats with little head support, so they won't work well for babies under six months of age.

◆ **Lightweight Strollers.** These strollers are our top recommendation: they're basically souped-up umbrella strollers with many convenience features.

WHAT'S COOL: Most offer easy set-up and fold-down; some even fold up similar to umbrella strollers. Many models have great features (canopies, storage baskets, high-quality wheels) at amazingly light weights (as little as eight lbs.). Graco and Maclaren probably make the most popular lightweight strollers.

WHAT'S NOT: Can be expensive—most high-quality brands run $150 to $300. The smaller wheels on lightweight strollers make maneuvering in the mall or stores easy . . . but those same wheels don't perform well on uneven surfaces or on gravel trails. Skimpy baskets are another trade-off.

◆ **Full-size Strollers.** Full-size strollers used to be called carriages or prams. Sort of like a bed on wheels—the seat lies flat and the leg rest pulls up to form a bassinet-like feature. Clearly, this feature focuses on newborns . . . but these strollers can then be configured for older babies with a seat that sits upright.

WHAT'S COOL: Full recline is great for newborns—they spend most of their time sleeping. Most combo carriage/strollers have lots of high-end features like plush seats, quilted canopies and other accessories to keep the weather out. The best carriage strollers and prams have a dreamy ride, with amazing suspensions and big wheels.

WHAT'S NOT: Hefty weight (not easy to transport or set up) and hefty price tags. Another negative: most Euro-style "prams" have fixed front wheels, which make maneuvering difficult on quick trips. Some carriage/stroller models can top $500, although entry-level carriage strollers start at $200. These strollers once dominated the market but have lost favor as more parents opt for "travel systems" that combine an infant seat and stroller (see below).

strollers

◆ ***Multi-function Strollers.*** These
strollers morph from infant carriages to toddler strollers, with either an infant car seat
adapter or bassinet accessory. With fully
reclining seats, these strollers can be used
from birth. Some multi-functions even have
second seat options, morphing from a sin-
gle to a double stroller. Examples include the UPPAbaby Vista and
the Britax B-Ready (pictured).

WHAT'S COOL: In a word, flexibility—parents who buy these
strollers love the ability to morph them into several different uses.

◆ ***Jogging (or Sport) Strollers.*** These
strollers feature three big bicycle-tire wheels
and lightweight frames—perfect for jogging or
walking on rough roads. The front wheel is
fixed to maximize glide.

WHAT'S COOL: How many other strollers can
do 15 mph on a jogging trail? Some have plush features like
padded seats and canopies—and the best fold up quickly for easy
storage in the trunk. This category was hip a few years ago, but is
now in decline: more popular are the all-terrain strollers (see below).

WHAT'S NOT: They can be darn expensive, topping $300.
Jogging strollers are a single-purpose item—thanks to their sheer
bulk and a lack of steering (joggers usually have fixed front wheels),
you can't use one in a mall or other location. On the plus side, the
flood of new models is helping lower prices. New, low-end jogging strollers run $100 to $150. The trade-offs to the new bargain
price models: heavier steel frames and a lack of features.

◆ ***All-terrain Strollers.*** The baby equivalent of
sport-utility vehicles, these strollers are pitched to
parents who want to go on hikes or other outdoor
adventures. All-terrain strollers are similar to joggers
with one big difference—the front wheel swivels.

WHAT'S COOL: Big air-filled tires and high clear-
ances work better on gravel trails/roads than standard strollers.
These strollers are great for neighborhoods with broken or rough
sidewalks. All-terrain strollers have many convenience features (baskets, canopies, etc.) as well as one key advantage over jogging
strollers: most all-terrains have swivel front wheels. That makes them
easy to maneuver, whether on a trail or at the mall. Pictured above
is the Phil & Ted's stroller.

WHAT'S NOT: All-terrain strollers are wider and heavier than other
strollers, which make them less useful in a mall or store with tight

aisles. And air-filled tires are great for trails . . . but a pain in the neck if you get a flat. If you really want to run with a stroller, all-terrains with a swivel front wheel are not the best choice (a jogger with a fixed front wheel is better). And let's not forget the cost—most all terrains are pricey, some topping $400.

◆ **Travel Systems.** It's the current rage among stroller makers—models that combine infant car seats and strollers. Century (now part of Graco) kicked off this craze way back in 1994 with its "4-in-1" model that featured four uses (infant carrier, infant

car seat, carriage and toddler stroller). Since then, just about every major stroller maker has jumped into the travel system market. Pictured here is the Graco Quattro travel system.

WHAT'S COOL: Great convenience—you can take the infant car seat out of the car and then snap it into the stroller frame. Voila! Instant baby carriage, complete with canopy and basket. Later, you can use the stroller as, well, just a stroller.

WHAT'S NOT: The strollers are often junk—especially those by mass market makers Cosco and Evenflo. Quality problems plague this category, as does something we call "feature bloat." Popular travel systems from Graco, for example, are so loaded with features that they tip the scales at nearly 30 lbs.! The result: many parents abandon their travel system strollers for lighter weight models after baby outgrows his infant seat. And considering these puppies can cost $150 to $250 (some even more), that's a big investment for such limited use. On the up side, better strollers brands such as Maclaren, Perego and Chicco have also jumped into the travel system market, offering alternatives to the heavyweight mass market strollers.

Safe & Sound

Next to defective car seats, the most dangerous juvenile product on the market today is the stroller. That's according to the U.S. Consumer Product Safety Commission, which estimates that over 11,000 injuries a year occur from improper use or defects. The problems? Babies can slide out of the stroller (falling to the ground) and small parts can be a choking hazard. Seat belts have broken in some models, while other babies are injured when a stroller's brakes fail on a slope. Serious mishaps with strollers have involved entanglements and entrapments (where an unrestrained baby slides down and gets caught in a leg opening) and lacerations when parents fold up the stroller and kids get their hands caught. Here are some safety tips:

strollers

1 **NEVER HANG BAGS FROM THE STROLLER HANDLE**—it's a tipping hazard.

2 **DON'T LEAVE YOUR BABY ASLEEP UNATTENDED IN A STROLLER.** Many injuries happen when infants who are lying down in a stroller roll or creep and then manage to get their head stuck in the stroller's leg openings. Be safe: take a sleeping baby out of a stroller and move them to a crib or bassinet.

3 **THE BRAKES SHOULDN'T BE TRUSTED.** The best stroller models have brakes on two wheels; cheaper ones just have one wheel that brakes. Even with the best brakes, don't leave the stroller unattended on an incline.

4 **FOLLOW THE WEIGHT LIMITS.** Most strollers shouldn't be used by children over 35 lbs.

5 **JOGGING STROLLERS ARE BEST FOR BABIES OVER ONE YEAR OF AGE.** Yes, some stroller makers tout their joggers for babies as young as six weeks (or six months) of age. But after consulting with pediatric experts, we suggest waiting until one year of age to run with baby in a stroller. Why? The neck muscles of infants under a year of age can't take the shocks of jogging or walking on rough paths (or going over curbs). Ask your pediatrician if you need more advice on when it is safe to use a jogger.

6 **FOLD AND UNFOLD YOUR STROLLER WHEN BABY IS NOT NEAR.** Simply because they are foldable, strollers have various pinch points where baby's fingers may get caught. While some stroller makers have included protective shields over those points, it's best to open and close strollers when your baby is not around—leave them buckled in their car seat or keep them a distance away while you set up or put away your stroller.

 Smart Shopper Tips

Smart Shopper Tip #1
Give it a Test Drive

"My friend was thinking of buying a stroller online, sight unseen. Should you really buy a stroller without trying it first?"

It's best to try before you buy. Most stores have at least one stroller set up as a floor model. Give it a whirl, practice folding it up, and check the steering. One smart tip: put some weight in the stroller seat (borrow a friend's toddler or use a backpack full of books that weighs about 15 lbs.). The steering and maneuverability will feel different if the stroller is weighted—obviously, that's a more real world test-drive.

Once you've tried it out, shop for price through 'net or mail order sources. Ask retailers if they will meet or beat prices quoted to you online (many quietly do so). What if you live in Kansas and the nearest dealer for a stroller you want is in, say, Texas? Then you may have no choice but to buy sight unseen—but just make sure the web site has a good return policy. Another tip: use message boards like those on our web site (BabyBargains.com) to quiz other parents about stroller models.

If you buy a stroller from a store, we strongly recommend opening the box and making sure everything is in there BEFORE you leave the store!

Smart Shopper Tip #2
What Features Really Matter?

"Let's cut through the clutter here. Do I really need a stroller that has electronic stability assist and anti-lock brakes? What features are really important?"

Walk into any baby store and you'll encounter a blizzard of strollers. Do you want a stroller with a full recline? Boot and retractable canopy? What the heck is a boot, anyway? Here's a look at the features in the stroller market today:

Features for baby:
◆ **Reclining seat.** Since babies less than six months of age sleep most of the time and can't hold their heads up, strollers that have reclining seats are a plus. Yet, the *extent* of a stroller's seat recline varies by model. Some have full reclines, a few recline part of the way (120 degrees) and some don't recline at all. FYI: just because a stroller has a "full recline" does NOT mean it reclines to 180 degrees. It may recline slightly less than that for safety reasons.

◆ **Front (or napper) bar.** As a safety precaution, many strollers have a front bar (also called a napper bar) that keeps baby secure (though you should always use the stroller's safety harness). Better strollers have a bar that's padded and removable. Why removable? Later, when your baby gets to toddler hood, you may need to remove the bar to make it easier for the older child to access the stroller. Some strollers have a kid snack tray, which serves much the same function as a napper bar.

◆ **Footrest.** Footrests can range from a simple strap extending between the two side bars of the stroller or as complex as a ratcheting adjustable footrest with leg support. FYI: If a stroller has a fully reclining seat, voluntary safety regulations require the stroller to have an adjustable footrest that can fold out to fully enclose the entire stroller seat—this keeps baby from sliding out.

◆ **Seat padding.** You'll find every possible padding option out there, from bare bones models with a single piece of fabric to strollers with deluxe-quilted padding made from fine fabrics hand woven by monks in Luxembourg. (Okay, just kidding—the monks

Guaranteed Frustration:
Baby gear warranties can leave you fuming

It's a fact of life: sometimes you buy a product that breaks only days after purchase. So, you pick up the phone and call the manufacturer and ask about their warranty. "Sure, we'll help," says the customer service rep. In no time, you have a replacement product and a happy parent.

Fast forward to real life. Most parents find warranties only guarantee frustration—especially with baby products like strollers and other travel gear. Numerous hassles confront parents who find they have a defective product, from unreturned emails to endless waits on hold waiting for a customer service rep.

Consider the process of actually registering an item. Filling out a warranty card often requires information that you can only find on the product box or carton. Some parents find this out the hard way . . . after they've hauled all the boxes off to the trash. Even worse: some baby product makers like Peg Perego actually request a copy of the sales receipt for their warranty form. Hello? What about gifts?

Then, let's say something goes wrong. Your new stroller breaks a wheel. That brand new baby monitor goes on the fritz after one week. If it is a gift or you lost the receipt, the store you bought it from may say "tough luck"—call the manufacturer. With many warranties, you have to return the defective item to the manufacturer at your expense. And then you wait a few more weeks while they decide to fix or replace the item. Typically you have to pay for return shipping—and that can be expensive for a bulky item like a stroller. And then you must do without the product for weeks while they fix it.

Dealing with the customer service departments at some baby product makers can add insult to injury. It seems like some companies can count their customer service staff on one hand—or one finger, in some cases. The result: long waits on hold. Or it takes days to get responses to emails. The U.S. offices of foreign baby product companies seem to be the worst at customer service staffing, while mass-market companies actually live in Switzerland). For seating, some strollers have card-board platforms (these can be uncomfortable for long rides) and other models have fabric that isn't removable or machine washable (see below for more on this).

◆ **Shock absorbers or suspension systems.** Yes, a few strollers do have wheels equipped with shock absorbers or suspension springs for a smoother ride. This is a nice feature if you live in a neighbor-hood with uneven or rough sidewalks.

such as Graco and Evenflo have better customer service.

And customer service can go from good to bad in the blink of an eye. Recalls can cause a huge surge in customer service requests—and many companies fail to adequately staff their customer service depart-ments during such events. Hence, even good companies can fall flat on their face during such episodes.

The bottom line: it's no wonder that when something goes wrong, consumers just consider trashing the product and buying a new one. And let's be realistic: paying $30 in shipping to send back a broken $50 stroller doesn't make much sense. Here's our advice:

Keep your receipts. You don't have to get fancy a shoebox will do. That way you can prove you bought that defective product. If the item was a gift, keep the product manual and serial number. Ask for gift receipts when possible.

◆ **If something goes wrong, email/call the manufacturer.** We're always surprised by how many consumers don't contact the manufac-turer FIRST when a problem arises. You might be surprised at how responsive some companies are at fixing an issue.

◆ **If the problem is a safety defect,** immediately stop using the prod-uct and file a complaint with the Consumer Product Safety Commission (cpsc.gov). Also contact the company.

◆ **Attack the problem multiple ways.** Don't just call; also send an email and perhaps a written letter. Be reasonable: allow the company one to two business days to reply to a phone call or email.

◆ **Let other parents know about your experiences.** The best way to fix lousy customer service? Shame companies into doing it better. Post your experiences to the message boards on our site (BabyBargains.com) and other parenting sites. Trust us, companies are sensitive to such criticism.

strollers

◆ **Wheels.** In reality, how smooth a stroller rides is more related to the type of wheels. The general rule: the more the better. Strollers with double wheels on each leg ride smoother than single wheels. Most strollers have plastic wheels. In recent years, some stroller makers have rolled out models with "pneumatic" or inflated wheels. These offer a smoother ride—but they are heavier and can go flat.

◆ **Weather protection.** Yes, you can buy a stroller that's outfitted for battle with a winter in New England, for example. The options include retractable hoods/canopies and "boots" (which protect a child's feet) to block out wind, rain or cold. Fabrics play a role here too—some strollers feature quilted hoods to keep baby warm and others claim they are water repellent. While a boot is an option some may not need, hoods/canopies are rather important, even if just to keep the sun out of baby's eyes. Some strollers only have a canopy (or "sunshade") that partially covers baby, while other models have a full hood that can completely cover the stroller. Look for canopies that have lots of adjustments (to block a setting sun) and have "peak-a-boo" windows that let you see baby even when closed.

What if the stroller you've fallen in love with only has a skimpy canopy? Or lacks a rain cover? Good news: after-market accessories can fill the gap (see box below).

Features for parents:

◆ **Storage baskets.** Many strollers have deep, under-seat baskets for storage of coats, purses, bags, etc. Yet, the amount of storage can vary sharply from model to model. Inexpensive umbrella strollers may have no basket at all, while other models have tiny baskets. Mass-market strollers (Graco, etc.) typically have the most storage; other stroller makers have been playing catch-up in the basket game. One tip: it's not just the *size* of the storage basket but the *access* to it that counts. Some strollers have big baskets but are practically inaccessible when the seat is reclined. A support bar blocks access to some baskets. Tip: when stroller shopping, recline the seat and see if you can access the basket.

◆ **Removable seat cushion for washing.** Let's be honest: strollers can get icky in a jiffy. Crushed-in cookies, spilt juice and the usual grime can make a stroller a mobile dirt-fest. Some strollers have removable seat cushions that are machine washable—other models let you remove *all* of the fabric for a washing. Watch out for those models with non-removable fabric/seat cushions—while you can clean these strollers in one of those manual car washes (with a high-pressure nozzle), it's definitely a hassle, especially in the winter.

◆ **Lockable wheels.** Some strollers have front wheels that can be locked in a forward position—this enables you to more quickly push the stroller in a straight line (nice for exercising).

◆ *Wheel size.* You'll see just about every conceivable size wheel out there on strollers today. As you might guess, the smaller wheels are good for maneuverability in the mall, but larger wheels handle rough sidewalks (or gravel paths) much better.

◆ *Handle/Steering.* This is an important area to consider—most strollers have a single bar handle, which enables one-handed steering. Other strollers have two handles (example: Maclaren as well as Perego's Pliko line). Two handles require two hands to push, but enable a stroller to fold up compactly, like an umbrella. It's sort of a trade-off: steer-ability versus easier fold. There are other handle issues to consider as well. A handful of strollers feature a "reversible" handle. Why would you want that? Initially, you can push the stroller while the baby faces you (better for small infants). Later, you can reverse the handle so an older child can look out while being pushed from behind. (Note: models with reversible handles seem increasingly rare in recent years; instead some strollers now have reversible *seats*. We'll note which have this feature later).

Another important factor: consider the handle *height*. Some handles have adjustable heights to better accommodate taller parents. However, just because a stroller touts this feature doesn't mean it adjusts to accommodate a seven-foot tall parent (at most, you get an extra inch or two of height). Later in this chapter, we'll mention which have height adjustable handles as we review stroller brands. Finally, a few stroller makers offer "one-touch fold" handles. Hit a

Handy stroller accessories

What if your stroller doesn't have a rain cover? One option is the **Protect a Bub Universal Rain Cover**, which runs $25.

You're in love with a fancy stroller. . . except for that skimpy canopy. What's the solution? Try the **RayShade** ($15) by Summer. This shade extends your stroller canopy and is excellent for blocking low-angle sun (take note, Californians). It also blocks ultraviolet rays and has a hidden bottle pocket. Also consider: the **SnoozeShade** ($35; pictured) which is a breathable shade that covers the entire stroller.

button on the stroller and it can be folded up with one motion.

◆ *Compact fold.* We call it the trunk factor—when a stroller is folded, will it fit in your trunk? Some strollers fold compactly and can fit in a narrow trunk. Other strollers are still quite bulky when folded—think about your trunk space before buying. Unfortunately, we are not aware of any web site that lists the size/footprint of strollers when folded. You are on your own to size up models when folded in a store, compared to your trunk (hint: take trunk measurements before you go stroller shopping). Not only should you consider how compactly a stroller folds, but also how it folds in general. The best strollers fold with just one or two quick motions; others require you to hit 17 levers and latches. The latest stroller fold fad: strollers that fold standing UP instead of down. Why is this better? Because strollers that fold down to the ground can get dirty/scratched in a parking lot.

◆ *Durability.* Should you go for a lower-price stroller or a premium brand? Let's be honest: the lower-priced strollers (say, under $100) have nowhere near the durability of the models that cost $200 to $400. Levers that break, reclining seats that stop reclining and other glitches can make you despise a cheap stroller mighty quick. Yet, some parents don't need a stroller that will make it through the next world war. If all you do is a couple of quick trips to the mall every week or so, then a less expensive stroller will probably be fine. However, if you plan to use the stroller for more than one child, live in an urban environment with rough sidewalks, or plan extensive outdoor adventures with baby, then invest in a better stroller. Later in this chapter, we'll go over specific models and give you brand recommendations for certain lifestyles.

◆ *Overall weight.* Yes, it's a dilemma: the more feature-laden the stroller, the more it weighs. And strollers are often priced via the Bikini Principle: the less it weighs, the more it costs. Yet it doesn't take lugging a 30-pound stroller in and out of a car trunk more than a few times to justify the expense of a lighter-weight design. Carefully consider a stroller's weight before purchase. Some parents end up with two strollers—a lightweight/umbrella-type stroller for quick trips (or air travel) and then a more feature-intensive model for extensive outdoor outings.

One factor to consider with weight: steel vs. aluminum frames. Steel is heavier than aluminum, but some parents prefer steel because it gives the stroller a stiffer feel. Along the same lines, sometimes we get complaints from parents who own aluminum strollers because they feel the stroller is too "wobbly"—while it's lightweight, one of aluminum's disadvantages is its flexibility. One tip for dealing with a wobbly stroller: lock the front wheels so you can push the stroller in a straight line. That helps to smooth the ride.

Smart Shopper Tip #3
The Cadillac Escalade or Ford Focus Dilemma
"This is nuts! I see cheap umbrella strollers that sell for $30 on one hand and then fancy designer brands for $900 on the other. Do I really need to spend a fortune on a stroller?"

Whether you drive a Cadillac Escalade or a Ford Focus, you'll still get to your destination. And that fact pretty much applies to strollers too—most function well enough to get you and baby from point A to point B, no matter what the price.

So, should you buy the cheapest stroller you can find? Well, no. There *is* a significant difference in quality between a cheap $30 umbrella stroller and a name brand that costs $150, $250 or more. Unless you want the endless headaches of a cheap stroller (wheels that break, parts that fall off), it's important to invest in a stroller that's durable.

The real question is: do you need a fancy stroller loaded with features or will a simple model do? To answer that, you need to consider *how* you will use the stroller. Do you live in the suburbs and just need the stroller once a week for a quick spin at the mall? Or do you live in an big city where a stroller is your primary vehicle, taking all the abuse that a big city can dish out? Climate plays another factor—in the Northeast, strollers have to be winterized to handle the cold and snow. Meanwhile, in Southern California, full canopies are helpful for shading baby's eyes from late afternoon sunshine.

Figuring out how different stroller options fit your lifestyle/climate is the key to stroller happiness. Later in this chapter, we'll recommend several specific strollers for certain lifestyles and climates.

One final note: name-brand strollers with cachet actually have resale value. You can sell that pricey stroller on eBay, at a second-hand store, or via Craigslist and recoup some of your investment. We'll note which brands have the best and worst resale values later in this chapter.

Smart Shopper Tip #4
Too tall for their own good
"I love our stroller, but my husband hates it. He's six feet tall and has to stoop over to push it. Even worse, when he walks, he hits the back of the stroller with his feet."

Strollers are made for *women* of average height. What's that? About 5'6". If you (or your spouse) are taller than that, you'll find certain stroller models will be a pain to use.

This is probably one of the biggest complaints we get from parents about strollers. Unfortunately, just a few stroller models have height-adjustable handles that let a six-foot tall person comfortably push a stroller without stooping over or hitting the back of the stroller with his or her feet. One smart shopping tip: if you have a tall spouse, make sure you take him or her stroller shopping with you. Checking out handle heights in person is the only way to avoid this problem.

The best stroller brands for taller parents: Maclaren and Peg Perego (particularly, the Pliko, which has height adjustable handles). The worst? Combi, a Japanese brand that has low-handle heights.

Smart Shopper Tip #5
The Myth of the Magic Bullet Stroller

"I'd like to buy just one stroller—a model that works with an infant car seat and then converts to full-featured pram and then finally a jogger for kids up to age four. And I want it to weigh less than ten lbs.. And sell for just under $50. What model do you suggest?"

Boy, that sounds like our email some days! We hear from parents all the time looking for that one model that will do it all. We call it the Myth of the Magic Bullet Stroller—an affordable product that morphs into seven different uses for children from birth to college. Sorry, we haven't found one yet.

The reality: most parents own more than one stroller. A typical set-up: one stroller (or a stroller frame) that holds an infant car seat and then a lightweight stroller that folds compactly for the mall/travel. Of course, we hear from parents who own four, five or six strollers, including specialty models like joggers, tandem units for two kids and more. First-time parents wonder if these folks have lost their minds, investing the equivalent of the gross national product of Aruba on baby transportation. Alas, most parents realize that as their baby grows and their needs change, so must their stroller.

Far be it for us to suggest you buy multiple strollers, but at the same time, it is hard to recommend just one model that works for everyone. That's why the recommendations later in this chapter are organized by lifestyle and use.

✂ Money-Saving Tips

1 **STOP! DON'T BUY THAT GIANT STROLLER.** Here's a classic first-time parent mistake: buying an expensive, giant travel system stroller (a.k.a, the Baby Bus), thinking you need all those whiz-bang features. But the huge bulk and weight of those strollers will have you cursing the thing before your baby hits six months. A better bet: get a basic stroller frame for $60 (more details on these later), strap in an infant seat and voila! You have transport for an infant for at least six months. Trust us, after you've hung out with your baby for a few months, you'll have a much better idea what your stroller needs are. As your baby nears the limits on an infant car seat, THEN you buy a regular stroller.

2 **WHY NOT A BASIC UMBRELLA STROLLER?** If you only plan to use a stroller on infrequent trips to the mall, then a plain umbrella stroller for $40 to $50 will suffice. One caveat: most plain umbrella strollers do NOT recline—you will not be able to use it until your baby is able to hold up his head (around six months). And they may not have any storage.

3 **CONSIDER A CARRIER FOR NEWBORNS.** Yes, a simple baby carrier (sling, wrap, front carrier, etc.) can be a much more affordable alternative to expensive strollers. Check our new carrier chapter (Chapter 10) for reviews of different types of carriers.

4 **CHECK FOR SALES.** We're always amazed by the number of sales on strollers. We've seen frequent sales at the Burlington Coat Factory's Baby Depot, with good markdowns on even premium brand strollers. Coupons are also common. Babies R Us offers occasional coupons in newspaper circulars as well as to parents on their mailing list. Another reason strollers go on sale: the manufacturers are constantly coming out with new models and have to clear out the old. Which leads us to the next tip.

5 **LOOK FOR LAST YEAR'S MODELS.** Every year, manufacturers roll out new models. In some cases, they add features; other times, they just change the fabric. What do they do with last year's stock? They discontinue it—and then it's sale time. You'll see these models on sale for as much as 50% off in stores and on the web. And it's not like stroller fabric fashion varies much from year to year—is there really much difference between "navy pin dot" and "navy with a raspberry diamond"? We say go for last year's fabric and save a bundle. See the Email from the Real World nearby for a mom's story on her last year model deal.

6 **SCOPE OUT FACTORY SECONDS.** Believe it or not, some stroller manufacturers sell "factory seconds" at good discounts—these "cosmetically imperfect" models might have a few blemishes, but are otherwise fine. An example: one reader told us Peg Perego occasionally has factory sales from their Ft. Wayne, Indiana headquarters. If you live nearby, call (800) 671-1701 for the latest schedule.

7 **DON'T FALL VICTIM TO STROLLER OVERKILL.** Seriously evaluate how you'll use the stroller and don't over buy. If a Toyota

Camry will do, why buy a Lexus? You don't really need an all-terrain stroller or full-feature pram for mall trips. Flashy strollers can be status symbols for some parents—try to avoid "stroller envy!"

8 **SELL YOUR STROLLER TO RECOUP YOUR INVESTMENT.** When you're done with the stroller, consign it at a second-hand store or sell it on Craigslist. You'd be surprised how much it can fetch. The best brands for resale are, not surprisingly, the better names we recommend in this chapter. Of course, the strollers with the best resale value are those that are in excellent condition. If you keep an expensive jogging stroller in your garage or on your deck, consider a cover. BuggyBonnets.com sells a $85 cover for single strollers, $110 for a double, made from heavy duty, water-resistant fabric.

9 **WAREHOUSE CLUB DEALS.** Yes, Sam's and Costco periodically sell strollers, including joggers. At one point before going to press, Costco was selling Schwinn jogging strollers from their web site (Costco.com) at 45% under retail. Of course, these deals come and go—and like anything you see at the warehouse clubs, you have to snap it up quickly or it will be gone.

10 **EBAY/CRAIGSLIST**. It's highly addictive and for good reason—these sites are more than just folks trying to unload a junky stroller they bought at K-Mart. Increasingly, baby gear retailers are using eBay to discreetly clear out overstock. Better to unload online the stuff that isn't moving than risk the wrath of local customers who bought the model for full price last week. An example: a reader scored a brand new Peg Perego for HALF the stroller's retail price through an eBay auction. Other readers regularly report

E-MAIL FROM THE REAL WORLD
Last year's fashion, 50% off

A reader emailed her tip on how she saved over $100 on a stroller:

"When looking for strollers you can often get last year's version for a big discount. I purchased a previous year Maclaren model online for $190. That compares to the $300 price tag for the current year model from Babies R Us. As far as my research could tell, the models are identical except for the color pattern. A quick web search can turn up a number of sources that are selling last year's strollers; colors are limited (dmartstores.com had the widest selection) but it is a great way to save over $100 for a very nice stroller."

saving $100 to $200 through eBay. Hint: many strollers sold online are last year's model or fashion. Be sure to confirm what you are buying (is it in the original box? No damage? Which model year?) before bidding. And don't forget Craigslist either. Yes, this site has both junk and jewels. Be patient and search carefully to find worthwhile stroller buys.

Resale Value: Best & Worst Brands

Which stroller brands have the best resale value? To find the answer, we poured over 4000 Craigslist ads for every major city in the U.S. and calculated resale value for both brands and individual models. We excluded ads for brand new, still in the box strollers (some retailers use Craigslist to unload unsold inventory). We focused on strollers that were in good or excellent condition with minimal wear and tear.

Best Resale (Brand). The top three brands for resale are Britax (65.26%), Baby Jogger (63.98%) and Bugaboo (63.90%). Hence, the average Britax stroller sells for 65.26% of its original retail price on Craigslist. All of these three brands have popular models that command a premium on the resale market.

Best Resale (Model). Among the top models for resale are the Baby Jogger Summit (a jogging stroller with an astounding 87.5% resale value) and Baby Jogger's City Select with second seat (79.55%). The Baby Jogger City Mini scores third at 75%. In general, we found double strollers scored at the top of the resale list—perhaps because they are somewhat rare and demand is high. Stores also stock fewer double strollers, making Craigslist a popular outlet.

Worst Resale (Brand). The stroller brands with the worst resale value are Graco (41.90%), Maclaren (41.43%), and Inglesina (33.31%). Graco is a mass-market brand whose strollers simply don't fetch much on a resale market. Maclaren has had its struggles with bankruptcy and safety recalls. Inglesina is a bit of surprise here—we're not sure what is driving this low resale, but folks appear to be willing to part with these models for very little cash.

Worst Resale (Model). Inglesina's Zippy (20.69%) and Trip (26.32%) scored at the bottom of our survey—on the plus side, they are great values to pick up second hand (the Zippy sold fold for just $74.50 on Craigslist, compared with a $360 retail value). The Peg Perego Pliko P3 (30%), Combi Cosmo (30.77%) and Maclaren Quest (32.22%) also came in with very low resale values.

Individual brands' resale value are noted in the next section, listed as *Baby Bargains Resale Rank*. Note: some brands don't have a resale ranking because we couldn't find enough of their strollers for sale on the secondary market to make a judgment. Index ratings are excellent, good, fair and poor. Excellent resale brands were in the top 25% of resale values; poor brands were in the bottom 25% of resale values.

Of course, you can look at these resale rankings two ways: as a buyer of a brand new stroller, you'll get the most resale value for brands that have a good or excellent rating. If you are looking for a used stroller, brands with a poor or fair rating are selling at a steep discount from their resale price—and that might make for some great bargains!

The Name Game: Reviews of Selected Manufacturers

So, how do we rate and review strollers? First, we do hands-on inspections in stores and at trade shows. That involves giving the stroller a test spin, checking the fold and more. Next, we listen to you, the reader. The stroller message board on our web site is one of the most popular forums, brimming with over 1000 posts a month. As always, parent feedback is our secret sauce.

One key point to remember: the ratings in this section apply to the ENTIRE line of a company's strollers. No, we don't assign ratings to individual strollers, but we will comment on what we think are a company's best models. Following this section, we will give you several "lifestyle recommendations"—specific models of strollers to fit different parent lifestyles.

The Ratings

A **EXCELLENT**—*our top pick!*
B **GOOD**— *above average quality, prices, and creativity.*
C **FAIR**—*could stand some improvement.*
D **POOR**—*yuck! could stand some major improvement.*

4moms (Origami) 4moms' Origami stroller's claim to fame is its power-folding feature—yes, the stroller actually folds by itself. Press a button on the handle and the stroller does the rest.

So this stroller is a conversation piece. But is it worth the $850 price tag? Weighing in at 32 lbs., it's too bad the folded stroller doesn't also levitate off the ground and into your trunk for that price.

The Origami comes with a few other bling-y features, including an LCD screen that includes a thermometer, speedometer, trip and lifetime odometers. Optional accessories include a cell phone charger ($40) which charges your phone when you push the stroller, Graco car seat adapter ($60), and "color kit" that lets you change the color of your stroller's fabric pad for $100.

Early parent feedback on the Origami has been mostly positive. The stroller has a smooth glide and can handle even gravel surfaces. And it is hard to discount the "wow" factor with this stroller—you'll be asked to demonstrate the automatic fold feature for friends, family and complete strangers.

The downsides: the lack of a reclining seat makes this stroller only appropriate for babies that can sit up on their own (6 months +). That's because the seat only has a slight recline. To use the stroller with a newborn, you have to buy the aforementioned Graco infant car seat adapter (and have a Graco car seat, of course). That seems like a glaring omission for an $850 stroller. Most of the Origami's competitors (UPPAbaby Vista, etc) include infant seating options . . . at a price $200 less than the Origami.

The other major flaw: the Origami's weight. Hauling this stroller in and out of a trunk qualifies you for a spot on the next U.S. Olympic weight lifting team. We realize the motor, batteries and gizmos to make the Origami do-it-itself-folding mojo require this added weight, but a stroller that tips the scales at 32 lbs. may be a no go for some moms. On the plus side, once folded, the Origami takes up less space than other full-size strollers in a vehicle trunk, thanks to its relatively smallish footprint. And the Origami's motor is self-charging, so you don't have to plug in this stroller to have it recharge the fold-up motor.

From a practical point of view, the stroller's storage basket is decent sized; there are also other storage pockets on the side of the seat. But there is no snack tray or bumper bar for the child.

New in late 2014, 4Moms will address the weight issue with the release of the Origami mini, a 16 lb. umbrella stroller which is the Mini Me of its flagship model. Same power folding feature, day-time running lights, etc. Price: $450.

So it is a mixed review for the Origami—kudos to 4moms for their innovation. If you're the kind of person that likes to draw attention at the park, then this stroller is for you. For everyone else, the Origami's weight and high price tag make it a niche stroller at best.

Finally, we've also been troubled to see some online reports of quality glitches—wheels that get stuck, a dead battery that prevents the stroller from opening, etc. For $850, we'd expect more perfection. As a result, we are ticking the grade down for the Origami. **_Rating: B-_**

Babyhome babyhome.es Spanish stroller maker Babyhome recently debuted their first model in the US, the Emotion. This lightweight ($250 to $350, 16.9 lbs.) stroller features a curved frame, rain cover, mosquito net, fully reclining seat, and maintenance kit and is car seat adaptable (Chicco, Graco, Maxi Cosi).

The stroller's unique feature: polyurethane wheels (with ball bearing suspension) give a smooth ride. Made in China, the Emotion comes in six solid color fashions.

Parent feedback on the Emotion is mostly positive—fans love the smooth glide and light weight. Critics knock the low to the ground profile, lack of cup holder and skimpy hood coverage. We like that the Emotion includes a rain cover and mosquito net.

Optional accessories include a cup holder, front bumper bar, rotating snack tray and canopy extender. That might make the stroller more user friendly—but we'd argue if you're paying $300 for a stroller, those should be standard. ***Rating: B***

Baby Jogger babyjogger.com Baby Jogger literally invented the jogging stroller category 30 years ago with the first stroller with bicycle tires designed for runners. Since then, the company has been through numerous ups and downs . . . including a bankruptcy back

Stroller Shopping Secret: Rear Wheel Width

Weight may be the most important factor to urban parents looking for a new stroller, but we suggest looking at one additional criteria: rear wheel width. Many new strollers have a wide spread between the rear wheels. The problem? Many urban parents have to negotiate tight spaces (grocery store aisles, subways, etc). A stroller with a wide wheelbase may not squeeze through small doorways and into tight elevators. Here is a look at the rear wheel widths for some popular urban strollers.

STROLLER	REAR WHEEL WIDTH
Bugaboo Bee	20.0
Stokke Xplory	22.0
Bugaboo Cameleon	23.0
Peg Perego Skate	23.75
Orbit	24.0
UPPAbaby Vista	25.0
Quinny Buzz	25.5

Our advice: go for the narrowest wheelbase you can find—23" and under is probably best (some doors are a narrow 24" wide).

in 2003 that led to new ownership. The company has since refocused on all-terrain strollers with swivel front wheels. Their new models have met with much success, despite the fact the company has drifted away from its "jogger" name.

The models. Baby Jogger has three main stroller models: the City Series, Summit and F.I.T.

The secret sauce to the City Series is the company's Quick-Fold technology: pull up on one strap and zip! The stroller collapses and folds. No complicated buttons or latches. No multi-step process. The Quick-Fold has super-sized Baby Jogger's sales of the City series, which boasts five models: the Mini, Mini GT, Elite, Versa and Select.

The tri-wheel City Mini (single $250, 17.1 lbs.; double $450, 26.6 lbs.) is Baby Jogger's best-selling stroller, featuring a full recline and large canopy. In the past year, the City Mini got a few tweaks: a slightly larger seat, an easier to access storage basket and an auto lock feature when the stroller is folded.

If you aren't sold on the tri-wheel set-up, there is a four-wheel version of the City Mini (dubbed the City Mini 4-Wheel) for $260. It is identical to the three wheel version, just one more wheel.

To appeal more to off-road users, the City Mini GT ($350, 21.5 lbs.) adds bigger, no-flat tires, as well as an adjustable handle bar with brake, a redesigned seat/canopy that provides more headroom, and an easier to access storage basket.

At the top end, the City Elite (single $400, 31.3 lbs.; double $650, 42 lbs.) features 12" air-filled wide tread tires and a parent console. While those air-filled tires make the Elite more of an all-terrain stroller, the trade off is added weight.

FYI: One major difference between the City models is weight capacity. The City Elite works to 75 lbs. single, 100 double. The City Mini's limits are 50/100 lbs.

Baby Jogger is also a player in the multi-function stroller market with its City Select, which is sort of like the Swiss Army Knife of strollers. It can be configured 16 ways, with an optional second seat. With a telescoping handle and foam tires, the Select (28.1 lbs.) costs $500 (plus $160 for the second seat). A bassinet accessory is $90. In the past year, Baby Jogger has made only small changes to the Select, upping the amount of seat padding yet keeping the price the same.

If you can't decide between the City Mini and the Select, there is a third option: the City Versa (23.7 lbs). This hybrid is a cross between those two models: the seat on the Versa reverses (like the Select), but the stroller doesn't expand to a double. You do get a full canopy and recline, an adjustable leg rest, all wheel suspension, hand brake and a flat fold. Price: $450.

New for 2014, Baby Jogger is debuting the Vue ($200)—it's claim to fame is a reversible seat on an umbrella stroller frame. The Vue also has a large canopy, adjustable leg rest, full seat recline (in either mode) and an optional bassinet. To be released in March 2014, the Vue prototype we viewed weighed in at 19.5 lbs, which stretches the umbrella stroller claim a bit. And the Vue will not have the Baby Jogger Quick Fold—instead you hit a latch on the side and fold the stroller over to the ground. But the reversible seat is impressive.

Trivia note: the Baby Jogger Vue is actually a stroller from Spain—the Njoy Bubble. You can see videos of how it works at *njoybaby.com*. Baby Jogger acquired Njoy in order to get access to their reversible umbrella stroller design patents.

If you want to actually jog with a Baby Jogger, the company offers the F.I.T. ($300, 25.4 lbs.), with a fixed front wheel, deep seat recline and aluminum frame.

For more serious all-terrain use, the Summit X3 comes in single ($430, 27.1 lbs.) and double ($650, 38.8 lbs.) versions. The Summit is Baby Jogger's top-of-the-line model, with 16" rear and 12" front air-filled tires, swivel front wheel that locks, suspension, and the same quick-fold technology you see on the City Series. The X3's handlebar has a front wheel lock feature, which is nice.

Finally, Baby Jogger has a hybrid jogging stroller/bike trailer model, the POD ($500). The POD is a chassis that allows you to add a stroller kit ($90; two small wheels up front), jogger kit ($65 for a 16" air-filled front wheel) or a bike trailer adapter ($45). No tools are needed for the conversion. At 30" wide, the POD can fit through most standard doors yet can accommodate up to two kids and features the same quick-fold technology found in Baby Jogger's strollers.

One final note: Baby Jogger sells a car seat adapter that works with most infant car seats, including Graco and Peg Perego.

Our view. Baby Jogger has been on a roll in recent years—innovative features (that Quick Fold technology is the star here), excellent quality and overall good pricing has been a recipe for success. You can see the brand's popularity here in their strong resale prices, among the highest in the category. *Baby Bargains Resale Rank: Excellent.* ***Rating: A***

Baby Trend babytrend.com Baby Trend's biggest selling stroller isn't really a stroller at all—it's a stroller frame . Here's an overview of the line:

The models. The Snap N Go is Baby Trend's claim to fame—basically, it's a stroller frame that lets you snap in most major-brand infant car seats. Presto! Instant travel system at a fraction of the price. The basic Snap & Go is $70 (less online); a double version that holds two car seats is $100. Be aware that while most infant car seats snap into the Snap & Go, others merely rest on the top bar. In either case, Baby Trend recommends using the supplied safety belt to

Different Versions Spark Confusion

Here's a common question we get at the home office: readers go into a chain store like Babies R Us and see a major brand stroller they like. Then, they visit a specialty store and see a similar model, but with some cosmetic differences . . . and a higher price tag. What's up with that? Big stroller makers like Graco have to serve two masters—chain stores and specialty retailers. Here's a little trick of the baby biz: stroller makers often take the same basic model of stroller and make various versions for different retailers. Hence, you'll see a Graco stroller with basic fabric in Babies R Us—and then the same model sold with fancier fabric in specialty stores. So is there any real difference besides the fabric color to justify the increase in price? Yes, sometimes the fabrics are upgraded (or there is more padding). But overall, you are basically seeing the same stroller. Our advice: if you can live with the basic version, go for it.

make sure the seat is secure.

The Snap N Go has been so successful it has spawned knock-offs from several competitors, namely Graco.

We should point out that, in many ways, the Snap N Go is now passé. Many stroller makers either come with car seat adapters or sell them as an affordable accessory—perhaps the Snap N Go is best for folks who are undecided on their stroller pick. In that case, the Snap N Go would be a good place holder.

Besides the stroller frame, Baby Trend also offers travel systems, double strollers and joggers. Baby Trend's travel systems combine their Flex-Loc or *Inertia* car seat with basic low-end strollers. Example: the Envy travel system is $150 (car seat and stroller). That's a low price, but the stroller (21 lbs.) is nothing fancy—steel frame, five-point harness and multi-position recline. You do get a decent canopy, one-hand fold and big basket.

In addition to a basic stroller, the company sells a smattering of other stroller models, including a Bugaboo knock off (Euro Buggy, $140) and the Stride Sport Stroller ($90-100).

Baby Trend is a big player in the all terrain/jogger stroller market—their flagship model is the Expedition. This steel frame jogger is loaded with features (reclining seat, five-point harness, parent tray with cup holders and ratcheting canopy) and is sold as a travel system ($200-$345) or separately ($120-$185).

New for 2014, Baby Trend is debuting the "Go Lite" collection of strollers. The flagship of this line is a riff on the BOB Revolution: the Baby Trend Quantum is a $350 aluminum frame tri-wheel stroller with removable snack tray, car seat adapter and extended canopy.

FYI: Baby Trend still sells the Sit N Stand stroller, a "pushcart" that combines a stroller with a jump seat for an older child, despite being sued by rival Joovy over a patent dispute. See Joovy's review for more info on this.

Baby Trend recently rolled out a redesigned Sit N Stand double that holds two car seats and has a napper bar that rotates away when not in use. It comes in both steel (36 lbs.) and aluminum (30 lbs.) versions that run $160 to $200. The redesigned single Sit N Stand will let you attach a car seat in front or back.

Our view. After writing about baby gear for 20+ years, there are still some companies that are mysteries to us. Baby Trend is Exhibit One.

The company rarely releases new stroller models, content to sell basically the same products year after year in chain stores like Babies R Us and Walmart. Despite quality that our readers charitably cite as average, the company seems to merrily chug along. Basically, these are strollers that are sold on price—if it breaks, that's your problem.

Baby Trend hit a speed bump in 2009 when it lost an $8.4 million verdict in a wrongful termination lawsuit. A jury found the company "acted with malice, oppression and fraud" in firing an employee who was a marketing executive. As a result of the verdict, Baby Trend filed for bankruptcy in 2010.

If that weren't enough, Baby Trend has also become embroiled in multiple patent lawsuits. Joovy has sued Baby Trend over the patent rights to the Sit N Stand stroller. And in 2010, Graco sued Baby Trend for allegedly violating the patents for its playpens. This was followed by a lawsuit in 2011 by Kids II that alleged Baby Trend infringed on its patents for a bouncer. For good measure, Baby Trend has also sued Dorel for alleged infringement on its patent for a car seat harness.

Even if you set aside Baby Trend's legal and financial woes, its products are becoming out of date. The unique niche once occupied by the Snap & Go has now been matched by competing stroller frames. And now many strollers are sold with car seat adapters, making the Snap & Go an unnecessary expense. As for Baby Trend's other strollers, there's not much to write home about. Bottom line: we'd avoid this brand until it resolves its problems. *Baby Bargains Resale Rank: Good.* **Rating: C-**

Bloom *bloombaby.com* The mini-boomlet of modern baby gear companies turned into a bust when the recession hit, taking with it a raft of companies that thought the market for $2000 cribs was ever expanding.

Yet a few companies somehow made it through these trying times. Among the survivors is Bloom, which is probably most famous for their Bloom high chair and Alma mini crib. And now Bloom adds strollers to its stable of products.

Count us among the skeptical when we toured Bloom's booth at a trade show and got the full court press for the new stroller. Does the world need another $800+ stroller?

But we have to admit: Bloom's new stroller, the babyZEN, is darn impressive. The stroller's flat fold system is something you have to see to believe (there is an online demo *video*, naturally).

Invented by the French designer who thought up the BEABA brand, the babyZEN features an adjustable frame, a reclining seat that can be swapped out for a lay-flat bassinet and a footprint when folded that can fit into the smallest compact car.

The babyZEN stroller is $800. The Yoga newborn nest (the bassinet) is $215.

Ok, there are some gimmicky features here, most notably a remote-activated headlight that is rather superfluous. But it's the little design touches that impressed us most: the babyZEN stands when folded and then can be wheeled about, thanks to small casters in the handle.

The negatives? Well, the seat recline is a series of zippers and catches, which seems overly complicated. And the weight (25.5 lbs) in the toddler mode is on the cusp of hefty.

Another bummer: the stroller comes in just two color schemes: monochrome (silver, grey) and something Bloom calls CMYK. For those not in print production, that stands for cyan, magenta, yellow and black—hence this model looks like something a Cirque du Soleil

E-MAIL FROM THE REAL WORLD
The Weight Game

"I saw the same stroller listed with two different weights online. How can the same model weigh five lbs. less on one site?"

Good question—call it the weight shell game. We've noticed some web sites play fast and loose with the weights of strollers listed on their sites. Why? What parents' value most in a stroller is LIGHT overall weight—and online sellers know this. So, why not cheat and list a stroller's weight . . . minus a few items like a canopy, basket or other amenities? Another explanation: stroller manufacturers often tweak their models from year to year, adding new features. This can add additional ounces, but some web sites "forget" to update the weight. Yes, it is deceptive—but there are ways around the problem. First, this book lists the true weight for most models. Also check the manufacturer's web site, which usually lists the correct weight.

costume designer might dream up.

There's been little real world feedback on this stroller, as of this writing. But we think babyZEN shows promise. **Rating: A**

BOB Strollers bobgear.com BOB has won accolades for their innovative joggers—you can tell these were designed by runners for runners. (Trivia note: BOB stands for Beast of Burden trailers, the company's original name—the owners decided BOB was easier to spell . . . and would avoid a lawsuit from Mick Jagger).

BOB's strollers are billed as "sport utility" strollers and that's an apt moniker, as their rugged design (polymer wheels to prevent rust, for example) and plush ride make these strollers best sellers despite their $300+ price tags. The BOB Sport Utility stroller sells for $300 (duallie: $400)and comes with polymer wheels.

FYI: BOB is now owned by Britax, after being acquired back in 2011. Among the first joint efforts between the brands is a revised car seat adapter that now works with Britax infant car seats. And Britax has debuted a BOB B-Safe version of its B-Safe infant car seat—same seat, just new fabric to match BOB's strollers.

The models. The best-selling BOB model is the Revolution, with its front swivel wheel, rear wheel suspension, multi-position canopy and seat recline, padded handlebar. While not as easy to fold as a Baby Jogger, the Revolution's two-step fold is a close runner-up.

BOB has tweaked the Revolution over the years to improve its features. The latest models feature an adjustable crotch strap, new multi-position canopy and a storage basket with easier access. Strollers with polymer wheels are referred to as the Sport Experience (SE; single $450, duallie $660) while those with smaller, aluminum wheels are called the City Experience (CE; single $470). We weighed the current Revolution SE at 24.9 lbs.

The BOB Stroller Stride model ($400 to $440) is basically a BOB Revolution with an added handlebar console and tension tubing for resistance exercise. In the past year, BOB gave these models a makeover with several small improvements. Among the headlines is a new universal accessory adapter that can be removed without tools. The adapter can fit a snack tray or BOB's infant car seat adapter ($60) and works with the Britax, Graco SnugRide, SafeSeat, and Peg Primo Viaggio.

If you are a serious runner, the BOB Ironman Stroller (single: $350 to $410, 21 lbs.; double: $480 to $560, 31.4 lbs.) is probably the pick of the litter, with smooth tires, stiffer shocks, suspension wheels and more. Plus the bright yellow color gives it great visibility.

New in the past year, BOB rolled out its first four wheel model, the Motion (23 lbs., $350). It features a height adjustable handle bar and air-filled tires, as well as a one-hand fold. The Motion strikes a

Bugaboo like pose, with smaller front wheels. A series of accessories (weather shield, travel bag, etc) are available. The Motion was an REI exclusive in 2013, but now is more widely available.

Our view: Parents give BOB excellent marks on quality and durability. Yes, these strollers are expensive, but worth it. Minor quibbles: the handlebars are not height adjustable, frustrating some taller parents. The seat recline on the Revolution is cumbersome, requiring you to adjust both from harness straps. That's much more complicated than Baby Jogger's Summit, which also boasts a quicker fold.

While the BOB Revolution and Ironman receive much love, folks

Shopping Cart Covers: Advice & Picks

Grocery store carts aren't exactly the cleanest form of transportation—yet once your baby outgrows her infant car seat, you will likely put baby in the little seat up front . . . and quickly realize that keeping the carts clean doesn't seem to be a high priority for most stores. Some stores have added in a wipes dispenser near the carts, but you can't get the gook off the fabric belts—that's just gross.

Ditto for restaurant high chairs—they can be germ factories.

To the rescue comes the shopping cart/high chair cover, basically a fabric seat that provides a clean and safe space for baby while you shop or dine. Here are our top picks:

◆ **Infantino.** Infantino's Compact 2-in-1 Shopping Cart Cover is made of polyester and comes with a sippy cup strap, teether and loop. At $25 to $30, it's one of the most affordable options and parents like the cute fabrics.

◆ **Itzy Ritzy.** These shopping cart covers are more fashionable than the ones you see in stores and run $68. Readers say Itzy Ritzy covers (itzyritzy.com; pictured) are easy to use and work on both regular grocery store carts and those large carts at Costco. Price includes a carrying case.

◆ **Bellingham Baby's** (bellinghambabycompany.com) shopping cart covers were recommended by readers for their reversible covers in cool fabrics. Covers include two toy loops plus pockets and are available in 17 fabric choices. Prices are about $68.

strollers

are more mixed on the new four-wheel Motion. The storage basket is hard to access and the model's overall bulk is an issue. The Motion isn't designed for all terrain use (its wheels are too small). . . and the strollers large size/bulk make it a no go for most mall trips. This model looks like a rare miss for BOB.

Overall, however, BOB has excellent quality and is among our top picks for all terrain strollers. *Baby Bargains Resale Rank: Excellent.* **Rating: A**

Britax *britaxusa.com* Best-known for its well-made car seats, Britax launched a stroller line in 2005 so it could compete in the travel system market.

The models. Britax offers three stand alone stroller models: the B-Agile (both in single and double versions), B-Ready, B-Nimble.

The B-Ready ($500–we've seen it discounted online in the $300's, 28.1 lbs.) is Britax's flagship stroller and their first stab at a modular stroller that works with an optional bassinet and second seat. Designed to integrate with Britax's infant car seat (the Chaperone), the B-Ready has 14 different configurations, much like the Baby Jogger Select and UPPAbaby Vista.

Out of the box, the stroller will work with Britax's infant car seats (a separate $50 adapter is needed for Graco and Chicco seats). The B-Ready features a seat that reverses to face forward or rear, full tire suspension, large storage basket and full seat recline. They've improved the stroller recently by adding a fourth recline position to the seatback as well as more durable foam filled rubber wheels.

Got two kids? A second seat ($150; $120 online) transforms the B-Ready into a double stroller. New for 2012, they've tweaked the B-Ready by adding four recline positions for the main seat including a more upright position, a deeper storage basket and foam filled rubber tires that never go flat.

The B-Nimble ($200, online as little as $163; 15.5 lbs.) is the B-Ready's much lighter cousin— it is infant car seat compatible and features a removable/reversible seat liner, cup holder and rain cover. It works with the Britax infant seat out of the box.

The last stroller in the Britax line-up is their riff on the Baby Jogger City Mini, the Britax B-Agile. It weighs in at 16.5 lbs. and runs $250 ($195 online). It features a one-hand quick-fold, large canopy and a no-rethread harness. Recently, Britax added a B-Agile double stroller to its lineup. This side-by-side version ($450 retail; $330 online) accommodates kids up to 50 lbs. each and can carry one Britax infant seat.

New for 2014, Britax is debuting the Affinity ($600, 27.4 lbs), a multi-function stroller with reversible seat. The Affinity fits all Britax car seats, as well as Chicco, Peg and Graco seats, and features a fully reclining seat, height adjustable handle and air-filled tires. The

Affinity includes a rain cover, but is designed for babies six months or older (when using the seat). Oddly, the Affinity will not come with a canopy—that is an optional accessory. In fact, you can fully customize the Affinity with six different fashions and a choice of three frame colors (white, black or silver).

Our view. Britax has struggled in this category, racking up five years of failure before finally getting it right with its current offerings. Why the struggle? Ironically, Britax's strength in car seats has been a weakness when it comes to strollers. That's because what works with car seats (strong engineering focus and innovation) doesn't necessary translate to the world of strollers, where success is often a meld of function, style and value.

As for the function part, the new Britax strollers are much closer to the mark. We liked the B-Ready's ability to morph into different configurations—many more than the comparable UPPAbaby Vista (which notably, runs $180 more than the B-Ready). And you can fold the B-Ready with the second (toddler) seat attached—that's something the competition can't do.

Critics, however, knock the B-Ready's overall bulk and weight (about two pounds heavier than the comparable Vista). To Britax's credit, however, they have made small tweaks to improve the B-Ready (example: new rubber wheels replaced the previous foam versions).

So we have the function and value, but what about style? That's probably Britax's weakness . . . and we aren't just talking about the B-Ready's paint-by-number fabric color choices. Britax strollers lack a certain je ne sais quoi when compared with Baby Jogger (see: Quick Fold, definition of) and UPPAbaby. And when you are trying to sell a $500 stroller like the B-Ready, you need some zing.

On a more positive note, the Britax B-Agile gets good marks on quality. The price (about $200) makes it a good deal. Parents like the smooth glide, large canopy and easy to adjust harness. We recommend the B-Agile as a credible alternative to the Baby Jogger City Mini.

As for the B-Nimble, it gets more mixed reviews than Britax's other offerings, with an equal number of fans and detractors. The Affinity wasn't out as of press time, so no parent feedback yet.

Bottom line: we recommend Britax's strollers. The B-Ready in particular is a credible and affordable alternative to the UPPAbaby Vista; and the B-Agile is a good bet compared to the Baby Jogger City Mini. *Baby Bargains Resale Rank: Excellent.* **Rating: A-**

Bugaboo bugaboo.com. Bugaboo. It's Dutch for "priced as if from a hotel mini-bar."

The models. Here's an unlikely recipe for success in the stroller biz. Take a Dutch-designed stroller, attach an $800 price tag and

strollers

voila! Instant hit, right? Well, chalk this one up to some creative design, marketing, and a dash of good timing.

Bugaboo's breakthrough success was the Frog, named as such for its small wheels in front that give it a frog-like look. The Frog ($760, now discontinued) was a clever hybrid of an all-terrain and carriage stroller, pitched to parents for its multiple uses. The Frog was comprised of three parts: an aluminum frame and bassinet that could later be replaced by a stroller seat (included with canopy and basket). It weighed about 20 lbs., which is rather amazing. (Although discontinued, used Frogs can still be found online on Craigslist, eBay, etc.).

Oh, and we forgot the fourth ingredient of the Bugaboo—hype.

The Bugaboo folks were in the right place at the right time. How did the Bugaboo become so hot? Sure, it was fashionable, but that doesn't quite explain it. Nope, the answer is Bugaboo had one of the great product placements of all time . . . it was the featured stroller on HBO's *Sex in the City*. The rest is stroller history. In no time, celebs like Gwyneth Paltrow were swishing their Bugaboos across the pages of *People Magazine*. The Bugaboo was the first baby stroller to cross paths with the white-hot supernova that is celebrity product placement.

It also didn't hurt that Bugaboo debuted during the boom in baby luxury products during the early 2000's, when dropping $800+ on a stroller wasn't a big deal.

Cleverly, Bugaboo played on its Dutch design roots . . . even though (shhh! don't tell anyone!) Bugaboo's are made in Taiwan, not Amsterdam.

Bugaboo's sequel to the Frog—the aptly named Cameleon (20 lbs.) runs $890. The Cameleon adds a more springy suspension on the front wheels, plus a slightly larger seat frame and higher chassis. Unlike the Frog, the Cameleon is available in a wide range of color combinations—you can choose from six base colors and nine top colors, mix and match. Also new: a height adjustable handle.

Bugaboo recently rolled out a slightly revised Cameleon, dubbed the Cameleon3 (C3 for short). At first glance, there aren't many major visible differences between the new and old Cameleon. But Bugaboo points out the C3 has an easier fold (with one-hand!), a larger storage basket with lid, quick release front wheels, improved brake and new mosquito net accessory. The price on the C3 is the same as the last model. Oddly, Bugaboo is also touting the C3's "refreshed design", which includes a more durable chassis. That seems to be a tacit admission that the old Cameleon lacked durability, which you think would come standard in a $900 stroller.

In addition to the full-featured Cameleon3, Bugaboo has one compact stroller in its line-up: the Bee ($650, 22 lbs.). Pitched to urban dwellers with its narrow width (20"; about four inches narrower than other Bugaboo's), the Bee has an over-sized canopy, reversible seat, and four-position seat recline.

Yet the Bee was never the runaway hit that the Frog or Cameleon were, so Bugaboo went back to the drawing board and launched a refreshed Bee back in 2010. Dubbed the Bee Plus , it features a wider, height adjustable seat, adjustable canopy height and upgraded wheels. The company seemed to listen to its critics when it dropped the original Bee's much-hated seat "wings."

Bugaboo's first double stroller is the unfortunately named Donkey. The unique feature here is a frame that can expand to accommodate a bassinet, storage basket or second baby seat. In its single or mono configuration, the stroller is 23" wide; for a duo, it expands to 29." Unfortunately, all this presto-chango goodness comes at a price, both literally and figuratively. The weight of the Donkey is a hefty 32 lbs. as a single and a whopping 40.3 lbs. as a duo (with the added second seat). Before you add your kids!

Bugaboo's newest model, the Buffalo (26.2 lbs., $1129), is the company's first all terrain stroller featuring foam tires and a one-piece fold. The Buffalo features an included rain cover, reversible seat, and is car seat compatible (adapters sold separately).

FYI: Bugaboo also sells a raft of accessories for its strollers such as cup holders (What? You thought that would be included?). Example: a $45 car seat adapter lets you attach most major brand infant car seats to the frame. That cup holder is $25, parasol $40, foot muff $130.

Our view. The rise and fall of Bugaboo at first blush looks like a tale that mirrors the 2000's economy: at first, parents (and grand-parents) quickly snapped up $1000 Bugaboo strollers. Then came the Great Recession, which took the wind out of Bugaboo's sails.

But some of Bugaboo's woes go beyond macroeconomics . . . and are more self-inflicted. The company's notorious slow and arrogant customer service is Exhibit One. When you spend this much on a stroller and something breaks, you expect white glove treatment from the company. Yet reader reports and online reviews again and again slam Bugaboo for indifferent customer service, long waits for parts and other hassles.

Quality issues have also dogged Bugaboo (plastic parts that break, inflated tires that go flat, etc.) and that's on top of some of the built-in design hassles of the strollers, particularly on the Cameleon. In 2011, Bugaboo recalled Bee strollers in UK for defective wheels.

Readers gripe that the assembly and folding on the stroller takes too darn long. To fold a Bugaboo Frog or Cameleon, you must first remove the seat—that's a major pain, especially for folks who live in the suburbs and plan to fold it up frequently to fit in a trunk (and you'll need a big trunk). Hence, setting up the Bugaboo requires re-attaching the seat to the frame. Sure, this takes 30 seconds or so, which isn't forever—but about 25 seconds longer than most strollers.

Bottom line: a Bugaboo is probably best for urban dwellers or folks who don't plan to frequently disassemble and throw it in a trunk. (The Bee is an exception—it is easy to fold and set-up).

Fans of Bugaboo love the strollers' smooth steering, ride and suspension. The multi-function aspect of the Cameleon also earns kudos, although this has been matched in recent years by the UPPAbaby Vista and even Britax B-Ready. And while we think the Donkey's amazing expandable frame is a key innovation, it's hard for us to suggest anyone spend $1500 on a stroller.

Given its quality and customer service issues, we will drop our rating for Bugaboo this time out. Except for a few well-heeled urban parents, the hassle and expense of Bugaboo makes this a questionable purchase. ***Rating: B***

Bumbleride bumbleride.com In a stroller market stuffed with look-a-like models in varying shades of navy, Bumbleride's niche is all-terrain and umbrella strollers with more than a touch of style. Started by a husband and wife team in San Diego, Bumbleride is a small stroller company with three basic models: Indie, Indie Twin and Flite.

The models. The Indie ($500, 20 lbs.) is a tri-wheel, all-terrain stroller with quick release 12" inflated tires, boot, adjustable handle, full recline and deep storage basket. Basically, the Indie is a more stylish version of the Mountain Buggy Urban Single or BOB Revolution. In the past year, the Indie got a new longer (and adjustable) footrest, a new included bumper bar and locks on the front wheel so it can be pushed in a straight line. The Indie now ships with a car seat adapter included in the box, which is great.

FYI: A twin version of the Indie runs $680 and now can hold two infant car seats. It weighs a rather hefty 32 lbs.

For 2014, Bumbleride plans to debut a four-wheel version of the Indie, called the Indie 4. Instead of the air-filled front wheel, the Indie 4 will have two small plastic wheels, similar to the Bugaboo Cameleon. The goal is a stroller that "bridges the gap between urban and off-road terrain" strollers, says Bumbleride. Price: $600, to be released in the second quarter of 2014. The prototype of the Indie 4 we saw weighed 23.1 lbs, although Bumbleride says they plan to shave some weight off the final version.

Finally, the Flite ($250, 14 lbs.) is a lightweight stroller with two handles (a la the Peg Pliko or Maclaren Techno), a big canopy, two recline positions and car seat adapter bar. We liked all the included accessories such as a rain cover and travel bag.

Also, Bumbleride has jumped on the sustainable wagon in the past year, rolling out eco-friendly fabrics across its entire line (50% of the exterior fabric is recycled PET plastic bottles; the interior fabric is made of 50% bamboo fabric).

FYI: As we were going to press, Bumbleride discontinued the Flyer ($400), a carriage stroller with a reversible handle.

Our view. Reviews for Bumbleride are mixed—the Indie probably gets the best marks from readers, who often compare it to the BOB Revolution. The Indie is three pounds lighter than the Revolution and fans like its easy fold, height adjustable handle, car seat adapter and more. But critics point out the Indie doesn't have as smooth of a glide as the Revolution and the Indie only has a partial seat recline. The canopy on the Indie also gets low marks for its skimpy coverage and gaps near the frame. And while the fold is easy, the Indie is very bulky when folded. Considering both strollers cost about the same, the advantage goes to the BOB Revolution.

The Flite also is a mixed bag. Readers like the compact fold and car seat adapter—plus the overall style of the stroller is a winner. Critics say similar strollers like the Maclaren Techno have a smoother ride and easier access to the storage basket (the Flite's puny basket is a loser). One big difference between this stroller and the Techno: the Flite doesn't have a height adjustable handle, so if you are short and your partner isn't, this could be an issue. And the Flite's seat recline requires two hands to operate.

So it is a mixed review for this brand. Customer service, design and fashion are good; but inconsistent quality drags down Bumbleride's rating a bit. *Baby Bargains Resale Rank: Excellent.* **Rating: B-**

Chicco chiccousa.com Chicco (pronounced KEY-ko) has a 50-year history as one of Europe's leading juvenile products makers. Along with Peg Perego, Chicco is one of Europe's biggest producer of baby gear and toys. When we first started writing about baby gear (way back in the early 90's), Chicco always played second fiddle to Peg, whose strollers outsold Chicco by a large margin. In recent years, their fortunes have switched: Chicco has seen a string of successes in America, with a popular infant car seat and several lightweight stroller models. Peg, meanwhile, has languished.

The models. Chicco's emphasis is on lightweight strollers designed for the mall—the company offers two compact models (Liteway, C6/Capri) and a full-size options (Cortina). In the compact category, the Liteway ($120 to $140, 17 lbs.) features two handles, rear wheel suspension, padded five-point harness, cup holder and a full recline. We liked the boot that tucks away when not in use. New in the past year, the Liteway has an enhanced version (the Liteway Plus, $180) that works with the Chicco infant seat. After you are finished using it with the infant seat, you flip back the stroller seat and it becomes a toddler stroller that has an umbrella fold and weighs 19.2 lbs.

Similar to the basic Liteway, the Echo ($100) which is a Target exclusive, features a four position reclining seat and adjustable leg rest. The main difference between the Echo and Liteway: the Echo has double wheels up front, while the Liteway has single wheels.

The entry-level C6 (also known as the Capri; $70 to $80, 11 lbs.) features a two-position seat recline, five-point harness and basic canopy . . . a bit like the Maclaren Volo, but almost half the price.

The Cortina, Chicco's marquee stroller, is sold separately ($140 to $180, 23 lbs.) or as part of a travel system ($300 to $350, paired with Chicco's excellent KeyFit infant seat). The Cortina features a more traditional design with height-adjustable handles and decent size basket. We thought it was well designed—we liked the one-hand fold and fully reclining seat. FYI: There is also an upgraded version of this stroller, the Cortina Magic, that runs $200 and features upgraded fabric, a slightly larger canopy and boot plus a reversible seat insert.

Chicco also offers a twin stroller, the Cortina Together ($300, 30 lbs.). This version of the Cortina is a front/back tandem stroller that holds two car seats and features an aluminum frame, a storage basket with trap door access, three-position handle and flat fold. New for 2014, Chicco is rolling out a new double version of its Echo, the Echo Twin ($190, 30.5 lbs.). This Target exclusive will be out in early 2014.

Rounding out the line is a stroller frame, dubbed the KeyFit Caddy ($100, 11 lbs.). As you might guess, it fits a Chicco KeyFit infant seat (which pops in with a click) and has a big storage basket plus a height adjustable handle. The frame only fits Chicco infant seats, however.

Chicco plans a major expansion of its stroller offerings in 2014, this time tackling the full-size, multi-function market. The new models are:

◆ *Bravo* ($250 stand-alone, $400 travel system, 22 lbs.) features a self-standing, quick fold. Release: April 2014.

◆ *Activ3/Tre* are Chicco's take on the tri-wheel, all-terrain market dominated by the BOB Revolution. The Active3 features height adjustable handle, swivel/lockable front wheel, extendible canopy, large basket and included car seat adapter. The Active3 ($300) also has 12" foam filled tires and a standing fold plus adjustable suspension. The Tre ($370) is an upgraded version of the Active3, with bigger 16" air-filled wheels, hand brake and upgraded fabrics.

◆ *Urban ($400)*. This Babies R Us exclusive will debut in April 2014 as a European-designed modular stroller with telescoping handle, aluminum frame, standing fold, large basket, quick release EVA tires, included car seat adapter for the KeyFit and a reversible seat. This 24.1 lb stroller also includes a clever seat that converts to a carry cot. The Urban is clearly aimed at the UPPAbaby Vista and is priced aggressively. This model will the be the one to watch in 2014.

Our view. "Cute and cheap" is how our readers sum up Chicco. Take the 11 lb. Chicco Ct0.6 (Capri)—it's half the price of a Maclaren and 40% lighter than the Peg Pliko. That makes it ideal for quick trips to the mall or airplane travel.

Detractors point out that Chicco strollers don't work well for tall folks, who often find the handle heights uncomfortable. And the canopies on many of their low price strollers don't offer much shade.

But that's the minority view: most readers say they are happy with their Chicco, especially those who mainly use the strollers for quick shopping trips.

So which Chicco strollers get the best marks? Readers give the full-featured Cortina very good reviews—fans cheer the easy steering, one-hand fold and padding (critics point out when folded, the Cortina is a bit bulky).

How about the lightweight strollers? Readers seem to like the C6 and Liteway equally. Detractors point out the Liteway isn't that light—at nearly 20 pounds, it stretches the definition of lightweight. The skimpy baskets also come in for criticism on the Liteway and C6. The new Liteway Plus gets good marks and is recommended. Bottom line: most parents are happy with the overall quality of Chicco—and the customer service is good.

Chicco's stroller frame receives good marks from parents, even if it is a bit pricey at $100 (other stroller frames are about $70). The height adjustable handle and snap-in capability for the Chicco KeyFit win kudos across the board.

Chicco's ambitious expansion into multi-function and all-terrain in 2014 will be interesting. Chicco has stumbled in the three-wheel market and never gained traction. We'll see if the new models fare better; of all the new strollers, the Urban is the one we like the best based on a prototype we previewed.

Overall, we think Chicco is a good brand and the prices are a decent value. If you like the look of Maclaren but don't have the bank account, Chicco is a good alternative. *Baby Bargains Resale Rank: Good.* **Rating: B+**

Combi *combi-intl.com* Japanese-owned Combi had its heyday in the '90's with a string of best-selling lightweight strollers, but the company has struggled in recent years. Combi has gone through several management changes and shifts in strategy, which has hurt its brand.

The models. Combi's focus is on lightweight, compact strollers. The company's flagship model, the Cosmo, is a good starting point. The Cosmo ($110 to $150, 13 lbs.) features a compact fold, full seat recline for infants, and removable napper bar plus it holds Combi's Shuttle infant car seat. The Cosmo E ($120) is a Babies R Us exclusive, basically the same as a regular Cosmo but with upgraded fabric.

Next is Combi's Cabria, which is basically a pimped out Cosmo. It features an extended canopy, larger basket, larger wheels, parent storage console and cup holder. This adds about a pound to the stroller (14.8 lbs.). Price: $160-$180. In the past year, the Cabria

strollers

got a few tweaks: bigger wheels, a bigger basket and cup holder.

Combi has quite a few models in the double stroller (side by side) category. The Twin Sport ($230 to $260, 22 lbs.), a side-by-side model that can fit one Combi infant car seat, features a removable napper bar, machine washable cushions, 165-degree reclining seats and a separate canopy for each seat.

The Combi Twin Savvy E ($200) is a Babies R Us exclusive and is similar to the Twin Sport, with somewhat less fancy fabric and padding. Finally, there is the Twin Cosmo ($213), which features a full recline, infant "safety boots," self-standing fold and large canopies.

Combi newest stroller is the Catalyst, a very un-Combi like stroller that weighs in at 28.1 lbs. This $300 stroller features a reversible seat, extendable handles, and a bassinet that morphs into a seat. It is car seat compatible with Combi's Shuttle infant seat plus adapters for other brands (Graco, Chicco). While this stroller is innovative, we were scratching our heads at why Combi would attempt to compete in the multi-function stroller market with a nearly 30 lb. model.

Our view. Combi's woes in the stroller market can be traced to one major problem: its infant car seat. Unlike competitors Perego and Chicco, Combi has yet to figure out this market (its weak Shuttle car seat has suffered from slow sales amid recalls and other issues). As a result, Combi has missed out on the entire travel system market.

Design snafus have also dogged the brand. Parents have complained for years about Combi's handles (too short) and storage baskets (too small, hard to access). You'd think Combi's designers would have better adapted these models to America after being here for 30 years. Instead, Combi appears to be just importing the same strollers it sells in Asia, with minimal changes for the U.S.

And while parents universally like Combi for their lightweight and easy folds, there always seems to be some fatal flaw that pops up . . . front wheels that are easily damaged when the stroller is folded up, an overall lack of durability, etc.

When you spend $40 on a bare-bones umbrella stroller, you might put up with some of these issues. But at the $100+ price level, that's a tough sell, especially when competitors like Chicco and Maclaren offer similar strollers without the hassles mentioned above. On the plus side, the new Combi Catalyst does earn mostly positive marks from readers, who like the built-in bassinet. But critics say it is too heavy and doesn't have a smooth push/ride, which you'd think you'd get for $300.

As for parent feedback, the most positive reviews for this line come for the Combi double strollers. The reviews for the Cosmo and Cabria are more mixed. *Baby Bargains Resale Rank: Poor.* **Rating B-**

Cosco *djgusa.com* Baby products conglomerate Dorel takes a divide and conquer approach to its stroller offerings. In mass-market discounters like Walmart, Dorel sells travel systems under the brands Cosco and Safety 1st. For chains like Babies R Us, it sells more upscale versions of its strollers under the Eddie Bauer brand. Finally, at the top end, Dorel uses its European sister brands (Quinny, Maxi Cosi) to sell strollers in specialty stores and chains.

Since Quinny and Maxi Cosi are marketed as their own separate brands, we review them separately. Below is a review of Cosco, Safety 1st and Eddie Bauer.

The models. Osco's niche is entry-price point strollers such as the Sprinter Go Lightly Travel System. This $110-$130 travel system combines the Cosco Designer 22 car seat and a no-frills stroller with one-hand fold and three-point harness. These travel systems are sold under both the Cosco and Disney brands.

Cosco also sells a handful of low-price umbrella strollers ($18 to $35) and what it calls "full-feature strollers" (the Umbria, for example) in stores like Sears and K-Mart for $35 to $90. But the main emphasis here is on travel systems.

Eddie Bauer and Safety 1st offer more options and upscale fabrics—these strollers are sold at Babies R Us and Diapers.com. A typical offering: the Eddie Bauer Destination travel system ($200). Like the Cosco travel systems, the Eddie Bauer offerings combine the Designer 22 infant car seat with a stroller with one-hand fold and large basket. Eddie Bauer and Safety 1st sell a dozen or so different models.

New in the past year, Eddie Bauer has rolled out a travel system with a tri-wheel stroller (Trail Hiker) paired with an infant seat that works to 35 lbs. Also new, Dorel now has a stroller frame, the Safety 1st Clic ($70, 13 lbs.). It features a large storage basket, two cup holders, a click-in feature for Dorel seats and a strap-in system for other infant car seats.

Safety 1st is Cosco's biggest stroller platform—and the company is introducing ten new models for 2014. The Saunter Sport ($140 travel system, 17.1 lbs) features a telescoping and self-standing fold. The UniLite ($100, 14 lbs) takes just about every infant car seat on the market (except Orbit and Britax) and features an umbrella fold. The Lift LX features a Baby Jogger-like quick fold and is a Babies R Us exclusive ($240 system with the OnBoard 35 car seat).

Safety 1st's marquee stroller is the AeroLite LX ($150 to $215), which is combined with the OnBoard Air infant car seat to make a travel system. This model features a curved frame, ultra compact fold, multi-position canopy and seat recline. There are multiple versions of this travel system ranging in price from $180 to $240.

Need to transport a baby and toddler? The Safety 1st Stand Onboard has a stroller seat and the ability to hold an infant car seat, plus a stand-on platform at the back to transport an older toddler. Price: $150, 24.8 lbs.

Our view. Let's be honest here—no one considers Cosco, Eddie Bauer or Safety 1st strollers to be best in class. Sold on price and paired with Cosco's middling infant car seats, these travel systems are aimed at folks on very tight budgets who can only spend $100 or so on a stroller and car seat. Yes, this is a book on bargains, but what we have here is a case where the cheap is no bargain.

Example: Eddie Bauer bills its tri-wheel strollers as "all terrain" models and gives them names like Trail Hiker, but the low-end plastic tires couldn't handle even the smoothest path. Quality woes dog Cosco, Eddie Bauer and Safety 1st's strollers—canopies that break, wheels that squeak, etc. Add in the low-end fabrics and skimpy padding and you can see how this bargain doesn't add up.

Take the Safety 1st Aerolite, as another example. Parents tell us the strollers' vaunted one-hand fold/step-up is a pain to use (the stiff release mechanism frustrates users) and design goofs like the wider rear wheelbase cause the stroller to get caught in tight spaces at the mall.

Bottom line: we aren't impressed with these strollers. Unless you are picking up one as a steal on Craigslist, we suggest skipping them. *Baby Bargains Resale Rank: Poor.* **Rating: C+**

Cybex *Cybex-online.com* German stroller brand Cybex had the misfortune of launching in the USA during the economic meltdown of 2009. As a result, Cybex hasn't made much of a dent here in the U.S. stroller market.

The models. These brightly colored models combined features similar to Maclaren at $200+ price points. But the white frames and white solid wheels turned off parents, who perhaps thought they'd quickly lose that pristine look after a spin in the mall parking lot.

So it was back to the drawing board for Cybex, which revamped its line to feature silver frames and improved features. Example: the Ruby ($150, 13.2 lbs.) has a foam handle, two-step fold and full canopy that is even height adjustable. An infant car seat adapter is available as an accessory ($25).

The Onyx ($260, 16 lbs.) features more padding and full seat recline. A double version of the Onyx is called the Twinyx (for children starting at six months of age; $450). The Callisto is Cybex's top of the line model ($350, 22 lbs.) with plush fabric and wheel suspension.

In the past year, Cybex has rolled out designer versions of its strollers, such as the Jeremy Scott "Food Fight." Don't fall in love with these looks if you don't have a serious bankroll, however—the designer Cybex versions run three times the retail price of the non-designer models.

Our view. Reader feedback on the Cybex has been thin, probably due to their poor sales. One mom who bought an Onyx posted to our stroller message board that she loved the stroller's canopy, high handles and decent steering. But the ride was rickety, especially on cracked sidewalks. Overall, she was impressed—but she only paid $65 for the stroller on Overstock.com. "It would absolutely not be worth it at the full $200 retail price point."

Other readers agreed, saying they liked but didn't love their Cybex. While most folks compliment the bright colors and overall features, critics knock the use of flimsy plastic (such as the canopy attachment) and too high prices. If you can find one of these strollers at a steep discount, go for it. *Baby Bargains Resale Rank: Excellent.* **Rating: B**

Eddie Bauer See Cosco.

Evenflo *evenflo.com* Evenflo's efforts in the stroller category have been hampered by their lackluster infant car seat sales—since most of Evenflo's strollers are sold as travel systems, competitors like Graco who have stronger infant car seats are enjoying much more success here.

The models. Most of Evenflo's strollers are what we'd call full-feature, first-time parent strollers—when folks think they need a large stroller with every bell and whistle to ferry baby. While these features are nice, they tend to add weight and bulk to Evenflo's strollers.

Evenflo's stroller offerings are much like that of *Cosco*—low-end travel systems where the company pairs its mediocre infant seats with bare bones strollers like the Journey. One box for one price ($125) at Walmart.

Evenflo's stroller models include the Journey, Featherlite and FlexLite. The Journey comes in a dozen or so variations (Journey LX, JourneyLite, etc.). They are basically the same stroller a 20 lb. model with large storage basket, standing fold and kid snack tray.

Perhaps the best thing about Evenflo strollers is their amazing parent trays complete with two cup holders with "automotive cup grippers" and a storage area with "privacy lid." If only Evenflo had put as much effort into the rest of the stroller as they did the parent tray.

Evenflo recently broke with its full-size stroller pattern to debut the Feather Lite 200. As the name implies, this travel system is 20% lighter than Evenflo's other offerings with the stroller clocking in at 15 lbs. It features a full recline and five point harness. Retail: $230. We saw a prototype of the Feather Lite and were impressed: you don't see too many affordable travel system strollers in the 15 lb. range.

Our view. About the best we can say about Evenflo's strollers is that they get slightly better marks from readers than similarly priced Cosco travel systems. But that is a low bar to cross. We aren't fans of Evenflo's infant car seats, which of course are paired with all these strollers sold as travel systems.

On the plus side, Evenflo has jettisoned the more heavier models it sold in years past. The company now focuses more on lightweight models at an entry price point. And we also give a shout out to Evenflo's customer service department, which earns good marks from our readers for promptly taking care of problems.

So, it's a mixed bag for Evenflo. **Rating: B-**

First Years thefirstyears.com Better known for their feeding accessories and toys, First Years (part of the Learning Curve family) also has an affordable line of strollers. Here's an overview.

The models. The super affordable Jet ($50, 11.4 lbs) is a good place to start: this no frills umbrella stroller features a simple design and basic basket. The compact umbrella fold and the price are the stars here—a basic, safe stroller for under $50. Who would've thought?

For another $20, the Ignite ($60, 15.8 lbs.) adds upgraded fabric, a bigger seat and partial seat recline. The Ignite features both a storage basket AND a "parent bag," an additional storage compartment near the handles.

The First Years also offers two more expensive models: the Indigo ($180, 22 lbs.) and the Wave ($400, 24 lbs,; aka the JJ Cole Broadway). The Indigo features a reversible seat, adjustable handle height and universal car seat adapter. The Wave's unique selling point is a seat that can swivel 360 degrees. It also has larger rear wheels and a seat that makes into a bassinet. You also get a universal car seat adapter. FYI: The Wave isn't being sold online as of this writing, so perhaps First Years is giving this model to JJ Cole as an exclusive.

In the past year, The First Years has released its first travel system: the Wisp ($200 to $300) combines First Years' Via infant seat with a 16.6 lb. stroller that has a removable child tray and rather tall handles.

New to the line, First Years debuted its first all-terrain stroller, the ATS. This $350 tri-wheel model features a fully reclining seat, rain cover, side storage bag and air filled 12" tires. Also new is the Burst Stroller ($200, 22.7 lbs.), a full-size stroller with four position partial seat recline, large canopy and super sized storage basket.

Our view. First Years has a winner with its stroller line—their affordable, lightweight strollers win kudos for both design and value.

Take the basic Jet and Ignite strollers—readers tell us these strollers are great for travel and quick outings to the mall. And yes, they cost just $50 and $60, respectively. Readers generally give the Jet and Ignite very positive reviews.

What is missing? Well, the seat recline for Jet and Ignite is only partial—so these strollers aren't designed for newborns but for older babies who can sit up on their own. The canopy coverage is rather skimpy. If you are on the tall side, the Ignite's handles would be a better bet than the Jet.

Other negatives: many of First Years models lack cup holders, which is an odd oversight. Yes, you can add an aftermarket cup holder—and considering the value of these models, that seems like a fair trade-off. While other stroller makers offer a raft of accessories so you can customize your baby's ride, First Years has zip. Nada. Even for its more expensive offerings.

While we recommend the affordable First Years Jet and Ignite models, the more expensive First Years models (Indigo, Wave/JJ Cole Broadway, ATS, Burst) earn lower marks from readers. If you really want to spend $200 to $400 on a stroller, there are better choices out there than First Years. The quality isn't there for these models, given the price tag.

We will recommend First Years, but only for the Jet and Ignite models. *Baby Bargains Resale Rank: Excellent.* **Rating: A**

Graco *gracobaby.com* Graco's main stroller niche is the travel system combining an infant car seat and stroller and aimed at first-time parents who want all the bells and whistles. The secret to their success is their excellent infant car seat, the SnugRide.

Graco is like the Honda of strollers—a mid-priced brand with decent quality, but not a lot of pizzazz. Graco leaves the low-end, opening price-point market to Dorel/Cosco.

Graco's line is huge, so let's get to the highlights:

The models. Graco divides their stroller line into three areas: lightweight, three-wheel and multi-child strollers.

The lightweight models include the Breeze, Modes, UrbanLite, Vie4, Dynamo Lite, FastAction Fold and LiteRider.

The three-wheel models include the FastAction Fold Jogger/Sport and Trekko.

In the double or multi child category, Graco offers the FastAction Fold Duo, Ready2Grow, Quattro Tour Duo and DuoGlider.

Then to make things even more confusing, Graco makes TWO different attachment systems for its strollers and infant car seats: Click Connect and Classic Connect. The newer Click Connect is a one-step process—when you snap the infant car seat into the stroller, you hear a click. The Classic Connect is a multi-step process: you connect the car seat to the stroller and then have to use a latch or straps to hold it to the stroller. Make sure you are matching the right Graco infant seat to the correct stroller.

Example: the Graco Snug Ride Click Connect 40 works in Graco Modes Click Connect stroller. Just to confuse you, some stroller models have two versions—the FastAction Fold strollers come in both Click Connect and Classic Connect versions.

And, adding in another layer of fun, some of Graco's strollers are exclusive to certain chains. Example: only Babies R Us carries the FastAction Fold Duo.

Whew. Deep breath. Let's look at the stand-outs in each category:

◆ *Lightweight*. Modes and Fast Action strollers are the stars here. The Graco Modes Click Connect stroller is 23.3 lbs. (which pushes the concept of light weight to the outer limits of reality) and features a reversible seat, one-hand standing fold and removable child tray. You can use Modes just as a stroller frame to transport the infant car seat (by removing the stroller seat). All told the Modes stroller converts into ten different configurations.

As with all Graco strollers, you also get Graco's generous parent tray with cup holders. Feedback on the Modes has been quite positive and we'd recommend it. Price: $250 as a stand-alone model or $370 as part of a travel system with the SnugRide Click Connect 35. Our only reservation about the Modes: at $250, you are getting up into Baby Jogger City Mini price territory. And the City Mini, while lacking the reversible seat, is six pounds lighter with an easier fold.

Speaking of Baby Jogger, Graco is hoping to conjure up some of that Baby Jogger Quick Fold magic with its new FastAction Fold LX stroller ($130, 20.9 lbs). As the name implies, this stroller folds in a single-step and stands when folded. It features a multi-position reclining seat, 3 or 5 point harness and all the standard Graco stroller features you'd expect (large storage basket, parent tray with cup holders, etc). It holds all Graco infant seats. Sold as a stand-alone model or as a travel system ($200).

Graco's other lightweight strollers have been in the line for several years. Example: the UrbanLite, a 20 lb. stroller with three positions, full recline, height adjustable handle, large basket and one-hand fold. The canopy on the UrbanLite fully covers the seat. Price: $270 as part of a travel system, $150 as a stand-alone model. Similar to the UrbanLite is the Dynamo Lite (17.5 lbs.), It features a full recline and large basket and will be sold as a travel system ($170-$200) or stand-alone model ($120).

New for 2014 is the Graco Breaze ($170, 17.5 lbs), a one-hand fold lightweight stroller with full recline, extended canopy and front wheel suspension. It is car seat compatible.

◆ *Three-wheel strollers.* Graco's main entry here is the FastAction Fold Sport ($150), a Baby Jogger City Mini knock-off that is a Babies R Us exclusive. This tri-wheel stroller features a multi-position reclining seat and large storage basket.

Graco also makes other tri-wheel strollers with air-filled tires under the FastAction moniker (FastAction Fold Joggers). Even though these strollers are billed as joggers, they really are designed for walking on trails, not running. The turnable/lockable front wheels on the FastAction Fold Joggers make the strollers more maneuverable, but less ideal for actual running.

Also in the three-wheel category is Graco's Trekko ($160 stand-alone, $300 travel system). This full-size stroller has a front wheel that can be locked and features a 180 degree rotating canopy, full seat recline, one-hand fold, rubber tires, and a height adjustable handle. And it works with any Graco infant car seat. Our only concern with this stroller: the rear-wheel width at 25.5" may make negotiating tight spaces difficult (most strollers have a 20-24" rear wheel width). Also this stroller clocks in at 26.9 lbs., about 10% heavier than the similar Valco Tri-Mode. FYI: The Trekko has "never flat" rubber tires, not air filled.

◆ **Double strollers.** Most of Graco's offerings here are tandem (front/back) doubles, such as the Ready2Grow. It features 12 seating positions, the ability to hold two infant seats, and a removable rear jump seat with harness that can hold an older toddler. The Ready2Grow runs $180 to $200 and weighs in at a hefty 32.4 lbs. This stroller seems squarely aimed at the Joovy Big Caboose market.

The DuoGlider ($150, 29 lbs.) is also a front/back tandem. Graco's claim to fame in this niche is "stadium seating," where the rear seat is elevated. Of course, you get all the standard features: huge storage baskets, removable canopies, etc. Cool feature: The DuoGlider holds two Graco infant car seats.

Graco's other tandem is the Quattro Tour Duo (32 lbs., $200-$230), which features a curvy frame, fancy cup holders, stadium seating, one-hand "gravity" fold, large basket and a back seat with full recline. The Quattro Tour Duo is about 20% smaller than the DuoGlider.

New to the lineup is a model that is similar to Baby Trend's Sit N Stand: the RoomFor2. This stroller holds a 50 lb. child in both front or rear jump seat and features a large basket, one-hand fold, parent tray and the ability to hold a car seat in front. The child in the rear can sit or stand. Price: $140, 24.7 lbs.

Finally in the double stroller category, Graco offers one side-by-side model: the FastAction Duo ($280), a Babies R Us Exclusive. This stroller is essentially a double version of the FastAction Fold Sport.

◆ **Misc.** Graco has a couple of other strollers that don't quite fit into the above categories.

Graco's entry in the stroller frame category, the Snug Rider, is a winner—this $70 frame holds the (what else?) Graco Snug Ride infant car seat with a secure lock-in feature and has a one-hand fold and basket. New in the past year, Graco rolled out a Snug Rider Elite: this $90 model has integrated cup holders, zippered storage and one-hand fold. It holds both Graco's Classic and Click Connect infant seats.

Travel systems are a major part of the Graco stroller line-up, where a Graco stroller (like the ones reviewed above) are paired with a Graco infant seat in one box. Graco does sell some travel systems that include older model strollers that aren't sold separately. An example is the Quattro Tour, a Hummer-like stroller that weighs 26+ lbs. empty. The Quattro features a one-hand gravity fold, fully reclining seat, and large parent storage tray that holds two drinks. The Quattro Tour Reverse (30.6 lbs.) features a seat that rotates to face forward or rear,

strollers

plus a three position recline, one-hand fold and large basket. It is sold as a travel system with the SnugRide 30 or 35 ($300).

There are a slew of other travel system models out there (Alano, Spree, etc)—most of these strollers are "full-feature" models that feature large storage baskets, parent trays and reclining seats.

Our view. Graco has slowly improved its stroller line over the past several years. The brand used to be known for selling mostly bulky travel systems with hulking strollers that weighed 30 lbs. empty. Today there are more three-wheel options and strollers that have slimmed down, weight wise.

The best options here are the Modes and FastAction Fold Sport strollers. Fans of the Modes like its ability to have baby face you or out—the ten riding configurations are a plus. The fact that the seat removes and you can use the remaining frame to snap in an infant car seat is another major plus. Critics of the Modes point out the stroller is still rather heavy and bulky—23.3 lbs with seat is light for Graco, but heavy when compared to the competition. The $250 Modes is pricey.

The FastAction Fold Sport is also a winner—a credible alternative to the Baby Jogger Mini at a price that's 40% less.

Of course, despite the generally positive reviews, Graco strollers aren't without their faults. Look at how some Graco strollers fold up . . . when folded, the front tray hits the ground, inevitably damaging or scratching it in a parking lot. Parents also complain about canopies that offer less than full coverage (note that several of Graco's new models include fully enclosing canopies). And the steering on most Graco strollers is only so-so. These strollers were designed for the mall or smooth sidewalks.

Graco strollers are bulky when folded—even the lightweight ones can eat up the entire trunk of an average sized car. Factor this into your decision if your ride is a small compact.

Bottom line: Graco's strollers are designed for the mall or other light duty shopping trips. Don't expect these strollers to do well in urban environs with cracked sidewalks. Stick with Graco's lightest weight models and set your expectations accordingly. *Baby Bargains Resale Rank: Poor.* **Rating: B**

Harmony *HarmonyJuvenile.com* Canada-based car seat maker Harmony is probably best known for their affordable booster car seats, sold in chain stores. The company is trying to expand outside that niche with their first stroller, the Odyssey.

The Odyssey Modular Stroller, is surprisingly cheap—$150 at Target. As the name implies: this is a modular stroller, which is aiming for the multi-function stroller buyer.

The unit includes a universal car seat adapter, reversible seat with 3-positions and bassinet conversion, height adjustable handle, and full canopy. The wheels on the Odyssey are EVA foam with larger 10" wheels in the rear and lockable 7" wheels in front.

That all sounds great, but there is one definite negative: it's heavy! Yep, the frame is 17.9 lbs. and the seat is a 10.7 lbs. making the stroller nearly 28 lbs. total. And you have to remove the bassinet from the frame in order to fold it all down flat.

Real world feedback on this stroller has been mostly positive. Critics, however, say it is too heavy/bulky. And the Odyssey's car seat adapter doesn't work with all car seats (Britax's B-Safe is an example of a non-compatible one).

The Harmony Odyssey is aiming at the multi-function market that is dominated by UPPAbaby's Vista and Britax's B-Ready, as well as the Baby Jogger Select. Those strollers sell for $500 to $700, so the Harmony looks like a steal. We like the clever design, including the seat that morphs into a bassinet for newborns.

But we wonder if Harmony is a bit out its league here—multi-function stroller buyers are most likely urban parents who care about the stroller's weight. Most of these strollers are sold in specialty stores or chains like Buy Buy Baby. Harmony's emphasis on bargain basement booster seats sold in Walmart and Target makes us wonder if they can succeed here. Harmony's goal of taking a modular stroller and making it affordable is laudable, but we'd guess that most Target shoppers are looking for simple, lightweight strollers designed for the suburbs.

And the fact the Odyssey weighs 10% to 25% than the competition may outweigh the bargain price. ***Rating: B-***

Hauck/I'coo *GTBaby.com* Grand Touring Baby is the US importer for German stroller maker Hauck, which sells its wares under both Hauck and a sub-brand, i'coo.

The models. The i'coo Photon ($500) is a multi-function stroller with a seat that elevates—yep, you read that right. The Photon's seat's moves up or down to adjust the eight (so it can be pulled up to a table at a restaurant, for example). The Photon's seat also morphs into a lay flat bassinet and reverses.

Under the Hauck brand, the Malibu ($216, 19.1 lbs.) features a curved, aluminum frame, four-way reclining seat, adjustable footrest and large basket.

The Hauck FreeRider ($400, 23 lbs.) looks like a riff on a Phil & Ted, with its second seat that rides behind the storage basket. This three wheel stroller features an adjustable handle, adjustable footrest and the ability to hold an infant car seat. In the past year, Hauck added an extra canopy for the second seat and a full recline.

New in the past year, the Hauck Torro is a $170, 17 lb. model with large canopy, cup holder and boot. The Torro features a one-hand seat reline.

Our view. This brand has had such little sales success in the U.S., it is hard to judge the quality here. What little feedback that is posted to our message boards or in product reviews is mostly positive, however.

The Hauck Malibu has the most feedback—and most readers are happy with it. Fans love the large canopy and multi-function design. But critics knock the extensive assembly, difficult two-hand fold and the lack of a cup holder.

Perhaps the biggest drawback to this brand is their European-ness. Hauck and i'coo are successful in Europe, but that doesn't always translate to the US. An example is the difficult and complicated fold on many of these strollers. Since Europeans walk more and drive less, we'd guess that collapsing the stroller to put it in a trunk isn't high on the design priority list for European parents. But for us, that is an essential—and when the competition is so much easier, Hauck/i'coo doesn't stack up well.

Bottom line: buying one of these strollers is a leap of faith, as there are few stores that sell it so seeing these strollers in person will be a challenge. *Baby Bargains Resale Rank: Poor.* **Rating: B-**

Inglesina *Inglesina.com* Given the success of fellow Italian stroller makers Peg Perego and Chicco, you'd think Inglesina would be another slam-dunk here in the U.S. Yet the company has struggled for several reasons. First, it lacks an infant car seat—that means Inglesina is frozen out of the big travel system market. Second, distribution—these strollers aren't sold in many big box stores, so seeing them in person takes quite a bit of effort.

The models. Inglesina has two umbrella-style models: Trip and Swift.

The Trip ($200, 14.9 lbs.) is a lightweight umbrella model with a four-position seat recline, adjustable footrest, cup holder and included rain cover. The Swift (13 lbs., $130) is a scaled down version of the Trip, but still has the same seat recline. It omits the cup holder and rain cover and has a less fancy canopy. FYI: the Trip and Swift are made in China.

Inglesina recently made some small improvements to the Trip: bigger wheels, improved suspension and a larger extended canopy. In the past year, the Trip got a bumper bar and rain cover with no increase in price.

The company plans to launch two new, full-size stroller models in 2014: the Quad and Trilogy. These replace the Avio ($500), which is now discontinued.

The Quad ($600) is an all-terrain stroller with front and rear suspension, a full recline, reversible seat and one-hand fold (that only works without the seat in place, unfortunately). The Quad weighs in at a hefty 26.1 lbs and will be released in March 2014. Included in the price is a cup holder, rain cover and boot. A optional bassinet is $250. The Quad is compatible with Combi infant car seats.

The Trilogy ($500) features a reversible seat, rain cover, one-hand, self-standing fold with seat (in either direction). The weight is 22.7 lbs.

Our view. We've always liked this brand, despite its lack of distribution and market success. The Trip and Swift are the most popular models and get good marks for quality. Fans like the tall handles and ease of use, but critics say the seats are too shallow for larger toddlers.

The Quad and Trilogy will be tougher sells, given their high price points. Both were not out on the market as of this writing, so no parent feedback yet.

Bottom line: Inglesina strollers are well made; we like all the included extras (cup holder, rain cover on some models) that cost extra elsewhere. *Baby Bargains Resale Rank: Poor.* **Rating: A**

InStep *See Schwinn.*

i'coo/Traxx *See Hauck.*

Jane Spanish stroller maker Jane (pronounced Hah-ney) tried and failed to crack the US market in the last decade. But they're back, to give it another go.

Jane's flagship model is the Powertwin Pro ($700), an all-terrain double tri-wheel stroller with turnable front wheel. The Powertwin features a handle-bar activated front disc brake and rear wheel suspension.

Jane has three other strollers: the Nanuq (an umbrella stroller for $250), the Rider (a full size model with reversible seat for $750) and the Trider Extreme (similar to the Rider, $790).

Feedback on the last version of the Powertwin that was sold in the US was mixed at best. Many complained of the stroller's weight and bulk, plus the storage basket is hard to access. Oddly, Jane doesn't look like it has changed the Powertwin in recent years.

These reintroduced strollers were new to the market as of this writing, so no feedback yet. **Rating: Not Yet.**

Jeep See *Kolcraft.*

JJ Cole JJ Cole's strollers are re-branded versions of strollers made by The First Years. The JJ Cole Broadway 360 ($400 to $450) is the same as the First Years Wave. The JJ Cole Monroe ($130) is similar to the First Years Ignite ($60), but adds a front bumper bar and snack tray.

See *The First Years for a review.*

We're not quite sure why you'd pay a premium for the JJ Cole version of these strollers—the Monroe is almost double the price of the Ignite, although it is nearly identical. We like First Years strollers—but at First Year's prices.

Joovy *joovy.com* Joovy was launched in 2002 by a former Baby Trend executive who secured the rights to the English pushcart better known as the Baby Trend Sit N Stand.

The models. Joovy re-christened this model as the Caboose Stand-on Tandem ($150, 26 lbs.). Compared to the old Sit N Stand, Joovy's Caboose features a higher handle height, foam handle, improved car seat attachment and nicer canopy. The company also brightened up the fashion.

Over the last few years, Joovy has refined the Caboose—now the seat recline doesn't interfere with the space for the toddler. And the infant car seat attachment sits higher than the previous model. FYI: the Joovy works with 13 infant seats, including the Graco SnugRide and Chicco KeyFit.

In recent years, Joovy has rolled out several spin-offs of the Caboose: the Caboose Ultralight, Big Caboose, Ergo Caboose and Big Caboose Stand On Triple.

The Caboose Ultralight ($240 to $270, 24.3 lbs.) is 20% lighter than the original Caboose and features a larger canopy and neoprene parent organizer. In the past year, this stroller got a fancier canopy and taller seat. A new rear seat accessory (Caboose Too seat) is now available for an additional $70. In the future, the rear seat may become an included accessory with the Ultralight for $299 total. FYI: There is also a Caboose Too Ultralight, which is similar to the Ultralight but adds a second seat (instead of a jump seat) in the back.

Got three kids? The Big Caboose ($350 to $380, 37 lbs.) has two seats plus a toddler jump seat/standing area. This model can also handle two infant car seats—so if you have twins and an older toddler, this would be one of the few models out there to hold all three tykes.

The Ergo Caboose ($350 to $400, 28.5 lbs.) looks like a pregnant Bugaboo—it features air-filled rear tires, ergonomic mesh seat with two-position recline, a longer frame with better access to the storage basket and a slew of accessories (rain cover, fleece canopy, etc).

New to the line is the Caboose VaryLight ($440, 34 lbs.)—this Caboose features a frame that expands, turning the stroller from a single to double stroller. The VaryLight is car seat compatible and features a one-hand fold, storage basket and front wheel suspension.

While the Caboose is Joovy's flagship model, the company has several other strollers. The ScooterX2 ($230) is a lightweight side-by-side twin stroller with a funky elevated handle and elliptical frame. It also features a deep (but not full) seat recline. Like all Joovy strollers, the Scooter X2 features an oversized canopy and large storage basket. Yes, there is a cup holder, perched between the two handles. FYI: There is a single version of this stroller, called the Scooter.

The compact, two-handle Groove ($190, 17 lbs.) umbrella stroller has a partial seat recline (150 degrees) and an extended canopy with sun visor plus six-inch wheels with suspension. The Groove Ultralight

($200) has much the same features to the Groove, but has a lighter weight frame (12.8 lbs) as well as smaller wheels and somewhat less seat padding.

Joovy's Zoom ATS ($250 to $270) is a jogger with fixed front wheel, no rear axle (so you can run without kicking the back), full canopy, car seat adaptor (seats click in) and parent tray. Yep, it is pricey—but it does include a rain cover. A version of this stroller (Zoom 360, $250 to $270) is available with a front swivel wheel.

Joovy's stroller frame is the Roo, which comes in both single ($100 16.2 lbs.) and double versions (TwinRoo, $120, 21.6 lbs.). Both feature a one-hand fold, parent organizer and work with Chicco, Graco and Peg Perego infant seats. Unlike other stroller frames, Joovy's Roo positions the infant car seat sideways. You can click the car seat into the frame and release it with the seat's release lever.

New in the past year is the Qool, available both in single and double (Too Qool) versions. The Qool ($550, 21.5 lbs) features a reversible seat, telescoping handlebar, four wheel suspension, large canopy, and an adjustable footrest. The seat offers a 140 degree recline. The Too Qool ($800, 36.5 lbs.) is a double, with the second seat in the back (like Phil & Teds). The Too Qool can be used with a bassinet or car seat adapter, both of which are optional accessories.

Our view. Of all the Caboose variations, we recommend the Joovy Caboose Ultralight as tops. Reader feedback on this model is mostly positive—the lighter weight makes it a worthy upgrade over the regular Caboose. Fans like the easy fold and compatibility with most infant car seats. Critics say infant car seats must be strapped down (there is no click-in lock). And even when collapsed, the Caboose takes up a large amount of trunk real estate.

Feedback on Joovy's other strollers has been generally positive. Readers like the Zoom, especially the 360 model. The Zoom is a great value, but a few parents criticized the weight (27 lbs.) and smallish seat, which means larger toddlers will quickly out grow it. The Groove has less feedback (but again, mostly positive).

As for Joovy's other offerings, the ScooterX2 also gets good marks for its easy fold, although it takes two hands. This stroller is a good choice for those looking at an affordable option for a side-by-side stroller.

The Joovy models that are least popular are probably its largest/heaviest strollers: the Ergo Caboose and Big Caboose. These strollers are large and bulky—and when weighed down with two or three kids, they can require Herculean efforts to push and maneuver.

Bottom line: it's unusual for a stroller company to have mostly positive reviews across nearly all its models, especially a line as large as Joovy's. Fans love the overall value and features like oversized canopies. We are raising Joovy's rating this year to reflect this. *Baby Bargains Resale Rank: Good.* ***Rating: A-***

strollers

Kinderwagon Shopping for a double stroller can often be a choice of lesser evils. In Column A, you have tandem (front/back) strollers that are expensive beasts, weighing slightly less than a young adult hippopotamus. A tandem's long wheel base can make them difficult to steer when fully loaded with kids and diaper bags. And you'll need a huge trunk to haul it around.

In Column B, you have side-by-side strollers, which tend to be lighter in weight. The trade-off is width—at 30"+, these strollers may not fit through doors or around shopping racks.

Into this void comes the Kinderwagon Hop, the first lightweight tandem that is the same width as a single stroller, yet can hold 50 lbs. of kid per seat. Invented by parents of multiples, the Kinderwagon Hop weighs just 21.8 lbs. and features stadium seating—the back seat is higher than the front. This prevents that inevitable fight between twins over who gets the view. (FYI: despite the German sounding name, Kinderwagon is actually based in Rhode Island and imports its strollers from China).

The Hop's back seat features a partial (130 degree) recline and the front seat is basically fixed. For $300, the Hop includes a large number of features that are often extras: diaper bag, cup holder and rain cover. When folded, the stroller is 47" tall, 11.5" deep and 10" wide—basically, long and narrow, which should fit well into most trunks.

Like many baby gear companies, Kinderwagon was started because two parents couldn't find what they were looking for, this time in the double stroller category.

Parent feedback on the Hop is positive, with kudos to the light weight and overall smart design. Negatives to the stroller include a rather stiff folding mechanism that takes some time to loosen up. The fold itself requires a few steps but can be done with one-hand. The lack of fully reclining seats means babies under six months will probably need head support to sit in the Kinderwagon Hop's seats.

And there is just a single canopy for the Hop—that means the front seat doesn't get full coverage.

In many ways, the Hop feels like a version 1.0 product. It is a good first effort, but small improvements would make the Hop better (example: the front napper bar isn't removable, so toddlers can't climb in/out of the stroller by themselves). The cup holder pops off too easily. And smaller moms may notice their visibility of the stroller's front blocked by the canopy.

Bottom line: the Kinderwagon Hop is an innovative and unique stroller, with a few rough edges. At $300, it is hardly a bargain—but for parents of twins (or two babies close in age), this may be the best choice for a lightweight and compact stroller. ***Rating: B+***

Kolcraft *kolcraft.com* Kolcraft is the exception to the rule that you need a successful infant car seat to succeed in the stroller market—

despite the lack of any travel systems, Kolcraft has survived, thanks to some clever licensing and innovation.

The models. Kolcraft sells strollers under three brands: Kolcraft, Jeep and Contours. Kolcraft is sold as entry-level models at chains stores like Walmart.

The best-selling strollers here are in the Jeep line— yep, an entire line of strollers based on the Jeep vehicle brand. Yes, a stroller with a toy steering wheel is cute . . . but can these strollers stand up against other brands in this price range?

The best selling Jeep is the Liberty Limited—a three-wheel stroller with turnable front wheel that can be locked in a forward position. This all terrain stroller fits many major brand infant car seats and features a reclining seat, height-adjustable five-point harness (Grow-With-Me) and more. At $170 to $200, it's no surprise this one has been a hot seller. Parent reviews have been generally positive on this model, albeit with a stray complaint about inflated tires that go flat and a too-short handle for tall parents.

Kolcraft sells several versions of the Liberty—the more expensive models add extra storage (a bag on the side of the basket), fancier padding and an electronic toy steering wheel.

Kolcraft also makes a raft of other Jeep models, including an umbrella style (Wrangler All Weather, 18.5 lbs., $40) and a more traditional lightweight model, the Cherokee Sport ($46), which is a best seller. The Wrangler Twin Sport is a side-by-side model for $110.

There are also a couple joggers: the Jeep Overland Limited ($180 to 210) and the Jeep Wrangler Sport ($350).

Kolcraft's other major stroller label is Contours, which features a bit more style than one would expect from a mass market brand like Kolcraft (bright red fabrics, curved tubular frames, etc.).

Contours has both single and double strollers. On the single side, the Contours Options 3 Wheel Stroller ($130 to $170, 26 lbs.) has an infant car seat adapter and reversible seat, so you can see baby while pushing. The Contours Lite stroller ($80, 15.5 lbs.) features a large storage basket, partial seat recline and a value price..

The Contours Bliss (25.3 lbs.) 4-in-1 stroller is new and the most expensive Kolcraft stroller—the $400 Bliss features a reversible seat that can convert into a bassinet. Yep, this is like a poor man's UPPAbaby Vista. At $400, the Bliss is pricey but includes an infant car seat adapter, a fold with or without the seat attached, cup holder and more.

Contours double stroller options are among our top picks in this category. The Contours Options LT Tandem ($250, 32 lbs.) is a good example. It has seats that can face each other—and the stroller comes with a car seat adapter (a second one is available as an accessory). An upgraded version of this tandem (the Contours Optima) is $300. New for 2014, the Contours Options Elite will debut in June for $300 and replace the LT—it features rubber coated tires, side storage basket access and seat back storage.

Our view. Dollar for dollar, these are the best affordable strollers on the market. Compared to other low-end brands (Graco, Cosco), Kolcraft shines.

The Contours Lite is a winner—we liked the affordable price tag and overall lightweight design. Critics, however note the seat doesn't quite sit upright, which bothers some older toddlers. The canopy's coverage is also a bit skimpy, the toddler tray and cup holder are in an awkwardly high position and the stroller doesn't offer a compact fold. But then again, it is just $66 on Amazon.

Readers also like the Contours Options 3 Wheeler (but be forewarned: the stroller can't be folded when the seat is in the rear-facing position) as well as Kolcraft's double strollers.

The Contours tandem strollers are also winners.

As for the Jeep line., we like the Jeep Cherokee Sport as a good, affordable stroller that is under $50. The Jeep Liberty three-wheeler isn't a bad option for an affordable all-terrain stroller, but it is showing its age. It needs to be updated to keep up with the competition.

Bottom line: for suburbanites who need a sturdy stroller with lots of storage for the mall, this brand fits the bill. *Baby Bargains Resale Rank: Fair.* **Rating: B+**

Lamaze *TheFirstYears.com* See *The First Years.*

Maclaren *maclarenbaby.com* Maclaren maclarenbaby.com Given this brand's bankruptcy and safety recalls, we do not recommend Maclaren strollers. *Baby Bargains Resale Rank: Poor.* **Rating: F**

Mamas and Papas *mamasandpapas.com* No, not the 1960's folk rock group. Mamas and Papas is the UK-based baby product manufacturer and retailer that landed in the U.S. in 2010. In Britain, the brand is like Graco, selling products across several categories. Unlike U.S. competitors, Mamas and Papas not only makes baby gear but also runs their own chain of stores in Britain.

The models. The flagship model here is the oddly named Armadillo, a "big little stroller" as the company bills it. The Armadillo ($250, 20 lbs.) features a wide seat, full recline, adjustable footrest, one hand fold, large basket and wheel suspension. Car seat adapters are available for the Chicco, Maxi Cosi and Cybex car seats.

In case you missed it, the Armadillo is clearly "inspired" by the Bugaboo Bee, down to the animal name and bright yellow canopy. On the plus side, the Armadillo is less than half the Bee's $650 price tag.

Mamas and Papas other major offerings is the Urbo ($500), a 22.3 lb. shiny aluminum model with reversible seat, large canopy and fully reclining seat. Infant car seat adapters are available for Graco and Maxi Cosi infant seats ($35 to $60).

New in the past year, the company debuted a revised version of the Urbo (called the Urbo 2) that adds front and rear wheel suspension, a reversible fully reclining seat and flip flop friendly brakes. The Urbo 2 ($575, 23.7 lbs.) has an optional bassinet ($215) and an easier fold (with the seat facing forward only, however).

The spider-like Mylo stroller is heavy (32 lbs.) and pricey ($600 to $800), but includes a carrycot, foot muff, fully reclining seat that reverses, telescoping handle and adjustable footrest.

The Sola ($400 to $420, 26.1 lbs.) is Mamas and Papas' riff on the Bugaboo Cameleon, with smaller front wheels and reversible seat. Like the Urbo, it has an optional infant car seat adapter and features adjustable handle height. The Sola has four wheel suspension, a lay flat seat and included rain cover. FYI: The Sola is Mamas and Papas best-selling model in the UK.

In the past year, Mama and Papas pared their line back quite a bit, discontinuing the three-wheel Luna Mix and a raft of lightweight strollers (Trip, Trek, Tour, Cruise, Voyage). You may still see these models sold on discount sites, however.

Our view. When Mamas and Papas invaded the U.S. a few years ago, they fell victim to one of the classic blunders of European stroller companies. The most famous of which is never get involved in a land war in Asia. But only slightly less well known is this. Never assume the stroller that sells well in the UK will appeal to Americans.

Hence, the first round of Mamas and Papas strollers brought to these shores were met with the sound of one hand clapping. They were too heavy, too expensive, had dinky storage baskets, lacked cup holders and were cumbersome to fold.

To their credit, Mamas and Papas regrouped and released the Armadillo. Despite being clearly derivative of other animal-named strollers, at least this stroller hits all the right notes—relatively light in weight (although at 20 lbs., they are pushing it), easy to fold and spacious in storage. Parent reviews of this stroller are positive.

Feedback on Mamas and Papas other models have been mixed. While fans like the overall features for the strollers, critics point out little problems are always popping up—a cup holder that doesn't stay in place, wheels that squeak or click after a month of usage. The fold of many models (like the original Urbo) is probably the biggest problem here—"user unfriendly" is how one parent described the fold on her Mamas and Papas umbrella stroller. "Good luck closing it," chimed another.

We are also somewhat perplexed with Mamas and Papas distribution strategy—many of these company's models are exclusive to Babies R Us. That seems to us to be a mismatch, as BRU's more mainstream customers aren't likely to throw down $500+ on an Urbo.

And why no car seat adapter for Graco for the Armadillo? Did they miss the millions of these infant seats being sold?

Bottom line: it is mixed review for Mamas and Papas. Kudos to the Armadillo for hitting the mark. But a miss for the Urbo, Mylo and Sola. The revised Urbo 2 was too new as of this writing to see whether its improvements merit another look. Overall, we're raising this brand's rating a half grade to reflect improvement, however. *Baby Bargains Resale Rank: Excellent.* **Rating: C+**

Maxi Cosi *maxi-cosi.com* Dorel brought its European subsidiaries Maxi Cosi and Quinny to the U.S. a few of years ago to bolster the brand's efforts in the upper end of the stroller market.

The models. Maxi Cosi's main focus in the U.S. is car seats, but they do offer one stroller: the Kaia ($200, 16 lbs.).

This lightweight umbrella stroller stands when folded and works with Maxi Cosi's Mico infant car seat (adapters are included). It also is sold as a travel system with the Mico.

The basket is smallish, but has decent access. Ditto for the canopy—not the largest on the market, but decent enough. The partial seat recline will work for most toddlers, but not for napping—hence Maxi Cosi suggests using this stroller (without the car seat) for babies six months and older.

One plus: the Kaia has a long distance (12") between the seat and leg rest, a plus for toddlers with longer legs. On the downside, the Kaia only comes in two colors: you better like black or red.

Our view. Maxi Cosi has jettisoned many of its heavier models that it sold in recent years. The Kaia is probably more in tune with the market—a higher-end umbrella stroller that weighs just 16 lbs.

Feedback on the Kaia has been mostly positive, although the limited canopy coverage and partial seat recline suggest this it is aimed more at parents with older toddlers for trips to the mall. *Baby Bargains Resale Rank: Poor.* **Rating: B**

Mia Moda *This brand is reviewed on the free side of our web site, BabyBargains.com/bonus.*

Mima *MimaKids.com* The Netherlands must have a college with a stroller design major—the small country has churned out such heavyweight stroller brands such as Bugaboo, Quinny, and Mutsy. Now, add Mima to that list, as it debuts in the US in 2014.

Actually, Mima is based in Spain, but designer Davy Kho hails from the Netherlands, so we'll still chalk this one up to the Dutch.

Mima's flagship stroller is the impossibly over-the-top Kobi, a stroller that sells for a whopping $1350 to $1700 (with a second seat). The stroller features an egg-shaped seat made from a material called EVA, which Mima says "provides a firm, protective 'shell' for your baby." The Kobi features an unique Z-shaped frame and five different riding configurations. Cool feature: a bassinet that morphs into a seat. What's missing? Well, a storage basket for one (the Kobi has a small storage compartment near its base).

The Kobi is a beast—the chassis alone weighs 23 lbs. Add in a seat and you've got a 35 lb. stroller.

The Kobi's cousin is the Xari ($1200), a stroller that has much the same function of the Kobi but is a bit lighter, features three recline positions and can be folded with or without the seat.

If this is too much stroller, Mima also offers the Bo ($300, 17.9 lbs.), an umbrella stroller with partial seat recline, adjustable leg rest and interchangeable color inserts. The leather-like finish on the Bo's fabric is an eye-catcher, but it also adds somewhat to the stroller's weight. The Bo looks and folds like other high-end umbrella strollers (such as Maclaren), with a latch on the back you push up and then fold over the stroller to the ground.

Mima just started shipping to the US as of this writing, so no parent feedback yet. Rating: **Not Yet.**

Mountain Buggy *mountainbuggy.com* Mountain Buggy got a second chance at the U.S. market when rival Phil & Teds scooped them out of bankruptcy in 2009. After moving the production of the New Zealand brand to China, Phil & Teds also updated Mountain Buggy's aging designs and lowered prices.

Mountain Buggy's forte is the all-terrain, tri-wheel stroller, with lightweight aluminum frames (21-24 lbs., depending on the model), 12" air-filled tires with polymer rims, fully reclining seats, height adjustable handles and one-step folds.

The brand's flagship model is the Urban Jungle ($375 single, 24 lbs.; $600 to $680 double—called the Duo, 36 lbs.). It has a front wheel that can swivel or lock into place, plus a raft of available accessories, including a car seat adapter, carry cot, rain cover and more. Unfortunately, the cup holder is an extra expense.

If you don't need the swivel wheel, the brand offers a fixed-wheel model: the Terrain ($500). It is designed more as a jogger with 16" wheels and a hand brake.

The Swift ($450, 21 lbs.) is a compact version of the Urban Jungle—it has smaller, 10" tires. In the last year, Mountain Buggy has added a higher canopy with extendable visor and bumper bar to the stroller.

Following the trend of tri-wheel stroller makers adding four wheel models (re: Baby Jogger), Mountain Buggy debuted their first four wheeler in the past year: the Cosmopolitan ($550, 26 lbs.). It features a reversible seat that turns into a lay-flat bassinet for newborns,

EVA/rubber tires (12" rear, 8" back), two step fold and large canopy.

Obviously, the Cosmopolitan is drifting away from Mountain Buggy's core market (note the lack of air-filled tires). This model is clearly aiming at the multi-function market dominated by UPPAbaby and Britax's B-Ready. One note: the Cosmopolitan has car seat adapters for Graco, Maxi Cosi and Cybex.

Along the same lines is the MB mini stroller ($350)—basically, this is a Swift that substitutes foam filled wheels for the air tires. This helps shave off four pounds in weight—the MB Mini is 17.5 lbs.

You can see Phil & Ted's influence on this line with the new +one Mountain Buggy ($650)—this inline stroller can hold two kids in a front/back position. Sort of like a tandem version of the Urban Jungle.

New for 2014, Mountain Buggy will launch what it claims to be the lightest weight stroller on the market—the Nano ($200, 13.1 lbs.). This travel stroller has universal infant car seat straps (to fit any infant car seat) and is clearly aimed at folks who do a lot of airplane travel. The Nano comes with a travel bag and doesn't need to be gate checked, claims Mountain Buggy (try explaining that to the airplane gate attendant, however).

Our view. Mountain Buggy generally gets high marks for quality and usability. Fans love the off road ability, although critics wish the canopy was larger. We've also seen a few complaints from heavy users on the durability of tires—some folks go through one or two replacement sets because the tread wears too quickly. If Mountain Buggy could offer heavy duty tires as an accessory, that might do the trick.

Early feedback on the Cosmopolitan has been positive. It will be interesting to see if Mountain Buggy picks up more fans as it moves away from its all terrain niche with the Nano and MB Mini. *Baby Bargains Resale Rank: Fair.* **Rating: A**

Mutsy *Mutsy.com* Dutch-bred Mutsy came to the U.S. in 2007 and sells a collection of high-end, multi-function strollers.

The models. Mutsy's flagship model is the 4Rider ($575, 33.5 lbs.), which has 10" single-spoke wheels, a car seat adapter and optional bassinet. The 4Rider Light ($545 to $580, 30.6 lbs.) swaps the 4Rider's air-filled tires for rubber versions.

The Transporter ($400, 24 lbs.) features a partially reclining seat, height adjustable handle and 10" rear wheels. Car seat adapters and a bassinet ($150) are available.

The latest addition to the Mutsy line is the EVO stroller ($400). This 26.6 pound, full featured stroller has full recline, reversible and removable seat, and includes an enclosed footrest and expansion canopy. It is available with a black or aluminum chassis. Large foam wheels, a large basket and a height adjustable handle round out the features.

New for 2014, Mutsy is launching the iGo, a model that will eventually replace the 4Rider. The iGo features a telescoping handle, a reversible seat and optional bassinet. Price: $530. At 22.8 lbs., the iGo is significantly lighter than other Mutsy strollers and definitely a step in the right direction.

Our view. On paper, Mutsy looks like a slam-dunk—multifunction strollers that just ooze cool Euro chic. Unlike other models that tout a faux "European-inspired" label, Mutsy is the real deal. These strollers are head turners.

Yet, so far, Mutsy has barely been a blip on the sales radar at baby stores. Why the washout? In a word: weight. These strollers are too darn heavy. Even the "light" version of the 4Rider is 30.6 lbs. That's just too much for American tastes.

It will be interesting to see how the new iGo does—finally, Mutsy seems to have understood that light weight is a must.

Fans of Mutsy cite the super-adjustable handles, plush fabrics and ease of use. We also liked the more affordable Transporter, although the seat recline requires two hands and the canopy is somewhat skimpy. Quality, overall, is excellent.

One negative note: Mutsy suffered a safety recall on the Evo in 2012—the space between the grab bar and seat bottom was too large, allowing an infant to pass through. Fortunately, no injuries were reported due to this hazard. *Baby Bargains Resale Rank: Good.* **Rating: B+**

Nuna *Nuna.eu* Dutch-based baby gear maker landed in the U.S. in 2013 and is the latest European stroller company to give it a go here. Apparently, Europe has an endless supply of these companies, all looking to expand in North America.

The problem with European baby gear makers is they simply don't get how Americans use a product like a stroller. Yes, European strollers have four wheels—and American strollers (for the most part) have four wheels. But the lifestyles of European parents are much different than here—their use of mass transit, where they walk . . . and even their need for cup holders. Example: Italian strollers don't have cup holders because when an Italian mom goes for coffee with her baby, she walks to a cafe, sits down and drinks coffee. We, on the other hand, drive to the nearest mall, hit the Starbucks for a coffee . . . and need a cup holder because we are walking and strolling. We're a busy nation and we're off to invent the next tech wonder gadget. Europeans? Not so much.

Hence, most European strollers bomb in the U.S. for several reasons. They are often heavy, cumbersome to fold (because you don't often fold them in Amsterdam) and generally lack features like cup holders.

The Nuna Pepp is a case in point. This $300 stroller aims to be a lightweight, super-maneuverable stroller for shopping the mall.

And at 21.8 lbs, it does avoid the trap of other European strollers that are way too heavy to haul in and out of a trunk. But still . . . the Pepp is 20% (four pounds) heavier than the best-sellers in this category like the Baby Jogger City Mini or Britax B-Agile.

And the Pepp's other specs are equally disappointing—there is no full seat recline (only partial). And the seat reclines with two zippers, which are difficult to re-zip without getting the fabric stuck, etc. That's why most U.S. strollers have simpler reclines. And the fold? That requires two hands and several steps. Again, Europeans must have extra time on their hands because the one-hand, one-step fold is what wins parents' hearts here.

We liked the height adjustable handle and extra sun visor for the canopy; but the canopy's overall coverage pales in comparison to the canopies on a BOB stroller, for example. The Pepp's car seat adapter (an extra accessory) will work with only the Maxi Cosi and Cybex seats. The Pepp has an odd, low-to-the ground profile—we wonder if taller parents will find it cumbersome to buckle in baby. And of course, there is no standard cup holder.

Undaunted by the tepid reception of the Pepp, Nuna is launching a new high end stroller in 2014: the IVVI LUXX. This $900(!) stroller comes with a carry cot and reversible toddler seat, large storage basket, fully enclosing canopy, foam wheels, adjustable footrest, telescoping handle, infant insert—basically, everything but the kitchen sink. The weight? 32.8 lbs. (seat plus frame).

Also new: the MIXX, a $600 stroller that includes car seat adapters, reversible seat, full recline, large canopy, large storage basket and an easy flat fold. Nuna said they are aiming for a 24 lb. final weight, although the prototype we viewed was 27 lbs.

Bottom line: there has been little parent feedback on this brand, given the low sales. Nuna needs to do more homework on the stroller market here if it wants to break through in the U.S. *Rating: C-*

Orbit orbitbaby.com Fans of *The Office* may remember the Orbit, after Dwight Schrute spent an entire episode trying to destroy the pricey travel system to no avail. While that episode may qualify as the best baby product placement in a TV series ever, it showcased the Orbit's quality to withstand the show's extreme road test (you can see the episode on Orbit's web site).

The model. What set off Dwight? It was Orbit's über expensive price tag ("$1200 is more than I spent on my entire bomb shelter!"). Actually, the Orbit runs $750-$940, including the infant car seat reviewed in the past chapter. And no, the Orbit doesn't come with a toddler stroller seat—that's an extra $225.

New for 2014, Orbit is rolling out a third generation of its travel system. Orbit says it has upgraded the stroller's steering, handling and fold (its faster). You can now customize your Orbit with various color packs and accessories, sold a la carte. There are now two cup holders.

Our view. The verdict? Folks who have the Orbit love it—the unique car seat base makes for simple, rock solid installation, as we noted in the last chapter. The engineering on the Orbit is top notch: parents like the stroller frame's simple one-hand fold and ergonomic handles. And the frame lets you shift the car seat in a 360-degree range of motion.

Downsides? Even though the infant car seat works to 30 lbs., most kids will outgrow it by height before they hit that weight limit. Some bigger kids will age out of the Orbit at six months—and that's a lot of money to spend for such brief usage. Yes, you can pony up another $225 for a toddler stroller seat—but that means a total investment of $1000.

As we noted in the Orbit car seat review, the infant car seat carrier is heavy (nearly ten lbs.) and bulky, making it a tight fit in smaller vehicles. Once your baby is near the weight limits of the seat, carrying the Orbit's 30 lb. weight (baby plus car seat) will be a hardy upper-body workout.

New to the Orbit line is the Double Helix stroller. This stroller holds two infant seats, two toddler seats or one of each. The cost: a whopping $1200 (for a model with two toddler seats). You can also buy a Helix kit if you already have an Orbit stroller for $750. The kit allows you to add a second seat to your existing stroller.

Our View. The take-home message: if you are looking for a travel system that is a conversation starter, then Orbit is your brand. Parents love the Jetsons-like look . . . and having a stroller/car seat that no one on the block has is appealing.

Critics knock the overall bulk and weight of the Orbit. Some folks found the Orbit's handle bars to be uncomfortable. And while most fans like the infant car seat/frame combo, there is noticeably less love for the toddler configuration, when the weight/bulk of the system begins to outweigh the Orbit's advantages.

The new G3 version of Orbit wasn't out as of this writing, so we'll have to see if the brand's continued tweaks to the system improve parent feedback. *Baby Bargains Resale Rank: Fair.* **Rating: B**

Peg Perego *perego.com* Peg Perego is the Italian stroller maker that was among the first European brands to land in North America, way back in the 1980's. The company traces its roots back to 1949 when its founder Giuseppe Perego created a carriage for his infant son.

Unlike most other European brands who long ago abandoned production on the Continent in search of lower labor costs in Asia, Peg Perego still makes all its strollers in Italy. (Okay, there was a brief time when Perego flirted with Chinese imports with one model—the

strollers

Aria—but that didn't go well and the company returned back to an all-Italian line).

That all-Italian mantra for Peg has been both a blessing and curse. On the upside, the company's fabrics are considered among the most fashionable (although, admittedly, other companies have since closed the fashion gap). Peg's reputation for quality is also excellent. In an era where parents are concerned about Chinese imports and their safety, recalls on Perego strollers are rare.

But . . . the made-in-Europe label has its price—in the last few years, Peg's strollers have jumped in price to compensate for a strong Euro. Many new Peg models run $500 or more . . . that's a tough sell in this economy.

This brand has had its ups and downs in the past decade. They missed out on the all-terrain craze, as well as the boom in tri-wheel strollers. You'd think Perego would be strong player in the multi-function stroller market, first pioneered by Bugaboo and then perfected by UPPAbaby, Britax and others. But they missed that one too.

Peg also lost a bit of its cache after unloading its overstock strollers in closeout discounters like Marshall's.

So can Peg get its mojo back? Let's look at their current line up.

The models. Perego has a lengthy list of strollers that includes single models, doubles and what they dub "systems," modular models that include an infant car seat. Below is the current model line-up. We'll break this down into single, double and systems.

Single strollers. Peg's line-up includes eight single strollers: the Uno, Switch Four, Pliko Four, Vela Easy Drive, Pliko Mini, Book, Book Plus and Book Pop Up.

The Uno ($370 to $400, 23 lbs.) features a Bugaboo-ish wheel design with smaller wheels up front and larger ones in the back. It includes a reversible handle so you can face baby, as well as a boot and height adjustable handle. The only bummer: when you reverse the handle on the Uno, you have the turnable wheels in back (rear-wheel drive), which is awkward.

The Switch Four ($500, 23.8 lbs.) has a 150 degree reclining seat, reversible seat, foot muff and rain shield.

The Pliko Four ($400, 18.7 lbs.) features all wheel suspension and ball bearings for a smooth ride. This latest generation Pliko features a two-handle design, 150 degree reclining seat, adjustable leg rest, adjustable height handle and removable/washable seat cushions. There is also a one-hand fold. Compared to past versions of the Pliko, this model has a more compact fold.

If you like the Pliko but are turned off by the weight, there is a Pliko spin-off called the Pliko Mini ($250, 14 lbs.), Peg's lightest weight stroller. The Mini features a three-position reclining seat, cup holder, adjustable footrest and height adjustable handle.

The Si ($220 to $300, 16.5 lbs.) stroller was discontinued in 2013, but then comes back to life in 2014 as the Si Switch. As the name implies, it will feature a reversible seat, can be folded with the seat in either direction and stands when folded.

The latest addition to the Perego family is the Book stroller ($400, 22.6 lbs.), which gets its name from its fold: yes, it folds up like a book (and stands when folded). The Book features wider front wheels with suspension and a wider seat (it can also hold a car seat). Peg Perego recently tweaked the Book basket to make it larger and more accessible. Other features include a height adjustable handle bar, fully reclining seat, ball bearing wheels for a smooth glide and one-hand fold. The Book is also sold as a travel system, paired with Peg's infant car seat.

The Book Plus ($500, 24.4 lbs) adds a reversible seat and can be folded with or without the seat. The Book Plus comes with a boot and rain shield. You can snap in a Perego infant car seat right to the chassis, which can be bought separately for $270 (you can later add the stroller seat).

New for 2014, Peg is expanding the Book line with two new offerings: the Book Pop-Up and Booklet. The Book Pop Up ($800, 25.6 lbs.) is similar to the Book, but adds a seat and bassinet that both pop-up when opened. You can fold the Book Pop Up with the seat facing either direction and it takes a Peg infant seat without an adapter.

The less expensive Booklet ($350, 19 lbs.) features the same Book fold, but the seat doesn't reverse and is three pounds lighter than the base Book model.

Double strollers. Peg makes two double strollers: the Aria Twin ($300 to $350, 17 lbs.), a side-by-side model and the Duette SW ($800, 32 lbs.), a tandem model. The Aria has a 60/40 configuration that holds a car seat in the larger space.

Got triplets? Peg even makes a triple stroller, dubbed the Triplette SW for $1000 (we've seen it online for less). It weighs a whopping 61 lbs!

Modular systems. Peg sells two modular models: the Switch Four Modular System and the Skate.

The Switch Four Modular System is like the single version described above, but adds a bassinet and infant car seat plus a raft of accessories (bassinet stand, child tray, rain cover, foot muff, etc). Price: $1100. While this model is discontinued, we still see it for sale on some sites online.

The Skate was introduced in 2008 with much fanfare—it featured a Bugaboo-like multifunction frame, a height-adjustable handle, four-wheel suspension, ball-bearing wheels for a smooth glide, three seat heights and (drum roll) a cup holder. But it also cost an outrageous $900 and weighed 33.7 pounds . . . 68% more than the Bugaboo. The Skate was a bust.

Peg has since tweaked the Skate to fix its shortcomings. The current version now weighs 28.8 lbs. and features an $800 price tag, which includes a bassinet, an improved fold and other refinements. Yes, there's even a storage basket now.

Our view. Peg Perego's DNA is making expertly tailored full-size strollers. And bless their hearts, they have made these things no matter how the stroller market has changed over the years. Call them dedicated, crazy or just Italian, Peg Perego is . . . Peg Perego.

The Peg strollers we think are the best are their lightest weight offerings—the Pliko Mini is probably our favorite here, with its compact fold and overall good design. We wish it folded up quicker, with fewer steps, however. The Pliko Four is also a good choice, as is the Si (now reborn as the Si Switch).

Fans of Perego like their overall quality, features like a standing fold (in some models), and made in Italy fabrics. Critics bristle at the price (the Pliko Mini is $250—for a lightweight umbrella stroller?). The storage baskets on many Peregos are small.

Peg's full-size strollers are a tougher sell, given their weight and price. The Book and Book Plus are the stars here, with fans liking the reversible seats. Both are credible alternatives to the UPPAbaby Vista and Cruz models. The Skate, however, is a bust.

As for the double strollers, we are less enthusiastic about the Aria Twin, which gets low marks from readers—there are better options out there than this. *Baby Bargains Resale Rank: Fair.* **Rating: B+**

Phil & Teds *philandteds.com* When the sales of its in-line, all terrain strollers took off a few years ago, Phil & Teds committed one of the seven deadly sins of business—it over-expanded. The company quickly rolled out spin-offs to its tri-wheel stroller . . . and then suffered when quality control snafus led to a series of embarrassing safety recalls.

If that weren't enough, Phil & Teds acquired competitor Mountain Buggy's business out of bankruptcy. Digesting that acquisition and the hangover from the past years' expansion efforts has dogged the brand.

Phil & Teds has rebooted its business by slimming down its line in recent years and launching revisions to its best-selling inline buggies. Here's an overview.

The models. Phil & Ted's brand mojo is a tri-wheel stroller with inflated tires that can morph from a single stroller to a double with a toddler seat accessory. Car seat-compatible or with an optional bassinet, a Phil & Ted in-line stroller can go from birth to the toddler years with ease.

Phil & Teds flagship stroller is the Navigator ($500). The stroller features a large canopy, one-hand fold, adjustable handle and is car seat compatible. The Navigator has a large number of accessories, from storm/sun covers, to a travel bag, cold weather boot, cup holder and more. New accessories for the Navigator: a Snug Carry Cot ($150) and a face-to-face seat ($50), where the baby faces you when pushing. You can also use the doubles kit (the extra toddler seat) and an infant car seat at the same time.

What sets Phil & Ted apart is their second-child seat ($90 to $100 extra; for kids six months and up), which can attach to the FRONT or BACK of the stroller (for comparison, Valco's toddler seat only attaches to the front). The rear seat configuration turns off some parents (safety hint: the child in the backseat has to be removed first to prevent tipping). And if you put a larger toddler in the back seat, the access to the stroller's storage basket is limited.

Feedback on the Navigator has been positive—parents tell us the stroller's all-terrain 12" air-filled wheels are perfect for both the mall and hiking trails, plus the wide seat accommodates children for many years.

If the Navigator looks too big for your tastes, Phil & Ted's has a new compact stroller—the Dot ($450, 26 lbs.). The Dot and the Navigator share the same basic features and accessories (with one exception: the Face to Face seat is a Navigator exclusive). Even though the Dot is more compact than the Navigator (a little over an inch in width), the seat size is the same. The Dot's width is a slim 23".

If a $400-$500 stroller is out of your budget range, the company sells a stripped down version of the Navigator, dubbed the Classic ($370, 24 lbs.). The Classic omits the height adjustable handle and has less fancy padding. But it still has a large canopy and one-hand fold. Reader reviews on the Classic are not as effusive as the Navigator or Dot, however—the trade-off of fewer features and less fancy padding for a lower price is too much, say critics.

Two other strollers round out the inline category at Phil & Teds: the Verve and Promenade. The Verve ($550, 28 lbs) drops the air-filled wheels for foam tires—and adds a fourth wheel up front. You still get the option of adding a second seat, but there are only seven seat configurations for the Verve (versus 26 for the Navigator). Hence, the Verve is more aimed at city dwellers than those who plan off-road adventures.

The Promenade ($600, 28 lbs) is also aimed at urban parents, with a reversible seat that converts to a lay flat bed, adjustable handle, adjustable footrest and foam tires.

If all these presto-chango features are too much for your tastes, Phil & Teds does make a simple lightweight stroller. The Smart ($250, 12 lbs.) has smaller wheels up front and bigger tires in back, and features a compact fold and one-touch brake, but no cup holder. In a recent update, the Smart got a reversible seat with a car seat adapter accessory ($29).

New in the past year, Phil & Teds plans to release its first true jogging stroller, the Sub 4 ($900). It will feature wishbone suspension, disc brakes and quick-release wheels. The seat is made from a variable density foam.

FYI: Phil & Teds also makes a Costco exclusive stroller, the S4 ($400). This stroller is a less-fancy Classic, with "aerotech" tires and an included doubles kit. Aerotech tires are not air-filled; instead they are a blend of EVA foam and rubber—the same tires that are on the Verve and Promenade.

Our view. These strollers are perfect for the outdoors—the air-filled tires are great for hikes, gravel paths or rough sidewalks.

Readers give Phil & Teds an enthusiastic thumbs up for a smooth ride and second-seat functionality. The height adjustable handle also wins raves. We like the little touches such as the flip-flop friendly brake pedal and new, bigger canopy. Cons: a few parents complain of tire blowouts (requiring the purchase of extra tubes). And why no included cup holder? For 500 bucks, the least Phil & Teds could do is include a place to hold a water bottle.

Critics wish there was wheel suspension on the Navigator for a smoother ride. And one trade-off of the inline design is the rather long distance from the front to back of this stroller, making it a tight fit in smaller elevators.

Phil & Ted's more urban-focused models (Promenade, Verve) receive good marks from readers.

In the stroller wars, Phi & Teds has been somewhat eclipsed in recent years by Baby Jogger and BOB—thanks to the former's quick fold and the latter's more affordable prices. A BOB Revolution Double runs about $100 less than a Phil & Ted's Navigator with second seat accessory, but is wider with its side-by-side seat configuration.

Bottom line: if you need to transport two kids and like the idea of an in-line, all-terrain stroller, then Phil & Teds is a good bet. *Baby Bargains Resale Rank: Excellent.* **Rating: A-**

Quinny *quinny.com* Quinny is Dorel's (Cosco, Safety 1st) Dutch subsidiary known for its stylish multi-function strollers.

The models. The Buzz (26.4 lbs.) is Quinny's flagship model—this clever tri-wheel stroller has an innovative "automatic unfolding" feature plus a sleek look with a fully reclining seat that can face forward or back toward the parent. Like the Bugaboo, the Buzz is a modular system, albeit sold separately: $580 for a stroller, $100 to $190 for a carrycot (Dreami) and $190 for a matching Maxi Cosi Mico infant car seat. There is even a two-tone fashion option, like the Bugaboo Cameleon.

New for 2014, the Buzz gains an extendable, zippered canopy

and an air-filled tire up front. The 2014 Buzz weighs 27.7 lbs and runs $600.

The Zapp Xtra ($350, 20.1 lbs.) is Quinny's lightweight stroller with compact fold and reversible seat. This model also accommodates a Maxi Cosi car seat (Mico or Prezi). Unlike the Zapp's European counterpart, the U.S. Zapp Xtra has a storage basket. A cup holder, however, is an extra $25.

The Moodd comes in a $700 version with a white frame or as an $800 multi-colored "Britto" model. The Moodd features one-touch automatic unfold, reversible seat and funky T-bar front attachment, which makes the stroller look like something out of the Jetsons. A separate car seat adapter accessory works with Maxi Cosi or other brand infant seats.

The final stroller in the Quinny line is the odd ball of the group—the Yezz, which is billed as an ultra light weight urban stroller. At 11 lbs, it certainly is among the lightest strollers on the market, but this $280 stroller sacrifices storage to get there: no under seat storage basket, no parent storage, cup holder, etc. The skimpy canopy won't block much sun. The Yezz has a funky frame and small, skateboard like wheels.

Our view. Quinny's hardcore fans love the sleek design and gee-whiz features like the Buzz's automatic unfolding trick. But Quinny has failed to achieve mainstream success here and a look at parent feedback gives you a clue why.

Take the Buzz. It lacks all the features most parents take for granted in a good stroller—easy, one-hand fold, generous canopy, a place to put a cup of coffee, kid's snack tray and so on. The Buzz has none of that. Instead, you get a stroller with 25.5" wide rear wheels. This makes negotiating tight spaces difficult. The Buzz's fold can be a challenge, with levers that are hard to push. Add in that 26 lb. weight and you can see why the buzz on the Buzz has evaporated.

The Zapp has similar faults. Yes, it is much lighter in weight than the Buzz, but it lacks the simple quick fold found in competitors like Baby Jogger. Instead—the Zapp requires multiple steps, buttons you have to push, and a bottom latch that must be wrestled with. The skimpy canopy and lack of cup holder is the final capper for a $350 stroller.

We've heard little feedback on the pricey Moodd . . . and the Yezz is an expensive, niche offering for those looking for the lightest weight stroller and not much else.

One universal issue for Quinny: the smallish seats may be a tight fit for older toddlers. A clue to this issue comes in the top age recommendation for these strollers: at just three and a half years and 50 lbs., bigger toddlers may outgrow these pricey strollers too soon. And even the 50 lb. weight seems optimistic, considering the small seat dimensions.

In Quinny's defense, we should point out that the company has

strollers

tried to address their strollers' shortcomings with recent upgrades and improvements. And feedback on the strollers (especially the Buzz) has improved in the past year. Still, these strollers seem like they are sold mostly on snob appeal than practicality. We can understand if folks are attracted to the look here, but be prepared to pay through the nose for a stroller that just doesn't perform as well as its peers. *Baby Bargains Resale Rank: Fair.* **Rating: C**

Safety 1st See Cosco.

Schwinn/Instep *instep.net* This brand specializes in jogging strollers and all-terrain models with turnable front wheels.

Instep is part of the Pacific Cycle bicycling conglomerate, which in turn is part of the Dorel/Cosco juvenile products empire. InStep uses Schwinn as a sub-brand—basically, Schwinn models are similar to InStep, with upgraded fabric and additional accessories.

InStep offers two types of strollers: fixed and turnable wheels. In the fixed category, there is the Flash ($130) with 16" plastic wheels and the similar Arrow, which has bicycle spoke aluminum rim tires ($240).

The most popular InStep stroller is the Safari ($140), which has a turnable front wheel (12" in front, 16" rear). The Safari has plastic rims.

Schwinn has two models: the swivel wheel single jogger (Turismo, $175), and the Arrow , a fixed wheel single jogger for $175 to $200. There's also a double version of the Turismo for $225 to $280. These all-aluminum joggers are some of the most affordable on the market.

Schwinn joggers come with pneumatic tires, parent tray with two cup holders, hand break, dual trigger fold, and spring suspension. Your child will also get a built-in MP3 speaker so they can hear the music too.

There isn't much difference between the Schwinn and Instep strollers—you are basically paying 20% more for the Schwinn name.

Fans of these strollers like the value and features . . . it's hard to find a full feature stroller like this for under $200. Critics point out that even though these strollers have "jogger" in their name, they really are designed more for casual walkers, especially the swivel wheel models.

FYI: Instep hasn't changed or updated its line-up in some time; in fact, their web site still lists its 2008 catalog as its most recent offering. *Baby Bargains Resale Rank: Poor.* **Rating: C (Schwinn); B (InStep)**

Stokke *stokkeusa.com* Stokke (pronounced Stuck-Ah) is a Norwegian based baby gear company that traces its roots back to 1932. As you might guess, Norway's influence on the world baby gear market has been slight, but Stokke has had modest success here in the US, especially in the high chair category with the Tripp Trapp.

Stokke's strollers, however, have never quite gained much traction. Exhibit A: The Stokke Xplory.

The futuristic Xplory might look like something George Jetson would have pushed his boy Elroy around in, but it failed to make a splash when it was introduced to the U.S. ten years ago. Here's an overview.

The model. Like the Bugaboo, the Xplory ($1100) is a modular system that includes a frame with rubber tires and a seat that can attach to the frame either forward or rear facing. The Stokke's key feature is its high-altitude seating. The pitch, according to Stokke, is to keep baby higher off the ground so they are away from exhaust fumes, slobbering Labradors, etc. (the target market is urban parents).

In addition to a generous canopy, adjustable footrest and a raft of accessories, Xplory has optional car seat adapters for Maxi Cosi, Perego and Graco (older models, not the Click Connect). What's missing? If you answered, "storage basket," you are correct—instead Stokke throws in a shopping bag that is attached to the front of the unit.

After not releasing a new model for several years, Stokke rolled out not one but two new strollers in the past year: the Crusi and Scoot.

The Crusi (26 lbs., $1250) clearly riffs on Phil & Ted's inline buggy, with the optional second seat riding below the main seat. The Crusi includes a bassinet and stroller seat which can face forward or rear. Unlike the Xplory, however, the Crusi's seat can't change height. (The handle, however is height adjustable). Very pricey at $1250, but at least you get a rain cover, bug net and cup holder. The second seat runs $300.

The Stokke Scoot is the lighter weight cousin to the Crusi—it weighs 23 lbs. and runs $500. While you get the same reversible seat as the Crusi, this model omits the optional carry cot or sibling seat. The basket is also smaller, as are the wheels.

Our view. So why haven't you seen the über rich pushing the Stokke Xplory around Greenwich Village? That's because for the most part, the Xplory has been a bust. First, the handle and most of the Xplory's frame is injection-molded plastic, not something you'd expect from a $1000+ stroller. The "plastic-y" feel turns off many, while the lack of a basket is another major negative. Instead the Xplory has a "shopping bag" that attaches to the frame . . . right.

For years, Stokke resisted having infant car seat adapters available for its strollers—and that hurt sales. While the brand relented and finally added them a couple of years ago, it was too little, too late.

And look at the fold for the Xplory—it folds into *four separate pieces.* You first remove the foot rest, bumper bar and seat before you fold the chassis. Really? We're guessing the same person in Norway who thought this was smart also considers boiled cod a delicacy.

Add in the hotel mini bar prices for accessories ($300 for a winter foot muff?) and you can see why the Stokke Xplory just doesn't make the cut.

The newer Crusi and Scoot have sold in such modest numbers that we've heard very little parent feedback.

Bottom line: Stokke is a pass. *Baby Bargains Resale Rank: Good.*
Rating: C-

Stroll Air stroll-air.com Polish stroller company Stroll Air offers yet another multi-function stroller that aims to compete with the UPPAbaby Vistas of the world.

The models. The Zoom ($530, 24 lbs.) is Stroll Air's flagship model. This modular stroller system comes with three components: aluminum chassis, stroller seat and bassinet. The Zoom includes a wind cover, diaper bag, umbrella, storage basket, mosquito net, boot and rain cover. That's a rather impressive list considering the price. Accessories include a stroller organizer/console ($30, holds bottles and drinks) and infant car seat adapter.

Like the Bugaboo, the Zoom features larger rear wheels and smaller front wheels. Unlike the Bugaboo, you can fold the Zoom with the seat on.

The Stroll Air My Duo ($730 to $800, 26 lbs.) is the brand's first side-by-side model with two independently reversible seats that fully recline, front and back suspension, adjustable footrest and more.

New in the past year, Stroller Air debuted a new single stroller, the CosmoS ($500, 22.4 lbs). This compact folding stroller features a reversible seat, extendable canopy hood, rain cover, diaper bag, mosquito net and more—all for $500, including a bassinet. FYI: The CosmoS is replacing the Zoom.

Our view. You'd think with all the included accessories, Stroll Air models would be a slam dunk for a bargain pick in this book. But you'd be wrong.

That's because the quality just isn't here. As one parent put it in an online review, "they include all the accessories to sell a crap product." And that was one of the kinder reviews. Quality woes dog this brand—canopies that won't stay open, wheels that stop turning, low quality fabric that rips, etc.

Stroll Air's retail distribution is very thin—as of this writing, it was available in just ten states. That means probably buying one of these strollers sight unseen, which is risky.

The CosmoS was too new as of this writing for any parent feedback.

Bottom line: Stroll Air needs to go back to the drawing board and beef up its quality. **Rating: D**

Summer summerinfant.com Best known for its video baby monitors, Summer added strollers to their stable of products in 2010. Here's an overview.

The models. Summer's first effort in this category was the

Prodigy travel system that paired a stroller with Summer's first infant car seat in 2010. That stroller would go on to earn Biggest Stroller Bomb Of The Year Award . . . if we had that award to give out.

The Prodigy looked like a Graco stroller circa 1998—bulky, heavy and ugly. And that was its better features.

Summer wisely buried that model and rebooted its stroller line with three new models: the Fuze, Spectra and 3D Lite.

The Fuze ($300, 25.4 lbs) features a reversible seat, full canopy, fully reclining seat, large basket, height adjustable handle, cup holder and drop down fold. An included car seat adapter works with Summer's Prodigy infant seat as well as those from Perego, Chicco and Graco.

The Spectra ($220, 19.8 lbs) looks similar to the Fuze, but lacks the reversible seat. The Spectra does have a full seat recline, full canopy, adjustable foot rest and self-standing fold.

The 3D Lite ($80, 12 lbs.) is a two-handled umbrella style stroller that features a full seat recline, pop-out canopy, easy access to the basket and cup holder.

Our view. Summer 2.0 is definitely an improvement—we like the lower prices and feature mix here. The 3D Lite is probably the pick of the litter—we liked the seat recline, although it does require two hands.

Parent feedback on these models has been sparse, as they were relatively new as of this writing. Early adopters of the 3D Lite have been positive in their reviews, but a few cited some quality woes (wheels that broke, etc) and design flaws (the canopy needs to be bigger and offer more coverage).

There's been less feedback on the Fuze and Spectra—we were a little surprised at the price points here. While Summer has done a decent job in spec'ing these models, the $300 price point of the Fuze puts it squarely in Britax B-Ready and Baby Jogger territory. We're not convinced Summer has the same level of quality as those players, but we'll have to see. Meanwhile, we're raise Summer's grade a half point to reflect the improved offerings. **Rating: B-**

Thule Chariot *ChariotCarriers.com* Outdoor gear brand Thule Chariot takes a different approach to the jogger market—they makes bicycle trailers that covert into jogging strollers. If you are an avid bicyclist who also wants to occasionally jog with baby, Thule Chariot offers six models of bike trailers with optional kits that turn the trailers into jogging strollers. Example: the Cougar ($585, includes strolling kit), which features plush harness straps, padded seats and adjustable suspension. A plus: the Cougar has expanded legroom for the kiddies.

New to the line is the Corsair bike trailer that features Thule Chariot's largest child cockpit, side air vents, padded seat and 20" removable wheels. Price: $500 to $675.

While this brand is pricey (some models run close to $800), we've been impressed with Thule Chariot's quality—no, they aren't cheap . . . but you'll be amazed by the ease of use and adjustments. (Yes, there is even a cross-country ski kit). The downside: these trailers/joggers are too wide to take into most stores, so this isn't a good solution for shopping. Obviously, unless you are a serious biker or runner, a Thule Chariot is probably overkill. But if you want a quality bike trailer that can morph into a stroller, this brand should be on the top of your shopping list.

FYI: The Chariot brand started off as a Canadian company. It was acquired in 2011 by Thule, a Swedish outdoor brand best known for its bike carriers for vehicles. **Rating: A**

Trends For Kids *This brand is reviewed on the free side of our web site at BabyBagains.com/bonus*

Truly Scrumptious by Heidi Klum Truly Scrumptious strollers are a Babies R Us exclusive that are made by two partners: Thea & Co and Cosco. Thea & Co is a Chinese-made stroller importer based in Brea, CA. See Cosco for more info on their strollers.

UPPAbaby *UppaBaby.com* UPPAbaby was started by Bostonians Bob and Lauren Monahan and launched in the last decade. Bob worked for First Years and Safety 1st in product development before striking out on his own; Lauren provides the PR and design mojo. Obviously, Bob and Lauren have kids, as you can tell from the well thought-out designs of their strollers.

The models. UPPAbaby has a hit with their flagship model, the multi-function Vista ($700 to $730, 26.3 lbs.). Made with an aircraft alloy frame, the Vista stroller system includes a bassinet and stroller seat, telescoping handle and easy fold. We liked all the included extras, such as a rain shield, mesh sunshade and bug cover. Plus the Vista uses rubber-like foam wheels that give a smooth ride, but don't go flat. Unlike the Bugaboo, you can fold the Vista with the seat attached.

In a recent update, the Vista got a few minor tweaks and upgrades, including an improved canopy with pop-down sunshade and easier-to-adjust harness. Also new: a $130 rumble seat for a second child (we've seen it for $95 online) that can be used when the Vista is either in infant car seat or stroller seat mode. The latest model includes a slightly taller seat and lower basket, plus a new push-button brake.

The biggest news in the past year was UPPAbaby's launch of an infant car seat, the *Mesa*, which will obviously work with the Vista. But if you don't want to go for the Mesa, UPPAbaby offers car seat adapters for Graco, Chicco and Peg infant seats. While the Vista does include a weather shield, mesh sunshade and bug cover there are few additional accessories available (travel bag, cup holder, all terrain wheels).

UPPAbaby's second offering is the G-Lite ($120 8.3 lbs.), a super lightweight umbrella stroller with a standing fold and mesh seat and seat pad. The G-lite doesn't recline, so it is best for babies six months and up. There is also an upgraded version of the G-Lite, dubbed the G-Luxe ($190, 11.9 lbs.). It features a standing fold, bigger wheels, and partial seat recline. In a recent update, the G-Luxe got a removable, washable seat pad and an improved canopy.

In the past year, the G-Lite and G-Luxe got new wheels, a new, easier closing mechanism, reinforced frame and removable washable seat pads. The G-Luxe will also have a three-position seat recline.

The newest addition to the UPPA line is the Cruz, positioned between the G-Lite and the Vista. It features a reversible seat (but no bassinet) and adjustable height handle. The weight is about 17 lbs., and price is $460. Car seat adapters for the Maxi-Cosi, Graco, Chicco and Peg Perego infant seats are available for $30 to $40. Accessories include a bumper bar ($30), snack tray ($40) and travel bag ($90). Interesting note: the travel bag guarantees against damage by the gorillas at the airlines. Just register the bag with UPPAbaby's TravelSafe Program before you leave on your vacation.

Our view. Parent feedback on UPPAbaby has been positive. Readers who like the Vista praise its quality, huge basket and high-riding seat and bassinet. The no-flat foam tires also win raves. The negatives include a basket that is a bit hard to reach with the bassinet attached—and the rear wheelbase (25″) on the Vista is rather wide, making the stroller harder to maneuver in tight aisles or doorways. Another bummer: the seat doesn't have a full recline, which irks some users. But . . . the footrest is adjustable (something the Bugaboo lacks) and the fold is much easier and more compact compared to the Bugaboo or i'coo Targo. Another parent told us she loved the stroller as a single, less so as a double (the attached toddler seat made the steering difficult). We blogged about that issue back in 2011.

Those criticisms aside, folks who have the Vista give it high marks for quality and durability. The company's customer service is also excellent. If you live in the city and need a durable, multi-function stroller (and can live with the weight/bulk), the Vista is a good choice.

The G-lite wins similar kudos, with fans citing its super light weight and included cushions. The lack of seat recline in the G-lite is one major negative, but folks with older toddlers say it is fine for them.

So, we will recommend UPPAbaby—no, the Vista isn't cheap. But at least for the money, you get decent value (example: the sun canopy is included for the Vista; a $40 add-on for Bugaboo Cameleon, which is already $200 more than the Vista!). *Baby Bargains Resale Rank: Good.* Rating**: A**

strollers

Valco *valcobaby.com* Australia-based Valco has made a splash in the all-terrain stroller market with their Tri-Mode EX, a tri-wheel stroller whose key selling point is expandability.

The models. The basic Tri-Mode EX comes in both a single ($500, 23 lbs.) and double ($700, 33 lbs.) version and features a five-position, fully reclining seat, large storage basket, aluminum frame, newborn insert and swivel front wheel that can be locked in a fixed position. The Tri-Mode has 12" air-filled tires.

That's nice, but what really has parents jazzed are Valco's add-ons: a bassinet ($200) and toddler seat ($80 to $100) that extend the use of this stroller. The bassinet is fine, but the toddler seat is really cool, turning the Valco into a double stroller. Valco's other accessories include a car seat adapter ($30 to $40) and foot muff ($65 to $120).

New for 2014, Valco is revamping the Tri-Mode frame, adding wheel suspension and an easier fold with self lock. The new Tri-Mode will also be somewhat lighter, landing at 21.3 lbs. Also new: a four-wheel version of the Tri-Mode with air tires at 25.1 lbs.

How does the Valco stack up versus its main competitors in the swivel wheel, all terrain category? Well the Valco is a touch heavier than the Mountain Buggy Urban Jungle, although Valco has reduced its weight in recent years to be more comparable. And folks seem to like the Valco's toddler seat configuration better than Phil & Ted, although there is a split opinion here. Fashion wise, Valco is a bit dull, with only four choices.

Besides the Tri-Mode, Valco has three other models: the Snap, Zee and Spark.

At a mere 13 lbs. for the single version, the Snap ($230 to $250) is a feature-packed three-wheel stroller. Included are a padded napper bar, extendable canopy, full recline, adjustable foot rest, extra compact fold, "flip flop friendly" brake and large basket. There is also a four-wheel version of the Snap (dubbed the Snap4, $280, 15.3 lbs.). Air filled tires are an option on the Snap4.

The Zee ($300 to $330, 17 lbs.) is a bit of a departure for Valco: this four-wheel in-line stroller features a compact fold, adjustable footrest, compact/standing fold and one-touch seat recline. The Zee also has a companion double stroller, called the Zee Two. This side-by-side double also has swivel double front wheels like the single version as well as two independent canopies. In the past year, the Zee gained a height adjustable handle and a canopy with two-position height adjustment.

The Spark ($500, 24 lbs.) is Valco's offering in the multi-function category now dominated by the UPPAbaby Vista. The Spark's seat morphs from bassinet mode (full recline) to a full seat that is reversible. Other features include air-filled 10" tires, an extended canopy and a storage basket with both rear and side access. A double version of the Snap (Snap Dual) runs $400 and weighs 21.7 lbs.

Valco's Matrix ($375, a tri-wheel model with air-filled tires) is discontinued, although you may see a few still available online.

Our view. Parent feedback on the Tri-Mode has been positive, with folks lauding the stroller's quality, maneuverability and sturdy ride. We've been impressed with how Valco has trimmed the weight on the Tri-Mode, as that was previously a major drawback. Readers love all the storage and air-filled tires, which make the Tri-Mode a better bet for folks who want to use it on trails or rough sidewalks.

Valco's other models also earn high marks on quality, ease of use and overall design. Perhaps the only complaint here is the lack of included cup holders or parent consoles—that's an extra $20-$40 accessory. And Valco's retail distribution is somewhat thin, concentrated in independent baby stores(not chains). That makes seeing one in person a challenge—example: Texas has just one retail dealer, as of this writing.

All in all, Valco is a winner. *Baby Bargains Resale Rank: Good.*
Rating: A

Our Picks: The Best Strollers

Lifestyle #1: Mall Crawl

You live in the suburbs and drive just about everywhere you go. Besides the mall, you take quick strolls around the block, which has paved sidewalks in good condition.

The ideal mall crawler stroller has small wheels that enable tight cornering in narrow aisles—it can't be too wide or bulky. As for weight, you'll be hauling this stroller in and out of a trunk several times a day . . . so anything over 20 lbs. is asking for trouble.

Trunk space is a concern when considering the fold of a mall stroller—some strollers are more bulky than others. If you have a compact car, take a second to compare the measurements of the folded stroller and your trunk. Other nice features for a mall stroller include a decent cup holder and good-sized basket. The canopy and accessories like a rain cover are a bit less important, since this stroller is used more indoors than out.

Common first-time parent mistake: buying a giant travel system, with matching infant car seat and stroller. These are common shower gifts and many folks fall for that coordinated look . . . and think their stroller should be built like a tank to protect a newborn from thermonuclear attack. But many travel system strollers are behemoths—and that huge weight and bulk make them impossible to use as baby gets older, not to mention wrestling it in and out of trunk.

Good. Ok, you have two choices here: get a stroller that is infant-car seat compatible or go for a stroller frame.

Good news: more stroller models now can fit other brand car seats (but check for compatibility), so you don't have to buy a giant Evenflo or Graco travel system. We note which strollers have car seat adapters in the reviews earlier in this chapter. A good example is the Baby Jogger City Mini (see below)—its car seat adapter accessory ($60) works with most major brand car seats.

Another option: buy a simple stroller frame, like the **Graco Snug Rider** ($70) or **Baby Trend Snap & Go** ($70). If you can't decide what main stroller you want just yet, this could be a placeholder. When your baby outgrows the infant car seat, you'll end up buying a good lightweight stroller like the ones recommended below.

FYI: When trying out different stroller frames, take a second and snap your favorite infant car seat into the various stroller frames in the store before purchasing. Some car seats will lock into place; others must be held with straps. Locking is best for safety, of course.

Finally, a caveat about over-use of the infant car seat for newborns in strollers. Pediatricians generally recommend limiting the amount of time newborns spend in an infant car seat—this is especially true for preemies or infants with certain medical conditions (ask your doctor for advice if there is a concern). While there is no hard and fast rule, it makes sense to take your baby out of the seat frequently so there is a change in position.

STROLLER ROUND-UP

Here's our round-up of popular lightweight models by the major stroller manufacturers.

Maker	Model	Weight	Price	Recline
Baby Jogger	City Mini	17.1	$250	Full
Chicco	C6 / Capri	11.0	$70-$80	Partial
Combi	Cosmo	13.0	$110-$150	Full
Cybex	Ruby	13.2	$150	Partial
First Years	Jet	11.4	$50	Partial
Graco	Breaze	17.5	$170	Full
Inglesina	Swift	13.0	$130	Partial
Kolcraft	Contours Lite	15.5	$80	Partial
Mtn Buggy	Mini	17.5	$350	Full
Peg Perego	Pliko Mini	14	$250	Partial
Uppa Baby	G-Lite	8.3	$120	None
	G-Luxe	11.9	$190	Partial
Valco	Snap	13.0	$230	Full

Better. Your baby has now outgrown the infant car seat and you are looking for a lightweight stroller. Among the better bets would be the **Chicco C6** (aka the Capri; $70 to $80, 11 lbs.; pictured) which features a two-position seat recline, five-point harness and basic canopy . . . it is a best bet for the mall. Yes, you read right—it is just $65.

We also like the **First Years Jet** stroller ($50, 11.4 lbs.)—it is bare bones, but has a compact fold and basic basket—and the taller handles may be just the trick for tall parents.

A bit more money but still excellent would be **UPPAbaby's G-Lite** ($120 8.3 lbs.). Compared to the other two mall strollers, the G-Lite has upgrades like a removable washable seat pad.

FYI: All of the above strollers have limited or no seat recline—hence, they are best for babies six months and older. The maximum weight capacity for the Jet and G-Lite is 50 lbs; the C6 is 37 lbs.

Best. Here's our top pick for the mall crawl: the **Baby Jogger City Mini** ($250, 17.1 lbs.). The Baby Jogger City Mini is an excellent tri-wheel stroller with oversized canopy and fully reclining seat. Baby Jogger's quick fold technology is amazing—you lift a strap in the middle of the stroller and zip! It's folded. An optional car seat adapter can turn a City Mini into a travel system if you wish.

strollers

COMMENTS

Quick-fold technology, extended sun canopy, tri-wheel.

Compact umbrella fold, decent-size basket. aka the Capri.

Affordable, compact fold, can be paired with Combi infant seat.

Two-step fold, one-touch brake; height adjustable canopy.

No frills, compact umbrella fold. Basic basket.

Full recline, extended canopy, front wheel suspension.

Skimpy canopy, no cup holder, two handle design.

Affordable, but seat doesn't sit upright. Skimpy canopy.

Single hand, fast fold, extended sun visor.

Height adjustable handle, lightest weight Pliko model.

Lightest weight. Standing fold, mesh seat, machine-washable pad.

Bigger wheels, improved canopy and seat recline.

Extendable canopy, adjustable footrest, compact fold.

Airline travel. Experienced parent rule #429: *never* gate-check an expensive stroller. Instead, if you plan to do much airline travel, go for a super cheap, lightweight model. Our suggestion: The ***Kolcraft Contours Lite*** ($80) has a good size canopy and removable snack tray. Or the above-mentioned ***First Years Jet***—either would be great . . . and easily replaced if the airline mangles it in the cargo hold.

Lifestyle #2: Urban Jungle

When you live in a city like New York, Boston or Washington D.C., your stroller is more than just baby transportation—it's your primary vehicle. You stroll to the market, on outings to a park or longer trips on weekend getaways.

BUGABOO SMACKDOWN!	The Bugaboo Cameleon ($890, 20 lbs.) is the reining champ of ultra expensive, three component strollers (combining a bassinet, stroller frame and seat). Whether you think it is a cleverly designed

CONTENDER	PRICE	WEIGHT	BUGABOO-ISH?
BABY JOGGER CITY SELECT	$500	28.1 LBS.	🥿🥿
BLOOM babyZEN	$800	25.5 LBS.	🥿🥿🥿
BRITAX B-READY	$500	28.1 LBS.	🥿🥿🥿
CHICCO URBAN	$400	24.1 LBS.	🥿🥿🥿
MUTSY 4RIDER LIGHT	$580	30.6 LBS.	🥿🥿🥿
PEG PEREGO SKATE	$900	28.8 LBS.	🥿🥿
QUINNY BUZZ	$960	24 LBS.	🥿
STROLL AIR ZOOM	$530	24 LBS.	🥿🥿
UPPA BABY VISTA	$700	26.3 LBS.	🥿🥿🥿

Weight is crucial for these parents as well. While you are not lugging a stroller in or out of a trunk like a suburbanite, you may find yourself climbing up subway stairs or trudging up to a fourth-floor walk-up apartment. It's a major trade-off here: full-featured strollers that are outfitted for the weather (full boot, rain cover) can weigh more than lightweight models designed for the mall. Basically, you want a rugged stroller that can take all the abuse a big city can dish out—giant potholes, uneven sidewalks, the winter from Hell . . . without the weight of a bulldozer.

In the past, carriage strollers or prams were the primary "urban jungle" stroller, but these have fallen out of favor for their bulk, weight and other disadvantages (prams typically have front wheels that don't turn).

---

stroller that embodies urban chic . . . or a sign of wretched excess, Bugaboo sure has been one thing: a design leader. Now competitors are nipping at Bugaboo's wooden shoes. We rate the contenders on a scale of one to three klompen! (Google it.)

COMMENTS/VERDICT

Swiss Army knife of strollers with 16 configurations. 2nd seat runs $160, bassinet is $90. **But it weighs 40% more than Bugaboo.**

Coolest alternative. Flat fold, adjustable frame, reclining seat can be swapped out for a lay-flat bassinet. Bassinet is $250.

Reversible seat, 14 different seat configurations. 2nd seat is $150. wheel suspension, large storage basket. Fashion is a bit dull.

Telescoping handle, alumnlm frame, standing fold, large basket, quick release EVA tires. **Reversible seat that converts to carry cot.**

Solid rubber tires. Includes car seat adapter, but bassinet is extra. Quality is good, but heavy weight makes this a tough sell.

Folds with seat, **includes accessories like car seat adapter,** rain cover and boot. But it is 45% heavier than Bugaboo. Expensive.

Price includes stroller, carry cot and infant car seat. **Extendable zipper canopy, air-filled front tire.** Full recline. Reversible seat. Tri-wheel.

Includes bassinet, reversible seat, adj. handle, plush padding, rain cover, diaper bag, umbrella. **Can fold with seat on.**

Pricey, but includes bassinet, height adj. handle, rain shield, mesh sun shade, rubber-like foam wheels. Bonus: $130 rumble seat for toddlers.

strollers

Multi-function strollers are now the rage for urbanites—these combine a chassis with stroller seat for older babies and a bassinet for newborns. Some models include the bassinet, others offer it as an optional accessory.

While multi-function strollers are nice, they do have one disadvantage. They're heavy (many are 20+ lbs.) and most don't fold compactly. When you are trying to ascend subway stairs with baby in one arm and a stroller in another, the last thing you need is a bulky stroller.

So we recommend a lightweight second stroller—but unlike a stroller for the mall, this one needs more weatherproofing for the city. Of course, if you live in a studio apartment, all you may have room for is the lightweight stroller.

Hence, we will break down our picks for the urban jungle into two categories: multi-function and lightweight, but weather proof:

Best (multi-function). The winner here is the *UPPAbaby Vista* ($700, 26.3 lbs., pictured), which includes a bassinet and stroller seat, plus many extras (rain shield, mesh sun shade, bug cover, etc). Readers love how functional this stroller is (you can fold it with the stroller seat attached, for example), plus

its smooth ride on no-flat foam tires is a must for urban dwellers.

If you plan to have two kids close in age, we'd suggest the *Baby Jogger City Select* ($500, 28.1 lbs.). It can be configured 16 ways with an optional second seat ($160). An excellent stroller with a quick fold.

Finally, a dark horse in the multi-function stroller race is the *Britax B-Ready* ($500, 28.1 lbs.). It also has the second seat option, but lacks the cool quick-fold of the Baby Jogger. The B-Ready works out of the box with the Britax infant car seat, which is a nice plus.

You'll note we didn't mention Bugaboo in the above picks—sorry, their $890 Cameleon just doesn't offer the same value and features as the others we mentioned. See the "Bugaboo Smackdown" box nearby for a look at how the Bugaboo stacks up to the competition.

Best (light weight). Our top pick is the *Baby Jogger City Mini* ($250, 17.1 lbs.; pictured).

There are two key reasons to go with the City Mini over an umbrella-type stroller: fold and canopy. Baby Jogger's "quick fold" is amazing—grab it by a strap on the seat and zip! It's folded in one simple step. That's a key advantage over many umbrella-type strollers, most of which require a parent to hit a couple of levers and then fold the stroller to the ground . . . not easy to do with a baby in your arms. Seconds count in the big city—and the Baby Jogger's quick fold is, well, quicker.

Ditto for the canopy. The City Mini has an awesome, giant canopy that completely shields baby from sun, wind and all the urban weather you can think of.

The **Britax B-Agile** ($250, 16.5 lbs) is also a top choice here—its curved back axle might be a better bet for taller parents. And the included car seat adapter for Britax seats is a great value (versus the extra $60 you'd shell out for a Baby Jogger adapter). We also like how easy it is to adjust the harness on the B-Agile, which can be done without the re-clipping that the City Mini requires. On the downside, the B-Agile has a foam handle versus rubber for the Baby Jogger—the rubber is probably more durable than the foam. There are also little differences that tip the scales to Baby Jogger—the hidden brake cables on the City Mini versus the exposed one on the B-Agile. The City Mini also has a deeper, more enclosed storage basket than the B-Agile.

Lifestyle #3: Green Acres

If you live on a dirt or gravel road or in a neighborhood with no sidewalks, you need a stroller to do double duty. First, it must handle rough surfaces without bouncing baby all over the place. Second, it must be able to "go to town," folding easily to fit into a trunk for a trip to a mall or other store. And what about snow? Most mall strollers simply don't work in snow.

The answer: an all terrain stroller with air-filled tires.

Good. Phil & Ted's Navigator ($500, 30.1 lbs.) is a tri-wheel stroller with swivel front wheel and air-filled tires. This new, upgraded model features a large canopy and one-hand fold. What's unique about the Phil & Ted's: a toddler seat accessory ($90-$100) that attach-

es to the front or back of the seat, giving you added flexibility if you have multiple kids. That's what makes Phil & Ted special: the flexibility to use the same stroller for newborn, toddler, BOTH toddler and newborn at the same time and two toddlers. Hence, this is a good bet if you are planning on having more than one kid. If not, consider one of the next two picks.

Better. Similar to the Phil & Ted's Explorer (in fact, they are owned by the same company), the **Mountain Buggy Urban Jungle** ($375, 24 lbs.) is our better pick in this category. The polymer spoke wheels won't earn fashion points, but at least they don't rust (helpful for folks who live near an ocean). Fans of Mountain Buggy love the way these strollers push and handle the most extreme weather (Snow? Sleet? Bring it on). We also like the stroller's overall weight (24 lbs.). Although it does have an infant car seat adapter accessory, there is no second seat option.

Best. The crown for best all-terrain stroller goes to the **BOB Revolution** stroller ($450-$470, 24.9 lbs.). It comes in two versions: polymer wheels (SE or Sport Experience) or aluminum alloy rims (CE or City Experience). The polymer wheels are a pound heavier (24.9 lbs.) than the aluminum option (23.9 lbs.); the aluminum version is about $10 more expensive. We love the new infant car seat adapter accessory ($60) that can be removed from the stroller without tools. Fans of BOB love the stroller's quality and durability. The only slight negative: the handle bar isn't height adjustable. So if one parent is much taller than the other, this might be an issue.

See the chart below for a comparison of all-terrain models.

Lifestyle #4: Exercise (Jogging & Sport Strollers)

If you want to exercise with a stroller, you have two choices: tri-wheel strollers with fixed front wheels, or a model with a front wheel that swivels.

Fixed-wheel jogging strollers with air-filled tires are best for folks who want to actually jog or run with a stroller—you can push them

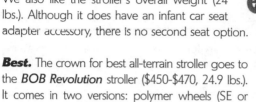

ALL-TERRAIN STROLLERS		How top all-terrain strollers compare—each of these	
MODEL	**WEIGHT**	**PRICE**	**BRAND RATING**
BABY JOGGER CITY ELITE	31.3 LBS.	$400	A
BOB REVOLUTION SE	24.9	$450	A
BRITAX B-READY	21.8	$500	A-
BUMBLERIDE INDIE	20.0	$500	B-
JEEP LIBERTY LIMITED	29.2	$170	B+
MOUNTAIN BUGGY URBAN	24.0	$375	A
PHIL & TED NAVIGATOR	28.0	$500	A-
VALCO TRI-MODE	23.0	$500	A

in a straight line. The disadvantage to these strollers: to turn them, you have to pick up the front wheel and move it. Hence, fixed wheel joggers aren't good for walking or shopping trips.

Strollers with turnable front wheels are NOT recommended for folks who want to run—even if the stroller has the option to lock the front wheel. That said, strollers with a swivel front wheel are great for folks who just want to walk the neighborhood or trails. So you need to ask yourself, exactly how do you plan to exercise with the stroller?

Another issue to consider: how young can your baby be and ride in a jogger? First, determine whether the seat reclines (not all models do). If it doesn't, wait until baby is at least six months old and can hold his or her head up. If you want to jog or run with the stroller, it might be best to wait until baby is at least a year old since all the jostling can be dangerous for a younger infant (their neck muscles can't handle the bumps). Ask your pediatrician for advice if you are unsure.

Another decision area: the frame. The cheapest strollers (under $200) have steel frames—they're strong but also heavy (and that could be a drawback for serious runners). The most expensive models ($300 to $400) have aluminum frames, which are the lightest in weight. Once again, if you plan casual walks, a steel frame is fine. Runners should go for aluminum.

Finally, remember the Trunk Rule. Any jogger is a lousy choice if you can't get it easily in your trunk. Check the DEPTH of the jogger when it is folded—compared this to your vehicle's trunk. Many joggers are rather bulky even when folded. Yes, quick release wheels help reduce the bulk, so check for that option.

So, which jogging stroller do we recommend? Let's break that down into two categories: power walking and serious runners. Note that all these strollers have fixed front wheels; if you want a stroller with a turnable front wheel (more suited to the mall or light

---

models are tri wheels with air-filled tires and front wheels that swivel.

COMMENT

12" AIR-FILLED TIRES, PARENT CONSOLE, QUICKEST FOLD ON MARKET.
POLYMER RIMS (OR ALUMINUM $20 EXTRA). CAR SEAT ADAPTER $50 EXTRA.
14 CONFIGURATIONS; OPTIONAL BASSINET AND 2ND SEAT.
ADJUSTABLE HANDLE, FULL RECLINE, BOOT AND BIG STORAGE BASKET.
ONE-HAND FOLD, PARENT AND CHILD TRAY, ADJUSTABLE FOOT REST. HEAVY.
MANY ACCESSORIES, SMOOTH GLIDE, FULL RECLINE.
WIDE SEAT, HEIGHT ADJUSTABLE HANDLE. OPTIONAL SECOND CHILD SEAT.
FULLY RECLINING SEAT, LARGE BASKET, TODDLER SEAT ACCESSORY.

duty outdoor activities), see the Green Acres section above.

Best (power walking). Jeep Overland Limited ($180-$210, 28 lbs.) has a fixed front wheel and a boatload of convenience features: parent tray that can hold two water bottles, compartment to store an mp3 player, height adjustable handle and an easy fold. Since it is heavy, we think this would be a better bet for

power walkers than serious runners, but the price is right: we've seen it discounted under $200 on Amazon.

Three mistakes to avoid when buying a jogging stroller

With jogging strollers available everywhere from Target to high-end bike stores, it is easy to get confused by all the options. Keep in mind these traps when shopping for a jogger:

◆ *Rust.* Warning: cheaper jogging strollers are made of steel—rust can turn your jogging stroller into junk in short order. This is especially a problem on the coasts, but can happen anywhere. Hint: the best joggers have ALUMINUM frames. And make sure the wheel rims are alloy, not steel. All-terrain strollers like Mountain Buggy use polymer wheels (in most models) to get around the rust problem.

◆ *Suspended animation.* The latest rage with joggers is cushiony suspensions, which smooth out bumps but can add to the price. But do you really need it? Most jogging strollers give a smooth ride by design, so no added suspension is necessary. And some kids actually LIKE small bumps or jostling—it helps them fall asleep in the stroller.

◆ *Too narrow seats.* Unlike other baby products, a good jogging stroller could last you until your child is five years old—that is, if you pick one with a wide enough seat to accommodate an older child. The problem: some joggers rather narrow seats. Great for infants, not good for older kids. We noticed this issue after our neighbors stopped using their jogging stroller when their child hit age three, but our son kept riding in his until five and beyond. Brands with bigger seats (like BOB) offer more long-term value. (As always, confirm seat dimensions before committing to a specific stroller; seats can vary from model to model).

Best (serious running). *BOB* Ironman ($350-$410, 21 lbs.) has all the quality features of a regular BOB, but adds adjustable tracking, stainless steel wheel spokes, new smooth 16" tires and bright yellow fabric. Thanks to an aluminum frame, this jogger weighs just 21 lbs. Second place goes to *Baby Jogger's F.I.T.* ($300, 25.4 lbs.), with a fixed front wheel, deep seat recline and aluminum frame.

Need a double jogger? Our advice would be the same: BOB would come first, followed by Baby Jogger.

Plan to take your jogger out in the cold weather? Instead of bundling up baby, consider a stroller blanket. One of our favorites is the *JJ Cole Bundle Me* (bundleme.com), which comes in several versions for $40 to $50. And what can you use to keep a blanket on your stroller? Try the *BlankyClip*, a $20 tension clip (blankyclip.com) cleverly disguised as a stuffed bear or duck.

Of course, you could have the opposite problem: you live somewhere where the summer weather is brutal. If your stroller seat fabric doesn't breathe, consider a *Cool Mee Seat Liner* from Meeno Babies (MeenoBabies.com). Their machine washable seat liner ($20-$35) is made of three-ply mesh material that promotes airflow to cool baby.

Double The Fun: Strollers for two

There are two types of strollers that can transport two tikes: tandem models and side-by-side styles. A tandem stroller has a "front-back" configuration, where the younger child rides in back while the older child gets the view. These strollers are best for parents with a toddler and a new baby.

Side-by-side strollers, on the other hand, are best for parents of twins or babies close in age. In this case, there's never any competition for the view seat. The only downside: some of these strollers are so wide, they can't fit through narrow doorways or store aisles. (Hint: make sure the stroller is not wider than 30" to insure door compatibility). Another bummer: few have napper bars or fully reclining seats, making them impractical for infants.

So, what to buy—a tandem or side by side? Our reader feedback shows parents are much happier with their side-by-side models than tandems. Why? The tandems can get darn near impossible to push when weighted down with two kids, due to their length-wise design. Yes, side by sides may not be able to fit through some narrow shopping aisles, but they seem to work better overall.

Double strollers can be frustrating—your basic choices are low-price duos from Graco or Kolcraft or high-price doubles like those from Maclaren and Baby Jogger. There doesn't seem to be much in between the low-price ($200 range) and the high-end ($400 and up).

strollers

***Best tandem strollers (front/back dou-
ble).*** Kolcraft *Contours Options LT Tandem*
($250, 32 lbs.) features seats that reverse to face
the parents or each other. This model features a
few upgrades over other tandems, including
adjustable leg rests and each seat can fully
recline. On the downside, there is no parent

tray (just one small cup holder) and no child snack trays or cup holders (you can add an aftermarket cup holder if need be). And, yes,
this stroller is heavy and quite bulky when folded—but so are most
tandem strollers. (FYI: A similar model to the Options LT that does
have a parent tray is the Contours Optima, $300).

Runner's up: Chicco has a winner with the ***Chicco Cortina
Together*** ($300, 30 lbs.). This front/back tandem stroller holds two
car seats and features an aluminum frame, a storage basket with
trap door access, three-position handle and flat fold. Readers love
the steering and overall quality of this stroller.

Another runner up in this category: the ***Joovy Caboose Stand-
on Tandem*** ($150, 26 lbs.). It really isn't a tandem, but a pushcart—
the younger child sits in front while the older child *stands* in back
(there is also a jump seat for the older child to sit on). This is a bet-

E-MAIL FROM THE REAL WORLD
***Biting the bullet on a
pricey twin stroller***

*Cheapo twin strollers sound like a good deal for parents of
twins, but listen to this mother of multiples:*

"Twins tend to ride in their strollers more often and longer, and
having an unreliable, bulky or inconvenient stroller is a big mistake.
As you suggest, it's a false economy to buy an inexpensive Graco
or other model, as these most likely will break down before you're
done with the stroller. My husband and I couldn't believe that
we'd have to spend $400 on a stroller, but after talking to parents
of multiples, we understand why it's best to just bite the bullet on
this one. We've heard universally positive feedback about side-by-
side strollers for their maneuverability, durability and practicality.
We've heard much less positive things about front-back tandems
for twins. These often are less versatile, as only one seat reclines, so
you can't use them when both babies are small (or tired). And
when the babies get bigger, they're more likely to get into mischief
by pulling each others' hair and stuff."

ter solution when you have an older toddler who doesn't want to ride all the time in a stroller . . . but still gets tired and needs a place to sit on long outings.

Best side by side strollers. For parents of two little ones on a tight budget, we suggest the *Jeep Wrangler Twin Sport Umbrella Stroller* (27 lbs., pictured) for $110. It's bare bones (no basket) but will get the job done with reclining seats and a compact fold.

If your budget allows, we'd suggest the *Graco Fast Action Duo* ($280, 33 lbs.). Yes, it is six lbs. heavier than the Jeep, but you get a storage basket, better canopies with sun visors as well as quick fold. A similar good bet here is the *Joovy Scooter X2* ($230, 28 lbs).

Is Grandma offering to buy your twin stroller? If so and the budget allows, we recommend the *Baby Jogger City Mini Double* ($450, 26.6 lbs., pictured), with its excellent extended canopies and quick fold.

Finally, for outdoor treks with two kids, we'd suggest looking at our top-rated all-terrain stroller brands (Phil & Ted, Mountain Buggy and BOB). They each make swivel wheel doubles that, while pricey, feature great quality and comfort.

Bike Trailers, Seats & Helmets

Bike Trailers. Yes, lots of companies make bike trailers, but the gold standard is *Burley* (burley.com; pictured left). Their trailers (sold in bicycle stores) are considered the best in the industry. A good example is the *Burley D'Lite.* It features a

multi-point safety harness, built-in rear storage, 100 lb. carrying capacity and compact fold (to store in a trunk). Okay, it's expensive at $630 but check around for second-hand bargains. And there is a $160 jogger conversion kit that turns a Burley into a jogging stroller (we've heard mixed reviews on this for its wobbly steering).

If the D'Lite is too expensive, consider Burley's newer Honey Bee at just $300 to $400. It comes out of the box with everything to attach it to a bike or convert it to a stroller. It's basically like their D'Lite, with seating for up to 2 kids and all of Burley's safety features.

A close runner-up to Burley in the bike trailer race is *Thule*

bike trailers

Chariot (thule.com). "These are the best engineered bike trailers I've ever seen," opined a reader and we agree. The basic Cheetah runs $400-$450.

Baby Jogger, the jogging stroller company reviewed earlier, has an entry in the bike trailer race as well—the POD. This model is sold as a chassis for $500—you can add a stroller kit for $90, jogger for $65 and bike trailer adapter for $45. The POD is 30" wide so it can fit through most standard doorways, yet still accommodate up to two kids.

What about the "discount" bike trailers you see for about $100? *InStep* makes a few of these models:, including the Quick N EZ ($125). InStep also makes four Schwinn bike trailers, which are upgraded versions of their regular line. Cost: $115 to $400.

What do you give up for the price? In general, lower priced bike trailers have steel frames and are heavier than the Burleys (which are made of aluminum). And the cheaper bike trailers don't fold as easily or compactly as the Burleys, nor do they attach as easily to a bike.

The key feature to look for with any bike trailer is the ease (or lack thereof) of attaching the trailer to a bike. Quick, compact fold is important as well. Look for the total carrying capacity and the quality of the nylon fabric.

So, should you spring for an expensive bike trailer or one of the $150 ones? Like jogging strollers, consider how much you'll use it. For an occasional (once a week?) bike trip, we'd recommend the cheaper models. Plan to do more serious cycling, say two or three times a week? Then go for a Burley or Thule Chariot. Yes, they are expensive but worth it if you really plan to use the trailer extensively. Hint: this might be a great item to buy second-hand on eBay or Craigslist.

Safety information: you should wait on using a bike trailer until your child is OVER one year of age. Why? Infants under age one don't have neck muscles to withstand the jolts and bumps they'll encounter with bike trailers, which don't have shock absorbers. Remember you might hit a pothole at 15+ mph—that's not something that is safe for an infant to ride out. Be sure your child is able to hold his head up while wearing a helmet as well. Your child should always wear a helmet while riding in a bike trailer—no exceptions. And, no, there is no bike trailer on the market that safely holds an infant car seat, which might cushion the bumps. Most trailers will accommodate children up to about age six.

Bike seats & helmets. When considering whether to buy a bike seat or a bike trailer, the low price of many bike seats (which start at $100) may be tempting. However, for safety reasons, we recommend a bike trailer.

Why? Bike seats are inherently less safe for baby than a trailer. That's because if you crash on a bike with a bike seat, both you and baby hit the ground. Even if your baby is wearing a helmet, that can still be ugly. Meanwhile, a trailer doesn't hit the ground the same way in a crash—and it is closer to the ground to begin with. Also: bike seats can make even the best of bikes unstable. That's because the additional weight of a child plus the bike seat can make a bike hard to handle even for experienced riders. Of course, bike trailers have their own issues—since they sit lower to the ground, they can be hard for motorists to see (always use an orange flag on the trailer). And they can be tippy, especially on tight turns. Since a trailer is wider than a bike, you have to be careful when negotiating tight spaces. That said, we still think bike trailers are a better (and safer bet) than a bike seat. As a result, we will no longer recommend bike seats in this edition.

One final tip: don't forget the helmet. If your child is strapped in securely to a bike trailer, she still needs a helmet that is properly fitted and adjusted. *Consumer Reports* does a good job rating and reviewing kid bike helmets: we agree that their most recent top pick (the Bontrager Solstice Youth helmet) is a good option. Price: $32. A few tips on helmets: sometimes it is hard to fit a helmet on a toddler. The best advice is to go to a bike store for help. One tip: add in thick pads (sold with some bike helmets) to give a better fit. Don't glue pads on top of pads, however—and adding a thick hat isn't a safety solution either. If your child cannot wear a bike helmet safely, put off those bike adventures until they are older. Be sure your child wears the helmet well forward on his head. If a helmet is pushed back and your child hits the ground face first, there is no protection for the forehead.

Diaper Bags

We consider ourselves experts at diaper bags—we got five of them as gifts. While you don't need five, this important piece of luggage may feel like an extra appendage after your baby's first year. And diaper bags are for more than just holding diapers—many include compartments for baby bottles, clothes, and changing pads. With that in mind, let's take a look at what separates great diaper bags from the rest of the pack. In addition, we'll give you our list of nine items for a well-stocked diaper bag.

Best Online Sources

Just because you have a new baby doesn't mean you have to lose all sense of style. And there is good news: an entire cottage industry of custom diaper-bag makers has sprung up to help fill the style gap. One good place to start: our message boards. Go to BabyBargains.com, click on the message boards and then to Places to Go (All Other Gear, Diaper Bags, etc). There you'll find dozens of moms swapping tips on the best and most fashionable diaper bags. Here's a round up of our readers' favorite custom diaper bag makers (most sell direct off their sites, but a few also sell on other sites):

Amy Michelle	amymichellebags.com
California Innovations	californiainnovations.com
Fleurville	fleurville.com
Haiku Diaper Bags	haikubags.com
Holly Aiken	hollyaiken.com
I'm Still Me	imstillme.com
Ju Ju Be	ju-ju-be.com
Kate Spade	katespade.com.
Kipling	kipling.com
Lexie Barnes	lexiebarnes.com
Oi Oi	oioi.com.au
One Cool Chick	onecoolchick.com
Reese Li	reeseli.com
Skip Hop	skiphop.com
Timbuk2	timbuk2.com
Tumi	tumi.com
Vera Bradley	verabradley.com

No doubt there are dozens more, but that's a great starting point. You can expect prices to be commensurate with style. Kate Spade can cost over $300 a diaper bag. But there are some great looking options for under a $100 too. One caveat: many of these manufacturers are small boutique companies. Often it may be the owner who's taking the order. . . and also sewing the bag! While we admire the entrepreneurship of these companies, many are so small that a minor event can put them off kilter. All it takes is one hurricane or a deluge of orders to turn a reputable company into a customer service nightmare. Check the feedback on these companies on our message boards before ordering.

 Smart Shopper Tips

Smart Shopper Tip #1
Diaper Bag Science
"I was in a store the other day, and they had about one zillion different diaper bags. Some had cute prints and others were plain. Should I buy the cheapest one or invest a little more money?"

The best diaper bags are made of tear-resistant fabric and have all sorts of useful pockets, features and gizmos. Contrast that with low-quality brands that lack many pockets and are made of cheap, thin vinyl—after a couple of uses, they start to split and crack. Yes, high-quality diaper bags will cost more ($50 to $150 versus $30 to $45), but you'll be much happier in the long run. High-end diaper bags (like those made by Kate Spade and other designers) can reach the $300 mark or more. Of course, many of our readers have found deals on these bags, so check out our message boards for shopping tips.

Here's our best piece of advice: buy a diaper bag that doesn't *look* like a diaper bag. Sure those bags with dinosaurs and pastel animal prints look cute now, but what are you going to do with it when your baby gets older? A well-made diaper bag that doesn't look like a diaper bag will make a great piece of carry-on luggage later in life.

Smart Shopper Tip #2
Make your own

"Who needs a fancy diaper bag? I just put all the necessary changing items into my favorite backpack."

That's a good point. Most folks have a favorite bag or backpack that can double as a diaper bag. Besides the obvious (wipes and diapers), put in a large zip-lock bag as a holder for dirty/wet items. Add a couple of receiving blankets (as changing pads) plus the key items listed below, and you have a complete diaper bag.

You can buy many items found in a diaper bag (such as a changing pad) a la carte at most baby stores.

Top 9 Items for a Well-Stocked Diaper Bag

After much scientific experimentation, we believe we have perfected the exact mix of ingredients for the best-equipped diaper bag. Here's our recipe:

1 **GET TWO DIAPER BAGS**—one that is a full-size, all-option big hummer for longer trips (or overnight stays) and the other that is a mini-bag for a short hop to dinner or the shopping mall. Here's what each should have:

The full-size bag: This needs a waterproof changing pad that folds up, waterproof pouch or pocket for wet clothes, a couple compartments for diapers, blankets/clothes, etc. Super-deluxe brands have bottle compartments with Thinsulate to keep bottles warm or cold. Another plus: outside pockets for books and small toys. A zippered outside pocket is good for change or your wal-

diaper bags

let. A cell phone pocket is also a plus.

The small bag: This has enough room for a couple diapers, travel wipe package, keys, wallet and/or cell phone. Some models have a bottle pocket and room for one change of clothes. If money is tight, just go for the small bag. To be honest, the full-size bag is often just a security blanket for first-time parents—some think they need to lug around every possible item in case of a diaper catastrophe. But, in the real world, you'll quickly discover schlepping that big full-size bag everywhere isn't practical. While a big bag is nice for overnight or long trips, we'll bet you will be using the small bag much more often.

2 EXTRA DIAPERS. Put a dozen in the big bag, two or three in the small one. Why so many? Babies can go through quite a few in a very short time. Of course, when baby gets older (say over a year), you can cut back on the number of diapers you need for a trip. Another wise tip: put whole packages of diapers and wipes in your car(s). We did this after we forgot our diaper bag one too many times and needed an emergency diaper. (The only bummer: here in Colorado, the wipes we keep in the car sometimes freeze in the winter! As they say, you don't know cold . . .)

3 A TRAVEL-SIZE WIPE PACKAGE. A good idea: a plastic Tupperware container that holds a small stack of wipes. Some wipe makers sell travel packs that are allegedly "re-sealable" to retain moisture; we found that they aren't. And they are expensive. For example, a Huggies travel pack of 16 wipes is $6. That works out to 38¢ per wipe compared to 2¢ per wipe if you buy a Huggies refill box of 384 from Kmart.

4 BLANKET AND CHANGE OF CLOTHES. Despite the reams of scientists who work on diapers, they still aren't leak-proof—plan for it. A change of clothes is most useful for babies under six months of age, when leaks are more common. After that point, this becomes less necessary.

5 A HAT OR CAP. We like the foreign legion-type hats that have flaps to cover your baby's neck and ears (about $10 to $20). Warmer caps are helpful to chase away a chill, since the head is where babies lose the most heat.

6 BABY TOILETRIES. Babies can't take much direct exposure to sunlight—sunscreen is a good bet for all infants. Besides sunscreen, other optional accessories include bottles of lotion and diaper rash cream. The best bet: buy these in small travel or trial sizes.

Don't forget insect repellent as well. This can be applied to infants two months of age and older.

7 **DON'T FORGET THE TOYS.** We like compact rattles, board books, teethers, etc.

8 **SNACKS.** When baby starts to eat solid foods, having a few snacks in the diaper bag (a bottle of water or milk, crackers, a small box of cereal) is a smart move. But don't bring them in plastic bags. Instead bring reusable plastic containers. Plastic bags are a suffocation hazard and should be kept far away from babies and toddlers.

9 **YOUR OWN PERSONAL STUFF.** Be careful putting your wallet or checkbook into the diaper bag—we advise against it. We left our diaper bag behind one too many times before we learned this lesson. Put your name and phone number in the bag in case it is lost.

Our Picks: Brand Recommendations

Here we go with our top picks for best diaper bag. We realize a diaper bag is a fashion choice and our tastes may not always agree with yours, but if one style by the following manufacturers doesn't appeal to you, check out the other options by that brand. You may find something else you like and you'll be getting commensurate quality.

Good. *Gerber* diaper bags (made by AD Sutton) are affordable and fashionable. At only $20 to $30 (often on sale), the Gerber Tote Diaper Bag features a large shoulder strap, a large zip front pocket with elastic bottle holders, two more front pockets and one in back. Plus there is a spacious changing pad. The polyester fabric wipes clean and the style is neutral in chocolate brown with green trim.

Better. The *Ju-Ju-Be* line of diaper bags gets raves from readers. Most of their designs are over $100, but the Be Hip is a great option at only $58 (Amazon.com). The messenger style bag comes with two outer front pockets, an insulated bottle pocket on the side, Teflon-treated outer fabric, anti-microbial treated inner fabric, a changing pad, and memory foam padded strap. A wide variety of colors and styles are available.

Best. Okay, you need more than a basic bag—but you don't want to spend the equivalent of a used car price on a diaper bag? Our

*(sidebar)* diaper bags

readers love the **Skip Hop** line of bags (skiphop.com). Skip Hop offers nine different designs, but our favorite is the Duo ($55). The Duo is their largest bag with eleven pockets including a cell phone pocket, magnetic closures instead of zippers and their cool Shuttle Clips, which allow you to clip it to a stroller. Yes, it has a shoulder strap too and changing pad, as you'd expect. Some parents say the bag holds less than they expected and the magnetic closures don't work as well if you stuff the bag really full. Those complaints aside, Skip Hop is a great option if you are looking for a full-size diaper bag with a bit more style.

The Bottom Line:
A Wrap-Up of Our Best Buy Picks

Wow . . . and you thought car seats were complex!

Here's the take-home message on strollers: match a stroller to your lifestyle. That means thinking about HOW you'll use the stroller. Mall? Park? Hikes? Read our lifestyle recommendations to match the right stroller to your needs.

Overall, the best strollers brands are UPPAbaby, Phil & Ted's and BOB. But even brands that get a lukewarm rating can have an occasional winner—witness Graco's twin strollers or Kolcraft/Jeep's affordable all-terrain models.

No matter which stroller you get, it is always smart to go for the lightest weight model you can find. Another key factor: rear wheel width, especially for urban parents. Some new strollers have wide rear wheel widths . . . making negotiating a narrow doorway or tight elevator darn near impossible.

For diaper bags, we like Gerber, Ju-Ju-Be and Skip Hop's offerings. Designer diaper bags are nice to get as gifts . . . but go for practical here and you'll be happier.

Next up: baby carriers—which are best for you, baby . . . and your back!

CHAPTER 10

CARRIERS

Carriers: Slings, Pouches, Front, Mei Tai, Hip, Backpack, Wrap Around

Inside this chapter

E ver wonder what a mai tai is? Here's your 411 on baby carriers, from mai tais to slings to frame carriers. We'll show you which style is best for what you need and give you the inside scoop on our best picks in each category. We'll also explore safety tips to wearing your baby as well as advice on how to be comfortable in any type of carrier.

Advocates of baby wearing from pediatricians to your next-door neighbor tout the benefits of closeness with your child. But even if you don't subscribe to attachment parenting, you have to admit carriers are darn convenient. When you have a baby who just won't take a nap and you've got dinner to get on the table, a carrier that gives you two hands free is a godsend. In this chapter, we'll look at the different types of carriers and they're uses,

Just to make it more confusing, though, it seems like there are 437 different carrier makes and models on the market, from simple slings to fancy backpacks. And we've noticed over the years that every single one of those models has a fan. Of course, the key is to find the right carrier for you. One idea: we like an instructional DVD on baby wearing called Tummy 2 Tummy (tummy2tummy.com). It covers different types of carriers and how to wear them—a good introduction to the world of carriers. Another tip: we recommend buying a carrier that either has a DVD with instructions or provides an instructional video on their web site.

Getting Started:
When do you need this stuff?

Many parents recognize the benefit of baby wearing and want to begin as soon as they bring their baby home from the hospital. So having a carrier available to new moms means you'll be shopping for this item in the last trimester of your pregnancy. There is no knowing if your baby will like the type of carrier you buy, so we recommend parents keep the original packaging and receipts in case you need to return it. Another note of caution: if you have a c-section, you may not be able to use your carrier immediately. And most carriers have a minimum weight requirement of about seven to eight lbs. (backpack carriers minimums are around 16 lbs.). So if you have a smaller baby, you won't want to use your carrier until your baby gains some weight.

Best Online Sources

The Baby Wearer

thebabywearer.com. The Baby Wearer is just the right resource for parents interested in "baby wearing." Yes, you've seen Guatemalan natives wearing their babies in PBS specials and you love the idea of that kind of closeness. And take it from us, there's nothing quite like it. But there are so many different options available today. So this is the site to visit when you're not sure if you want a sling, a wrap, a hip carrier and so on.

Here you'll find articles, reviews, product listings, ads, you name it. The main emphasis seems to be on sling-type carriers, not so much front carriers. There are a couple of great charts that offer detailed comparisons for carriers. In fact, there is so much here, you could spend days on the site. If you're a newbie to baby wearing, be sure to start with the basic articles as well as the glossary of terms. Then you can join chats and message boards or click on product links. Our biggest criticism of the site: there's a lot of advertising here. And the site is very jumbled. You're probably smart to take their recommendations with a grain of salt and verify reviews with other sites before you buy. ***Rating: B***

No Better Deal

nobetterdeal.com. This web site was recommended by some of our frugal readers as a great source for baby carriers and slings. When we last visited, they had 32 different carriers including the

Peanut Shell ($20, reg. $50), several ErgoBaby styles (Original $63, reg. $115), Baby K'Tan ($22, reg. $60), Baby Hawk ($88 Oh Snap!, reg. $150) and more. This site is clearly selling closeouts, so you'll be limited on colors and inventory. If you see something at a good price, it pays to snap it up.

What Are You Buying?

Carriers come in several flavors: slings, hip carriers, front carriers, mei tais, wrap arounds and frame carriers. Here's a look at each:

◆ **Slings and Pouches.** Slings allow you to hold your baby horizontally or upright. Made of soft fabric with an adjustable strap, slings drape your baby across your body and uses rings to connect the strap (see picture). The first slings were made by NoJo, but many other manufac- turers have jumped into the sling market. Whichever brand you choose, devoted sling user Darien Wilson from Austin, Texas has a great tip for new moms: "The trick for avoiding backache when using a sling is to have the bulk of the baby's weight at the parent's waist or above."

Some parents complain that there isn't much between your baby's head and a collision with a wall, furniture, etc. It's true you have to watch where you're going and what you're doing, but sling aficionados say once you get the hang of it, slings are simple to use.

Slings come in padded and unpadded versions in a variety of fabrics. They may also be called Rebozos (they tie together instead of using rings).

Pouches (pocket slings; pictured) work in a similar way to slings across mom's body, but they are really just one continuous piece of fabric with an area of fabric that forms a pouch or pocket. No tying or looping fabric through rings.

◆ **Mei Tai or Asian Carriers.** This type of carrier is made up of a fabric rectangle with straps at each corner. The bottom straps tie around your waste while the top straps go over your shoulders and attach to the carrier or are tied together.

◆ **Wrap Around Carrier.** These are like those Guatemalan carriers we mentioned earlier. They are basically made by wrapping a long (three to six meter) piece of fabric around and around your body forming a pouch around baby. Wrap arounds can be positioned to go around the shoulders and waist for better support. But there is a learning curve—wrap around carriers require some practice for correct use.

◆ **Hip Carriers.** Hip carriers are a minimalist version of the sling. With less fabric to cradle baby, they generally work better for older babies (over five or six months). Baby is in a more upright position all the time, rather than lying horizontally. And like a sling, the hip carrier fits across your body with baby resting on your hip.

◆ **Front (Soft) Carriers.** Front carriers are basically a fabric bag worn on your chest. Your baby sort of dangles there in an upright position either looking in at you (when they're very young) or out at the world (when they gain more head control). Some front carriers will convert to a back carrier. Structured soft carriers have more rigid padding so they maintain their shape even when not in use.

◆ **Frame (or backpack) Carriers.** Need to get some fresh air? Just because you have a baby doesn't mean you can never go hiking again. Backpack manufacturers have responded to parents' wish to find a way to take their small children with them on hikes and long walks. The good news is that most of these frame carriers are made with lightweight aluminum, high quality fabrics and well-positioned straps. Accessories abound with some models including sunshades, diaper packs that Velcro on, and adjustable seating so Junior gets a good view.

More Money Buys You . . .

When you spend more money on a carrier, you generally get more luxurious fabrics like from organic cottons to washable silk. Some manufacturers also add embroidery or ruffle accents. Patterns can also cost more than basic solids.

Safe & Sound

In 2010, the Consumer Product Safety Commission issued a warning to parents about sling use for infants under four months of age. At least 14 deaths have been associated with the use of slings in the last 20 years. Here are the CPSC's tips for using a sling:

◆ *Premature infants and those with low birth weight (including twins or infants with breathing issues such as a cold) should not be placed in a sling.*

◆ *Make sure the infant's face is not covered* and can be seen at all times regardless what type of carrier you're using.

◆ *Frequently check on your baby to make sure he is breathing.*

◆ *Check the graphic below.* This shows both the correct way (chin up, face visible, nose and mouth free) and the improper way to wear your baby.

| **Right** Chin up; Face visible; Nose and mouth free | **Wrong** Baby's face is covered | **Wrong** Baby is too low | **Wrong** Baby is hunched with chin touching chest | **Wrong** Baby's face is pressed tight against wearer |

Smart Shopper Tips

Smart Shopper Tip #1
Try More than One
"My friends are all experienced moms and they have very different opinions on what carrier I should by for my baby. Why can't I get any consensus from them?"

The best carrier works for you *and* your baby. That's why we suggest you buy one or two styles that interest you and keep the packaging/receipts. That way, if your baby loves the Ergo soft carrier, but hates the Maya Wrap sling, you're covered. Or you may find that certain carriers are more comfortable—like wrap-arounds, which can be infinitely adjusted for the right fit. Finally, some of our readers own more than one type of carrier. Certain carriers work better with infants but not so great with toddlers. Some carriers are too hot to wear in the summer.

Smart Shopper Tip #2
How Does It Work?

"My new carrier came in today. I was so excited until I tried to get it to work. What am I doing wrong?"

Great question. Here's how you find out. Before you even buy a carrier, check the manufacturer's web site for instructions. We prefer sites that have videos you can watch. Some even send a DVD with the product. And as a last resort, check YouTube to see if any moms posted helpful videos on how to use your carrier. If you notice the manufacturer only has written instructions, beware! It can be as bad as an IKEA shelving unit.

Waste of Money

"All these carriers look the same; a sling is a sling, a front carrier is a front carrier. Can't I just buy the cheapest one I find in the store or on the 'net?"

You could, but you might also be wasting your money. Cheap carriers are typically made with scratchy fabrics, little or no padding, no waist belts for parents, and so on. The key is to find a carrier that is comfortable for both you and your baby. A carrier that lacks support will be quickly discarded.

The Name Game: Carrier Reviews

Here are our reviews of baby carriers. We've divided them into different categories (slings/pouches, front carriers, mai tais, wrap arounds, hip carriers and frame carriers). You'll find that manufacturers often make more than one type of carrier so they'll appear in different categories. While we've attempted to include weight ranges, some manufacturers only list their maximum weights. Most manufacturers also have online videos as well as written instructions included with their products. If they don't have videos, customers often post videos to YouTube to help other parents. Finally, we can't stress enough that you should always practice putting on your carrier and taking it off before you put your baby into it. Some carriers are complex and need practice to use.

Slings and Pouches

BabaSling

Joovy.com
Price: $90 to $130
Weight Range: 7.7 to 33 lbs.
Comments: The BabaSling allows you to carry your baby in five different positions (three carrying positions, two breastfeeding positions). Heavy duty "ski buckles" are used to secure and adjust the sling. The shoulder straps are padded as well as the sides of the sling. BabaSling has organic fabric options as well as lighter weight, warm weather styles (the BabaSling Lite). Overall, parents are happy with the BabaSling, although a few have complained that it's too tight. If you need more adjustability, a ring sling may be a better bet. Joovy's web site has instructional videos. As a side note, there is a similarly named Australian sling on the market We have not reviewed this sling. The Joovy version has a Joovy logo on the front. *Rating: B*

Baby K'Tan

babyktan.com
Price: $50 to $60.
Weight Range: 8 to 35 lbs.
Comments: The best thing about a Baby K'Tan carrier: it rests on both shoulders. That's right, unlike usual slings, which lay across your body and put the weight on one shoulder, the K'Tan distributes the weight evenly. Another plus: it works like a mei tai, but you don't have to do any wrapping or knotting and you don't have all that excess fabric. However, when baby is placed in certain positions, a sash must be tied around baby and your waist for additional support. Great videos on the web site tell you how to choose the correct size, how to use the carrier and how to remove it as well. Fabrics are all cotton except for the Breeze version which is a mesh fabric for hot weather. One disadvantage: readers tell us the Baby K'Tan works best for young or small babies. Once you get beyond 20 lbs., the K'Tan may be too small. Another reader praised their double sling which comes in five sizes including XL. *Rating: A-*

Balboa Baby Adjustable Sling by Dr. Sears

BalboaBaby.com
Price: $50 to $60.
Maximum weight: 8 to 35 lbs.
Comments: Dr. Sears was the original advocate for "baby wearing." He worked for years with NoJo

(owned by Crown Crafts) who manufactured his version of a sling. Now he's moved on to a new manufacturer, Balboa Baby, which is making his approved slings. This sling is basically a pouch with a contoured and padded strap that slips through an adjustable ring system. There is elastic and padding around the edges that help create the pouch and a small front pocket for storage. Parent feedback is mixed on this sling: fans liked the comfortable padded strap while others complain that if they don't position baby just right, the sling becomes quite uncomfortable. Check YouTube for videos to help you position your baby correctly. Parents also noted it works best for small infants. Once they hit 15 lbs. it's difficult to wear for long periods. *Rating: B*

HOTSLINGS ADJUSTABLE POUCH

HotSlings.com

Price: $65

Weight Range: 8 lbs. to 35 lbs.

Comments: They were here; they were gone; they're baaack! Yep, HotSlings has been revived. So how have the new owners changed HotSlings? Their new adjustable slings (called AP or adjustable pouches) come in two sizes which can adjust to fit nine size ranges based on a measurement across your body from shoulder to hip. The fabric now has higher thread counts and they're using more durable buckles (no rings here) than in the past.

HotSlings AP comes in nine fabrics for $65. Reviews are mostly favorable, although some moms complained that the sling was too small; others recommended waiting until baby can hold her head up. While all carriers have information on how to use their product safely, we like HotSlings safety motto: Visible & Kissable. Easy way to remember how your baby should be seated in the sling. *Rating: B+*

MAMMA'S MILK

mammasmilk.com.

Price: $50 to $95 depending on fabric.

Maximum weight: 35 lbs.

Comments: Made of stretch cotton, the Mamma's Milk slings are probably the simplest style of sling available. They are infinitely adjustable and use Aplix (a stronger version of Velcro) to keep the sling in the correct position for the parent. Comfortable foam padding is included in the area where toddlers' legs rest. Most of the designs are made of cotton stretch fabric, although they also offer one solar veil option, three organic fabrics and two beautiful silk fabrics (dry clean only). Videos are available online as well as photos to help you use and adjust your sling. Feedback is positive. *Rating: A*

Maya Wrap

mayawrap.com

Price: $75

Weight Range: 8 to 35 lbs.

Comments: Maya Wrap has consistently been recommended to us by readers who love its flexibility and comfort. Helpful instructional videos are available on their web site and a DVD is included with your purchase. The rings are made of ¼" anodized aluminum, the fabrics are 100% cotton hand-loomed and are only made of one layer of fabric (there is padding at the shoulder area for comfort). As a result, the Maya Wrap is quite lightweight. It comes in four sizes with at least 15 fabric options. Reader feedback on the Maya Wrap is positive, although some parents complain about the long piece of fabric that hangs from the rings when the sling is being used. If you want to avoid a lot of extra fabric, you can size down your wrap so the hanging fabric is shorter. Another complaint: it can be painful to use with older babies or for long periods of time.r. **Rating: A**

New Native Baby Sling

newnativebaby.com

Price: $42 to $54.

Maximum weight: 35 lbs.

Comments: New Native's focus is eco-friendly slings made from mostly organic cotton. This sling is styled as a one-piece pouch with no adjustments. Check the size chart carefully since you can make the sling smaller, but not larger. That lack of adjustment is a negative here and parents complain that the sizes run small. An infant support pillow can be purchased separately to improve fit for both preemies and newborns. Online instructional videos are available. Recently, we noticed New Native has a factory seconds option with carriers priced as low as $20. **Rating: B-**

The Peanut Shell

thepeanutshell.com

Price: $30 to $50.

Maximum weight: Adjustable: 8 to 26 lbs.; Classic: 8 to 36 lbs.

Comments: Peanut Shell was one of our readers' favorite slings a few years back, but the company changed ownership and the new owners completely re-launched the line. They now offer two sling options: the Adjustable ($55), and the Classic ($39).

The Adjustable is a one size fits all sling with a cool safety strap and catch plus padded rails in a stretch cotton fabric. The Classic comes in two sizes (S/M and L/XL), includes a pocket for storage and has only light leg padding.

carriers

Parents definitely have mixed feelings about the Peanut Shell Adjustable. For some it works great, but others complain that it is difficult to use, can't safely accommodate a newborn and is hard to adjust. Parents like the Classic version better as long as you get the correct size. So it's a mixed review for the Peanut Shell. **Rating B**

WALKING ROCK FARMS SLING BABY SLING

abaybe.com
Price: $58.
Maximum weight: 35 lbs.
Comments: Readers love the Sling Baby Sling because it's so easy to use—-no rings, no knots or ties, no tails of fabric hanging down. The strap works like a duffle bag strap—just slide it one way or the other to lengthen or shorten. It's so easy to adjust, maker Walking Rock claims you can hand baby off from one parent to the other without waking your baby. The Sling Baby is available in three fabrics: micro fleece for cold climates, pique air flow fabric for warm climates and "all-climate" Ponte Roma knit. Unfortunately, this sling appears to only be available directly from the abaybe.com web site. **Rating: A-**

ZOLOWEAR ADJUSTABLE POUCH

zolowear.com
Price: $49 to $69
Weight Range: 8 to 40 lbs.
Comments: Unlike the ring-design of Zolo Wear's sling (see below), the company's adjustable pouches are a single loop of fabric with a shaped pocket for baby. True to the name, the pouches can be adjusted by using four button holes. The advantage to this: no long tail of fabric. A free instructional DVD is included with the pouch. Reader feedback on the adjustable pouches has been sparse, but given the company's overall reputation, we will recommend them. **Rating: B**

ZOLOWEAR SLING

zolowear.com
Price: $60 to $125 depending on fabric.
Weight Range: 8 to 35 lbs.
Comments: Zolo Wear's mojo are cool fabrics: cotton (including organic), silk brocade and breathable mesh. Yep, it's the gorgeous silk material (machine washable) that catches your eye. Designed with a front ring, these slings include a front pouch and come in four sizes and two styles (pleated or classic–it's just a style difference). The Zolo Wear sling can be used with baby in six different positions. Check their web site for sales, plus there is a factory outlet. Reader feedback on Zolo Wear

is positive, although a few moms told us it takes a bit of practice to use the sling. An instructional video is included plus you'll find videos and illustrations on their site. If you're trying to choose between a pouch or a traditional sling, the web site offers a comparison of their pros and cons under their FAQ section. **Rating: A**

Front Carriers

BABY BJORN COMFORT
BabyBjorn.com
Price: $140 to $200
Weight Range: 13 to 31 lbs.
Comments: Baby Bjorn is the 800-pound gorilla in the carrier category. This Swedish import comes in five flavors: Original (and Original Spirit in brighter colors or Original Organic), Comfort, Air, Synergy and Active (also available in organic fabric). We'll review the line in three parts, starting with the Comfort.

Unlike the original Baby Bjorn carrier which is sized for newborns, the Comfort is intended for older babies up to small toddlers. It's a beefier carrier with its own ergonomic waist belt, a necessity when you're carrying around a heavier child. As with all the Baby Bjorn carriers, the Comfort allows baby to face in or out. Two leg positions are available: the narrower position with the child's legs dangling or a wider position allows older babies to face inward if they still prefer that position.

The fabric on the Comfort is organic cotton, and (like all the Bjorn carriers) meets the European Oeko-Tex standards for health hazardous substances. Readers are very complimentary of the Comfort. They tell us they love the waist belt and thick padded straps since they help parents carry a larger child longer. Just as with all their carriers, you can easily transfer a sleeping baby from the Comfort to the crib without waking baby.

We've noticed the Comfort is selling online for as little as $140, but this carrier is no longer on the Baby Bjorn site. We suspect they may be phasing it out in favor of the new One, so you may not see it for sale much longer. It is a great improvement over the Original so we'll give the Comfort a bit higher rating this time out. **Rating: A-**

BABY BJORN ONE
Price: $200
Weight Range: 8-26 lbs. forward facing; up to 33 lbs. inward facing and as a back carrier (over one yr.).
Comments: $200? For a carrier? The Baby Bjorn One is pitched as the Ginsu Knife of baby carriers—-it works for infants. And toddlers. As a front carrier—facing in or out.

And as a back carrier.

So does it live up to all the hype? Yes, it does.

The clever design feature of the Bjorn One is its ability to morph from a carrier that works for the smallest infants, then for larger toddlers. Like the Bjorn Comfort, the One has a waist belt for lumbar support and to distribute the baby's weight on your hips. The carrier has a newborn height position that utilizes a simple zipper to position the baby high up in the carrier and facing inward. No need for a separate infant insert.

Then at about four months—and here's the One's secret sauce—you can unzip the seat and your baby drops down lower in the carrier. This makes the carrier more comfortable for parents as baby gets bigger. An audible click on the buckles let's you know when the carrier is attached properly.

Once your baby hits five months, you can position your baby to look outward and then at 12 months you can convert the One to a back carrier. To use as a backpack carrier, you'll need to adjust it into the wide leg position. Just open the zipper on each side to change from normal to wide leg. You'll want to load your child into the carrier in the front position, then slide the carrier around to your back.

Even though the $200 price tag seems steep, let's look at what it would cost to buy a carrier that morphs into all these uses. A basic front carrier (that works for infants) runs about $75 to $125. To get a carrier that also works for toddlers and as a back carrier, you'd have to shell out another $100 or more. So that makes the One seem reasonable, especially if you are an attachment parenting fan and want to carry your baby beyond the newborn stage.

So what are parents telling us about the One? Most are enthusiastic about it. They love the flexibility and find the waist belt quite comfortable. While some complain it took a while to figure out how to get the carrier on in all positions, others noted that it is easy to adjust and transfer between different size parents. Baby Bjorn has hit a home run with the One. ***Rating: A***

BABY BJORN ORIGINAL, ACTIVE, MIRACLE

Price $50 to $80, depending on the fabric.

Weight Range: Original: 8 to 25 lbs.; Active: 8 to 26 lbs.; Miracle: 8 to 26 lbs.

Comments: The Original is easy to use and adjust (baby can ride facing forward or rear). Best of all, the front of the Bjorn snaps off to put a sleeping baby down in a crib.

The Active ($190) adds lumbar support and wider straps for longer walks.

The Miracle builds on some of the features of Bjorn's other carriers including the Comfort (see separate review). The Miracle has an adjustable waist belt for starters, and includes a unique measuring tape adjustment inside the carrier so you can make sure the seat is a best fit for your child. For parents, the adjustable weight belt combines with infinite adjust shoulder straps allowing parents to evenly distribute the weight on shoulders and waist, or take weight off either the waist or the shoulders. This makes the fit even more customized. Also, the waist belt flexes as it pivots meaning it stays flat on the stomach and doesn't dig in. The Miracle is available in three price points: the basic at $185, the organic at $199 and the mesh at $220. Not cheap certainly and considerably more than the Mamas and Papas Morph with similar features.

Baby Bjorn consistently gets high ratings from parents who purchase front carriers—-they like the ease of use and the fact that baby can face outward eventually. But detractors point to the high price and limited use (babies outgrow it fast–the three reviewed here only go up to 25 lbs.). Plus size moms, as well as moms with larger breasts, complain the Bjorns are uncomfortable because babies sit so high. Back/neck strain is a common complaint of Bjorn users (the Active and Miracle generate fewer complaints on this, thanks to the lumbar support). Some babies also don't like the Bjorn for whatever reason. We recommend keeping the receipt just in case you have a picky baby. ***Rating: B***

BABYHAWK OH SNAP!
BabyHawk.com
Price: $130 to $150
Weight Range: 15 to 45 lbs.
Comments: A soft structure carrier similar to the Ergo, the Oh SNAP! has triple padded top straps and a foam core bottom strap with adjustable webbing and buckles. BabyHawk also offers customizing options. Choose a main fabric and a strap color or you can use your own fabric. And the site does have some ready-made Oh SNAPs! for $115 to $130. All their carriers are made in the US.

The only complaints we heard about this carrier were from petite or small framed women who couldn't get a comfortable fit because the waist belt was too wide across their backs. For average size women, this carrier should work just great. ***Rating: A-***

BABY TREKKER
babytrekker.com
Price: $150 (free shipping to US, Canada).
Weight Range: 8 to 50 lbs.
Comments: Baby Trekker was first recommended to us by our Canadian readers who raved about this made-in-Canada, multi-use carrier. Yes, it works as your typical front carrier with baby facing in when young and out when older. But the carrier also has a cool

nursing option and a backpack position allows baby to either face your back or out to see the world (though not until your baby is at least three months old or 15 lbs.). Special safety straps in the carrier are for use when baby is under 16 lbs. to keep her from slipping out of the leg holes. The Trekker stores in its own attached pocket making it easy to pack in your diaper bag. All colors except navy are organic cotton. We liked the extra padding under every buckle for baby's comfort. Canadians also like the fact that it is easy to use when baby is dressed in a snowsuit—not a problem for Florida readers, but you get the idea. An instructional video is available on YouTube. ***Rating: A***

BECO GEMINI

BecoBabyCarrier.com
Price: $130.
Weight Range: 7 to 35 lbs.
Comments: Unlike Beco's Butterfly 2 carrier, the Gemini allows baby to face forward. It comes with head support, waist belt, adjustable chest strap and adjustable base. This base alternates to allow for small infants facing mom, then, when baby gets bigger, facing out. Unlike the Butterfly 2, you don't need a separate infant insert. And you can also adjust the carrier so baby rides on your back or hip. Reader feedback on the Gemini is positive. Yes, it is pricey, but a bit less than the Butterfly 2. ***Rating: A***

BELLE BABY CARRIER

Web: BelleBabyCarriers.com
Price: $110 to $130.
Weight Range: 8 to 35 lbs.
Comments: Looking for a lightweight, easy to pack carrier? Belle Baby carriers forgo all the extra padding to make a lighter, cooler carrier that allows baby to face both in and out. Based in California, they are available in four organic cotton/hemp designs as well as four classic (polyester) options. A removable head support comes with the carrier for sleeping babies.

We liked the ergonomic design and how the densely padded straps cross in the back like the Baby Trekker. Buckles are similar to what you see in quality backpacks. An independent waist belt puts the weight on your hips, not your back. ***Rating: A-***

BOBA CARRIER 4G

BobaFamily.com
Price: $120 to $125
Weight Range: 7 to 45 lbs.
Comments: For parents who want to begin baby wearing immediately with their newborn, our readers recommend the

Boba Carrier 4G. The beauty of this carrier: you can use it for newborns with a special integrated insert. And it works with children seven to 45 lbs. as a front or back carrier. No, you can't face baby out (and that's really the only negative here) but it has pretty cool accessory foot straps that attach to the adult waist belt for toddlers being carried on the back. Compared to similar carriers like the Ergo, parents liked the longer body and less bulky straps on the Boba. FYI: As we were going to press, Ergo debuted the 4G version of this carrier—it features a lowered shoulder strap connection, slightly wider seat and stronger buckles. The sleep hood is also lighter and longer. ***Rating: A***

BRITAX BABY CARRIER
BritaxUSA.com
Price: $75 to $140
Weight Range: 8 to 32 lbs.
Comments: The Britax Baby Carrier's key feature is Britax's CarryLong System, a padded waist belt and shoulder straps that claim to "distribute weight across shoulders, back and hips for maximum extended wear comfort." The carrier includes a multitude of features: padded leg openings; easy on/off design with one hand buckles and snaps; easy adjust front harness straps; "easy-adjust waist belt" (22" to 56"); bib; adjustable head support; leg loops sized for small infants. Whew! Clearly, Britax did their homework.

Of course, all these features come at a price: $130. That's about 30% more than a basic Bjorn but less than the Bjorn Miracle.

So is it worth it? Feedback is positive. Parents really seem to like the high weight limit—the Britax Baby Carrier can be used up to 32 pounds, versus the Bjorn carriers which only go up to between 22 and 26 pounds (except the Comfort at 31 lbs.). Bottom line: you can use this carrier longer than Bjorn. The carrier's light weight (3 lbs.) also comes in for praise. Overall, parents tell us the carrier's comfort and back support is superior . . . so we'll recommend the Britax Baby Carrier. Pricey, but an excellent offering. ***Rating: A***

CATBIRD BABY PIKKOLO
CatBirdBaby.com
Price: $130.
Maximum weight: 8 to 40 lbs.
Comments: Maker Catbird Baby started off with a mei tai carrier, but recently expanded into a soft carrier with buckles. The straps are shorter than a mei tai, addressing a common complaint with those carriers. The Pikkolo can be used front and rear facing, on the back and on the hip like a mei tai. They offer it in only one size and recommend their original mei tai if you are very petite or large. The Pikkolo comes with an attached hood, memory foam straps, chest strap to use in the piggyback position and instruction booklet.

Fabric options are limited (one solid, two patterns), made of brushed cotton canvas. Reader feedback on the Pikkolo has been very positive—the hybrid style of a soft carrier with mei tai like options makes it a favorite. Our only complaint: we wish they had videos on their site to show parents how to use the Pikkolo. *Rating: A*

ERGO 360°

ErgoBabyCarrier.com
Price: $160
Weight Range: 8 to 35 lbs.
Comments: The Ergo 360° is Ergo's first carrier that allows a baby to face out. The new 360° is made with a structured bucket seat that prevents baby's legs from dangling (this is a concern for hip dysplasia).

The Ergo 360° has three positions: as a front carrier, hip carrier or even as a back pack. It comes with a wide waist belt which can be worn high when baby is little and adjusted down to carry the weight of older babies and toddlers. The forward facing carry is recommended for babies six months old and older.

The Ergo 360° will be available in spring 2014 for $160—considerably less than the Baby Bjorn One ($250). We previewed the Ergo 360° and were impressed, but we'll wait to assign a rating until we see parent feedback. *Rating: Not Yet.*

ERGO BABY CARRIER

ErgoBabyCarrier.com
Price: $115 to $165 depending on fabric.
Weight Range: 7 to 45 lbs. (7 to 12 lbs. with optional newborn insert, priced separately)
Comments: Made by Hawaii-based ERGOBaby, the Ergo carrier has won kudos on our boards for its ease of use (you can wear it in front or back or on the hip) and less strain on the back. While most front carriers put the strain on your shoulders and back, the Ergo comes with a padded hip belt that takes the strain off your upper back. Best of all, you can use it from birth (with a newborn insert, $25 to $38) up to an amazing 45 lbs. (toddlers)—most front carriers can only be used for a short time (the Bjorn limit is 25 lbs.). And the Ergo can be used as a hip carrier. One important caveat: you cannot face your baby out when wearing it in the front position; baby always rides facing you. On the plus side, Ergo offers five versions: Original, Performance (special light-weight fabric), Travel (no bells and whistles), Organic, and Designer (exclusive prints).

Ergo recently released its newest carrier, the ERGOBaby Bundle of Joy. It is a set that includes a baby carrier and matching infant insert for $130 to $163 depending on the fabric, priced less than buying them separately.

Feedback on the Ergo is overwhelmingly positive. In fact, the only negatives parents note are a bit of a learning curve and the fact that you have to buy the infant insert or wait till baby is 12 lbs. Otherwise, they praise lack of back pain and the comfortable straps and belt. **Rating: A-**

KINDERPACKS
KinderCarry.com
Price: $164
Weight Range: Infant version is 8 to 50 lbs..; Standard is 18 to 50 lbs.; Toddler is 25 to 50 lbs.; Preschool is 35 to 50 lbs.

Comments: Kindercarry offers yet another version of the Soft Structured Carrier (SSC): the Kinderpack. This carrier is sort of an amalgamation of other styles with a structured body but straps that work a little like a mei tai. Except they don't tie, they buckle. Anyway, the real selling point is that they are very wide so they support legs rather than leave them dangling and they can accommodate large kids. They come in four sizes. The newborn size has an adjustable base that changes the crotch width to accommodate infants. The standard version works for babies starting at 20 lbs., the toddler is for 25 lbs. and up and the preschool model works starting at 35 lbs. (if you can carry your child at that point!).

All the carriers are rated up to 50 lbs. although its doubtful you could carry a child that size. Kinderpacks come with buckles on the contoured straps and waistband, a hood, and contoured body panel made of canvas and twill. Handy videos help explain how to use your Kinderpack. Parents comment that they like Kinderpacks but would mainly recommend them for older children. Feedback is very positive so we'll give them our recommendation. **Rating: A**

MAMAS AND PAPAS MORPH CARRIER
MamasandPapas.com
Price: $139
Weight: 8 lbs. to 27 lbs.
Comments: Mamas and Papas first carrier, the Morph, has straps that go on just like a jacket, not over your head, and snaps and zips together. Another plus: the Morph allows parents to adjust the shoulder straps and waist strap easily for a great fit. The carrier comes in two sizes (sm/med and med/lg) and additional harnesses are available ($65 each). One hand adjustable straps and waist belt are wide and well padded with lumbar support built in.

Putting baby in the harness is simple too. The "pod" (structured pouch for baby) has adjustable sides and slides into the front belt then snaps to the harness straps. The pod also includes a head rest and dribble cloth. Baby can be positioned facing in or out. Cost for the complete set of harness and pod runs $139 and comes in five colors.

So what do we think of the Morph? We're impressed. It has features similar to Baby Bjorn's $200 Miracle at a much better price. Most parents like it although a few noted it's more complicated than the company claims. Their favorite feature is how easy it is to transfer baby from one person to another (if you buy another harness). **Rating A**

MAXIMOM
4CoolKids.com
Price: $65 (single), $100 (twin), $140 (triple).
Weight Range: newborn to 35 lbs. per child
Comments: We've had several readers email to
extol the virtues of the MaxiMom carrier. One moms said, "it does everything short of making dinner. It can be used as a front carrier facing forward or backward, backpack facing forward or backward, emergency high chair, sling and can be used for a child up to 35 pounds. Here's the great part: MaxiMom is designed to also be used with multiples!" If you plan to use it for multiples, the weight limit is 35 lbs. per child. **Rating: A**

MOBY GO
MobyWrap.com
Price: $73
Weight Range: 15 to 45 lbs.
Comments: The Moby Go is a structured soft carrier
manufactured by the folks who gave us the Moby Wrap. Intended for older babies from 15 to 45 lbs., the Go has straps that cross at the shoulders to distribute baby's weight similar to the Pikkolo carrier. The carrier includes a padded waist belt and uses buckles to secure baby. You can loosen the straps to remove baby without having to unbuckle it. One complaint: this carrier does not allow for back carrying like other soft carriers. Older babies might prefer a back carry position to the front carry, especially since baby can't face out either.

Parental feedback is rather new for this carrier, but parents who have tried it really like it. It's much easier to put on, take off and adjust than the Moby Wrap. We'll give the new Moby Go a recommended rating. **Rating: A-**

PETUNIA PICKLE BOTTOM SIGHTSEER & TOURGUIDE
Petunia.com
Price: $70
Weight Range: 8 to 22 lbs.

Comments: Comments: If you are a fan of Petunia Pickle Bottom diaper bags, you can now buy a front carrier in coordinating fabrics. The Sightseer "slips on like a t-shirt" according to the web site and uses buckles to secure it. Buttons allow the carrier to be adjusted for very young babies (8 to 11 lbs.) as well. There is no parent waist belt, which likely explains why it only goes up to 22 lbs. We're betting it gets uncomfortable at the high end of the weight range. The Sightseer does allow baby to both face in and out. Feedback from readers was slim, but those who have used it were not impressed saying it wasn't comfortable to wear.

The TourGuide is basically the same as the Sightseer except for the fabric: it is made from recycled materials. The shell is recycled polyester and the liner is recycled nylon. That's unusual since most "eco-friendly" carriers are organic. Other than that limited feedback on the TourGuide was also not positive.

As a side note, there are Ergo carriers (see review earlier) made with Petunia Picklebottom fabrics. ***Rating: C***

STOKKE MYCARRIER

Stokke.com
Price: $220
Maximum weight: 7.7 to 33 lbs.
Comments: : After seeing the $250 price tag mentioned above, we're betting we lost quite a few dear readers before we even got to the comments section. For those of you still with us, yes, that is quite a hefty investment—the pitch is the MyCarrier by Stokke also works for kids as a backpack carrier up to 33 pounds (about three years of age).

The carrier comes with one harness and two pouches. The first pouch works facing in from birth then facing out at about four months. The second pouch is for kids that can sit up on their own and are at least 28 inches tall.

The harness includes a support belt for parents as well as two pockets for keys, etc., a chest clip and an integrated sunshade/sleep support. Carabiners are used to attach the pouches to the harness as well as quite a few buttons and zippers. In fact, you might be a bit overwhelmed when you first try to put together your MyCarrier. To help, Stokke has posted detailed how-to videos on its site for the MyCarrier. After watching these, however, we can guess some folks will still be flummoxed by the carrier's ease of use, or lack there of.

The back carrying position seems to be the MyCarrier's secret weapon. Stokke includes an aluminum support bar with the carrier (this is installed down the back of the carrier for extra support). Again, the online video is helpful. This added feature is a real must have when you want to use this carrier with older children. Now that Baby Bjorn has come out with the One which has similar features, the Stokke faces some tough competition

As you might expect from eco-focused Stokke, the carrier uses only organic fabrics. Yet, for this amount of money, we kept looking for gold leaf accents on the MyCarrier. They also make a MyCarrier Cool with breathable fabric ($200-$220). Parent feedback has been mixed. Some parents complain about a lack of padding in the shoulder straps, and it can be difficult to put on. Others, however, liked that the carrier doesn't require an infant insert and grows with the child. Overall we think the Stokke has enough negatives to assign them only an average rating. **Rating: C**

Mei Tai or Asian Carriers

BabyHawk
babyhawk.com
Price: $85 to $135.
Weight Range: 8 to 40 lbs.
Comments: BabyHawk offers quite a few options if you want to custom design your own mei tai. Start with a strap color (6 options) and main body color (over 40), and then decide whether you want extra long straps ($5), a pocket ($10), toy rings ($5 each) or reversible fabric ($10). Without all the extras, a basic BabyHawk is $85. If you just want to buy an in stock mei tai, we saw 13 options available when we last visited.

BabyHawk makes two types of mei tais: one for smaller babies up to 40 lbs. and the other for older babies to 15 to 45 lbs (called the Oh Mei!). This allows for a more customized fit

We like all the unique fabrics including Amy Butler designs as well as florals, Asian prints, and geometrics. Like other mei tais, BabyHawk can be used in front, back or on the hip. Readers most like the customization options (but be forewarned: customized BabyHawks are non-returnable) and the comfortable fabrics. On the other hand, some readers complained that the straps were too long . . . and it takes a while to figure out how to use these carriers. **Rating: A**

Catbird Baby Mei Tai
CatBirdBaby.com
Price: $75 to $96
Weight: 8 to 40 lbs.
Comments: Looking for an affordable mei tai option? Catbird Baby (we review their front carrier, Pikkolo in the front carrier section) makes a lower priced option of their well loved mei tai for a mere $75. It's the same as the original version but does not have the hood (a padded headrest instead) and

is only available in three solid colors. The rest of Catbird Baby's designs use graphic and floral fabrics with sold color straps. Baby faces in when used as a front carrier and can also be carried on the back or hip (after five or six months of age). Catbird also sells a support belt ($25) so carrying older babies is more comfortable. Fans of mei tais give the Catbird Baby excellent reviews and the lower price of the solid color versions leads us to rate them highly. **Rating A-**

ELLAROO MEI TAI

ellaroo.com
Price: $90.
Weight Range: 8 to 35 lbs.
Comments: Ellaroo's version of the mei tai gets rave reviews from readers. Fans like the short learning curve and the fact that either mom or dad can wear it—it easily adjusts to different sizes and body types. Baby can face in or out in the Ella Roo or on the back as with most mei tais. Shoulder straps are lightly padded and there is a padded headrest as well. All carriers are made of 100% organic cotton and must be hand washed/hung dry. They are made in Italy. The only complaint: The Ella Roo takes some time to put on or take off so check out their video instructions on the web site. **Rating: A**

KOZY CARRIER

kozycarrier.com
Price: $90.
Weight Range: 8 to 40 lbs.
Comments: Kozy Carrier's web site touts that this mei tai-inspired carrier has no buckles or rings—just tie it on. You'll notice it has wide shoulder straps with light padding, a lightly padded curved head support and is reversible. Extra long straps are available as an option. All Kozy Carriers are made to order so you can customize them to your taste: pick a base fabric (natural, black or canvas) and a solid or print accent fabric. Like other mei tai carriers, baby can be worn in front (facing in or out), on the side or on your back and used for infants up to toddlers. You'll need to check the web site for instructions on how to use the carrier. Reader feedback has been quite positive on the Kozy Carrier. **Rating: A**

TOGETHERBE FREEHAND MEI TAI

TogetherBe.com
Price: $72
Weight Range: Newborn to 35 lbs.
Comments: Looking for an attractive, comfortable mei tai option? Our readers recommend the Freehand Mei Tai by TogetherBe. With ten graphic fabrics and a

couple solid color options, these mei tais have great style plus they are reversible and affordable. Readers also praise how easy these carriers are to use and adjust no matter who is wearing them. They can position your baby in front (facing in only), on your back or on the hip. Priced on the low end for this type of carrier, they have padded shoulder straps and head support, use stretch twill fabrics and include "Grow With Me Triangles" that "allow the carrier to fit your baby perfectly." Finally, all Freehand's mei tais are made in India at a fair trade sewing house. All this adds up to a great mei tai option so we'll recommend Freehand's mei tai. ***Rating: A***

Wrap Around Carriers

BOBA WRAP

BobaFamily.com

Price: $38

Weight Range: 7 to 35 lbs.

Comments: Boba Wrap gets universally positive feedback from readers. At a mere $48, it's priced very affordably. Made of cotton with a bit of spandex for stretch, this wrap is relatively easy for newbies to get the hang of. The key is to make sure you get a very snug fit to yourself before you put baby in. That spandex makes it really work, but if it's too loose when you put baby in, it will begin to sag and hurt your back. The online videos and instructions are helpful since you tie this wrap rather differently from similar products. We especially love the "helpful tips" section of the instructions plus the numerous safety reminders. Parents note that the fabric holds its shape well even after long term use although it can be a pain for beginners to use. ***Rating: A***

ERGO WRAP

ErgoBaby.com

Price: $80

Weight Range: 7 to 45 lbs.

Comments: Wrap carriers have long had a big drawback: you can get it tight enough to support baby for awhile, but eventually it stretches out with use. Ergo, maker of the Ergo Baby Carrier, think they've solved the problem. They call their new Wrap a "hybrid": strong like a woven but with added stretch equally in all directions. They claim this will cause the wrap to rebound back to its original shape after every use. And you can remove and put your child back in the carrier multiple times without re-wrapping. Baby can be wrapped into six different positions, plus the carrier folds into a pocket. The new Ergo Wrap is scheduled to debut in stores in early 2014. We'll assign a rating once we get parent feedback. ***Rating: Not Yet.***

GYPSY MAMA WRAPSODY

gypsymama.com

Price: $68 to $86.

Maximum weight: 35 lbs.

Comments: Gypsy Mama makes three Wrapsody wraps in different fabrics: the Wrap DuO (can be used in water $68), The Breeze Wraps (cotton gauze, $80), and the Stretch-Hybrid (like t-shirt material, $86, pictured).

The Breeze wraps are the lightest weight but not stretchy and are made of fabric hand dyed and batiked in Bali. It folds down into a built in storage pocket, making it easy to toss in the diaper bag. Gypsy Mama recommends the Stretch-Hybrid wraps ($84) for beginners as they are "more forgiving of sloppy wrap jobs." The fabric is similar to a t-shirt and is very soft for both newborns and older kids.

The Wrap DuO is made to use in the water and on land for babies until they reach about 35 lbs. in the water or 25 lbs. on land. Made of high tech sports knit, it's intended to keep mom and baby cool on those hot summer days.

Online instructions (both videos and printed) were clear and easy to follow. We recommend the Breeze for parents in hot climates or for summer wearing. ***Rating: A***

MOBY WRAP

mobywrap.com

Price: $48 to $160.

Weight Range: 8 to 35 lbs.

Comments: Moby Wraps are one-size-fits-all carriers designed to allow moms to adjust the fit by how tight they wrap the baby. The wrap uses three sections of fabric for extra security. The lack of padding means its not bulky to wear or store. They use cotton stretch fabric to get a close fit to the body. The Original version sells for $48 and comes in solid colors. Fabrics get fancier with cute patterns($56), UV fabrics ($56) and even a Major League Baseball line ($63) in case you want to support your favorite team. Organics are $63 but the most expensive options are the Dolcino styles made with organic yarn from Germany for up to $160.

You can expect some shrinkage when you wash the Moby Wrap, although they add extra fabric to account for that. A downside: it takes a bit of time to learn to use it, and even once you have it figured out, the Moby Wrap takes some time to put on. Although they include an instruction book with each wrap, you'll want to check YouTube for video help as well. The Moby Wrap can be used for both front and back wearing. Parent reviews are mostly positive, with the exception of the learning curve. Plus size moms will love the Moby Wrap as it can be adjusted to any parent's body type. ***Rating: B+***

Vatanai

vatanai.cz

Price: $105 to $135.

Weight Range: 8 to 35 lbs.

Comments: Manufactured in the Czech Republic, Vatanai wraps have a world wide following. In the US, they are sold on PieceofCloth.com. Vatanai slings are made of lightweight cotton and are recommended for warm climates. They can be tied in eight different ways from cradle carries to hip to backpack style. They claim to have a unique "cross-wise stretch" that makes them easier to tie plus a three year guarantee. While instructions are included, check YouTube for videos to help you the first few times. These wraps are available in four sizes from 4 to 5.5 meters of fabric. **Rating: A**

Hip Carriers

Cuddle Karrier

cuddlekarrier.com

Price: $60

Maximum weight: up to six years of age.

Comments: Cuddle Karrier won't win any design awards for their web site, but their hip carrier is the Swiss Army knife of carriers. It converts from carrier to shopping cart restraint, high chair cover . . . and four more uses. The Cuddle Karrier adjusts and repositions with just one hand (the online video is helpful to see this). One caveat: you may need a waist belt to make the Cuddle Karrier work most comfortably. Oddly, the site doesn't sell this accessory, but you can use a regular belt threaded through the crotch strap. **Rating: B-**

Hip Baby

abaybe.com

Price: $82 to $92

Maximum weight: 44 lbs.

Comments: We mentioned Walking Rock Farm's sling earlier in the chapter, but their hip carrier is the company's biggest seller. The Hip Baby comes in three types of fabric: Inprints, which is a lycra knit with heat reducing lining; Cooler II, a waterproof fabric with breathable lining; and Air Flow, a special water proof athletic fabric. Walking Rock touts their strap for its length and no-slip padding. A few readers complain the strap digs into their necks, despite the padding. The Hip Baby adjusts pretty much the same way all-hip carriers work with a backslide adjustment. All in all, this is a good choice among hip carriers. **Rating: B+**

Mei Hip

ellaroo.com

Price: $90.

Maximum weight: 35 lbs.

Comments: Ellaroo's Mei Hip carrier wins rave reviews from our readers. It has a waist strap that you buckle on first, then a strap that wraps around the back, cups the shoulder and clips to the carrier in front. The straps are wide and very long—an advantage if you're tall but annoying to some parents. Both straps can be tightened by pulling on the loose ends (that sounds like a flight attendant talking!). One frustrating aspect: we heard from parents that directions weren't included in their order. Finally, Ellaroo has added videos to their web site so parents can see how to use the hip carrier. *Rating: A-*

Original Hip Hammock

swankeltd.com

Price: $54.

Weight Range: 15 lbs. to three years of age

Comments: The Original Hip Hammock was designed to make the usual baby-on-the-hip carry easier on moms' backs. Attach the waist belt, slide your baby into the seat, then wrap the shoulder strap around your back and snap to the front of the carrier. In a nutshell, it is similar to a messenger bag. The Hip Hammock only works with children who are at least 15 pounds, so it's not for newborns. FYI: avoid the Playtex version of the Hip Hammock—readers didn't like it much and it was involved in a recall, both in 2005 and again in 2013. *Rating: B*

Scootababy Hip Carrier

scootababy.com

Price: $120.

Weight Range: 12 to 37 lbs.

Comments: Scootababy makes just one product: a hip carrier that's a bit like a mei tai and a bit like a sling. It positions baby to sit on your hip (although you can use it as a back pack or front carrier too) by using a wide, padded strap that goes around your back and over the shoulder. The wide, padded waist belt provides added support and the body of the carrier is shaped to fit your baby. Videos on the site are helpful. Overall, parents rave about their Scootababy hip carrier. The only downside: price. At $120, Scootababy is considerably more expensive than other hip carriers. *Rating: A-*

Frame (Backpack) Carriers

Reviews of frame/backpack carriers are on the free side of our web site at BabyBargains.com/bonus. Brands reviewed include Deuter Kid Comfort III, Kelty Transit 3.0 Child Carrier, Kokopax Carrier and Tough Traveler Kid Carrier

Our picks: Brand recommendations

Here are our top carrier recommendations:

In the sling category, we have a tie: the *Mamma's Milk* baby sling and the *Maya Wrap*. Parents love the simplicity of the Mama's Milk and the flexibility and comfort of the Maya Wrap.

In the front carrier category, our top pick this year is the *Pikkolo* from Cat Bird Baby. It's really a mash-up of a front carrier and a mei tai with buckles instead of long ties. It's also more flexible than other front carriers—it can be used in front facing both in and out, on the back and as a hip carrier. Our runner up favorite is the *Ergo* with it's padded ergonomic hip belt. A big caveat: baby can only face toward the parent in an Ergo.

What about a recommendation for the soft structured carrier sub category? We do have a top pick for those of you who don't mind that baby can't face front but would still like to have baby on your back when he's older: the *Boba Carrier 3G*. This one can be used as a front carrier comfortably by babies without a special insert and goes up to 45 lbs. as a back carrier.

As for hip carriers, some parents only need a carrier that offers a hands-free option with baby riding on the hip. Our top choice here: the *Mei Hip* from Ella Roo. Great fabrics and padding make this a stylish and comfortable hip carrier.

Mei tais or Asian carriers have really made inroads in the carrier market. Our top pick for this category is the *BabyHawk*. The customization options, great fabrics and ease of use made this mei tai a favorite. The *Ella Roo* mei tai is our runner-up in this category.

Wrap carriers also have front and back carrying flexibility. Our favorite here is the *Wrapsody Baby Breeze* gauze carrier. If you get hot when wearing your baby, this is the coolest, lightest fabric on the market.

Finally, frame carriers. For those committed to long hikes with baby, a frame carrier is a great option. Our favorite is the *Kelty TC 3.0*. It's comfortable for parents and baby, easy to use and reasonably priced. If you've just inherited a bit of money from a long lost uncle, the *Deuter Kid Comfort III* would be an excellent choice here. It's got everything you could ever need: adjustability, storage and great safety features. It's just ridiculously expensive.

CHAPTER 11

What Does it All Mean?

How much money can you save if you follow all the tips and suggestions in this book? Let's take a look at the average cost of having a baby from the introduction and compare it with our Baby Bargains budget.

Your Baby's First Year

ITEM	AVERAGE	BABY BARGAINS BUDGET
Crib, mattress, dresser, rocker	$1420	$1285
Bedding / Decor	$350	$222
Baby Clothes	$655	$301
Disposable Diapers	$750	$400
Maternity/Nursing Clothes	$1300	$550
Nursery items, high chair, toys	$545	$225
Baby Food/Formula	$1015	$350
Stroller, Car Seats, Carrier	$730	$490
Miscellaneous	$620	$500
TOTAL	$7415	$4323
TOTAL SAVINGS:		**$3092**

WOW! You just saved $3000. We hope the savings makes it worth the price of this book. We'd love to hear from you on how much you saved with our book—feel free to email, write or call us. See the "How to Reach Us" page at the back of this book.

What does it all mean?

At this point, we usually have something pithy to say as we end the book. But, as parents of two boys, we're just too tired. We're going to bed, so feel free to make up your own ending.

And thanks for reading *Baby Bargains*.

APPENDIX A

Registry Cheat Sheets

SAMPLE REGISTRY

Time is tight—we know. So to help juice your baby registry, here are the Baby Bargains Registry Cheat Sheets.

These sample registries follow our Good, Better, Best recommendations earlier in the book. If you need more detail about a particular recommendation, see the index to find a full review. Enjoy!

Good

Item	Baby Bargains recommends	Price
Crib	IKEA Sniglar	$70
Mattress	Lullaby Earth Super Lightweight	$160
Dresser	Ikea Hemnes Chest	$129
Changing pad	Summer Infant Contoured Changing Pad	$16
Glider Rocker	Dutailier Ultramotion Glider	$390
Bedding	Sleeping Partners Tadpole sheets (4)	$60
Wearable blanket	zzZipMeSack	$36
Breast pump	Medela Swing mini-electric	$150
Bottles	The First Years Breastflow Starter Set	$18
High Chair	Fisher-Price Space Saver	$50
Bathtub	First Year's Infant to Toddler Tub with Sling	$29
Potty seat	Fisher Price Precious Planet Potty	$30
Audio monitor*	VTech Safe & Sound Digital Audio Monitor	$30
Video Monitor	The Infant Optics DXR-5	$99
Play Yard/Bassinet	Joovy Room2 Portable Play Yard	$150
Bouncer	Fisher Price RainForest bouncer	$60
Humidifier	Crane EE-5301	$40
Swing	Kids II's InGenuity Portable Swing	$65
Safety gate	KidCo's Safeway Gates (2)	$120
Thermometer	Safety 1st Gentle Read Rectal Thermometer	$6
Infant Car Seat	Graco SnugRide 30	$100
Convertible Seat	Cosco Scenera	$40
Stroller	First Years Jet stroller	$40
Diaper Bag	Gerber diaper bag	$20
Carrier	Mama's Milk baby sling	$50
Clothing	Wait until after showers; see page 202.	
TOTAL		**$1958**

Better

Item	Baby Bargains recommends	Price
Crib	Baby Cache Heritage	$425
Mattress	Moonlight Slumber Little Dreamer	$170
Dresser	Baby Cache Heritage 4-Drawer	$600
Changing pad	Summer Infant Contoured Changing Pad	$16
Glider Rocker	Little Castle Cottage Chase	$825
Bedding	Land of Nod sheets (4)	$100
Wearable blanket	zzZipMeSack	$36
Breast pump	Ameda Purely Yours	$180
Bottles	Mam bottle starter set	$20
High Chair	Graco Blossom	$150
Bathtub	EuroBath by Primo	$40
Potty seat	Fisher Price Precious Planet Potty	$30
Audio monitor*	VTech Safe & Sound Digital Audio Monitor	$30
Video Monitor	Samsung's BabyVIEW (SEW-3036WN)	$180
Play Yard/Bassinet	Chicco's Lullaby LX Play Yard	$190
Bouncer	Graco Sweet Peace	$175
Humidifier	Crane EE-5301	$40
Swing	(Graco Sweet Peace, see above).	
Safety gate	KidCo's Safeway Gates (2)	$120
Thermometer	Safety 1st Gentle Read Rectal Thermometer	$6
Infant Car Seat	Britax B-SAFE	$135
Convertible Seat	Diono Radian RXT	$220
Stroller	UPPAbaby's G-Lite	$120
Diaper Bag	Ju-Ju-Be Be Hip	$55
Carrier	Pikkolo baby carrier	$130
Clothing	Wait until after showers; see page 202.	
TOTAL		**$3993**

Audio monitor is optional—you can get either audio or video. You most likely will NOT need both!

See the next page for the best picks.

registry cheat sheets

SAMPLE REGISTRY

Best

Item	Baby Bargains recommends	Price
Crib	Munire Urban	$600
Mattress	Naturepedic Organic Cotton Lightweight	$260
Dresser	Munire Urban Double Dresser	$800
Changing pad	Summer Infant Contoured Changing Pad	$16
Glider Rocker	Dutailier upholstered glider	$1200
Bedding	Carousel bedding sheets (4)	$120
Wearable blanket	zzZipMeSack	$36
Breast pump	Medela Pump In Style Advanced	$250
Bottles	Avent Classic Infant Starter Set	$30
High Chair	Fisher-Price Healthy Care	$90
Bathtub	Puj Tub	$44
Potty seat	Fisher Price Precious Planet Potty	$30
Audio monitor*	VTech Safe & Sound Digital Audio Monitor	$30
Video Monitor	Samsung's BabyVIEW (SEW-3036WN)	$230
Play Yard/Bassinet	Graco Pack N Play Classic	$109
Bouncer	4Moms MamaRoo	$200
Humidifier	Air-O-Swiss 7135 Ultrasonic Humidifier	$180
Swing	Fisher Price My Little Lamb Cradle 'n Swing	$120
Safety gate	KidCo's Safeway Gates (2)	$120
Thermometer	Safety 1st Gentle Read Rectal Thermometer	$6
Infant Car Seat	Chicco KeyFit 30	$190
Convertible Seat	Britax Marathon	$215
Stroller	Baby Jogger City Mini	$250
Diaper Bag	Skip Hop Duo	$55
Carrier	Boba Carrier 3G	$120
Clothing	Wait until after showers; see page 202.	
	TOTAL	**$5301**

Grandparents

Item	Baby Bargains recommends	Price
Crib	Dream on Me portable crib	$160
Mattress	Sealy Soybean Foam-Core	$150
Bedding	Sleeping Partners Tadpole sheets (4)	$60
High Chair	Cosco Flat Fold	$34
Thermometer	Safety 1st Gentle Read Rectal Thermometer	$6
Safety gate	KidCo's Safeway Gates (2)	$120
Convertible Seat	Cosco Scenera	$40
	TOTAL	**$570**

APPENDIX B

Advice for multiples

Yes, this year, one in 32 births in the US will be twins. As a parent-to-be of twins, that can mean double the fun when it comes to buying for baby. Here's our round-up of what products are best for parents of multiples:

◆ **Cribs.** Since twins tend to be smaller than most infants, parents of multiples can use bassinets or cradles for an extended period of time. We discuss this category in depth in Chapter 2, but generally recommend looking at a portable playpen (Graco Pak N Play is one popular choice) with a bassinet feature as an alternative.

Cool idea: a mom of twins emailed us about the **Leachco Crib Divider** for $35 that lets you use one crib for twins. Available on BabiesRUs.com.

Baby's Dream offers a great crib for parents of twin: the Cube ($500) converts to two twin platform beds.

◆ **Nursing help.** Check out **EZ-2-NURSE's pillow** (800-584-TWIN; sold on Amazon). A mom told us this was the "absolute best" for her twins, adding "I could not successfully nurse my girls together without this pillow. It was wonderful." This pillow comes in both foam and inflatable versions (including a pump). Cost: $70.

Walmart has a breastfeeding collection with **Lansinoh** products (including their amazing nipple cream). Check the special displays in the store or on their web site at walmart.com.

Yes, nursing one baby can be a challenge, but two? You might need some help. To the rescue comes **Mothering Multiples: Breastfeeding & Caring for Twins and More** by Karen Kerkoff Gromada ($18.95). This book was recommend to us by more than one mother of twins for its clear and concise advice.

FYI: Skip buying a glider-rocker if you plan to nurse your twins. The large nursing pillows won't fit! Instead, go for a loveseat.

◆ **Car seats.** Most multiples are born before their due date. The smallest infants may have to ride in special "car beds" that enable them to lie flat (instead of car seats that require an infant to be at least five or six pounds and ride in a sitting position). The car beds then rotate to become regular infant car seats so older infants can ride in a sitting position.

Some hospitals sell infant car beds—they can be used for premature infants up to nine pounds. The key feature: a wrap-around harness to protect a preemie in an accident. FYI: ALL premature infants should be given a car seat test at the hospital to check for breathing problems—

ask your pediatrician for details.

Another idea: check with your hospital to see if you can RENT a car bed until your baby is large enough to fit in a regular infant car seat.

◆ **Strollers.** Our complete wrap-up of recommendations for double strollers is in Chapter 8 (see Double the Fun in the lifestyle recommendations). In brief, we should mention that the **Chicco Cortina Together** accepts two Infant seats ($300).

Another top pick for tandem strollers: the **Kolcraft Contours Options II Tandem** ($250, 32 lbs.). Cool feature: the seats reverse to face the parents or each other. This model features a few upgrades over Graco, including adjustable leg rests and each seat can fully recline (only the back seat of the Quattro Tour Duo reclines fully).

For side-by-side strollers, we suggest the **Jeep Twin Sport All Weather Umbrella** (27 lbs.) for $93. We also liked the **Baby Jogger City Mini Double** ($450, 26.6 lbs., pictured), with its excellent extended canopies and quick fold.

◆ **Deals/Freebies.** Chain stores like Babies R Us and Baby Depot offer a 10% discount if you buy multiples of identical items like cribs. Buy Buy Baby has a similar program—and they even allow you to use one of their 20% coupons in addition to a 10% twin discount (for the second item only).

The National Mothers of Twins Clubs (nomotc.org) has fantastic yard/garage sales. Check their web page for a club near you.

Don't forget to check out the freebie list on our message board, updated frequently: babybargains.com/freebies.

Another good source: Twins Magazine is a bi-monthly, full-color magazine published by The Business Word (twinsmagazine.com).

◆ **Miscellaneous.** For clothes, make sure you get "preemie" sizes instead of the suggestions in our layette chapter—twins are smaller at birth than singleton babies.

One of our readers with multiples sent us an extensive list of tips from her experience with twins. Go to BabyBargains.com/twins to download this free PDF.

index

index

index

index

index

index

index

index

index

BabyBargains.com

What's on our web page?

◆ *Updated blog with news and safety recalls.*

◆ *Download ebooks for your Kindle, iPad or Nook.*

◆ *Message boards with in-depth reader feedback.*

◆ *The latest coupon codes and freebies!*

◆ *Corrections and clarifications.*

◆ *Links to our Facebook page and Twitter feed.*

◆ *Subscribe to read reviews online!*

BabyBargains.com
Email: authors@babybargains.com
Phone: (303) 442-8792

More great books!

Expecting 411

Clear Answers & Smart Advice For Your Pregnancy
The Insider's Guide to Pregnancy & Childbirth! $14.95
As seen on Rachael Ray
Go to Expecting 411.com for details!

Baby 411

Clear Answers & Smart Advice For Your Baby
Questions and answers for new parents with detailed advice from an award-winning pediatrician. Sleep, nutrition, growth and more! $14.95
Co-authored by Dr. Ari Brown
Go to Baby411.com for details!

Toddler 411

Clear Answers & Smart Advice For Your Toddler
Temper tantrums? Potty training? Picky eaters? Here's the missing manual for toddlers! $14.95
Co-authored by Dr. Ari Brown
Go to Toddler411.com for details!

our other books

Order online
WindsorPeak.com
or call toll-free to order: **1-800-888-0385**
More info on our books is on WindsorPeak.com

If this book doesn't save you at least

$250

off your baby expenses, we'll give you a complete refund on the cost of this book!

NO QUESTIONS ASKED!

Just send the book and your mailing address to

Windsor Peak Press • 436 Pine Street, Suite T Boulder, CO, 80302.

If you have any questions, please call
(303) 442-8792.

Look at all those other baby books in the bookstore—no other author or publisher is willing to put their money where their mouth is! We are so confident that *Baby Bargains* will save you money that we guarantee it in writing!